Early Years

HODDER
EDUCATION
AN HACHETTE UK COMPANY

Orders: please contact Bookpoint Ltd, 130 Milton Park, Abingdon, Oxon OX14 4SB. Telephone: (44) 01235 827720. Fax: (44) 01235 400454. Lines are open from 9.00–5.00, Monday to Saturday, with a 24 hour message answering service. You can also order through our website www.hoddereducation.co.uk.

British Library Cataloguing in Publication Data

A catalogue record for this title is available from the British Library

ISBN: 9781444156676

First Published 2012

Impression number   10 9 8 7 6 5 4 3 2 1

Year   2016 2015 2014 2013

Hachette UK's policy is to use papers that are natural, renewable and recyclable products and made from wood grown in sustainable forests. The logging and manufacturing processes are expected to conform to the environmental regulations of the country of origin.

Cover photo © Richard Laschon–Fotolia.com

Typeset in 10/12 Bembo Std by Datapage (India) Pvt. Ltd.

Printed in Italy for Hodder Education, an Hachette UK company, 338 Euston Road, London NW1 3BH.

Contents

Contributors

About the editor

Francisca Veale BA (Hons) Social Pedagogy, PGCE, MA (Ed.), PhD, SEDA accredited teacher in HE, PQ Social Work Practice Teacher, PQ Counsellor and Supervisor has been the programme leader and senior lecturer for the Early Years Foundation Degree and the BA (Hons) Early Years Education and Care for Bournemouth University for many years. She was a mentor and assessor for the Early Years Professional Status (EYPS) for five years. Previously, she has taught early years FdA and BA courses for Plymouth University. She also works as an independent off-site social work practice teacher for a number of universities in the south-west, and has conducted research with social work students in England. Initially, she worked for many years with children and families as a social pedagogue in Germany and in England, and was the manager of the Weymouth and Portland Children's Centres, before dedicating herself to teaching, research and writing.

About the contributors

Dr Cath Arnold MEd, PhD, QTS has worked in the Early Years field for the last 35 years, as a teacher, family worker and researcher. She has worked at the Pen Green Centre for the last 24 years, recently as an Early Years Consultant. She is fascinated by how young children learn, and teaches and writes about early education and working with parents.

Kathy Brodie MA, EYPS, DTLLS is a lecturer in Early Childhood Studies Degree and Foundation Degree courses at Stockport College. She has worked in childcare, in both private and state sectors, as a Special Educational Needs Coordinator (SENCO) and EYP. She delivers tailored training to settings, through Kathy Brodie Early Years Training. She writes regular updates and articles for practitioners on her website www.kathybrodie.com.

Tina Bruce BEd (Hons), MA, CBE is Honory Professor at Roehampton University, a leading international expert on early childhood and a best-selling author. She a is Vice-President of the British Association for Early Childhood, and a Trustee of the Froebel Council.

Louise Dryden BEd (Hons), MA in Primary Education, Cert Ed, PG Cert Learning & Teaching in HE is an educationalist, specialising in early years language and literacy. Working at London Metropolitan University for over ten years, she lectured on undergraduate and postgraduate programmes. At the beginning of her career, Louise taught young children in inner-city nurseries and primary schools, before moving on to lecture in further education colleges, where she trained adults to work in childcare settings. Louise has a particular interest in developing adult students' academic skills.

Professor Ann Farrell DipT(EC) (BKTC) (Brisbane Kind TC), BEdSt (University of Queensland), MEdSt (University of Queensland), PhD (University of Queensland) is Professor of Early Childhood and Head of the School of Early Childhood at Queensland University of Technology, Brisbane, Australia. Her research and teaching expertise are in research ethics, children's rights to protection and participation, childhood and families studies, and children in the legal and criminal justice systems. She has authored more than 100 scholarly publications as well as numerous technical reports for government and peak bodies in early childhood education and care. Ann was also awarded an honorary doctorate from Gothenburg University in October 2012. She serves as an 'IntReader' (researcher of international standing) for the Australian

Research Council, as an expert assessor for Australia's National Health and Medical Research Council and as a member of an expert interim panel for the Tertiary Education Quality and Standards Authority (TEQSA) in Australia.

Dr Ros Garrick BA (Hons), PGCE, PG Cert Teaching & Learning in HE, MA Education, PhD is Principal Lecturer Early Years at Sheffield Hallam University. Ros has more than 20 years' professional experience as an early years teacher and teacher adviser and has taught on a range of undergraduate and postgraduate courses. Ros undertook doctoral research into the mathematical development of three- and four-year-olds while lead teacher of a large, inner-city nursery class and more recently she co-directed a study of young children's experiences of the Early Years Foundation Stage (EYFS), a study that informed Dame Clare Tickell's review of the EYFS.

Penny Greenland BA Hons, MBE began her career as a dancer and choreographer, then as an actor and theatre director. In 1985 she founded JABADAO, a charity offering movement play projects with people of all ages. From 1998, she led an eleven-year action research project exploring the ways we support our youngest children's physicality in early years settings. She is author of *Hopping Home Backwards: Body Intelligence and Movement Play* (JABADAO 2000), editor and contributor to *What Dancers Do That Other Health Workers Don't* (JABADAO 2000) and contributor to *Early Childhood: A Guide for Students*, Tina Bruce (Sage 2009). She is currently Director of JABADAO and teaches CPD courses in early years settings across the country. She was awarded an MBE in the 2001 New Years Honours List for Services to Dance.

Dr Eleni Kanira BA (Hons), PGCE, MA, PhD is a PhD graduate of the University of Warwick and a Senior Lecturer in Early Childhood Education at Birmingham City University. She trained and worked as an early years and drama teacher. Her research interests draw on the uses and applications of drama as an impetus for children's meaning-making in play and across the curriculum.

Alison McLeod PGCE, CQSW, PhD has worked as a teacher, social worker, social work manager and lecturer, and is currently a freelance childcare consultant. She has done research into communicating with children and promoting children's participation, and is the author of *Listening to children: a practitioner's guide* (Jessica Kingsley 2008).

Penny Mukherji BSc, MSc, SRN is a Senior Lecturer at London Metropolitan University and teaches child health topics on the Early Childhood Studies Scheme. Penny has had many years' experience teaching early years practitioners on Higher Education courses and helped to set up the Sector-Endorsed Foundation Degree in Early Years at London Metropolitan University. She is an experienced early years author.

Dr Ioanna Palaiologou BA (Hons), MEd, PhD, PGCHE, CPsychol Chartered Psychologist is a lecturer and researcher in the Centre for Educational Studies at the University of Hull. Ioanna is currently leading the Master's in Early Childhood Studies and is the Academic Coordinator for Research Students Support within the Faculty of Education. She is a chartered psychologist of the British Psychological Society, specialising in child development and learning theories.

Linda Pound MA (ed), Cert ed has worked in three universities and was an LEA inspector responsible for the early years for almost ten years. In addition, she has been head of a nursery school and deputy head of a primary school. In her current role as an education consultant, she provides training for early years practitioners around the country and overseas. Linda writes extensively for a range of audiences and on a range of topics. She published two books last year: *Teaching Mathematics Creatively* (co-written with Trisha Lee and published by Routledge), and *Influencing Early Childhood Education* (published by Open University Press). She is currently working on a series of study guides for early childhood studies to be published by Hodder Education.

Tracy Rydin-Orwin BSc (Hons), CPsychol, DClinPsy, AFBPSs is a chartered clinical psychologist. She works within the NHS in Devon in perinatal infant mental health. She is passionate about primary prevention and early intervention to support infant mental health within family relationships. She has been actively involved in strategic developments in Devon for perinatal infant mental health and lectures to different professional groups on attachment and perinatal infant mental health. She is also a research supervisor for Doctorate Clinical Psychology trainees carrying out their theses in perinatal infant mental health.

Joy Scadden BA (Hons) French & Sociology, NVQ4 TDLB, FAETC is an experienced practitioner, having worked in the childcare sector for over 20 years. As well as being a lecturer on the Early Years Foundation Degree (EYfd) and Early Years Professional Status (EYPS) programmes, she owns three nursery settings and a training centre in West Dorset, delivering apprenticeships and training programmes up to Level 5.

Lyn Trodd BA (Hons), PGCE, MA, EdD is Head of Multi-Professional Education at the University of Hertfordshire. Her professional background is in teaching and childcare. Her research interests include self-efficacy in children and practitioners and professional learning for children's centre leaders. Lyn is the National Chair of the Sector-Endorsed Foundation Degree in Early Years Network (SEFDEY).

Karen Ward BEd (Hons), MEd spent 23 years teaching in primary schools, working across the age range in a variety of posts, before moving to Birmingham City University to take up the post of Senior Lecturer in Early Years. Her research interest is behaviour in the early years, the policy to practice context and the ways in which practitioners can support children in this important area of development.

Dr Margy Whalley MA, PhD is Director of the Research, Development and Training Base at the Pen Green Centre. She was the founding head and has worked there since 1983, during which time she has been involved in the design and development of a knowledge-sharing programme which involved parents in their children's learning, a programme which has now been adapted regionally, nationally by local authorities and internationally by those developing integrated services. Margy has managed multi-disciplinary early years services and is involved in research, training and consultancy work in the UK and internationally. Her most recent development and research at Pen Green is the Early Years Training Centres National Network, a two-year project funded by the Department for Education to establish a national network of Early Years Teaching Centres and to identify new ways in which outstanding centres can train and support staff in local early years settings and improve outcomes for children and families in their reach areas.

Preface

This exciting new book is essential for practitioners studying at Levels 4 and 5, covering a wide range of topical Early Years subject areas written by authors who have many years of experience in the field. As well as offering the necessary information and support required by students, this book also provides lecturers with salient material suitable for teaching. The reflective exercises are particularly relevant as discussion points for group work in the classroom and can also be undertaken individually.

The book contains up-to-date references to the reformed Early Years Foundation Stage (DfE, 2012) and research of current literature and peer-reviewed journal articles. Within each chapter the authors present a holistic perspective of their subject area, which encompasses historical development from traditional to contemporary theory and practice in early years, as well as recent policy and legislation. This approach encourages 'joined-up' thinking, endorsing an integrated and interdisciplinary way of working, thus promoting high-quality childcare. Further to this, practitioners are inspired not only to reflect on and evaluate their own practice, but also that of their setting through the introduction of new and different ways of working, illustrated by case studies and good practice examples.

The chapters are bright, and structured consistently, making them accessible and designed to engage the reader with the topic. This will inevitably encourage wider reading, and signpost the way to further resources appropriate to the level of study.

The authors have been selected to offer a range of perspectives; from experienced practitioners, lecturers and childcare providers, to well-known and prolific early years writers. Most have published books and journal articles at the same or a higher level of academic standard, and all share a passion to continue to improve the quality of early years practice. This book encapsulates their knowledge, experience and passion which, it is hoped, will in turn prompt the practitioner to research further, and in more depth, by locating 'original sources' to learn more about particular subject areas. It is hoped that these practitioners will lead for change and contribute to a high-quality early years experience for the children in their care.

Study skills for higher education

Louise Dryden

Introduction

Starting a new course of study is an exciting prospect, and enrolling on a Foundation Degree programme opens a new chapter in your professional and academic career. As a new student you will be enthusiastic about returning to study but perhaps a little apprehensive about the challenges that lie ahead. This chapter will help you to recognise the expectations of higher education programmes (at Levels 4 and 5), and aims to prepare you for the months ahead, by building on the study skills that you already possess. Establishing study habits, exploring individual learning preferences and honing academic literacy skills will help to make your Foundation Degree or Higher National Diploma (HND) a meaningful and enjoyable experience.

Learning outcomes

This chapter will help you to:
- Reflect on and evaluate your previous study experiences.
- Be confident in your ability to organise your study effectively.
- Understand the expectations of higher education study at Level 4 and Level 5.
- Acquire a range of note-taking skills.
- Increase your academic reading skills.
- Understand the importance of careful planning, leading to successful assessment outcomes.
- Be able to write for a range of different purposes.
- Recognise the importance of correct referencing, and avoid plagiarism.
- Recognise the importance of critical and analytical skills in enabling you to demonstrate your deeper understanding of a topic.
- Be familiar with the processes which enable you to become an independent researcher.

Transition into higher education

The move to studying at degree level requires that you take on greater responsibility for your own learning. Previous study, perhaps at A Level or National Diploma level, will have prepared you for this transition. You will have recognised that at Level 3 better grades were awarded for work where you moved away from being purely descriptive towards demonstrating your ability to explore and discuss the material. Higher education takes you further along this route. As an adult learner, at college or university, you will need to take responsibility for your own learning journey. Lecturers will certainly be there to guide and support you, but you will be expected to be independent and self-regulated in a way that may be new to you in the student role.

You already possess a number of academic skills which you will be able to transfer to this new programme of study. Study is part of a spiral curriculum where existing skills and prior knowledge and understanding are built upon and deepened. You will already have developed a range of transferable study skills, such as the ability to understand and grapple with new concepts or organise and express your ideas verbally and in written form, and you will know how reading enhances your own learning.

Lectures at degree level require a higher level of engagement on the part of the individual learner. Every lecture will be important, and often there is little time for repetition, so ensuring good attendance enhances your chances of doing well on your degree programme. Taking ownership of your own developing understanding is the key to success. Listening attentively and making notes are not going to be enough; discussion and debate with fellow students will heighten your ability to understand and analyse the subjects you are studying.

Sadly at this time in our educational history, most students have the additional burden of financing their studies. It is essential that you organise exactly how you intend to pay your tuition fees before you start your programme so that your attention is not diverted from your studies. At the time of writing, there are some opportunities available for those working in childcare for grants and support from local authorities and employers, and these bursaries should be investigated well in advance of the start of the programme.

Andragogy – being an adult learner

Returning to study as an adult will probably be very different from your previous educational experiences. **Andragogy** (an idea revived by Knowles, 1980, 1990) is a term used to explain the way in which adult learning may differ from **pedagogy** (learning as a child).

Knowles (1990) considered that adult learners want to know *why* they are learning things. This theory recognises that adult learners, unlike children, have a pool of experience to draw upon, and that they want to link their studies to their existing knowledge and social roles. Adult learners like to be more independent and in control of their own studies; they are intrinsically motivated and wish to be given options and have their views respected. To this end, Knowles (1990) suggests that a practical, problem-centred curriculum is most appropriate for adult learners, one where they will be able to see immediate benefits in their personal and professional life.

Reflective task

Rate these statements from 1 to 5, where 1 = most important and 5 = least important.

Knowles (1990)	Rate these statements 1–5	
Self-concept	Take responsibility for your own learning.	
Experience	Use your previous experiences (personal and professional) as resources for your current studies.	

Readiness to learn	Your studies should include developing your general life skills.	
Orientation	Your studies should focus on problem solving and practical application.	
Motivation to learn	Motivation should be intrinsic (for self-satisfaction) as opposed to extrinsic (to reap rewards).	

Table 1.1 Based on Knowles, 1990: 57

Do you consider that Knowles is right in his assumption that adult learning is different from the way children learn?

Some critics suggest that there is a conflict of ideas here – that the adult student's supposed focus on practical application could be seen as extrinsic, rather than intrinsic, motivation. Would you agree?

Your Foundation Degree programme will certainly be designed to help you make strong connections between theory and your existing knowledge, and current childcare practices. Frequently coursework will require you to analyse these connections directly, with the result that you should be able to recognise some shift in your working practices, alongside a deeper understanding of child development and teaching and learning strategies.

Time management

Embarking on a new course requires you to step back and carefully consider your current lifestyle and the various commitments which fill your waking hours. You do need to be realistic about how much time you have available – perhaps you need to fit in a busy work schedule alongside college attendance, private study, and home and family commitments.

Reflective task

1. Use this grid to indicate how you spend your time currently. Include work, home, social and sporting activities.

	Early morning	Morning	Afternoon	Evening
Monday				
Tuesday				
Wednesday				
Thursday				
Friday				
Saturday				
Sunday				

Table 1.2 Timetable

2. Now use another colour or highlighter pen to show how you can adjust your current schedule to accommodate your studies. Put in the periods of attendance at lectures alongside opportunities for private study, such as reading and research in libraries. Remember that this timetable will need further adjustment when coursework deadlines are looming.

You will need to experiment in order to find the timetable that best suits your lifestyle and body clock. For example, if you are studying for a master's degree while holding down a full-time teaching post, early mornings may be a very productive time, especially as your mind is clearer after a good night's sleep. However, many students with parental responsibilities find it best to study after their children are in bed. However, this makes for very long days, and lack of sleep can become a problem. If you are a parent it is a good idea to arrange for a partner or family member to help out at weekends, freeing up some quiet time for study, especially when you have an assessment deadline approaching. If you do not have any immediate family who can help, try to find someone who is willing to care for your children for a few hours, perhaps someone for whom you can return the favour when your schedule is quieter.

It is important to recognise that your return to study also affects the people around you. You should ensure that your close family understand the process you will be going through, and that you make time for them so that they do not feel neglected. If you are working, your relationship with your colleagues also needs consideration; you may need to ask them to take part in work-based projects or swap shifts with you. Be aware that you may encounter envy from those around you who feel that they have had fewer opportunities for career advancement.

Managing stress

It is important to recognise that studying will become stressful at times; there are few students who do not consider abandoning their studies at some point in their course. When you recognise that you have reached such a crisis point, take a break, phone a friend (preferably a fellow student) and try to consider rationally what has caused you to become despondent. Exercise is also a good stress reliever; if you already go to the gym or swim make sure that this appears on your timetable. If you are not used to making time for exercise, going out for a walk can help to clear your head.

Colleges and universities usually offer a variety of student support services; these can range from help with academic writing and financial advice, to counselling for anxiety and personal issues which may arise while you are studying. These services are there to help relieve the pressures that sometimes occur during your studies and they are all strictly confidential; your programme tutors do not need to know that you have sought help unless you choose to tell them.

Planning for study

Planning is a crucial aspect of any successful project. It can be argued that successful study consists of 80 per cent organisation and just 20 per cent inspiration. If you make careful preparations, the process should be less arduous. The difference between home cooking and cordon bleu cuisine is the attention to detail; the staff in professional kitchens meticulously prepare the individual elements of a dish in advance, so that chefs are able to concentrate on the final processes which make their food exceptional.

There are a number of important study practices that you can establish at the very beginning, which will save you many hours on your journey towards graduation. Establishing effective study habits as you embark on this new programme will enable you to concentrate on the more enjoyable and creative aspects of study. First, it is helpful to find a study space and a place to store your materials. You may have a room with a desk and shelves that can house your files and books; however, for most people this is an impossible luxury. Some people have amazing powers of concentration and are able to study amid the hurly-burly of a family living space, while others need a quieter, more tranquil atmosphere. Some students may share a bedroom with a sibling or partner, and resort to writing essays sitting on a bed, balancing a laptop on their knees. Whatever your personal circumstances and preferences, you need to experiment until you find the conditions which suit you best. Remember, you can always go and use the library and the computers at your college or university if you need to work in a quieter environment – with the added benefit that you can ask library staff for help, for example with referencing.

Reflective task

Use this chart to consider your previous study habits. Answer the questions to consider what helped or hindered your success.

School and college	Did you find it easy to organise your time?	Did you find it easy to organise your materials?	What was most challenging?	What strategies helped you to be successful?
Coursework				
Essays				
Exams				
Presentations				
Practical tasks				

Table 1.3 Study habits

Considering the answers you have given, was there a pattern to your previous experiences?

How can you change your habits to help you as you embark on your new course of study?

It is important that you store your notes and research materials systematically. It helps to separate information by subject; this will enable you to effectively 'file' information in a way that will be easy for you to retrieve at a later date. If several modules cover similar ground, then there is no reason why you should not store them together, especially if a new module builds on your knowledge and understanding from a previous one.

Some materials are best stored electronically, for example lists of useful websites. Again, you should organise them in such a way that you can access them quickly. You may decide to list them alphabetically or organise them by subject matter – or it may even be useful to do both. At the beginning of each new module, it is helpful to make an audit of your existing knowledge. Consider what you already know about the subject and check to see if you have any books or articles which are related to the topic.

Being part of a learning community

You will make some good friends during your programme of study, people who have similar interests and share your passion for working with children. You will soon find yourself engaging with particular students with whom you have a special affinity, although working as a group is also important. Find one or two people who you feel work in a similar way to you and build a special relationship with them. You may wish to have a study buddy – someone you can discuss your work with, read alongside and even share books with. Once you have built up trust with one another, you can each take on the role of a 'critical friend'. A critical friend will give honest feedback, providing praise and supportive criticism in equal measure.

Listening to feedback and advice can be difficult. It is hardest when you feel that you have put a great deal of effort into something and it appears not to have been acknowledged. It is best to listen to or read the feedback and review the advice privately, taking time to really understand what the person is telling you. You may not agree with them but you will have had the opportunity to consider a fresh perspective on your work.

Studying

Tutorials

A tutorial may be a new experience for you; it is a private opportunity for you to meet with a tutor to discuss your understanding of a module or to prepare for a piece of assessment. You may feel a little daunted at first but tutorials are the perfect time for you to get individual support and feedback of a type not available during lectures. It is best to prepare for the tutorial: go armed with a few questions or perhaps the plan for a piece of work you are doing, and *always* make notes during the discussion.

Lectures

It is always a good idea to prepare for lectures in advance. You should look at the module handbook, find out what the topic is and, whenever possible, do some preparatory reading. Most colleges and universities have virtual learning platforms now, which provide access to a great many useful files and documents relating to your course and the individual modules. If you have begun to think about the lecture topic before you arrive, you will be much more receptive to the content when the lecture begins. You will have had an opportunity (perhaps on the bus) to recollect your existing knowledge and to consider what you would like to get out of the session – you may even have framed some questions that you would like to ask. All this will help you to be much more participative in the whole learning experience.

How to make the most of a lecture: taking notes that work for you

Reflective task

Find a set of notes that you have taken recently from a lesson, lecture or a staff development event. Looking back at these notes:
- How useful are they in retrospect?
- Do you think that they are an accurate record of what happened?
- Have you captured all the important facts and some of the details?

There are a number of different note-taking techniques; it is a good idea to experiment with several of them until you find the method that best suits your learning style. Below are several different techniques for your consideration.

Dictation

The biggest mistake that many students make is to try to write down everything that is said. The problem with this method is that, in the race to get it all down quickly, the writer is not able to focus on the material being imparted, nor can they fully participate in the lecture. Many students use this method as they fear they might miss something important, and consider scribing everything as an insurance policy against missing vital information. The problem with this method is that they are not using the lecture to make sense of the material, they are relying on doing this on their own after the lecture.

Lecturer's slides

Some lecturers publish their PowerPoint® slides or notes on the virtual learning platform before the lecture takes place. This is a very effective method of taking notes, because the student can print these off in advance and then just annotate the sheets while fully participating in the lecture.

Linear

Linear notes are the most commonly used method. These notes use headings and subheadings to separate out different material (thoughts, concepts etc.). These can be made more effective by the use of colour to distinguish specific content or levels of importance. Phrases and key words or concepts can be quickly written down, and most students develop their own shorthand which enables them to put down the gist of an idea without writing it in full.

The Cornell method (Pauk and Owens, 2011) is similar to the linear method but the student divides the page vertically into two columns. The student highlights a particular aspect or key idea in the left-hand column and expands on the ideas in the right-hand column. These notes can be returned to after the lecture and further additions can be made.

Diagrammatic

Taking notes using a diagrammatic technique, such as mind maps (Buzan, 2006) or pattern notes (Burns and Sinfield, 2008), encourages the student to make links between ideas and concepts in a non-linear manner. This method encourages greater participation in the lecture and nurtures a creative approach, where the student seeks to make sense of new material by making connections with existing ideas and concepts.

Using a laptop

Some students find it beneficial to make lectures notes on a laptop, although this does require excellent touch-typing skills if it is to be truly effective. This method can interfere with the student's ability to actively participate in the lecture, and obviously necessitates using a linear style of note taking. However, this method is often encouraged by those supporting students with specific learning difficulties such as dyslexia.

Taping lectures

In some instances students may seek permission from the lecturer, and their fellow students, to make voice recordings during lectures. This can free them to actively participate in the lecture but it requires a large time commitment, since for every hour of lecture they will need at least another hour to replay the taped material and make notes.

Making the most of lectures

Your tutors take the time to prepare their sessions very carefully; most will begin by explaining what material they are aiming to cover during that particular lecture, and they will discuss how this links to the overall learning outcomes for the module. The tutor's opening statements will set the scene for what is about to follow, and you should listen out for 'signposts' and summaries that they provide during the lecture. Tutors usually stress the most important points they are making and often repeat or rephrase these key pieces of information several times.

Many tutors will intersperse their lecture with opportunities for you to engage in debate with your fellow students. These exercises encourage you to be an active participant in the learning process (see below). Some lectures include seminar sessions which enable you to take part in discussions relating to preparatory reading you have been asked to do. Again these activities encourage an active engagement on your part; be sure to do the required reading, so that you can make the most of the debate that follows.

It is very useful to take the time to summarise what you have learnt at the end of the lecture. You can do this by jotting down a couple of sentences at the bottom of your notes, or use the journey home to reflect on the information you have gathered. These activities allow you to consider any questions that remain unanswered, so that you can ask for clarification during the next lecture or tutorial. It is also very important that you review the notes you have taken; this will give you the opportunity to check that they are meaningful, and enables you to fill any gaps which you did not have time to expand on during the lecture. This process will enable you to feel confident when referring back to the lecture notes at a later date.

Listen, think and debate

Make sure that you are as active as you can be during a lecture:
- Listen carefully.
- Think about what is being said.
- Check your understanding.
- Use every opportunity you are given to discuss ideas.
- Make links whenever possible to previous knowledge and experiences.
- If you have a retiring nature or are lacking in confidence, you may not wish to make contributions to general class discussions, but do ensure that you make the most of opportunities to express your ideas in small-group work.

Working in groups

Most lecturers will organise their lectures to include varying amounts of student participation. These group tasks and discussions encourage you to be an active rather than a passive learner. They will help you to engage fully in the curriculum and encourage you to examine the subject matter, debate the issues and consider the opinion of others. These types of exercises help you to explore new ideas and will be helpful when you review your understanding of a topic for assessment purposes.

You should take full advantage of these opportunities to discuss, debate and analyse material with your fellow students – practising these debating skills will help you to write balanced arguments in your written assessments. While you should listen carefully to what other students have to say, it is important that you are also an active participant. Sharing information is an integral part of working in groups. Some students can be anxious about proving their competence and may feel compelled to hog the limelight, while others only want to listen, trying to keep their ideas and knowledge to themselves. Everyone in the group needs to get an opportunity to voice their opinions or suggestions, and if one extrovert personality dominates a group, it is up to the other group members to try to ensure that there are equal opportunities for all.

Often lecturers will ask for a spokesperson to feed back to the large group after a group discussion. Try to take on this role when you can, even if you find it makes you feel a little nervous. Feeding back in this way gives you the chance to practise important skills, including the ability to summarise and succinctly explain new information. These skills will really enhance your ability to write discursive essays.

This is known as *attribution*. You need to give clear details of where you found (sourced) the information so that the listener or reader can verify your supporting evidence or follow up the topic for themselves. Poor referencing can lead to allegations of plagiarism, which is the suggestion that you have used other people's ideas as if they were your own. Plagiarism is taken very seriously in academic circles and can lead to suspension from your studies. This is why it is so important that you reference your work effectively and correctly.

There are two ways in which references support your academic writing. In the main body of your essay or report, you provide *citations*. These are partial references which provide minimal information, such as author(s) name and the date of publication. The full *reference* information will be displayed at the end of your writing. This needs to include all the information you have gathered such as the title of the article, book, chapter etc. as well as publication details, whether it is published online or in book form. In longer pieces of work like dissertations, an additional section termed a *bibliography* is often included. This demonstrates that further reading has been undertaken which has not been directly referred to in the work but which has contributed to the writer's understanding of the subject.

Quotations require the brief citation information (author(s) and date of publication) plus the exact pages on which they occur, and the quoted words need to be inside quotation marks. Short quotes can be incorporated into the sentence they are being used to support. However, quotes longer than a sentence should appear in their own paragraph, but you must signpost very clearly which paragraph they are supporting (the one above or below). It is not a good idea to directly quote lengthy sections of other authors' work, as this suggests to the examiner that you have not analysed or fully understood the material for yourself. It is much better to demonstrate your comprehension by putting the ideas into your own words.

When using (citing) the ideas and theories of other authors, you should clearly identify the source. You can write this in two ways:

- either immediately indicate your source, for example 'author (date) suggests that…'; or
- give the information and put the citation in brackets at the end, for example 'It is suggested (author date)…'.

Frequently you will need to cite *secondary sources*, as discussed earlier. This is when you have found the information you need in a piece written by another author. For example, you want to discuss ideas relating to Maria Montessori but, rather than going to her original material, you have read about her theories in a more recent publication. You need to clarify this by indicating the source of your information, for example:

- Montessori (cited in Pound, 2008) considered…

Where you have the year of publication by the original author who has been cited in another source you write, for example:

- Bronfenbrenner (1979, cited in Pound, 2008) discussed…

Quotations

It is usually better to paraphrase an author's idea, making sure that you indicate the reference clearly. However:

- Ask yourself why you feel the need to use the author's exact words. Sometimes it *is* appropriate, particularly if it would be hard for you to express their idea as clearly.
- Do not use long quotations in your essays – one sentence or phrase should be sufficient.
- Always lead into a quote (using words such as 'suggests', 'concludes', 'believes', 'explains' etc.) and ensure that you make it part of your discussion.

- Do not just leave a quote dangling in the middle of the page, leaving the reader to decide which paragraph it belongs to and what point you are making with it.
- Always include the page number(s) and date of the work.
- Always explain or link how the author's idea or theory is related to the topic you are writing about or how it is applicable to your practice. A quote should not substitute your own words, explanations or critical analysis.

References require the full details of the source: the author(s), publication date, title and publisher information, and are listed in the reference section in alphabetical order by author surnames. They are set out in the following way:

Reference checklist

- Author(s) (and or editor(s))
- Date of publication; edition where relevant
- Title of book, article, essay or chapter
- Contributor's name and chapter title if in edited volume
- Publisher information if in book form (town and publishing house)
- Journal title, date and page numbers if article
- Web address for online materials and date when accessed

Examples

	In the main body of your essay	In the reference section
One author	Copus (2009)	Copus, J. (2009) *Brilliant Tips for Students*, Basingstoke: Palgrave Macmillan.
Two authors	Peck and Coyle (2005)	Peck, J. and Coyle, M. M. (2005) *Write it Right*, Basingstoke: Palgrave Macmillan.
More than two authors	Judge *et al.* (2009)	Judge, B., Jones, P. and McCreery, E. (2009) *Critical Thinking Skills for Education Students (Study Skills in Education)*, Exeter: Learning Matters.
A chapter from an edited book	Mukherji (2005)	Mukherji, P. (2005) 'The importance of health', in Dryden, L. *et al.*, *Essential Early Years*, London: Hodder Arnold.
A quote from another source within a chapter	Lalonde (1974, cited in Mukherji, 2005)	Mukherji, P. (2005) 'The importance of health', in Dryden, L. *et al.*, *Essential Early Years*, London: Hodder Arnold. (i.e. Lalonde will not appear in the reference)
Newspaper article	Furedi (2004)	Furedi, F. (2004) 'Plagiarism stems from a loss of scholarly ideals', *Times Higher Education Supplement*, 6 August.
Journal article	Dryden *et al.* (2003)	Dryden, L., Hyder, T. and Jethwa, S. (2003) 'Assessing individual oral presentations', *Investigations in University Teaching and Learning*, vol. 1, no. 1, pp. 79–83.
Internet	Stainthorp (2003)	Stainthorp, R. (2003) 'Use it or lose it' [online]. Available from: http://www.literacytrust.org.uk/Pubs/stainthorp.html (accessed 6/10/2004).
Acts	Children Act 1989	Children Act 1989, London: HMSO. Available from: http://www.legislation.gov.uk/ukpga/1989/41/contents (accessed 20/01/2012).

Table 1.4 Referencing

Referencing online resources

Referencing online resources is a complex task. Material on the internet does not always provide all the information required for accurate citations. For example, many articles appearing on the internet will not have a date, and in this case you will need to read the material carefully to try to ascertain how recently it was written (see my earlier comments on the currency of legislation and statistics). Some reputable national organisations will have interesting information posted on their websites but it might not always be clear when the piece was written or whose views are being expressed. You will also need to decide whether you think the authors are providing an unbiased, balanced opinion. Reputable organisations and websites usually state at the end of their homepage 'Last updated' and a year which can be used as the year of publication.

Cite Them Right (Pears and Shields, 2010) explains how to cite accurately from websites. You need to give the date you 'accessed' the text from the internet and give as much information as possible about the source, authors and date. Also, your college or university will have referencing guidance and examples on their virtual learning platform.

Academic writing

Written language is different from spoken expression where gesture and tone amplify and support our ability to communicate and where we are able to respond to the listener. Written communication has to be very concise, to ensure that the reader understands the message we are trying to convey. Punctuation and grammar are vital to good written communication, and punctuation in particular takes the place of the pauses and emphasis found in verbal expression.

One of the best ways to improve your academic writing is in fact reading. The more you read, the better your own written style will become; gradually you will find yourself adopting some of the techniques and phrases that you find in journal articles and textbooks, and these will help you to develop your own written 'voice'.

Planning an essay

Planning essays can appear a frightening prospect when you begin your studies; however, with careful preparation essay writing can become a very satisfying, skilful activity. There is a commonly held misconception that writers can just sit down with a pen, or at a keyboard, and the words just flow onto the page. This is a totally unrealistic expectation for almost all of us.

To help you recognise the importance of planning in the writing process, consider how the author set about preparing this chapter. The task could have felt overwhelming as the author was asked to write 10,000 words on the subject, but planning for such a big piece of writing would make it feel manageable. The author began by making a list of the main issues that help students to study on the programmes currently taught. She then gathered material from various sources, including lecture notes, and visited a library to look at some study guides written by other authors. Having completed all this preparation, the author got an A3-sized piece of paper and began to make an enormous mind map, placing the title of the chapter at the centre of the page, adding a series of spokes labelled with the main areas to discuss (such as time management, transition to higher education etc.), and then adding numerous branches from each of these spokes, which contributed further detail. This document helped to develop confidence that there was a structure for the chapter, in order to start typing out the headings that could be used to organise ideas. Finally the author began to flesh out the individual paragraphs.

Planning and drafting

However experienced a writer is, planning is *the* most important tool; the second is drafting and redrafting, and the final skill is editing and proofreading.

Preparing to write an essay

The very first thing you need to do when starting to plan an essay is to ensure you really understand the task that is required of you. Highlighting key words in the essay title helps you to focus on the most important aspects of the question, and enables you to check that you understand the task. Another useful exercise is to try rephrasing the question in your own words and then make sure that your version mirrors the original.

Once you are clear about the task, you can begin to gather the material you need. It is always a good idea to brainstorm everything you already know on the topic and also revisit your lecture notes from the relevant module(s). Make a list of questions which will help you to read around the subject and fill in the gaps in your knowledge. Then, search through any books or articles you already have, skimming and scanning for relevant information which can support your discussion. Make time to search for new material online or in your college library. Thorough preparation as described earlier in the chapter will save you time in the long run.

Once you have gathered sufficient material, you can draw up a plan with a mind map or linear notes, using major headings to organise the ideas. Once you have made the plan, add the sources you are planning to use to support the different sections; this technique will enable you to see where you have sufficient theoretical support, and where you may need to do more research. Once the plan is almost complete, you need to consider the most effective (rational) order in which to write up the ideas; your essay needs to build an 'argument' which flows, smoothly leading the reader from one idea to another, and counterbalancing different perspectives where appropriate. At this point you should number the headings or spokes on your plan to show the order in which you are going to address the individual sections.

Drafting an essay

First draft: using the careful preparation described above, writing your essay should be relatively easy. Each of the major ideas you have on your plan will be expanded into prose, in a series of paragraphs. Each individual paragraph should contain a number of sentences analysing one central idea, and importantly, the opening sentence of each of these paragraphs should signpost to the reader what you are about to discuss in the sentences that follow. Remember that one sentence does not constitute a paragraph, however long it is. If you find yourself composing a string of sentences, find ways to tie them together into a paragraph. This is where your detailed planning will help you to organise your ideas, showing you how to relate a series of points into a coherent paragraph. On the other hand, be sure to avoid producing very long paragraphs; divide them into shorter, logical sections with perhaps three or four sentences at the most.

Organising the essay

An essay should have three major sections. An introduction, the main body where the discussion takes place and a conclusion that brings the essay to a satisfying end. It is quite acceptable to compose the introduction *after* you have written most of the essay. It is your opportunity to explain to the reader how you are going to tackle the assessment task. The conclusion indicates to the reader that the essay is ending, summarising your thoughts on the topic. It should not bring in new material, nor should it repeat statements you have already made. It can suggest new avenues that you would like to research in future or make recommendations for the consideration of others in the field.

Throughout the planning and writing process you must consider the word limit set for the particular piece of work. You should always write at least the minimum number of words; if you do not, it suggests that you have not done enough research. On the other hand, cutting down very large essays which far exceed the word limit can be a hard task, and sometimes important information gets culled if you do this in a hurry. You can better control this aspect by allocating approximate word limits to the sections on your original plan; then, while you are composing the essay, keep an eye on the word count available on your computer.

Other organisational features

Cover page – you need to follow the instructions given to you by your particular institution. Usually the cover page needs to include the course and module information, the title of the piece you have written and your candidate (student) number. Normally you will be told not to put your name on your work – your assignment will be *blind-marked*, which means that the marker cannot identify you while they are assessing your work.

Pagination – again you need to follow the guidance your college provides, but it is always best to have the pages numbered. Some institutions ask you to put your candidate number on each sheet; use the 'header and footer' tool for these additions.

Reference list – you need to list all the sources you have used in the main body of your work in alphabetical order. The reference list is not part of the word count.

Appendices – these include any additional evidence, relevant documents, field notes, observations etc. which you have used to support your discussion. They are *not* a repository for all the material that you have not had time to discuss. Each appendix must always be directly referred to at least once in the main body of the text and should be numbered (at the proofreading stage, see below) to reflect the order in which they first appear in the essay. Appendices are not part of the word count.

Abbreviations – the names of organisations and documents can be referred to in abbreviated form, but you must give the full title the first time you mention them, with the abbreviation or acronym in brackets; for example: Foundation Degree (FdA).

A glossary – this is a list, in alphabetical order, of the terms and abbreviations you have used in your essay.

The second draft is your opportunity to step back from the original composition and explore how well you have explained yourself. Try to put yourself in the position of the reader and examine how clearly you have organised the material and how well the argument flows; make adjustments, moving sections and paragraphs around until you feel happy that you have a cohesive discussion. Linking paragraphs often helps the flow of your work, using words like *therefore, moreover, consequently, however.*

The third draft is where you consider the technical aspects of your essay. At this stage you need to ensure that you have expressed your ideas in the very clearest manner possible. Check for over-long sentences, which may confuse your reader, and use punctuation carefully to divide complex sentences into manageable phrases.

Proofreading is your last task. This is where you make final adjustments, looking not at the content but at the spelling (typing errors) and punctuation, and check that all citations and links to appendices are correct. You may like to ask a friend, relative or colleague to read through your work; they do not need to understand the subject to help you with this process.

Tips for reducing the word count

- Check that *everything* you have written is directly relevant to the essay title.
- Reread the assessment criteria and learning outcomes for the module. Use these as a checklist.
- Check to see if you have repeated yourself; the same supporting material may have been used in several places – decide where it is most relevant.
- Proofread your work carefully and look out for places where you could use one word instead of three!
- If you are really desperate, try turning sentences around so that they use fewer words.

Critical and analytical skills

Writing essays at degree level requires that you demonstrate a depth of understanding; it is not enough to just show your knowledge of the topic under discussion. In previous study programmes, particularly at school, it may have been enough to show that you had learnt a series of facts about the subject, but at this level you need to show 'ownership' of the material. This requires you to demonstrate analysis and synthesis.

Your essays (and presentations) should show that you have studied the subject matter and that you are now in a position to identify and clarify the underlying concepts and issues relating to the topic; this takes your work from being purely descriptive to being analytical. This skill requires you to collect evidence by reading widely so that you explore the ideas of a number of relevant theorists. You can then use these different sources to generate a discussion, which enables you to debate important aspects of the subject. Where there are conflicting views or counter arguments you should provide a balanced argument supported by the evidence you have gathered.

In educational essays you are at liberty to include some evidence from your own work experiences, synthesising the theoretical elements of your study with your practical experiences. You may voice your opinion from time to time, but you must be wary of generalising or making assumptions based purely on your own limited experiences or research. Be sure to evaluate your ideas and support them with substantial evidence; usually your opinions need to be supported by reference to other authors.

Preparing for seminars and presentations

Seminars are an opportunity for you and a small group of fellow students to engage in a rich discussion on a particular aspect of your subject, and are most frequently based on specific reading material which you are required to prepare in advance. It is crucial to the process that all the participants have indeed done the preparatory reading; if they have not, they will benefit less from the exercise. Sometimes the groups are organised so that the members take it in turns to lead the discussion; when it is your turn, prepare questions to elicit discussion from your fellow students. You can for instance choose an interesting or controversial idea, or perhaps read aloud a short extract from the text, which you believe will prompt enthusiastic debate.

Full participation in this type of seminar opportunity should give you some rich material for your essays, helping you to look at the topic in detail and enabling you to scrutinise your ideas and formulate your own opinions. You may need to defend your opinions during the seminar, and this in itself is an extremely useful exercise, helping you to scrutinise your supporting evidence and listen to the opinions of others. You can take some notes in seminars in much the same way as you do in a lecture, so that you can reflect on the discussion at a later date.

Presentations

Presentations are frequently part of the assessment requirements for a module; these can take many forms. You may be asked to prepare an individual presentation (for example to discuss a child case study) in front of your peers and tutor. For formal assessment purposes it is usual for two examiners to observe the presentation so that sufficient evidence is available to attribute marks.

Planning a presentation

Check that you fully understand the requirements of the task. Read the instructions carefully and, as with essays, underline or highlight the key words. You will have a short time to display your understanding of a given topic and there will not be time to waste on material which is not directly relevant to the task.

Presentations need exactly the same type of careful planning as essays. Scrupulous attention to detail during the early stages of preparation will save you time later and help you to have a clear structure to your piece. First, brainstorm your existing knowledge of the topic, then make a list of the type of supporting evidence you require. For some presentations you will need to gather primary evidence (such as your own observational notes or interviews with practitioners) as well as secondary evidence, doing further reading to widen your theoretical understanding.

Once you have gathered all your material, you can plan the presentation using the diagrammatic format you prefer (as discussed in relation to essay plans above). Generally, you can decide on about five main points that you wish to make and use these as headings to organise your talk. A presentation, like an essay, should have an introduction, a main body and a conclusion. The introduction will explain how you plan to discuss the topic, indicating the (five) major points you are going to make, and the conclusion will signal that you have come to the end of the presentation, leaving the audience with a final thought or observation. Poor presentations tend to stop abruptly, as though the presenter has run out of ideas; the conclusion can tie up the loose ends and should provide a neat ending.

Supporting aids

Attractive supporting materials will enliven your presentation. It is currently common practice to use PowerPoint® slides to display points on a screen. If you use this method remember that you should not have too much material on one slide; use a large font size, about 25–30 point, so that you are not tempted to write too much on a line, which would leave your audience squinting from a distance. It can also be helpful to use other props such as artefacts, illustrations, books etc. which you can show or even demonstrate to your audience. On some occasions you may be asked to design a poster presentation, where you display your material creatively on an A3-sized sheet. Again, selecting the major points and making them prominent features on the poster will add clarity to your presentation.

Delivering the talk

You will be given a time allocation for your presentation; around ten to 15 minutes, according to the weighting it contributes to your module assessment. You will need to practise your timing, as a small amount of material takes a surprisingly long time to present verbally. Timing is normally very strict (treated like essay word limits), so if you overrun you will be stopped before you have presented all your material, which will affect your grade. You can practise alone with a stopwatch, or find a 'critical friend' who will time you and provide you with some supportive feedback on your presentational style.

Ensure that you present your talk using a lively, enthusiastic style, engaging your audience through eye contact, using an appropriate tone of voice with sufficient volume for the size of the room. A little appropriate humour can enliven your talk, and do not forget to smile!

As with essays, you are required to reference your sources on your handouts or PowerPoint® slides, as well as provide a reference list with your presentation.

Presenting to an audience

- Speak clearly.
- Try to look as if you are enjoying yourself – enthusiasm is catching.
- Try to make the delivery lively; you can use humour.
- Always face the audience and maintain as much eye contact as possible.
- Try not to rush – you will make mistakes and become flustered. Speak slowly and clearly.
- Use your visual aids to help the audience; they should not be a distraction.
- Wear something that makes you feel good and helps to boost your confidence.
- Most importantly, remember that the audience are your peers. They are going to be receptive to your ideas, without being critical.

Group presentations

Students are sometimes required to work with other students to plan presentations as part of their assessed coursework. This can be a very effective learning opportunity, where you work collaboratively with your fellow students, share knowledge and understanding and utilise the particular talents and expertise of individual group members. These situations can also have their drawbacks.

Reflective task

Consider the pros and cons of working with one or more fellow students on a group presentation. In the third column consider how any difficulties might be addressed.

Advantages of working collaboratively	Negative aspects of working collaboratively	Possible ways of avoiding or resolving the negative issues

Table 1.5 Working in a team

You will probably have considered the opportunities that are afforded by sharing the task with others – such as sharing information, dividing up the tasks and playing to the particular strengths, skills and talents of the individual members of the group. The downside is that some members of the group can be less enthusiastic or active, and sometimes if one member has a personal or family crisis this can affect the whole group enterprise.

Collaborative work should be a positive experience, enabling group participants to share ideas, knowledge and skills, but sometimes certain individuals see group work as an opportunity to sit back and let others do the work. This needs to be addressed by the group at the start of the exercise.

It should be made clear to everyone that the tasks will be shared, engaging the strengths and talents of particular members of the group. A timeline should be drawn up, with several interim points scheduled when progress can be monitored. Marking schemes may have an element of self-assessment which gives an opportunity for individual members to consider their own contribution alongside the contribution of those they were working with. Tutors should be made aware of particular difficulties which the group has, despite their best efforts, failed to resolve.

Sharing group presentation tasks

- Discuss the task carefully.
- Share out the tasks fairly.
- Produce a timeline and set manageable, short-term targets.
- Communicate effectively, meeting as a group if possible.
- Clarify the scope of the individual tasks carefully.
- Organise visual aids, such as PowerPoint® slides, posters etc.
- Have a practice run-through before the presentation.

Next steps

As you proceed through the Foundation Degree, academic expectations will be increased. During the second year of the degree, the assignments will become longer and you will need to demonstrate deeper levels of understanding and a greater ability to analyse the material. You should read more widely as you will have had the chance to become familiar with the professional literature appropriate to the discipline, and you will also be more confident in selecting appropriate sources for material on statistics and current legislation. You should be more critical of your own academic writing skills, and be using the literature you access to help model the way in which you express your ideas.

Conclusion

This chapter has provided practical guidance on study skills you may find useful. Even the most confident of students needs some advice during their degree. You will find a number of very good study guides listed below should you wish to read about study skills in greater depth. There is something very satisfying about completing a good piece of work, and learning to enjoy the assessment aspects of your course as much as the content is part of this.

Evaluate your...

Confidence

- Have you decided how you will fit your studies into your busy schedule?
- Do you understand how to benefit from attending lectures and tutorials?
- Have you decided on a style of note taking that suits you best?
- Do you know how to reference material from books and the internet?
- Do you recognise the importance of meticulous organisation in planning for essays and presentations?

Further reading

Copus, J. (2009) *Brilliant Tips for Students*, Basingstoke: Palgrave Macmillan.

Cottrell, S. (2008) *The Study Skills Handbook* (3rd edn), Basingstoke: Palgrave Macmillan.

Dryden, L., Hyder, T. and Jethwa, S. (2003) 'Assessing individual oral presentations', *Investigations in University Teaching and Learning*, vol. 1, no. 1, pp. 79–83.

Dryden, L., Mukherji, P., Forbes, R. and Pound, L. (2005) *Essential Early Years*, London: Hodder Arnold.

Furedi, F. (2004) 'Plagiarism stems from a loss of scholarly ideals', *Times Higher Education Supplement*, 6 August.

Judge, B., Jones, P. and McCreery, E. (2009) *Critical Thinking Skills for Education Students (Study Skills in Education)*, Exeter: Learning Matters.

Peck, J. and Coyle, M. M. (2005) *Write it Right*, Basingstoke: Palgrave Macmillan [available in Kindle edn].

Stainthorp, R. (2003) 'Use it or lose it' [online]. Available from: http://www.literacytrust.org.uk/Pubs/stainthorp.html (accessed 6/10/2004).

Wyse, D. (2007) *The Good Writing Guide for Education Students* (2nd edn), London: SAGE.

Websites

Burns and Sinfield (2012) *Essential Study Skills: Succeeding at University: Quick Steps to Success*. Available from: http://www.youtube.com/watch?v=JMvvnNsZenM&feature=relmfu (uploaded by SAGE Publications on 6/3/2012).

Open University: http://www.open.ac.uk/skillsforstudy

Palgrave Macmillan: http://www.palgrave.com/skills4studycampus

Becoming a reflective practitioner
Lyn Trodd

2

Introduction

If you are currently studying for a degree in Early Years, one of your hopes may be that people see you differently once you have the degree. If you are already working as an early years practitioner, you may feel ready to assume more challenging responsibilities in your work with children. Whatever your situation, you will have certain expectations and aspirations for the future. As Maslow's hierarchy of needs (1967) illustrates (see Figure 2.1), human beings yearn for much more than just safety and comfort.

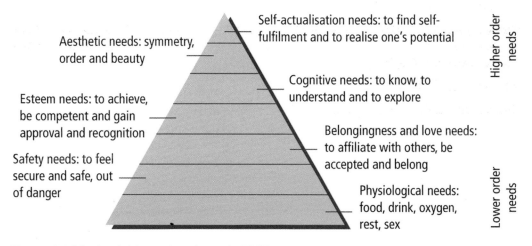

Figure 2.1 Maslow's hierarchy of needs (1967)

Maslow argues that once our basic needs are satisfied we tend to have 'growth motivations' or 'metamotivations' (Maslow, 1967) to achieve our potential and do our best. One of the main ways to become the best you can be in your early years work is to become a 'reflective practitioner'. According to Schön (1983, 1987), being reflective is one of the defining characteristics of professional practice.

In this chapter you will explore the concept of reflective practice as a way to develop yourself and your practice, and so create the best possible opportunities for children's learning and development. The structure of the chapter is based on a holistic view of human consciousness – it arises from processes of being, becoming and belonging. Theories of reflection, reflexivity and critical reflection are outlined. The interplay between an early years practitioner's relationships, and reflection and reflective practice are explored and the day-to-day reality of reflective practice is discussed.

Learning outcomes

This chapter will help you to:

- Understand reflection, reflexivity, critical reflection and reflective practice.
- Know some models and frameworks for reflection and critical reflection.
- Begin to apply the concept of reflection to your professional interactions and development of your practice.
- Learn how to give and receive feedback.
- Understand the role of the mentor.

Being a reflective practitioner

What is reflection?

Students are sometimes perplexed when they get back an assignment and the marker has written a comment such as 'Develop a more reflective approach' or 'Your work is mainly descriptive and lacks reflection'. It is difficult to respond to this developmental feedback if you do not understand what writing reflectively looks like. Although there are some differences of opinion about aspects of reflection there are some characteristics which most people agree on.

A simple working definition of reflection is that it is a 'looking back' on experiences so as to learn from them and construct knowledge about yourself and the world. It is accepted that reflection is occurring when you are:

- trying to make sense of an experience and find the meaning or significance in it
- looking at something in detail and thinking about why it is as it is
- thinking intentionally and purposefully and seeking to answer questions and find solutions
- developing and challenging your understanding by asking yourself searching questions about your experiences, thoughts, ideas, attitudes, values and theories
- seeking the truth, acknowledging difficult realities and taking everything into account.

It is a process that goes beyond ordinary thinking and obvious answers, and is a way of reprocessing your existing feelings, experiences and knowledge in order to learn from them, create new understanding and engender change. Thus it helps you decide what to do next time and how to do it.

When your tutor gives you feedback that you need to write more *reflectively*, consider whether your writing tells the reader the facts of what happened OR explores, explains and considers the possible implications, causes and potential improvements that could be made. Ask yourself whether it relates the whole story OR chooses to focus on the most significant elements of the story and to relate them to an idea or theory.

Scenario

Read these two excerpts from Sophie's professional practice log. Apart from the length, can you identify the difference made by being reflective?

Excerpt 1

The room leader said it was my turn to read a story to the children. This was a new experience for me. I had not done this before. I chose a book from the book box. As the time drew nearer I felt more and more nervous. The other practitioners stayed in the room. They tidied up and began to prepare some things for the following day. I managed to get the children to sit down and I launched into the story. When I got to the end of the book the story didn't make sense and I realised that the last two pages were missing. Disaster!

Excerpt 2

The room leader said it was my turn to read a story to the children. This was a new experience for me. I had not done this before. *Looking back, I should have been more assertive and said I needed more time to prepare. Not only would that have given me confidence but I could have made the story more interesting by linking the story to something within the children's experience.* I chose a book from the book box. *Several of the children knew the book really well and at first I felt sorry that I did not have a special new book for them. However, it occurs to me now that there is a place for the children to see adults choosing a book to read as a kind of modelling or observational learning.* As the time drew nearer I felt more and more nervous. The other practitioners stayed in the room. They tidied up and began to prepare some things for the following day. *I can understand them doing this but I would have liked to have read the story in a quiet room with no distractions for the children.* I managed to get the children to sit down and I launched into the story. *Part of me wanted to wait until everyone was ready but on the other hand I was worried the children who were waiting might get restless. I am going to watch how the other practitioners do this because it was not easy.* When I got to the end of the book the story didn't make sense and I realised that the last two pages were missing. Disaster! *What I should have done (apart from check the book beforehand) is to ask the children to tell me the ending or to make one up for the rest of the group. That way they would have had to use their imaginations or their memories and we could have had some fun and learned about the structure of stories at the same time.*

Excerpt 1 above is mainly descriptive. It describes what happened but the points are not linked. It refers to Sophie's feelings but does not question how her actions led to the turn of events or consider how things could have been different. It is written entirely from Sophie's perspective.

Excerpt 2 is more reflective. It describes the events but it considers each stage of what happened in order to make sense of it. Sophie recognises that by reflecting on what happened she can learn from it and improve her story-reading skills and her practice. She also links her reflections to her knowledge of learning. Sophie shows awareness of the reasons for the behaviour of others. She is able to stand back from what happened and recognises how one thing led to another and how, with hindsight, she could control events better next time.

The 'genre' of reflection

Sometimes the barrier to being reflective is because you have not yet learned the 'grammar', 'vocabulary' and genre of reflecting. The first thing to acquire is a degree of comfort in talking about your own views and writing in the first person. One way that can help with this is to read a passage that is reflective or reflexive written by someone else. Another is to 'interview yourself' about an experience by first of all drafting the questions the significant other in your mind (your tutor? your boss?) would want to ask and then answering them. In addition, if you take every possible opportunity to engage in discussions of early years theories or practise with colleagues in a practice, training or study context, you will hear yourself thinking – a process that is very helpful to developing your 'voice'.

It is difficult to be reflective if you communicate in the passive voice – for example, 'It *was decided* that the role-play area *would be converted* into a vet's surgery' – because, by talking or writing in this 'report style', you depersonalise what you are saying and remove a key feature of reflectiveness, an element of accountability for actions. When you speak or write in the first person, referring to yourself as 'I' or 'we', you give your listener or reader the chance to access your perspectives, thoughts, feelings and arguments, which is fundamental when communicating reflections.

It may feel much safer to hide behind other people's views. There may be cultural, gender or personality influences that may be constraining you from talking about your views. However, by *reflecting* on these possibilities and becoming more self-aware, you are taking the first step to breaking free from such constraints. If this is an issue for you, you might like to find out more about the 'imposter phenomenon' (Clance and Imes, 1978; Clance and O'Toole, 1987), in which people, especially high-achieving females, have a prevailing sense of unworthiness and lack of entitlement to a 'voice'.

Certain sentence structures are likely to be used in reflection. You are likely to offer an interpretation of events, such as:
- *In my view* the reason why the children did not like my efforts to turn the role-play area into a travel agent's shop was that few of them have ever been into one.
- *Looking back, I realise that …*
- *Perhaps the reason for this is …*
- *Having read about this, I now know that the most significant aspect was …*
- *What I learned about this will change the way I …*
- *What stood out for me was …*
- *I think there are connections between … and …*

Reflection is often a response to questions you ask yourself, such as:
- What is really happening here?
- Why am I doing this? Who will benefit from it?
- How will I know I am being effective? What are the criteria I am using to judge whether I am being effective? Where did those criteria come from?
- How is what I experienced different from what I expected? Why did I expect it to be that way? How can I improve?
- If I could do it again, what would I do differently?
- What do I feel about it? Why do I feel like that?

Once you have gained some expertise in reflecting in the first person, ask your tutor to show you an example of reflecting in the third person so that you can use it as a model to master that genre too.

Why is reflection important?

Perhaps you find yourself asking why there is such an imperative for early years practitioners to be reflective, something Sweet (2006: 12) calls 'reflection dogma'. If you are asking this, you are asking a critically reflective question! Doubts and queries about the value of reflection exist. Although there is an assumption that reflection is beneficial because it brings about improvements in your practice, the evidence for this is often assumed as common sense (Zeichner and Liston, 1987). As Atkinson (2003a) argues, just as diagnosis does not automatically lead to treatment, so reflection does not necessarily lead directly to changes in practice. However, in their research study, Korthagen and Wubbels (1995: 66) found that *reflective* student teachers:

- are able to structure situations and problems
- use a questioning approach when evaluating their experience
- are clear about what they want to learn
- can describe and analyse experience and interaction well
- have strong feelings of personal security and self-efficacy.

Although Korthagen and Wubbels (1995) are much less confident about evidence for a causal relationship between reflection and changes in practice, their research found that once reflective students became reflective teachers they had better interpersonal relationships with pupils and colleagues than other teachers and also they developed a higher degree of job satisfaction and were less likely to experience 'burnout'.

However, there are many other reasons why reflectiveness is seen as so important.

Reflection and the quality of provision for children

The learning and development of children in an early years setting depend heavily on the quality of the work by the practitioners in it. As an early years practitioner you have to take responsibility for the way you work with children, families and colleagues, in the same way as those in other professions do, such as doctors and lawyers. Like other professionals you have to work fairly autonomously, and any outside monitoring of your actions is largely retrospective. As you tend to take decisions on a minute-by-minute basis, there is no one policing your work. Your manager cannot tell you what to do in every situation. She has to rely on your professionalism and your own sense of responsibility for the quality of your work. As a reflective practitioner you will be professional and competent, and will continuously seek to improve your practice. The importance of reflection, continuous professional development and training for practitioners in early years is highlighted in the EYFS (DfE, 2012a).

Throughout both your studies and your training your aim should be to develop a reflective and critical approach to working with children that will continue throughout your career. This will enable you to manage change by thinking critically, drawing on evidence to ensure the validity and currency of your practice in the future. Early years practitioners who have learned to think critically and reflectively will question assumptions and actively challenge accepted values and practices if they are no longer relevant or beneficial to children. This questioning and reflection are an important part of ensuring that children's real needs are met. This is why reflection is associated with high-quality provision in early years settings. Reflecting on your skills, attitudes, knowledge and experience, and the strengths and weaknesses of different aspects of your setting's provision will cause you to think about how you work, what you can develop further and how you can improve. It is worth noting that it is a process that supports the development of the Self-Evaluation Form (SEF) when you are preparing for Ofsted.

Reflection and tacit knowledge

Fish and Coles (1998) used the metaphor of an iceberg as a way of explaining the role of reflection in professional practice. The tip of the iceberg is the visible aspect of practice but it is the larger, submerged part of the iceberg, the invisible aspects, which influence, shape and buoy up the visible aspects of practice. Under the waterline is tacit knowledge (Polanyi, 1967), which is composed of practice expertise, intuition and understanding, and that is held so unconsciously that it is hard to surface and communicate to another person. Eraut (1994) points out that one of the benefits of making tacit knowledge explicit through reflection is that working with others becomes easier because team members can communicate their expectations and assumptions effectively. To continue with Fish and Coles's iceberg metaphor (1998), the large mass under the waterline is diminished and so less likely to scupper effective working. This is particularly important in interprofessional teams when team members may have different terms of reference because of their professional backgrounds.

Reflexivity

Another very important aspect of reflection is an awareness of yourself – especially your own thinking. A central part of reflective learning is about the uncovering and questioning of assumptions or informal theories. Schön (1983) argued that 'surfacing' assumptions and learning is an important dynamic in personal growth and self-awareness. You can learn to treat yourself as an 'object of knowledge and evaluation' and develop your self-awareness by making sense of your actions and thus your ability to act in a professional, safe and consistent manner. Eventually this mindset, or habit, becomes an important aspect of critical reflection – it is sometimes described as reflexivity (Usher and Edwards, 1994). You can develop your own self-awareness through reflection on the explicit or implicit feedback that you receive from your work with young children, their families and your colleagues which will facilitate the development of reflexivity. There are many sources of such feedback and later in this chapter we will look at some of them.

Reflexivity and the development of a personal narrative of identity

In an interview for a new post you may be asked, 'Tell us about something you have done as an early years practitioner that makes you feel proud.' It may seem like an easy warm-up question but the minute you start to speak you are informing the interviewer about your values and principles and telling a story of your professional identity. The interviewer will interpret what you choose to say as an indication of your priorities and interests. When you talk with others, when you write in your practitioner log or write an essay, blog or tweet, you are telling stories about your practice. When you recollect or reread what you were thinking, the stories you told help to make your thinking explicit to yourself and others as a key way of developing your reflexivity. It is a way of listening to yourself think and contributes to your subjective self-conceptualisation in your professional role – how you see your identity as an early years professional practitioner.

Critical reflection

As you progress through your degree you will be asked to write *critical* reflections. This is because critical reflection is perceived as a higher order of thinking, appropriate for the later stages of your qualification. It may appear confusing that, just as you have become confident and comfortable with writing *reflectively*, further demands are placed on you. Being critically reflective is much easier if you know what it is. However, this is not as straightforward as it sounds because we tend to use the terms reflection, reflexivity and critical reflection interchangeably and indiscriminately. Even Dewey (1933: 9) appears to do this when he refers to reflection as 'assessing the grounds [justification] of one's beliefs', meaning scrutinising the assumptions that are used as a basis for action. As we will see, Dewey's view of *reflection* makes a good characterisation of *critical reflection*.

Critical reflection refers to thinking that makes connections between your frames of reference or taken-for-granted knowledge and understanding, and the decisions, expectations and choices you make as a professional practitioner. You may reconsider your views on what you feel and why, what you see and why, what you know and why, what you believe and why and so on, and crucially reconsider the outcomes of all of these things in terms of the actions you take. It is hard work and sometimes uncomfortable, but it can lead to shifts of perspective that can change and improve your practice. It can cause you to be properly responsive to the children and families with whom you work and trigger creative problem solving.

Reflection and learning

Another important reason to develop your capacity for reflection is that the main learning tool used by practitioners and students is reflection. Dewey (1933: 78) states: 'We do not learn from experience. We learn from reflecting on experience.'

Deep learning (Entwistle, 1991) involves the critical examination of new material and reflection on experiences, connecting them to the concepts and principles you already know, so that you understand them and can apply them and seek the meaning of them. Whereas, surface learning (Entwistle, 1991) involves instrumental learning of disconnected facts and passive acceptance of experiences.

Mezirow (2000) argues that learning that facilitates greater awareness of the influences on one's own thinking, by developing the capacity to reflect critically on the lenses we use to filter, engage and interpret the world, encourages autonomous thinking. He suggests transformations occur in four possible ways:

- by elaborating existing frames of reference
- learning new frames of reference
- transforming points of view
- transforming habits of the mind.

Thus reflective learning, for Mezirow (2000), creates a 'perspective transformation', which enables you to become self-directed and more emancipated from the influence of your assumptions, beliefs and cultural context because you are more aware of them.

Reflection and adult learning

It is often argued that there is a difference, even polarisation, between pedagogy – the science of education – and andragogy – a particular approach to adult learning. In common parlance, pedagogy is sometimes used to signify children's learning characterised by an instructional and directive approach. In contrast, andragogy is taken to refer to self-directed learning by adults. See Chapter 1 for further discussion of this. In fact, we talk about early years pedagogy referring to an approach which is absolutely NOT instructional and directive, so the territory of pedagogy and andragogy is confusing and contested. One distinction that is fairly well accepted, however, is that adults are capable of taking much more responsibility for their learning and being more reflective about the processes through which they learn than children, although there are those who would disagree with that assertion too.

Extend your knowledge

Read further about andragogy and reflect on the differences between how you learn today as an adult in comparison to when you learned at school as a child during the various stages of your education:

- Usher, R., Bryant, I. and Johnston, R. (2002) 'Self and Experience in Adult Learning', in Harrison, R., Reeve, F., Hanson, A. and Clarke, J. (eds.), *Supporting Lifelong Learning*, London: Routledge-Falmer/ Open University.

Reflecting and professional autonomy

Reflecting on your practice helps to put you in control of any changes that should be made. Self-knowledge and awareness help you to monitor and control your behaviour better. By becoming more self-aware you can become more self-controlled in your professional role. Identifying what needs to be changed and your own professional development requirements empower you, give you ownership of your practice and make your job more satisfying. A practitioner with a reflective mindset is much less likely to be complacent and much more likely to challenge the way things are done. Reflection helps with change and stressful situations as well as providing learning that will help when that same situation is encountered again. When practitioners are reflective they take a step back from a challenge or difficulty and by doing so they are usually able to be more rational about it and to see underlying causes and understand things from other people's points of view, and so are better positioned to take responsibility for their actions.

This aspect of professional autonomy has been identified as the defining feature of being a professional, both in the mind of practitioners and also in the mind of society (Atkinson, 2003b; Furlong, 2003; Hoyle and John, 1995). Katz (1985), for instance, is one of many writers who view having autonomy as an expectation of being a professional. She includes autonomy in her list of eight criteria of professionalism in the field of working with young children. It is usual for professional autonomy to be justified by society by the lengthy, specialised training undertaken by professionals, which validates them to use their discretion in the relevant area of expertise and to be trusted to behave altruistically in the best interests of children, families and society.

Recently a different view of professional autonomy has been developed. Greater awareness of the influences on your own thinking, by developing the capacity to reflect critically on the lenses you use to filter, engage and interpret the world, encourages autonomous thinking. Another way to conceptualise it is to see it as choosing the values and principles by which decisions and actions are taken, as a professional, and being aware of the process of learning from experiences as well as an ability to make critical judgements (Chene, 1983). Autonomy is seen as the ability to determine *how to work* rather than what to do – to understand what is right and wrong for oneself, rather than to have independence in decision making. According to Mezirow (2000), autonomy is being able to be self-directed and more emancipated from the influence of one's assumptions, beliefs and cultural context because one is more aware of them.

A positive feature of this view is that it appears to reflect current reality in which the state seeks to control what early years practitioners do through the publication of standards, curriculum guidance and through the implementation of the latest Ofsted framework. A critically reflective mindset predisposes you, as an early years practitioner, to becoming more aware of the values and principles that shape your practice so you are better able to choose and take responsibility for how you behave in your professional role.

Becoming a reflective practitioner

As we have seen, reflection, reflexivity and critical reflection are essential skills and mindsets for someone working in early years. Your aim should be to become a reflective practitioner, which is the expectation expressed in the EYFS (DfE, 2012a). It is worth noting that you will always be in a state of *becoming* a reflective practitioner. There is no end point at which you can say to yourself, 'Right, I have got there now. It's time to turn to other things.'

Schratz and Walker (1995) explain this as a tendency for learners to move through a capability cycle or continuum. Their theory is easier to understand when it is applied to a practical situation as follows in Table 2.1.

Imagine you are learning to drive a car from scratch...	Schratz and Walker call this stage:
You get a lift from a friend. Driving looks easy. You do not know what the fuss is about. Lessons are a waste of money really.	Unconscious incompetence
As you take your first driving lessons you discover driving is more difficult than you thought. You recognise you are an incompetent driver. You have to think hard to know which gear to move into and which lane to be in at any given moment.	Conscious incompetence
You pass your test and know you have met the required standards for driving. You begin unsupervised driving, enjoy giving friends and family lifts, and take pride in driving safely and well.	Conscious competence
You drive safely and well and are relaxed when you arrive at your destination. You no longer think about your driving technique and you take your skill for granted.	Unconscious competence 1
You arrive at your destination having travelled around three roundabouts and two zebra crossings BUT you can't remember a thing about the journey. Did you go through a red light? Did you go too fast down that 30mph road?	Unconscious competence 2 OR Unconscious incompetence again?

Table 2.1 (Adapted from Schratz and Walker, 1995)

The 'unconscious competence' of expertise may quickly become 'unconscious incompetence' (Schratz and Walker, 1995: 106), unless it is regularly refined and updated by learning. Being reflective about what you do is a safeguard against lapsing into unconscious incompetence and complacency.

Reflective task

Can you identify a time when your unconscious competence turned out to be unconscious incompetence?

Models of reflection

There are many models or frameworks of reflection and it would serve no useful purpose to try to list and describe all of them here. Not everyone accepts that such models or frameworks are needed or valid. It is best to see them as tools for you to use to reflect, or alternatively as maps that represent reality but are not reality. Models and frameworks of reflection can provide a structured way to process and assimilate our experiences, which are often unclear and confusing. They can provoke valuable questions to ask ourselves and help us to make sense of our world.

Fundamentally, all the models of reflection share similar elements: they take careful note of an incident, strive to understand it, learn from it and then modify the actions that were taken.

Dewey and the process of reflection

Dewey (1933) saw an important distinction between impulsive actions, routine actions and reflective actions. Impulsive actions are based on trial and error. Routine actions are shaped by 'prejudices, that is, prejudgments, not judgments proper that rest upon a survey of evidence' (Dewey, 1910: 4–5). Reflective action is shaped by 'the active, persistent and careful consideration of any belief or supposed form of knowledge in the light of the grounds that support it' (Dewey, 1933: 9), without which, practice is based on random considerations.

Dewey (1933) did not believe that reflection needs to follow a set sequence of stages. However, his theory describing the process of reflection can be summarised broadly as follows:
1. You recognise that a problem or thought-provoking event has happened.
2. You try to interpret the event using existing knowledge and understanding.
3. You use your intelligence and skills to describe and explain the event thoroughly.
4. You use your thoughts from point 3 to change your perceptions and expectations.
5. You alter your approach or thinking in order to improve or change things.

When students read a description of Dewey's stages in reflection, it often reminds them of Piaget's notion of schemas and the processes of adaptation, assimilation, accommodation, equilibration and organisation (Piaget, 1954). Just as Piaget thought that children actively construct knowledge and understanding as they manipulate and explore the world, Dewey thought that individuals develop, deepen and evaluate their knowledge and understanding through reflection.

However, Dewey's theory of reflection can be criticised for emphasising and simplifying the superiority of reflective actions over impulsive and routine actions (Furlong and Maynard, 1995), as if it is always easy to recognise and distinguish the differences in the messiness of lived experiences. It is sometimes seen as being unduly judgemental and dismissive of unreflective practice, and seeing it as having much less moral and ethical value.

Nonetheless, it is important to see Dewey's thinking in its historical context. He was a man of his time who was fiercely critical of unquestioning teaching of rote learning and who could see the links between education and experience, and important issues such as progress, democracy and emancipation. For Dewey reflection is fundamental to achieving these higher purposes.

Schön's theories of reflection

Knowledge-in-action

Schön's model (1983) represents a process that begins with the practice wisdom and common sense that are used in work contexts. Schön (1983) called this underpinning theory translated into action 'knowledge-in-action'. It is often the knowledge about which Polanyi (1967: 4) wrote: 'we can know more than we can tell'. In many ways this is rather like a tacit schema of practice that has been developed thus far. It is the knowledge that is revealed in the way a practitioner approaches problems and carries out tasks. It is very difficult to surface *knowledge-in-action* and make it explicit in words. It is usually derived through observational learning by another person that is offered as feedback or through reflection-on-action.

Reflection-in-action

When a surprise or problem or unexpected issue is encountered that cannot be dealt with using practitioners' knowledge-in-action, the practitioner may seek other answers and solutions in order to understand and manage it. This *reflection-in-action* is informed by the practitioner's knowledge and experience. It occurs in the moment, at a time Schön (1983) calls the 'action-present', while the surprise or problem or unexpected issue is being addressed and when practitioners are thinking what to do as they are doing it, also known as 'thinking on your feet'. The practitioners' *reflections-in-action* guide the ongoing and immediate decisions so that they think in a new way and adjust what they do to meet the needs of the circumstances.

Reflection-on-action

Later *reflection-on-action* occurs when practitioners look back on events, think about what occurred and ask questions in order to understand their experiences and modify their schemas of practice accordingly. It is often a conscious process and sometimes documented.

Double-loop learning

In collaboration with Argyris, Schön developed a theory that practitioners have mental maps or *theories-in-use* that guide their actions, which are different from the theories they say they espouse. *Theories-in-use* are implicit in actions but *espoused theories* are the narratives we use to say what we do or what we would like others to think we do.

Furthermore, goals, values, plans and rules tend to be used in practice rather than questions. Argyris and Schön (1974) describe this as *single-loop learning*. However, when the variables that govern practitioners' actions are scrutinised and questioned, *double-loop learning* occurs, which offers a powerful force for change (Argyris and Schön, 1974).

Schön's ideas about reflection in professional learning are very influential; however, they too have been criticised as being applied too loosely and being based on evidence gathered in professional development sessions about critical cases rather than in everyday practice where a 'routine situation comes to be perceived as problematic' (Eraut, 1994: 13). In response to being criticised for being unrealistic about practitioners' capacities to engage in all his reflective processes at the same time, Schön went on to make distinctions between reflection during actions (*reflection-in-action*) and after actions (*reflection-on-action*) and he acknowledged that some professional actions take place over a period of time (Schön, 1983).

Reflective task

Journal an account of a time when there was a health and safety incident that occurred when you were working with young children. Narrate the account to a student colleague explaining:

- how you felt; what YOU did; why you did it; how you knew what to do (or not) – *reflection-*in-*action*
- why the incident happened; whether you did the right thing; what you could have done differently; what you would do next time – *reflection-*on-*action*.

Together discuss whether it is easy/possible/realistic to reflect-**in**-action.

Greenway and Rolfe

Greenway (1995) proposed a simple model of reflection, a three-stage cycle as shown below.

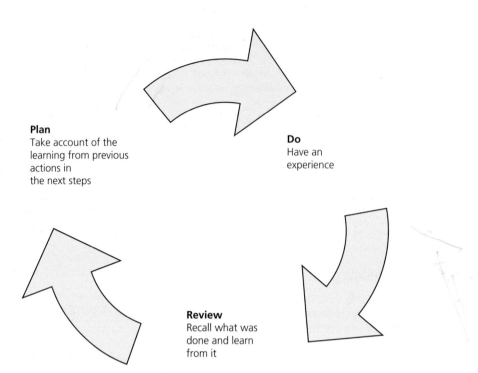

Plan
Take account of the
learning from previous
actions in
the next steps

Do
Have an
experience

Review
Recall what was
done and learn
from it

Figure 2.2 Greenway's reflective cycle (1995)

As early years practitioners you will recognise Greenway's model of reflection in the way you approach child-initiated learning when children 'Plan, Do and Review' their learning. It is an approach used in the High/Scope curriculum (High/Scope Educational Research Foundation, 2003) and also promoted in the Early Years Foundation Stage in which practitioners are advised to 'Model the plan-do-review process yourself' (Early Education, 2012: 7).

Rolfe *et al.* (2001) suggest another very simple framework for reflective practice based on Borton's (1970) developmental model. It asks three questions:

- **What?** (Describing the experience.) What were the gains and losses, feelings and thoughts, issues and outcomes?
- **So what?** (Theorising about what has been learnt.) So what have you learned about yourself, others, possible improvements etc?
- **Now what?** (Identifying the next steps.) Now what can you do so that more can be learned and things can be better?

At first sight, practitioners are bound to appreciate the attractive simplicity of the models from Greenway and Rolfe. However, they provide tools for reflection rather than helping you to understand what reflection is by describing the processes involved.

Kolb's reflective cycle

Kolb's reflective cycle (1984) shares many characteristics with those of Dewey, Schön, Greenway, Rolfe and others. It is widely used, perhaps because it counters any suggestion that reflection is merely academic navel-gazing. What distinguishes it is the emphasis on trying out or testing the learning that occurs as a result of reflection within the reflective cycle. For Kolb (1984), it seems reflection is not complete until 'active experimentation' has occurred.

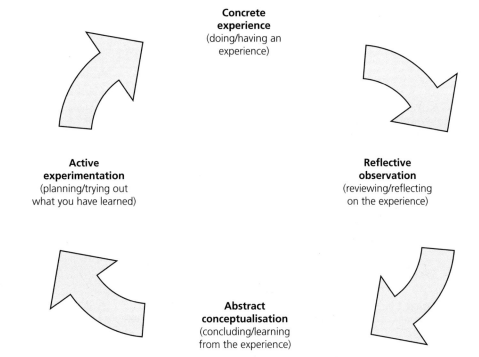

Concrete experience
(doing/having an experience)

Reflective observation
(reviewing/reflecting on the experience)

Active experimentation
(planning/trying out what you have learned)

Abstract conceptualisation
(concluding/learning from the experience)

Figure 2.3 Kolb's reflective cycle (1984)

Like the proverb 'To know and not to act is not to know', Kolb's view is that reflection is realised in the action that it creates.

However, Kolb's model has also been criticised, because it gives little detail about the actual process of reflection, and lacks an evidence base. It is sometimes seen as rigid and sequential in its nature, and simplifying learning from reflection unduly (Smith, 1996).

Reflective task

Try out Kolb's model by applying it to a difficult situation that has occurred recently with a colleague or with a parent of a child in your setting. Describe the event(s). Reflect on them. Identify what you learned. How did you use what you had learned?

Gibbs's reflective cycle

Gibbs's reflective cycle (1998) is used by many practitioners who find it works for them. Gibbs's cycle and also a model proposed by Boud (2001) are unusual in that they make feelings an explicit dimension of their models of reflection, and therefore include 'Feelings' in their frameworks.

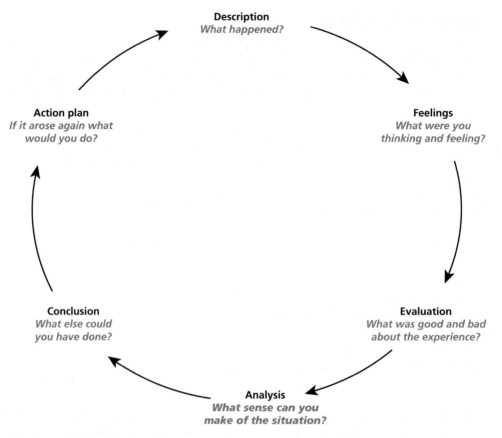

Figure 2.4 Gibbs's reflective cycle (1998)

Unlike Kolb's model, Gibbs's cycle is more specific about the processes of reflection, and so it is often seen as more helpful and useful for people working with children and families, especially with regard to engaging in reflection that has a positive impact on practice.

Reflective task

Now apply Gibbs's model to the same difficult situation that has occurred recently with a colleague or parent of a child that you described above.

- Describe the event(s).
- What were you feeling and thinking?
- What was good and bad about it?
- What sense can you make of it?
- What else could you have done?
- How did you use what you had learned?
- Has Gibbs's model added anything to your reflections on your chosen situation?

Critical reflection

Some models or frameworks aim to facilitate *critical* reflection from which you gain an understanding of the assumptions that dictate your responses. The intention is that you see yourself and your practice as situated in a bigger picture or context. You become more aware of your values, biases and beliefs and the inevitable gap between what you say you believe in (your espoused theories) and what you actually do.

One model of critical reflection is known as the DATA process (Peters, 1994). It suggests you should:

D **D**escribe the problem, task or incident that needs to be looked at and possibly changed.

A **A**nalyse the description, looking at assumptions that were made at the time and also any that are being made about how to respond now.

T **T**heorise about a range of ways to respond to the problem, task or incident.

A **A**ct using one or more of the theories above.

Reflective task

D Can you remember your own first day at school when you were a child?

A What were the beliefs and values from the school that influenced your experiences on that first day?

T How would you meet children's needs on entry to a new setting now? What has changed? Why has it changed? How could it be improved further?

A How could the improvements you describe be put in place?

A rather different approach to critical reflection has been described by Brookfield (1995), who suggests that in order to achieve a balanced view of your practice you should look at reality from four different perspectives.

Figure 2.5 Brookfield's critically reflective lenses (1995)

- **Assumption analysis** refers to your own viewpoint (personal reflections – typically carried out using a reflective diary).
- **Contextual awareness** includes your colleagues' viewpoints (reflections resulting from mentoring, professional conversations, engagement in professional development and communities of practice).
- **Imaginative speculation** would encompass the viewpoints of learners (reflections drawing on feedback from children).
- **Reflective scepticism** refers to the viewpoints offered by theoretical literature (reflections as a result of reading about subjects linked to your practice, which challenge your thinking and help you to see how what you do fits into wider trends).

These are four critically reflective lenses to look through and ask yourself, 'What were the assumptions made by each perspective?' Brookfield (1995) suggests that critical reflection consists of:

- analysing assumptions to explore how they affect what you do
- considering how society and culture influence your assumptions
- imagining another way of thinking to challenge your existing one (counter-intuitive thinking)
- being reflectively sceptical about anything that is taken as a universal truth or certainty.

Reflective task

Think about the first day for children in your setting:

- What assumptions do you make about the needs of children on their first day in your setting? Where do these assumptions come from?
- What views do your colleagues have of children and their needs in their first day in the setting? Where do these views come from?
- Are these views different from those of parents? Where do you think the parents' views come from?
- What assumptions do the children make? Do they assume that they only need to attend once? That you and your colleagues live at the setting and do not go home at night?
- What about the assumptions in theories of child development and concepts of childhood? How do they underpin your expectations of children on their first day in a new setting?

Another approach to critical reflection is critical incident analysis (Blade and Wolf, 1990). This approach is similar to case-study research. The critical incident you analyse does not need to be a dramatic or negative event. It is an incident you think or feel is significant. Perhaps it gave you pause for thought and raised new questions in your mind or perhaps it made you look differently at your behaviour, beliefs, attitudes, values, interactions or working practices. It might be something that went especially well or was very difficult or demanding, or had an unexpected consequence or reaction from others. You examine a typical incident or example – one that illustrates a general point – and identify problems or issues to explore further. An example would be to investigate the experience of a child with a mobility difficulty when he or she plays outside. You might be able to identify barriers to inclusion that could be removed. This process should also help to increase your awareness of any knowledge-in-action and hidden assumptions that you might hold about mobility difficulties.

Because Critical Incident Analysis has been widely used in healthcare and medicine when things go wrong and in the aircraft industry when a fatal or near-fatal event occurs, it is easy to see the word 'critical' as meaning evaluating in order to identify what needs to be improved, i.e. what is deficient or problematic. In fact, critical incident analysis works in much the same way as critical reflection, where you are trying to achieve a balanced view of your practice. Compare this to a theatre critic, who is just as likely to report that a play or concert is unmissable (and why), as he is to report that it is a waste of the ticket money (and why).

The examples of models or frameworks above are not a definitive list of approaches to critical reflection, but they do help to illustrate how you can explore the informal theory that guides and shapes your practice. You may find it hard to describe or articulate this informal theory, even though you use it all the time – you probably perceive it as common sense.

In addition to informal theory, there is a whole body of formal theory that you use to guide your practice. For example, you may expect to describe children's development in a linear, sequential way because many theorists such as Freud, Piaget and Erikson have described developmental change in stages. If you have used a developmental checklist in the last few weeks, your assumptions were underpinned by Freud, Piaget and Erikson's theories of development!

Using a learning journal, blog or diary

As an early years practitioner, you regularly use the professional skill of observation of children, and this means that you are well aware that a factual narrative can be a rich source of analysis and reflection. In the same way, a regular journal can be a very useful source of evidence for your professional and personal development action plan. It can help you to become more self-aware and reflective and can provide evidence of progress to develop your self-esteem, professionalism and confidence (Boud, 2001). You may find that you need to keep this journal entirely private in order to enable you to write it in a frank and honest way and remain true to yourself. An example of a journal entry is shown below:

---

10 August 2012

It is so frustrating that I can't get on with my interviews for my research on what parents think about homework for children younger than 7. I really should have planned things better and carried out the survey before the term ended and everyone disappeared for the holiday. Talking to my sister Louise today I realised that people have different ideas about what actually constitutes homework. Louise thinks that homework includes my niece, Georgina, pairing up socks and counting them in twos as well as learning the two times table by heart (as set by her teacher). Maybe I should have defined what I meant by homework more clearly before starting…

Portfolio building

Obviously, assessment methods vary considerably across the wide range of foundation and undergraduate early years degree courses. However, many courses will require some element of portfolio building as part of the assessment process, and skill in creating a portfolio is essential in order to gain Early Years Professional Status and Qualified Teacher Status. The work-based assessment aspect of your programme is a very significant feature. Generally, a list of learning outcomes is provided by your university or college. You should be able to meet many of the learning outcomes using evidence generated from your existing work role or from your placements. This evidence will need to be collected together and organised in a portfolio. The process of creating, organising and cross-referencing a portfolio is a challenging task. If you have already taken an NVQ you will have some experience of portfolio building. Many students take great pride and pleasure in ensuring that their portfolio is of a high quality.

You will need to be determined, alert to opportunities and very organised in your pursuit of evidence. Your university or college tutor will advise you about what constitutes valid and acceptable evidence for your portfolio. Generally there is a requirement that evidence is sufficient (for the learning outcome or competence being claimed) and authentic (directly attributable to the candidate). Usually the portfolio will include witness statements, signed observations of you, child observations, supervisor reports, 'products' such as policies and other working documents, photographs, minutes of meetings, letters, reports, videos, reflective accounts, work plans and samples of children's work.

Next steps

Top tips for starting your portfolio

- Decide how you will organise your portfolio NOW.
- Colour coordinate the file or select a particular font or type of paper. Having your own distinctive style can encourage your sense of ownership of your portfolio.
- Decide where the learning outcomes and evidence will go and how you will separate them – using dividers or index tabs.
- Design and set up a template or pro forma on your laptop or computer that can be used to record your evidence.
- Spend half an hour each week reviewing your portfolio and planning how to get the necessary evidence – what you have, what you still need.
- Talk to your mentor, line manager or critical friend to hear their ideas about how you could provide the evidence needed.
- A potential employer may be interested in seeing your portfolio. Bear this possible audience in mind as you create it.

Belonging and reflective practice

It would be wrong to characterise reflection and reflective practice as mostly individualistic or solitary. If you are fortunate enough to belong to a community of practice in your workplace or a professional learning community while you attend a course, you have the opportunity to reflect alongside fellow practitioners. Currently both of the terms 'community of practice' and 'learning community' are widely used in education and care, sometimes interchangeably (Samaras *et al.*, 2008). Wenger's view (2008: para 1) is: 'In a nutshell: communities of practice are groups of people who share a concern or a passion for something they do and learn to do it better as they interact regularly.' Kemmis (1982, cited NCSL, 2008b: 8) describes a learning community as: 'a self-reflective community of practitioners – theorists committed to critically examining their own practices and improving them'. Many practitioners nowadays extend the definition of a learning community to include everyone in the setting: children, parents, practitioners and all other adults. Reflective practice is rooted in participation and partnership. Arnold and Whalley continue this theme in Chapter 14 in this book. Research by Hatton and Smith (1995) showed that interaction with another person, which involves talking with, questioning or confronting that person, promotes reflection by facilitating a safe environment in which you can risk disclosing your views and revealing your experiences. When you are able to do this you have the opportunity to take a step back from your actions, ideas and beliefs, and hold them up for scrutiny, seeing them through the eyes of an early years colleague. Reflecting on your practice is an element which is core to professional supervision and has become a statutory requirement within the EYFS (DfE, 2012a). See also Chapter 5, page 116, about reflective practice and supervision.

Reflective stories of practice are constructed through engagement with others who are members of your professional community in a social and interactive process in which you internalise and externalise stories you tell and hear about yourself as an early years practitioner. The people who tell stories about you, and to whom you tell stories of your practice, co-author your reflections. This is because people convert the stories of other speakers about themselves into the first person particularly if the other speakers are what Sfard and Prusak (2005: 11) call: '*Significant narrators,* the owners of the most influential voices … carriers of those cultural messages that will have the greatest impact on one's actions'.

Feedback

The feedback you gain from the sources in your professional context can influence and sustain your reflections on your practice. Before we consider some of the 'significant narrators' and givers of feedback who might be available to you it is worth exploring Johns's framework of reflection (2000) as a way of structuring shared reflections.

Johns's framework for reflection

Johns's framework for reflection (2000) recognises the value of the role of others in guiding and encouraging reflective practice. Johns (2000) argues for a highly structured approach to reflection because, rather like an agenda for a meeting, it helps participants to collaborate. Johns (2000) designed the framework with nurses in mind, so the details that follow have been adjusted slightly to work for early years practitioners. The framework has as its central feature five key cues or provocations, with each one intended to lead to a series of questions.

1. Description of the experience
- Phenomenon – describe the here and now experience
- Causal – what essential factors contributed to this experience?
- Context – what are the significant background factors to this experience?
- Clarifying – what are the key processes for reflection in this experience?

2. Reflection
- What was I trying to achieve?
- Why did I intervene as I did?
- What were the consequences of my actions for:
  - myself?
  - the child/family?
  - the people I work with?
- How did I feel about this experience when it was happening?
- How did the child feel about it?
- How do I know how the child felt about it?

3. Influencing factors
- What internal factors influenced my decision making?
- What external factors influenced my decision making?
- What sources of knowledge influenced/should have influenced my decision making?

4. Could I have dealt with the situation better?

- What other choices did I have?
- What would be the consequences of these choices?

5. Learning

- How do I now feel about this experience?
- How have I made sense of this experience in light of past experiences and future practice?
- How has this experience changed my ways of knowing:
    - empirics – scientific
    - ethics – moral knowledge
    - personal – self-awareness
    - aesthetics – the art of what we do, our own experiences.

Johns (2000) sees his framework as part of a system of guided reflections that would support a community of practice and mentoring relationships. Its emphasis is on reflecting about real-world practice issues, using structured formats such as logs, diaries, blogs, feedback and portfolios as supportive materials. For Johns (2000), *sharing* reflections on learning experiences gives greater understanding of those experiences and faster learning from them than reflecting as a single individual.

Reflective task

Draw up two lists showing where you might obtain evidence to help you assess your effectiveness in:

- your job role
- your professional development or student role.

Discuss what you have written with a fellow student or early years colleague.

Your lists probably included feedback received from your line manager when you were last appraised or observed, as well as comments from children, parents, peers, family, friends, tutors and other students. It might also be interesting to ask for feedback from colleagues whom you manage while reflecting on the effect of any power dynamic that is likely to exist.

The important thing is to see the feedback as a gift from someone who has your best interests at heart – to invite it and welcome it.

As well as learning to receive feedback constructively (Cottrell, 2008) you may need to develop your skill in giving feedback to someone else. The principles are generally the same. You should check that:

- the receiver wants and is ready to receive the feedback
- there is an appropriate length of time to discuss it fully
- the context is conducive, relevant and non-threatening
- the feedback has been heard correctly
- the feedback is expressed in descriptive rather than evaluative or judgemental language
- the feedback is delivered in a 'sandwich' or layered approach.

The feedback 'sandwich' or layered approach is:

- a statement of intention to be helpful and supportive
- positive comments and acknowledgement of strengths
- an area for development
- an opportunity for the receiver of feedback to comment
- a restatement or summary and thanks
- the receiver of the feedback has the last word

Figure 2.6 The feedback 'sandwich' or layered approach

Unfortunately, now you are aware of this widely used approach, you will expect positive comments to be followed by areas for development!

Being and having a critical friend

Fellow learners on your degree programme can be a valuable source of feedback too, particularly if you enter into an informal contract as 'study buddies' or 'critical friends'. The fullest definition of a critical friend, and the one quoted frequently by writers on the subject, is:

> *A person who asks provocative questions, provides data to be examined through another lens, and offers critiques of a person's work as a friend. A critical friend takes the time to fully understand the context of the work presented and the outcomes that the person or group is working toward. The friend is an advocate for the success of that work.*
>
> (Costa and Kallick, 1993: 50)

A critical friend can be seen as someone who not only has a different perspective on your actions, your opinions or your work, but also assists you to see the familiar in a new light. A critical friend's viewpoint assumes even greater credibility if it is informed by an understanding of the situation.

As suggested earlier, 'critical' can appear to have unhelpful, negative connotations, and 'friend' could imply a lack of professionalism, but together they describe a role that combines the elements of non-judgemental support, benevolent support and assistance implied by 'friend' and, at the same time, provision of an external perspective and challenge implied by 'critical'.

A critical friend is someone who has 'a licence to help', who brings a particular perspective which is informed by an understanding of the situation, but who maintains an element of detachment. They build and maintain a relationship of trust, balancing friendship and critique, with the emphasis on being a *friend* to the person and a *critic* of the actions of that person. A critical friend aims to motivate and reassure, and seeks to enable those they work with to become more self-sufficient and skilled at self-improvement.

The overall aim of a critical friendship is to support improvement through empowerment, by demonstrating a positive regard for people, and providing an informed critique of processes and practices. In carrying out this role, the higher education critical friend will observe, listen and learn, demonstrate positive regard for their colleague/fellow student, help to identify issues and explore alternatives, offer sources of evidence and/or expertise, work collaboratively and encourage collaboration and the sharing of ideas, and offer a thoughtful critical perspective. However, he or she will not assume a directive role, offer solutions to problems or provide 'quick fixes', rush to judgement, have hidden agendas or impose their own agendas.

Reflective task

Think about the role, function and benefits of a critical friend as described above. Now write down three ways that a fellow student or early years colleague could have helped you to improve a recent report or assignment or difficult situation at work by being a critical friend.

Mentoring

Schön (1987: 309) describes the 'reflective practicum' as a setting or environment which is designed for practice learning and is a 'bridge between the worlds of university and practice'. The student practitioner learns by doing, while being coached or mentored in order to engage in and improve his or her capacity to reflect-in-action, where possible through reciprocal reflection-on-action with their coach or mentor. Schön (1987: 171) saw the 'reflective practicum' or work-based learning as offering 'high interpersonal intensity' in which the coach or mentor is crucial.

You will find that individual courses have different requirements in terms of mentoring. You may have both specific mentoring arrangements and also more informal ones. A workplace mentor can be a very useful source of feedback. The mentoring relationship will vary from learner to learner and will be shaped by the expectations of both mentor and 'mentee' or protégé. It is difficult to define mentoring other than in a very general sense, but fundamentally it is a process that enables the mentor to use their experience to help the mentee to learn more quickly, more reflectively or more deeply than they would have done otherwise. In general, the skill of mentoring 'involves primarily listening with empathy, sharing experience and learning (usually mutually), professional friendship, developing insight through reflection, being a sounding board, encouraging' (Clutterbuck, 1991, cited in Gardiner, 1998: 77).

Colwell (1998) noted that mentorship has a crucial role in the socialisation processes of an individual into workplace culture. Dialogue, challenge, critical examination and reflection on practice can also be part of a mentoring relationship. Pollard (2002: 381) establishes the link between reflection and mentoring in the context of teaching:

> Reflection is the process through which teachers become aware of the complexity of their work and are able to take actions which impact positively on this. Mentoring provides a stimulus, drawing on accumulated professional knowledge and experience, which can help teachers to reflect with purpose and focus. Taken together then, reflection and mentoring help to inform and build a culture of professional learning.

In your education and training to work with children you may have come across Bruner's analogy of 'scaffolding' learning (1975). Scaffolding is a process in which students are given support until they can apply new skills and strategies independently (Rosenshine and Meister, 1992). Being mentored can be seen as a way to scaffold your learning as an early years professional.

A good mentoring relationship is dynamic and evolving, based on trust and mutual respect. It can be extremely valuable for the mentor and mentee to draw up an informal contract, outlining how the mentoring relationship will work. This will help you both to agree your expectations, and to establish any specific goals, as well as setting boundaries. You may need to decide how frequently and for how long you will meet and the kinds of topics and activities you will discuss within the mentoring relationship.

If you work in a school setting it is possible that someone on the staff has already had a great deal of experience being a mentor to teaching practice students or newly qualified teachers. Quite often, however, your mentor is new to the role and may feel quite daunted by it. They may feel responsible for you and your success on your degree programme. What matters when you are looking for a mentor is that they take on the role freely and gladly, that they wish to see you succeed and that they can support you but also challenge you – in much the same way as a critical friend. It is an added bonus if your mentor can use their influence to open doors for you so that you can gain further experience. You can support your mentor by sharing information about your programme, your assignments and your work-based portfolio. Mentors often report that they pick up new ideas and improve their own practice through the mentoring relationship. One of their motivations for being a mentor may be that they were helped by someone who was a mentor to them when they were starting out in their career.

Figure 2.7 While you are being mentored you are also learning how to be a mentor

One of the more difficult aspects for mentors and mentees is that in some early years degree programmes the mentor supports the student but also assesses them in the workplace. The mentor can feel that there is a conflict of roles in such circumstances. Remember that the mentor is accountable to your organisation for the supervision of your practice and must try to ensure that you work with children in a safe, sensitive and effective way, as well as liaising with your university or college tutors.

Mentoring is a key way in which you become socialised into your role as a practitioner. Törnebohm's view of socialisation (1986) explains how reflection can influence a participant's capacity to learn, practise and respond to change. Törnebohm (1986) compares professional socialisation to a process whereby you acquire a lens which filters your attention to selected features of the professional world so you think about it in particular ways. This lens changes your observable professional behaviour and your individual internal view of the world and so influences what you pay attention to and how you use your knowledge of theory and practice, as well as your evaluations of what is good and bad practice, which problems you notice and how you decide to solve them. In turn, your internal world view influences your practice.

Conclusion

Early years practice remains a national priority and is viewed by successive governments as a tool for social engineering so that health, happiness and children's potential learning are maximised, and crime, poor parenting and low achievement are minimised. Faced with this pressure to facilitate a cure for society's ills through your work and the ever-changing demands of early years practice, reflective practice can help you to maintain some professional control and autonomy and provide you with professional development and resilience.

I hope you agree that reflection, reflexivity and critical reflection help you to be a much better early years practitioner because you become:

- more open to other perspectives
- self-aware
- in control of your own way of working
- a more effective learner
- self-monitoring
- a source of your own development
- resilient.

These are vital skills and habits to have.

Evaluate your...

Reflective response to reading

As you read the other chapters of this book, apply this framework for reflection (Rolfe *et al.*, 2001), asking three questions:

- What? (Retelling what you have read.)
- So what? (Identifying the meaning and implications of what you have learned.)
- Now what? (Identifying the next steps for you as a result of what you have read.)

How far does new learning influence your early years practice?

Further reading

Cottrell, S. (2008) *The Study Skills Handbook* (3rd edn), Basingstoke: Palgrave Macmillan.

Ghaye, T. (2011) *Teaching and Learning Through Reflective Practice: A Practical Guide for Positive Action*, Abingdon: Routledge.

Lindon, J. (2010) *Reflective Practice and Early Years Professionalism: Linking Theory and Practice*, London: Hodder.

Moon, J. (2004) *A Handbook of Reflective and Experiential Learning: Theory and Practice*, London: Routledge Falmer.

Paige-Smith, A. and Craft, A. (eds.) (2008) *Developing Reflective Practice in the Early Years*, Maidenhead: Open University Press.

Pollard, A. (2008) *Reflective Teaching: Evidence Informed Practice* (3rd edn), London, New York: Continuum.

Reed, M. and Canning, N. (eds.) (2010) *Reflective Practice in the Early Years*, London: SAGE.

Robins, A. (ed.) (2007) *Mentoring in the Early Years*, London: Paul Chapman Publishing.

Thompson, S. and Thompson, N. (2008) *The Critically Reflective Practitioner*, Basingstoke: Palgrave Macmillan.

3

Listening to young children
Alison McLeod

Introduction

Why should a whole chapter of this book be given over to listening to children? Early years staff may well feel that they listen to children all day and that listening is just a matter of common sense. Unfortunately, the evidence suggests that many people who work in education and care settings are poor listeners: they do not try to understand the perspective of the young people they are working with, they do not routinely ask them what they think or how they are feeling. The result is likely to be that children's needs are less well met than they might be. In a worst-case scenario, abuse or neglect could go undetected: children have died when professionals who might have listened to them have failed to do so.

This chapter will explain what true listening means, why it is important and how we can learn to be more attentive to children. This knowledge can help early years staff to hear the voices of the young people they work with more clearly and can make their interventions more effective. Listening is a core skill, perhaps the most important skill of all those that people in the children's workforce need to learn.

Learning outcomes

This chapter will help you to reflect on your own practices and attitudes around communicating with young children, seeking to understand their perspective, finding out their wishes and feelings, and promoting their age-appropriate autonomy. By the end of the chapter you should have some knowledge and understanding of:

- The meaning and value of 'listening' as it applies to adults working with children in early years settings.
- The history of children's rights.
- Law and policy relating to the voice of the child: the *Convention on the Rights of the Child* (United Nations, 1989); the Children Acts of 1989 and 2004; *The Common Core of Skills and Knowledge for the Children's Workforce* (CWDC, 2010a); the Childcare Act 2006; the *Statutory Framework for the Early Years Foundation Stage* (DfE, 2012a).
- Research findings which throw light on how adults can best communicate with young children, elicit and understand their views.
- The practical application of these research findings in early years settings.

Why should we listen to children?

Listening means more than keeping half an ear open while children are playing so as to be able to intervene if it sounds as though things are getting out of hand. The kind of listening referred to here is an active process. It involves the adult going out of their way to try and find out what the child thinks and how they feel. It encompasses careful observation and assessment of children's development, demeanour and behaviour, as well as hearing what they say and trying to puzzle out what they may mean. Kjørholt *et al.* (2005) describe listening as a sensitive awareness of another person which should be an integral part of all the time a worker spends with a child. Similarly, Lefevre (2010) sees listening as the central means of achieving empathy – the ability to step into someone's shoes and see things from their point of view. She points out that 'as well as listening to the words, workers also need to listen "with the third ear", that is, to what is not being said, to what may be being thought and felt and to the wider social and cultural context of the communication' (Lefevre, 2010: 135).

Getting inside the head of a child with limited communication skills presents particular challenges but nevertheless remains crucial if children's individual needs are to be met. An adult may have to take the initiative in setting up situations where children can share their views and this may involve providing children with materials or equipment to promote their self-expression; in some cases interpreters or specialist communication systems may be required.

There is a pragmatic reason for finding out the views of the children we work with: we do not want to waste our time, and if we fail to ask what individual children want we may not be able to guess the best way to help them. For example, Paige-Smith and Rix (2011), researching early intervention programmes with children with Down's syndrome, discovered that when the children chose activities for themselves they were more interested in them, engaged more fully and learnt more from them than when adults selected activities for them. More importantly, perhaps, if we regularly encourage young people to share their triumphs and their worries with us, and demonstrate that we will take these seriously, they are more likely to tell us if they are being ill-treated, bullied or neglected, and this then will allow us to take steps to safeguard their welfare. Not to ask about their concerns, or failing to act when they do share them, 'entraps them in lethal silence' (Freeman, 1999: 52).

Reflective task

- Read the report on the death of Peter Connelly (Haringey Local Children Safeguarding Board, 2009).
- Identify missed opportunities when professionals could have listened to Baby Peter but failed to do so.
- Reflect on what you could have done, had you been in their position, to ensure that Peter's voice was heard.

There are other benefits claimed for listening to children. Think how you feel when someone listens attentively to your opinion and takes it seriously. Then consider how you feel when someone contemptuously rejects your contribution to a debate. It is no different for a child, even a small one. When we genuinely consult with a young person it enhances their self-esteem and helps them to build a positive sense of their own identity (Eide and Winger, 2005). There are examples of how this works from many spheres. Kinney (2005), for example, reported on a project seeking the views of children in an early years setting in Scotland. The experience of being heard respectfully by adults who were prepared to make changes to the way the setting was run in response to their views led the children to become more confident, to listen better to staff and to each other, and to be more assertive on entry to primary school. The consultation also led to improvements in the way the setting was run.

Butler *et al.* (2002) found that children consulted about their parents' divorce felt more in control and hence less distressed than those who were not. Munro (2001) argues that children in public care cope better and feel under less stress if they are involved in the planning for their own care at an appropriate level. Sinclair (2000) observed that being consulted improves children's problem-solving skills, while Gilligan (1999) provided evidence that the ability to work out solutions to problems makes children more resilient: it helps them weather the storms of life. Furthermore, Hillman (2006) asserts that children need to practise making choices from an early age so that they can learn how to make good ones.

Reflective task

- Think back to your own childhood.
- Recall an occasion when adults failed to take account of your wishes when making a decision.
- How did that make you feel?
- How would you have preferred the adults to have responded at the time?

Because there is so much evidence that it enhances children's well-being if adults listen to them, and that it can also improve delivery of services, it can be argued that it is an obligation on childcare staff to seek children's views. This is why some writers regard listening as not just a skill but an ethical issue. Kjørholt *et al.* (2005: 178) concluded that: 'listening is first and foremost about an ethic of openness to and respect for the other'. In other words, childcare staff should listen to children because it would be wrong to do anything else.

The voice of the child through history

There is another reason why professionals should consider the views and wishes of young people seriously, and that is because the law says we must. The voice of the child is central to the concept of children's rights. This is because those who are 'seen and not heard' can be oppressed: wrongs cannot be put right unless those who suffer them can express their grievances and demand change.

This begs the question: are children oppressed? We may not feel they are now; however, historically they certainly have been. Under British (and Australian and US) law up until the 19th century, children were treated as possessions of their parents rather than as people in their own right. Attitudes changed gradually through the 20th century. The *Declaration of the Rights of the Child* published in 1924 by the League of Nations (the precursor of the United Nations) was an important milestone (Fuller, 1951), but it was not about children's right to be heard, rather about their right to protection and to services to meet their basic needs: adults were expected to act on the child's behalf. Further laws were introduced increasing rights to services and protection for children, but the right of children to self-determination was slower to gain favour. It was not until the 1970s that the idea of respecting children as people capable of making their own decisions began to be recognised in law. In England the Children Act 1975 gave children their first legal right to a voice when it included the clause: 'The Court must ascertain and give due consideration to the wishes and feelings of the child.' A decade later a committee advised the government on changes required to childcare law:

> The idea that the child belongs to his family, to the extent that it denotes ownership, is no longer accepted as valid ... a child is an independent person with a complete and separate identity ... He should only be protected to the extent he is less than fully capable of self-determination.
>
> (Social Services Committee, 1984: para 16).

In 1986 a landmark legal decision known as the Gillick judgment or Fraser ruling (made in a case where a mother challenged the local health authority's right to give contraceptive advice to her under-age daughters without her knowledge), gave the competent child the right to make their own decisions, even when these conflict with the wishes of their parents. 'Parental right yields to the child's right to make his own decisions when he reaches a sufficient understanding and intelligence to be capable of making up his mind on the matter requiring decision' (House of Lords, 1986).

1989 was a key year for children's rights. The *Convention on the Rights of the Child* (United Nations, 1989) was passed and has since been ratified by almost every country in the world. Article 12 says:

> States parties shall assure to the child who is capable of forming his or her own views the right to express those views in all matters affecting the child, the view of the child being given due weight in accordance with the age and maturity of the child.
>
> (United Nations, 1989)

The same year, in England and Wales the Children Act 1989 was passed with all-party support, the key sections being Section 1(3)(a): 'A court shall have regard in particular to the ascertainable wishes and feelings of the child concerned (considered in the light of his age and understanding)', and Sections 22(4)(a) and 22(5): 'When any decision is made about a child who is, or may be, looked after by a Local Authority, the child's wishes and feelings must be ascertained and given due consideration (having regard to his age and understanding)'. The Children (Scotland) Act was passed in 1995 and contained a similar clause.

This requirement, that children's views must be taken into consideration before decisions are made which may affect them, has been incorporated into subsequent childcare legislation and guidance in the UK. The Family Law Act 1996 said children's wishes and feelings must be considered in divorce cases; the Adoption and Children Act 2002 extended the same expectation to adoption cases; the Children Act 2004 added family support and child protection services to the list, and associated guidance required local authorities to consider children's views when developing policies. Of particular relevance to early years workers is the Childcare Act 2006, which stipulated that local authorities must consider the views of children five years and younger when providing services for them.

Guidance supporting these laws stressed the importance of staff who work with children having the skills necessary to elicit children's views. *The Common Core of Skills and Knowledge for the Children's Workforce* (CWDC, 2010a) names the first essential skill for childcare workers as 'communication and engagement', further breaking this down into skills of listening and building empathy, summarising and explaining, consultation and negotiation, plus knowledge of how communication works, sources of support and the importance of respect. Similarly, the *Statutory Framework for the Early Years Foundation Stage* (EYFS) (DfE, 2012a) identifies 'communication and language' as one of the three prime areas of children's development, and in the associated guidance it is spelt out what staff can do:

> **Make time to listen to children respectfully and kindly, and explain to all the children why this is important. Children will then know that they will be listened to when they raise injustices.**

(Early Education, 2012: 14)

It is thus very clear that the law expects professionals to seek the views of children, both individually and as a group, when planning and delivering services and before any decision is taken which will have an impact on an individual child. This applies to children of all ages, even the very young, although there is a get-out clause, in that, having ascertained the children's views and given them 'due consideration', the views can then be discounted if the child is not of sufficient age, maturity or intelligence to understand the matter at issue. Some would argue that this is unjust, and that even young children are more than capable of making their minds up on issues affecting their lives and should be allowed to make unwise choices: 'At the core of a rights-based philosophy is the acknowledgment that those with rights will sometimes do things we think wrong' (Freeman, 1999: 53). On the other hand, others believe that the child's right to participate in decisions can potentially conflict with their right to be protected and that judgements about what is in the best interests of the child's welfare should take precedence over the child's wishes, which may in any case be complex and contradictory (Schofield, 2005).

Kjørholt (2005) further argues that there are other values (for example, respect for others) which should be placed above the value of self-determination. Thomas (2002: 46) concludes that 'every person has full human rights, but that the exercise of those rights varies with the circumstances'. So, for example, an adult unconscious following an accident has a right to care and protection that they did not previously need, whereas they will temporarily be unable to exercise the right to self-determination that they took for granted only the day before. Similarly a young child has the right both to care and protection *and* to self-determination, but the former takes precedence when a judgement can be made that to follow their own wishes would put them at significant risk. Professionals working with young children have to make daily decisions balancing these sometimes difficult priorities.

Reflective task

Examine your own views on children and autonomy. How much say should a four-year-old have in the following decisions?

- Parents are divorcing. Both parents want the child to live with them.
- A dentist recommends cosmetic treatment for crooked teeth. The child has had the treatment explained and says he/she does not want it.
- The child's parent has a new job 50 miles away and wants the family to move. The child does not want to leave his/her friends.

Supposing the child were nine or 15, how much say do you think they should have?

You can consider these questions on your own or you could discuss them with colleagues.

Barriers to hearing children's voices

It is clear, then, that for practical, ethical and legal reasons children's voices should be heard by the professionals who work with them, but does this actually happen in today's workplace? In 1991 Wittmer and Honig studied teachers in early years settings and found that they did not encourage children to express their thoughts, rather they limited and controlled the contributions they could make to class discussion. Might practice have improved since? Sadly, for the most part, the answer would appear to be 'No'. There is now a substantial body of more current literature on the topic of listening to children in a wide range of settings and in a number of countries, and its overall findings make disappointing reading.

Shemmings (2000) studied the attitudes of different UK professionals working in the field of child protection and found many quite opposed to children being allowed autonomy even in minor matters. Auberry and Dahl (2006) interviewed young children receiving family support services and found they had little understanding of what these services were for and limited involvement in relevant decisions. Archard and Skiveness (2009) researched the attitudes of social workers in England and Norway and found them quick to dismiss children's views where they conflicted with those of adults. Winter (2010) found that young children in care lacked information, explanations and opportunities to express their feelings and felt that their social workers did not really listen to their concerns.

The findings on consulting with young children about the delivery of early years services are no more positive. Te One (2006) studied practice in New Zealand and found that consultation with children was mainly carried out on the adults' terms and amounted to little more than window dressing. In the same year, Linsey and McAuliffe (2006: 405) identified only 'pockets of good practice' in Britain. Four years later the situation was little improved according to Day (2010). In fact, as Kelley (2006) demonstrates, even though the government's rhetoric encourages consultation with children, when the Department for Education and Skills, as it then was, consulted with children in care about one of their own policies (creation of a national computer database containing children's personal information) and the young people raised objections, their views were simply ignored. Involving children in policy formation, Kelley (2006: 37) concludes, is 'a radical idea, one which opens up exciting possibilities … but it is also profoundly challenging'. Why should this be?

Reflective task

Why don't adults always listen to children? What gets in the way? Take a moment to think about what sorts of barriers get in the way of early years staff habitually hearing and respecting the views of the young children they work with.

You may have thought of a range of different reasons why professionals fail to hear children's voices. Garbarino and Stott (1992: 15–17) identify four areas critical to effective communication, in each of which problems may arise. These are:

- the child's 'competence'
- the child's 'orientation'

- the adult's 'competence'
- the adult's 'orientation'.

The first is the child's 'competence': he or she may not yet have learnt to speak or may have limited language development; some children do not speak English; others have disabilities such as hearing loss or a learning difficulty which can impede their ability to express themselves; or the child may not understand the question at stake. The second set of barriers can be created by the child's 'orientation' or attitude towards communication with the adult: this might just be a shy child, or perhaps one who has been taught that children should be 'seen and not heard' and so finds it difficult to grasp that staff seriously want to know what he or she thinks. The child may say what they think the adult wants to hear in an effort to please them; in some cases children may have learnt to distrust all adults or may even have been specifically told not to pass on certain information.

Scenario

Stephen's scarf

This story illustrates how when a child is reluctant to talk about an experience it may require careful and sensitive handling from an adult to find out what has happened.

Three-year-old Stephen arrived at nursery on a hot summer's day with a thick woollen scarf tied around his neck. When a member of staff went to help him take off his outdoor clothes Stephen held on tight to his scarf, saying 'I'm not allowed to take it off.' The staff member was surprised by this response but left the scarf and observed Stephen for a while. She saw that he was more subdued than usual, did not seem to be his usual outgoing self and kept putting his hands to his neck, so she decided that she should investigate further. 'That scarf's too hot for a day like this, I can see you're uncomfortable,' she said. 'Let's hang it up on the pegs until you go home.' Stephen allowed her to take it off and she was shocked to see that it had been hiding red marks all round his neck. 'Your neck looks sore,' she commented quietly. 'Yes,' said Stephen, 'Daddy strangled me.'

Other barriers to effective communication are located within the adult. There can be problems with the adult's 'competence': not all adults are skilled at listening to children. 'Competent' adults observe children and interpret their play and behaviour; they create situations where children can express their views and feelings using appropriate props; they use language and concepts at a level that children can understand and respond to; they take account of individuals' special needs. The adult who lacks these skills will find it harder to discover what children really think.

Finally there is the question of adult 'orientation' or attitude: an adult who does not believe that it is possible to find out what young children think, or who thinks it does not matter, or who simply cannot be bothered to try and find out will discover very little. Finding out the perspective of young children is time-consuming, and paperwork and procedures can get in the way (Winter, 2009). There is also the question of erosion of adult power. Kinney (2005) found some children's centre staff were threatened by a consultation exercise because of the possibility that their established practices would have to be changed in response to the views of the young people who used the service.

However, after considering the evidence on how best to communicate with children as well as the many barriers that can prevent adults from hearing children's voices clearly, Garbarino and Stott conclude:

We believe that when adults adopt an empathic orientation to children and demonstrate the highest possible level of competence, the process of adult–child communication can succeed well beyond conventional expectations, expectations that are based on a devaluing of children and less than optimal adult performance.

(Garbarino and Stott, 1992: 317)

Knowledge, skills and values for listening to children

We have seen that it is an expectation from government that childcare staff should be competent at communicating with children. 'Good communication is central to working with children. [This] is not just about the words you use, but also about your manner of speaking, body language and, above all, the effectiveness with which you listen' (CWDC, 2010a). Practitioners will want to know, however, exactly what it is that will make their listening effective. Michelle Lefevre, in her useful book on communicating with children (2010), divides what is required into *knowing, doing* and *being*, corresponding to the three domains of knowledge, skills and values.

Knowledge

Firstly most authorities agree that early years staff need to understand child development. Even if you feel very knowledgeable about child development it can be helpful to remind yourself what level of linguistic and cognitive development can be expected of children of different ages.

Reflective task

Ages and stages

- Get a copy of *From Birth to Five Years* (Sheridan, 2008) or a similar text listing developmental milestones.
- Identify all items relating to language or cognition.
- Think of some children you know of different ages between birth and five years.
- Do their levels of speech and understanding coincide with the stages laid out in the book? In which areas are they ahead of the 'average' child and in which areas are they behind?
- What does this tell you about the use of developmental charts?
- Make links to the EYFS (DfE, 2012a).

You may well have concluded from this exercise that developmental charts can only give you a rough guide to any individual child's development, so consulting with them needs to be done in a discriminating way. Children grow and change at different rates, never coinciding exactly with the construct that is the 'average' child. In fact the risk of seeing children as having something 'wrong' with them if they do not conform to the average leads some commentators to argue that studying child development theory is not useful for childcare practitioners at all. If you would like to learn more about this view, read Taylor (2004).

Our understanding of children's linguistic and cognitive development owes much to the work of Piaget (1959), whose writing remains influential despite the passage of time. He identified stages in children's ability to think about the world around them, describing pre-verbal children as at the 'sensorimotor' stage. In other words they explore the world through their senses and movements, having no language with which to think about experience. Once children begin to learn language, representational thought becomes possible. However, most preschool children are still 'pre-operational' according to Piaget (1959), seeking answers to problems through trial and error rather than logical thought. Piaget (1959: 99) argued that a young child could not understand abstract concepts and was 'shut up in his own point of view', unable to see the world from the perspective of others.

Piaget's body of work has come under fire in more recent years. It has been demonstrated that even young children can understand abstract concepts if they make sense of them in terms of their own experiences. For example, a four-year-old who has suffered a bereavement can come to understand what 'death' means (Donaldson, 1978). Similarly, preschoolers can see things from another person's point of view, provided that they can relate that person's experience to something comparable in their own life (Cox, 1991). Nevertheless, Piaget's central finding is still accepted: children under five make sense of new information by reference to what they have already learned about the world.

Since young children understand things through practical experiment and the evidence of their senses rather than through abstract thought, and because their own life experience has been limited, there are many things in the outside world which they cannot make sense of. This has important implications for early years staff who should avoid abstract concepts when they communicate and root explanations in children's day-to-day practical experience. Concrete demonstrations of what is being discussed will make it easier for a child to understand.

Scenario

Making an explanation practical

Jenny was a four-year-old in foster care who was very confused about what had happened in her life: not surprisingly since she had moved in and out of care repeatedly when her mother, who was mentally ill, had been unable to care for her. The family support worker helped the child to understand what had happened by using play figures for Jenny, her mother, a doctor, the social worker and the foster carer, together with little houses for her home, the foster home and the hospital. She acted out the mother being ill, the doctor saying she must go to hospital and then with a toy ambulance she took the mother to the hospital. It was like a light coming on for Jenny as she saw the figure that represented herself left alone at the house. She exclaimed: 'But who's going to look after the baby?' The worker brought the social worker round in his car, Jenny popped her own figure in the back and it was 'driven' round to the foster home. Understanding what had happened helped Jenny to settle into her foster home. Until she was offered this practical demonstration of her experiences she had been unable to make sense of them.

Another set of ideas which has influenced our understanding of child development is attachment theory, first conceived in the mid-20th century by John Bowlby (Bowlby, 1969, 1973, 1980), but much refined since. Attachment theorists see the quality of an infant's relationship with the parent or carer as the key to their social and emotional development. The nature of the relationship with this primary carer is described as creating an 'internal working model' or psychological template for future relationships. It is argued that a warm and consistent relationship with the parent/carer enables the child to feel secure and valued, to explore the environment and to develop a conscience. Insecure attachments have been found to be associated with delayed language and cognitive development and difficulty trusting adults, and different patterns of attachment have been linked to different patterns of language use. For example, a child who has been inconsistently parented is likely to talk more, express more emotion and demand more attention but he or she may have difficulty understanding cause and effect and developing logical thought. A child whose parent/carer has been consistently cold and rejecting, on the other hand, may withdraw from human contact and will often communicate less, even though cognitively he or she may perform well (Howe *et al.*, 1999; Crittenden, 2005).

Extend your knowledge

Find out more about attachment theory.
- Search in your library under 'attachment theory'.
- Find a text explaining what the theory is about.
- See how many implications you can identify from this theory for early years practice.

Tip: you could try looking for books by David Howe, Vera Fahlberg, Brigid Daniel or Sally Wassell, all of whom have written accessible introductions to the topic.

See also Chapter 6 and Chapter 7 about attachment theory.

One of the important insights gained from attachment theory is the way in which children's learning and development take place in the context of *relationships*: we know that they will thrive better if their key relationships are loving and reliable. Many writers argue that this will apply to their relationships with teachers or carers as well as with parents. Day (2010) confirms through her research with young children in day care that they make better progress where they have continuity of relationships and argues that this is because familiar, stable adults act as 'secondary attachment figures'. This view has significant implications for the way early years settings should be organised: it implies that each child needs a member of staff who maintains a special relationship with them, and is the theoretical justification underlying the requirement within the EYFS that settings operate a 'key person' or 'keyworker' system (DfE, 2012a: 7).

Skills

The first thing we must do if we want to find out children's views is 'Stop, look and listen!' Adults are much too ready to jump in with preconceived ideas, setting the agenda for an interaction by asking questions rather than holding back and seeing what the child wants to talk about. There is a danger that this will discourage the child from saying what is on their mind. *Observation* is one of the early years worker's most fundamental skills. This may be the only way of deducing the views of the child who has no language, but it is also the key to a holistic assessment of children who can talk. 'Children express themselves, sometimes without being aware they are doing it, in a range of ways, only one of which is language' (McLeod, 2008: 70).

Scenario

Observing children's play: Camilla's doll

The childminder was concerned about three-year-old Camilla but it was hard to put her finger on what might be wrong. She was small for her age and always seemed to be hungry. She clung to her mother when she was dropped off at the childminder's and it was hard to get her to settle, but then she threw tantrums when her mother came to pick her up again and did not seem to want to go home. It also irritated the childminder that Camilla's mother was an erratic timekeeper who was often late to drop the child off or to collect her. The childminder began to get a clue as to what the problem might be when she observed Camilla playing with a doll. Camilla spent some time playing at feeding the doll, dressing it and singing to it, but then she appeared to lose interest. She threw the doll into a pram, saying, 'You lie there and shut up! I'm going down the pub.'

Early years workers should observe children's behaviour and demeanour, watch their play and learning, check their growth and development, ask their parents or carers about their progress and make opportunities for children to talk about their concerns before starting to question them about their views. It is easy to misunderstand what young children say: there is evidence that even familiar teachers misinterpret up to 10 per cent of what children in early years settings say to them (Melton and Thompson, 1978). There is also a risk, though, of jumping to the wrong conclusion when observing children's behaviour (Yarrow and Waxler, 1979), so evidence taken from a range of sources will help you to arrive at a more reliable interpretation of what the child is trying to communicate.

Another important aspect of communication is *body language.* While we observe them, children will be observing *us* – our demeanour, facial expression, tone of voice – and they will be drawing conclusions about our intentions. Sensitivity to non-verbal cues starts very young. This is probably a survival mechanism: non-verbal cues help us to distinguish quickly between friend and foe. It has been estimated that less than 10 per cent of the meaning communicated in an interaction is contained in the words used: the rest is transmitted through body language, behaviour and tone of voice (Lefevre, 2010: 45). Early years workers who want to listen to children must therefore cultivate open body postures, encouraging expressions and calm tones of voice, and must control gestures such as looking at their watch, which may suggest their mind is on other things.

Every child is different and the worker needs to be sensitive to the individual child's needs. This means coming to understand how he or she communicates and what specific difficulties they might have with communication: physical, linguistic or social. The child's family background can influence the way they interact with adults in authority: have they, for example, been told to keep a respectful silence, memorise what the teacher says to them and not to rudely intrude with their own ideas? *Cultural sensitivity* to children from different social, ethnic and religious groups will help the practitioner to communicate with them more effectively. Understanding the impact of racism and being aware of one's own assumptions and preconceptions can help the worker avoid misunderstandings.

Questioning children can have unintended consequences. The questioner tends to control the agenda of the conversation and some types of questions close down the range of available responses. Young children are generally keen to please adults and will tend to second-guess what the adult is looking for and they may give the answer they think the adult wants. However, the skilful practitioner will be selective in the type of question he or she uses so as to have the best chance of finding out what the child really thinks. There is an important distinction between 'closed' and 'open' questions. A 'closed' question is one which invites only a limited range of answers, and often only one 'right' answer (What day is it today? Which of these two is bigger?). An 'open' question, on the other hand, has the potential to elicit a much wider range of responses (What did you do at the weekend? How are you feeling today?) Open questions open up a conversation and stimulate children to think for themselves whereas closed questions focus the discussion and narrow its scope; they lead children in directions chosen by the adult and discourage them from extending their thinking. It follows therefore that where possible people working with children should try to increase the proportion of questions they ask that are open.

Allerton (1993) studied the sorts of questions asked by staff in an early years setting and found that the most effective way of eliciting new information from children, and also of making them think, was to ask what he called 'verbal reflectives'. This is a type of completely open question in which the adult shows interest in what the child has said, inviting them to say more by reflecting back what the child has said, but does not try to direct what they should say next (Child: I went to the park. Adult: You went to the park, did you?). It takes practice to use verbal reflectives and make them sound natural; however, it is worth practising: Allerton (1993) found that such questions led to more extended and varied responses from the children and were a much more effective way of finding out about children's views and experiences. It also enhanced the children's learning: 'When the adult listens and the child "thinks on her feet" the child is able to exercise cognitive skills – to question, hypothesise, reflect, wonder, project' (Allerton, 1993: 47). A link can be made here with the concept of 'sustained shared thinking' 'where two or more individuals "work together" in an intellectual way to solve a problem, clarify a concept, evaluate activities, or extend a narrative' (Siraj-Blatchford, 2009: 78), which has been found to lead to more effective learning for young children. Where one has a specific issue one wants to address it may be necessary to ask direct questions in order to get relevant answers; however, best practice is to start with open questions where possible and only move on to the more closed ones next (Home Office *et al.*, 2002).

What matters most, perhaps, is that staff adopt a *holistic approach* in which they seek to understand the child's meanings from a range of angles. The Italian educator Carlina Rinaldi (2005) writes about the 'hundred languages of childhood', in other words the many ways in which children can communicate their thoughts and feelings, without necessarily using the spoken or written word at all. 'Listening,' she says, 'is not easy. It requires a deep awareness and at the same time a suspension of our judgements and above all our prejudices' (Rinaldi, 2005: 20). Rinaldi advocates a practical approach to hearing children's voices, which involves staff providing children with materials and activities through which they can express themselves, and interpreting the children's meanings through their actions rather than just through their words. Asking the views of others who know the child and pooling one's observations adds to the assessment.

Reflective task

'Open' and 'closed' questions

- Make a list of open questions that you might ask of a child, and a second list of closed ones.
- Consider when each type of question might be appropriate.
- Read further about adults questioning children: Siraj-Blatchford, I. and Manni, L. (2008) '"Would you like to tidy up now?" An analysis of adult questioning in the English Foundation Stage', *Early Years: An International Journal of Research and Development*, vol. 28, no. 1, pp. 5–22.

Values

The *Common Core* (CWDC, 2010a) talks about knowledge and skills, but Lefevre (2010) adds another category: values. Effective communication, she argues, is not just about what you know and what you do, but about who you are and what you believe. 'Success in communicating with children seems directly linked to the strength of workers' personal beliefs that achieving mutual communication is their responsibility' (Lefevre, 2010: 68–9). If staff do not seem genuine but are just 'going through the motions' of asking the children what they think, the children will not be fooled. To quote a young person interviewed in the course of research into the experiences of children in care: 'If they treat you like a kid you resent telling them something, but if you're treated like an equal then you want to share things' (McLeod, 2008: 73). Issues of power impact on all interactions, and as an adult and a professional you will be bigger, older and (perhaps!) wiser than every child you work with. This leads to a power imbalance which can skew all communications between you and the child, so you may need to work hard to give some power back to the child. In an early years setting staff might argue that the children they work with are too young to be allowed to be in control and indeed this is true: adults have to be responsible for children's safety. However, this does not mean controlling all aspects of their behaviour or choices of activities. Showing respect for these young people as human beings of equal value involves letting them initiate conversation and control its direction, offering them safe and appropriate choices and assisting them in their turn to develop responsible behaviour which is respectful towards others. This is what child-centred practice is all about.

Next steps

Observation and reflection exercise

- Ask a colleague to observe you interacting with a child.
- Afterwards seek feedback from them about what they saw you do.
- Reflect on what you could have done to make your listening to this child more effective.

Best practice in listening to young children

Although, as we have seen, practice in listening to children in Britain today does not always measure up to the high standards we might aspire to, there exist many good examples of practice from which we can learn. The conclusion of this chapter will consider what best practice might look like. Many practical ideas for how to promote children's language and communication skills are furnished in the guidance to the EYFS (Early Education, 2012). However, while this is necessary for early years staff, it is not sufficient if we are to be as effective as we can be in hearing children's voices. The guidance could be criticised for giving so much attention to helping children to communicate better, but rather less to what we can do to listen better. What follows are ideas for early years settings and their staff who want to improve how they listen to children.

Relationship-based work

Young children learn to understand the world, manage their own emotions and behaviour and express their views through the medium of significant adults. While their parents or other primary carers will remain the most influential, when they spend time in early years settings, care and education staff will be increasingly important to them too. Children are more likely to develop the closeness and trust which enhance communication and allow for confidences if they have a continuing relationship with an adult who is special to them (Winter, 2009). The EYFS (DfE, 2012a) recognises this when it requires settings to operate a keyworker system.

In many settings keyworkers will also have opportunities to form relationships with parents and may assist them by modelling good listening habits for them to emulate, allowing gains in the early years setting to transfer to the home.

Treating each child as an individual

A member of staff may be responsible for a whole group of children but must not forget that each one has a different experience and different needs. Opportunities need to be created for one-to-one time with each child so that their special strengths and difficulties can be identified and also so that they have the chance to speak out if they have something on their mind. It is important that staff leave preconceptions behind and are open to whatever the child may tell them and try to conceal shock at hearing the unexpected as this may discourage children from communicating more (Home Office *et al.*, 2002). When offering children, whether individually or as a group, options to choose between it is necessary to be clear about what the choices entail, and these will need to be explained simply and clearly, in concrete ways which make sense in terms of children's experience (Jewett, 1995).

Some children have very particular needs. While they point out that not all disabled children have impaired communication and urge that you should 'see the child as a child first and disabled second', Stalker and Connors (2003: 27) give useful advice on maximising the chances of eliciting their views. They used games and activities (including diagrams, cards, word choice, a 'lifeline', cartoons, unfinished sentences, maps and a magic wand) to engage disabled children. Where there were particular communication difficulties they took advice from parents first, and employed British Sign Language, Makaton, word boards, a special computer program or an interpreter.

Children who come to an early years setting speaking little or no English face a different set of challenges. It is a daunting prospect to be placed as a small child in a strange environment where nobody speaks your language. The mother tongue is an important part of any child's cultural identity, should be celebrated wherever possible and never denigrated. The EYFS says that settings 'must take reasonable steps to provide opportunities for children to develop and use their home language in play and learning' (DfE, 2012a: 7). Settings can allow children who speak the same language to play and talk together in their own language, interpreters can be provided or volunteers from the local community can be brought in to assist. However, each of these approaches can have drawbacks: children who stick with others from the same minority group can be 'ghettoised' and fail to interact with others; interpreters may lack training, misunderstand and mistranslate; a child who has difficult information to impart may be inhibited from doing so by the presence of a relative or neighbour. Chand (2005) considers these and other issues and concludes that, while some method of hearing what the child wants to say must be found, the best solution is for there to be a member of staff who speaks the child's language. He particularly warns against using children as interpreters where their parents do not speak English as a practice that is both inefficient and inappropriate (Chand 2005).

Clark and Moss (2001) make complementary recommendations for communicating with the children of asylum seekers, who often have had traumatic histories and are living in temporary accommodation. It is crucial for staff to work closely with parents/carers and community members to seek the best ways of supporting these children and ensuring they are heard.

- Think about children you work with now, have worked with in the past or might work with in the future who have special needs (for example, children with a learning disability, those whose language is delayed or speakers of English as an additional language).
- Consider what methods, techniques and resources you use to ensure their needs are met and their voices are heard.
- Could you do more to support them?
- If so, make a plan for how to extend your learning on this topic.

Seeing things from the child's point of view

Good listening requires empathy – the ability to put oneself in the other person's shoes. This can be difficult with a child whose communication skills are limited, which is why careful observation is so important. An interesting technique for making it easier to appreciate the child's point of view is put forward by Paige-Smith and Rix (2011: 30). They observed toddlers playing, made notes and then rewrote the notes as a first-person narrative, so instead of writing 'Andrew picked up the ball', for example, they wrote 'I picked up the ball'. They then used these narratives in discussion about the children's development with the parents and found that the use of the first person made it much easier for parents to see things from the children's perspective: 'the power of children's voices can result in changes in adults' understandings'. This is a technique that could well be adopted for use in early years settings.

Extend your knowledge

The National Children's Bureau (NCB) has developed a range of practical resources for listening to children. Go to the website, download and read their eight leaflets: NCB (2011) *Listening as a way of life*. Available from: http://www.ncb.org.uk/ycvn/resources/listening-as-a-way-of-life.

Creating practical opportunities for communication

Research findings make it clear that children with limited language skills can express themselves, but they are more likely to do so if actively encouraged by adults and given practical tools to do it with. Kinney (2005) used 'survey sheets' with pictures of different activities, and children were invited to attach 'happy face' stickers next to their favourites; she also used figures of staff and a model of the centre to prompt discussion. Paige-Smith and Rix (2011) took photos of the children engaged in activities and asked them to point at a picture to show what they wanted to do next. Photographs and videos are also used by the New Zealand educationalist Margaret Carr (2001) as a means of understanding children's learning processes through an illustrated narrative of their progress. These can be used with the children themselves, with staff and with parents as a tool for assessment and an aid to understanding the child's perspective. Read further examples of photo or video observations in Chapter 10, and sharing of photographic work with parents in Chapter 14.

Digital photography has opened up many new opportunities for finding out children's views, because of the possibility of creating instantly an easily recognisable visual image of the place, person or thing being discussed. Clark (2005) describes, however, how one professional resisted the use of digital photography for finding out children's views allegedly on the grounds of expense, but really because they were uncomfortable with the technology. This, she says, is 'a good example of how adults may need to take the leap to be co-learners with children in order to listen effectively' (Clark, 2005: 46).

A multilayered approach

There is always a risk in adult–child communication that adults will make assumptions and rush to unjustified conclusions based on their own expectations. The way to guard against this is to assess holistically and to come at the child's perspective from as many angles as possible. An influential piece of research into the views of children in an early years setting was carried out by Clark and Moss (2001), who studied the views of children under five attending day care on a 'community campus' in inner London. Their methods involved observation of the children in the setting and group discussions with the children asking them what they liked and did not like about the nursery. The children were given cameras and asked to take pictures of what they saw as important. Then they were asked to take the researchers on a 'tour' of the site: 'a child-led way of talking which is far more alive than the sterile interview room' (Clark and Moss, 2001: 28), after which they made and discussed maps, models and drawings of their experiences in the centre. The researchers also carried out role-playing exercises around nursery life, with the children using play figures and the researchers asking the children to make up stories about them. Finally parents and staff were interviewed to find out their views of the children's perspectives. The mass of data collected was pieced together to form an overall picture of the children's perspectives which was then tested through further discussion with the participants.

Because it involved so many little pieces of information, together creating a bigger picture, Clark and Moss called their method the 'Mosaic' approach and this has been adopted in numerous consultation exercises with young children since (Kinney, 2005; Day, 2010). The strength of the Mosaic approach is the richness of the information it generates; the drawback is that it is very time-consuming. However, the authors argue that:

> ... listening to young children cannot be a rushed activity ... Negotiating meanings involves staff taking time out to reflect on their own perceptions ... Keeping children's perceptions central requires patience, constantly engaging children to check meanings have not been assumed.
>
> (Clark and Moss, 2001: 64–5)

Extend your knowledge

Read the article:

- Day, S. (2010) 'Listening to young children: An investigation of children's day care experiences in Children's Centres', *Educational and Child Psychology*, vol. 27, no. 4, pp. 45–55.

Then consider the following questions:

- What do you think of Day's comments regarding the possible negative impact on children of attending day care?
- How could you, in your work setting, adopt some of Day's approaches to finding out children's views?

A whole-organisation issue

It will be clear by now that listening to children is not something that one member of staff can easily do on their own without support from the organisation within which they work. One-to-one work to find out what is troubling an individual youngster requires staff time, as do in-depth consultation exercises with groups of children. Adequate staffing has to be financed, therefore decisions about what tasks an individual member of staff has time to undertake must be taken at the top of an organisation, or even at a national level where policies are agreed about the funding of public services. Staff need training if they are to listen effectively (Kinney, 2005). A setting that truly respects children – 'a caring community of mutual recognition and listening '(Kjørholt *et al.*, 2005: 178) – is different in nature from one that does not. In short, what is required is a listening organisation.

Respecting others and hearing their voices must be put into practice at many different levels, and will be built into the underlying structures of a listening organisation. A keyworker system ensures a particular member of staff has opportunities to identify each child's unique perspective, while team reviews of the child's progress will ensure that the observations of other staff members are also taken into account. Listening will become part of children's whole learning experience: 'Children need a curriculum which encourages them to think, choose, plan, challenge and feel valued, to articulate what they think and express how they feel' (Pugh and Selleck, 1996: 125). Many children's centres help children whose language development is delayed, or for whom English is an additional language, to learn to express themselves through structured group work as, for example, in 'chatterbox clubs' where parents and children attend together and engage in music, crafts and messy play, with the aim of improving children's concentration, listening and attention, confidence and interaction skills. Activities can be devised which teach children to listen to each other, such as 'circle time' where each child in turn has a chance to speak while the rest of the group pays attention (Lown, 2002). Some programmes, for example the 'pyramid' scheme (ContinYou, 2012; see also Roe, 1994 and National Children's Bureau, 2011), focus particularly on supporting and encouraging the shyest and most withdrawn children to gain the confidence to speak, using words, music and trust games in a small group. While some of these techniques have been developed for primary school-age children, they can be adapted for use in the early years.

The listening organisation will also want to find out and take seriously the views of parents and carers and will have structures in place to ensure this happens. For example, there may be a parent on a board of governors and a parent can contribute to interviewing new staff. Parents should feel welcome at the setting, know they are viewed as partners in their children's education and that staff will always be ready to lend them an ear. Where parents are not fluent English speakers the setting will find ways of making sure their voices are nevertheless heard.

It is also clear that staff will listen best if they feel that they in their turn are respected by their managers and that their own views are taken seriously: they will know this informally through the conversations they have daily with colleagues, but formal structures such as supervision, appraisal and governance should also have built into them an opportunity for staff's views to be taken forward about the setting and how it is run.

Next steps

Is your work setting a listening organisation?
- Identify in what respects your workplace lives up to the ideal of a listening organisation and in what respects it falls short.
- Are there any ways in which you can make suggestions or put forward proposals to improve listening practice in your workplace?
- Perhaps this is an issue you could bring up for discussion in a supervision or in a staff meeting.

Conclusion

Listening is the key to child-centred, ethical, safe and effective early years practice. Listening at its best is not just something one staff member does to one child, but an openness to others that characterises all the work of an early years setting, from the way children learn, through the involvement of parents, to the experience of the employees who work there and the way resources are used. Effective listening requires staff to have both knowledge and skills, but perhaps more importantly a respectful attitude towards young people and a genuine wish to empower them. It is not just a matter of common sense, but something that needs to be studied and practised: 'No-one can fully appreciate classical music without some teaching: we can go on courses on how to listen to music and emerge able to get much more out of the great classics than before. The same goes for listening to children' (Ross, 1996: 92). This chapter has aimed to show that there are many things you can do to make your listening more effective.

Evaluate your...

Learning

Can you answer the following questions? Go back over the chapter to find any answers you are not sure of.

- Identify at least three reasons why it is important for staff in early years settings to listen to the children they work with.
- What piece of legislation says that local authorities in England and Wales must consult with children who receive early years services and give consideration to their views?
- Why is listening sometimes described as an ethical issue?
- Describe five or more practical ways in which an early years setting can demonstrate that it is a 'listening organisation'.

Further reading

To extend your knowledge of this topic, you can read the following books:

Jones, D. (2003) *Communicating with Vulnerable Children*, London: Gaskell.

Lefevre, M. (2010) *Communicating with Children and Young People: Making a Difference*, Bristol: Policy Press.

McLeod, A. (2008) *Listening to Children: a Practitioner's Guide*, London: Jessica Kingsley.

Siraj-Blatchford, I. and Manni, L. (2008) '"Would you like to tidy up now?" An analysis of adult questioning in the English Foundation Stage', *Early Years: An International Journal of Research and Development*, vol. 28, no. 1, pp. 5–22.

Traditions, influences and trends in early years education and care

Linda Pound

Introduction

This chapter will explore some of the factors which have influenced early childhood care and education in the past – and which continue to do so today. Four main areas will be explored, namely:

- the historical legacy offered by the pioneers and traditions of early childhood education and care
- the changing views of children and childhood
- legislation and policy
- international influences.

Finally the chapter will consider some of the trends and tensions which face practitioners. Throughout the chapter, further reading and research as well as critical reflection on policy, theories and practice will be encouraged since these aspects of professionalism are felt to be essential elements of effective practice.

Learning outcomes

This chapter will introduce, explain and invite you to read further and critically evaluate your own working practices. It will consider ways in which your practice might be improved by reflecting on national and international policy and initiatives. It addresses the following learning objectives:

- Increased awareness of the aspects of theory, policy and practice which underpin the cultural beliefs of early childhood practitioners.
- Enhanced understanding of the ways in which policy decisions arise and impact on practice.
- Exploration of the threats and opportunities offered to effective early childhood care and education in the 21st century.

The traditions of early childhood care and education

The study of the traditions of early childhood care and education has an important role to play. It can enable practitioners to evaluate, predict and respond to trends in the care and education of young children. But it can also enable those involved in the field to influence trends and policies. Psychotherapist Kramer (1995: x) suggests that 'a culture should know where its beliefs originate'. Many factors, in addition to the historical origins of provision, shape our views of what constitutes good-quality care and education in our complex society:

- social theories (such as beliefs around smacking or 'naughty steps')
- media stories (such as the response to the Bulger case, the role of punishment)
- family and cultural traditions (whether independence or dependency on others is of more value; whether three-year-olds ought to be regarded as babies or seen as responsible schoolchildren)
- legislation (such as the age at which children ought to go to school, what form the curriculum should take or the welfare and safeguarding of children).

Extend your knowledge

Urie Bronfenbrenner (1979) was the first theorist to articulate a clear view about what he termed the 'ecological system', which surrounds and supports children's development. Although he describes these factors differently he is concerned with the social and cultural aspects which shape children's lives.

- If you are not already familiar with Bronfenbrenner's ecological theory of human development, find out about it. His seminal text is *The Ecology of Human Development: experiments by nature and design* (1979), but you will find a short overview in Pound, L. (2009) *How Children Learn 3: Contemporary thinking and theorists*, London: Practical Pre-School Books. There are also a number of Google references to him (see, for example, http://www.psychologicalscience.org/observer/getArticle. cfm?id=1881).
- With a child (or children) you know well in mind, try to work out what should be included in the relevant microsystem, mesosystem, exosystem and macrosystem (see page 148 for definitions of these terms). Who, for example, form the child's inner circle or microsystem – 'the objects to which he responds or the people with whom he interacts on a face-to-face basis' (Bronfenbrenner, 1979: 7)? Ask yourself similar questions about the other systems.
- Bronfenbrenner also identifies what he terms the 'chronosystem'. Again, try to find out more about this.
- Reflect on what this theory means for your practice. It has been suggested that 'the theory has helped tease out what is needed for the understanding of what makes human beings human' (Bronfenbrenner's obituary in the *LA Times*, cited in Pound, 2009: 11).

The development of theories related to children's learning and development

What is sometimes overlooked is the fact that theories develop over time and ideas grow out of one another, but most theories are not wholly replaced by those which are developed later. While it is possible to categorise theories chronologically (Pound, 2011), many early ideas have persisted. In this way the ideas of theorists such as Pestalozzi and Rousseau, who regarded children primarily as innocent creatures, were developed and extended by progressive 19th-century thinkers such as Friedrich Fröbel. The early part of the 20th century saw the development of highly influential approaches within the field of early childhood – including Isaacs, McMillan, Steiner and Montessori. It also saw the growth of broader theories based on the psychoanalytical ideas of Freud, constructivist theories of Piaget and behaviourist theories of Pavlov and Skinner. Both constructivist and behaviourist thinking led to new theories which placed an emphasis on the social context. Albert Bandura, essentially a behaviourist, developed social learning theory.

Piaget's constructivist theories have been supplemented by those of Lev Vygotsky who is probably the best known of the social constructivists. In the 21st century, postmodern thinking challenges many existing ideas, in seeking to deconstruct concepts of schooling, childhood and development.

Extend your knowledge

- If any of these theorists or theories are not familiar, take some time to find out about them.
- Take some time to consider the ways in which different views and approaches continue to influence your thinking and practice.
- Identify how your practice is influenced by traditional theorists. Write down examples from your practice and link to the corresponding theorist.
- Identify where these theories are used in the EYFS (DfE, 2012a).

The impact on society of theories related to children's learning and development

MacNaughton (2003), who shares many of the postmodernists' views, categorises theories and theorists according to her view of their impact on society:

- **Conforming to society**. MacNaughton (2003: 121) describes approaches which support conformity as those which set objectives to support the development of skills which are considered necessary to achieve 'national economic, social and political goals'. The underlying philosophy is that these represent the traditional skills and values of the dominant culture. This can be seen around the world in many forms and MacNaughton gives a variety of international examples, including England's Early Years Foundation Stage (EYFS).
- **Reforming society**. Many of the theories that underpin models of early childhood education are fitted into this category by MacNaughton. She identifies the key philosophies as a belief that education is primarily concerned with the development of autonomous free-thinking adults and a desire to reform the values of society to support the development of 'freedom, truth and justice' (MacNaughton, 2003: 155). Fröbel, Montessori, McMillan and Dewey are identified as key theorists promoting this approach and the key elements include play, exploration, informality and adults' reliance on observation.
- **Transforming society**. Key to this view of education is the work of the Brazilian educator and social activist Paulo Freire. MacNaughton (2003: 182) suggests that his view of education seeks to:
  - transform the individual into a morally, intellectually and politically engaged actor
  - transform society and its values to extend the possibilities for justice in public life.

For MacNaughton (2003) the approaches which can be described as transformative are those which strive for equality – feminists, anti-racists and social reconstructionists.

Mezirow (2000) takes a different view of transformation – referring to transforming learning. He refers to Bruner's four modes of making meaning (1996), which begin with intersubjectivity, as babies and carers achieve shared attention and attune to one another's emotions and intentions. Gradually, infants learn to link words, events and behaviour to particular situations. They then link these meanings to the rules and habits of the culture. Finally for Bruner comes meaning through inference or logic. Mezirow (2000) adds a fifth mode of meaning-making which involves becoming critically aware of one's own assumptions or expectations and those of others. For Mezirow this marks the ultimate transformation – a stage not arrived at before adolescence.

Reflective task

Categories can only ever offer a broad guide. For example, Moss (2001) regards the approach adopted in Reggio Emilia in northern Italy as falling into the category of postmodern effective education and therefore presumably would see it as being transformatory. However, Browne (2004) and others have criticised work in the Reggio Emilia settings as being insufficiently anti-discriminatory.

- If you are not familiar with the well-publicised and much-praised work in Reggio Emilia, take some time to look it up (see, for example, http://www.reggiochildren.it).
- Can any approach transform society without addressing issues of social justice?
- Think of a range of approaches to early childhood care and education. How would you categorise them? Why?
- Think about examples from your practice, or the work of your colleagues and setting, which have influenced or transformed developments in the local community.

Children and childhood

The development of pedagogical approaches can inevitably be linked to views of childhood. Hendrick (1997) outlines the way in which increasing regulation of children's lives in the 19th century, through strengthening labour laws and the introduction of compulsory schooling, led to a situation in which children came to be seen as the concern of the state. Three categories are particularly relevant to current trends in early childhood care and education:

- **The child-study**. The introduction of compulsory schooling in 1870 and growing concern about the effects of 'poverty and its possible political consequences' (Hendrick, 1997: 47) gave rise to interest in scientific surveys. Child study 'served to position the social, educational, psychological and racial importance of childhood and of children, in terms of education, social welfare and mental and physical health' (Hendrick, 1997: 49).
- **Children of the nation**. Recruitment for the Boer War led to the realisation that the state of the nation's health was nothing short of parlous. Rachael and Margaret McMillan were among those who focused on welfare measures such as school meals for poor children and school medicals. Others saw children as holding 'the key to the kingdom of the morrow' (Hendrick, 1997: 50, citing reported words of a contemporary medical journalist Dr Kelynack). Hendrick (1997) suggests that in the early years of the 20th century children and childhood were being positioned as the tools for national development.
- **The child of the welfare state**. If children are tools of the nation then it becomes important to see their welfare as a national responsibility. This point of view was underlined by wartime evacuation; theories of maternal deprivation and the Curtis Report (Children Act 1948) which drew widespread attention to the shocking conditions to be found in many Children's Homes.

John Bowlby is a familiar figure in the history and traditions of early childhood care and education. He developed the theories of maternal deprivation, drawing his attachment theories from studying orphaned children (Bowlby, 1969). As the Curtis Report indicated, conditions in Children's Homes were extreme and it was on these children that Bowlby based his claims about maternal deprivation – presented in 1951 to the World Health Organization. These theories, in turn, led to changes in nursery provision in the 1950s. The full-time places provided during wartime to enable mothers to work were mainly changed to part-time places. This chimed with Bowlby's views on attachment, but had the added political advantages of taking women out of the job market and thus creating more jobs for men in post-war Britain (Riley, 1983).

Classic research

John Bowlby's theory of attachment was based on research carried out during the Second World War on homeless and orphaned children. Although widely challenged by feminist groups on political grounds and by many other researchers on cultural and methodological grounds, his work remains highly influential. If you are not familiar with this work, you can find out more:

- For a brief overview see *How Children Learn* (Pound, 2005), pp. 44–6.
- *Key Times for Play* (Manning-Morton and Thorp, 2003) is very accessible and offers helpful insights into how the theory can be put into practice.
- There are a number of videos online featuring Bowlby himself and outlining his work. See, for example, http://www.youtube.com/watch?v=VAAmSq2GV8.

Mary Ainsworth (1913–99) built on Bowlby's work in attempting to analyse the responses of babies at around one year of age when separated from their mothers in experiments which Ainsworth termed 'strange situation'. The work has been influential but has been heavily criticised for failing to take account of cultural differences in patterns of mother–child attachment (Singer, 1998).

The impact of sociology

James *et al.* (1998: 9–10) highlight the impact of the discipline of sociology on understandings of childhood. They suggest that sociology has raised a number of issues:

- The concept of 'multiple realities' of childhood carries the risk of undermining standards of concern for children. Where, for example, does child labour fit into this model? Is, for example, physical abuse justifiable because it is regarded as an everyday reality in some cultures?
- The insights into children's childhoods (such as the work of Iona and Peter Opie, first published in 1959) may increase adult control rather than merely illuminate children's views.
- Identifying minority groups may actually undermine the rights of some children as diversity *within* groups is overlooked.

Reflective task

James *et al.* (1998) raise some challenging questions which would repay some critical reflection. Spend some time reflecting on the questions and statements in the list above. Write down one or more examples from your practice.

Threats to childhood

Throughout history, children and childhood have been regarded as a problem. Brooks (2006) describes the anxieties of ancient Greek thinkers, 12th-century moralists, enlightenment philosophers and 18th-century social reformers. Some of the views we hold today are a legacy from the past. In his compelling book *The Invention of Childhood*, Cunningham (2006) suggests that in contemporary thinking there is no agreement on what childhood is. He lists a range of contradictory concerns – the problems of childhood obesity, heavy marketing of sweets, crisps and burgers; concerns about risk and danger; bullying other children and terrorising neighbours; growing up too fast; not taking enough responsibility; mental ill-health; self-harm; evil in some eyes but innocent in others – and so on (Cunningham, 2006).

In her well-publicised book *Toxic Childhood*, Palmer (2006) lists the changes that have occurred in children's lives over the last 20 or 30 years. It includes diet; amounts of exercise and access to fresh air; sleep; emotional stability and security; interactions with adults at home and within the wider community; and the ethos of schools and preschool provision. One of the potentially toxic influences she cites is the impact of technology or screen-time (Palmer, 2006). She is not alone in this. Steiner Waldorf educators have long urged caution but so have such notables as Professor Susan Greenfield, Robin Alexander and groups of speech therapists (Pound, 2011: 39).

Contemporary research

There is extensive research on the impact of television on young children's language development. The Literacy Trust (http://www.literacytrust.org.uk) offers an overview of some of this, and Nursery World's website (http://www.nurseryworld.co.uk) includes an article by Rosie Roberts entitled 'Speech delay: early words'. However, the full analysis of an American national study, although not an easy read, is worth looking into as it presents robust and interesting evidence. The full reference for the paper presented is: Zimmerman, F. and Christakis, D. (2005) 'Children's television viewing and cognitive outcomes', *Archives of Pediatrics and Adolescent Medicine*, vol. 159, no. 7, July, pp. 619–25.

Some contemporary writers (e.g. Palmer, 2006) also argue that television viewing may contribute to the development of aggressive attitudes in children. If you are not familiar with the work of social learning theorist Bandura, see Gray and MacBlain (2012: 93–7). Bandura's study of young children's aggressive response to seeing an adult behave aggressively is widely quoted but is also criticised since it is based on violence towards a doll – an act which critics claim cannot be compared with violence towards humans.

Layard and Dunn (2009) acknowledge concerns about commercial pressures, exposure to violence, increased emotional stresses (including those imposed by current approaches to education). However, they also highlight the material well-being of most children including that offered by the world of technology. They point out that children are more educated and more healthy as well as being 'more open and honest about themselves and more tolerant of human diversity in all its forms'; and 'more concerned about the environment' (Layard and Dunn, 2009: 1). The report itself, drawn from children's own views, highlights the strong emphasis which children of all ages place on love and friendship.

This is reflected in a report produced by Ipsos MORI (2011). An earlier UNICEF study (2007) was critical of the levels of well-being among British children when compared with a number of other countries worldwide. Ipsos MORI (2011) undertook a follow-up study which focused on children in Spain, Sweden and the UK. The findings highlight very different views of what constitutes deprivation. Parents in Spain felt deprived if they had insufficient time to spend with their children. In Sweden deprivation was linked to not having anywhere that children could play and roam safely outdoors. Deprivation in the UK was linked to material goods. The report concludes, however, that what children in all three countries really want is time with family and friends; opportunities to be out and about (with or without money); and the secure sense of who they are which comes from loving relationships. The report makes much of the importance of making British children resilient in resisting pressures to consume – something that Spanish and Swedish families appeared to be more able to do.

Extend your knowledge

Many writers have expressed concern about the growing commercial pressures placed on young children. See, for example:

- Kenway, J. and Bullen E. (2001) *Consuming Children*, Buckingham: Open University Press.
- Linn, S. (2005) *Consuming Kids: Protecting our children from the onslaught of marketing and advertising*, New York: Anchor Books.
- Media Education Formation: http://www.mediaed.org/cgi-bin/commerce.cgi?preadd=action&key=134-cfc-d&preadd=action.
- Ken Robinson's view of the education system, *Changing education paradigms*: http://www.ted.com/talks/ken_robinson_changing_education_paradigms.html.

Look around your setting and identify how you are using commercial products and resources and what message this sends out to children in your care and to their families.

Also, can you think of examples where children and their families bring in branded goods or other commercial items, which might put pressure or certain expectations on other children and their families?

Scenario

Staff in a children's centre noticed that the toys and books children brought from home were often commercially produced offshoots of television programmes or films. After much discussion, staff agreed to create a collection of such toys to help children feel at home, surrounded by familiar materials and resources. Although many parents welcomed the idea, some members of staff remained unhappy about actions which they felt played into commercial forces. They believed it to be their role to protect children from interests which they regarded as being imposed by inappropriate marketing and advertising.

What's your view? Explain why.

Policy and legislation

The focus of this section will be on the development of the EYFS, Sure Start and the Every Child Matters (ECM) agenda. In this section the policy and legislation referred to pertain particularly to England and to Northern Ireland. In Scotland and Wales, where the legislative chambers have been able to make their own decisions, some interesting variations have arisen. In Wales, for example, the foundation phase runs through to the end of what would be Key Stage 1 in England, when children are seven years of age. In Scotland, the framework for provision for children up to the age of three has closely involved Trevarthen and his views on young children (Trevarthen and Marwick, 2002; Learning and Teaching Scotland, 2005), and has therefore a markedly different flavour than the more politically influenced *Birth to Three Matters* (DfES, 2002). Its emphasis is on 3Rs (relationships, responsive care and respect) rather than six or seven areas of learning development which the EYFS is organised around.

EYFS – how did we get here?

In 1995, the Conservative government introduced a nursery voucher scheme. Nursery providers who were seen to be teaching to a prescribed set of outcomes were eligible to accept the vouchers which were sent directly to parents. Although the scheme was very short-lived, being ousted by the incoming Labour government, the outcomes (SCAA, 1996) have lived on. They were divided into six by now very familiar areas of learning, aligned to the national curriculum:

- personal and social development
- language and literacy
- mathematics
- knowledge and understanding of the world
- physical development
- creative development.

In 2000, what were then termed desirable outcomes (SCAA, 1996) were transformed and extended into the early learning goals (QCA, 2000). The same six areas of learning were maintained, although some of the names were changed slightly. Emotional development was added to personal and social development; communication was added to language and literacy; and mathematics became mathematical development. These outcomes were aimed at children aged over three, while for younger children *Birth to Three Matters* (DfES, 2002) was developed.

The first version of the EYFS was created in 2007 – addressing the learning and development of children from birth through to the end of the reception year (QCA, 2007) and revised in 2008 by the Department for Children, Schools and Families (DCSF). The new EYFS (Department for Education/DfE, 2012a), while retaining the chronological coherence, has refocused on the needs of very young children by underlining the importance of 'prime areas' – addressing emotional needs, the primacy of talk and the fundamental importance of physicality in supporting learning and development. To the remaining 'specific areas' has been added a seventh area of learning and development. Literacy has been added, as distinct from the prime area of communication and language. There has been much reassurance that dividing prime and specific areas of learning is not intended to reduce consistency across the foundation stage – in other words both younger and older children should continue to have full access to all areas of learning and development – prime and specific.

The content aspect of this framework is in sharp contrast to the way in which early childhood curricula have developed in other parts of the world. However, the pedagogical guidance is more in line with international approaches – focusing on the uniqueness of individual children, the importance of positive relationships and of enabling environments (Early Education, 2012).

Sure Start?

The creation and development of Sure Start are described in great detail and with great candour by its ex-director Eisenstadt (2011). She describes the development of Sure Start as 'a case study of policy development under the New Labour government of 1997' (Eisenstadt, 2011: 3). It is interesting to note that leading the initiative was Norman Glass, a senior Treasury official. He had been impressed by the findings of studies in America, such as the influential High/Scope research, which claimed that, for every dollar spent on early childhood services, seven or later it was claimed nine dollars could be saved. Such savings were believed to arise from lessening the cost of dealing with special educational needs, substance abuse, early pregnancy, unemployment and delinquency (Epstein, 2011) – and improving the life chances of children deemed to be at risk of failure. There are of course parallels with the work of pioneers such as Robert Owen, Maria Montessori and Margaret McMillan – all of whom believed that by focusing on the needs of young children, lives could be changed (Pound, 2005 and 2011). The needs were different from those faced by families today but the principle that they should be addressed for the good of the child, the family and the nation remain.

Reflective task

Consider the tensions between the good of the child, the family and the nation. Think, too, about whether or not you agree with the statements below:

It is inequality itself that results in poor outcomes, not poor outcomes determining life chances ... The root cause of poor outcomes is not poverty per se but the difference in incomes between the most well-off and the least well-off ... Countries that are more equal ... deliver better outcomes for all citizens across the income distribution.

(Eisenstadt, 2011: 140)

Education may be seen as about valuing and nurturing each child's individuality but it can also be regarded as the tool of a 'political culture that seems to value children only for their economic potential'.

(Brooks, 2006: 334).

The 1997 Labour manifesto floated two distinct sets of aims. One was to provide all children with the early education that High/Scope and other similar studies had shown to be so beneficial. The other was and still is the provision of childcare to enable parents to work. What was not included in the manifesto but quickly became part of its implementation were multi-professional working and early intervention (Eisenstadt, 2011). The introduction of Early Excellence Centres highlighted the importance of integrating education and care but advice about 'joined-up' or integrated services, including health and employment, was to come later.

The government was keen that the Sure Start initiative should be evidence based. The list drawn up by Glass (1999, cited in Eisenstadt, 2011) highlighted characteristics of services that seemed to make a difference. Building on the success of High/Scope, Sure Start was to include *work with children and parents*. However, as Eisenstadt (2011) points out, there are many other points of difference. Sure Start was to *avoid stigmatisation* of families – while High/Scope actively and overtly sought out very poor children. However, initially from 1999, Sure Start children's centres were only opened in so-called areas of deprivation. In 2006 they started offering 'universal services' to all children under five and their families regardless of their socio-economic backgrounds. Whereas High/Scope had focused on educational outcomes, Sure Start was to be *multifaceted*. Indeed High/Scope's much-vaunted successes in employment, avoidance of imprisonment etc. were simply long-term benefits which arose from its educational focus. *Local needs* were to be addressed by Sure Start, whereas High/Scope had a single highly defined approach. According to Eisenstadt (2011), Glass was keen to see *persistence* in the programme, something which High/Scope's longitudinal studies had shown the benefit of. This was to prove something of a stumbling block for Sure Start. The government wanted a speedy demonstration of results which essentially would take generations to achieve.

Moreover, Sure Start programmes presented particular difficulties of evaluation. The emphasis on local need meant that there were many variables. Interventions or services were not randomly allocated as robust research would require but were open to all families in any particular area. Sure Start's aim had been to integrate services but since the extent to which fragmentation was addressed in any area was very patchy there was no reliable way of doing this. Furthermore, no clear pilot programme was run and within 18 months of starting the programme the number of children's centres was doubled – meaning that there was little possibility of finding areas with which data could be compared.

Scenario

In order to realise the ambitions of Sure Start programmes four issues need to be addressed (Eisenstadt, 2011: 102). The first was affordability, and the remaining three were 'choice and flexibility for parents', availability of childcare, and quality of childcare. Consider the following scenario.

A mother has secured a job working from 3pm to 6pm five days a week at a local supermarket. In order to take up the job she needs the local Sure Start children's centre to offer her three-year-old a corresponding place. While this clearly addresses the issue of choice and flexibility for the parent, what are the issues about availability and quality of childcare? Would you be prepared to offer this child a place?

Eisenstadt (2011) identifies two important achievements arising from Sure Start: the establishment of an expectation that services for young children are important, and an infrastructure to support more widespread and less piecemeal provision. However, she underlines some problems:

■ Because Sure Start was politically driven it was under pressure to show rapid gains, but without mechanisms for gathering better and more reliable data.
■ The government of the day tried to go too fast – setting up too many centres too quickly.
■ The integration of services, particularly health, should have been addressed more quickly and more robustly.
■ There should have been greater clarity about desired outcomes for children and families.
■ There was a need for improved staffing structures and pay levels, as well as strong and well-qualified leadership for all centres.

Contemporary research

The *Effective Pre-school and Primary Education Project* or EPPE (Sylva *et al.*, 2010) findings about the importance of well-qualified staff and the importance of the home learning environment (Melhuish *et al.*, 2010) influenced developments at Sure Start. If you are not familiar with the EPPE project you can look up the findings on http://eppe.ioe.ac.uk/eppe/eppepubs.htm.

How do you encourage and support families to integrate learning with their children in their own home?. What other ideas could you promote after having read Melhuish *et al.* (2010)?

Does every child still matter?

The Every Child Matters (ECM) agenda became an integral part of the Children Act 2004, and represented the government's efforts to provide seamless children's services. Its five outcomes were identified as necessary to ensuring well-being in childhood and later life, by keeping children:

■ healthy
■ safe
■ enjoying and achieving
■ making a contribution to the community
■ in situations of economic well-being.

Furthermore, the Children Act 2004 established the duty of professionals to work together and share information to enable children to achieve the five outcomes. Children's services were restructured in an effort to ensure that all professionals engaged in aspects of education, child protection and health would, together with all other relevant agencies, work together towards these five common goals.

Knowles (2009: 2) argues that social justice is 'the single most important principle that underpins the Every Child Matters agenda'. She highlights the requirement placed on schools by the Labour government to:

- address the individual needs of children and their families
- work in partnership with parents and children to create appropriate services
- offer a range of multi-agency and extended services to cater for the needs of community groups
- keep children safe from harm, and healthy
- pay heed to children's voices.

However, Barker (2011) draws attention to strategic changes that have come about since a coalition government took office in 2010. The first is an undermining of a planned approach to children's services in favour of an approach which is 'less state interventionist, more libertarian' (Barker, 2011: no page numbers). One early step in the apparent process of marginalising the ECM programme was to rename the Department for Children, Schools and Families (DCSF), the Department for Education (DfE). In August 2010 an internal DfE memo was leaked which suggested that the phrases 'Every Child Matters' and 'the five outcomes' were to be replaced with the phrase 'help children achieve more' (Chandiramani, 2010; Puffett, 2010). Any undermining of the ECM agenda has been denied and there is a suggestion that there is to be a series of radical reforms to schools, early years provision and child protection (referred to in previous legislation as 'safeguarding'). Barker (2011) asserts that the Secretary of State for Education, Michael Gove, maintains that, since so many people have difficulty in identifying the five outcomes and that they are 'unimpeachable gospel', simply 'what every teacher will want to do', they are, by inference, not worth listing. His reference to teachers underlines another worrying indication of the possible future of children's services, since the ECM agenda is by no means simply the work of schools. Its whole rationale depends on building multi-professional support (Barker, 2011).

Barker (2011) also warns of the impact of the radical reforms already floated. These include the creation of free schools and academies, answerable only to the Secretary of State for Education, a reduction in money for the school building programme, and movement towards targeted rather than universal services in Sure Start and children's centres. But there is also a high emphasis on school readiness (see Chapter 5). To this list of potential threats to services which place children and families at their heart must be added the removal of ring-fencing of the funds for children's centres, in the context of straitened budgets within local authorities. As Eisenstadt (2011) has pointed out, targeted services may miss their intended target, since around half of the children growing up in poverty do not live in identified poor areas.

Another serious worry is that there is little public acknowledgement that outsourcing services for children may not be of quite the same order as privatising refuse collection. In the area of safeguarding, for example, public accountability and consistency are of utmost importance. While the vast majority do not require safeguards of such an order, we should not forget that young children are among society's most vulnerable members and that it is they who will shape our tomorrows.

Shared responsibility?

Although there was no recognised single qualification for early childhood professionals when Labour embarked on its ambitious programme, there had been widespread interest in multi-professional training for some time. In an article entitled 'Towards multi-professional co-ordination: the rationale of an in-service training course', Condry (1981) described the creation at Roehampton Institute in London of a multi-professional diploma course. He described multi-professional working as 'implicit' within the work of Margaret McMillan and went on to describe the Plowden Report (Central Advisory Council for Education, 1967) as seeking to address the difficulties which arose from the diversity and apparently random nature of early childhood provision and services at that time. The 1980s saw a surge of interest in multi-professional working with the setting up of Pen Green Centre for under-fives and their families in 1982 (Whalley, 1994). Degree courses in early childhood and childhood studies have proliferated since that time.

Margy Whalley was herself highly influential, as she had been in Corby in establishing the Pen Green Centre, but increasingly on a national scale. Her work undoubtedly influenced the establishment of the Sure Start programme, early excellence centres and children's centres, and she created and led the pilot and initial National Professional Qualification for Integrated Centre Leadership (NPQICL) courses.

There is not only a duty to work together as established in the Children Act 2004, there are also many benefits of multi-agency or multi-professional working. It can help to minimise disruption and duplication for families; professionals may be more flexible and adaptable; and the fact that different people with different training, backgrounds and beliefs come together to support families should mean more creative and effective solutions (Gasper, 2010). However, this depends on teams developing shared vision and respect for one another and for each member of the team to be reflective and actively seeking to improve services. An Australian study (reported by Gasper, 2010) identified some factors which constrain effective multi-agency working. It was found that colleagues were more likely to consult and share information with those from the same professional background. At worst this led to withholding of information on the grounds of confidentiality and professional competitiveness. In relation to health professionals there were some specific worries among other professionals, according to Gasper (2010: 71), citing the work of Kaye Colmer:

- a demand from the health team that they required separate and 'more complex' professional development opportunities
- a (worrying) sense from the health team that their intervention was of greatest significance.

This remains a difficult area, perhaps particularly in the area of health but in the spirit of ECM, practitioners should be active in seeking to develop opportunities for multi-agency work wherever possible. Changes take time. In 2003, Lord Laming undertook an inquiry into the death of Victoria Climbié and reviewed his recommendations in 2009 following the death of Baby P (Peter Connelly). In both reports he underlined the vital importance of multi-agency working and information sharing in order to ensure children's well-being and safety. The Common Assessment Framework (CAF) was introduced in 2006 (DfES, 2006b), but it is still not used consistently or consistently well – despite obvious advantages to families.

Next steps

- Which agencies have you had contact with in the last 12 months?
- What information did you share?
- How did you involve the child and the parents?
- What were the successes and what were the barriers?

Multi-professional working

Early in this chapter the work of Bronfenbrenner (1979) was considered. His obituary in the *LA Times* suggests that before Bronfenbrenner:

> ... child psychologists studied the child, sociologists examined the family, anthropologists the society, economists the economic framework of the times and political scientists the structure ... As the result of Bronfenbrenner's groundbreaking concept of the ecology of human development, these environments – from the family to economic and political structures – are viewed as part of the life course, embracing both childhood and adulthood.
>
> (cited in Pound, 2009: 11)

Sadly, while it may be true that it is now possible to take a broader view of work with children and families, in practice multi-professional working remains very patchy. There are some excellent examples of highly effective practice – settings where there is good interaction between different professional groups. However, across the whole field of early childhood care and education much remains to be done.

What we should perhaps be aiming for are 'communities of practice ... groups of people who share a concern or a passion for something they do and learn how to do it better as they interact regularly' (Wenger, 2006). Wenger (2006) describes the way in which sharing information, practice and stories enables 'communities of practice' to problem-solve, to seek information and benefit from the experiences and practice of others, to map or document information and to identify gaps in understanding. Sure Start, early excellence centres and children's centres have supported better interaction between practitioners in the fields of care and education. An understanding of the importance of higher qualifications (Sylva *et al.*, 2004) and courses such as Early Years Professional Status (EYPS) and NPQICL have improved the situation and brought closer the model of social pedagogy.

However, much remains to be done. Thirty years on from the pioneer in-service courses we still have not achieved viable multi-professional training. Despite repeated demands in official documents (Laming, 2003 and 2009) and arguments from practitioners and theorists (Anning *et al.*, 2006) for closer working over many years, there is still much to be done. Although education practitioners with different training and different philosophies are beginning to come together, there is not yet any consistent model of shared beliefs between professional cultures.

Scenario

The service providers' forum of a children's centre decided to tackle higher than national levels of childhood obesity in their area. The figures for their area indicated that there was a gap of 3 percentage points between the national and local incidence of childhood obesity. The approach they used is known as 'turning the curve' and is fully outlined in Friedman's book *Trying Hard Is Not Good Enough* (2005). Members of the forum identified some of the possible reasons for the high levels. These included:

- an increase in the population of black African families, a group where obesity rates are increasing
- a noticeable increase in numbers of cheap fast food shops in the area
- affordability of fresh foods
- unhealthy lifestyles and no local authority strategy
- lack of basic skills in family cooking
- poor snack choices to pacify children.

Their strategies for 'turning the curve' included:

- increased promotion of the fruit and vegetable scheme for targeted families through midwives and family outreach workers
- development of some published ideas for healthy picnics to be available in local parks and in the café in the centre
- the creation of a weaning group in the café at the centre
- promotion of local walks: leaflets were freely available but the promotional material needed to be circulated.

All professionals within the forum agreed on the issues and together came up with strategies that they could all promote in various ways. Do you have similar issues in your setting that you could explore with other professionals in a similar way?

International perspectives and influences

In addition to the impact of its history and of legislation, practice in Britain has undoubtedly been influenced by international perspectives. This is not a new process. Europeans such as Friedrich Fröbel, Maria Montessori and Rudolf Steiner all left an indelible mark on early childhood education and care – not just in this country but around the world. Today the process continues. In this section three current approaches are examined – forest schools, the New Zealand curriculum Te Whāriki, and the work undertaken in Reggio Emilia. It is important to remember that no matter how admirable the work with young children found in other countries and cultures, practice cannot simply be lifted from one context to another. The views of families and professionals, and the expectations and beliefs of society determine the extent and ways in which different approaches influence practice elsewhere.

It would be wrong to omit High/Scope from any discussion of international influences. As we have seen, it has been highly influential in England in raising the profile of the importance of early childhood. As one of the many Head Start programmes developed in the USA, it is High/Scope research which has led the way in securing influence around the world.

Classic research

If you are not familiar with the research, led by David Weikart (Schweinhart *et al.*, 2005), which underpins the High/Scope approach look for the following:

- http://www.highscope.org
- Epstein *et al.* (2011) 'The High/Scope Approach' (see Further reading below).

This research, like the EPPE project, is longitudinal. It remains a highly respected piece of research because it used randomised sampling. Families did not choose to attend a particular type of nursery – they were allocated so that the original samples of children could be compared.

Forest schools

This is widely regarded as an international influence on current practice. The first recognised forest school in Britain was established at Bridgewater in 1995. After a visit to Denmark, members of staff at Bridgewater College were inspired by seeing young children enjoying the freedom offered by a forest environment. However, forest schools have a long history in this country. Fröbel was himself a trained forester and his emphasis on outdoor provision sprang from his belief in the power of nature. The practice of both Margaret McMillan and Susan Isaacs reflects Fröbel's philosophy. All were influenced by the work of 18th-century writer Jean-Jacques Rousseau. The Order of Woodcraft Chivalry was devised in 1916 by Ernest Westlake. His ideas were expressed in progressive terms as 'religion, ritual, tradition, discipline and mystical expression all coming together in a radical movement opposed to the given social structures' (van der Eyken and Turner, 1969: 134). The forest school established on Westlake's founding principles in the New Forest was open until 1938 and inspired such notable schools as Dartington and Bedales, which are still operational (Pound, 2011).

Over the last decade or so a wide network of forest schools has developed – not only in obvious rural locations but in some tiny corners of crowded urban spaces where trees and shrubs have been squeezed in to recreate something of the forest. The benefits are numerous but a particularly strong emphasis is placed on children's personal and emotional development and well-being. The benefits of positive social and collaborative interaction as well as greater awareness of the need to take responsibility for the care of the environment are at the heart of forest school work (Blackwell and Pound, 2011). And, of course, the importance of physical competence is underlined. One of the great achievements of the forest school movement in this country has been not simply giving risk-taking a higher profile, but in persuading parents and staff that this is desirable. This is underlined by Louv's (2006) research and writing, which also highlight the health aspects of increased oxygenation and above all the spiritual benefits of being in and part of nature.

Despite such laudable intentions, forest schools are not without critics. In Scandinavia, concerns are expressed about the potential marginalisation of young children. The view has, for example, been expressed that 'childhood has no place in modern society' (Gullov, 2003, cited in Tovey, 2007: 87) and that perhaps forest schools are contributing to the marginalisation. Children, Gullov argues, are being tided away into forgotten and hidden corners. Tovey (2007) suggests that a greater integration of the work by forest schools with the early childhood heritage of outdoor provision in the form of gardens is needed. This she hopes will encourage 'wilder, more challenging and riskier aspects of the forest [to] become an integral part' of everyday practice (Tovey, 2007: 96).

Finally, one criticism is that in choosing to call these areas 'schools' an unhelpful emphasis is placed on instruction, in contrast to the Scandinavian use of the term kindergarten. The latter term means 'children's garden' or 'garden of children'. Nicol (2007) also suggests that Fröbel's intention in creating the term was to call to mind something closer to 'a paradise garden' – a very far cry from 'forest school'. This argument could be countered, as Rinaldi (2007: xix) does in defence of Reggio Emilia's use of the word school by seeing it as 'an attempt to hold the meaning of school open for interpretation and discussion'.

Te Whāriki

Te Whāriki, the New Zealand early years curriculum framework introduced in 1996, is internationally known and praised. Indeed Smith (2011) refers to its 'gospel-like status' and quotes the words of Norwegian teachers referring to it as their 'bible'. Smith (2011) acknowledges the many strengths of the document. She highlights the sense of professionalism, the shared language and sense of ownership which it offers – and perhaps less predictably, emphasises the way in which it has made 'what teachers do with children more visible' (Smith, 2011: 157). There is a danger in a practice that is so widely admired that there may be insufficient critical reflection. Smith explores this idea and suggests that the way to ensure this is to offer high-quality training for practitioners (both in- and pre-service) with clear theoretical foundations. Sadly, as in Britain, current resourcing of early childhood provision in New Zealand is not strong (OECD, 2004).

One of the many things that is admired about Te Whāriki is its rootedness in biculturalism, a focus that many UK practitioners could learn from. Ritchie (2005: 122) describes its foregrounding of Maori culture and language and emphasises the importance of developing learning 'around shared interests in the socio-cultural contexts of home, community and centre'. However, she also draws attention to failures in practice which stem from having insufficient Maori staff members and an unequal understanding of the cultures represented within the setting. She offers an example of food sharing, normal among Polynesian families, but not allowed within all settings.

Te Whāriki's focus on *how* things are learned rather than on *what* is learned has influenced primary school practice in New Zealand with the inclusion of a set of Key Competencies in the primary curriculum. There have, however, been criticisms. Some fear that early childhood practitioners have too little subject knowledge (Hedges and Cullen, 2005) and that this limits the extent to which teachers are able to extend children's interests and understanding.

Reggio Emilia

While the curriculum adopted in Reggio Emilia is similarly well known and as admired as that of New Zealand, there are many important differences. Te Whāriki was developed as part of a move to integrate different types of early childhood provision. In Reggio Emilia there is no written curriculum, and practice developed not, as in New Zealand, through government initiative but through the determination of a group of parents, mothers in particular. Malaguzzi, the teacher to whom the innovative work in Reggio Emilia is generally attributed, was inspired by parents. At the end of the German occupation of their town during the Second World War, parents occupied buildings that they wanted to safeguard for early childhood provision for their children. Malaguzzi writes that the first nursery in the town:

> … was created and run by parents … in a devastated town, rich only in mourning and poverty … [and funded from] the sale of an abandoned war tank, a few trucks, and some horses left behind by the retreating Germans.
>
> (Malaguzzi, 1993: 42)

This beginning is a vital factor – parents and community remain key to the success of the approach. In addition, Moss (2001: 136) describes how the wartime experiences which led to the development of early childhood provision in Reggio Emilia sprang from a drive to resist the conformity which had led to the Fascist regime. Instead, Reggio parents nurtured 'a vision of children who can think and act for themselves' (Malaguzzi, 1993). Moss (2001) goes on to suggest that the absence of a written curriculum reflects the firm belief that the values which underpin Reggio's approach can only be *lived*. Its beginnings can therefore be seen to have shaped the pedagogy and ethos.

The decision to employ *atelierista* (or an artist in residence) in all Reggio settings has placed a clear emphasis on the importance of the learning environment, which they describe as the 'third teacher'. Particular attention is paid to spaces, materials, colours, light, microclimate and furnishings (Clark, 2007). The emphasis on the visual has also contributed to the publicity achieved through worldwide tours of Malaguzzi's *The Hundred Languages of Children* exhibition.

Despite the fact that critical reflection is seen as highly important, with parents, the *pedagogista* (or educator/teacher), staff discussion among themselves and documentation of learning all being key features of practice, there are criticisms. Browne (2004) suggests that although a central tenet of work with young children in Reggio Emilia is encouragement for children to challenge adult ideas, visiting educators seeking to understand the Reggio approach are not afforded the same encouragement. Browne (2004) is particularly critical of the lack of clear policy on issues of equality, as she cites concerns voiced by visitors to Reggio about an apparent unwillingness to address gender issues and quotes a parent who expresses anxiety about the increased cultural mix which is seen as bringing problems.

Next steps

Identify areas of your work which might have been influenced by: the Reggio Emilia approach, High/Scope, the Te Whāriki and/or forest schools ideas.

Which area of your practice could you develop further by using some of the ideas from these models of pedagogy?

Tensions and trends

It is difficult to know where early childhood care and education are heading since there are many conflicting views and approaches. Concern is often expressed about the politicisation of early childhood (Pound and Miller, 2011) but all decisions about the care and education of young children are inescapably political. Whatever the decision, young people's lives and society's future are inevitably shaped for good or ill.

The government's reasons for providing services for children are varied. They include:

■ equality for women
■ perceived need to increase the labour force, by enabling women to work
■ efforts to eliminate child poverty and educational disadvantage
■ recognition of the role of early education in enhancing children's well-being and life chances
■ acting in the 'public good' (OECD, 2006: 7) by supporting early childhood care and education.

These categories are not mutually exclusive. They do not have the same aims and this may mean a loss of focus and clear direction. Eisenstadt (2011) describes in detail the impact of the shift in emphasis which changing political agendas had on the development of Sure Start.

The commodification of early childhood care and education

Commodification refers to the increasingly widespread practice of treating the care and education of young children as a commodity, like anything else that can be purchased in a shop, such as the proverbial tin of beans. This involves both schoolification and disembodiment of their care and education. The OECD (2006: 13) describes the 'schoolification' of early childhood care and education:

> Research suggests that a more unified approach to learning should be adopted in both the early childhood education and the primary school systems, and that attention should be given to transition challenges faced by young children as they enter school. The search for a more unified approach has generated different policy options. France and the English speaking world have adopted a 'readiness for school' approach, which although defined broadly focuses in practice on cognitive development in the early years, and the acquisition of a range of knowledge, skills and dispositions. A disadvantage inherent in this approach is the use of programmes and approaches that are poorly suited to the psychology and natural learning strategies of young children. In countries inheriting a social pedagogy tradition (Nordic and Central European countries), the kindergarten years are seen as a broad preparation for life and the foundation stage of lifelong learning. Facilitating transitions for children is a policy challenge in all systems. Transitions for children are generally a stimulus to growth and development, but if too abrupt and handled without care, they carry – particularly for young children – the risk of regression and failure.

Extend your knowledge

The paragraph above from *Starting Strong II* (OECD, 2006) sets out the tensions between a 'school readiness' approach and the 'social pedagogy tradition' or 'education in its broadest sense' (*Community Care*, 2012). If the term social pedagogy is new to you, go to http://www.infed.org/biblio/b-socped.htm for an overview. There are further references on the site. Take some time to extend your understanding of this approach since it is vital in understanding the issues surrounding the debate and the potential limitations of a 'school readiness' approach. What consequences might this have for your early years practice?

It has been suggested that 'the tide of social pedagogy ... is swelling' (*Community Care*, 2012). Social relationships, dialogue and critical reflection are valued and are often achieved through activities which demand physical engagement such as expressive arts or outdoor challenges. Moreover 'risk-taking [is seen] as an educational objective which clashes with the considerable priority given to health and safety' (*Community Care*, 2012). These are familiar ideas to many early childhood practitioners in the UK but sometimes seem difficult to achieve. The social pedagogy website draws attention to the need for training not only for practitioners but for local and national policymakers.

This links to another trend identified by Tobin (2004). He writes of 'disembodied' education by which he seeks to underline the way in which the brain is favoured over the body, and skills over feelings; consequently, he sees the 'schoolification' agenda as having contributed to the disembodiment he describes (Tobin, 2004). An overemphasis on phonics, on sitting still on a carpet or at a computer are recognisable elements of teaching for 'school readiness', which, at worst, can undervalue the importance of the role of the body in learning and understanding (Blakeslee and Blakeslee, 2007). This raises the question of how appropriate the relatively young age of an introduction to statutory schooling in the UK is. However, the debate about disembodied education challenges the notion that privileging the brain over the body is appropriate at any age (Claxton, 2008 and Robinson, 2010). Read more about school readiness in Chapter 5.

Time spent in being instructed allows little time for free-flow play. Paley (2004) argues that placing an ever greater emphasis on what she calls 'academics' leaves less time for play. She describes these practices as rewriting theories of child development. They are indeed a long way removed from the play argued for by Isaacs and McMillan and still safeguarded today by Steiner practitioners. Paley suggests that in curtailing the amount of time available for play, practitioners have limited the development of children's play and rendered it less effective. Paley (2004: 22) describes a 'social curriculum', with an emphasis on 'good play and the sort of talk that follows'. She suggests that these 'take time and deep thought'. She continues:

> Today fantasy play is at the barricades with fewer and fewer teachers willing to step up and defend the natural style and substance of early childhood, the source of ... vocabulary building and image decoding and Socratic questioning.
>
> Though fantasy propels the child to poetic heights over and above his ordinary level and was considered the original pathway to literacy it is now perceived by some as an obstacle to learning. We are allowed to nourish play only so long as it initiates reading, writing and computing ...
>
> We who value play must do more than complain of unwanted drills and steal away our time. We must find time for play and keep daily journals of what is said and done during play if we are to convince anyone of its importance.
>
> (Paley, 2004: 32–33)

Another trend has been the 'corporatisation' or 'marketisation' of early childhood services. The ethics of placing services for children in the marketplace have been questioned (Urban, 2008). Eisenstadt (2001) suggests that the ministers involved in the setting up of Sure Start came to regret a reliance on private services. There is an echo of the Australian programmes which have 'seen education as a commodity and early childhood teachers and practitioners accountable for effective delivery' (Pound and Miller, 2011: 166) in the payment-by-results schemes being piloted.

Is what works good enough?

Governments are frequently heard to say that practice should be based on 'what works'. However, without strong and agreed 'ethical and democratic principles' (Pound and Miller, 2011: 166) it is difficult to agree on whether or not things are working. Reliance on outcome measures has come to be seen as a sound measure of effectiveness; however, as the sign rumoured to have been on Albert Einstein's study wall says, 'not everything that counts can be counted and not everything that can be counted counts' (Stewart, 2011). A variety of terms such as accountability, value for money and monitoring are bandied about but the measures selected are not always those that will make a difference. Sure Start offers a clear example – as shown above it was clear that the data wanted by government could not be made available with the speed that political expediency demanded. Eisenstadt (2011: 155) describes 'finding the right set of measures that deliver the right kind of data that will inform practice without being overly bureaucratic' as 'a significant challenge'. Similarly the High/Scope outcomes which so impressed Norman Glass and his treasury colleagues were not those anticipated by Weikart and his colleagues (Schweinhart et al., 2005).

In New Zealand criticisms arising from outcomes were seen as an indication that the approach had matured. In Reggio Emilia, however, there is resistance to external evaluation. They believe that their focus on critical evaluation and the close involvement of parents and community ensure that provision is monitored and that practitioners are accountable. Over-reliance on external evaluations, in their view, takes away professionalism.

Conclusion

This chapter underlined the factors which shape beliefs and practice. The way in which historical events impact on practice and policy is explored. Views of childhood held by practitioners and public alike are changed by media influences and by contact with the rich diversity of family and cultural traditions in Britain today. International practice which has also been shaped by similar factors continues to encourage us all to reflect on why we do what we do and to consider what we might take from other ideas – always recognising that theories and practices cannot be simply transferred from culture to culture, from country to country.

In the latter part of the 20th century, as pressure grew to work to a prescribed curriculum framework, the ideas and thinking of pioneers such as Fröbel and the McMillan sisters were seen as having less relevance. In the 21st century there has been a renewed understanding of the need to know where our beliefs originate. The legacy and insights of important thinkers such as Lev Vygotsky and skilled and reflective practitioners such as Susan Isaacs and Margaret McMillan are, once again, becoming valued in their own right (Pound, 2011). They can offer today's practitioners a vital starting point for their own thinking and reflection. As Nutbrown et al. (2008: 181) state: 'There is no better tribute to those who have gone than to remould, revisit and revise their ideas for a new today.'

Evaluate your...

Beliefs and their impact on your practice

- Discuss with colleagues and parents their views of childhood. You might do this by considering what your 'ideal child' might look like and to what extent children match up to this.
- Analyse what is said and written about children. Words which crop up frequently can provide a window on your thinking – and that of your colleagues.
- What do you believe to be the key elements of your practice? Compare your views with those of your colleagues. What are the mismatches and similarities?
- Review your daily evaluations. Are children being given appropriate amounts of attention and time? It is sometimes the case that quiet or undemanding children are overlooked by staff. Is this the case in your setting?
- Having read this chapter, do you think your view of children and childhood has changed? If so, why?
- What new ideas and inspirations has this chapter provided you with and how do you think you could incorporate these or try new ways of working with children?

Further reading

Bennett J. (2011) 'Early childhood education and care systems: Issue of tradition and governance' (rev. edn), in Tremblay, R. E., Boivin, M., Peters, R. de V. (eds.), *Encyclopedia on Early Childhood Development* [online], Montreal, Quebec: Centre of Excellence for Early Childhood Development and Strategic Knowledge Cluster on Early Child Development, 1–5. Available from: http://www.child-encyclopedia.com/documents/BennettANGxp2.pdf (accessed 20/6/2011).

DeLoache, J. and Gottlieb, A. (2000) *A World of Babies*, Cambridge: Cambridge University Press.

Early Childhood Research & Practice (ECRP) Journal. Available from: http://ecrp.uiuc.edu.

Epstein, A., Johnson, S. and Lafferty, P (2011) 'The High/Scope Approach', in Miller, L. and Pound, L. (eds.) *Theories and Approaches to Learning in the Early Years*, London: SAGE.

European Early Childhood Education Research Journal (EECERJ). Available from: http://www.eecera.org/journal.

Holland, P. (2004) *Picturing Childhood*, London: I. B. Taurus and Co. Ltd.

5

The early years curriculum and pedagogical strategies to support learning and development for children

Francisca Veale
with contributions from Joy Scadden

The test of successful education is not the amount of knowledge that pupils take away from school, but their appetite to know and their capacity to learn.

(Sir Richard Livingstone, 1941)

Introduction

This chapter explores the emergence of the current curriculum for early years and identifies pedagogical strategies for practitioners to support children in their learning and development. The review of the curriculum in England by Tickell (2011) drew on evidence from early years research and practice making recommendations and proposing changes to the curriculum. The changes were intended to create a curriculum which is fit for purpose, in the sense that children learn and develop in a safe environment, where their welfare and well-being are central and they are supported by suitably trained and knowledgeable practitioners (Tickell, 2011). Also, the reports by Allen (2011) and Munro (2011) influenced Tickell's review (2011), as they focused on children's welfare and well-being, highlighting the importance of early intervention for enhancing children's life chances and giving better outcomes for children in later life.

The reformed Early Years Foundation Stage (EYFS, DfE, 2012a) and its areas of learning are discussed with particular emphasis on pedagogical strategies that early years practitioners need to embrace in order to engage children in learning opportunities and to support their development. Particular emphasis on the importance of play and fostering creative practice are encouraged in the chapter. The concept of pedagogy is discussed: pedagogy views the child in a holistic manner and aims to develop children as whole people, and not just intellectually or academically. The contentious issue of school readiness and the implications for children's transitions are debated.

The role of adults in facilitating children's learning and development is examined for early years practitioners, as well as for parents and carers in the home learning environment, by drawing on seminal research studies such as *Researching Effective Pedagogy in the Early Years* (REPEY) (Siraj-Blatchford *et al.*, 2002) and *Effective Provision of Pre-school Education* (EPPE) (Sylva *et al.*, 2004). The importance of quality provision in early years and suitable monitoring tools for quality in childcare settings is demonstrated.

Learning outcomes

This chapter will enable you to:

- Enhance your current knowledge and understanding of the curriculum.
- Gain a wider view of different curriculum models and international influences on the EYFS.
- Learn about pedagogical approaches that enable children's learning with particular emphasis on learning through play.
- Explore creative ideas and methods when working with children.
- Think about the role of adults in supporting children's development in the setting and in the home.
- Consider school readiness while planning for children's transition and working with parents.
- Review the quality monitoring systems in your setting.
- Debate the importance of practitioner support and supervision.
- Reflect on and evaluate your practice.

What is a curriculum?

The term 'curriculum' is often interpreted and understood in different ways, which has led to some negative responses from practitioners and the media, particularly when the early childhood frameworks have been introduced in recent years. The media have described the EYFS (DfE, 2012a) as the 'nappy curriculum' (Woods, 2012), questioning the need for a curriculum that will stifle creativity and freedom and that focuses on the 'three Rs' rather than play. This clearly demonstrates the media's lack of understanding of the term and most definitely the ethos of the EYFS (DfE, 2012a).

A curriculum in its simplest form is a plan or a course. However, in today's society this term is mainly used in an educational context to describe something:

- based on a body of theory about teaching and learning
- targeted to the needs and characteristics of a particular group of learners
- outlining approaches, methods and procedures for implementation.

In examining the curriculum it is the outcomes that are required of that plan and how these outcomes are achieved which are important. Further to this, the curriculum provides a context for the quality of education.

In her report, Rumbold (1990: 10) described the curriculum as 'concepts, knowledge, understanding, attitudes and skills that a child needs to develop'. However, it also needs to be considered *who* determines these concepts, knowledge, understanding, attitudes and skills, and *for what purposes* the curriculum models are used.

Traditional curriculum models

Originally, curriculum models were designed for schools to provide teachers and learners with a clear structure of what has to be delivered, and how, and what students need to learn. Tyler (1949) described three different models of curriculum design:

- The **product-driven curriculum** considers the nature and structure of knowledge, learners' needs, as well as society's needs. For example, learners need to have sufficient numeracy and literacy skills to enable them to participate successfully in the workforce and contribute to the economy. Therefore, learners' needs become secondary to the need of the economy, as the 'product' is to produce a qualified workforce.

- The **process-driven curriculum** recognises that learners are self-directed in their desire to learn – they negotiate with teachers and parents what needs to be learned and how tasks are decided. The assessment process is formative, tailored to the individual need with coursework that offers open-ended opportunities. This participatory pedagogical style of learning invites learners, parents and teachers to make shared decisions.
- The **objectives-driven curriculum** is based on the terms of consumer choice rather than pedagogy and it gives learners the autonomy to choose the course and modules they wish to study. The assessment process is based on competency and criterion-referenced summative competencies which are subdivided into a number of elements. The teacher is seen as a guide to the learner with regard to what to learn and which subject to study.

Similarly, Smith (1996, 2000) described three types of curriculum. In the **product curriculum** the objectives are set, a plan is drawn up and implemented, and the outcomes are measured. The **process curriculum** is based on general principles and 'meaning-making' as it relies on the interactions between teachers and learners, and depends on what happens in the classroom. Preparation and evaluation are important, but the education may be viewed as 'informal'. The **praxis curriculum** can be seen as a development of the process curriculum, which requires informed teachers who are 'free thinkers' and who view the curriculum as dynamic and continually evolving.

Reflective task

- Identify which type of curriculum model is followed in the EYFS.
- Research different curriculum models relevant to early years, for example New Zealand's Te Whāriki approach or the Italian Reggio Emilia approach to the curriculum. Compare these by identifying their advantages, disadvantages, and implications for your practice.
- Identify early years theories within the models.

Historical roots of the early years curriculum

The early years curriculum we are familiar with today in England has been developed as a result of a significant shift in the adult concept of childhood. Historically, children were viewed as contributors to the family, either in a financial sense or as carers for younger siblings or elderly relatives. Indeed, during the Victorian era, families were encouraged to have large numbers of children to ensure that there were enough 'survivors' in those times of high infant mortality to contribute their labour. Industrialist and social reformer, Robert Owen (1771–1858) worked hard to change this view of child labour and is attributed as the founder of infant childcare in the UK (Kwon, 2002). At his New Lanark mills he established his own revolutionary curriculum, combining care and education, greatly influenced by the work of the Swiss pedagogue and educational reformer Johann Pestalozzi (1746–1827). Likewise, Margaret McMillan (1860–1931) believed in the power of education as a means to reduce childhood poverty, providing advice on nutrition, health and well-being to parents, and going on to establish an 'open-air' nursery school in Deptford in 1903 (Kwon, 2002).

Owen's and McMillan's contributions to the history of childhood with the creation of childcare and education are undeniable, but the start of the playgroup movement is attributed to Belle Tutaev, according to Kwon (2002). In 1961 Tutaev organised a playgroup for her own young daughter in a draughty church hall, reminiscent of so many similar settings since. These groups not only provided an opportunity for mothers to meet up with other mothers, but also the children were encouraged to 'learn through play' according to the traditional Piagetian approach.

A different, more liberal and progressive approach was taken by A. S. Neill, who can be seen as one of the pioneers of a child-centred approach to teaching and learning. His philosophy was based on the idea that a school should be made to suit the child, rather than the other way around, by allowing children to make free choices about what they want to learn and how. Neill called this approach 'free schooling' and he launched his first free school in 1921 in Germany. He later moved to England and opened the Summerhill School in Suffolk in 1927. The school provides opportunities for children to use their imaginations, to make their own free choices and to think freely, and it involves them in democratic decision-making processes within the school. The Summerhill School still operates today, as a boarding school, but its pedagogical approach caused a political storm in 2000, following its poor Ofsted report in 1999.

In 1931, the Hadow Report (Gillard, 2006) proved to be the first official acknowledgement of 'progressive' educational methods, putting the child at the centre. In 1944, the minister for education, Richard A. Butler, launched the Education Act which established primary education in law. The need for a child-centred approach was further reinforced by Plowden (1967) in her review of primary education in 1967. Later, Gillard (1987) argued that the Piagetian approach came through very strongly in the Plowden Report, which emphasised the need for teachers to be facilitators, supporting children to experiment and learn through play.

However, despite such important reviews being undertaken by Plowden in 1967, Rumbold in 1990 and Ball in 1994, it was not until 1997 that we started to see a surge in changes to early years, with the launch of the *Effective Provision of Pre-school Education* (EPPE) project (Sylva *et al.*, 2004). A 'new age' of early years research and policy followed, particularly from centres such as Pen Green and the Thomas Coram Institute, thereby demonstrating change, regeneration and the beginnings of the development of a curriculum specifically for early years.

In response to the EPPE (Sylva *et al.*, 2004) findings and in line with the government's strategy to improve social inclusion and reduce childhood poverty, two early years curricula were launched: the *Curriculum Guidance for the Foundation Stage* (QCA, 2000) and the *Birth to Three Matters* framework (DfES, 2002). The *Birth to Three Matters* (DfES, 2002), greatly influenced by research from New Zealand and its Te Whāriki early years curriculum, at last recognised the importance and value of a child's development in these early years. Unfortunately, however, the introduction of the *Curriculum Guidance for the Foundation Stage*, followed by the *Birth to Three Matters* framework, left many practitioners confused and overwhelmed, because these two curricula were not integrated. In particular, providers who offered childcare from birth to five years old found it difficult to link the two curricula and maintain a consistent focus on areas of learning and development for children.

Further to the introduction of *Every Child Matters* (ECM) in 2003, the Children Act 2004 specified the way forward for children's services in the UK, introducing a children's commissioner to champion children's and young people's views and interests. This required local authorities to appoint a director of children's services, and a number of specific obligations with regard to safeguarding and integrated working. Furthermore, the creation of an integrated framework and inspection processes (DfES, 2004a), consolidated by the Children Act 2004 and the Childcare Act 2006, specified the duties of local authorities to implement childcare services to support the ECM (DfES, 2003) strategy. This, however, required a new statutory framework for early years, and laying out a new structure for the regulation and inspection for early years services. Ofsted's new regulation and inspection framework (for September 2012) is discussed later in the chapter.

In 2008 the Early Years Foundation Stage or EYFS (DCSF, 2008a) was launched. Essentially this framework amalgamated all the fragments of guidance and legislation around early years, as well as providing a nationally acknowledged curriculum for birth to five years. Finally, there was some cohesion, based on evidence-based research (Sylva *et al.*, 2004), as well as learning from a wide range of recognised and established approaches, such as the Italian Reggio Emilia and the New Zealand Te Whāriki approaches. The EYFS (DCSF, 2008a) framework was welcomed by the majority of practitioners in early years, because it appeared more accessible and workable for practice than the *Curriculum Guidance for the Foundation Stage* (QCA, 2000) and *Birth to Three Matters* (DfES, 2002). However, there still appeared to be miscommunication regarding its contents and function, as well as a lack of training and support in place prior to implementation.

From this point onwards, we see the publication of some significant reports and reviews which will have a major impact in early years practice and strategy in forthcoming years. To summarise, in December 2010 Frank Field MP published his review on poverty and life chances (Field, 2010); then in January 2011, Graham Allen MP published his review of early intervention (Allen, 2011); and finally in March 2011, Dame Clare Tickell published her review of the EYFS (Tickell, 2011), resulting in the reformed EYFS (DfE, 2012a). You can read further about traditions and trends in early years education in Chapter 4 of this book.

Historical summary

The development of the early years curriculum in England

■ Nursery Education: The Desirable Learning Outcomes (SCAA, 1996)

This signalled a shift to more formal approaches to learning in the early years. Playgroups became preschools and reception teachers in particular found that they were at the sharp edge of change. The Desirable Learning Outcomes (DLOs) moved away from the child-centred approach to a prescriptive and often adult-led curriculum.

■ Curriculum Guidance for the Foundation Stage (QCA, 2000) and Birth to Three Matters (DfES 2002)

A sound set of principles for effective early years provision which emphasised the importance of play and active learning. In theory, the child was at the centre of the curriculum, but in practice the Early Learning Goals often made practitioners use adult-led approaches.

■ Early Years Foundation Stage (DCSF, 2008a)

A conscious attempt to set the principles that informed those guidelines in the foreground, by putting the child firmly back at the heart of practice. Adults and children are seen as critical partners in the learning process where adults model and 'scaffold' skills.

Reflective task

■ Until the introduction of the EYFS in 2008 there was no integrated statutory curriculum for early years children from birth to five years. What are the advantages and disadvantages of a statutory curriculum in early years?

■ Research further and find out why A. S. Neill's Summerhill School was so controversial in 2000, and why Ofsted did not approve of the approach.

■ In her review, Tickell (2011) recommended that the government extend the exemptions from these early learning goals to all settings within the Steiner Waldorf Foundation. Why do you think this is?

■ Read the following article and identify the similarities between the different curriculum models: Soler, J. and Miller, L. (2003) 'The struggle for early childhood curricula: A comparison of the English Foundation Stage Curriculum, Te Whāriki and Reggio Emilia', *International Journal of Early Years Education*, vol. 11, no. 1, pp. 57–68.

The reformed EYFS curriculum 2012

The reformed EYFS (DfE, 2012a) was launched in April 2012 following an extensive review undertaken by Tickell (2011). Having been implementing the EYFS framework for three years, practitioners were asked to contribute to the consultation process. Although the EYFS framework was generally well received, there were undoubtedly improvements to be made. The review built on the positives from the previous EYFS (DCSF, 2008a), namely the consistent framework across the early years age groups and the emphasis on high quality, and made recommendations for practical improvements. A significant one was a reduction in the number of early learning goals from 69 to 17 with the aims of making the early years profile 'much more manageable' and having 'clearer links into the National Curriculum' (Tickell, 2011: 58).

There is a focus on a smooth progression and transition to school, reinforced by the phrase 'school readiness' used within the EYFS (DfE, 2012a) and actively promoted through the work of UNICEF (2012a) as stated on their website:

> Our work on behalf of school readiness rests on three pillars: children's readiness for school; school's readiness for children; and families' readiness for school. Together, these pillars bolster children's likelihood of success.

However, in their article '"Wasted down there": policy and practice with the under-threes', McDowall Clark and Baylis (2012) voice their concern that this emphasis on transition to school and future academic achievement will simply reinforce the view that the care of under-threes is insignificant, thus deterring the more highly skilled practitioners such as EYPs from working with this age group.

In preparing children for school, practitioners are urged to build strong relationships, 'working in partnership' with parents and carers, by discussing their children's progress and development at every opportunity. This partnership should be driven by a relationship with the 'key person' in the setting, a role which is given particular prominence in this EYFS (DfE, 2012a). The introduction of the progress check at age two will provide practitioners and parents with a timely opportunity to review their child's development, identifying strengths as well as any 'significant emerging concerns', promoting early intervention as endorsed by Allen (2011).

A revision of the areas of learning has launched the 'prime' and 'specific' areas of learning. Tickell points to the work of Siegel (1999: 92, cited in Tickell, 2011), which underlines the 'impact of experience on inborn genetic potential' to justify their introduction. The '**prime areas**' cover personal, social and emotional development; physical development; communication and language development – all of which are emphasised as significant areas of learning for the under-threes (DfE, 2102a). The 'prime areas' follow through to the under-fives, but added to these are the '**specific areas**' of literacy; numeracy; understanding of the world; and the new expressive arts and design to encompass imaginative play, music and dance, so named to move away from the traditional 'junk modelling' concept of creative play (DfE, 2012a).

In her rationale for the split between the 'prime' and 'specific' areas of learning, Tickell (2011: 97) quotes the work of Hall (2005) who identifies 'experience-expectant' (prime) learning and 'experience-dependent' learning (specific). In the period of experience-expectant learning the brain is ready to accept all kinds of stimulation from the surrounding environment and indeed expects it. During the experience-dependent period the brain develops based on cultural expectations, for example the expectation of society for children to learn to read and write around the age of five years. This expectation is significantly supported by curriculum requirements, based on contemporary political agenda.

Further to this, Tickell (2011) highlights the characteristics of effective learning which run through all the areas of learning, emphasising the role of play in the learning process. These characteristics, or methods, of learning existed in the previous EYFS (DCSF, 2008a), but were unexploited or perhaps misinterpreted by practitioners.

The characteristics of effective learning are defined as (DfE, 2012a: 7):
- *Playing and exploring* – children investigate and experience things, and have a go.
- *Active learning* – children concentrate and keep on trying if they encounter difficulties and enjoy achievements.
- *Creating and thinking critically* – children have and develop their own ideas, make links between ideas, and develop strategies for doing things.

The importance of play in the learning process has been long acknowledged, particularly by theorists such as Tina Bruce, but has often been lost or misinterpreted in past frameworks which have been product driven, such as *Nursery Education: Desirable Learning Outcomes* (SCAA, 1996), which moved away from a child–centred approach. Even as long ago as 1967, the Plowden Report identified the significance of play in the process of learning. How children learn is examined more closely in the next section of this chapter.

The relationship between the areas of learning and development and the characteristics of effective learning is illustrated in the *Development Matters* document (Early Education, 2012: 4) with the following diagram:

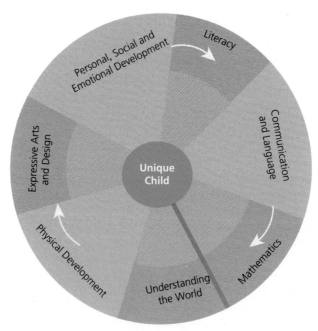

Figure 5.1 The characteristics of effective learning (Early Education, 2012: 4)

The characteristics of effective learning (Early Education, 2012) associated with the EYFS's emphasis (DfE, 2012a) on children's well-being and involvement in their learning can be linked in practice by applying the Leuven scales (Laevers, 1997).

In addition to the changes in the learning and development requirements, there are changes to the welfare requirements, most of which are clarified and streamlined to reduce miscommunication and unnecessary bureaucracy. The adjustments to the welfare requirements covering child protection and safeguarding in settings are very welcome and strongly supported, following the outcomes of the Vanessa George case (Plymouth Safeguarding Children Board, 2010). You can read more about the welfare requirements in Chapter 13 of this book. Furthermore, the EYFS (DfE, 2012a) adds the requirement for sound staff inductions, training and supervision. Again this is another welcome improvement, further supported by the recommendations of the Nutbrown Report (2012), which proposed that newly qualified practitioners should receive mentoring for at least the first six months of their employment. Indeed, Nutbrown (2012) suggests that the government should supply induction and training modules which could be accessed by everyone working in the sector. The new requirement of professional supervision is further explored later on in this chapter.

Reflective task

- What areas of the EYFS are you comfortable with and why?
- Consider the advantages, disadvantages or potential issues which may arise with the progress check at age two.
- How will you ensure that you and your colleagues have a good understanding of the characteristics of effective learning? How will you demonstrate this in your assessments?

Extend your knowledge by reading about the Leuven scales for well-being and draw up some key ideas about who could implement these in your practice:

- Laevers, F. (1997) *A Process-Oriented Child Follow-Up System for Young Children*, Leuven University, Belgium: Centre for Experiential Education.

How children learn – the child in context

Bronfenbrenner (1979) illustrated that the child does not exist in isolation, but is surrounded by their family, carers and friends, as well as being part of the community where they live and where socio-cultural values and norms are transmitted (see figure 7.1, page 148). The *Every Child Matters* (DfES, 2003) agenda acknowledged the fact that children need to be seen in the context of their families and communities, and addressed this in the five outcomes framework, specifically the 'making a positive contribution' and 'social and economic well-being' outcomes. Indeed, Watson (2006) goes further and asks practitioners not only to be concerned about children's welfare and well-being as originally outlined in *Every Child Matters* (DfES, 2003), but to work with children in a more holistic approach that promotes their 'spiritual' well-being. She highlights that children should be listened to, given a voice, participate and be actively involved in the decision making about their lives, as well as their 'spiritual' needs being met, which she describes in terms of values, norms, cultural and belief systems which children and their families and their communities hold (Watson, 2006: 253). The curriculum has to include the diverse backgrounds and cultures children and their families come from and address their individual needs in an inclusive manner which takes into consideration the whole child.

Viewing early years care, education and school as part of the child's environmental context was highlighted in the *Early Years Learning And Development: Literature Review* (Evangelou *et al.*, 2009), stating that children's learning and development is:

> … **located within nested social contexts (Bronfenbrenner, 1979). Thus development is constrained and elaborated by cultural contexts and by the architecture of the brain. These nested social contexts include the impact of close family on development and therefore underscores the vital role of parents in supporting children's learning.**
>
> (Evangelou *et al.*, 2009: 2)

The EYFS (DfE, 2012a) acknowledges the influence of families and communities on children, and emphasises that early years practitioners need to strengthen working in partnership with parents and children's carers. The EYFS (DfE, 2012a) areas of personal, social and emotional development, understanding of the world, and communication and language offer ample opportunities to provide equality of opportunity, as well as acknowledging diversity. This can be achieved by including children (and their families and communities) in planning for learning and development activities by listening to their lives and worlds.

An often used example is the Italian Reggio Emilia approach (Malaguzzi, 1993), which views the pedagogue's role as 'co-educator' (children and pedagogues learn from each other) and 'co-researchers' (children and pedagogues explore and research together). Children's learning takes place alongside the educator/pedagogue, as well as including the parents and the community, who all become part of the learning. Again, this has been incorporated in the 'characteristics of effective learning' of the EYFS, where under 'playing and exploring – engagement' children should experience encouragement of 'finding out and exploring; playing with what they know; being willing to have a go' (Early Education, 2012: 5), thus facilitating children's learning.

Furthermore, the environment is seen as the 'third teacher' in children's learning in the Reggio Emilia approach and the Te Whāriki early years curriculum. The design of indoor and outdoor spaces, natural resources and educational equipment available to children, the use of colour, space and lighting in settings, as well as a creative, inclusive and diverse atmosphere and ambience, are all seen as important and integral elements to providing quality early childcare that enhances children's learning and development in a holistic manner.

In the UK, the Pen Green Centre (see Chapter 14 in this book) is a good example of how the above-mentioned models are applied in practice and how parents and the community are being included. Parents are acknowledged to be the child's 'first educator' and are actively involved. Early Excellence Centres like the Pen Green model and the UK Sure Start Children Centre's approach are also rooted in the American High/Scope and Head Start approaches (Bronfenbrenner was a founding member of Head Start) of the 1960s. High/Scope and Head Start's focus was on equality of opportunities in the educational and vocational systems, with the intention being to reduce the cost to society and the economy. The convincing argument has been that apparently for every dollar spent on early years education and prevention, the economy would save seven dollars (Schweinhart *et al.*, 2005).

Reflective task

- How do you involve parents, carers and families in children's learning?
- What do you know about the communities your children live in?
- How do you utilise the EYFS characteristics of effective learning in your practice?
- Plan for an activity that could include, for example, the grandparents and possibly local community services or community groups.

Learning through play – engaging the senses

In English preschools, play is an integral part of the curriculum, founded on the belief that children learn through self-initiated free play in an exploratory environment (Bruce, 2006). Free play is especially the norm in the traditional English nursery curriculum, following Rousseau, Fröbel, Owen, McMillan and Isaacs. They all saw play as the 'work of the child' and a part of the educational process. The Plowden Report (Plowden, 1967) suggested that play is the principal means of learning in early childhood:

> **In play, children gradually develop concepts of causal relationships, the power to discriminate, to make judgements, to analyse and synthesise, to imagine and formulate.**
>
> (Plowden, 1967: 193)

The Early Years Learning and Development: Literature Review (Evangelou *et al.*, 2009) identified the most important aspects to young children's learning and development as:

- warm relationships
- contingent responsiveness by adults
- conversation
- play.

Similarly, the 'characteristics of effective learning' in the EYFS (DfE, 2012a) place a great emphasis on children's 'playing and exploring' and 'active learning' as well as 'creating and thinking critically' in the process of their learning. This implies that children are not simply to be sat down and 'taught' knowledge, but instead are seen as active learners who explore the world around them.

Traditional theorists, like Rousseau, Steiner, Piaget, Bruner, Vygotsky, Fröbel and Pestalozzi, to name but a few, all developed educational theories which convey that children explore the world themselves because of their innate curiosity and thirst for knowledge. Montessori first suggested that children do not perceive play as work and, if it is conducted skilfully, children can learn through play. Children make sense of their experiences while experimenting and exploring, that is, through 'schemas' which lead to assimilation and later to accommodation (Piaget and Inhelder, 1969). These are two aspects of the cognitive adaptation of the individual to their environment, because this interaction between the child and their environment invites them to explore and it facilitates imagination (Fröbel, Steiner), as well as stimulating the senses and leading to physical balance (Rousseau).

Similarly, Athey (2007) viewed play as an integral part of the curriculum and sees the focus as being on the development of schemas (or patterns of repeated actions) in children's play and development. According to Athey (2007), as children repeat actions over and over again in their play, the accumulation of schemas, developing later into concepts, will enable a child's learning and development. Additionally, Bruce (2006) argues that play comes from within the child and in particular free-flow play is a vital part of learning and experience. In order to determine exactly what constitutes quality play, Bruce (2006: 113) has identified '12 features of play' (see Chapter 17), which can be used to assess play provision (see Chapter 9).

Recent writing by Goswami (2011) describes children's learning as an experience-based and multi-sensory process which is individual to each child and the context or environment they are exposed to. Play with creative and natural resources as well as role play or imaginary play can stimulate multi-sensory learning which can bring out the spectrum of children's abilities. Effective practitioners not only need to be able to facilitate these learning opportunities, but also need to be confident in making observations and identifying children's multiple intelligences (Gardner,

1983) and not just their cognitive abilities. Goswami (2011) also states that learning takes place in incremental steps as the brain will extract and represent structures that it is presented with, even when it is not taught directly, and emotional information is prioritised by the brain and receives privileged access to learning. Previous research by Goleman (1999) found that emotional intelligence is more important than cognitive and academic intelligence for children and adults to succeed in life. The notion of multiple intelligences and emotional intelligence is supported by current educationalists, such as Claxton (2006), who highlights that learning takes place in many forms: through *immersion* in experience, though *imitation*, through *imagination*, through *intuition* and through the *intellect*. Claxton (2006) criticises an educational curriculum that favours the intellect and neglects the continuing development of the other areas of learning.

Practitioners need to offer stimulating and enabling environments for children's senses to be invited to take in new information and for learning to take place. Warm, trusting relationships with pedagogues, carried out with unconditional regard for the individual child, their needs and their interests, are essential for the child to feel safe and to want to explore and learn. Practitioners need to plan for learning activities through playful and creative approaches that stimulate all the senses and offer opportunities for incremental learning at the individual child's level of readiness to learn. However, 'the significant question is not *whether* a child is ready to learn but *what* a child is ready to learn', according to Whitebread and Bingham (2011: 2) and they challenge Piaget's theory that children need to be cognitively 'ready' before they can learn. Instead, Vygotsky's (1978) learning theory is much favoured today as children are recognised to be able to socially construct their knowledge, understanding and learning, progressing from the zone of actual development (what they can already do) to the zone of proximal development while being supported (scaffolded) by more experienced peers as well as adults.

Moyles and Worthington (2011) criticise current early years practice which does not give children enough encouragement to take responsibility for their own learning within the curriculum, and they suggest that the curriculum should embrace more opportunities for children to learn through play. Indeed, of interest is a study by McInnes *et al.* (2011) who researched the differences in practitioners' understanding of play, as well as children's perceptions of play, and how this influenced the pedagogy in planning for children's learning. In a later study, Howard and McInnes (2012) emphasised the importance of practitioners being able to understand children's view of what they consider to be play, so as to be able to facilitate playful situations which children want to engage with and which can increase the developmental potential of play. Furthermore, they found that children's emotional well-being was increased when an activity was perceived by children as 'play' rather than learning (Howard and McInnes, 2012). It could be concluded that emotionally well-balanced children are open and 'ready' to learn when their senses are playfully engaged in activities.

Extend your knowledge

Read the following journal article: McInnes, K., Howard, J., Miles, G. and Crowley, K. (2011) 'Differences in practitioners' understanding of play and how this influences pedagogy and children's perceptions of play', *Early Years: An International Journal of Research and Development*, vol. 31, no. 2, pp. 121–33.
- Ask yourself what your understanding of play is.
- What do your colleagues think play is?
- What are parents' attitudes towards play versus active learning?
- How can you bring together play and exploring in your pedagogy?

The role of the pedagogue in supporting children's learning and development

The EYFS (DfE, 2012a) stipulates a robust pedagogy that recognises the sophistication of young children's thinking and the complexity of early learning and development, and the four themes and principles describe the conditions necessary for lifelong learning and apply equally to learners of all ages. Pedagogy is often defined as the 'art of teaching children', and in early years practice it is seen as important to get 'the balance right between guided and self-initiated learning' (Evangelou *et al.*, 2009: 12). Earlier studies such as the REPEY (Siraj-Blatchford *et al.*, 2002) and the EPPE project (Sylva *et al.*, 2004) found that effective pedagogues would use a combination of adult-led and child-led activities in their child-centred practice. However, the research by McInnes *et al.* (2011: 122) discusses the challenges of direct instruction versus free play, and they found, when examining early years practice, that 'practitioners tend to focus on children's behaviour rather than analysing their own'. Earlier studies observed similar evidence in which early years practitioners were readily able to identify children's behaviours and children's progression, but were reluctant to reflect on their own professional behaviour and how this might influence and affect children's learning and development (Moyles *et al.*, 2002). Similarly, Stephen (2010: 17) discovered that practitioners found the question challenging and difficult to answer when asked 'how they acted to support children's learning and how they knew that children were learning'.

Roberts-Holmes (2012) discusses that, even though the EYFS places emphasis on planned and purposeful play, at the same time it also requires measurable results and an accountability from practitioners for children's outcomes. However, Rogers and Evans (2008) see this as contradictory to spontaneous and intrinsically motivated child-led play. Even though traditional and current theory and thinking about children's learning focuses on child-centred play, studies found a 'lack of evidence' that would support the effective relationship between play and learning (Smith, 2010, cited in McInnes *et al.*, 2011: 122). This might be one of the reasons why practitioners feel less confident in using play activities to facilitate children's learning, because they work in a product-orientated rather than a process-orientated pedagogical approach which produces 'easy' to document evidence of children's progression. Even though the previous and the current EYFS curricula guidance emphasises the importance of play and a play-based curriculum, McInnes *et al.* (2011) found that many practitioners:

> ... admit to a lack of knowledge regarding play and how play relates to pedagogy and therefore the reality of practice is somewhat different, with a mismatch between what practitioners say and what they do. Studies have repeatedly shown that practitioners are not comfortable with play, child-led activities and allowing children choice (King 1978; Cleave and Brown 1989; Bennett *et al.*, 1997; Pascal 1990). ... In reality, a lack of understanding of play, combined with a mistrust of child-led activities and reluctance to give children choice and control, results in an overreliance on adult-led activities with adults having control and choice.
>
> (McInnes *et al.*, 2011: 122–3)

Alternatively, Petrie *et al.* (2009) draw on European research which identifies the key principles of pedagogy as having the child and their development as a whole person in focus, and practitioners having a relationship with the child in a non-hierarchical environment that they share together. Consequently, pedagogy is not solely about teaching children to learn, but preparing children for life, with a more holistic approach that looks at their development as people, and includes children's families and communities. Therefore, early years practitioners who engage in effective pedagogical practice need to consider the following (Petrie *et al.*, 2009: 4):

- As professionals, pedagogues are encouraged to constantly reflect on their practice and to apply both theoretical understandings and self-knowledge to their work and to the sometimes challenging demands with which they are confronted.
- Pedagogues should be both practical and creative; their training prepares them to share in many aspects of children's daily lives, such as preparing meals and snacks, or making music and building kites.
- Pedagogy builds on an understanding of children's rights that is not limited to procedural matters or legislative requirements.
- There is an emphasis on teamwork and valuing the contributions of others – family members, other professionals and members of the local community – in the task of 'bringing up' children.

Pedagogical strategies and approaches which have been discussed in the literature and substantiated by various research projects and studies appear to favour practitioners co-constructing play activities and scaffolding any potential learning opportunities. Rose and Rogers (2012) see the role of adults in early years settings as being a critical reflector, a carer, a communicator, a facilitator, an observer, an assessor and a creator. One can see how the role and the expectations of what childcare practitioners and early years pedagogues are required to do to provide quality childcare and education has grown over the past decades. The curriculum for early years has grown and become more demanding in the sense that people working with children have to have a very wide and in-depth knowledge and understanding, not only about children but also about the influences from the family and environment. Reflective practice and working in partnership with children's families require many more skills than just reading up on children's developmental stages.

Extend your knowledge

Undertake further reading and research about the role of pedagogy in children's early learning and development by reading the following:

- Moyles, J., Adams, S. and Musgrove, A. (2002) *Study of Pedagogical Effectiveness in Early Learning (SPEEL)*, Research report 363, London: DfES.
- Stephen, C. (2010) 'Pedagogy: The silent partner in early years learning', *Early Years: An International Journal of Research and Development*, vol. 30, no. 1, pp. 15–28.
- Wood, E. (2010) 'Reconceptualising the play–pedagogy relationship: From control to complexity', in Brooker, L. and Edwards, S. (eds), *Engaging Play*, Maidenhead: Open University Press.

Reflect on your practice and identify areas where you apply effective pedagogical strategies that offer playful learning and developmental opportunities which are centred on the children in your care. How can you link this to the EYFS?

Pedagogues as learning companions to co-construct children's learning

Current thinking about facilitating children's learning and development in early years suggests that practitioners need to apply effective pedagogical approaches that combine the notion of children's curiosity to learn through play with guided adult interactions that support and enhance learning and developmental opportunities. This requires practitioners to move away from the expectation of product-orientated learning and school readiness to a more holistic approach that offers meaningful and enjoyable learning experiences suited to children's abilities and interests and aimed at meeting their personal, social and emotional requirements in order to enhance their social competencies for life. The EYFS (DfE, 2012a) looks at the unique child in a holistic manner in the prime and specific areas, but it all depends on what practitioners do with this framework. Only when practitioners allow themselves to view the world through a child's eyes, to listen to children through a child's ears and to make sense of the world around them from a child's perspective, can they become a 'learning companion' to the child. This 'learning companion' is similar to Reggio Emilia's concept of the pedagogue being the co-educator and co-researcher. Likewise, Pestalozzi (cited in Brühlmeier, 2010) considered children's learning as a natural and holistic process in which children explore and learn the environment through their 'heads, hands and hearts'. Children should be able to follow their individual interests and come to their own conclusions. The role of the educator is to enable spontaneous rather than directed or guided learning for the child, thus offering holistic experiences.

Indeed, Claxton (2007: 14) advises educators and pedagogues to show children that they continue to learn, too, because if teachers always present themselves as 'endlessly omniscient' and 'Know-Alls', they deprive children of learning for themselves. Therefore the idea of co-construction of learning and knowledge-building between pedagogues and children should be aimed for and can be achieved in all areas of the curriculum through creative and playful activities. Inviting children to experiment indoors and outdoors with water, sand, building blocks, bricks, natural materials, paint or recycled materials will raise their curiosity, and the adult can explore alongside the child what would happen 'if'. Working from this premise, what the child observes and describes in their own words indicates to the practitioner what the child already knows or how the child interprets and constructs new learning. The next step can lead to the pedagogue increasing the child's knowledge and understanding by describing their observations and interpretations, and comparing and contrasting, and together with the child critically thinking about the different perceptions.

This pedagogical approach combines Vygotsky's theory of extending children's competence (1978) and Bruner's scaffolding (1996) with the didactical method that invites a dialogue between the adult and child: as an interactive way of discovering new knowledge and understanding through the process of asking questions and finding answers together. In this process the role of the adults, or the pedagogues/teachers and parents, is not to be the ones who have and transmit pertinent knowledge (product-orientated), but to invite the young child to formulate questions and find answers for themselves. This process-orientated approach enables the child to gather new insight and new knowledge appropriate to their individual developmental stage. The pedagogical aim in early years education is not to 'test' for the 'right' answers, but instead to enjoy and have fun asking questions and exploring everyday life and the world around them with curiosity. Playing and exploring, or solving problems and finding answers, which enables children to successfully complete a task based on their personal competence, will enhance children's self-efficacy (Bandura, 1986). Indeed, self-efficacy can assist children to deal with conflict and solve problems, as well as master difficult situations independently. Moreover, self-efficacy influences children's trust in their own abilities and promotes self-esteem which in turn develops greater resilience, better social competencies and overall improved life chances.

Claxton (2007) encourages pedagogues to go further and not just engage children in knowledge implementation, but in knowledge-creation processes by getting them interested and getting them actively involved in extending their own learning capacity. He suggests that play and learning opportunities should be:

- **rich**: there is much to be explored
- **challenging**: the topic contains real difficulty

- **extended**: there are time and opportunity to go into it in depth
- **relevant**: the topic connects with learners' own interests and concerns
- **responsible**: learners have some genuine control over what, why, how and when they organise their learning
- **real**: solving the problem or making progress genuinely matters to someone
- **unknown**: the pedagogue does not already know the 'answer'
- **collaborative**: most learners enjoy the opportunity to work together.

(adapted from Claxton, 2007: 12)

Collaborative co-construction of knowledge between pedagogues and children as learning buddies or learning companions can make the process of learning creative, fun, relevant and meaningful at the same time. Together they can explore, ask questions, imagine what might be, make new connections, critically think and reflect on what they have learned today, and share it with parents, families and communities. Practitioners need to be not only creative and enthusiastic, but also collaborative, a critical friend and provocateur, who shows interest in the children, and has knowledge and competencies which can be shared with the children. A suitable method of learning together is sustained shared thinking (SST).

Scenario

The following scenario exemplifies how a childminder, or a child's keyworker, can use the pedagogical approach to become a learning companion and co-construct children's learning and development, leading to sustained shared thinking and working in partnership with parents, which will be explored further in the following sections of this chapter.

Alfie

Vicky has undertaken several observations of Alfie (28 months old) since he moved through from the baby group and after meeting with his mother during his transition period. She is building up a holistic picture of Alfie's development, his likes and interests. Today, he is playing with sand, trying to 'build' sandcastles using the bucket and spade in the sand tray. The sand is dry so the sandcastles do not stand. Alfie is disappointed. Vicky has been playing with him and talking to him encouragingly about 'patting' and 'pouring' the sand. Noting his desire to build a sandcastle, Vicky tells Alfie she is going to fetch a jug of water. While pouring the water into the sand Vicky explains what she is doing and talks to Alfie about 'building sandcastles' and how the water will make the sand grains 'stick' together. Vicky shares with Alfie how she builds sandcastles when she goes to the beach. She encourages Alfie to 'shovel' the 'wet' sand into his bucket, and at the same time she starts to build a sandcastle alongside with another bucket and spade. Their play develops into a 'sandcastle competition' punctuated with lots of laughter and 'ooohs' and 'ahhs'. Later that afternoon Vicky tells Alfie's mother about the sandcastle competition. The mother tells her that at the weekend they had been to the beach and built sandcastles and collected seashells. Vicky asks Alfie's mother if she could let Alfie bring in some of the seashells to add to his sand play and she asks if there were any photos to add to his learning journey. Vicky resolves to plan a beach theme into Alfie's next steps and also give him opportunities to try 'building' with other textures and materials such as soil and small stones.

Sustained shared thinking and thinking about thinking

Co-constructing children's learning experiences through playful learning that builds on the child's interest, supported by open-ended questions from the pedagogue, was found to be a pedagogical effective approach in the REPEY study (Siraj-Blatchford *et al.*, 2002). Enhancing the communication and collaboration between the practitioner and child further, by encouraging children to expand their thinking and expression, can be achieved through sustained shared thinking (SST), according to Siraj-Blatchford (2007). SST has been defined as an experience in which two or more individuals engage in activities together in an intellectual way to explore a new idea, to solve a problem, clarify a concept, evaluate an activity, or extend a narrative. All participants in this process must contribute to the ideas and communicate their thinking with each other so that it can be further developed and extended potentially over a period of time and across different learning environments (Siraj-Blatchford *et al.*, 2002). The EYFS has incorporated the approach of SST, which is understood to enhance children's learning because children feel that they are given attention, that somebody is showing an interest in them and that their individual experiences are valued. The EYFS (DfE, 2012a) encourages SST in particular through the characteristics of effective learning (Early Education, 2012), namely active learning, playing and exploring, creating, and thinking critically. Again, it depends on practitioners and how they implement the curriculum in practice, because practitioners often find it a challenge to use SST with under-threes by underestimating the abilities of babies and toddlers. In their research, McDowall Clark and Baylis (2012) challenged practitioners' preconceptions about the abilities of very young children to engage in SST. They found evidence that babies are very 'skilful communicators who engage in sustained shared thinking', contrary to the common perception that babies are 'weak and dependent' (McDowall Clark and Baylis, 2012: 237).

Siraj-Blatchford and Manni (2008) reviewed the forms of questions practitioners use in early years settings, because during the REPEY study and the consequent EPPE projects it became apparent that:

> **94.5% of all the questions asked by the early childhood staff were closed questions that required a recall of fact, experience or expected behaviour, decision between a limited selection of choices or no response at all. Only 5.5% were open-ended questions, which provided for increased encouragement (to speculate and trial and error) and/or potential for sustained, shared thinking/talking.**

> (Siraj-Blatchford and Manni, 2008: 5)

Consequently, they recommend that pedagogues need to reflect on their practice and undertake further training in asking open questions which invite children to engage in a conversation and can lead to SST. In addition, practitioners need to learn to 'listen' to children. Listening to children's experiences involves listening to their views and opinions, as well as their needs and wishes. SST can assist in the process of listening to children, and it is important that children are involved in planning a curriculum that meets – above and beyond anything else – their needs.

The REPEY and EPPE studies and consequent research all found that more highly qualified practitioners, in particular those at graduate level, are generally better at supporting SST by using open and extending questions.

Some good examples of sustained shared thinking, which practitioners can use, are:
- **Tuning in:** Listening carefully to what is being said, observing body language and what the child is doing.

- **Showing genuine interest:** Giving their whole attention to the child, maintaining eye contact, affirming, smiling, nodding.
- **Respecting children's own decisions and choices by inviting children to elaborate:** Saying things like 'I really want to know more about this' and listening and engaging in the response.
- **Recapping:** 'So you think that …'
- **Offering the adult's own experience:** 'I like to listen to music when I cook supper at home.'
- **Clarifying ideas**: 'Right, Darren, so you think that this stone will melt if I boil it in water?'
- **Suggesting:** 'You might like to try doing it this way.'
- **Reminding:** 'Don't forget that you said that this stone will melt if I boil it.'
- **Using encouragement to further thinking:** 'You have really thought hard about where to put this door in the palace – where will you put the windows?'
- **Offering an alternative viewpoint:** 'Maybe Goldilocks wasn't naughty when she ate the porridge?'
- **Speculating:** 'Do you think the three bears would have liked Goldilocks to come to live with them as their friend?'
- **Reciprocating:** 'Thank goodness that you were wearing your wellies when you jumped in those puddles, Kwame. Look at my feet, they are soaking wet!'
- **Asking open questions:** 'How did you … ?' 'Why does this … ?' 'What happens next?' 'What do you think?' 'I wonder what would happen if … ?'
- **Modelling thinking**: 'I have to think hard about what I do this evening. I need to take my dog to the vet because he has a sore foot, take my library books back to the library and buy some food for dinner tonight. But I just won't have time to do all of these things.'
- **Using positive questioning:** 'I don't know, what do you think?' 'That's an interesting idea.' 'I like what you have done there.' 'Have you seen what X has done – why?' 'I wondered why you had … ?' 'I've never thought about that before.' 'You've really made me think.' 'What would happen if we did … ?'
- **Making sense words:** 'I think', 'I agree', 'I imagine', 'I disagree', 'I like', 'I don't like', 'I wonder'.

(summarised from Siraj-Blatchford, 2005)

Similar to SST and the collaborative learning between pedagogues and children, Claxton (2007: 8) focuses on *how* children learn more than the *what* or *how much* they learn, and he encourages pedagogues to challenge children's thinking and talk with them about how they are learning by using questions such as:

- How did you do that?
- How else could you have done that?
- Who did that a different way?
- What was hard about doing that?
- What could you do when you are stuck on that?
- How could you help someone else do that?
- What would have made that easier for you?
- How could you make that harder for yourself?
- How could I have taught that better?

Note the last question, which encourages co-learning between children and pedagogue, and stipulates reflection and evaluation of the process of teaching and learning. The types of open-ended questions, as suggested by Siraj-Blatchford or Claxton, also have the purpose to encourage children (and adults) to think critically about their thinking, which is known as meta–cognition. Steiner, DeBono, the SPEEL study (Moyles *et al.*, 2002) and recent publications by Hargreaves

(2005) have highlighted the value of learners considering their own learning, evaluating how and what they have learned, and making sense of it. The EYFS (DfE, 2012a) places emphasis on children's ability to think critically and Hargreaves (2005: 18) suggests how teachers and early years pedagogues can facilitate this:

Much of what teachers do in helping students to learn how to learn consists of strengthening their meta-cognitive capacity, namely the capacity to monitor, evaluate, control and change how they think and learn.

Reflective task

- Observe colleagues and identify how their knowledge and understanding of SST actually support SST when working with children.
- How do you ask questions? (You might use peer observations.)
- What opportunities do you offer children for SST?
- How do you extend children's capacity to learn and their meta-cognition?
- How do you use SST and the results of SST in planning for individual children's needs?
- How do you involve the child's family in SST?

Extend your knowledge

Read the following journal articles:

- Siraj-Blatchford, I. (2007) 'Creativity, communication and collaboration: The identification of pedagogic progression in sustained shared thinking', *Asia-Pacific Journal of Research in Early Childhood Education*, vol. 1, no. 2, pp. 3–23.
- Siraj-Blatchford, I. and Manni, L. (2008) '"Would you like to tidy up now?" An analysis of adult questioning in the English Foundation Stage', *Early Years: An International Journal of Research and Development*, vol. 28, no. 1, pp. 5–22.
- Claxton, G. (2007) 'Expanding young people's capacity to learn', *British Journal of Educational Studies*, vol. 55, no. 2, pp. 1–20.

School readiness

Initially it may be useful to define the term 'school readiness', yet a simple, clear definition of this concept has been hard to establish. Indeed, historically within early years there had been a reluctance to provide a definition (Salufa *et al.*, 2000). Now, however, there are many which shift according to cultural and political perspectives. Originally, definitions were founded on a maturational approach, drawn from the work of Gesell *et al.* (1974), whereas some recent definitions consider the 'goodness–of–fit' between the child and the environment, thus maximising developmental outcomes for the child (Graue, 1992). Educational definitions too have changed, moving away from preparing children for primary school by simply supporting literacy and numeracy skills, to a more holistic social pedagogic approach that provides a broader approach, supporting life skills and the child's family. Interestingly, UNICEF (2012a, 2012b) states that for it 'school readiness' is defined by the characteristics of 'transitions' and 'gaining competencies' across the three dimensions mentioned previously: 'children's readiness for school; school's readiness for children; and families' readiness for school'. However, Petrie (2005: 179) warns that what she calls the process of 'schoolification' raises pedagogical expectations in early years practices which can be detrimental for young children in their formative years.

This holistic approach taken by UNICEF (2012b) with regard to school readiness and the significance of the transition process highlights the debate which has existed about the differences between child readiness and school readiness, academic ability and social ability, as further noted by Kennedy *et al.* (2012). Moreover, we can see influences of Bronfenbrenner's ecological approach in that all involved with children are taking a role and responsibility within the transition process, which he defined as occurring 'whenever a person's position in the ecological environment is altered as a result of change in role, setting or both' (Bronfenbrenner,1979: 26).

Reflective task

Consider these two quotes and discuss the different emphases:

We need to ensure 'school readiness' for children who arrive in reception class 'unable to form letters or even hold a pencil'.

(Gove 2011)

Rushing young children into formal learning of literacy, mathematics etc as young as possible is misguided. This leads to a situation where children's basic emotional and cognitive needs for autonomy, competence and relatedness are not being met.

(Whitebread and Bingham, 2011: 4)

Having read these quotes, and by undertaking your own research, how would you define 'school readiness'?

Supporting transitions to Key Stage 1

One of the main objectives of the EYFS (DfE, 2012a) is to promote 'school readiness' through its teaching and learning methodology. A significant feature of this is the assessment process which must now be formally summarised by practitioners at age two, in order to support early intervention, and then by teachers at the end of reception class. However, before this, we must not forget the importance of the transition from nursery to school which, if not managed sensitively, can be traumatic for children. Kennedy *et al.* (2012: 20) refer to the 'stress, uncertainty and emotional discomfort, as children must relinquish some of the security of the familiar and readjust to the uncertainty of the new'. Further to this are the stress and anxiety experienced by parents, which in turn inevitably exacerbates the feelings of the children.

The relationships between all involved are vital to ensure smooth transitions and these were strongly promoted in the previous EYFS (DCSF, 2008a) through the positive relationships theme. Communication as always is the key and, although not always straightforward, this is something that a nursery setting or childminder will inevitably find easier than a school simply due to sheer scale. Furthermore, in the nursery setting, the 'key person' role provides that pivotal point for relationships. Shields (2009) in her study examined parents' views of their relationships with their child's nursery setting and then, once at school, with their primary school teacher. Not surprisingly, the findings showed that parents felt their relationships were fostered by nurseries, but this was not the case in schools, which resulted in parents feeling less involved in their child's learning (Shields, 2009).

Extend your knowledge

Read the following extract from Shields's conclusions (2009: 247) and ask yourself how you can support children's transitions and communicate effectively with parents.

The findings demonstrate the complex nature of preschool to school transition for parents. While close, supportive relationships between parents and staff are prioritised by nurseries, parents perceive that such bonds are less important for schools, which has a negative impact on their perception of the school, and results in them feeling less closely involved in their children's learning.

...

The Early Years Foundation Stage has been designed to promote continuity between the settings experienced by young children. One of its key principles is that parents are children's first educators, and that settings must work with them as partners. Future research is needed to evaluate the impact of the EYFS on schools' practice when working with parents. Such research should prioritise the voices and experiences of the parents themselves, as they are currently missing from much research on Early Years settings.

Research transition procedures in your setting and in other settings by reading and comparing to the good practice example from *Southwark's Transition and Assessment Record and the Integrated Child Support Service 0–5 Component Transitions Protocol,* referred to and discussed by Kennedy *et al.* (2012: 24).

What can you learn from this example and how can you improve your practice?

In her review Tickell (2011) acknowledged the difficulties experienced by primary school teachers in the transition of children from the EYFS curriculum to Key Stage 1. Moreover, in his chapter 'Play and pedagogy: A conflict of interest?', Rogers (2011) points to the pressures experienced by reception class teachers in trying to reconcile the differences in approach between the EYFS and the National Curriculum. He refers to it as 'a conflict of interests' (Rogers, 2011: 14). Tickell (2011) did not go as far as recommending an extension to the EYFS up to age six, as did the Cambridge Primary Review (CPR) (University of Cambridge, 2009), but she did want to see improved compatibility between the two curricula and that the EYFS delivered in reception class should be valued. Therefore, in the 2012 EYFS (DfE, 2012a), there has been a revision of the assessment process, with the introduction of the Early Years Foundation Stage Profile. The EYFS (DfE, 2012a: 11) states that the EYFS Profile must reflect:

- ongoing observation
- all relevant records held by the setting
- discussions with parents and carers, and any other adults whom the teacher, parent or carer judges can offer a useful contribution.

The EYFS Profile will be an assessment of the child's learning and development against the early learning goals and will show whether the child is *meeting* the expected level of development, *exceeding* the expected level of development, or if the level of development is not yet met but *emerging*. This assessment process will not only advise and inform the Key Stage 1 teacher of the child's level of development, but will also identify the need for any additional support.

The CPR (University of Cambridge, 2009: 16) also makes a call for England to 'fall into line with international practice' by raising the school starting age to six or seven and provides evidence that indeed the Key Stage 1 curriculum may be damaging to children's learning. So this begs the question as to whether or not we should be placing so much emphasis within the EYFS on 'school readiness'.

The CPR believed that primary schools could deliver play-based learning through to age six successfully and quoted a case study which described the experience of a school where the children were experiencing ineffective transition to year 1 and their learning was regressing. As a result of the change in teaching method to a play-based approach, 'the children are happier and standards have gone up, particularly for boys' (University of Cambridge, 2009: 17).

Read the Cambridge Primary Review (University of Cambridge, 2009) and consider the advantages and disadvantages of extending the Foundation Stage to age six.

Involving the family and the home learning environment

Supporting families in their child's transitions has become more important than ever, because parents and carers need not only reassurance but knowledge and understanding of what is expected of their child and how it might affect the child's well-being. Consequently, working in partnership with the child's family and communicating with them has to be established right from the start when children attend preschool provision. In the early days of childcare parents or grandparents were either actively involved in running the provision themselves in playgroups, or they left the childcare to trained and paid professionals in nurseries. In the latter scenario, parents did not get involved because they paid somebody else to look after their children, and might not have had the time, or they felt that they should not interfere in the professionals' job. However, the *Start Right* report (Ball, 1994) highlighted the importance of involving parents in children's learning and education, because it was acknowledged that parents are interested in their children's progression and that they do want their children to do well. Parents are seen as the child's first educator, and one should also add to this that grandparents often have a pivotal influence in children's learning and development. Working in partnership with parents has become one of the cornerstones since the introduction of the first curriculum for the Foundation Stage (QCA, 2000) and the subsequent early years curricula, all stating that parents are to be seen as central partners in their child's education and that practitioners need to work effectively with parents to achieve best outcomes for children. Examples of good practice where parents and professional were working together can often be found in Sure Start Children's Centres, because parents feel more encouraged to be part of their child's learning and development (Morrow and Malin, 2004). The government published *The Impact of Parental Involvement on Children's Education* (DCSF, 2008g) and *Supporting Families in the Foundation Years* (DfE and DoH, 2011) to provide practitioners with further support and guidance.

The impact of the home learning environment (HLE) with regard to children's learning, development and the predictability of their adult outcomes has been investigated by a number of researchers (Sylva *et al.*, 2004; Feinstein, 2006; Siraj-Blatchford and Siraj-Blatchford, 2009; Siraj-Blatchford, 2010). The EPPE (Sylva *et al.*, 2004) study had found that children who grew up in an encouraging and supportive HLE achieved better cognitively and academically (mathematics and literacy), than children who came from a disadvantaged background. Moreover, subsequent studies highlighted that a family's socio-economic status or social class was not a predictable factor with regard to the quality of the HLE, because it appeared to be more important *what parents do rather than who they are* or what background they come from (Sylva *et al.*, 2010; Siraj-Blatchford, 2010). Also, children benefit from being cared for or having regular contact with their grandparents, as these 'children showed benefits associated with higher co-operation and less anti-social behaviour' (Siraj-Blatchford and Siraj-Blatchford, 2009: 47).

Recent research by Neumann *et al.* (2012) investigating emergent literacy based on a joint mother–child writing environment confirmed that parents play a vital role in children's early reading and writing skills. They highlight that parents can use the home as well as the surrounding environment (for example, going shopping) to encourage and support (scaffold) children's literacy skills which are seen as 'important predictors of future reading ability and long-term academic outcomes' (Neumann *et al.*, 2012: 1350). Children often imitate and replay everyday experiences, such as shopping, in the role-play area in early years settings. This presents an ideal opportunity for practitioners and parents to work together, to jointly encourage and support children's learning in all areas from literacy to mathematics, to communication and language development, for example by the child creating a creatively designed shopping list.

Another recent study by Vandermaas-Peeler *et al.* (2012) used cooking sessions as a form of encouraging parental support of numeracy for four-year-olds, and they recommend that parental awareness needs to be raised with regard to opportunities which can support early mathematics in activities with children at home. Likewise, Worthington (2006) encourages practitioners to be more creative in exploring mathematical concepts with children, and be open-minded about children's early graphical illustrations which might be misinterpreted for early writing instead of early mathematics. Practitioners draw on children's experiences in their everyday home lives and in return parents or grandparents can be encouraged to get drawn in to the experience of the setting. The concept of SST can be extended to include, and share with, the child's family, when used in the setting as well as the HLE. This can facilitate longer-lasting episodes of SST which in turn enhances children's learning in a more holistic way. Also, projects like those in the Reggio Emilia approach, which children and their families can be actively involved with, at the setting as well as at home, for example using photographic or video diaries which can be shared, offer sample scope for working in partnership with parents and sharing opportunities for sustained shared thinking. You can read more about working with parents in Chapter 14 of this book.

Reflective task

- How do you encourage involvement by parents in their children's learning at the setting *and* at home?
- Design a project that can involve children, their families and the setting. Try to be creative, think outside the box, use everyday experiences, involve children and parents right from the planning stages and identify together how you can enhance all areas of learning and development.
- Explain the concept of SST to children and families in terminology that is 'jargon-free' and understandable for all involved.

The use of information and communication technology in early years

Children are growing up in an environment that surrounds them with electronic information and communication technology (ICT) equipment, gadgets and toys. Interactive games such as

Nintendo Wii often get the whole family, including grandparents, together and involved in activities which can promote communication, language, social interaction and physical movement. Technology is part of children's everyday life and, consequently, practitioners need to incorporate this into planning and implementation of children's learning and development. The use of ICT in early years is an area of learning in the EYFS (DfE, 2012a), in order to prepare children for school and offer them better opportunities for later work life. Today, most early years settings have computers, digital cameras, computer animate games, remote controlled battery operated and electronic toys. This can present a challenge for practitioners in so far as they need to be familiar with the equipment to be able to assist children to use the technology appropriately and to extend children's learning. Research (Plowman and Stephen, 2007) indicates that children require adult guidance and support rather than being left to 'play' with these resources randomly.

A recent study by Wild (2011) conducted a computer-based literacy task with young children aged five to six years, based on the earlier mentioned SST pedagogical strategies example (Siraj-Blatchford, 2005). The study found that children showed much greater potential for SST by working together on a computer-based literacy program than on traditional paper-based worksheets (Wild, 2011: 224). Also, the collaborative approach and working in small groups enhanced children's communication with each other and supported the literacy activity at the same time.

Conversely, an earlier study by Plowman and Stephen (2005) with three-to four-year-olds showed limited collaboration and SST when using computer-based programs. In their subsequent study, Plowman and Stephen (2007) used computer-based activity with preschool children supported by guided interactions from adults to facilitate collaboration and opportunities for SST, which proved more successful. However, none of the research studies elaborated on the practitioners' knowledge and skill-based competence with regard to ICT.

The question might need to be posed as to whether or not the staff in the preschool settings felt confident in using computers alongside SST in the Plowman and Stephen (2005 and 2007) studies; and if the staff in the research by Wild (2011) had Qualified Teacher Status (QTS). This would be noteworthy, because as the REPEY and EPPE study had shown, a better quality of teaching and learning takes place where practitioners are qualified to graduate level, which also might imply that they have sounder ICT skills, as would be expected at this level. It also needs to be acknowledged that often practitioners and parents have concerns about the use of ICT in early years, as they feel it might be too early to introduce young children to the equipment and children should just enjoy playing and using their imaginations. Other views are critical with regard to the implication for children's health, from physical posture-related issues and possible repetitive strain injuries to lack of exercise and poor concentration. Palmer (2007) warns that children's language development is negatively impacted by the overuse of computers, as their brains are so used to quick and flicking images on screens that the brain is not able to slow down or cannot focus on slow learning such as reading and writing.

However, when working with children with special educational needs and disabilities the use of ICT and digital resources is not only helpful but often a lifeline for children to communicate with the world around them and express their ideas. There are many resources available for practitioners to use, for example Learning and Teaching Scotland (2003) has produced creative resources to use with children who have language and communication difficulties.

The use of ICT should not be reduced to special occasions when camera or video equipment is taken out of locked cupboards or when a specific educational activity is introduced on the computer. Children should have the opportunity to access this equipment whenever they like so they can experiment and problem-solve for themselves, for example how to take photos and how to upload these to the computer and how to print pictures. As demonstrated in the Mosaic approach (Clark and Moss, 2001), children like to play and explore the world and capture their view of it with the help of photographic tools. The Mosaic approach is a useful method to 'listen' to children by gaining a glimpse of how they see the world around them, and children can become active partners in planning for their learning and development.

Morgan and Siraj-Blatchford (2009) published a very useful book about the use of ICT and how practitioners and parents can work in partnership. It gives practical examples about how to use ICT indoors and outdoors, as well as in creative ways, such as in role play, for explorations, or making movies, all of which can encourage creativity, imagination, communication, collaboration and SST in the setting as well as in the HLE. Furthermore, Hayes and Whitebread (2006) also published a book and journal articles on how to use ICT to facilitate children's learning.

Scenario

The following case study was provided by an experienced practitioner and manager, Nicky. It shows how ICT can be used in an outdoor environment to encourage cognitive learning of emotional literacy and to support children's confidence within group situations by using ICT equipment.

Walkie talkies

A box of ICT resources was put outside, including cameras, walkie talkies and an iPad. Two children, Katie and Sarah, each took a walkie talkie from the box and started to talk into them and press various buttons. A practitioner noticed that they were not familiar with how to use these and proceeded to show them. Katie and Sarah soon mastered the use of these, enabling them to talk to each other. The practitioner moved away from the children to give them some time to explore using the walkie talkies. During this time another child, Zac, joined Katie and Sarah, asking if he could have a turn. Katie and Sarah were engaged in conversation using the walkie talkies, ignoring Zac. Sarah shouted into her walkie talkie and Katie started laughing into hers. Zac asked again if he could have a turn, but Sarah said 'No'.

The practitioner used this opportunity to explore their feelings, asking them all questions, such as, how are you feeling? Sarah and Katie were feeling 'happy' because they were having fun with the walkie talkies, but Zac was feeling 'sad' because he had not had a turn.

The practitioner picked up an iPad and proceeded to open an application that builds awareness of others' feelings. All three children were instantly intrigued by this and joined in together to listen to the emotion and match it to the picture on the touch screen. With initial practitioner support the children were encouraged to take turns. Then the practitioner moved away from the group to enable them to work together, to communicate and to share without adult intervention. Sarah, Katie and Zac continued to take turns with the iPad, with Sarah noticeably telling Zac that it was his turn.

Katie then offered Zac the walkie talkie she was holding, showing him the button that he needed to press to get it to work. All three children continued to use the walkie talkies and iPad together – sharing, taking turns and conversing in a small-group situation, while also developing their knowledge regarding different emotions.

Additional activities to extend learning further
- Children can use the camera to capture their own emotional faces.
- Create an emotions board with the photos the children have taken, to use within this learning situation as an additional resource.
- Load the photos taken onto a digital photo frame and share with parents to promote further discussion at home.

Reflective task

Ask yourself and evaluate:

- Are your ICT resources simply there for children to 'play' with or do you use them as an integral part of your everyday practice, indoors and outdoors?
- How are ICT resources used as part of the assessment of children's learning and development?
- How confident do you feel when using electronic resources in general, and computers in particular?
- How confident are your staff in using ICT resources?
- What are your staff's and parents' attitudes towards ICT in early years?
- How can you involve parents and make use of the HLE when using ICT?
- Undertake wider reading to get more ideas and feel confident in using ICT effectively.
- You might wish to organise training or a workshop for you and your staff on how to use ICT creatively. You also could invite parents or grandparents to attend to learn alongside each other.

Try to get the child's perspective by getting down to their level (on all fours) and use a video camera to film what you see and how you perceive the world around you from a child's level of height.

Creative ways and approaches to learning in early years

In an era of so called *intelligent* information and communication technology children need to be nurtured from an early age to become curious learners and to maintain their imagination and creativity. Creating and thinking critically (DfE, 2012a) require divergent thinking, thinking outside the box, where multiple answers are seen as opportunities, not necessarily linear but more in DeBono's sense of lateral thinking processes. To enable this, children need creative opportunities to explore their environment and they do not need 'knowledge that is funneled into them'. Educationalist Ken Robinson (1999) produced a report for the NACCCE (National Advisory Committee on Creativity and Cultural Education) in which he blames school and education systems which make children not more intelligent but more 'stupid', as they progress through what he calls the 'educational factory'. He references a longitudinal study which tested 'genius' potential in children using their creative abilities. At kindergarten age 98 per cent of children showed great creativity and indicated 'genius' tendency, whereas by the age of eight to ten this figure had dropped down to 50 per cent, and even further down in later tests (Land and Jarman, 1998). According to Ken Robinson (1999), when children leave school all they have learned is that 'the answer is at the back of the book, but you are not allowed to look and copying is cheating'. Ken Robinson (1999) requests in his report for the government that more creativity needs to be allowed and fostered in the education system.

Reflective task

- Think about what you **can** do with a paperclip and write it down in one minute.
- Now think about what you **cannot** do with a paperclip and write it down in one minute.

You can do the same exercise with children in your care and compare their answers with your answers.

- Watch the video clip: *Changing Education Paradigms*, at http://www.youtube.com/watch?v=zDZFcDGpL4U (11 minutes).

How can you maintain your own and children's level of creativity and 'genius' potential?

You also might wish to read the Robinson report about creativity: Robinson, K. (1999) *All Our Futures: Creativity, Culture and Education*, London: National Advisory Committee on Creativity and Cultural Education.

Creativity needs to be seen as an integral part of any curriculum. As Mindham (2005: 81) states, practitioners and pedagogues should view children not solely as 'in need of an education', but should encourage and emphasise the skills in which children excel in particular in the early years with activities inviting imagination and creativity. The area of expressive arts and design in the EYFS (DfE, 2012a) can incorporate many aspects of creativity from storytelling, role play, drama, music, dance to arts and crafts, as well as exploration and experimentation, where children's curious minds and imagination provide endless opportunities. This should not be restricted to the indoor environment. Much exploration can take place in the natural environments of gardens, parks and forests. A nursery's playground should provide natural resources and materials (instead of plastic slides and Wendy houses), such as pine cones, wooden logs, sticks, leaves, mud, sand, sea shells, robes, pots and pans for creative musical sessions. These materials can be supplemented with mirrors, crayons, bin liners and recycled materials which invite children's imagination and creativity more than many so-called 'education' resources. Through exploration and the innovative use of resources children use their senses and engage in social interaction with others through play.

The creative use of resources can enable children to learn and develop in the prime areas as well as the specific areas of the EYFS (DfE, 2012a). As Worthington (2006) highlighted, children often express mathematical concepts in very creative ways which can get overlooked by practitioners. For example, practitioners could include the use of mathematical concepts in everyday activities with children while they explore and play, for example in counting steps, shells, the colours of the rainbow; or by making music, clapping and counting the rhythm; using rhyme. All of these activities can be creative, and support language development and mathematical understanding at the same time.

Research has shown that when children interact in social situations with peers, such as when playing, they learn to use socially competent behaviours and positive social skills which can reduce the risk of behavioural and emotional problems in later stages of development (Newton and Jenvey, 2011). Also Bruce (2011) states, children's play and children's creativity are integral parts of children's learning and development as a whole person. In particular, children with complex needs, behavioural or learning difficulties can use play and creativity to learn through their 'senses and movement', and they can 'express themselves in more ways than one' (Bruce, 2011: 8). Play and creativity are inclusive activities which offer opportunities for all children to take part regardless of their age, culture, gender, or physical, emotional and intellectual abilities. Read more about creativity and play in Chapter 17 of this book.

There is not one cohesive definition of what constitutes creativity as it is often down to the interpretation of the creator. However, many educationalists agree that creativity promotes children's independence and encourages them to use their imagination and thinking outside conventional or predictable patterns, as well as problem posing and problem solving. Research studies have shown that preschool children are very creative in the sense that they can imagine many uses for an item other than its obvious purpose (Land and Jarman, 1998). Whereas, when children get older their creative thinking declines and they can only think in expected patterns, for example that a paper clip can only be used to clip paper together and nothing else.

> When children are being creative they go further than the information given to create something new and original for them. For young children, the process of creativity – which includes curiosity, exploration, play and creativity – is as important as any product they may create.
>
> (Duffy 2010: 20)

Craft (2008: 1) suggests that practitioners should engage in 'possibility thinking' with children by going beyond the 'what is' to the possible, or to the 'what could be', or 'what if'. This can be applied to all areas of children's learning and experiences, from imaginative play to scientific enquiries and experimentation at the setting, inside and outside, as well as in the home. This is supported by Bruce (2011: 22) who argues that, without sensitive engagement with children and their families, 'emergent possibilities for creativity that are in every child do not develop or can be quickly extinguished'. Indeed, Craft (2008: 3) highlights the important difference between 'creative practice' which uses imaginative approaches when working with children; and 'practice which fosters creativity' by encouraging children's ideas and possibility thinking. Craft (2008: 3) gives examples from her research in early years settings of how to foster creativity, as follows:

- **Posing questions:** Children's questions; both those posed aloud and others implied through actions, were closely documented by practitioners with a concerned, deep knowledge of each individual. Questions were treated with respect and interest, nurtured and celebrated. Question posing often occurred in imaginative play.
- **Play:** Children in these settings were offered opportunities to play over extended periods of time. Children were highly motivated and engaged, deeply interested and very serious in their playfulness, engaging closely with one another's ideas and experience, imagining all kinds of scenes, encountering and solving problems.
- **Immersion:** The children were deeply immersed in a caring, positive, loving environment in each setting. In each case this was combined with overt cognitive challenge.
- **Innovation:** Children in these three settings made strong and playful connections between ideas in their own ways, and were encouraged to do this. Practitioners sought to further the children's growing understandings, offering provocations to stimulate connection-making.
- **Being imaginative:** Through imagining and being imaginative, children were able to be decision makers about the quality of ideas, content of their learning tasks, and ways of conducting them.
- **Self-determination and risk-taking:** Children were enabled in taking risks, working in safe, secure and supportive environments in which they were expected to exercise independence (agency) in making decisions and where their contributions were valued. Adults encouraged learning from experience as both empowering and generative. Each adult worked hard not to rush children.

(Craft, 2008: 3)

Educational theories often promote both adult-initiated and child-initiated strategies for enhancing young children's self-expression and creativity. To foster children's potential, adults need to fully understand how children explore the world around them, what representation means and how to communicate with children, thus to assist children in expressing their experiences and learning. By fostering creativity and listening to children, adults can learn from the children's creative ideas and should include children in planning for children's individual needs. Edwards and Springate (1995) highlighted that practitioners should not rush children's creativity, and it should not be restricted by timetabled sessions or limited space for children to express their creativity. Children should be given the opportunity to return to their creative creations and continue or progress their creative engagement. As in the Steiner Waldorf approach, children need to be able to access natural and inviting materials which can include recycled materials, as well as having light spaces and harmonious colours to nurture creative expression. And as in the Reggio Emilia approach, children need to have opportunities to display their creative works and share them with others in a non-judgemental environment where uniqueness and freedom of expression are accepted. In all their creative representations and demonstrations children need to be actively involved in decision-making processes of what and how they wish to articulate themselves and where they wish to seek their inspirations from.

> **Creative teaching is an art; it involves practitioners in using their imagination to make learning more interesting, exciting and effective to ensure that all children want to become involved and enthused about learning. ... Creative teaching involves taking risks, leaving the security of structured lessons behind and learning from the children.**
>
> (Duffy, 2010: 23)

Practitioners and families need to cooperate in offering inviting creative experience opportunities and get excited about these together with the children, thus facilitating freedom of expression and process-orientated rather than product-orientated learning and development. Workshops or sessions that invite parents or grandparents along to explore their own creative potential alongside their children can often readdress preconceived ideas about what creativity should look like or be.

Creative expression in all of its forms, which involve all the senses, can assist children in posing problems as well as solving problems and being innovative, which are all essential skills for life. Freedom of expression and non-judgemental acceptance of children's creative creations and communications will build confidence and self-esteem because they discover themselves and the world around them in an atmosphere of encouragement and acceptance. Listening to children and offering children opportunities to document and exhibit their creative practice and projects by using, for example, photography and video in the process mean that children become documenters of their own learning, development and unique innovations. A useful method for involving children in documenting their creativity is the Mosaic approach (Clark and Moss, 2001), which again can be extended to the HLE.

Reflective task

Evaluate your practice and ask yourself:

- What are your definition and perception of creativity?
- What are your colleagues' understandings of and approaches to creativity?
- What are your parents' expectations of what creativity should be?
- How do you 'nurture' creativity?
- What are the differences and similarities between play and creativity?
- Think about creative activities indoors and outdoors.
- How can you embed creativity as discussed above in the curriculum areas of expressive arts and design, creating and thinking critically, as well as playing and exploring?

Read further about creativity:

- Tims, C. (2010) (ed.) 'Creative learning in the early years is not just child's play...': Born creative, London: DEMOS. Available from: http://www.demos.co.uk.

Monitoring quality in early years through assessment of teaching and learning

The Rumbold Report *Starting with Quality* (Rumbold, 1990) and the Royal Society of Arts Report *Start Right* (Ball, 1994) both stressed the importance of quality in early years education. Earlier projects to measure and improve quality in early years, such as the *Effective Early Learning* (EEL) project (Bertram and Pascal, 1997), focused on the adult–child interaction, using the Laevers (1997) adult engagement scale. But it was not until the publication of the *Effective Provision of Pre-school Education* (EPPE) project (Sylva *et al.*, 2004) that the direct relationship between the quality of preschool settings and the intellectual and social development of children from age three and four years was clearly identified. Summarising, good–quality provision was associated by Sylva *et al.* (2004) with:

- integrated centres, nursery schools and nursery classes
- staff with higher qualifications, especially if a good proportion of the staff are trained teachers
- pedagogy that includes 'interaction traditionally associated with the term "teaching", the provision of instructive learning environments and "sustained shared thinking" to extend children's learning'
- a balanced approach to the education and social development that regards these as complementary.

In order to monitor and evaluate the quality of the settings which participated in the project Sylva *et al.* (2004) used the *Early Childhood Environment Rating Scale* (ECERS), an auditing tool developed in the USA by Harms *et al.* (2004). ECERS belongs to a group of scales developed to assess provision for children from birth to 12 years. Relevant to early years are the *Infant/ Toddler Environment Rating Scale (ITERS-R*)*, which is designed to assess group programmes for children from birth to two and a half years of age, and the *Early Childhood Environment Rating Scale (ECERS-R*)*, which assesses centre-based provision for children between the age of two and a half and five years (Harms *et al.*, 2004, cited in Sylva *et al.*, 2010). The scales have been revised over the years as indicated by *R**. An extended version of ECERS was later developed for use in the ongoing EPPE project (Sylva *et al.*, 2010) and assessed the provision for children aged three to five years in the areas of literacy, mathematics, science and the environment, diversity (race, gender and individual learning needs). The focus was on the assessment of the quality of curricular provision, including pedagogy, and the domains aimed at fostering children's academic development (Sylva *et al.*, 2010).

The different forms of ECERS, including a version for childminders called the *Family Child Care Environment Rating Scale (FCCERS)*, as well as the Laevers scales of adult engagement and child involvement (1997), have all been used extensively over the last ten years as reliable and credible measures of quality in early years research.

When preparing for an Ofsted inspection, centre managers and their staff have reported that they found ECERS-R, and the extended version developed by Sylva *et al.* called ECERS-E (extension), useful quality measurement tools in preparing the Self Evaluation Form (SEF), according to Sylva *et al.* (2010).

Also, many local authorities have their own quality management and quality measurement tools and accredited quality schemes encouraging early years practitioners to improve their overall practice. The DCSF published a document to support local authority early years consultants and leaders of early years settings to improve the quality of their provision, called *Early Years Quality*

Improvement Support Programme (EYQISP) (DCSF, 2008e). The key principles highlighted in the guidance document are built on (DCSF, 2008e: 6–7):

- the role of effective leadership in securing and improving quality
- a continuous cycle of self-evaluation, improvement and reflection, thus empowering practitioners to see themselves as learners, seeking improvements in their practice, reducing inequality and narrowing the achievement gap
- a system of support and challenge which is transparent and agreed by all
- strong partnerships between the local authority, settings and each setting's community.

These key principles are explored through the following five elements (DCSF, 2008e: 6–7):

- strengthening leadership for learning – focusing on the key role of leaders in building capacity and ensuring high-quality learning development and provision
- developing practitioner learning – focusing on the needs and highlighting/developing strengths of practitioners who support and extend children's learning and development
- facilitating partnerships for learning and development – focusing on working in partnership with parents/carers, children, other settings and partner professionals to support children's learning and development
- supporting progress, learning and development – focusing on using observations to assess and understand children's learning and development, both in the home and the setting, and translating observations of children at play into an assessment of each child's progress to help and support them further
- securing high-quality environments for learning and development – focusing on the enabling environment (including the physical and emotional environment), which promotes children's well-being, nurtures children and fosters positive relationships between children, parents and adults, and where children are valued for their uniqueness and individuality.

Quality and improvement of early years practice are further discussed in Chapter 15, page 351, of this book, supported with illustrations of the EYQISP quality improvement diagram (DCSF, 2008e) and the SPEEL wheel (Moyles *et al.*, 2002).

Extend your knowledge

Read further:

- DCSF (2008) *Early Years Quality Improvement Support Programme (EYQISP)*, Nottingham: DCSF. Available from: http://www.school-portal.co.uk/GroupDownloadFile.asp?GroupId=716966&Resource ID=2635260.

The EYQISP guidance document can provide you with lots of useful tools and tips to improve your setting's quality. Look at the illustration in Chapter 15 (see figure 15.11 on page 351) and evaluate what your setting's quality looks like. Go to page 12 of the EYQISP document, where you will find a range of reflective questions which will assist you in evaluating the quality of your setting. Then go to page 14 and use the Quality Improvement Cycle to plan for your setting's provision.

Furthermore, most of you are probably very familiar with SEF and the different forms of ECERS. You might like to read further about improving the quality in adult–child interaction and draw on international research. Read some of the chapters available on google books of the following book:

- Laevers, F. and Heylen, L. (2003) *Involvement of Children and Teacher Style: Insights from an International Study on Experiential Education*, Leuven University, Belgium: Leuven University Press.

The role of Ofsted

The Office for Standards in Education (Ofsted) has no formal or statutory role in determining the curriculum, although it is party to national curriculum developments and provides advice based on inspection evidence. Ofsted's approach is predicated on how well children are achieving in relation to the curriculum specified at the time. Ofsted has made regulatory changes to align with the reformed EYFS (DfE, 2012a) and since September 2012 the new Ofsted regulation aimed to:

- help to minimise risks to children when in registered early years provision
- allow greater autonomy to providers to manage their own service
- strengthen registration arrangements
- continue with rigorous enforcement for those who cannot or will not comply with requirements.

The inspection system does not determine curriculum arrangements, but does provide evidence-based feedback which can influence curriculum policy. Based on a survey, Ofsted published their report in February 2011 which evaluated the impact of the EYFS on the quality of provision and developmental outcomes for young children from birth to five years. Some of the key findings with regard to provision and outcomes for children are summarised below (Ofsted, 2011b: 3–4):

- Outcomes in personal, social and emotional development (PSED) were satisfactory or better in all the childcare providers visited by Ofsted and they found that the key to good outcomes was the routines that practitioners established and the high expectations that they had of children's behaviour.
- Children's PSED was better where the providers were clear about the stages of learning and development and specifically planned activities to cover all aspects of this area of learning.
- Outcomes for communication, language and literacy were good or outstanding in two-thirds of the settings, because practitioners were specifically planning opportunities to develop children's speaking and listening, and early reading and writing skills.
- The childcare providers visited, particularly childminders, tended to focus on children as individuals rather than consider the specific needs of different groups, other than those with identified additional needs, in which case they knew how to access external support or advice.

These survey reports are published regularly by Ofsted on their website and provide invaluable guidance for improving practice. The July 2012 Ofsted guidance on preparing for your next inspection, the *Evaluation schedule for inspections of registered early years' provision*, is available on the website (Ofsted, 2012). Ofsted inspections since September 2012 focus very much on opportunities provided for children's personal, social and emotional development and their general progress in learning. Ofsted (2012) will make an overall judgement based on these three factors:

- how well the early years provision meets the needs of the range of children who attend
- the contribution of the early years provision to children's well-being
- the leadership and management of the early years provision.

Inspectors are looking at how well the setting meets the needs of the individual children and will grade the setting using detailed descriptors based on all aspects, with particular attention paid to children requiring additional support. The inspectors will be looking for evidence of the setting and practitioners 'working in partnership with parents', how children's progress is communicated to parents and of course how well the setting prepares the children for school ('school readiness').

New features of these inspections (Ofsted, 2012) are a strong emphasis on safeguarding and children's welfare and promotion of well-being (see Chapter 13 in this book). The inspectors will be questioning the 'key persons' to ascertain their knowledge of their key child's progress, as well as observations being undertaken with the setting's manager to gauge identifications of the setting's strengths and weaknesses and plans for improvements, thereby assessing leadership and management. Therefore, the quality of the overall setting is very important and some of the quality management tools discussed in the earlier section can assist you in improving practice and provision as well as getting better Ofsted reports.

Hopkin *et al.* (2010) undertook an analysis on the quality of early years education as measured by Ofsted inspections and compared these to the ECERS-E and ECERS-R measurement tools to see whether or not Ofsted judgements on quality could predict outcomes for children. They found that:

> ... low correlations may be because Ofsted rates settings in terms of achieving minimum standards, whilst the other measures just rate the quality of aspects of the service provided, but it remains somewhat surprising that Ofsted ratings were not more highly correlated with these quality indicators.

> ...

> However, when we considered other child outcome measures, again ones that are widely considered in academic research, we were able to demonstrate a positive relationship between quality and outcomes for some of these measures, although Ofsted inspection judgements did not predict any of our outcome measures.

> (Hopkin *et al.*, 2010: 83–4)

Recently, Mathers (2012) within her study *Improving Quality in the Early Years* identified the stakeholders (parents, children, practitioners and policymakers) within the early years sector, and researched their individual perceptions of the concept of 'quality'. Furthermore, Mathers (2012) examined the tools that have been used to measure quality and thus guide the various stakeholders such as the Ofsted grades and ECERS (Harms *et al.*, 2004), as well as other quality improvement schemes. Not only does she note the fact that the quality improvement schemes are initiated based on the Ofsted grades, but she also highlights the purposes and vested interests that each quality measure may serve (Mathers, 2012).

Reflective exercise

The EYFS states: 'A quality learning experience for children requires a quality workforce' (DfE, 2012a: 7).
- Is it reasonable to expect all childcare providers regularly to evaluate the quality of their work?
- How do you do this in your setting?
- What does it say in the EYFS about evaluation and reflection?
- How does this fit with the Ofsted inspection framework?

Read further and evaluate your approach to quality in your setting:
- Hopkin, R., Stokes, L. and Wilkinson, D. (2010) *Quality, Outcomes and Costs in Early Years Education*, London: National Institute of Economic and Social Research. Available from: http://www.niesr.ac.uk/pdf/Quality%20Outcomes%20and%20Costs%20in%20early%20Years%20Education.pdf.

Reflective practice and supervision in early years

The old EYFS (DCSF, 2008a) introduced reflective practice in early years which is a concept that has been used in other disciplines such as social work and health for many years, in order to improve practice. Reflection is linked to evaluation of what works and why, so as to increase effectiveness and accountability (see Chapter 2 in this book). The reformed EYFS (DfE, 2012a) has now introduced supervision alongside appraisals to provide quality in early years and to achieve better outcomes for practitioners and the children in their care. Supervision of practitioners has been practised for many years in social care and health. In supervision, practitioners reflect and evaluate on their practice and identify effective practice, or areas of improvement, on a regular basis. Practitioners need to explore their feelings, their knowledge and effective practice continuously in order to provide good-quality services for children and their families. Reflection and supervision are to be understood as tools also to be used to inform the planning and effective implementation of the curriculum.

Munro's review (2011) of safeguarding children emphasised the importance of self-reflection, in particular through regular supervision of practitioners' work, in order to identify and raise any concerns regarding children's welfare at an early stage. Equally, the Allen (2011) report enforced the importance of early intervention and prevention to keep children safe and promote their well-being, as well as helping children to achieve better outcomes in later life. The Tickell (2011) review of the EYFS recommended the use of regular supervision to enhance early years practice by identifying children's needs at the earliest possible stage, as well as acting swiftly and professionally in responding to potential safeguarding issues. The progress check at age two, as recommended by Tickell (2011), should be on the agenda of supervision sessions when practitioners, together with their line managers, discuss how best to support children's development, and how to relate the information to the children's parents. Supervision has now been consolidated in the reformed EYFS (DfE, 2012a) as a requirement for all staff working in early years. Supervision is also considered a tool to enhance job satisfaction, reduce stress, encourage staff retention and motivation of the workforce (Skills for Care and the Children's Workforce Development Council, 2007).

The main difference between appraisal and supervision is that appraisals usually take place only once or twice a year, whereas supervision should take place more frequently, usually every four to six weeks, depending on staff's contractual hours. As with appraisals, supervision sees staff performance and training needs assessed, but in regular supervision effective practice and accountability of work are reviewed in more depth and in relation to the children and families practitioners work with. Children's and families' needs are discussed and professional practice support and guidance are part of the supervision process. Supervision is to be understood as a two-way process where practitioners come prepared with issues they wish to discuss with their line manager and where the line manager has agenda items they wish to address with the staff member. Sound leadership skills are required for successful supervision processes to take place and supervisors need to attend training and read about how to conduct effective supervision.

The Children's Workforce Development Council (CWDC, 2010b) described the four functions of supervision as: line management, professional supervision, continuing professional development (CPD) and coordination of integrated practice.

Summarising, the CWDC (2010b: 8) stipulates what supervision should be:

- Supervision is a planned, accountable, two-way process, which should support, motivate, assist and ensure all workers develop good practice.
- Supervision outcomes should directly benefit children and families, improving the service they receive.
- Supervision is a key factor in better safeguarding practice.
- The supervision process must provide a supportive learning environment for reflecting on practice, assessing risk and making decisions.
- Supervision outcomes should ensure workers are confident and competent in their own role, are able to develop integrated working, improve their performance and learn from practice.

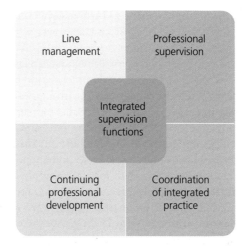

Figure 5.2 The four supervision functions (CWDC, 2010b: 7)

- Line managers should be confident in their ability to provide high-quality supervision, and are accountable for supervision practice.
- Responsibilities for the different functions of supervision need to be clear, balanced and agreed, to avoid duplication if people have more than one supervisor.
- Managers need to be clear how supervision will be provided in integrated management arrangements.
- Senior managers are responsible for ensuring that supervision is given priority. Time and resources must be embedded in effective policy for integrated supervision in the trust.
- Supervision should be underpinned by a Children's Trust strategy and policy based on agreed principles, values, language and expectations.
- Supervision is a fundamental part of leadership and management at all levels.
- All Children's Trust partner agencies should undertake regular evaluation and audit their own supervision strategy and practice.
- Change to integrated supervision arrangements should be planned and owned by all the people it affects.

It needs to be acknowledged that the introduction of formal and regular supervision can raise anxieties for staff who might feel they are being controlled. Staff might not be able to see the benefits of supervision and their accountability within this process. Supervision is aimed at providing good-quality practice and the best outcomes for children, as well as job satisfaction for the practitioner. On the other hand, managers, supervisors and nursery owners are concerned about the additional time (and money) it takes to provide regular supervision to staff which they fear will bring up the cost of childcare. However, in children's centres and other children's services regular supervision and case discussions about the children are already an integral part of practice. Further reasons behind the concerns by practitioners and line managers about supervision are possibly because it is another new change and they might require further training in order to enable them to undertake effective supervision.

Supervision can be seen as a combination of reflective practice and appraisal. Together the practitioner and line manager can reflect on what has been working well and where there are areas of improvement or further development. Active listening skills are crucial, together with an atmosphere of trust and openness which encourages staff to explore and solve problems together. Formal supervision needs to take place in a quiet, safe and confidential environment, which is free from interruptions and can last around one hour, depending on what is discussed. A brief written supervision contract should be agreed and signed by both parties at the beginning of employment which lays out the ground rules of confidentiality, regularity of supervision and the roles of both supervisor and supervisee. Standard items on the supervision agenda should be any personal (staff welfare) and everyday work-related performance issues, on which to provide guidance and support. In this way, supervision can be used as an all-year-round performance monitoring tool, and support can be identified as and when required to assist practitioners to do their job, for example by role modelling good practice, or offering training and CPD opportunities. Also on the agenda in supervision are discussions about individual children's cases, or matters with regard to their parents/carers, as well as any welfare, early identification and safeguarding issues. Consistent working approaches for the whole team, as well as when working with other agencies need to be addressed at supervision as appropriate. Formal supervision notes should be written up and two copies, signed by both parties, should be kept by each party for future reference, so as to be able to refer back at the next supervision as well as for input into annual appraisals.

The benefits of good supervision for all stakeholders are illustrated in Table 5.1 below.

Benefits for EY practitioners and managers	Benefits for children
• Role and accountability clear • Boundaries clarified • Pressures/decisions shared • Confidence and competence enhanced • Reflection facilitated • Focus on children and families maintained • Creative practice supported • Diversity valued • Learning needs identified • Feelings addressed • Team working enhanced	A well-supervised worker is more: • Focused, clear and prepared • Observant and attentive • Alert to strengths, needs and risks • Aware of power issues • Able to involve children's perspectives • Consistent • Child- and family-focused • Able to make a fuller assessment and plan for individual provisions
Benefits for the setting	**Benefits for parents/carers**
• Greater consistency • Facilitates internal communication • Shared responsibility for problems • Setting goals, values and policies disseminated • Improved consultation processes • Increased transparency and openness • Staff more connected to big picture • Facilitates change management • Lower rates of turnover, sickness • Lower rates of grievances/complaints • Effective multi-agency working and communication	A well-supervised worker: • Is clearer about their role • Understands parents' roles • Communicates better with parents • Has an accurate expectation of parents • Is more able to resolve conflicts with parents • Is supported in acting as a keyworker • Is more confident in multidisciplinary discussions with other agencies

Table 5.1 Benefits of effective supervision (adapted from CWDC, 2010b: 38)

Next steps

Supervision in early years

- Discuss with your line manager the arrangements and expectations for your supervision.
- If you are a line manager, identify who is providing you with supervision.
- If you are a line manager, or somebody who will be in charge of undertaking supervision with practitioners, evaluate your knowledge and skills about the supervision process and identify any further training needs.
- Discus as a team the benefits of supervision.
- Identify how supervision can be integrated to inform the planning and implementation of the early years curriculum for individual children and groups of children.

Conclusion

This chapter has explored and discussed the emergence of an early years curriculum and the changes it has undergone over the last decade. Different curriculum models and their purpose have been discussed. Questions were asked about the relevance and effectiveness of product-driven versus process-driven approaches to implementing the curriculum with its implications for practitioners and a child-centred versus an adult-led approach in early years.

We discussed how children learn influenced by the environment and context of their lives by identifying the roles pedagogues can take as 'learning companions' to co-construct children's learning and to enhance their development as a whole person. The concept of effective pedagogy in early years and the fostering of creativity in children through playing and exploring, together with the approach of sustained shared thinking (SST) and active listening to children were highlighted, which need to be taken into consideration when planning and implementing the curriculum.

The influence of the child's environment, and consequently the importance of working in partnership with parents and including the home learning environment (HLE) as part of understanding and learning from children and families, needs to be taken into consideration when planning for the individual child.

Finally, the effectiveness and quality of early years practice in implementing the curriculum through pedagogical strategies to support learning and development for children were discussed by drawing on research studies and good practice. The new requirement for early years settings to provide regular supervision to all staff was explained and the benefits for children, families, staff and the setting were outlined with the goal of improving and enhancing practice, and providing quality childcare.

Practice

Individually or as a team reflect on your current practice of planning for and implementing the curriculum. Evaluate what works and what needs to be changed to facilitate children's learning and development. You might like to use a SWOT analysis to help you identify the areas you are good at (strengths), the areas of improvement (weaknesses), and to look for opportunities, and consider where there are potential threats or barriers.

Consider the following reflective and evaluative questions:

1 What pedagogical methods do you use to plan for children's learning and development?
   a How do you plan for the prime areas of learning?
   b How do you plan for the specific areas of learning?
2 How do you listen to children and include what you learn about their views and experiences in planning for the curriculum?
   a How do you involve children in the planning and implementation of the curriculum?
   b How do you involve parents?
3 How do you link your observation of children to the curriculum areas and profiling of the child's progression?
4 How do you monitor the effectiveness and quality of your assessment tools and teaching and learning resources?
5 How do you document and use the progress check at age two to provide information and opportunities for collaboration with parents and other services?

Further reading

Allington, S. (2011) *Transitions in the Early Years: A practical guide to support transitions between early years settings and into Key Stage 1*, London: Practical Pre-school.

Beckley, P. (2012) (ed.) *Learning in Early Childhood*, London: SAGE.

Craft, A. (2010) *Creativity and Education Futures: Learning in a Digital Age*, Stoke-on Trent: Trentham Books Ltd.

Craft, A. (2011) *Creativity and Early Years Education*, London: Continuum.

Hall, K., Cremin, T., Comber, B. and Moll, L. (eds.) (2012) *The Wiley Blackwell International Research Handbook of Children's Literacy, Learning and Culture*, Oxford: Wiley Blackwell.

Rose, J. and Rogers, S. (2012) *The Role of the Adult in Early Years Settings*, Maidenhead: Open University Press.

Wood, E. (2010) 'Reconceptualising the play–pedagogy relationship: From control to complexity', in Brooker, L. and Edwards, S. (eds), *Engaging Play*, Maidenhead: Open University Press.

Keep up-to-date by regularly checking the following websites:

http://www.education.gov.uk

http://www.foundationyears.org.uk

http://www.ofsted.gov.uk

Working with babies (birth to 12 months)

Tracy Rydin-Orwin

6

Introduction

Government legislation has determined that the social and emotional health of children is the responsibility of all agencies (health, social care and education, including the early years), supported by the *Every Child Matters* (DfES, 2003), *The National Service Framework for Children, Young People and Maternity Services* (Department of Health, 2004), the Public Health White Paper *Choosing Health* (Department of Health, 2004), and *Supporting Families in the Foundation Years* (Department for Education and Department of Health, 2011) documents. They all highlight the importance of the family environment, and parenting in particular, in determining key outcomes for children. This development starts prenatally but is greatly influenced by the early experiences of the infant with its primary carers, in particular its mother. The mental health of the infant is determined by the parent's ability to respond sensitively to the infant's needs. The first few years of life are an important and vulnerable time. Infants are learning a great deal about themselves, their world and the people within their world.

Until the introduction of the *Birth to Three Matters* (DfES, 2002) framework there was very little recognition of the importance of providing stimulating and meaningful environments for play and learning opportunities for babies and very young children. Optimal conditions for early learning environments are where an infant can experience both unstructured and structured play, with it being both adult and child led (Göncü and Gaskins, 2006; Wood, 2010a; DCSF, 2010c). These examples of how the use of the outdoors not only for children but also for infants has influenced current practices in early years, with play now being established as the key way in which children learn (QCA, 2000). Furthermore, findings from the *Effective Provision of Pre-School Education* (EPPE) study support environments in which 'potentially instructive play activities' are accompanied by well-designed adult interventions in children's learning (Sylva *et al.*, 2004). The introduction of the 'key person' (DCSF, 2008a) has acknowledged the facts and findings from research that highlights the importance of building trusting relationships and attachment with children from the earliest stages of their life to enhance positive developmental outcomes. While the debate on the nature and value of play for children and for their learning continues to engage many commentators (Wood, 2010a), the benefits of play for children's physical, intellectual, social and emotional well-being are no longer in doubt.

This chapter will explore developmental aspects of infancy and why early attunement is important, with respect to brain development, sensory processing and later attachment. It will also encourage practitioners to reflect on the importance of early support and interventions, and how they can apply this to their setting, as well as enabling carers to increase their understanding of their infant's emotional needs.

Learning outcomes

This chapter will introduce some key issues relating to the social and emotional development of infants (under 12 months), provide resources to enable you to extend your knowledge further, and guide you to critically evaluate your practice around the following learning outcomes:

- To ensure that all those working with infants have an awareness of the latest research leading to an understanding of the physical and emotional development of these infants.
- To have an understanding of why it is important to have good parent–infant attunement.
- To have an understanding of the issues of sensory processing and how the environment has an impact on infants.
- To have an understanding of the development of the social and physical brain in infants.
- To have an understanding of infant development and the role of play.
- To feel able to use this information to support sensitive interactions with infants which encourage the development of child-initiated and appropriate learning opportunities and environments.
- To have the resources and to feel confident to use the tools given to support parent–infant attunement.

Infancy and early attunement

Babies do not exhibit the classic symptoms of mental illness and disorder and thus the importance of mental health services is not understood. Babies demonstrate through crying, poor feeding and sleep disturbance that they are tense and anxious, distressed and fearful. These emotions need to be responded to with love and empathy. Supporting families to provide this response is essential in order to reduce the incidence of mental health problems and their consequences in later life.

(Young Minds, 2004: 1)

Parents want to protect their children from harm. In their role as protectors they tend to think of the obvious provisions of food, warmth, and protection from illness and danger. But what if we consider safety from the child's perspective? For a child, a very real sense of danger can be brought about by situations that seem innocuous to an adult. In response to perceived threat, a distressed infant or child will naturally express his or her need for comfort and security. The way in which a parent responds to such signals teaches a child about the predictability and safety of his or her world. With time, children learn whether they can count on a parent to provide comfort and security. This, in turn, affects their expectations that the world is either a safe or a dangerous place to be.

Research in the field of attachment suggests that a child's sense of safety and security is as important to emotional and social well-being as actual safety is to physical well-being. The development of a sense of protection is directly related to the quality of the parent–infant relationship. Empirical research over the past three decades has confirmed our intuition about the critical importance of early relationships, and how a parent's role as an attachment figure might be one of the more important factors for a child's future emotional well-being.

Reflective task

Self-assess your experience, knowledge and understanding about babies and infants. Ask yourself the following questions:

■ What experience do you have in working with babies?

■ How do you plan activities for/with babies?

■ What did you enjoy most when working with babies and what where the challenges?

■ Identify the gaps in your knowledge and understanding by writing down questions. This can assist you in recognising where you need to extend your knowledge further after having read this chapter.

The emergence of attachment research

Attachment is a commonly used term with many different meanings between professionals. People tend to be familiar with the notion of bonding but less so with the idea of attachment. In fact, the two are quite different. The term bonding refers primarily to the emotional bonds that form between parents and their children, initially as a result of the events surrounding birth. By contrast, attachment focuses on the child's feelings and behaviour towards the parent over a period of time. John Bowlby and Mary Ainsworth are commonly associated with attachment research and theory development. Ainsworth defined attachment as:

> … an affectional tie that one person (or animal) forms to another specific individual. Attachment is thus discriminating and specific. Like 'object relations,' attachments occur at all ages and do not necessarily imply immaturity or helplessness. To be sure, the first tie is most likely to be formed to the mother, but this may soon be supplemented by attachments to a handful of other specific persons. Once formed, whether to the mother or to some other person, an attachment tends to endure. 'Attachment' is not a term to be applied to any transient relation or to a purely situational dependency transaction. Dependency relations vary according to the exigencies of the situation. Attachments bridge gaps in space and time. To be sure, attachment behavior may be heightened or dampened by situational factors, but attachments themselves are durable, even under the impact of adverse conditions.

(Ainsworth, 1969: 2)

Prior to the early 1900s there was little research on attachment, with the belief that infants neither needed nor were capable of giving human love (Karen, 1994). John Locke and John Watson, both behaviourists, believed that infants were born 'blank slates' and it was the environment that shaped them. They advocated that infants should be treated as young adults and that motherly affection was dangerous (Karen, 1994). In contrast psychoanalysts placed a high importance on loving relationships in order for the infant to develop healthy social–emotional behaviours (Bowlby, 1969). In the 1940s Spitz (1945) carried out a study looking at infants within a hospital setting. For the first three months infants received care and breast milk from their mothers, then they were separated from them, only receiving medical and physical care provided by the nurses. It was not long before there was an observable decline in the infants' development. After just three months' separation, the infants' motor development had completely stopped and they had become passive, not trying to sit up or roll over. The effects of social–emotional deprivation continued to be observed after the infants were placed back into loving homes (Spitz, 1945). This effect was also observed in Hungarian orphanages by Dr Pikler (1945).

Other researchers observed the behaviour of animals in natural and laboratory settings. Arling and Harlow (1967) carried out experiments using rhesus monkeys to gain an understanding of the conditions in which the development of human infants was affected and to come up with some preventative measures.

These studies and observations formed the basis of later theories of attachment by John Bowlby, a highly influential British child psychiatrist, who was the first to put forward a formal theory of attachment in 1969. He stated that:

> Human beings of all ages are found to be at their happiest and … able to deploy their talents to best advantage when they are confident that standing behind them are one or more trusted persons who will come to their aid should difficulties arise. The person trusted provides a secure base from which his (or her) companion can operate.
>
> (Bowlby, 1973: 6)

Bowlby believed that children's difficulties could be traced back to what either happened or did not happen to them as infants and young children. Based on his earlier research, Bowlby believed that for an infant and young child's mental health development it needs to 'experience a warm, intimate and continuous relationship with his mother (or permanent mother-substitute), in which both find satisfaction and enjoyment' (Bowlby, 1951: 11). Mary Ainsworth expanded and confirmed many of Bowlby's ideas by observing parent–infant interactions in the field and in a laboratory setting.

Extend your knowledge

Undertake further background research about attachment by reading:

- Arling, G. L., and Harlow, H. F. (1967) 'Effects of social deprivation on maternal behavior of rhesus monkeys', *Journal of Comparative and Physiological Psychology*, vol. 64, no. 3, pp. 371–7.
- Ainsworth, M. D. (1969) 'Object relations, dependency, and attachment: A theoretical review of the infant–mother relationship', *Child Development*, vol. 40, pp. 969–1025.

What were the key findings and what can we learn from them? How can they be related and applied to your practice when working with infants?

Trust and the quality of attachment

Infants are totally reliant on their carers for every aspect of their needs. Therefore, attachment involves two components in the parent–infant relationship: the child's need for protection and comfort, and the parent's provision of timely and appropriate care in response to these needs. The infant that has its needs met in a responsive and consistent manner by its carer will develop trust and will quickly adapt and become familiar with the adults who consistently provide it with the responsive and sensitive care it requires. Erikson's first stage in his theory of psychosocial development (1963) is 'trust versus mistrust', which occurs during the first year of life, with attachment and the infant's temperament highly intertwined. According to Erikson:

> The first year of life is a critical period for the development of a sense of trust. The conflict for the infant involves striking a balance between trust and mistrust. This primary psychosocial task of infancy provides a developmental foundation from which later stages of personality development can emerge … Resolution of the trust/mistrust conflict is manifest in a mature personality by behaviours that basically exhibit trust (of oneself and others) but maintain a healthy amount of skepticism.
>
> (Erikson, 1963: 246)

An infant will also develop a trust in its ability to successfully elicit a response from its caregivers to get its needs met. This ability to trust someone begins at birth and lasts throughout life. Conversely, mistrust of others develops when an infant is not responded to in a consistent and sensitive manner, thus making it unsure whether or not carers will respond and whether it has the ability to elicit a response, affecting its ability to resolve other conflicts in the later stages of psychosocial development.

> The general state of trust, furthermore, implies not only that one has learned to rely on the sameness and continuity of the outer providers, but also that one may trust oneself and the capacity of one's own organs to cope with urges; and that one is able to consider oneself trustworthy enough so that the providers will not need to be on guard lest they be nipped.
>
> (Erikson, 1963: 248)

Categories of attachment

Ainsworth and Bell (1970) developed the strange situation paradigm, a laboratory method used to measure the quality of attachment between carer and child. This procedure involves several separations and reunions between an infant or young child and their carer or a friendly stranger. The way the infant behaves at reunion with the carer is the main indicator of the quality of attachment. From this simple but very powerful naturalistic experiment, Ainsworth and Bell (1970) identified three general attachment patterns.

A **secure** pattern involves a positive response on the part of the child during reunion with the parent. These children use their parent as a secure base and are able to explore their environment, visually checking or returning to their mother when needed. They interact with the stranger if the mother is close by and shows approval; and get upset when the mother leaves the room, but are happy and easily comforted when the mother returns. The majority of children fall into this category.

In contrast, an **avoidant** (or **anxious-avoidant**) child does not seem to be bothered by a parent's absence and will often snub the parent on reunion. Such a child's attachment is insecure, because they do not seem interested in interacting with adults, showing no emotion, and have given up trying to elicit a response from the people in their world. They no longer trust in themselves or their mother and 'it seems very likely to us that maternal behaviour plays a large part in influencing the development of qualitative difference in infant–mother attachment' (Ainsworth *et al.,* 1978: 137).

Another form of insecure attachment is the **anxious** (or **anxious-resistant**) attachment style which is characterised by infant distress and anxiety upon separation and the child's reluctance to explore his or her environment even in the presence of the parent. The anxious child also does not respond to the parent's attempts at soothing and is resistant to reuniting with the mother. It is suggested that this is a result of inconsistent parenting style, responding to the child on the parent's terms rather than those of the infant (Mooney, 2010).

A fourth category was later added by Main and Solomon (1986, 1990) for children who seem to have no strategy for coping with separation or reunion. These children are considered to be **insecure-disorganised** with respect to attachment.

- Reflect on your practice and try to recognise some of the above suggested attachment categories in the infants you care for.
- What do you know about the parent–infant relationship?
- As a key worker how can you substitute some of the attachment the infant might miss out on with their parent/carer?

The parent–infant relationship and attachment

Parents who are consistently available, sensitive to their child's signals, and receptive to and accepting of the child's distress tend to have securely attached children. Parents of insecurely attached children tend to be less responsive to their children's signs of distress and need for comfort and protection. These parents are unavailable either physically, psychologically or emotionally, being insensitive or unpredictable in their parenting style. When a parent does not respond appropriately to a child's need for comfort, it is not necessarily the fault of the parent. There are instances when a parent, because of their own grief or needs, simply is not capable of being sensitive to his or her infant's needs in a particular situation. Other parents simply are not able to read a child's signals and thus respond inappropriately. These four major infant attachment patterns have been shown to be independent of a child's temperament. In other words, attachment style concerns the relationship between the child and carer rather than the personality of either. This means that a child might show insecure attachment with one carer and secure attachment with another.

Attachment behaviours occur when an infant is emotionally distressed, physically hurt or ill. In response to a threat to safety a child will stop his or her activity and seek close contact with carers. Attachment behaviours also include efforts to maintain contact with the carer by, for example, clinging to them or sitting on their lap, and any other behaviours that signal needs for comfort, such as crying. The presence of a secure attachment relationship with the primary carer forms the foundation for later social competence and confidence, as the infant has built up an expectation that their needs for soothing, comfort and protection from danger will be met in a timely and sensitive manner (Braungart-Rieker et al., 2001). Research has found that children with secure attachments will have improved self-regulation and self-reflective capacities (Fonagy, 2001), and this will enable them to have greater resilience than children who have insecure attachments (Belsky and Fearon, 2002; Edwards et al., 2006; Moss et al., 2006; Newman, 2002).

Patricia Crittenden (1999) developed the field of attachment theory, taking a slightly different angle from Bowlby's secure base, suggesting that attachment was a system against danger and avoidance from harm. Subsequently, Crittenden (2006a) developed the Dynamic-Maturational Model (DMM) of attachment, seeing it as a continuum – a maturational process. It is concerned with the interactive effects of genetic inheritance and person-specific experience strategies in keeping safe. This is a lifespan developmental theory of attachment and adaptation based on the need for protection from danger (danger being the primary organiser of behaviour) and the need for a reproductive partner (Crittenden, 1995). These self-protective patterns of behaviour are learned through interaction with protective figures, and symptoms are functional aspects of the dyadic strategy, for example acting out or inhibition, are as a consequent to a strategy, for example anxiety behaviours. Crittenden (2006a) believes that an individual's strategy will change when it no longer fits the context, they have alternative responses to offer or both people in the dyad believe and feel that it is safe to behave in different ways. The DMM does not recognise a disordered attachment, instead seeing self-protective organisation and adaptation even under conditions of great fear and danger. Crittenden (2006a) describes children's behaviour as attempts to 'reorganise' using variants of the secure and insecure patterns. Therefore, maltreated children will strategically organise their behaviour in order to reduce further maltreatment. Crittenden (2000) talks about two types of information processing: cognition – the basis for learning theory, and affect – being tied to arousal. These two forms of information processing lead to two basic attachment strategies. Type A (avoidant), whereby the child organises around experienced outcomes that they expect to reoccur in the future, minimises negative feelings, does what they expect will be reinforced and avoids doing what they expect to be punished for. Type C (ambivalent) children are motivated by feelings which are tied to intensity of stimulation and processing through the limbic system. These children focus on feelings as a guide to their behaviour. Crucial feelings are negative, in a gradient of increasing arousal. On the other hand, Type B (secure attachment) children are able to integrate cognition and affect, with an open, direct and reciprocal communication of expectations and feelings. They therefore have a balanced strategy.

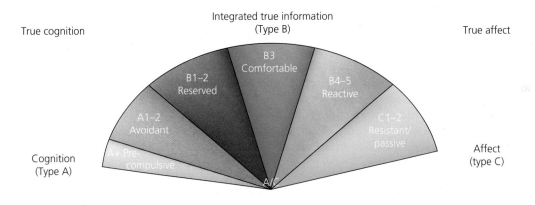

Figure 6.1 A Dynamic-Maturational Model of patterns of attachment in infancy

Infant characteristics contribute to the parent–infant relationship; experiences provided by the carer are the primary determinants of infant attachment patterns. According to attachment theory, the most important factor in the development of attachment style is an infant's experience of carer response in times of distress, with fear acting as a powerful organising affect for children's behaviour (Crittenden, 2006a).

The term 'carer sensitivity' is now used in attachment research to indicate the extent to which mothers and fathers demonstrate reflective functioning and mind-mindedness with their children and their capacity to link awareness of their child's or their own internal state to behaviour (Fonagy and Target, 2005). For example, a child has a tantrum in the shop (behaviour) because he was tired and hungry (physical state) and the parent had been dragging him around all day and he was sick of it (mental state). Therefore as a 'key person' it is important that you act as a 'secure base', increasing your sensitivity, availability, responsiveness and resilience, particularly those skills based on self-esteem, self-reflexivity and self-efficacy.

Extend your knowledge

Undertake further research and reading about attachment disorders, such as:

- Hornor, G. (2008) 'Reactive attachment disorder', *Journal of Pediatric Health Care*, vol. 22, no. 4, pp. 234–9.
- Zeanah, C., Scheeringa, M., Boris, N., Heller, S., Smyke, A. and Trapani, J. (2004) 'Reactive attachment disorder in maltreated toddlers', *Child Abuse & Neglect: The International Journal*, vol. 28, no. 8, pp. 877–88.
- Crittenden, P. M. (2006) 'A dynamic-maturational model of attachment', *ANZJFT*, vol. 27, no. 2, pp. 105–15.

Undertake further research and reading about reflective functioning by reading Fonagy, P. and Target, M. (2005), 'Bridging the transmission gap: An end to an important mystery of attachment research?', *Attachment and Human Development*, vol. 7, no. 3, pp. 333–43.

Parenting styles and attachment

The Resources for Infant Educarers (RIE) approach was founded by Magda Gerber in 1977 in the United States, originating from the work that had been carried out in an orphanage established by Dr Pikler in Hungary in 1945. Pikler (1945) observed that when the infants had a few primary carers, with the same carers always giving their full attention to the infants during all daily care routines, the infants became securely attached to those carers, were able to actively participate in their daily care and were easily transitioned into a family home when adopted at around the age of three years. This respectful approach was developed further in the United States, by Piaget, Erikson and Forrest with whom Gerber collaborated, forming the RIE approach. The philosophy underpinning the RIE approach is to provide infants with a few primary carers, who can be parents and other adults that consistently respond to the infants' needs. Infants were allowed to cry but they were never left to 'cry it out'. The infants were always responded to in a positive and supportive way, with their needs consistently met and their feelings always acknowledged and validated. RIE encourages the adult to tune into the non-verbal cues of the infant through observation and to respond in a sensitive manner, thus offering both security and freedom to the infant within the relationship and promoting the development of a secure attachment. RIE encourages the adult to speak to the infant before doing an activity. Hammond (2009: 13) states that 'when an adult speaks quietly about what is happening and waits for a response, the child does not need to be on alert that a change could be coming at any moment unannounced'. Infants learn to trust their environment more easily if they are never taken off guard by sudden changes.

McMullen *et al.* (2009: 22) suggest that empathic and sensitively responsive carers transmit messages to babies 'about what it means to be responded to with kindness and compassion'.

> If you pay half attention-which nobody does, it's usually much less-but let's say you give half attention all the time, that's never full attention. Babies are always half hungry. But if you pay full attention a little bit of the time, then you go a long way. That's what I would recommend; to be fully with a child, then let her be.
>
> (Gerber, 1998, cited in Mooney, 2010: 40)

Similarly, Dr Brazelton also observed infants and developed a strengths–based and preventative approach when working with infants. In 1973 he created the Neonatal Behavioural Assessment Scale (NBAS), which can be used to assess a newborn's visual, audio and tactile responses to different stimuli. He identified three types of infant based on their temperament and personality traits: average, active and quiet. Through the assessment parents are given insight into their infants' temperament, self-soothing strategies and preferred ways of being handled, and also how competent their infant already is. He wanted to encourage parents to see their infant as unique, by highlighting their strengths, enabling parents to then respond in a sensitive and appropriate manner. It has been found that after the assessment parents are more sensitive and responsive to their infant's behavioural cues at one month, and it continues throughout the first year (Brazelton and Sparrow, 2006). Brazelton (1992) also recommends that daily routines become times of social interaction between the carer and infant, making them a time for communication and fun. These times are great for learning from the infant their cues for signalling 'I want more' or 'I have had enough'. He also observed that infants sleep more lightly and wake more during the night before they are about to achieve a major developmental milestone, for example rolling over, sitting up or walking (Brazelton, 1992). Giving parents this information before it occurs allows them to understand the reasons for the change in behaviour and respond appropriately. Brazelton also believes that infants should not be left to 'cry it out'.

Attachment Parenting by William and Martha Sears (2001) continued with this philosophy of sensitive responsiveness to the infant and recommended a technique called babywearing which is carried out within many cultures. This is when the infant is worn on their parent's body throughout the day. There are seven facets to Attachment Parenting, which are called the 'Baby Bs'. These are: birth bonding, belief in baby's cries, breastfeeding, babywearing, bed-sharing, balance and boundaries, and beware of baby trainers (Sears and Sears, 2001). Responding to an infant's cries is one of the most important aspects of this approach, as this is the infant's way of communicating with the adults in their world. Sears and Sears (2001) recommend responding in some way every time an infant cries; especially with very young infants as they are learning to trust their parents and carers.

> **Meeting your baby's needs in the early months means that solid communication patterns will develop. With time you can gradually delay your response and gradually your baby will learn to accept waiting a little bit as she learns non-crying language and develops self-help mechanisms.**
>
> (Sears and Sears, 2003:6)

The approach also encourages parents to observe their baby's non-verbal cues and to recognise the pre-cry cues, enabling parents to respond early. This teaches infants that they do not have to fully cry to obtain a response. Sears and Sears (2001) found that early responsiveness reduced infant crying in the second half of their first year and, conversely, if the infant was not responded to they were more likely to cry more. Sears and Sears (2001) advocate the importance of understanding the infant's perspective in order to respond appropriately. If an infant can trust their parent to understand, respect them and meet their needs they are more likely to listen to the parent for what to do when. This will then permeate into their life, making them respectful, responsive and sensitive adults.

Parenting style has a significant impact on a child's attachment behaviour. Infants' attachment classifications have been predicted prior to birth simply from mothers' attitudes about the upcoming birth of their child. Numerous studies have shown that maternal behaviours in the home predict attachment at one year better than infant behaviours. These findings point to significant parental influence in the development of attachment patterns. Bowlby (1969) considered sensitivity within an infant's early attachment relationship to be crucial to its development and later positive outcomes, and this view is supported by current research findings (Feinstein and Sabates, 2006) and government reports (Allen, 2011; Field, 2010).

Putting this all together, you can think of the process of attachment as a kind of dance between infant and parent. In other words, attachment is not solely concerned with a carer's behaviour towards an infant. How the infant signals and responds to the carer is a critical part of the process. The infant's signal is responded to in a particular way by the parent, which in turn is interpreted by the child, depending on the nature of the parent's response, the infant and his or her behaviour. Very early on infants learn how to manage their distress or regulate their emotions depending on their carer's responses. Whenever infants feel anxious or in danger, their attachment systems will be activated. Thus, in this complex dance, different styles of attachment develop. Infants learn to expect certain responses from their carers based on the reactions of their carers over time. By the end of the first year of life, a child's expectations or internal working models of relationships with carers are established and may prove difficult to change, and general parenting style and parents' attachment histories may significantly influence their children's and even future generations' attachment outcomes.

Next steps

The government has recognised and acknowledges the messages from research about the importance of attachment for infants and young children. Consequently early years settings are expected to have a 'key person' system in place to nurture and support infants' personal, social, emotional and cognitive development. Reflect on the following points and discuss with your fellow students or your team:

- As a 'key person', how can you start the process of tuning into infants?
- How can you help others to tune into infants?
- Identify children that you have worked with that would be classified in the different attachment patterns.
- What sort of behaviours did they exhibit and how did you respond to them? Reflect on your role to promote secure attachments with the children you work with.
- What observations do you make and decide as noteworthy or share with the infant's carer? Do you only record the 'basic needs' (feeding, nappy change), or do you identify their personal and emotional developmental progression and well-being?
- Undertake further reading and research into Main's and Crittenden's classifications of attachment. Compare and discuss the differences and the relevance to your practice.

Brain development in infant years

It is important to understand how the brain's development from pre-birth and in the first 12 months influences and shapes the infant's personal, social, emotional, physical and cognitive growth and development. Sensory development and attachment are closely linked, as are language development and relationship building with other people and the world around the child.

There are three main parts to the brain. First, the reptilian brain (brain stem), which is the most ancient part of our brain, and is crucial for survival as it controls our bodily functions, such as breathing, digestion, regulation, hunger, temperature and our fight, fright or flight impulses. Then there is the mammalian brain which is also known as our emotional brain and evolved over 200 million years ago. This is responsible for our social behaviour, care of others, nurturing, playfulness and bonding. It also helps to control our fight or flight impulses. The mammalian brain will also activate an infant's separation distress, rage or fear.

Finally, there is the cerebral cortex (Primate Brain). This is the newest part of our brain in evolutionary terms. It amounts to around 85% of the brain mass. Although this is the higher brain, it can be easily influenced by the lower brain in times of stress. An emotionally responsive parent can have a dramatic impact on this part of an infant's brain development. The cerebral cortex is responsible for our creativity and imagination, self-awareness, problem solving, kindness, empathy, emotion, reasoning, complex thought and our ability to reflect upon things. During infancy the lower brain will control the infant's impulses, as the cortex is not developed enough to be able to inhibit the mammalian brain. The cerebral cortex is important for developing good stress systems which are important in supporting good mental health.

The first two years in an infant's life are critical for brain development. When a baby is first born their cerebral cortex is still quite immature. All the neurons in the cortex are produced before birth, but they are poorly connected. Within the brain stem and spinal cord the synaptic connections occur prenatally as they are required to support life, whereas the synaptic connections in the cerebral cortex occur postnatally, in a massive burst of synapse formation, called the exuberant period. At the peak of the exuberant period the cerebral cortex creates two million new synapses every second. These new connections enable the infant to attain many of their milestones, such as colour vision, pincer grip, strong attachment to their parent. The synaptic exuberance varies in different parts of the cerebral cortex, beginning in the primary sensory regions, for example the visual cortex, and later in the temporal and frontal lobes, which are involved in the higher cognitive and emotional functions. By the age of two years the cerebral cortex contains a hundred trillion synapses with the synaptic exuberance reaching its peak between four and eight years of age.

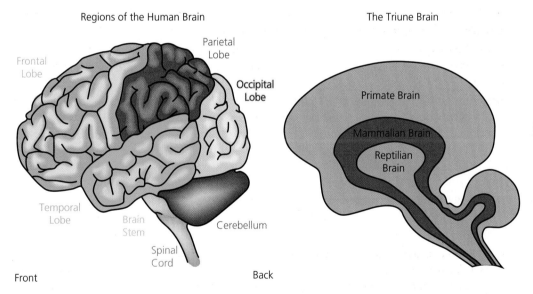

Figure 6.2 Regions of the human brain

Another process that occurs postnatally is the myelination of the neurons, which is required for efficient electrical transmission of messages around the body and brain. The lack of myelin around the neurons is the reason why infants are unable to process information as quickly as adults. Myelination of the cerebral cortex begins in the primary motor and sensory areas, for example eyes, ears, nose, skin and mouth, and then progresses to the higher order or association regions that control the more complex integration of perception, thought, memories and feelings. The majority of myelination occurs in the first two years of an infant's life, with the more complex areas in the frontal and temporal lobes continuing to be myelinated into the individual's twenties. This process of myelination appears to be hard–wired, with 'cells that fire together, wire together' (Hebb, 1949). The myelination sequence appears to be predictable in healthy children; only malnutrition appears to influence this process. Subsequently, pruning of neurons that are not used occurs, which streamlines the infant's neural processing, making it quicker and more efficient. It is also important to consider that even at two weeks post-conception there is brain development occurring within the foetus, with most of a human's lifetime supply of brain cells being produced between the fourth and seventh months in utero. Infection, lack of oxygen, malnutrition, taking of psychotropic drugs and alcohol can alter the migration of neurons and have a profound impact on the functioning of the brain. The synapses that are retained are those which are in most common usage during the child's development. The level of energy used by an infant's brain is low at birth, with a rapid rise between infancy and early school years; then there is a gradual decline between the middle childhood and adolescence years. There is a genetically guided process of brain development which is designed to 'capture' experiences and incorporate them into the brain. Likewise, new experiences help to trigger new brain growth and refine existing structures.

Extend your knowledge

Extend your knowledge and understanding about the brain, by reading:

- Curran, A. (ed. Gilbert, I.) (2008) *The Little Book of Big Stuff About the Brain*, Bancyfelin: Crown House.
- LeDoux, J. (1998) *The Emotional Brain*, London: Weidenfeld & Nicolson.

There are a number of videos online featuring Carl Sagan talking about the brain. See, for example, http://www.youtube.com/watch?v=owefQheNqwo.

Summarise some of the key messages and how they relate to your early years practice.

Let's not neglect the brain

Brain development is interactive, it reflects the co-action of nature and nurture. The orbitofrontal cortex begins its critical period of growth from the last quarter of the first year to the end of the second year. Relational trauma at this time interferes with the organisation of the orbitofrontal regions – the brain's central emotion regulating system – and compromises such functions as attachment, empathy, the capacity to play and affect regulation. As the maturation of the orbitofrontal regions occurs completely postnatally, their development is positively or negatively shaped by early relationship-based experiences.

Researchers use the term 'global neglect' to refer to deprivations in more than one domain, for example language, touch and interaction with others. Children who were adopted from Romanian orphanages in the early 1990s were often considered to be globally neglected; they had little contact with carers and little or no stimulation from their environment – little of anything required for healthy development. One study found that these children had significantly smaller brains than the norm, suggesting decreased brain growth (Perry, 2002). This type of severe, global neglect can have devastating consequences. The extreme lack of stimulation may result in fewer neuronal pathways available for learning. The lack of opportunity to form an attachment with a nurturing carer during infancy may mean that some of these children will always have difficulties forming meaningful relationships with others (Perry, 2001a).

But these studies also found that time played a factor – children who were adopted as young infants showed greater recovery than children who were adopted as toddlers (Rutter, 2000). This highlights the importance of appropriate early sensory stimulation and its influence on the brain's ability to think and to regulate bodily functions, as well as the powerful interaction between early stimulation and emotional nourishment. The core environment which provides appropriate early sensory stimulation during early development is relationships with other people, which was the intention of Sure Start (Department for Education and Employment, 1999). The sensitive carer is acting as an auxiliary cortex to begin with, in terms of affect regulation. The system that is being shaped by relationship–based attachment experience is the same one that will eventually regulate the expression of aggression (Crittenden, 2008).

The impact of neglect and the effect of poverty on a child's development were highlighted in the reports by Field (2010) and by Allen (2011), which argued for early identification and early interventions supporting children, to meet their needs and offer them better life chances in adulthood. The impact of neglect on a child's brain development is graphically illustrated in the scan of children's brains below:

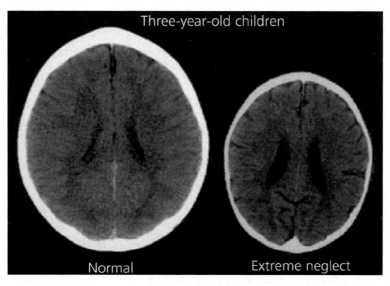

Figure 6.3 Brain development for three-year-old children

"This image illustrates the negative impact of neglect on the developing brain. The CT scan on the left is from a healthy three-year-old child with an average head size (50th percentile). The image on the right is from a three-year-old child following severe sensory-deprivation neglect in early childhood. The child's brain is significantly smaller than average and has abnormal development of cortex (cortical atrophy) and other abnormalities suggesting abnormal development of the brain."

Proper Attribution of This Work:

Academic citation: Perry, B.D. *Childhood experience and the expression of genetic potential: what childhood neglect tells us about nature and nurture*, Brain and Mind 3: 79–100, 2002.

'Windows of opportunities' in the first year: developmental issues

One of the main characteristics of the human brain is its plasticity. This is the brain's ability to change behaviour based on experience. Research distinguishes between 'sensitive periods' and 'critical periods' of development (Bear, Connors and Paradiso, 2001). The difference is important for recognising what infants and toddlers need early in life. **Critical periods** represent a narrow window of time during which a specific part of the body is most vulnerable to the absence of stimulation or to environmental influences. Vision is a good example: unless an infant sees light during the first six months, the nerves leading from the eye to the visual cortex of the brain that processes these signals will degenerate and die. A **sensitive period** represents a window within which the effects of environmental stimulation on brain structure and function are maximised. Sensitive periods represent a less precise and often longer period of time when skills such as acquiring a second language are influenced. The kinds of skills acquired during sensitive periods are those that some people are better at than others. But, if the opportunity for learning does not arise, these potential new skills are not lost forever. After the closing of the sensitive period, some level of plasticity is nevertheless retained; windows of plasticity do not shut suddenly or firmly – learning is still possible, although it is harder (Thomas and Knowland, 2009). Individuals learn new languages at many different times in their lives.

The early brain research highlights birth to three years of age as a sensitive period for development and learning in all areas. Within the auditory domain there are different sensitive periods for different facets of speech processing and other periods relating to basic aspects of music perception, motion perception and face processing (Thomas and Knowland, 2009).

Birth to six months

In the first three months of an infant's life the developmental issue is physiological synchrony and the carer's ability to comfort and regulate the infant's affect. In these first few months infants are unable to regulate emotions on their own. They need the relationship with their primary carer to help them deal with their arousal. The ways in which carers regulate their infant's physical and emotional arousal, or deal with their joy and distress, will have profound implications for their neurological, physiological and psychosocial development. Crittenden (2006a: 3) defines adult sensitivity in play as 'any pattern of behaviour that pleases the infant and increases the infant's comfort and attentiveness and reduces its distress and disengagement'. Maintaining infants in an alert and attentive state requires that adults hold infants comfortably, in a position where the infant can easily see the carer's face. Infants' bodies also need to feel supported so that they are not worried about falling, to enable them to engage in a 'conversation'. The carer needs to match the rhythm and synchrony of the infant's movements, keeping the infant in an alert state, but not overexcited. Infants become distressed when their biological rhythms are disrupted, for example when feeling sleepy, hungry etc. When carers are unpredictable in what they do and the infant perceives them as intrusive, or when they fail to respond, infants will find this particularly distressing. Infants who are silent, passive and visually avoidant with their gaze when the carer's behaviour is aversive, or who were distressed and then become passive, are more distressed than the infants who protest (Tronick, 1989).

Turn-taking between the infant and its carer within simple play sequences and synchrony of affect is the developmental issue between three to six months of age. Infants need to be positioned in such a way that enables them to actively contribute to the interaction, for example not on their backs.

Babies appear to have a biological need to feel understood and develop the social part of their brains (Fonagy *et al.*, 1995). Therefore, one of the most dramatic abilities of a newborn infant is their readiness for social interactions with other people and what might be going on in the minds of others. Trevarthen and Aitkin (2001) refer to this as 'purposeful intersubjectivity'. The early social environment directly influences the final wiring of the circuits in the brain, particularly the pre-frontal cortex. Gerhardt (2004) talks about the human infant needing to be invited to participate in human culture. She highlights the first step in this process as getting the infant hooked on social interaction. To do this infants need to feel secure in their body position thus enabling them to make the social interaction highly pleasurable. These social interactions are responsible for the future socio-emotional development of the individual. Therefore, infants are not passive in their relationships with others; they are active participants, interpreting and responding.

During parent–infant dyadic interactions, the parent acts as a hidden regulator of the infant's endocrine and nervous systems. This influences the biochemical activation of gene-action systems which programme the critical period of brain growth. A newborn's senses are still developing, with a newborn's vision being the least well-developed sense. In the first few weeks of life, infants are especially attracted to particular kinds of visual stimulation. For example, apart from people's faces, they will look intensely at patterns that have strong clear contrasts, such as a stripy black and white design. At this early stage infants are attracted to the edges or boundaries of visual pictures and patterns, compared to the internal portions of a pattern, as they have poor contrast sensitivity and can only see patterns when they are composed of highly contrasting elements (Kurtz, 2006). Newborns do not perceive a richly colourful world. Infants' colour vision is mature by two to three months of age, and by eight months their vision is comparable to adult vision. Infants are attracted to moving stimuli and by two to three months of age they can track slowly moving objects smoothly.

For infants up to six months of age, the most significant sensitive periods are in the areas of vision, vocabulary and emotional development. It is particularly important to pay attention to vision and emotional development at this stage, as these shut so early.

Six to 12 months

Infants between six and nine months of age form a person-specific attachment with one or two carers and their interaction is becoming more complex. Within play, infants require variation and extending of the sequences. This requires regulating of the infants' arousal and attention, turn-taking and a recognition of simple interpersonal patterning (Crittenden, 2006a). Between nine and 12 months of age the developmental issue moves to reciprocal communication around objects of joint attention – this requires confidence in the previously established dyadic, turn-taking process. Adults who are too unresponsive or too controlling still need their infants' direct attention. This will interfere with the ability of the infants to explore their surroundings without feeling alone. Infants will start to express their negative feelings as aggressive behaviour and will be developing the ability to struggle with their carer for what they want. Towards the end of the first year, infants will use their attachment figure for social referencing in new situations.

Critical periods for infants of this age are for speech and emotional development, as the connections for sight are now primarily established. Within the brain there is a hierarchy of systems, from perceptual/motor to abstract systems. Sensitive periods are mainly found in perceptual and motor systems – there is less evidence for them in the higher order systems for abstract thought (Thomas, 2010). He believes that learning multiple languages, being a musician or a gymnast are important skills that need to be learned early, as they rely on low-level perceptual and motor skills. Also, children are unable to learn abstract skills before they master perceptual skills (Thomas, 2010).

Children who are helped to regulate their arousal by a sensitive carer will learn to regulate themselves physiologically, emotionally and cognitively (Perry and Szalavitz, 2006). They are able to think about and reflect on feelings, resulting in them being less reactive, less impulsive, more reflective and more thoughtful. 'Co-regulation appears to lie at the heart of attachment, the ability to self-regulate, and the gradual growth of social cognition, empathy and interpersonal skill' (Howe, 2011: 25). Diamond and Fagundes's research (2010) investigated how mind states and the neurological systems or brain structures that underpin them can affect the body, and vice versa. As a result, well-regulated, securely attached infants tend to have less reactive stress systems. For the infants that have experienced abuse, neglect or trauma and therefore have not had their feelings or arousal levels regulated, their nervous systems become hypersensitive. This makes them easily aroused and dysregulated, even by small amounts of stress. If there is joy in the play, mutual gaze, fun in singing, pleasurable experiences and jointly shared pleasure when a new skill is acquired within the dyadic parent–infant relationship, it will enhance the infant's attachment and ability to think about feeling and regulate affect, which will continue into adulthood (Schore, 2001).

> **The central question is whether or not the adult can maintain the infant in an alert and attentive state and/or provide comfort that transforms infant distress to comfort and attention.**
>
> (Crittenden, 2006a: 38)

Perinatal mental health problems are common, can be serious, and can have lasting effects not only on the mother but also on her children. The impact on the future lives of children includes impaired brain development, difficulty with concentration, attention and emotional regulation, delays in communication skills, and long-term mental health problems, often associated with drug misuse and offending behaviour (Buchanan and Hudson, 2000).

Reflective task

- After having read this information about the growing and developing brain and the 'windows of opportunities', examine and reflect on your practice when working with infants.
- Read Sue Gerhardt (2004) *Why Love Matters: How affection shapes a baby's brain,* and identify how you can provide a loving and caring relationship and a safe environment for infants.
- Discuss and share your newfound knowledge with your team.

Sensory processing and integration

When in utero, we are literally bathed completely in the mother's environment. Every sight, sound, touch, scent and vibration – every sensation – is coming from that mother's world, a bath of sensations. At just six weeks, the embryo's sense of touch has already begun to develop, and is the most mature of all the senses at birth. The mother's uterus provides constant deep pressure; it is this pressure which provides the growing foetus with information to their muscles and joints.

Although sounds and noises are muted, the foetus is able to hear from around 28 weeks, which will provide them with essential information about the voices of their primary carers. Bathed in the amniotic fluid the foetus will experience movement patterns that they will use once born, and they will practise these until there is no more room for movement. The foetus's senses of taste and smell are also functioning at around 28 weeks. The visual system is the one sensory system that is most underdeveloped, and it undergoes a huge amount of development in the early weeks and months of life.

After birth, the 'bath' changes, yet all of the infant's senses continue to be bathed in a continuous set of sensations, most of which derive from the primary carer. Nothing is more soothing, reassuring or pleasurable than when the infant is bathed by the mother's touch, gaze, scent and taste – the baby is calm, warm and happy. As we get older, this somatosensory bath takes different forms: the hug, the smile and the handshake. When someone gazes at you, smiles at you, when somebody puts his or her arm around you, when you dance or touch, there is a connection back to our original somatosensory bath. These actions serve as shortcuts to the feelings of our original somatosensory bath.

From the moment infants are born they are beginning to learn about interpreting the information and sensations from their bodies and the environment in order to live, learn and play in the world. We all need to be able to do this if we are to be able to move our bodies and engage effectively and efficiently with the environment around us. The theory that underpins this knowledge was developed by an occupational therapist called Dr Ayres. Ayres (1972) describes sensory integration as a neurological process that enables the individual to organise the sensations from their own body and the environment, and therefore enables the individual to use their body efficiently and effectively with the environment. It is a process occurring in the brain that enables us to make sense of our world by receiving, registering, modulating, organising and interpreting information that comes to our brains from our senses. The brain processes all the information received by our senses, usually at an unconscious level, organises it and allows us to respond appropriately, for example to move efficiently, to attend and listen, to learn new skills.

Ayres (1972) described three further senses: proprioception, vestibular system and kinesthesia, and their importance for learning about our bodies and how they enable us to move in the world around us. These are in addition to the five senses we typically think of. Proprioception is the ability to know the position of our body and limbs in space (without actually having to look at it or be consciously aware of it) and enables us to move around our environment without bumping into other people and objects. It creates memories necessary for automatic, learned movements like walking, and provides us with an inner map of our body. It is essential in enabling us to anticipate and plan movements, so that we can move around our environment effectively. An example of this is an infant who is positioned on their tummy with their hands outstretched on the floor supporting themselves in the upright position. Sensory information from the muscles and joints, for example their hands and arms in relation to the floor, enables them to begin to think about what they need to do in order to move their body to reach for the toy – this is called kinesthesia.

Our vestibular system (the movement system) is part of a complex set of structures within the inner ear that helps us with our unconscious awareness of our position and movements in space. It helps us to stand up against gravity and balance. An example of this is the infant's ability to begin to sit up and maintain a balanced position for play. Initially this is difficult for infants as their vestibular and visual systems are developing, but as they become more mature it is easier for them to do this without having to consciously think about it, enabling them to use their hands for play. The sensory feedback via the vestibular system is developing in conjunction with the required motor control for such activities. It is the vestibular sense that is being activated when a child is being rocked to sleep (which has a calming effect) and when they are being bounced and played with (a more alerting activity). Information from the vestibular system can alter our state of arousal, influences our muscle tone, balance, eye movements and coordination, and affects our emotional state and levels of attention (Ayres, 1972).

If we understand how infants are beginning to learn how to process sensations from their world, we can begin to consider how and when an infant may need some stimulation, such as play, or when they need nurturing. This will also be helped if we are sensitive to the cues that infants provide us with. In previous sections we have explored the concept of the carer/parent as the emotional regulator for the infant. This includes helping the infant to filter out excessive sensory input to avoid sensory overload, and being mindful of how much stimulation to provide.

Reflective task

- How do you, or can you, create environments which stimulate the infant's senses?
- Evaluate the resources and provision you offer for babies in your setting.
- How are the babies in your setting able and allowed to 'explore' indoors and outdoors?

Stimulating the senses and the role of adults

Infants and young children need to be able to actively play in a variety of environments, with a variety of toys and activities in order to learn and develop. It is only through active participation and exploration that infants learn about themselves and the environments in which they live. We know from research that babies and young children who have not been afforded this opportunity are significantly disadvantaged in later life, for example Romanian orphans, and that it may not be possible to gain these skills later. Ayres (1989) also states that the infant needs to be able to effectively interpret the information from the senses in order to be able to engage in higher-level tasks, such as coordinating the two sides of the body for activities like playing with a toy or feeding, or concentrating and attending to an activity, and engaging in academic learning.

Infants who have difficulty receiving, interpreting and responding effectively to sensory information may find it difficult to maintain a calm/alert state, which may have a negative impact on the development of relationships, learning self-regulation and learning new skills. These infants may find activities such as feeding, bathing and dressing distressing or difficult, appear not to mould when being cuddled and have difficulty establishing sleep/wake cycles appropriate to their age. It is important to point out, however, that any one of these signs in isolation does not necessarily indicate sensory processing difficulty, and further assessment by a suitably qualified therapist is necessary to determine any dysfunction.

Our tactile system (our sense of touch) is also our 'first language' with the outside world, helping us to feel calm, nurtured and safe. Being held, swaddled and massaged enables an infant to begin to be able to calm themselves, as an example of self-regulation. It provides us with the beginnings of our body scheme and supports our physical and emotional development. Research shows us that touch and environmental stimulation support the development of the infant's central nervous system, and is 'most essential in a nurturing and healing environment of the infant and child' (Blackwell, 2000: 37).

Babies and young children also instinctively know how to make activities that they are doing just difficult enough for them to be challenging, but still achievable: this can be called 'the just right challenge'. It is this challenge, along with an inner drive to succeed in their environment, that helps babies and young children to achieve mastery in the activities that they engage in. This, in turn, supports development of their self-esteem and confidence, enabling them to go on and seek further challenges that promote their development.

As individuals we all have different preferences in relation to the stimulation that we enjoy and do not enjoy as much. For example, some people like lots of noise or movement, while others like less of a particular type of activity or stimulus. Infants and young children are exactly the same, and it is up to parents/carers to work out what type and amount each individual child likes. All of us come somewhere along a continuum ranging from very sensitive to external stimulation to not particularly sensitive at the other end.

If you feel a child is having more difficulties than you would expect for a child of that age, gaining a better understanding of the infant's likes and dislikes can enable you to further support their development. Good partnership working and information sharing with the infant's parents/carers, as well as with other professionals, such as the health visitor or occupational therapist, can assist you with your observations and understanding of the infant's abilities and needs.

The aim is to create the best match between the adult ('key person') and the infant's sensory processing needs, the activities and the environment. Early years practitioners need to be able to observe, understand and interpret infants' behaviours, so as to be able to respond in a way that meets the infant's needs, enhancing the adult–infant relationship.

When carers understand the meaning of their infant's responses to sensations and experiences, along with their own, they are able to anticipate and plan activities to make their interactions sensitive. Early sensory stimulation is important as it influences brain development and our ability to regulate bodily functions. It also has a powerful impact on the interaction between early stimulation and emotional nourishment. For infants their core environment during these early developmental years is the relationships they have with other people. As adults, we have learned how to filter out information that we do not need to respond to, and to focus on what is important; however, infants' brains have to learn to control what sensory information they take in and how they will respond to that information. Understanding how infants experience and react to different sensations can help us to determine the best activities and environments for nurturing an infant's growth, learning and development of happy relationships.

Reflective task

An infant is struggling to focus on activities, has frequent peaks of arousal and appears to be vigilant within the environment. How would you think about this infant in terms of attachment, brain development and their sensory processing and integration? Write down a few possible issues and arguments and discuss with your team or group of students.

- Reflect upon the impact our senses have on our emotional development and regulation, for example touch, movement, sound, vision and smell.
- Think about how you use sensations to maintain a calm/alert state.
- Discuss what sort of body language we display when we are in a calm/alert state.
- Discuss the importance of a calm/alert state for learning and for engaging in relationships with others.

Scenario

In a training group for Early Years Professionals, the group was asked how they thought infants experienced the world, in particular why they thought infants cried when people suddenly peered into their prams. The group leaders then handed out pairs of glasses that had been made to imitate the vision of a newborn infant. The members of the group paired up and took it in turns to wear the glasses, while the other person talked to them and moved in and out of their visual field. Afterwards, each person was asked how it felt to see the world as an infant and whether any of their other senses had become more acute. Participants found that the lack of visual clarity meant that their hearing became more acute and when people suddenly moved into their visual field it surprised them and had the potential to be quite frightening. The exercise highlighted why infants often become distressed when people unexpectedly move into their limited visual field. Understanding from an experiential perspective how newborn infants experience the world enabled participants to be reflective about their practice with infants and to adapt the way in which they gave verbal cues before moving in close to infants.

Conclusion

This chapter explored the developmental aspects of infancy and why early attunement is important with respect to brain development and sensory processing. It explored how sensitive attunement, warmth and synchrony in very early interactions with infants are associated with later secure attachment (Braungart-Rieker *et al.*, 2001). It has raised your awareness about the importance of identifying and intervening in the early years. Hopefully it will enhance or change your practice and make you proactive in promoting the importance of early attunement and advocating for the infant.

Evaluate your...

Practice

- Would you change your practice to incorporate the information on attachment, brain development and sensory processing and integration? If so, in what ways?
- What would be your role in promoting early attunement in your setting?
- What activities do you undertake to promote early attunement within your setting with infants, staff and parents?
- How would you identify if an infant had a sensory processing difficulty and how would you address this?
- How would you identify if an infant had an attachment difficulty and how would you address this?
- Find out what documents and policies your setting has to promote the emotional well-being of infants.
- Identify gaps in practice that do not incorporate information regarding attachment, brain development and sensory processing and integration, when working with infants.
- Develop an action plan for improving your setting's practices and discuss with your team.

Further reading

Brazelton, T.B. and Sparrow, J. (2006) *Touchpoints: Birth to Three: Your child's emotional and behavioral development*, Cambridge, MA: Da Capo Press.

Crittenden, P. M. (2008) *Raising Parents: Attachment, parenting and child safety*, Cullompton: Willan Publishing.

Fogel, A. (2011) *Infant Development: A topical approach*, Hudson, NY: Sloan Publishing.

Gerhardt, S. (2004) *Why Love Matters: How affection shapes a baby's brain*, Hove: Brunner-Routledge.

Goddard Blythe, S. (2005) *The Well Balanced Child: Movement and early learning*, Gloucestershire: Hawthorn Press.

Howe, D. (2011) *Attachment across the Lifecourse: A Brief Introduction*, Basingstoke: Palgrave Macmillan.

Sunderland, M. (2007) *What Every Parent Needs To Know*, London: Dorling Kindersley.

Websites

The Child Trauma Academy: http://www.childtrauma.org/

Zero to Three: http://www.zerotothree.org

Children's personal, social and emotional development
Kathy Brodie

Introduction

If early years settings foster children's personal, social and emotional qualities they are surely opening doors for them to live a life of personal fulfilment whatever their other achievements.

(Dowling, 2010: 8)

This chapter explores young children's personal, social and emotional development. The chapter discusses the good practice that can support child development and considers some of the issues that may hinder or delay development. Some of the contemporary research and traditional theorists help to justify current thinking. It is important to note that no one area of any child's learning and development stands in isolation, and that a child's development should always be considered holistically. This is especially true of personal, social and emotional developments, which are closely intertwined and almost inseparable.

This chapter first examines and explains in depth each of the three qualities of personal development, social development and emotional development. Then, some of the key factors that may have a negative effect on a child's development are considered. The conclusions are reflections of the types of good practice that support children's development.

Learning outcomes

At the end of this chapter, you will be able to:
- Distinguish between the different aspects of personal, social and emotional development.
- Identify theorists who have contributed to our understanding.
- Reflect on your own practice and how it can support young children.
- Consider some factors which negatively affect development.

Context

The early years curriculum for England, the Early Years Foundation Stage (EYFS), which became statutory in 2008, clearly put personal, social and emotional development as a crucial area of development for young children, coming first in the six areas of learning and development (DCSF, 2008a). Sylva *et al.* (2004) influenced the EYFS with the biggest longitudinal study of early years provision in Europe at the time, the Effective Provision of Pre-school Education (EPPE). The research demonstrated that the positive social, behavioural and cognitive effects of a good-quality preschool could still be seen at the end of Key Stage 1, which is up to three years later (Sylva *et al.*, 2004). This clearly illustrates the significant effects of good practice on the lives of young children and how important it is that early years practitioners understand and appreciate this.

Since then, the Tickell Review (Tickell, 2011) has identified personal, social and emotional development as one of the central or 'prime areas' of learning. Practitioners and parents further supported this during the public consultation period, when 89 per cent of practitioners and 81 per cent of parents supported a focus on personal, social and emotional development (Tickell, 2011: 92). The Tickell Review concluded that 'successful personal, social and emotional development is essential for young children in all aspects of their lives' (Tickell, 2011: 93). It also recognised that this area of development is interrelated with, and interdependent on, the other prime areas (physical, communication and language). The Tickell Review (2011) has been based on research and evidence, including the review of research completed by Evangelou *et al.* (2009). This project focused on updating the original research for the EYFS and investigated the evidence related to children's cognitive, social, emotional and brain development. Evangelou *et al.* (2009: 5) found that, 'talking about feelings' was beneficial for the development of social and emotional aspects of learning, but also that there was a large overlap of all the areas of learning and development. It is this overlap that means that children's development should be considered holistically, which has been incorporated in the EYFS (DfE, 2012a).

In this chapter, the unique elements of personal development, social development and emotional development have been investigated individually. This has enabled an in-depth discussion for each area. Reference has been made during the text of the interrelated aspects.

Personal development

Personal development is the sense of 'self' and encompasses self-esteem, self-confidence and personality. As children grow and develop they also begin to get a sense of 'others' and have empathy, ultimately becoming independent thinkers.

Sense of 'self'

The EYFS defines self-confidence and self-esteem as children 'having a sense of their own value, and understanding the need for sensitivity to significant events in their own and other people's lives' (DCSF, 2008c). Although closely related, self-esteem and self-confidence do have significant differences. Self-esteem is how we feel about ourselves, the self-perception. Low self-esteem results in negative attitudes towards oneself and a pessimistic attitude towards life. However, a healthy self-esteem fosters a mastery disposition and an acknowledgement of personal failings, without being unduly self-critical.

Good self-esteem is important in the early years of childhood, because it means that children are more willing to 'have a go' and approach new experiences in a positive manner, as recognised in the 'characteristics of effective learning' (DfE, 2012a). It also means that children are more likely to persevere with experiences that may be difficult for them. Dowling (2010) asserts that a child with good self-esteem is well placed to start learning. Self-esteem is strongly linked with resilience, defined as the ability to overcome or minimise the effects of adversity. Newman (2004) suggests that coping mechanisms can be learned through managed exposure to risk and that the long-term aim should be for effective adult adjustment, rather than the total elimination of all childhood difficulties.

Another definition of resilience has been given by Sylva *et al.* (2010), who were examining the evidence of attainment at school, when compared with the background of the children. They define resilience as doing 'better than predicted' (Sylva *et al.*, 2010: 188) in numeracy and literacy. Furthermore they found that there were four significant factors that affected resilience, the strongest of which was self-regulation, which measures independence and concentration. So, if a child had good self-regulation, such as being able to independently select equipment, persevering and not getting easily distracted, then they had better resilience and were more likely to do better than predicted in their primary education. The other three factors considered – gender, home learning environment and ethnic group – had less noticeable effects on resilience during a child's time at primary school.

Self-confidence is affected by how children are treated by others. For example, a word of encouragement or valuing a piece of work will raise a child's confidence, motivating him or her to try again. This is a virtuous circle, success building on success; however, the reverse is also true. Children who have their confidence undermined, by being told that they are less able than their classmates, for example, are less likely to continue trying and give up. In a classic study, Barnsley and Thompson (1988) researched the relative ages of children in the hockey league in Canada. They found that there was a far larger number of children who were born in the first half of the school year, i.e. the older and physically more capable children of each school year, represented in the teams than you would statistically expect. They termed this the 'relative age effect' (RAE). Their explanation was that 'by doing better, these older children achieve more success, receive greater rewards for their endeavours, and thus are more likely to remain in minor hockey for a number of years' (Barnsley and Thompson, 1988: 168). The success enjoyed by the older children gave them more self-confidence, but the negative experiences of the younger children meant that they were more likely to drop out of the team. This effect is even more important with very young children, because they have yet to learn that being successful may take several tries, so their self-confidence needs to be supported and nurtured by caring, sensitive adults.

How children behave under different circumstances depends on their temperament, which can be described as the 'inborn tendencies for individual children that shape their reactions and behaviour towards a more established adult personality' (Lindon, 2003: 200). It has been suggested that temperament has genetic links and that some babies, when born, can be said to be difficult, whereas others have a more relaxed temperament, or are 'easier'. Gerhardt (2004) terms these babies as being highly reactive or less reactive, respectively. Although the underlying reasons for different temperaments are diverse, from a difficult birth to drinking during pregnancy, the baby needs 'very good parental management to keep them free from stress' (Gerhardt, 2004: 68). This means that the people around the child, who care about them and care for them, mould a child's temperament. As they grow and experience life, children learn behaviour according to their experiences and the positive or negative reactions they receive from adults around them. This means that practitioners in nurseries and settings will have a role in forming the temperament of the children in their care.

Children will learn to have a sense of 'self' and what it means to be 'themselves' by the experiences and support they have from the adults around them. The home learning environment will largely influence this, but practitioners in nurseries and settings will have significant effects too. Encouragement, support and positive reinforcement will help children have good self-esteem and good self-confidence.

Sense of 'others'

As children develop they have to move from being highly self-centred, which is necessary for survival, to being aware of the needs, feelings and emotions of others. This is termed empathy and is closely linked to social and emotional development. Hughes and Dunn (2000) found that the empathy displayed by four-year-olds was directly, and significantly, correlated to their cooperative play with others. This demonstrates the importance of children socialising with other children, and how the social aspects of learning influences personal development. Lennon and Eisenberg (1987) had found that there was no gender difference in displays of empathy, although sometimes the methods used to measure empathy tended to favour girls over boys. This is an area which is still vehemently debated, and seems to be related to the measures and methods used to judge levels of empathy. As neuroscience progresses, more biological explanations are being discovered. For example, Pfeifer *et al.* (2008) reveal how activity in the mirror neuron system in a child's brain, located in the pars opercularis, directly correlates to empathy and interpersonal skills, which are essential for effective social interactions.

Without empathy, children are unable to put themselves in someone's place or to appreciate another's point of view. This can lead to egocentric behaviour, which leads to poor social interactions because playing together means understanding, and responding to, the other child's intentions. Children with good empathy tend to have a large social circle and can mix with a range of different children.

Scenario

Ellie (four years old) and Chloe (two and a half years old) both go to the same nursery. In this setting all the children play together, with free-flow play from one room to the next. Although Ellie has many friends of her own age, she is often seen playing with Chloe and helping her. When the craft materials had been put on a shelf that was too high for Chloe to reach, Ellie said, 'Do you want the green paper, Chloe? I'll get it down for you.' She proceeded to get down the paper and glue that Chloe needed. Then Ellie sat next to her and showed Chloe how to spread the glue – 'Look, copy me. Not too much, now! Now put the paper on top. That's right!' Ellie spent a long time sitting with Chloe, helping her with the glue and the paper, until Chloe decided the picture was finished. Both girls went to play elsewhere while the glue dried.

Ellie is demonstrating her excellent 'sense of others'. She has identified Chloe's needs and has acted appropriately to meet those needs. She knows how much support to give, without rushing Chloe or taking over the activity. You can also identify the words that the practitioner uses when supporting children ('Not too much, now!') that Ellie has used in her support of Chloe, demonstrating how Ellie has learned from the adults around her.

Becoming independent

As children grow and mature they naturally seek independence, whether this is to do up the zip on their coat ('me do it!') or to have a biscuit on demand. Becoming independent of carers and the environment is an important part of becoming who they are – their own personality. Indeed, Dowling (2010: 51) cites it as 'an essential life skill', which needs to be developed in all its forms: social, emotional, intellectual, environmental and cognitive.

One way of measuring the independence of children is to make their thoughts visible, by using methods such as the Mosaic approach, developed by Clark and Moss (2001). It is a method for children to express their opinions and thoughts about the early years setting, using cameras, video cameras and dialogue with practitioners. Practitioners can listen to the children's views and support their independence by providing areas they enjoy playing in. It also allows children to demonstrate those areas in the setting where they struggle to be independent, such as coat pegs that are too high, or taps that are too stiff. In a similar manner, practitioners who are tuned into schematic learning can encourage children's independence by providing materials and equipment that facilitate the schema.

Factors which shape children's personality

It has been postulated that it is children's experiences in life that shape and mould their personality. Gerhardt (2004) describes some of the roots of personality development from influences at home. She discusses how repressing feelings can lead to proneness to disease and how depressed parents can create children who get 'stuck with negative feelings' (Gerhardt, 2004: 131), and how personality disorders in parents can lead to disorganised babies, who cannot manage their own feelings. Gerhardt (2004: 56) also discusses how 'corrosive cortisol' (a hormone produced by the hypothalamus) during pregnancy can affect a baby's ability to handle difficult situations and stress later on in life. Fortunately, good parenting can mitigate some of these negative effects.

But it is not just influences in the home that affect children. Hill (2011) assessed how consumerism in Western society has affected children and their identity. She concluded that 'Younger children are being enticed, encouraged and seduced into adopting an identity older than their developmental age' (Hill, 2011: 350). She cites the examples of children trying to achieve a perfect body, as defined by the media, which will be unattainable for the majority of children, and how identity is expressed through material goods: 'identity formation is closely aligned with branded images that infiltrate deep into the psyche of children and youth' (Hill, 2011: 358). Consumerism and images which children are constantly exposed to can also affect the child's social identity and their social standing with peers. By not having the 'right' or latest branded goods children can be made to be feel inferior by their peers, intentionally or otherwise. These sorts of pressures can affect a child's self-esteem and self-confidence.

The commercialisation and sexualisation of childhood have been recognised for some time and in 2011 Reg Bailey was asked to review this in England. The review team found that there was an increase in sexualised content on TV, in music videos, on the internet and even on children's mobile phones. They also conceded that the world is more commercialised and that it is inevitable that companies will try to attract children as consumers of their products. The Bailey Review recommended that media and commercial literacy resources should always include 'education to help children develop their emotional resilience to the commercial and sexual pressures that today's world places on them' (Bailey, 2011: 72). The Bailey Review (2011) also made 14 recommendations that aim to ensure that children are protected from external pressures. Although measures such as these give limited protection to children, it is difficult to assess how these pressures influence children and shape their emerging personalities.

Personality and personal development are rooted in a child's earliest experiences as a baby. From the very start, they are bound tightly with issues of self-esteem, attachment, stress and temperament – to name a few. These can be affected by family factors, such as depression and personality disorders, and societal factors, such as consumerism.

Reflective task

- Read the Bailey Review (2011) and see if you agree with the recommendations. What would you recommend to protect children in the modern world?
- How will it be different for the next generation?
- Investigate how commercialisation of children is different around the world. Do other countries advertise to children in the same way? What regulations are there elsewhere?

Social development

Social development is interacting, learning and communicating with other people. It is the importance of relationships, sense of community and culture in which we grow up and how these affect our view of the world.

Social learning theory

Theories about children's learning vary enormously in their view on social interactions and their place in constructing children's knowledge. Piaget's theories (Piaget and Inhelder, 1969) were constructivist, meaning that the learning is 'constructed' or built on personal experiences. He believed that learning was moved on when children came across a new experience or idea, which altered their view on the world. His theories were based on children learning from direct experiences. He suggested that children's learning progressed in four distinct stages, where each stage had to be completed before the next could be started. Learning is achieved through 'assimilation and accommodation' (Piaget and Inhelder, 1969: 5). Assimilation is when knowledge is acquired, and accommodation is how the internal schema is modified to fit the experience. For example, a child may find out that this white bird is called a duck (assimilation). When he is told that the brown bird is also a duck, he has to change his knowledge from 'all ducks are white' to 'ducks can be white or brown' (accommodation). For Piaget the learning experience was about experience rather than social interactions.

Vygotsky (1978), however, theorised that children learn from their social experiences, both social interaction and language interactions. He described how children learn from social interactions with others who are more advanced, the 'more knowledgeable other' (MKO). The MKO may be a member of the peer group, teacher, parent or other family member. His theory was that the MKO assists or supports a child's learning from what they can do, 'zone of actual development' (ZAD), through to the 'zone of proximal development' (ZPD). The ZPD is the gap between what a child understands or can do by themselves (ZAD) and what can be further achieved with support from the MKO. For example, a child may be able to put his or her own coat on (ZAD), but struggles with the zip. With help and guidance from their teacher, the child learns how the zip fits together before it is pulled up. By having support through the ZPD, the child can learn how to independently zip up their own coat. Vygotsky argued that cognitive and social development were inseparable, each depending on the other, but that, 'each stage of the child's development is characterized by modes of social activity that are of particular significance at that stage' (Vygotsky, 1978 cited in Minik, 1997: 123).

Another significant difference between Piaget's and Vygotsky's theories was the role of culture in child development. Vygotsky thought that the cultural artefacts and surroundings affected and shaped a child's learning and development, but Piaget took little account of the child's background or previous experience.

A more contemporary theorist is Bandura (1976), who proposed social learning theory. The theory is that children learn from imitating behaviour, which has been modelled by others, whether this is desirable or not. During his research into aggression, children watched an adult being violent towards a 'Bobo doll'. When the same children were allowed to play freely with the same doll, they demonstrated the same violent tendencies that they had previously witnessed. They had 'learned' from observing the modelled behaviour that this was the expected behaviour. However, the circumstances have to be right for the behaviour to be learned. First, the child needs to be paying attention and be able to retain the information received. Then, the behaviour needs to be reproduced. Finally, there has to be motivation to imitate the behaviour. Motivation can be modified through reinforcement (rewards) or punishment, thus reinforcing or stopping the behaviour. So just witnessing violence does not necessarily result in violent behaviour, although under the right circumstances it may do. The sort of behaviour that children witness around them and the types of social interactions they have affect their own personal behaviour and social interactions.

Children have many different types of social interactions – with their parents, grandparents, siblings, nursery, school, library, bus driver and so on. Bronfenbrenner (1979) suggested in his ecological systems theory that all forms of social interaction are interconnected. He theorised that there are five systems, which nest inside one another, with the child at the centre. Bronfenbrenner (1979) named these systems, from the child at the centre, radiating outwards:

- **Microsystem** is the child's direct family and siblings.
- **Mesosystem** is the interface between family and school, community.
- **Exosystems** are the systems that are beyond the child's control, but will still affect the child's life, such as the employment status of parents, availability of libraries.
- **Macrosystem** is the culture and demographic where the child lives.
- **Chronosystem** is the changes that happen over time, such as the child starting school, siblings leaving home.

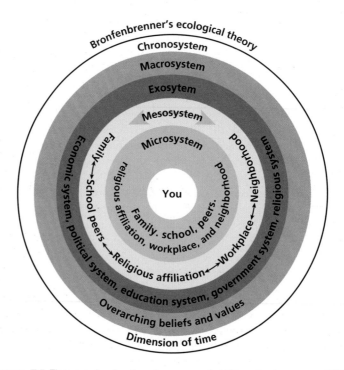

Figure 7.1 The ecological systems model (Bronfenbrenner, 1979)

The further away from the centre (child) that the social interaction sits, the more passive the interaction is. For example, a parent (microsystem) will have many, direct social interactions with their child, and the child will be able to help construct these interactions, but the child will have less control over what happens in school (mesosystem). In addition, external factors that are beyond the child's ability to control may still have an effect on their social development. For example, the slowing down of the global economy may mean that one parent loses their job, so spends more time with the child at home. However, because there is less family income, the child will not be able to attend their preschool any more. This will change the sort of socialisation the child has. Bronfenbrenner (1979) suggested that all these systems, working together, created the environmental context of the child's development and that the systems could not be separated.

The social context of human development can be analysed by comparing and contrasting the interactions between the different systems.

Friendships

Children's friendships, just as with adults' friendships, can be complicated and diverse. Learning the social skills required to form friendships is equally complex (Gottman, 1983). The nature of the friendship can depend on the context (at nursery, in the home or at school), the emotional state of each child and the relationship between the children (for example, whether they are siblings or not). Each child responds differently to making friends, depending on their personality. Those children with good self-confidence and an outgoing personality are more likely to make friends almost effortlessly, whatever the circumstances – at the park, in nursery or at a birthday party. Quieter or shyer children may have more difficulty engaging with other children. In addition, research shows that the critical age for making friends and engaging in play together is before the age of three (Maguire and Dunn, 1997). For those children who have experienced pretend play with a friend or sibling, the foundations of social understanding and social developments are constructed during this period. This underlines the importance of children mixing socially, even when very young or as babies. There are other benefits as well. While researching the role of conversation and socio-cognitive development, Cutting and Dunn (2006: 84) found that pretend play supported not only social development, but also emotional understanding and 'theory of mind' abilities. Theory of mind (Newton and Jenvey, 2011) is being able to understand how others may feel in a situation (empathy) and being able to understand that others may feel different emotions from oneself.

However, once friendships or social networks have been generated they are not static, but change as children grow older. In their work with three- and four-year-olds, Johnson *et al.* (1997) found the social networks were fluid, with little regard for gender. However, as the children got older, it was more likely that the social groups would be defined by gender: 'gender becomes important for social network structure over time' (Johnson *et al.*, 1997: 401). By the age of four years, social structures are more cohesive and well defined. Therefore, the optimum time for children to develop good social interaction is between the age of three and four years old. Roberts and Strayer (1996: 466) suggest that there is a 'functional difference between genders in the relation of empathy and prosocial behaviour', concluding that boys needed to understand empathy before they could fully develop prosocial behaviour. So it is likely that those children whose personalities include empathy are more likely to display positive social behaviour as well. In contrast, Ostrov and Keating (2004) propose that it is the context that makes the difference, with boys gravitating towards situations where their status will be enhanced by using aggressive behaviour, rather than prosocial behaviour. However, girls prefer situations where social bonds are strengthened within the group. This means that social development benefits from having a variety of social interactions, from small groups to large groups, from quiet time to boisterous activities and with some opportunity to mix with children of a different age.

There is much discourse on whether social development for young children is better in mixed-age groups, or whether children socialise better with peers of their own age (Winsler *et al.*, 2002; McClellan and Kinsey, 1999; Roazzi and Bryant, 1998; Dunn *et al.*, 1996; Howes and Farver, 1987; Ellis *et al.*, 1981). Many of the arguments for mixed-age groups stem from the theory that the older children model or construct more sophisticated play for the younger children. One of the few areas of consensus is that a child's social development is complex and difficult to isolate from personal and emotional development.

Indeed, the authors of the Researching Effective Pedagogy in the Early Years (REPEY) project suggest that good-quality early years programmes, such as High/Scope, have more important social outcomes than academic outcomes (Siraj-Blatchford *et al.*, 2002). They go on to say that early childhood social and behavioural development is directly linked to the pedagogic practices that the children observed. The experiences and opportunities that practitioners provide for young children and babies support their social and behavioural development. Often it is the quality of the interaction between practitioner and child that improves social development.

Some theorists, such as Vygotsky, Bandura and Bronfenbrenner, see social development as being vitally important for a child's global development. For other theorists, such as Piaget, social development is considered to be independent of cognitive development.

There has been plenty of research over the years about how children form friendships, how this affects their development and how this overlaps into the personal and emotional aspects of development. It is a complex and constantly evolving area of research.

Contemporary research

- Denham, S. A., Kalb, S., Way, E., Warren-Khot, H., Rhoades, B. L. & Bassett H. H. (2012), 'Social and emotional information processing in preschoolers: indicator of early school success?' *Early Child Development and Care*, pp. 1–22.

This American research is based on the premise that children who are socially competent when entering school will have better classroom adjustment. That is, socially competent children will be able to cope better with the demands of the school classroom, such as cooperation, and have a self-directing and positive attitude towards school. The research investigates social information processing (SIP) patterns and compares these to academic readiness.

- Cozolino, L. (2006) *The Neuroscience of Human Relationships: Attachment and the Developing Social Brain*, London: W. W. Norton and Company.

Cozolino investigates 'a deeper understanding of the interwoven tapestry of biological, psychological, and social processes that comprise human life' (2006: 4). The book explores the ideas around social relationships, the links between neurobiology and social interactions, and the idea that socialisation is necessary for children.

- Brooks, D. (2011) *The Social Animal: A Story of How Success Happens*, New York: Random House.

This very accessible and amusing book illustrates the pitfalls and highlights of social development. It refers to classic and contemporary research, but uses a series of stories to illustrate the points very well.

Reflective task

- Consider your own social networks, both virtual and actual.
- How has each of your social networks supported you and developed your personality, cognitive and emotional development?
- Can you see similar examples in the friendship circles of the children in your care?
- What sort of disadvantages may there be in social groups?

Emotional development

Emotional development is about understanding, expressing and controlling feelings. For young children this also means giving them strategies to manage and verbally express their feelings.

Attachment theory

Attachment theory has grown from the research work by John Bowlby and Mary Ainsworth. Bowlby's research approach (1969, 1983) was contrary to Kleinian methods (Klein, 1932), which were very popular at the time, because he believed that families and mothers were as important to the research as the behaviour of the child. He proposed that supporting the mother would help her to understand the child better and so be more sympathetic towards the child (Bretherton, 1992). As a result of this, Bowlby uncovered some interesting and previously undocumented patterns of behaviours between mothers and their babies. One of the areas he studied was the effect of a child being separated from his or her mother at a young age. As a result of this work he came to believe that the family experience was the 'basic cause of emotional disturbance' (Bretherton, 1992: 760), which was a belief at odds with some of his colleagues. In 1950, Mary Ainsworth had joined Bowlby at his research centre in London, where she studied the relationships between babies and their mothers. In 1958 Bowlby published the first of three seminal papers on attachment theory and how the experiences of early childhood affect children. These formed the basis of his three books: *Attachment* (1969), *Separation* (1973) and *Loss* (1980).

Bowlby explained how children form attachments with the main carer and how important this was to the child's future development. He defined a child as having an attachment to someone when 'he is strongly disposed to seek proximity to and contact with a specific figure', and attachment behaviour as the 'various forms of behaviour that a child commonly engages in to attain and/or maintain a desired proximity' (Bowlby, 1983: 371). Attachment theory describes both the behaviour and the long-term attachments that children make. Bowlby (1969, 1983) described several characteristics of attachment behaviour. These included the child wanting to maintain close proximity to the main carer, following a familiar adult (after the age of nine months), showing alarm at an unfamiliar face (after the age of ten months) and actively seeking attention from the main carer (Bowlby, 1983: 198).

Ainsworth and Bell (1970) expanded this research to include the 'strange situation' dilemma, where an infant was left briefly by their mother, but with a stranger in the room. The behaviours of the children were investigated, particularly the infant's behaviour when the mother returned. The different behavioural responses were classified according to attachment theory. Ainsworth found that there was a range of behaviours, as expected, but that the attachment behaviour depended on the conditions, with the behaviours being 'heightened in situations perceived as threatening' (Ainsworth and Bell, 1970: 64).

Three distinctly different behaviours were observed:
- **Secure attachment**. These children are in the majority for a normal sample of children. They are likely to be distressed after a short separation, but will be comforted by their main carer and return to play.
- **Anxious–avoidant attachment**. These children will avoid the main carer after a separation and will even prefer to go to a stranger.
- **Anxious–resistant attachment**. These children will sometimes seek proximity to the main carer or sometimes resist contact. They may be more violent, or more passive, than the average infant.

Further work using the strange situation research by Main and Solomon (1986) suggested that there was a fourth attachment behaviour, namely **insecure–disorganised** and/or **disoriented** attachment. This is where the child seems to have inconsistent responses to the carer's absence and return. Sometimes the child was avoidant, sometimes resistant and sometimes apprehensive.

The vital emotional, and physical, importance of secure attachment is discussed poignantly by Perry and Szalavitz (2006), who describe cases from first-hand experience where poor attachment has resulted in a failure to thrive and grow due to a lack of emotional bonding and nurturing in the very early years. In the most extreme case this led to the unfeeling murder of two young girls by a young man who had failed to make any attachments with his family members while growing up (Perry and Szalavitz, 2006: 101). These are extreme cases, but they demonstrate what can happen when attachment is not secure, and emotional development is disrupted.

Classic research

John Bowlby's theory of attachment was based on research carried out during the Second World War on homeless and orphaned children. His work has been widely challenged by feminist groups on political grounds and by many other researchers on cultural and methodological grounds. However, his work remains highly influential. Here are some places to find out more:

- For a brief overview see *How Children Learn* (Pound, 2005), pp. 44–6.
- *Key Times for Play* (Manning-Morton and Thorp, 2003) is very accessible and offers helpful insights into how the theory can be put into practice.
- There are a number of videos online featuring Bowlby himself outlining his work; see, for example, http://www.youtube.com/watch?v=VAAmSq2GV8.

'Key person' role

It is a statutory requirement that a setting has a 'key person' for every child who attends the setting (DfE, 2012a). This will look different from setting to setting. For example, in a large nursery each practitioner may be allocated a number of 'key children', whereas a childminder will be the 'key person' to all the children in their care, and a reception class teacher will take the role of the 'key person' for the whole class.

The role of the 'key person' is to secure high quality care and learning experiences for young children (DfE, 2012a) and is closely related to good attachment. Grenier *et al.* suggest that children need 'familiar and trusting relationships in order for them to develop emotional well-being' (2008: 50) and that the indiscriminate care of children by a number of adults can lead to 'anxiety, aggression or withdrawn behaviour' (2008: 49).

It should also be recognised that the 'key person' role can be emotionally demanding for the practitioners who work with the children and families. Elfer and Dearnley (2007: 278) explored this with head teachers and their staff and they concluded that there was 'emotional complexity' as well as intense demands made of the staff. To support staff successfully, there must be systematic reflective practice and staff should have time to 'think about and process the individual feelings evoked by their emotional work with the children' (Elfer and Dearnley, 2007: 278). In nurseries and settings where practitioners spend even longer in direct contact with children, the emotional drain can be enormous.

There is often discussion around attachment and the 'key person' and concerns that a baby may somehow start to prefer their 'key person' to the primary carer. This can make practitioners unsure of having loving, close relationships with the children in their care. However, this has not been shown to be the case in practice or in research. In fact, as Attachment theory shows, the more caring the relationship, the better. Page (2008 cited in Nutbrown and Page, 2008) talks movingly about how working with babies and young children should have an element of love and this would actually reassure mothers that their child is being cared for as they would themselves – with love and care. Page (2008 cited in Nutbrown and page, 2008: 184) calls this 'professional love' and advocates that all babies are entitled to professional love as part of their nursery or setting experience. Rogers (2004) has explained something similar in psychoanalytical therapy – unconditional positive regard. The definition he uses is 'outgoing positive feelings without reservations' (Rogers, 2004: 62), meaning that the therapist is caring towards the client at all times, not just when the client displays 'good' behaviour. In studies it was found that when psychoanalysts used unconditional positive regard with their clients, the outcomes for the clients were much better than when it was not used. This supports Page's view (2008, cited in Nutbrown and Page, 2008) that practitioners should care for and love children unconditionally.

Reflective task

- How do you select a 'key person' for the children in your care?
- Are the children allowed to choose their own 'key person'? Would this make a more natural bond between them?
- How does the 'key person' role differ if you work in the baby room or in the preschool room?

Multiple intelligences

For many years the idea of 'intelligence' came from Intelligence Quotient (IQ). This could be measured and resulted in a single number that described whereabouts on the intelligence continuum that person was. Binet and Simon (1905, cited in Gardner *et al.*, 1996) devised intelligence tests for children in 1905 on behalf of the French government. This was so those children who had genuine learning difficulties could be separated from those children who were difficult to teach because of their poor learning disposition or background. Unusually for the era, the tests were arranged in age bands, so there were tests that an average four-year-old, six-year-old, eight-year-old and so on should be able to complete. This would put the child into a mental age band. So if a child with a chronological age of eight years could only complete the test for the four-year-olds, but none beyond that, then the child would be deemed to have a mental age of four, and vice versa.

Jean Piaget worked with Simon in Paris in the early 1900s, standardising tests for children. It was during this time that he began to realise that it was more important to understand the thinking behind the child's answers – the why and how – rather than just obtaining the correct answers. From this he developed many theories on the working of a child's mind and intellectual development. His overarching theory was that children have four stages of intellectual development. These are the sensorimotor stage, pre-operational stage, concrete operations and formal operations (Piaget and Inhelder, 1969). His main contention was that whatever their intelligence or background, children will pass through the four stages, in that order.

However, a criticism of Piaget is that he only tested one sort of intelligence, 'logical-mathematical' (Gardner *et al.*, 1996: 114). Gardner (1983) challenged the view of a single intelligence, which can be measured using an IQ test. He suggested that human beings have multiple intelligences and that these will be in different stages of development at any one time. In his book *Frames of Mind*, Gardner (1983) suggests there is a family of seven main intelligences:

1 linguistic
2 musical
3 logical-mathematical
4 spatial
5 bodily-kinesthetic
6 intrapersonal personal intelligence (introspective, one's own feelings)
7 interpersonal personal intelligence (looking outwards to others' feelings).

Gardner (1996) later added an eighth, naturalistic intelligence, to his list.

Children display the range of intelligences and these should be valued. For example, some children may display a talent for making music or keeping a beat, whereas others may be physically able and have good hand–eye coordination.

Emotional intelligences

In 1990 Salovey and Mayer published two research papers which investigated people's abilities in a range of seemingly unrelated areas, hypothesising these were, in fact, related by a common core of 'emotional' intelligence. At this time they defined emotional intelligence as 'the ability to monitor one's own and others' feelings and emotions, to discriminate among them and to use the information to guide one's thinking and actions' (Salovey and Mayer, 1990: 189). They explained this as a Four Branch model, which describes emotional intelligence as the ability to:

- accurately perceive emotions (in others and oneself)
- use emotions to facilitate thinking
- understand emotional meanings
- manage one's own emotions.

Daniel Goleman (1996), who argues that emotional intelligence is not only important, but is more important than IQ, extended their work. When pupils at schools in the United States took part in emotional literacy classes, designed to improve the emotional intelligence of the children, they found that the children were better able to recognise their own emotions, were more able to manage their own anger, be more responsible and empathetic and were better at handling relationships (Goleman, 1996).

However, Roberts *et al.* (2001) questioned the assertion by Mayer *et al.* (1999) that there is such a thing as emotional intelligence. Roberts *et al.* (2001: 223) suggested that there is emotional conformity and that the emotional 'intelligence' of a person depends on the method of measurement and protocol used, so it could not truly be termed an 'intelligence'. Mayer *et al.* (2004) responded by declaring that a more accurate research scale answered some of the criticisms, but also that, not unreasonably, this is early days in the research of emotional intelligence and there may be more yet to be discovered.

Emotional intelligence and children's development

Controlling desires and not acting on impulse can be one of the most difficult things for a growing child to learn. Goleman (1996) relates an experiment, where a group of four-year-old children were given a choice: you can either have one marshmallow now, or, if you decided to wait, you can have two marshmallows when the researcher returns in a few minutes. Just to make things even harder, the marshmallow was left in front of the child while the researcher left the room (Goleman, 1996: 81). Some children took the marshmallow immediately, while other children distracted themselves and had two marshmallows as the reward. The progress of both groups of children was investigated 14 years later, with startling results. The children who had been able to delay eating the marshmallow were more socially competent and able to deal with the emotional roller coaster of life. The children who had been unable to resist temptation were more likely to get upset, less socially secure and still unable to delay gratification. This experiment demonstrates how control over emotions can have a significant impact on all areas of life, and how the lessons learned in the early years can persist into later life.

Thus, it is important that teachers and practitioners understand how vital emotional intelligence is for young children. Ashiabi (2000) suggests that children are more emotionally sophisticated than teachers allow for. The children who display accurate positive and negative feelings are more likely to have a 'secure relationship and an affectively balanced relationship with their caregivers' (Ashiabi, 2000: 82) and the reverse is also true – those children who do not have secure relationships tend to display emotions which are not accurate to their feelings. It is suggested that this is because children in secure relationships have help regulating their feelings from their carers. Children who have negative experiences while with their carers, and therefore do not have secure relationships, may exhibit social incompetence. This is closely allied to attachment theory and the types of attachments children may, or may not, have developed in early childhood. Children with secure attachments will be more able to express and control their feelings, compared with children who display insecure attachments. Siraj-Blatchford *et al.* (2002) describe how Schweinhart and Weikart (1997) found that emotional security was linked to the type of disposition that children had. Those children who had been given lots of direct instruction, and not been allowed to build up their own mastery disposition, had more emotional impairment than those children with a good mastery disposition.

Returning to neuroscience again, Albright *et al.* (2000) suggest that the emotional and cognitive parts of the brain are located in proximity, in the ventral and dorsal anterior cingulate. This means that the two areas work in tandem and that both emotion and cognition benefit by learning to regulate or control this area of the brain. They hypothesise that 'children who are well advanced in emotional regulation should be at a specific advantage in regulating cognitive conflict' (Albright *et al.*, 2000: 46).

When it comes to gender differences, Warren and Stifter (2008) found that boys and girls were equally emotionally self-aware, but that it was whether their environment was supportive socially which was important. A limitation of their research was that the research was completed with children on their own, so there were no observations of naturalistic behaviour in social groups. It has been suggested that boys should be encouraged to take part in emotional problem solving in the early years, so emotional conflicts can be more easily resolved in later years (Mercurio, 2003).

Reflective task

- How is the children's emotional environment supported in your setting?
- Are boys encouraged to demonstrate and describe their emotions as well as girls?
- How do you show that you value children's emotional intelligence as well as their linguistic or mathematical intelligence?
- Do you encourage/support good emotional awareness in the language you use with the children, for example by describing your own emotions?

Research has shown that there are many forms of intelligence, which are equally important and inseparable. Gardner *et al.* (1996) investigated the individual and their circumstances. They demonstrated how the culture and context affect children's intelligences and how imposing IQ tests, which do not explore these, are missing an important aspect of child development. Goleman (1999) showed the importance of being emotionally intelligent and how this can underpin all the other intelligences throughout life.

Extend your knowledge

Investigate your own emotional intelligence. You can do tests online, for example: http://www.bgfl.org/ bgfl/custom/resources_ftp/client_ftp/ks3/ict/multiple_int. Or try the book: Daniel, M. (2010) *Self-Scoring Emotional Intelligence Tests (Self-Scoring Tests)*, New York: Sterling Publishing.

Are you surprised at the results?
- How can you use this information to help you as a practitioner?
- How does this compare to your colleagues' emotional intelligence?
- What does this imply for effective team working and working with parents?

Next steps

Personal, social and emotional development is a prime area in the Statutory Framework of the EYFS (DfE, 2012a: 6), which states that 'the three prime areas reflect the key skills and capacities all children need to develop and learn effectively'.
- How will you ensure that you will support the personal, social and emotional development of all children in your care?
- Will some children require more support than others?
- Look at each element of the personal, social and emotional development statement on page 5 of the Statutory Framework. Are there any areas you feel could be better supported?
- Is each area given equal support? For example, are children encouraged to manage their feelings as much as they are encouraged to develop respect for others?

The new *Development Matters* document (Early Education, 2012: 4) states that the prime areas are 'fundamental, work together, and are moved through to support development in all other areas'.
- How can you ensure that personal, social and emotional development underpins all other aspects of child development?
- List some other areas of development that could be supported by personal, social and emotional development. For example, expressive arts and design (Early Education, 2012: 43) 'joins in singing favourite songs' would be supported by 'have confidence in their own abilities' from the Statutory Framework (DfE, 2012a) for personal, social and emotional development.

Review your policies on supporting children with special educational needs.
- How do you evaluate, assess and identify areas of children's development?
- What is the procedure for supporting a child who is currently not meeting their developmental stage?

Evaluate your own skills and knowledge.
- Do you require further training on specialist areas of personal, social and emotional development? For example, supporting a child who has witnessed domestic violence.

Factors that may affect personal, social and emotional development

There are many factors that may affect the personal, social and emotional development of children. Some areas for consideration when working with children in the early years have been highlighted here, but this should in no way be considered an exhaustive list.

Home learning environment

Siraj-Blatchford and Siraj-Blatchford's knowledge review (2010), based on the best research evidence, quantitative data and validated experience in the UK, demonstrates the importance of the home learning environment. In this extensive review they found that providing parents with strategies to support children's learning at home reduced underachievement. This included children 'being read to, going to the library, painting and drawing, playing with letters and numbers, singing songs and reciting poems and rhymes' (Siraj-Blatchford and Siraj-Blatchford, 2010: 33). The review also highlights how factors such as good nutrition, supporting self-esteem and developing resilience can raise children's attainment. Similarly, children's underachievement was reduced where health services, family and parenting services supported families with attachment and bonding issues, relationships with siblings and children's self-regulation.

But what happens when the home life is disordered or there are mental health issues? The effects of these are complex and unique to each situation and some children will be more affected than others. For example, there is research to show that postnatal depression in mothers can negatively affect the behavioural and social development of children (Murray et al., 1999). These children may be quiet or withdrawn and unwilling to engage in play with other children, missing out on vital opportunities to make friends.

Similarly, parents who abuse alcohol or drugs potentially put the home learning environment at risk. This can simply be through the lack of consistent care and attention or it may have more significant, long-term effects. West and Prinz (1987) found that, where children had suffered because of their parents' drinking or drug taking, they externalised problems. This means that the children displayed aggression or refused to comply with instructions. However, they also found that not all children suffered in this way and that the outcomes for each child depended on their particular circumstances (West and Prinz, 1987). The corollary to this is that the negative effects of parental drug or alcohol abuse may be mitigated by other factors. In addition, Zeitlin (1994) found that the children of alcohol-abusing adults were at risk, not only from behavioural problems, but also from a range of cognitive and emotional problems as well.

An often hidden factor of the home learning environment is homelessness. It can be very disruptive for children if the family have to stay with relatives or friends, moving frequently from place to place, with no settled address. This may not be obvious to practitioners who work in nurseries or settings, often because the family are reticent to share the information due to embarrassment or fear of labelling. However, children who are homeless can display behavioural problems, lack of compliance and problems with expressive skills (Koblinsky et al., 2000). These can have negative effects on the children's social and emotional development.

Other risk factors

Some of the other factors include being abused, or being exposed to abusive situations, such as domestic violence. Goldsmith *et al.* (2008) found that this could have long-term repercussions, particularly for behavioural development. Some factors are beyond the control of the parents, such as a child having to attend a paediatric outpatient clinic. In their research Glazebrook *et al.* (2003) found that there was an increased likelihood of emotional and behavioural disturbances in children who attend paediatric outpatient clinics. These examples underline how important it is to have close working relationships with parents and to ensure that as much information is shared as possible. If practitioners have prior knowledge of the background of a child, then greater support and understanding can be given in nurseries and settings.

Special educational needs may affect a child's personal, social and emotional development. For example, children who are oversensitive, or under-sensitive, to sensory stimulation, such as being touched or sounds (sensory regulatory disorder or dysfunction), will not enjoy being cuddled or listening to music. They may also suffer from behavioural difficulties as they get older (DeGangi *et al.*, 2000). Being unable to enjoy these experiences may affect the social development of children.

Positive male role models

There are still very few men working in childcare and attending childcare courses in the UK. This means that children are missing a male role model in nursery. Goldschmied and Jackson (2004) suggest that the staff team should include men, so there is a range of abilities and skills in the team. This is an ideal opportunity for children to see men in a caring and supportive environment, especially if there is no male role model at home. The lack of men in childcare could be due to negative cultural and social assumptions about men wanting to work with children, although these assumptions are, and should be, challenged. Sadly, abuse cases where women have been found to be the perpetrators have helped to shatter the widely held belief that it is only men who harm children, not women.

There are some more positive practices that are emerging in early years practice. Children's books are becoming more gender non-specific (using animals, for example) or are displaying people in less gender-specific roles and there are now many visual resources that show men in non-traditional roles, such as nursing. These help children to challenge assumptions and explore their own feelings about role models. Practitioners can also use them as a starting point for discussions about 'typical' roles for boys and girls, men and women.

Reflective task

Review the books and images you have on display at your setting.
- Are the roles displayed traditional and gender-stereotypical ones?
- Do you use books that challenge children about their preconceptions of the roles of men and women?
- How could you provide male role models more effectively in the setting?

Socio-economic factors

The type of socio-economic household that a child grows up in has been shown to affect personal, social and emotional development. Caspi *et al.* (2000) found that children growing up in a deprived neighbourhood affected children's global development. It has also been shown, over longitudinal studies in the UK, that the lower the father's social class, the more likely that the children will have social and emotional adjustment problems (Marmot, 2010). To improve the emotional health, cognitive and social skills of children, Marmot suggests that the expenditure on intervention programmes is 'focused progressively across the social gradient' (2010: 95), balancing the see-saw of social inequality, where the personal, social and emotional development problems go up as the social class comes down. Sylva *et al.* (2010: 189) are emphatic about how to reduce the negative impact of social circumstances, and they state 'good early experiences lay the foundation for children to thrive'. This is supported by Siraj-Blatchford and Siraj-Blatchford (2010: 34) who found that there was some evidence to suggest that targeting families who are socio-economically disadvantaged would be beneficial. They recommended that further intergenerational research with regional and minority ethnic groups would provide more evidence of the effect of socio-economic status.

Bronfenbrenner (1979) discusses how weak links both within and between the different systems (microsystem, mesosystem, macrosystem, exosystem and chronosystem) make each system less effective. For example, he cites how home visits from preschool to the child's home strengthened the links between microsystem and mesosystem. Conversely, where parents and preschools do not work together to form strong links, there is a 'developmental impact' on the child (Bronfenbrenner, 1979: 218).

Social and Emotional Aspects of Development (SEAD)

Social and Emotional Aspects of Development (SEAD) (DCSF, 2008d) is a National Strategies guidance document which promotes social and emotional development. It is the first in a series of programmes that support children's personal, social and emotional development throughout their life at school. The SEAD programme is specifically designed to flow through to *Social and Emotional Aspects of Learning* (SEAL) (DfES, 2005a) in Reception class and then through a child's whole school life.

The guidance starts with personal, social and emotional development of young children and how practitioners and parents can support this. The remainder of the SEAD document is designed to fit with the four themes of the EYFS (DfE, 2012a):

- Unique child
- Positive relationships
- Enabling environments
- Learning and development.

Each section investigates and discusses how the EYFS can support children, illustrated with practical examples. There is a reflective analysis page for each section, with ideas for discussions with practitioners. For example, how would you find out what activities the fathers at your setting would like? (DfES, 2005a: 28). The 'key person' and emotionally enabling environment are covered in detail and there is a very useful audit tool included in the appendices.

The SEAD guidance can be used as introductory guidance for new practitioners or as a springboard for discussion at staff meetings, particularly the 'Reflect and note' sections. It is very relevant to the EYFS (DfE, 2012a), even though it draws heavily on the Principles into Practice cards of the 2008 EYFS (DCSF, 2008c), because it encapsulates good practice for personal, social and emotional development in the early years.

Practitioner's own emotional health

The work that most early years practitioners, teachers, childminders and educators do every day can be physically and emotionally draining. Practitioners are expected to be endlessly patient and caring, even if they are at the end of a long, difficult shift. Many practitioners are based in one room, all day, with the same children. There may be two or more practitioners in one room together all day, who will be expected to work with one another efficiently and effectively. On the other hand, a childminder may not see another adult all day, but will only have children to interact with. The practitioner may have to support a child who is the subject of abuse or be caught in the middle of a family break-up. Practitioners are expected to be creative, observant, professional, loving, practical and empathetic. All of which can drain the practitioner's own emotional reserves.

In addition, practitioners will have their own families and circumstances to manage. It can be particularly difficult to be working with young children all day and then come home to start all over again with your own children, for example. Children can be very good at picking up on the emotional atmosphere in a setting, so it is essential that practitioners' emotional health is a priority. This means that effective coping strategies should be used. For example, this could be recognising our own limits or emotional state (DCSF, 2008d) or having a friend who can give support when needed.

There could be very serious consequences of not recognising this issue. Good practitioners may leave the profession, due to lack of support. Practitioner's modelling of emotions, such as being patient or being polite to a fellow practitioner, will be the children's guide. If the practitioner is unable to show these emotions, the children will be unable to learn them. Even worse, the children may assume that it is acceptable to be rude to a colleague or to be rough with the toy boxes. This is not an easy task. Dowling (2010: 215) recognises this, stating 'in fostering young children's personal, social and emotional development staff need to invest more of themselves than in any other aspect of work'.

Reflective task

In your setting:
- Do you feel welcomed and included?
- How can you make your induction processes inclusive?
- How often do you discuss your own attitudes and practice?
- Who do you discuss this with?
- In what ways are you supported during your work with the children?
- How are differences of opinion resolved between staff members?
- How can you support other staff?
- What external support networks are available?
- How can you get to meet practitioners in similar circumstances?
- When do you unwind or relax?

Conclusion

The personal development, social development and emotional development of young children are difficult to separate. In the conclusion to their research, Caine and Caine (1991: 66) state that 'emotions and cognition cannot be separated', while Gmitrováa and Gmitrovb (2004: 269) suggest they are 'integral'. For example, the emotional development of a child will affect their personality and their social competence.

In this chapter we have seen how an infant and young child's personality is formed, partly from genetics and partly from external factors such as attachment issues, family circumstances and the pressures of society. There is some debate as to how socialising affects children's development. Piaget paid little heed to social aspects of learning, whereas Vygotsky and Bandura considered them vitally important.

Similarly there has been a myriad of research around friendships, the overlapping of personal and social development and the effects these may have on a child's cognitive development. There has been much exploration around cognitive development, and the idea of multiple intelligences in relation to children. IQ tests do not demonstrate the importance of emotional development or how this can affect other aspects of intelligence.

Finally, some reflection points on how, as practitioners, you can support and help children with their personal, social and emotional development.

- Consider the type of emotional environment you provide in your setting.
- Children should be allowed to take some emotional risks, to build resilience.
- Be aware that by praising a child you may be implicitly criticising another.
- Take account of the relative age effect: children who look older or are more physically able may be mistaken for being older and have more expectations thrust upon them.
- Forming temperaments starts at the youngest age and is influenced by circumstances and people around the child.

In conclusion, the personal, social and emotional development of children is a very complex area. The great strides being made in neuroscience at the moment are helping us to understand some of the neurological developments in very young children. However, it would seem that the best thing we can do for the children in our care is to give them unconditional love and support.

Evaluate your...

Knowledge on personal, social and emotional development

- How do you show children that you value their own sense of identity?
- In what ways do you support the self-esteem and self-confidence of the children in the setting?
- How do you encourage children to be independent?
- What behavioural strategies do you have in place to ensure children socialise?
- How would you recognise a child who has emotional problems?
- Who can support the setting when a child is experiencing social and emotional difficulties?
- How can you reduce the negative effects of commercialisation and sexualisation of children in your setting?
- How do you support your own emotional well-being?

Further reading

Lindon, J. (2010) *Understanding Child Development: Linking Theory and Practice* (2nd edn), London: Hodder Education.

Moritz Rudasill, K. and Konold, T. (2008) 'Contributions of children's temperament to teachers' judgments of social competence from kindergarten through second grade', *Early Education & Development*, vol. 19, no. 4, pp. 643–66.

Powell, T. (2012) 'The impact of being homeless on young children and their families', NHSA Dialog, *A Research-to-Practice Journal for the Early Childhood Field*, vol. 15, no. 2, pp. 221–8.

Thwaites, J. (2008) *100 Ideas for Teaching Personal, Social and Emotional Development (100 Ideas for the Early Years)*, London: Continuum International Publishing.

Wood, J. (2007) 'Academic competence in preschool: Exploring the role of close relationships and anxiety', *Early Education & Development*, vol. 18, no. 2, pp. 223–42.

Physical development

8

Penny Greenland

Introduction

Physical development is about the body (every child's first home) and about movement (every child's first language). More complex and far reaching than the acquisition of motor skills (like crawling, walking, jumping and pencil grip), physical development begins with a child's ability to take in information through the senses in the body, and progresses through a magnificently complex and interweaving series of processes that create not only skilful and expressive movement, but also a sense of potency and equilibrium in the world. Given the right conditions, physical development culminates in a vibrant relationship with the feeling of life itself and the ability to embody all that we are and all that we do. If we aim for anything less, we do our children a disservice. The new placement of physical development as a prime area of the Early Years Foundation Stage (EYFS) (DfE, 2012a) provides an opportunity to rethink the way we support young children's physicality, in the knowledge that it is a vitally important underpinning for all their development and learning.

Learning outcomes

This chapter offers:

- An overview of different theories about physical development – drawing on both academic study and somatic approaches – to underpin a review of the physical development curriculum.
- An understanding of physical development as a series of unfolding processes, rather than a series of separate physical goals.
- A set of principles for reviewing the physical development area of the curriculum.
- An example of a tested developmental framework that aims to provide broad support for children's developing physicality in early years settings.

Feelings about children's physicality

Perhaps physical development is the area of the curriculum that we most take for granted, with a generalised sense that it will simply happen of its own accord. It harbours many (often unspoken) anxieties for early years practitioners, settling around safety issues and classroom management. These gaps and anxieties were revealed by a two-year consultation (1998–2000) carried out across the early years sector by JABADAO (Greenland, 2006), and again in the in-depth evidence-based action research project (2002–9) that followed (Greenland, 2009). Early years practitioners expressed a lack of basic knowledge about physical development and were quick to recognise a tendency to push physical activities outdoors, believing movement play indoors would get out of hand, be too noisy and disrupt other activities. Indoor movement activities were described as highly controlled and adult led, organised in groups, equipment based (slides, climbing frames etc.) or involving mostly small movement of hands and heads.

Practitioners also spoke about their personal discomfort with being on the floor with children and with joining in spontaneous, child-led movement play. Many said they felt guilty if they were 'just' engaging in movement play with children, concerned that this would not be perceived as a learning activity and anxious about what parents or colleagues would think (Greenland, 2006 and 2009).

Scenario

Amanda (baby room practitioner) is lying on the floor looking into the mirror with Shelley, 11 months. They are cooing and babbling together. Kegan, 10 months, crawls onto her legs and lies down on his belly. He is snuggled and content. Although Amanda recognises his obvious pleasure she can't stop thinking: 'What will people think if they come in and find me "lying about"? How can I justify this as a learning activity?'

Reflective task

With the emphasis given to the intellect in our culture, it can be hard for early years practitioners to set aside the prejudices and hidden constraints that often surround the body and physicality in a learning context.
- How do you feel about children's physical play?
- Are there aspects of physical activity that you feel anxious about?
- What do you do when you feel anxious?

Learning from theory

Traditional research and theory development

Establishing a clear understanding of the theory of physical development is an essential starting point for developing practice. Theories (developed from observations, assumptions, suggestions and principles) allow us to place our opinions and practice in a wider context. They help us to reflect on what we do and why. Theory about physical development has been developed by a range of different specialists, including developmental psychologists, kinesiologists and motor developmentalists. Focused research is relatively new, beginning in the early 20th century. It is significant that it has largely been motivated by a desire to understand cognitive development better, rather than to study the moving body in its own right.

However, alongside academic study, dancers and body workers have also undertaken serious and detailed research into human physicality from a different perspective. This work identifies further movement patterns and illuminates their emotional content. Somatics is the study of the body from within, a practical exploration of the principles of sensory, motor and perceptual development drawing primarily on the felt experience of the body (Hanna, 1976). There is much to learn from somatics, especially with regard to planning for early years settings as, above all, it is about the study of *being a body* – something babies and young children know all about and adults have often forgotten.

Maturational theory

Much of what we know about physical development is based on the work of Gesell (1928), McGraw (1935), Shirley (1931) and Bayley (1935). Their detailed observational work offered a maturational theory of physical development, assuming that as particular regions of the brain mature they allow or enable new sensory, motor and cognitive functions to appear. Physical development, therefore, was described as a universal sequence of movement patterns that always occurred in the same order and at the same age (although some stages might be skipped). Importantly, this process was deemed to be resistant to external influences – it was thought that it would take care of itself. Their theory also suggested 'nodal' stages – periods when children have a high degree of mastery over their environment with accompanying high mood; and 'out of focus' stages – when they have low levels of mastery and a troubled mood (like the notion of the 'terrible twos'). Although this theory is largely felt to be outdated now, it is still very much present in the minds of many parents and practitioners, and often used in readily available non-specialist advice for parents. It is compelling and simple and quite prevalent.

Extend your knowledge

Learn more about Gesell's maturation theory and identify the ways in which it influences current thinking and practice.

Developmental task theory

In the mid-20th century the work of Robert Havinghurst (1948–52) initiated a key development in thinking. Developmental task theory (Havinghurst and Levine, 1979) suggested that the movement patterns (or tasks) in the developmental sequence are linked to one another in such a way that each pattern is a building block for the next. Thus, successful achievement of each pattern leads to success with later patterns – and happiness; unsuccessful achievement or gaps lead to difficulty with later tasks, social disapproval – and unhappiness. Why is this so important? This is an activity-dependent view of development suggesting that we can use knowledge of how the developmental sequence occurs to predict future success or failure, and to do something about it. Therefore, if practitioners understand the developmental sequence well enough and take a developmental approach to the support of physical development, it is possible to support or construct experiences that minimise gaps in the developmental process, creating sure foundations for future learning and life.

A variety of current intervention programmes (such as Brain Gym and Sensory Integration) have been developed with this theoretical perspective at their core. Each has its own 'take' on how to ensure that significant developmental movement patterns are well established; each offers an intervention (specific movement activities or exercises) to achieve this.

It is difficult to find hard evidence of the effectiveness of many of these programmes, although The Institute for Neuro-Physiological Psychology (INPP) has published many detailed reports (Jändling, 2003; Preedy *et al.*, 2003). Some educators and health professionals feel that this work is based on an oversimplified theory of brain development. At the same time, there is considerable anecdotal testimony from families and individuals who have used movement programmes to address specific challenges, who feel this has been of considerable benefit to them (JABADAO, 2000). Somatic practitioners feel strongly that each movement pattern affects the others. Their evidence is drawn from the experience of getting to know them in the body, rather than from observation or intellectual analysis.

Extend your knowledge

Research different approaches to developmental task theory. You might start with Brain Gym (http://www .braingym.org.uk) and Sensory Integration (Ayres, 2005), and also look at the INPP Intervention Programme (http://www.inpp.org.uk/intervention-adults-children).

■ Explore criticism made of these approaches as well as statements of value.

■ How might your new understanding influence your practice?

Information processing theory

This theory, a form of developmental task theory, specifically addresses the sensory aspect of physical development. First appearing in the 1960s, it illuminates the way individuals take in, process and organise sensory information. It examines the 'kinesthetic' senses in particular – touch, proprioception (sense of where the body parts are in relation to one another) and the vestibular sense (broadly, the sense of balance). Ayres (1972), an occupational therapist working in the 1970s, developed Sensory Integration, a theory and practice focused on the potential to reduce learning disabilities such as dyspraxia, audio-language dysfunctions, poor hand–eye coordination, tactile defensiveness, visual and tactile perception issues. Her work is potentially of great relevance to the way we construct physical opportunities for babies and children in early years settings (Ayres, 2005). She suggested that every child has an inner drive to develop sensory integration through participation in meaningful sensorimotor activities (Ayres, 1972). She pointed to the excitement, confidence and effort observable in children's movement play as proof of this drive, and her focus was always on eliminating barriers that erode a sense of mastery, meaning, satisfaction and self-direction – not merely on the reduction of a developmental delay or learning disability (Ayres, 1972). Accordingly, her practice demanded that any sensory or movement intervention be contained within self-directed, meaningful activity for the child and not offered solely as an adult-led intervention.

Developmental milestone theory

Other theorists working in the mid- to late 20th century have suggested that the movement patterns in the developmental sequence, although indicators of the rate and extent of development, are not predicative of future functioning. Piaget's work (1950s–70s) can be seen within this developmental milestone theory. Here, the movement patterns are taken to be a continually unfolding series of linked processes, not specific patterns occurring at specific times. Crucially, there is no focus on intervention that might address gaps, but there is emphasis on sensorimotor development in the first two years. This theory most closely equates with the EYFS curriculum (DfE, 2012a), which asserts that 'children develop and learn in different ways and at different rates', but does not offer any guidance on identifying developmental gaps, or addressing them, through movement. It states, 'Practitioners working with the youngest children are expected to focus strongly on the three prime areas, which are the basis for successful learning in the other four specific areas' (DfE, 2012a: 6).

Piaget (1972) theorised that physical activity supports emerging mental activity and that between the ages of two and seven verbal language starts to replace sensorimotor activity as the primary learning mode and way of expressing thoughts and feelings. It is important to note this subservience to things of the intellect after two years of age. This continues to be very common in educational thinking. Physical activity (when not about 'letting off steam') is often treated as a way to boost verbal language development, concept formation (in, on, under etc.) or cognitive learning.

Somatic practitioners take a different view, suggesting that movement is essential in its own right (Johnson, 1995), forming the basis of our developing sense of self, our well-being and our learning throughout our lives.

Extend your knowledge

If you want to know more about somatic approaches, these are excellent books to read:

- Bainbridge-Cohen, B. (2008) *Sensing, Feeling and Action* (2nd edn), Berkeley, CA: North Atlantic Books.
- Johnson, D.H. (2000) 'Intricate tactile sensitivity: A key variable in western integrative bodywork', in Saper, C. and Mayer, E. (eds.), *The Biological Basis for Mind Body Interactions*, The Progress in Brain Research Series, vol. 122.
- Juhan, D. (2002) *Job's Body: A Handbook for Bodywork*, New York: Barrytown Ltd.

Ecological theory

This is another development of milestone theory. Based on work by Nicholas Bernstein (1967) and developed by Kugler *et al.* (1980), ecological theory states that each child is biologically programmed to strive for motor control and movement competence along a given sequence, but constraints within the individual, the environment and the task itself modify how development takes place, making it a highly individual process for each child. Development is further influenced by a drive to achieve things in the most efficient way possible (Kugler *et al.*, 1980), using the least amount of energy required. This provides a possible answer for, among other things, why babies might bum-shuffle instead of crawl. Not identified as a piece of the unfolding motor sequence, but used by many children to get about before they walk, could bum-shuffling simply be a more energy-efficient solution that fits the child's temperament and environment better than crawling?

Scenario

Ella (14 months) is bright as a button – very communicative, dedicated to sorting objects and putting them in and out of containers. She shows great interest in pencils and paper and frequently requests what she needs to 'write' and 'draw' things that are important to her. She is very interested in how the world works, especially in her ability to use the remote control to turn her brother's television programme off.

Ella was referred to a physiotherapist because she was not walking and because her feet and ankles 'are turned out'. There was growing concern about whether there was something 'wrong'.

Ella had never engaged in tummy time, belly crawling or crawling. She always liked to be upright with her hands free to do things. She quickly became a very efficient bum-shuffler. It supported her, from an early age, to get to and do the things she loved best. Her muscles and tendons had developed to support this, so when she eventually became interested in walking, she lacked the core stability that earlier belly crawling and crawling would have provided.

Ecological theory suggests that early years practitioners need to support physical development in the context of a child's life as a whole, being able to identify the influences on their development and offer relevant support.

Bioecological theory

Bronfenbrenner's bioecological theory (1979) focuses on the context for development – the microsystem (family, nursery, neighbourhood and peers); mesosystem (interaction between those microsystem contexts), the ecosystem (the wider social atmosphere), macrosystem (beliefs, attitudes and practices in the wide culture) and the chronosystem (the events of one's life) (see figure 7.1, page 148). This has huge implications for early years practice. Children absorb and interpret the values and behaviours in their surroundings and adjust their behaviour accordingly. Bioecological theory suggests that, far from physical development taking care of itself, the values of the people around – the things they say and imply about movement and physicality – have a fundamental effect on the way physical development takes place. This requires us to reflect upon what these (often hidden) values might be within our settings and check that they match our intentions for our children.

Research undertaken by JABADAO (Greenland, 2006) illuminated the context surrounding physical practice in early years settings. Practitioners almost always had an unwritten code for acceptable and unacceptable body and movement behaviour, with many kinds of movement deemed unsuitable – especially spinning, sliding, falling, boisterous jumping and full-on body contact between children during other activities. Certain body behaviours consistently attracted adult approval – being still, being upright, moving with 'control' and precision. Certain body behaviours (especially indoors) consistently attracted adult disapproval – wriggling, spinning, tipping off balance, sliding, climbing, moving with free flow, boisterous movement indoors, being in close physical contact with another child without a practical reason to do so. Lying on the floor was only acceptable for certain activities and tables were used for many activities when the floor could have provided a more child-centred learning environment. Full-bodied, spontaneous movement play was generally only supported in the outdoor environment (with little adult involvement), or using big equipment (such as a slide) in very controlled groups indoors. 'Rough and tumble play' (Holland, 2003) was advocated in early years literature as part of rounded provision, but practitioners often found it difficult to support.

The basis for current theoretical thinking

In the 1990s and early 2000s new dialogue between educators and neuroscientists added to the theoretical debate. Prior to this, it was believed that the wiring of the brain, and its functioning, was mostly 'programmed' by the individual's genetic blueprint. Now, the emerging view is that while the main circuits may be prewired (breathing, control of heart beat and reflexes), other basic pathways are quite rudimentary at birth, containing trillions of finer 'unprogrammed' potential connections. These connections appear to be dependent upon stimulation from the environment and experience in the environment to complete the structure of the brain (Greenough et al., 1987). This raised the question about what kind of stimulation babies and children need to support their physical development.

The early research (Diamond et al., 1964) suggested five crucial factors for sound development – diet, physical activity, challenge, newness and 'love' (which was actually physical touch or stroking). Greenough *et al.* (1987) subsequently suggested that these experiences were things that are almost inevitably going to be part of the infant's environment, not things that must be supplied as extras – the brain expects and needs the things that are going to be there. There is considerable food for thought for the physical development curriculum contained within this research. It establishes the significance of physical activity for the development of the brain as well as the body, but it also invites reflection on the kind of physical activity we offer. Opportunities for problem setting and solving, sociable intermingling and touch all appear to be vitally important components, and not just adult-led exercise or expressive movement.

Reflective task

- What kind of physical experiences do you think children need for sound development?
- Are the children in your care getting what their experience-expectant brains expect and need?
- What factors in the child's home environment influence the physical experiences available to them?
- Do you talk with the parents about the kinds of movement experience that are important for their child's development? What support do you offer to parents for relevant opportunities?

Summary of what the theory might tell us

Early theory suggested that motor development is a predetermined sequence that more or less takes care of itself. Later theories are more flexible about how the sequence occurs (around specific ages but with some potential variance in the sequence), but each generally supports the view that there is little that early years practitioners need to do apart from providing lots of opportunities for babies and children to be physically active, watch out for significant gaps in the sequence – and get specialist help if this is the case.

Some theories emphasise links between movement patterns in the sequence, suggesting that the provision of enhanced sensory or movement activities can make a significant difference to development. This implies that early years practitioners ought not to be leaving understanding of developmental movement to specialists, but need to be knowledgeable themselves, as the potential for supporting learning and development problems is profound.

Neuroscience tells us about the importance of sociable, problem-solving movement activity as vital experience for development; and describes babies as experience-expectant organisms seeking what ought to be a natural part of their environment to fine-tune neurological development.

Contemporary theory also emphasises the influence of the context. The environment, the values of those around, and the character and dispositions of the individual child all play an important part in how physical development takes place. This invites a thorough and candid review of the values that we impart to children and the potential effect this has on their development.

Reflective task

- Which theoretical construct most closely fits the approach in your setting?
- How is this understanding shared across the staff team in a clear way?
- How could a clearer understanding of the theory help you to develop your practice?
- What training implications are there for your staff team?

Next steps

Create a clear simple statement that articulates the foundations of your physical development curriculum.

Learning more about movement

Early years practice and the support of physical development

Physical development is not a series of goals, but a series of interweaving, overlapping processes that continue throughout a lifetime. Children are prompted to move by their biology. They move for many reasons, not just to acquire physical skills – 'moving and handling'. They move to find and maintain a sense of self, to learn about the world around them and to connect to the feeling of life itself, as well as to become efficient movers. Developmentally, the very act of moving prompts the development of their body, brain and nervous system, which in turn usually provides the capacity for new skills and abilities to emerge. These processes are endlessly complex, interweaving with one another in any one movement. As we support babies and young children we need to be able to separate and support each of these with a sound understanding of all the many aspects of a child's physicality.

Here are some things to look out for and support. Note interweaving processes are not presented in any particular order.

Moving to develop the feel of things and a subjective sense of self

The kinesthetic senses (touch, proprioception and the vestibular sense) provide us with what Damasio (1999) calls the simple sensory qualities of existence: what it feels like to be a body and what experience feels like. This is at the centre of an individual's existence throughout their lives. The earliest movement experiences are concerned with beginning this process, while establishing a core sense of self in the world through bodily felt, subjective experience. As a baby moves she rubs up against herself and the world, each movement and touch bringing new information about where she is and who she is. This underpins her capacity to feel at home in her own skin, to feel right in the world, and ultimately, to build her sense of being settled, comfortable and in touch with herself. Nothing will be more important to her future life than this.

What babies and children need from us

General

- Time to just be a body – free from any external goals or tasks – to be free to move in whatever ways their physicality allows and their curiosity demands
- Clear uncluttered space indoors and out
- Minimum restrictions to free movement (from equipment, environments or hidden values)
- Safe places to move and be moved, in lots of different ways
- Time on the floor (on backs and tummies) and time in loving arms

- Both familiarity and newness in their movement play
- Opportunities for lots of repetition
- Opportunities to create and solve physical challenges
- Opportunities to move with others
- Caring adults to partner, mirror, value and celebrate their exploration

Specific
- Focused opportunities to be seen and acknowledged for who they are (rather than who you would like them to be)
- As they become able, opportunities to make representations of their growing sense of themselves through movement play – performance, dances, pictures, stories and music

Moving to organise sensory information and develop perceptual abilities

Perceptual skills, just like motor skills, are learned. The infant receives and processes incoming sensory information through all their senses. At first, the information has no meaning, but through repeated experience, and by comparing information with previous experiences, infants and young children build their capacity for perception. They understand what is happening outside themselves and develop the ability to make an appropriate physical response. The child must learn to organise sensory information as well as to receive it (Ayres, 1972).

What babies and children need from us

All the general conditions plus:

Specific
- Many opportunities for repetition
- Opportunities to organise their own movement play that challenges their tactile, proprioceptive and vestibular senses (as well as taste, sound, vision and smell)
- Adults who know how to create delight-filled, meaningful, whole-bodied opportunities to explore these kinesthetic senses
- Adults who know how to identify gaps in sensory processing

Moving to connect the parts of the body and the feel of the whole

Watch a tiny baby moving and it is abundantly apparent that a fully felt sense of the body as a whole, interconnected entity is not yet present. It is movement that stimulates this process, with specific developmental patterns at work that will not only initiate early patterns but support all subsequent ones. When we support the earliest opportunities to engage with the developmental movement process, we are also supporting the sound development of all later skilled movement.

Hackney (2000) describes the way the movement patterns are involved in connecting up the body. Based on the somatic work of Irmgard Bartenieff ('Fundamentals'), Hackney (2000) groups some of the movement patterns from the developmental sequence into six areas, identifying their role in connecting up the body – breath, core to edge, head to tail, upper-lower, body-half and cross-lateral patterns. She identifies how each of these patterns supports both physical and emotional development, how each builds on the last and integrates with the next. Her work provides the potential to understand important, but often missed, aspects of infant movement and how these underpin future learning and well-being.

The EYFS curriculum (DfE, 2012a) speaks of the importance of physical development in well-being and confidence. This is not simply derived from the satisfaction that effective motor skills bring, or from the establishment of our body boundaries, the defining of our personal space or the development of a sense of time – all things the physical development curriculum has traditionally been concerned with. Somatics teaches us that the movement patterns in the developmental sequence underpin every aspect of our lives, our feelings and our capacity to think about things. The early patterns – rolling, crawling, yielding, pushing, reaching, grasping and pulling – underpin the secure development of these capacities, our will, the capacity to yield, the ability to make flexible responses, the ability to reach beyond our immediate grasp and the capacity to understand complex relationships. The way we develop and organise our movement continues to influence and reflect the way we operate in the world throughout our lives.

What babies and children need from us

All the general conditions plus:

Specific

- Adults who are delighted by, know about and support, the detailed process of physical development in a developmental perspective

Moving to build relationships

Building relationships with people and things around them is a key aspect of movement play for babies and young children. Using their primary language, movement, they are free to hold in-depth conversations long before (and long after) verbal language is available to them. This can be seen from day one in the tiny movements (and accompanying sounds) that pass between infant and mother (Malloch and Trevarthen, 2010). This rich and small dance holds as much communicative content as any words, and will build and extend to become a lexicon of non-verbal patters that unconsciously accompany all our interaction (Loman, 1996; Sossin and Birklein, 2006). Young children, if encouraged, will also delight in movement play in conscious and expansive ways to interact and bond with those around them.

What babies and children need from us

All the general conditions plus:

Specific

- Committed, uninhibited people to play with
- Resources that enable children to create new challenges in their play

Moving to create tactile experience

As you have already read in the previous chapter about babies by Rydin-Orwin, touch is the first sense that we acquire in the womb. It is the interface between our body and the world. By rubbing up against the world we learn about ourselves, each other and the world itself. The sense of touch originates on the bottom layer of the skin (the dermis). Filled with many tiny nerve endings, this provides information about anything the body touches, carrying information to the spinal cord and on to the brain, where the feeling is registered. The skin registers three different types of sensation: pressure, temperature (heat/cold) and pain.

The sensory activity of the skin is a major factor in our development. Research undertaken at the start of the 20th century exploring infant mortality in orphanages identified a 'disease' called merasmus, a Greek word meaning wasting away (Juhan, 2002). High numbers of infant deaths were found to be the result of insufficient touch stimulation, because there were too few carers to provide it. The highest number of fatalities were recorded between the seventh and 12th months. When staffing levels were increased, allowing infants to be held and played with, mortality rates plummeted. Further studies confirm that tactile stimulation associated with tender loving care is crucial to sound development and well-being. Bowlby (1979) suggests that physical contact is the ultimate form of 'the infant's most tangible, concrete indicator of safety', a central concept in attachment theory (Brennan *et al.*, 1998: 410). Research by Ainsworth and colleagues in the early 1970s found that the quality of touch rather than the quantity of touch is the primary ingredient in the formation of secure attachments (Ainsworth and Bowlby, 1991).

Levine (1960, cited in Juhan, 2002) researched concrete physiological changes that could be attributed to stimulation during infancy. In almost all cases, fondled rats developed more rapidly than isolated ones: they achieved motor coordination earlier, gained weight faster, and had a stronger resistance to disease, as well as a brisker, more efficient metabolism. Levine (1960, cited in Juhan, 2002) concluded that this was due to accelerated maturation of the central nervous system, specifically through increased myelin production (the fatty substance that promotes efficiency of the nerve pathways). A 1965 study (Gardner, 1972, cited in Juhan, 2002) of a child who was not handled for 15 months due to her mother's anxiety about disturbing a feeding tube, shows that sudden increase in handling (during a period of hospitalisation) resulted in a dramatic increase in development. The symptoms of tactile deprivation were the same as malnutrition: retarded bone growth, failure to gain weight, poor musculature and coordination, immunological weakness and general apathy. See the impact of neglect as illustrated by the scan image of the brain on page 133.

Montague (1971, cited in Juhan, 2002), interested in the manner in which tactile experience or its lack affects the development of behaviour, contends that the raw sensation of touch as stimulus is vitally necessary for the physical survival of the organism. He claims that it is as important as oxygen, liquid, food, rest, activity, sleep, bowel and bladder elimination, escape from danger and the avoidance of pain. Juhan (2002) sums up this research: 'Touch is food. Vital food.'

What babies and children need from us

All the general conditions plus:

Specific
- A rich diet of safe, appropriate touch, from people and the ground beneath them
- Experiences that offer full-bodied touch, such as rolling down hills, lying on their backs and bellies, bouncing on the bed and contact with other surfaces (the slide, the water in the swimming pool, the bark of a tree), as well as cuddles
- To be able to say no to touch as well as yes, and to have this completely respected
- Adults who know how to balance the creation of an environment that is full of tactile experience, with safeguarding children from harm

Reflective task

Think about – and list – all the different ways that babies and children in your setting get this vital touch nourishment, whether or not this is the focus for the activity. Do children have opportunities for whole-body touch as well as specific activities involving hands and feet?

Next steps

Make sure that you have a Touch Policy that is not only concerned with safeguarding but also reflects and articulates your understanding about the significance of touch for development.

Moving to gain a sense of where the limbs are, to develop the foundations for coordinated movement and to feel at home in the body

Proprioception is taken from the Latin word 'proprius' meaning one's own. It is the name given to the sense of where the limbs are in relation to one another. It is one of the senses that contributes to creating the felt sense of the body and its actions. Proprioception is what you use if you want to place your finger on the end of your nose, or pick up a cup and bring it to your lips. It originates in sensory receptors found all over the body – chiefly in muscles, joints and tendons, but also in connective tissue. There are three kinds of receptors: some detect length, stretch and rate of stretch in muscles; others detect these same in tendons; the third detect changes in movement and pressure in muscles. Receptors provide information as muscles stretch or contract, joints bend or straighten and ligaments, tendons and connective tissue stretch. This information is heightened when the body parts in question are working harder. Pulling, pushing and stretching actions give the strongest feedback. Proprioception underpins coordination. All changes of body position send proprioceptive messages to the brain for storing, sorting and sifting. The experience of the feel of things in our limbs, compared with the memory of previous experience, helps us to judge what level of force to use (not pushing too hard with a pencil as you write or draw; not gripping a ball too tightly). It helps us to plan how to carry out an action or maintain postural stability in new or challenging situations, like walking along a wall or standing on one leg with eyes closed. Without well-developed proprioception lots of everyday tasks become frustrating and difficult.

What babies and children need from us

All the general conditions plus:

Specific
- Full-bodied pushing, pulling, stretching, hanging, buffeting-about play
- Play that experiments with use of force, strong and light
- Some children might like to throw themselves down on the ground – splat!
- Rough and tumble play

Moving to develop a sense of balance and equilibrium

The vestibular sense tells us which way is up, how our body is oriented in relation to up, and how our body is moving in space. It is commonly thought of as the sense of balance. Balance is the mechanism through which we build a relationship with gravity and the ground – this is a hidden but primary relationship. The vestibular sense also helps us to adjust the eyes when the head changes position. Knowing 'which way is up' is vital to our sense of self and sense of well-being, as well as to efficient movement . All movement that includes spinning, tipping and being off centre is practice for the vestibular system. Movement is detected by an organ in the inner ear in vestibular sacs (which monitor the position of the head with respect to gravity) and semicircular canals which detect other movement of the head. In the semicircular canals, the motion of the fluid as the body spins or tips causes gelatinous lumps (cupulas) to bend one way or the other, which in turn causes hair cells to bend and send signals. There are three canals oriented at roughly 90° to one other, thus providing information in all three dimensions. When the vestibular system is well developed it provides feedback that enables the child to maintain the balance of the whole body in a dynamic relationship between the constant shift of their body's centre of gravity through space, providing a sure and steady sense of self in a moving world. This underpins a felt sense of balance and flexibility, and the capacity to be ready to respond to whatever might arise in an unpredictable environment.

What babies and children need from us

All the general conditions plus:

Specific

- Involvement in spinning, tipping, rolling, falling movement play, gentle or boisterous
- To move and be moved on and off balance
- To be supported to take safe risks with their balance
- To go very slowly and carefully with spinning, rolling etc. if it challenges their sense of safety

Moving to develop motor skills

A child will seek experiences that allow them to develop three kinds of motor skill: stability, locomotion (these two round up as 'moving' in the EYFS curriculum) and manipulation (includes 'handling' as described in the EYFS curriculum). These do not develop separately from one another, nor does one kind of motor skill complete before the next starts. They develop, over time, in a complex interweaving fashion that starts in the womb and continues all our lives.

Stability (and gravitational security)

Movement that seeks to establish stability is the most basic human movement; it is a cornerstone for our physical development. The development of stability takes place in direct relationship with the force of gravity – the gentle and constant force that helps to build bone density and muscle strength. We are earthbound creatures until we learn to work against gravity's pull. Our relationship with gravity is a formative one; how this early exploration goes plays an important part in underpinning our sense of security in all the other relationships we will have.

On a physical level, movement to gain stability involves any movement, or part of a movement, that is concerned with gaining and maintaining balance in relation to gravity and culminates in the ability to shift the relationship of the body parts in many ways and still remain in a chosen position. Early development includes reaching, twisting, turning, pushing, pulling, rolling, developing control of the head and neck, the trunk, sitting balancing on hands and knees then up to standing. Once upright, it includes bending, swaying, lifting, balancing on one foot, rolling, going head over heels, walking along a narrow surface, upside-down positions, complex balances and dodging.

It is within gravity that we also gradually develop a sense of equilibrium: more than balance, this is a grounded stability in the world. As Ayres (2005) suggests, gravitational security is so vital to our emotional health that nature has given us a strong inner drive to explore and master it. It is only when we start to develop a sense of security moving against it and within it that we can start to come away from the floor, or out of the security of caring arms, and learn to 'stand on our own two feet'.

As the child becomes more skilled at each motor task the element of balance takes less attention and effort, but children (and adults) may return frequently to 'play' and explore balance and equilibrium at all stages of their lives.

What babies and children need from us

All the general conditions plus:

Specific
- Very limited use of equipment that restricts movement as this develops, especially baby seats
- Lots of time on the floor, on back and tummy, essential for uncurling the spine and developing the necessary body shape and strength
- Lots of support, encouragement, soothing and understanding as the demands of new positions and stances make life very hard for a while
- A safe environment in which to take safe risks as they reach for new abilities

Mobility

These are the most obvious pieces of physical development – the movements that adults tend to celebrate as some of the most noticeable and remarkable aspects of child development. The first travelling movements are horizontal: scooting across the floor pulled along by the arms, belly-crawling (with the belly remaining in contact with the floor), then crawling. Upright travelling begins with supported walking, progresses to cruising around the furniture, then walking with light support, walking alone with much arm involvement and a wide stance, and finally walking alone with a narrower stance and arms less involved in maintaining balance. This provides the foundations for running, jumping, hopping, galloping and skipping.

What babies and children need from us

All the general conditions plus:

Specific
- Lots of time spent on movement that develops stability and gravitational security
- Not to be constantly rushed to the next stage of development
- Clear floor space (toys and clutter can significantly impede a child's ability and desire to move horizontally across the floor)
- Celebration of early mobility, not just the so-called milestone movements (sitting, crawling, walking)

Manipulation (including handling)

Manipulation requires the ability to apply and absorb force to and from objects, in directed ways, usually using hands, feet or mouth, but sometimes using other parts as well. It develops in close conjunction with stability and locomotion – the body has to be able to be controlled in many ways before manipulation skills can begin. It is a whole-bodied activity – children are involved in both fine motor manipulation and gross motor manipulation. 'Handling' is just one aspect of the manipulation spectrum. It has a very strong focus in the early years curriculum, with many links to readiness for school, for example pen grip. It is important to remember that this is just one aspect of the manipulation spectrum, and the one most closely linked to academic and indeed sedentary pursuits.

Early development of these motor skills centres on reaching, grasping, releasing and opening of the hand. (The hand is closed in the baby and only slowly opens with the early patterns that uncurl and connect the body, centre to edges.) Manipulation requires the ability to twist the wrist or ankle (young children sometimes use their feet as well as their hands to retrieve and manoeuvre objects), plus the flexible and dexterous use of the thumb and forefinger working in opposition. These early skills provide the foundations for later whole-body manipulation activities, including throwing, catching, kicking, trapping and striking, and also manipulation activities that use just the hands, often called fine motor skills, including cutting, writing, painting, doing buttons and laces.

Although manipulation skills tend to develop later than stability and locomotion, their foundations are present in the earliest movement patterns. Given the emphasis on pen control and writing in the British education system, it is worth noting that the whole body – fingers, wrist, arm, shoulder, trunk, and the sense of connection between them – is involved in, and must be sufficiently developed to support, writing.

What babies and children need from us

All the general conditions plus:

Specific
- Time on the floor involved in all the early movement patterns
- Adults who will play whole-bodied reaching, grasping and releasing games – not just with hands
- Encouragement and support as they practise the exacting tasks that require precision and accurate hand–eye coordination

Moving to acquire physical mastery

Once the basic motor skills are in place, children go on to acquire specialised motor skills that refine their ability to carry out particular activities for particular purposes – this may be in an activity, games, sports or dance context. Some very young children can be very focused on physical mastery, often with clear desires about the type of skills they are interested to acquire. These desires are often influenced by what is going on in the world around and a desire to achieve specific end results (like working the television remote, or playing football with Dad). Teaching, coaching or instruction is not relevant to the early movement patterns; helpful adults ensure the environment is conducive and the exploration valued, but they do not direct activities that teach the patterns. However, Miller (1978) found that instruction can enhance the development of specific skills more than practice in free play alone.

What babies and children need from us

All the general conditions plus:

Specific
- Support to develop specific physical skills that children show they are interested in acquiring

Moving to tell you who I am; moving to be seen

An important aspect of physical development is the child's need to communicate who they are, using the most direct human language they have. Movement precedes words and conveys rich and deep information from the mover to the watcher. A child's movement is as unique as their fingerprint. The way the early movement patterns emerge, the way the body parts connect to each other, the phrasing and shaping of every movement are formed out of their unique experience; it is both a universal and a totally individual language.

Children communicate readily and naturally in movement. As they develop the capacity for verbal language they acquire two means of expressing their feelings and thoughts, but adults tend to focus on verbal skills. Stern (1985) suggests that the emergence of verbal language can render some parts of our experience *less* shareable with ourselves and others as it drives a wedge between two simultaneous forms of our experience – lived and as we speak about it – causing a split in the experience of self. Moving and being witnessed (not assessed or observed but witnessed) are a fundamental desire. We all, babies and children included, long for others to see us, to share how we feel, to respond to us directly. Movement play supports this like no other activity. It also bridges the different aspects of our experience – felt and spoken – a vital underpinning for the development of literacy. Intellectual literacy is enhanced by physical literacy.

What babies and children need from us

All the general conditions plus:

Specific
- Opportunities to move for others
- Adults who are prepared to set words aside because they trust, and can engage in, the language of movement as readily as young children
- Adults who can witness movement play, involved as equals, noticing how they are moved by what they see, not simply working out what intervention to make next (assessment needs to happen too, but not all the time)

Moving to embody life and learning

By nature, we human beings strive to embody everything that we do – to feel our lives stir in our bodies as well as in our thoughts. We work things out in our bodies as well as in our heads (Greenland, 2000). This does not mean that we have to move all the time; it does mean we need ready access to the sensations in our body as well as the thoughts in our head throughout our lives, not just as the focus for the first two years.

What babies and children need from us

All the general conditions plus:

Specific
- An education culture and a curriculum that appreciate how we learn in our physicality throughout our lives, not just in the early years

New emphasis on health

The government green paper *Every Child Matters* (Department for Education and Skills, 2003) established 'staying healthy' as the first of five education outcomes deemed to be crucial to well-being in childhood and subsequent life. *Choosing Activity: A physical action plan* created by the Department of Health (DoH, 2005), set out government plans to increase participation in physical activity across England. It was inspired by rising concern about declining levels of involvement in physical activity, calculating the cost of inactivity to be £8.2 billion annually with obesity costing an additional £2.5 billion (alongside a human cost in terms of mortality, poor health and quality of life). The action plan identified early years providers as partners: ideally placed in the community to offer accessible, year-round services that could reduce obesity levels in pupils, parents and the wider community (DoH, 2005). Thus it became a responsibility for early years settings to be part of the wider initiative and this became a part of the physical development curriculum.

In creating these aims the Department of Health (2005: 6) stated that only a 'culture shift' would achieve the required increase in physical activity levels: 'This will only be achieved if people are aware of, understand and want the benefits of being active.' The plan set an aspirational target of a year-on-year increase of 2 per cent, converting approximately 21 million people to active living. The pre-plan consultation noted that no other country had achieved this: Finland, Canada and New Zealand, the most successful countries at that point, had only achieved around 1 per cent increase in participation per annum. Despite this knowledge, the plan did not encourage, or recognise, the need for new thinking about how we involve people, or about the hidden ways we currently stop people moving. Here was a real opportunity to develop some new ways of thinking about young children's involvement in their own physicality in order to establish patterns for life. Instead, a bold and active plan for more of the same was created.

In early years settings there is the opportunity to do things differently. Young children want to embody everything they do. Their instinct is to move almost all the time. It is adults who often stop or constrain them. If we find ways to support children's natural desire to embody their lives, the guidance about a specific amount of activity per day becomes irrelevant. Children will almost always do more than adults plan for. If the learning environment is set up to accommodate and – more importantly – value full-bodied movement indoors and out, children will be able to be the fully physical creatures their nature demands.

The challenge to adults is to think afresh: to stop thinking of organised physical activities, or even outdoor time 'to let off steam', and find ways, within the constraints of the spaces currently available, to support day-long physicality.

Reflective task

Make two lists.

- In the first, list all the opportunities you actively organise for babies and children to engage with their physicality, and put the aims for each alongside.
- In the second, list all the things that you see children doing of their own accord (alongside other activities, as an activity they organise for themselves or in spite of you), and add what you think this might be fulfilling for their learning and/or development.

Reviewing provision

Principles for reviewing physical development provision

Cultural and personal values influence every aspect of the way we think about children's physicality and the resources, experiences and environment we offer. In turn, it is these values that children interpret to establish the ways they inhabit their bodies, their body behaviours and the way they feel about being physical. This remains largely unacknowledged, happening outside discussion, debate or policy.

Here is a set of principles that might inform reflection and review.

The body is a child's first home – the place where the subjective sense of self develops, the vehicle through which they experience the feeling of life itself. Thinking about the body (before any specific kinds of movement), therefore, needs to lie at the core of the physical development curriculum.

Physical development involves many processes, visible and invisible, sensory and motor, physical and emotional. It is not simply concerned with the acquisition of motor skills or attitudes to self-care.

There is a sequence of movement patterns (Hackney, 2000; Bainbridge-Cohen, 2008) that underpins physical development. Each pattern within this sequence is involved in supporting many aspects of development, all at the same time:

- creating, processing and learning to organise sensory information
- growing connections in the brain and nervous system that create the capacity for new functioning
- uncurling the body and developing the shape and strength for an upright stance
- building a felt sense of the body and the feel of things
- establishing a core subjective self
- building the feeling of a connected body
- developing motor skills of three sorts (stability, mobility and manipulation).

The way the sequence of movement patterns emerges is strongly influenced by many factors, including genetics, the environment, the child's body, the child's temperament and interests, the task itself and the values (displayed in the actions and responses) of the people around them

There is considerable evidence to suggest that the movement patterns build, one upon the other, in ways that may influence a child's capacity to learn. Understanding the sequence and the way the body supports learning (as well as being able to offer additional support to complete each stage) is likely to have a significant effect on a child's future learning and life chances.

To support the unfolding sequence of movement patterns, babies and children need lots of opportunities to move spontaneously and freely in ways of their own choosing, to move in company with others and to move in ways that allow them to both repeat activities and to create and master new challenges.

Babies come into the world as experience-seeking creatures; they need certain kinds of experience for sound development. These experiences are usually readily available in the child's normal environment. Sound development is not reliant on creating 'enriched environments' based on toys and equipment. However, attitudes to the body and physicality in our culture may get in the way of babies and children getting what they need, as adults constrain and restrict their natural drive to move in particular ways.

Babies and children are the best planners of their own purposeful movement play. They are biologically driven to move in ways that will support their development; they do so with verve and commitment. They are endlessly resourceful in creating physical opportunities for themselves.

It is vital that we consider movement – physicality – in its own right, not simply as a support for other things like cognitive learning and exercise.

Reflective task

Analyse the opportunities children have for full-bodied physical activity in your setting.

List the principles that underpin these opportunities. How do these compare to the principles above?

A developmental framework

Developmental Movement Play (DMP) (Greenland, 2006) is an approach created to help early years practitioners work with the principles above. It was developed and tested over a seven-year period (2002–9), by movement specialists from JABADAO and early years partners from 26 early years settings. It is established in many settings across England and has shown considerable value for children (Greenland, 2009).

DMP is a developmental, child-led, play-based movement approach which aims to support children's ready ability to promote their own physical development and to embody their learning. It suggests that the contexts we create for children – and especially the values we impart – are as fundamental to the development process and to children's future learning as the physical experiences we enable. Indeed, they are inextricably linked. In this approach the child is the expert in the ways they need to move, and parents and early years practitioners support them to get what they need – safely – and to value this part of their experience and learning. DMP sets out to support the body and bodily felt experience as a child's first home, to support sensory-motor experience as a child's first and primary information about themselves and the world, and to support movement as a child's first and primary language.

The DMP programme (Greenland, 2009) suggests the following ways to bring about change:
- Place child-led movement play at the core of the curriculum rather than adult-led or adult-initiated activity.
- Train staff in a developmental movement approach so that they can observe and support developmental movement as an underpinning for all learning; and know what to do if a child has gaps or barriers in the sequence of movement patterns.
- Use a five-part framework as a simple way to create environments and experiences that ensure developmentally significant movement is fully valued and supported, indoors and out. (1. Floor play on backs and tummies. 2. Belly-crawling play. 3. Crawling play. 4. Push-pull-stretch-hang-buffet-about play. 5. Spin-tip-roll-fall play.)
- Make an indoor, clear space a movement play area, available to all children at all times as part of a setting's everyday provision.
- Ensure the outdoor space supports the five ways of moving; avoid naming the outdoor space as the only place where full-bodied movement should happen.
- Recognise that developmentally significant movement occurs as part of everything children do, not just in special activities, and change the environment to facilitate maximum physical involvement in everything (e.g. put tabletop activities on the floor).
- Make partnerships with parents, involving them in new understanding about the importance of early movement, and find practical ways that children can get what they need at home, as well as in early years settings.
- Promote a fully inclusive approach that avoids a phase-stage basis, or any suggested ages at which certain movements should occur. Replace this with an informed knowledge of the sequence of movement patterns and support each child to progress along it in their own way.

Next steps

If you want to find out more about JABADAO's Developmental Movement Play approach, visit the website http://www.jabadao.org to find research material, courses and projects you can become involved in.

Conclusion

Making physical development one of the three prime areas of learning (DfE, 2012a) invites new thinking and practice. Physical development underpins all aspects of learning and development – its significance is much wider than the development of motor skills and self-care behaviours. It is the area in which we can help children to embody their lives, not just to be efficient movers.

In the wider society, concern is building about decreasing involvement in physical activity, and in growing levels of obesity – early years settings are required to be part of the solution. Only a radical development of current thinking will make the impact that is needed. Settings need to review the values that they are imparting, check that they are not stopping children from being as active as they want and need, and help parents to do the same.

This requires knowledgeable, committed practitioners who love to move with children and love to move for themselves.

Evaluate your...

Practice

At some point in our lives we all end up sounding like our parents and wonder how that happened. We pick up certain ways of thinking and certain phrases in spite of ourselves. What do you think your children might say in future – with regard to movement and body behaviours – because of the things that they hear in your setting? Do you like this list or are there things you would like to change?

What is the balance between adult-led, adult-initiated and child-led physical activity in your setting? Are you achieving what you mean to achieve? If not, what is getting in your way?

Think about your setting with reference to the five kinds of movement as suggested by the JABADAO programme:

1 Floor play on backs and tummies
2 Belly-crawling play
3 Crawling play
4 Push-pull-stretch-hang-buffet-about play
5 Spin-tip-roll-fall play

Are these all well catered for?

Carry out observations to identify how your children are engaging in each of these kinds of movement. Separate the opportunities you provide consciously and the ways children devise of their own accord (e.g. crawling down a corridor; lying on their tummies on the reading corner sofa).

Are there plentiful opportunities in each area? Are there any gaps? How might you fill them?

What do you learn about how the children want to use the resources you offer that may alter how you think about your setting?

Further reading

Bainbridge-Cohen, B. (2008) *Sensing, Feeling and Action*, Berkeley, CA: North Atlantic Books.

Gallahue, D. L., Ozmun, J. C. and Goodway, J. (2011) *Understanding Motor Development: Infants, children, adolescents, adults* (7th edn), New York: McGraw-Hill.

Greenland. P. (2009) *Developmental Movement Play: final report.* Leeds: JABADAO

Hackney, P. (2000) *Making Connections: Total Body Integration Through Bartenieff Fundamentals*, Oxon: Routledge.

Juhan, D. (2002) *Job's Body: A Handbook for Bodywork*, New York: Barrytown Ltd.

9

Indoor and outdoor play
Ros Garrick

Introduction

Article 31 of the Convention on the Rights of the Child (United Nations, 1989) recognises the international right of children to enjoy relaxation and play as an essential right of childhood. This international recognition of play is reflected in a number of campaigning organisations that work to make this right a reality in children's lives. For example, Play England (2007) has a Charter for Children's Play that includes a statement on the need for schools at all levels to provide space and time for children to play with their friends. Turning to early childhood education and care, current government policy in England places a high value on play as an element of its framework for learning, development and care, as outlined in the Early Years Foundation Stage (EYFS) (DfE, 2012a). This framework explains that 'Play is essential for children's development, building their confidence as they learn to explore, to think about problems, and relate to others' (DfE, 2012a: 6). There is a similar focus on play in the curriculum frameworks of many countries internationally, for example in New Zealand's Te Whāriki curriculum framework (Ministry of Education, 1996).

Psychologists working in the field of child development, such as Whitebread (2012), support this privileging of play within the early years curriculum, and have identified a range of ways in which play can support early learning and development. However, early years educators and researchers have also raised questions about the relationship between children's play, which often takes place with peers, and prevalent approaches to teaching and learning that focus on objectives for individual children (Wood, 2012). The EYFS framework (DfE, 2012a: 6) states that 'Each area of learning and development must be implemented through planned, purposeful play'. However, play that is important to some children, for example gun play, as discussed by Holland (2003), may not fit easily with this prescription; and there are also issues as to whether the 'planned purposeful play' of adults will be perceived as play by children.

This chapter sets out to examine the nature of young children's play in a particular cultural context and to consider the place of play within the early years curriculum. It raises some challenging issues and questions relating to play in early years settings. The chapter also aims to support practitioners to reflect on how they can apply their knowledge and understanding of play to enhance young children's experience of play in early years settings, and to support their learning and development.

Learning outcomes

After reading this chapter you will be able to:

- Explain some of the ideas of early years educators who have pioneered a play-based curriculum in early years education.
- Discuss the findings of researchers and theorists who have examined the nature and role of play in early childhood, including its meaning for children.
- Outline the different ways in which play has been categorised.
- Recognise the key features of learning environments and how these can be developed to support early learning and development.
- Review the distinctive features of free-flow play.
- Describe the opportunities for play-based learning and development in outdoor environments with reference to forest school and nursery garden traditions.
- Consider the issue of risk in children's play and varying attitudes to risk across time and cultures.
- Explain some diversity and inclusion issues relating to play in early years settings.
- Draw on your knowledge and understanding of play to reflect on your role in promoting young children's learning and development.
- Apply your knowledge and understanding of play to develop and enhance play opportunities for young children.

The value of play

From the 19th century onwards, pioneering figures in the history of early years education, including Friedrich Fröbel, Margaret McMillan and Rudolf Steiner, have developed arguments for the value of play for children's learning and development. They established very different approaches to play which are reflected in the similarities and differences in their arguments for the value of play.

Researchers, working within a range of academic disciplines, have proposed further claims for the value of play; these include researchers from the disciplines of education, developmental psychology and the new social studies of childhood. Often, arguments about the value of play are specific to particular kinds of play. For example, researchers have hypothesised that physically vigorous exercise play, seen in young animals as well as children, makes an important contribution to children's physical fitness during periods of rapid physical development involving bone and muscle growth (Smith, 2010b). Recognising the diversity of perspectives on play and the variety of types of play, the section below considers arguments for the value of play made by some of the pioneers of early education and by theorists working from different disciplinary perspectives. Following this, we will identify six categories of play and related claims for the value of specific kinds of play.

Classic theorists and pioneers of play in early education

There is a long-established tradition of play being recognised as a key feature of the early years curriculum across Europe, the United States and beyond. Key educators in the history of early education and care have promoted play within their curricula. By critically reviewing the ideas of these pioneers, including the kinds of play promoted, we can develop our own understanding of the value of play today and develop a rationale for play in our own settings.

Reflective task

As you learn more about the work of these early educators consider:
- What are the elements with continuing relevance for your own practice in terms of supporting young children's learning and development?
- What are the elements with continuing relevance in terms of the meaning of play for children themselves?
- Which elements are interesting historically but have less relevance today?
- How do you see the role of the adult in children's play?

Friedrich Fröbel (1782–1852)

Fröbel developed his educational practice and theories about the role of play in young children's learning and development during the first half of the 19th century. He opened his first kindergarten for young children in Germany in 1837 with an innovative curriculum. Rejecting traditional rote learning and academic goals, the new curriculum focused on early socialisation, shaped by Fröbel's integrating concern for children's spiritual and moral development. It included outdoor experiences, for example gardening, as well as adult-led songs, dances and finger plays. Fröbel designed a structured sequence of educational play materials, the Gifts, which included geometric bricks and pattern activity blocks introduced in a sequence, each with a symbolic meaning.

Although Fröbel intended that the Gifts be used in structured ways, he valued young children's self-directed activity and creativity. Therefore, he changed the early didactic approach, informed by observation of his kindergarten teachers at work. Fröbel's radical educational theories and emphasis on the value of play inspired many followers across Europe, Japan and North America. They raise questions about the relative value of creative play with open-ended materials in contrast to more structured play for didactic purposes.

Extend your knowledge

You can find out more about Fröbel's work and continuing influence on thinking about play:
- For a brief overview of the Fröbel kindergarten tradition and Fröbel's' influence on outdoor play, see Garrick, R. (2009) *Playing Outdoors in the Early Years* (2nd edn), London and New York: Continuum, p. 15.
- For a detailed review of Fröbel's influence on contemporary thinking about play and the early years curriculum, see Bruce, T. (2012) (ed.) *Early Childhood Practice. Fröbel today*, London: Sage.
- A number of online resources explain different aspects of Fröbel's work, with relevant images. See, for example, a video about Fröbel's life and influence: Fröbel Kindergarten Gifts Early Childhood Education History of Toys at: http://www.youtube.com/watch?v=LNBzmCKLNdU.

Margaret McMillan (1860–1931)

Like Montessori, Margaret McMillan had a varied career with an integrating focus on working with children in the poorest areas of large cities. Growing up in both the United States and Scotland, McMillan developed her innovative educational ideas and practice in England during the last decades of the 19th century and the early 20th century. Following experience as a school board member of Bradford's elementary schools, McMillan moved to London. Here, with her sister, Rachel, she set up a children's clinic, camp schools for older children, and subsequently the first nursery school: for children from 18 months to seven years. The distinctive focus of the school on its garden grew from the McMillan sisters' concern for the poor physical health of young children growing up in poverty and from awareness of the power of outdoor experiences to transform lives.

Alongside sensory flower and herb gardens, the nursery garden offered varied opportunities for play, including adventurous physical play. It also offered exploratory play with natural materials and discarded household objects, as well as play with a wide range of construction materials (Steedman, 1990). The diversity of this outdoor environment and the range of outdoor play experiences on offer raise questions about the quality and range of outdoor play experiences available to many children growing up in cities today.

Extend your knowledge

You can find out more about the life, work and writing of Margaret McMillan:

- To see images of the McMillan nursery garden and read her book about the nursery school, see information on the University of Roehampton [online] http://core.roehampton.ac.uk/digital/froarc/mcmnur (accessed 29/7/12).
- To read a brief overview of Margaret McMillan's life see the Spartacus Educational [online] http://www.spartacus.schoolnet.co.uk/Wmcmillan.htm (accessed 29/7/12).
- Carolyn Steedman has written an authoritative biography of Margaret McMillan: Steedman, C. (1990) *Childhood, Culture and Class in Britain: Margaret McMillan*, Rutgers: Rutgers University Press. The chapter 'Gardens' is a challenging text but it provides a detailed account of the development of McMillan's thinking about the value of outdoor play.
- Her original work was published: McMillan, M. (1919) *The Nursery School*, London: J. M. Dent & Sons.

Rudolf Steiner (1861–1925)

Steiner was an Austrian philosopher and educationalist who founded his first school in 1919 for the children of factory workers and more affluent families. He opened a kindergarten for children from three to six years in 1926, and the model spread quickly through Europe, the United States and beyond. A Steiner kindergarten focuses on young children's social, emotional and physical development, rather than more formal academic work. There is also a spiritual dimension to the curriculum. Steiner argued that children will learn academic skills more easily following a period of development in a secure and caring environment, with rich opportunities to engage in creative play and everyday domestic activities, including crafts.

The learning environment of a Steiner kindergarten is distinctive, with a predominant use of soft materials and pastel colours; and with furniture, toys and equipment made from natural materials. Steiner education emphasises the provision of natural outdoor areas for play in all weathers (Drummond and Jenkinson, 2009) and open-ended play materials to promote children's use of their imaginations. As a result, Steiner play environments contrast with many settings that strive to offer realistic toys and role-play areas, representing the detail of children's worlds. This raises questions about the relative value of these contrasting approaches to promoting imaginative play. The adult role in the Steiner Waldorf approach is also distinctive. Teachers are non-interventionist during play, mainly offering specific help in response to children's requests (Steiner Waldorf Education, 2009).

Looking at the heritage left by the writings and practice of these innovative early years educators, Bruce (2010) has extrapolated ten shared principles of early childhood practice. There has been wide agreement about these principles and they have been important in influencing the development of the EYFS (DfE, 2012a) in England. However, it remains important to remember differences as well as commonalities in the ideas of these historical figures, for example in relation to how the environment for play is organised and the role of adults in children's play. Wood and Attfield (2005) explain some continuing difficulties for the development of agreed principles relating to play in early childhood education, in particular principles that are securely underpinned by theory and research. Having considered three important figures in the history of early childhood education, we now turn to consider how contemporary research is informing debates about the value of play in early years education and care settings.

Contemporary research

Play in early years education has traditionally been studied from the perspective of developmental psychologists, who set out to identify, for example, the kinds of play that are characteristic of children at different ages. Psychologists have identified developmental pathways in areas such as physical development, which practitioners can observe in children's play. In recent decades, researchers from different disciplinary perspectives have critiqued the dominance of this approach to studying play. The section below introduces the work of two contemporary researchers, who seek to understand the value of young children's play, one from a psychology perspective and one from sociology.

David Whitebread

As a contemporary psychologist, with experience as an early years teacher, Whitebread (2012) has a particular interest in play and early years education. He argues that research from the last 30 years challenges some of the earlier findings of developmental psychology, which sometimes underestimated children, and shows young children's capabilities in a range of areas often observed in play contexts. Whitehead's research focuses on independent learning and children's self-regulatory abilities, seen as essential to children's development as effective learners. Studying children aged three to five years in Foundation Stage settings, Whitebread (2012) observed such behaviours most often where children played together in small groups, for example during problem solving as a part of construction play and during imaginative role play.

Extend your knowledge

You can find out more about the perspective of developmental psychologists on play, including play in educational settings by reading Whitebread, D. (2012) *Developmental Psychology and Early Childhood Education: A Guide for Students and Practitioners*, London: Sage.

■ See Chapter 4 for a discussion of key research focused on children's play, development and learning.

■ See Chapter 7 for a discussion of young children's self-regulation in play contexts.

William Corsaro

Corsaro is a contemporary sociologist, working within the new social studies of childhood, with a particular interest in understanding the meaning of play for children themselves. He has worked extensively in Italy and the United States, using ethnographic methods to study children's experiences of their nurseries. As an ethnographer of nursery life, Corsaro joins in, observes and talks with children about their play, and has developed his theory of interpretative reproduction from these studies. This is a complex theory, but at the centre is Corsaro's account of the innovative and creative ways in which children draw on their experiences of the adult world to address their own peer concerns. Corsaro documents how young children interpret and reconstruct the world around them through play.

Extend your knowledge

You may want to find out more about Corsaro's research into children's play experiences:

■ Read Corsaro, W. (2011) *The Sociology of Childhood* (3rd edn), London: Sage, pp. 152–7. This provides a fascinating account of the play routines of toddlers in an Italian nursery.

■ Read Grooms, K. (2003) 'A childhood of their own', *A Child's Life,* vol. 25, no. 2. Available from: http://www.indiana.edu/~rcapub/v25n2/corsaro.shtml (accessed 24/7/12). This short article describes Corsaro's research into young children's experience of play in Italian nurseries.

Categorising types of play

Theories of play, for example the theories of Corsaro and Whitebread, are different from facts; they offer us explanations about the nature and/or value of play from the viewpoint of particular points in history and from particular cultural perspectives (Nolan and Kilderry, 2010). Theories can support our reflection, and we can draw on these to clarify our views about the value of different kinds of play in our settings. First, however, it is useful to identify the kinds of play that young children enjoy.

Reflective task

■ Observe six contrasting episodes of play in an education and care setting, involving children from birth to five years. Record these episodes of play as short narrative observations or through sequences of photographs.

■ Create your own categories to distinguish between these different types of play.

■ Share your categories with members of your group and agree five categories that represent all the types of play recorded.

■ Compare your agreed categories to the categories of play in Table 9.1. These are categories proposed by educationalists and theorists.

■ Which set of categories do you find most helpful, and why?

Table 9.1 sets out four frameworks that categorise play. It includes the categories identified as relevant to playing and exploring within the EYFS (DfE, 2012a), and as outlined in the *Development Matters* (Early Educations, 2012) guidance.

Smith (2010b)	Whitebread (2012)	Early Education (2012)	Caillois (2001)
Forms of play	The five types of play	Playing and exploring	Categories of play
Physical activity play: • exercise play • rough and tumble play	Physical play	Finding out and exploring objects, events and people … through physical development	Dizziness
Object play	Play with objects	Finding out and exploring objects … through all areas of learning	
Pretend play	Pretence/socio-dramatic play* • using language to develop pretend scenarios and narratives	Finding out and exploring objects, events and people … through all areas of learning • pretending • representing • acting out a role/experiences	Imitation
	Symbolic play* • playing with language		
Probably not play: • games with rules • exploration of objects • stereotypical behaviours, e.g. rocking • work that may include playful elements, e.g. scaring birds from crops	Games with rules		Competition
			Chance

Table 9.1 Categories of play

(* These two types of play are interlinked.)

The different sets of categories of play represent different disciplinary perspectives. Categories in the first two columns come from the work of developmental psychologists; the third column presents an educational perspective, while the fourth column presents a sociological perspective. The first three writers are primarily interested in play in childhood, while Caillois (2000) reminds us that there are continuities in play as found across human cultures and between child and adult cultures.

Whitebread's typology (2012), in column 2, is used below to introduce five scenarios of early years settings showing five different kinds of play. The more commonly used term 'pretend' is used for play that Whitebread (2012) labels pretence/socio–dramatic play. An invitation to reflect on the value or functions of the particular category of play follows each scenario.

Physical play

9

Scenario

Michael was four years old and attended a childminding setting four days a week. He enjoyed all kinds of physical play, including rough and tumble play with his childminder and the younger children, fine-motor practice, particularly building models from junk materials, and active exercise play. Michael's favourite activity was football, usually played in the back garden.

One sunny spring morning, Michael had persuaded the younger girls, Maisie and Iram, to join his game. He shouted to the girls, 'Me, me. Pass it to me' and then 'I'm shooting in the goal.' Later in the morning Michael played football with his childminder. He kicked the ball backwards and forwards to Tim for nearly half an hour. 'I'm going to hit it really hard,' he announced and then 'Goal! … You're Chelsea. I'm Hull.' When Tim saved the next goal, Michael praised him, 'Oh good save, Tim.'

Reflective task

- Identify children you have worked with who enjoy football or other physically active play.
- What physical skills have you observed during children's active exercise play?
- What evidence of children's developing knowledge and dispositions for learning have you observed during this play?

Many young children, like Michael, choose to spend time engaged in active exercise play with and without objects, for example running, jumping, hopping, kicking, throwing and climbing (Whitebread, 2012). Surprisingly, researchers have neglected this kind of play in comparison to other kinds (Smith, 2010b). However, from the available research, Smith (2010b) suggests that there is relatively strong evidence for the positive effects of such play on strength and endurance, and some evidence for the impact on motor skills and economy of movements. While Michael has developed a high level of physical skills and endurance, he is also developing stores of knowledge about football as a cultural practice and positive dispositions towards physical activity, including sport. This is important to his current and future health and well-being.

Extend your knowledge

Several resources support understanding of young children's physical play and/or the ways in which practitioners can promote such play.
- For a detailed account of developmental research into children's physical activity play, see Chapter 6 of Smith, P. (2010) *Children and Play*, Chichester: Wiley-Blackwell.
- A study of physical activity play in English early years setting includes some useful recommendations for practice. See Brady, L., Gibbs, J., Henshall, A. and Lewis, J. (2008) *Play and Exercise in Early Years: Physically active play in early childhood provision*, London: Department for Culture, Media and Sport.
- A US video provides information about the relationship between physical activity play and children's health, and some interesting examples of practice. See Move, Play and Learn – Physical Activity in North Dakota Child Care Programs [online] http://www.youtube.com/watch?v=4XtaotPsu4M&feature=plcp (accessed 28/7/12).

Object play

Scenario

At two years old, Leon had recently started at Little Pandas, a private nursery close to the offices where his dad worked. He had taken some time to settle into his new routine but was happiest during play in the small nursery garden. What Leon particularly enjoyed was pushing one of the two red wheelbarrows around the garden. Josie, his keyworker, had recently introduced spades for filling buckets with autumn leaves. Leon's favourite game now was to fill the largest bucket with leaves, tip it into his wheelbarrow, and then push the wheelbarrow to the end of the garden. Here, he emptied the leaves into a large tractor tyre. This game seemed to go on forever, only interrupted when reluctantly he had to give up his wheelbarrow to one of the other children.

Reflective task

- Identify children you have worked with who enjoy play with objects but are not using toys such as construction sets to represent their ideas.
- Make an observational record of a child engaged in this kind of play.
- What aspects of development and learning is this kind of play likely to develop?
- How could you support children to play with these or similar objects in more sustained and/or more complex ways?

Children begin to play with objects as babies, for example playing with commercial rattles, soft toys or with more varied everyday objects in a treasure basket. As children become mobile, like Leon, they often choose to move groups of objects from place to place, for example carrying favourite toys in a bag or pushing them in a wheelbarrow. Athey (2007) studied young children, aged three to four years, attending a nursery class, as well as their younger siblings. She observed many similar examples of play, categorising play such as Leon's wheelbarrow pushing as a transporting schema. Athey (2007) also observed play based on other repeated action patterns, for example a containing schema, having observed children like Leon repeatedly filling containers. She drew on the ideas of Piaget in identifying these repeated action patterns. Piaget (1896–1980) was one of the first researchers to identify the significance for young children's thinking of their early play with objects, labelling play of this kind as sensorimotor play. Athey (2007) and those who have extended her pioneering work have identified an important role for adults in supporting children's progress from early play with objects to the use of objects to represent aspects of their world, for example using a construction set to make a house, and on to more abstract thinking.

Extend your knowledge

You can draw on several resources to extend your understanding of object play and the ways in which adults can support development and learning in this area.

- See Athey, C. (2007) *Extending Thought in Young Children: A Parent–Teacher Partnership* (2nd edn), London: Paul Chapman. This includes an account of action schema. Focus on Athey's examples of motor level play, which often focus on play with objects.

- Community Playthings [online] includes a video with interesting examples of children engaged in object play. Available from: http://www.communityplaythings.co.uk/products/blocks/index.html.
- See Hughes, A. M. (2006) *Developing Play for the Under 3s*, London: Fulton. This offers detailed information about how to develop object play in the form of treasure baskets and heuristic play sessions.
- Watch the video 'Jack's heuristic play with his treasure basket' [online] http://www.youtube.com/watch?v=uCW7jZlWZ18&feature=related (accessed 28/7/12).

Pretend play

Scenario

At five years old, Nazia was one of the oldest children in the foundation unit of her village school. Nazia often showed her profile to her mum, and enjoyed talking about photographs of the things she liked most at school. Nazia's parents owned the village shop and she loved playing at shops with her friends, Ian and Lizzie. 'That's me,' she said excitedly, 'and I were doing a shop with Ian. You put things on a table and then you make a shop. Then you put a roof on. Cos our teacher helps us do that. Then we get the wooden triangles and pretend they're fish. They go on the shelf there. We pretend the crystals are like money. You see the shelf. I got the food down and Ian paid me twenty pounds.'

Reflective task

- Identify children you work with who enjoy pretend play.
- Make an observational record of a small group of children engaged in this kind of play.
- What aspects of development and learning is this episode of play likely to develop?
- How could you promote more sustained and/or more complex pretend play in your setting?

Researchers have identified pretend play as a persistent interest of young children historically and across cultures, although varying in frequency and in the extent to which it is culturally valued (Corsaro, 2011). Summarising findings from a range of recent studies, Smith (2010b) reports evidence of the functions of pretend play in supporting a range of aspects of development, including young children's increasingly complex narrative skills; their cognitive and language development; early literacy skills; and theory of mind development. Whitebread (2012) reports additional evidence of the value of pretend play in supporting young children's social and emotional learning, including emotional self-regulation.

Extend your knowledge

A number of resources can help to extend your knowledge and understanding of pretend play.
- See Smith, P. (2010) *Children and Play*, Chichester: Wiley-Blackwell, Chapters 8 and 9, for a detailed account of developmental perspectives on pretend play.

- For an account of how adults can support pretend play, see Kitson, N. (2010) 'Children's fantasy role play – why adults should join in', in Moyles, J. (ed.) *The Excellence of Play* (3rd edn), Maidenhead: Open University and McGraw-Hill.
- See Rogers, S. and Evans, J. (2007) *Inside Role-Play in Early Childhood Education: Researching young children's perspectives*, London: Routledge. This book reports an important study which examined role play in a reception class from child and practitioner perspectives.
- Several examples of pretend play can be found on the DVD by Siren Films: *Pretend play: twenty months to seven years.*

Symbolic play

Scenario

Harry was three years old and attended Sycamore Children's Centre. He loved creative play of all kinds, particularly play with language, and often made up words, chanted rhymes or devised jokes based on funny-sounding words. Recently, after a story about wizards, he had become fascinated by wizards and magic. As soon as he arrived at the centre each day, Harry went straight to the dressing-up trolley to find the wizard's cloak, and he wore this throughout the session. On this day, half way through the morning, some of his friends gathered round him as he announced he was about to do some magic tricks. Harry waved his wand with a flourish and chanted his new spell:

Abraacdabra, abracadoo. Make me be a dog.

Abraacdabra, abracadoo. Make the toy box be a gnu.

Abracadabra. Make the trolley be a gnu.

Make Jon be a gnu.

Harry waved his wand with one last flourish and everyone clapped.

Reflective task

- Identify children you have worked with who enjoy play with language.
- Make observational records of any language play that you hear.
- How could you encourage language play in your setting?

Children below the age of one commonly play with sounds as they babble when alone, seemingly for their own pleasure. Ruth Weir documented how her two-year-old son played with sounds, words and phrases as he lay in his cot just before going to sleep and on waking (Smith, 2010b). Later on, some children, like Harry, begin to enjoy more complex play with language, devising jokes and playing with rhymes. Research suggests that children who enjoy play with language are developing a foundation of language skills and phonological awareness that underpins later literacy development (Whitebread, 2012).

Extend your knowledge

Symbolic play includes children's play with a range of symbol systems, alongside play with language. Further areas include play with musical sounds, drawing, painting, collage, numbers and writing. A number of authors have reviewed the ways in which symbolic play can support the development of areas of learning and development.

- For a fascinating account of children's drawings as children move from home to school and then through school transitions, see Anning, A. and Ring, K. (2004) *Making Sense of Children's Drawings*, Maidenhead: Open University.
- Find summarised evidence relating to play and literacy development in Christie, J. F. and Roskos, K. A. (2009) 'Play's Potential in Early Literacy Development', *The Encyclopedia on Early Childhood Development* [online] Montreal, Quebec: Centre for Excellence for Early Childhood Development. Available from: http://www.child-encyclopedia.com/documents/Christie-RoskosANGxp.pdf (accessed 27/7/12).
- For information about children's musical development and how to support it during early childhood, see Pound, L. and Harrison, C. (2003) *Supporting Musical Development in the Early Years*, Maidenhead: Open University and McGraw-Hill.
- To gain a detailed understanding of language play, see Chapter 2 in Whitehead, M. (2009) *Supporting Language and Literacy Development in the Early Years* (2nd edn), Maidenhead: Open University and McGraw-Hill.

Games with rules

Scenario

At four years old, Georgio's favourite game was Monopoly, which he played with the older children who came to his childminder's house after school and in the school holidays. He was very proud that, with just a little help from Lucy, his childminder, he had been able to buy Park Lane, the most expensive street in London, and fill his street with houses and even a hotel. Georgio had visited Park Lane once with his nana who had pointed out the hotels. When he was at Lucy's house just with the younger children, he sometimes asked if he could get the Monopoly set out and play with Little Ted, his favourite soft toy. Lucy let him sit up at the dining table away from the younger children and sometimes the game went on for an hour or more. He always won, of course!

Reflective task

- What games with rules are offered in your setting? Consider active games like 'What's the time, Mr Wolf?', board and card games, as well as electronic and computer games.
- Make observational records of children who are involved in games of this kind.
- How do these games support learning and development?
- Would you categorise Georgio's activity as play or the games that you observe as play? Explain your reasons.

Whitebread (2012) includes games with rules as a fifth category of play, while Smith (2010b) suggests that games with rules are probably not play at all because they are governed by external rules. Smith, however, does acknowledge that the boundary between games and play is not clear. Some recognised forms of play, such as peek-a-boo with babies, have a rule structure, as do episodes of role play, where children themselves set the rules. Smith (2010b) also points out that children play computer games according to externally set rules, again making the play status of such games ambiguous. However, it seems likely that children like Georgio who enjoy games with rules would describe their activities as play.

There is further research (Whitebread, 2012) which suggests that children are highly motivated to make sense of their social worlds and are therefore often fascinated by games with rules. Although adults may use games to teach specific skills, for example counting skills, studies suggest that games with rules are particularly valuable in terms of supporting children's social development. Children often play games with rules in social groups, and sometimes actually pretend to have a play partner, as with Georgio above. However, electronic games-playing can be a solitary activity and the value of this kind of play is contested.

Extend your knowledge

Two resources can support you in developing your knowledge and understanding of this area of play.

- See Kalliala, M. (2006) *Play Cultures in a Changing World*, Maidenhead: Open University and McGraw-Hill, for a definition of play that excludes competitive games with rules defined by adults. However, Chapters 4 and 5 focus on child-led games with rules that Kalliala sees as a popular and enduring element of children's peer cultures.
- Find out about the positive features of well-designed digital games for children from birth to three years and the potential issues raised by poorly designed games in a detailed review: Lieberman, D. A., Fisk, M. C. and Biely, E. (2009) 'Digital games for young children ages three to six: From research to design', *Computers in the Schools*, vol. 26 no. 4, pp. 299–313.

Free-flow play

As well as the five categories of play considered above, Bruce (2010) identifies a further type of play, described as free-flow play, with 12 features. A key feature is its child-led nature. Free-flow play, according to Bruce (2010), is play driven by intrinsic motivation, contrasting with play planned by adults to meet external goals. It is useful to compare the features identified by Bruce with the three essential 'characteristics of effective learning', as identified in the EYFS (DfE, 2012a) and outlined in the guidance (Early Education, 2012). Table 9.2 identifies some elements of match and you may be able to identify more.

Characteristics of effective learning (Early Education, 2012: 5)	Selected features of free-flow play (Bruce, 2010: 284)
Playing and exploring – engagement	It actively uses previous first-hand experiences, including struggle, manipulation, exploration, discovery and practice.
Active learning – motivation	It is intrinsically motivated: children cannot be made to play.
Creating and thinking critically – thinking	It is about possible, alternative worlds, that lift players to their highest level of functioning, freeing them from the here and now. This involves being imaginative, creative, original and innovative.

Table 9.2 Free-flow play and effective learning

Each scenario above shows children leading their own play, driven by intrinsic motivation, although adults take on a supporting role in several scenarios. A further characteristic of free-flow play is that, where adults are involved in the play, they remain sensitive to children's own purposes and act to support these. Josie, Leon's keyworker in the Object play Scenario above, provides an example of an adult who is sensitive to a child's purposes in play.

For Bruce (2010), free-flow play represents children who are functioning at their highest level, drawing on and integrating a range of previous experience. Nazia in the Pretend play Scenario above provides an example of a child engaged in free-flow play that integrates pretend and object play with home experiences. Nazia's creative play was also sustained over several weeks. Kalliala (2006: 18) explains that when children play spontaneously in this way, with great pleasure and with intensity, we can describe them as being in a state of 'flow'.

Rogers's study of role play in a reception class (2010) found relatively few examples of children engaged in play as satisfying as Nazia's shop play. This is because practitioners' intentions for teaching and learning frequently clashed with those of children. Rogers (2010) highlights some key dimensions of play where children need control if they are to develop their play in purposeful and sustained ways. She suggests that, if free play is to become an actuality in early years settings and not just a myth, children need opportunities to make choices in terms of:

- what they play with: the materials and resources
- where they play: the location within the setting
- who they play with: children and adults as playmates
- what they play: any outcomes of the play
- when and for how long they play.

The section on the learning environment below returns to the issue of children's control in relation to these key aspects of play.

Reflective task

- Identify an episode of free-flow play from your experience of practice. This will be an episode where children seemed to play at their highest level and in a sustained way.
- Analyse this episode of play in terms of children making choices, as identified above. Identify the choices that children were free to make and any limitations on children's choices.
- Review the opportunities you provide for children to make choices in relation to their play.
- What is the role of the adult in this play?

Rather than representing an additional category of play to those identified in Table 9.1 (see page 189), the range of features seen in free-flow play establishes it as a broader category of play. It potentially incorporates all five categories of play discussed above. The next section considers the early years learning environment and how it can support a range of kinds of play, including free-flow play.

Extend your knowledge

The following sources will extend your knowledge and understanding of free-flow play.
- For more about free-flow play, see Bruce, T. (2010) 'Play, the universe and everything!' in Moyles, J. (ed.) *The Excellence of Play* (3rd edn), Maidenhead: Open University and McGraw-Hill.
- For a discussion of free-flow play outdoors and the contrast with more structured forms of outdoor play, see Chapter 7, Tovey, H. (2007) *Playing Outdoors: Spaces and Places, Risk and Challenge*, Maidenhead: Open University Press.

The 12 features of play (Bruce, 2006: 113):

1 Using first-hand experiences
2 Making up rules
3 Making props
4 Choosing to play
5 Rehearsing the future
6 Pretending
7 Playing alone
8 Playing together
9 Having a personal agenda
10 Being deeply involved
11 Trying out recent learning
12 Coordinating ideas, feelings and relationships for free-flow play

These features can be useful to educators who are determined to value play and promote quality play.

Read in more detail about the '12 features of play' by Bruce in Chapter 17 of this book.

Learning environments

The physical environment

In England, the EYFS (DCSF, 2008a; DfE, 2012a) categorises the learning environment of an early years setting as the indoor environment, the outdoor environment and the emotional environment. Another way of categorising environments is to contrast the physical environment of a setting with the social environment. This section will focus initially on the physical environment of settings, including both indoor and outdoor play provision. It then moves on to consider the social environment. The section begins with two scenarios, showing contrasting physical learning environments. This is followed by a related reflective task.

Scenario

Mayberry Foundation Unit

Ricky was four and a half years old and one of the older children in Mayberry Foundation Unit, a large unit with over 80 children. The unit's learning environment comprised three main areas: the Foundation 1 base area, the Foundation 2 base area and a shared outdoor area. Ricky spent much of the day in the Foundation 2 base area. This included a central carpeted area for whole-class teaching; shelves with construction toys, number games and jigsaws; a book corner; a computer area; tables and chairs where children worked on literacy and numeracy tasks; a mark-making table; a role-play shop; and a table with changing interactive displays. Ricky always tried to complete his work as quickly as possible as this meant he had longer for play, especially in the Foundation 1 base area or outdoors. The outdoor area was a large playground, surrounded by metal fences, with a small area of grass. Ricky loved the large blocks in the Foundation 1 base area, particularly for building spaceships with his friends. When his mum asked him about school, however, Ricky often seemed cross, 'Me and Leo were flying to the moon but Mrs Khan said it was Green Group's turn for shopping. She said I had to do my shopping list.'

Scenario

Westwold Kindergarten

Zachary was four and a half years old and in his last term at Westwold Kindergarten. He was in a room for three- to five-year-olds that opened out onto a medium-sized suburban garden. The indoor area was set out with bays, divided by low shelves and screens, but with a medium-sized central area. The bays included sand and water play areas, a dressing-up corner and a creative area for mark-making, art activities and work with reclaimed materials. Zachary had a small group of friends who regularly spent time building vehicles of different kinds in the centre of the room, bringing clothes horses, large blocks, small chairs and large pieces of fabrics to make their bus; and then smaller items like conkers and shells for the money and tickets on the bus. Often the play flowed outdoors as, for example, the children pretended they had arrived at the seaside and headed for the large outdoor sandpit. The garden also included a paved area, grassy areas, small flower and vegetable gardens and a small clump of birch trees at the end of a path.

Reflective task

- Identify the features of the two scenarios that relate to a learning environment that you know well for children between two and five years.
- Which of these settings is well designed to promote free-flow play?
- Think back to Rogers's research (2010) and consider the extent to which the indoor and outdoor learning environments of the two scenarios offer children control of:
  - what they play with
  - where they play
  - who they play with
  - any outcomes of the play
  - when and for how long they play.

Educators and architects working in Reggio Emilia in Northern Italy have highlighted the concept of the learning environment as 'the third educator' alongside the classroom's two teachers (Gandini, 2012: 339). Gandini (2012) highlights flexibility for children to shape their play as an important attribute of effective environments, particularly environments that support children's creative play. In England, Broadhead and Burt (2012) carried out a study of three- to five-year-olds playing in a school early years unit; they drew similar conclusions about the importance of flexible play environments for promoting children's sustained engagement in play matched to their interests. In the two Scenarios above, the settings offer different levels of flexibility in terms of the availability of blocks, screens, fabrics and natural materials that children can combine to support their individual and groups interests. In the Westwold Kindergarten Scenario, the opportunities for children to engage in more play that flows between indoors and outdoors further increases children's sense of control. In the Mayberry Foundation Unit Scenario, the more adult-structured role-play shop offers less flexibility, particularly where the play is directed by an adult.

Environmental and developmental psychologists similarly emphasise flexibility as an important dimension of the environment. Maxwell (2007) has devised a rating scale to assess those features of indoor and outdoor environments that affect young children's competence and learning. The dimensions of the scale link closely to the ideas of Gandini (2012) and Broadhead and Burt (2012) discussed above. For example, Maxwell (2007) highlights how opportunities for children to move materials and resources, such as child-sized furniture, can enhance their sense of control.

Maxwell *et al.* (2008) introduced a range of moveable resources outdoors during an intervention study, including blocks, tyres, tree stumps, piping and fabric, referred to as 'loose parts'. This led to significant increases in children's constructive and pretend play. Maxwell's rating scale (2007) also highlights privacy as a feature that increases opportunities for children to exercise control, in this case in relation to social experiences. She advises that practitioners provide spaces for children to be alone or play in small groups, and offer opportunities for children to create their own private spaces through construction with moveable resources (Maxwell, 2007).

Outdoor play: forest schools

The scenarios above are based on early years settings that offer important continuities with the indoor and outdoor environments developed by the pioneers of early education. The garden, in particular, was an essential feature of the kindergarten and nursery tradition as developed by Fröbel and Margaret McMillan.

More recently, the forest school concept, developed in Scandinavian countries that place a high cultural value on outdoor experience, has been introduced into the UK. While practitioners in some UK settings now provide daily access to woodland or forest areas, more frequently practitioners take children on weekly visits to woodland or forest areas. In urban areas this may be parks that include opportunities to experience large trees, shrubs and associated wildlife. Visits last half a day or a day and usually continue across the year, giving children experience of the forest environment in all seasons. The programme usually includes adult-led games and activities relating to the natural world of the forest; and some children also enjoy opportunities for free play, out of sight of adults, and with the natural materials of the forest as resources for imaginative play (Tovey, 2007). The scenario below shows how one foundation stage unit interpreted this more recent outdoor play tradition.

Scenario

Forest school visit

Ayesha was four years old and attended a nursery class at Greenhill Primary School where she went on weekly visits to Badger Wood on the outskirts of town. She was very excited each week to recount what she had done, particularly when snack time involved cooking something over a fire that she had helped to build. After one successful visit, Ayesha explained the highlights of the visit to her dad: 'We played good games. Eyes tied back, I mean blindfolded. You get took to a tree and when you've feeled it you've got to go and find it again … We play another game where you have to find something soft, hard, sharp, pretty and something round. Can't remember all the others … Then you sit down and you show them … I like it because it's fun. We learn about plants. We learn letters. We go on a walk and we have our snack there.'

Reflective task

- How does the forest school experience compare to outdoor experiences on offer in your setting or one you know well?
- What are the potential strengths of a forest school experience for young children?
- What are the potential limitations of the forest school experience when only weekly access is possible?

Extend your knowledge

- Find out more about the differences between gardens and forests as environments for outdoor play. See Chapter 5, Tovey, H. (2007) *Playing Outdoors: Spaces and Places, Risk and Challenge*, Maidenhead: Open University Press.
- Blackwell and Pound explain the history of forest schools and discuss their strengths and potential limitations. Blackwell, S. and Pound, L. (2011) 'Forest schools in the early years', Chapter 9, in Miller, L. and Pound, L. (eds.) *Theories and Approaches to Learning in the Early Years*, London: Sage Publications.

The social environment

The EYFS framework (DfE, 2012a) in England states the importance of social relationships for children's learning and development; this includes both peer interaction and adult–child interaction in the context of play. It advises a changing balance over time in the extent to which children lead the play and in which adults guide development 'through warm, positive interaction' (DfE, 2012a: 6). There are different viewpoints on the most appropriate role for an adult during children's play, in part depending on the age of the children and the nature of the play. Steiner kindergartens, for example, emphasise the importance of providing mixed-age family groupings of children with extended time for play, free from adult intervention. However, they identify an important role for adults in maintaining an 'attentive presence' (Drummond and Jenkinson, 2009: 35), discreetly observing children's play to deepen understanding of their development. Discussing treasure basket play for babies, Hughes (2006) emphasises the importance of an adult role in developing resources and in sensitively observing babies' play with objects, but not in interaction. She suggests that interaction is likely to distract babies from sustained engagement with objects. However, drawing on her research with toddlers and young children at a slightly later stage of development, Athey (2007) proposes a significant role for adults in interaction with children during play. She argues that skilful adults support children's development from early sensory play to representational play and then on to abstract thinking. A key initial strategy, advised by Athey (2007) is to talk to children about their play in the context of play, following children's lead and their interests.

A recent influential study of early years education across a range of settings for three- to five-year-olds (Siraj-Blatchford *et al.*, 2002) has confirmed the value of sustained peer interaction during play for children's learning and development as well as the potential benefits of sustained adult–child interaction. The authors refer to both as 'sustained shared thinking' (Siraj-Blatchford *et al.*, 2002: 46). Findings indicate that, in the most effective settings, children spend about half their time engaged in self-directed play; however, adults regularly interact with children during such episodes of play, for example extending play through open questioning and/or by taking on a role in imaginative play. Effective interactions of this kind were relatively infrequent in this study, suggesting that this is an important area for staff development in many settings. Read further about good practice examples of SST in Chapter 5, pages 99–100. Recently the *Every Child A Talker* (ECAT) project (DCSF, 2008i) has provided extensive guidance for practitioners on strategies to support adult–child talk, including in the context of play.

Reflective task

- Undertake further reading in relation to ECAT strategies used in the context of play.
- Review the Object play Scenario. How would you engage with Leon to encourage sustained shared thinking in the context of a young child's play with objects?
- Review the Pretend play Scenario. How would you engage with Nazia and her friends to encourage sustained shared thinking in the context of representational play with objects and pretend play?

Diversity and inclusion issues

Play has been recognised as an essential element of the early childhood curriculum historically and is now recognised in many curricula internationally. There is, however, a danger that adults think about childhood play in a nostalgic way, ignoring the complex issues that educators face in developing a pedagogy of play that can support the interests of all children. In recent years, researchers working from post-developmental perspectives have identified some significant diversity and inclusion issues in relation to young children's play.

Scenario

Potion play

Gina, Ally and Shazia were best friends at Ducklings Nursery and, in summer, loved mixing potions, making rose-petal perfumes in the nursery garden. There were various coloured petals to be found under the climbing roses in the special corner behind the shed. There was also a plentiful supply of jugs, bowls, spoons, whisks, sieves and a big bucket of water. The girls usually played without interruption in this area but there was a new boy at nursery, Addae, who seemed curious about the play. One afternoon, Addae ventured into the potions corner and announced, 'I'm going to make some of that stuff for my mum. It's her birthday.' 'Not here,' said Ally, standing and scowling at him. 'It's a girl's game, girls only here.' Addae had three big sisters and thought he knew how to deal with bossy girls: 'Great,' he said, 'I'm pretending to be a girl today,' and he sat down to play.

Addae's dilemma here, to challenge Ally's attempt to exclude him from the play or just leave, reminds us that play presents young children with many difficult social challenges. While some children, like Addae, are socially resilient, perhaps because of growing up in a large or extended family, others will find the experience of exclusion undermining.

Reflective task

When we reflect on children's play, it is important to acknowledge the diversity of the children we work with and the challenges this presents for inclusive play.
- Identify any issues in your setting that relate to gender, where one group of children excludes others from play. This could be explicit, as in the scenario above, or a more subtle form of exclusion.
- How do you and your colleagues address issues of this kind and how effective are your strategies?
- Are the children in your setting aware of other differences, for example differences of age, ability/disability, ethnicity or social background? In what ways do these differences affect play?

Contemporary research

Löfdahl (2010), working within the new social studies of childhood, has studied the play of three- to five-year-olds in Swedish preschools through interviews, informal conversations, video recording and field notes. Her observations indicate that children are often unkind to others, with some children using power to define the content of play, as well as who can play and in what roles. While Corsaro (2011) mainly highlights the constructive features of children's peer cultures, Löfdahl's examples (2010) raise issues for practitioners seeking to develop inclusive play environments. For example, she recounts an example of two girls who position themselves as successful at drawing, while denigrating the efforts of another child who subsequently leaves the room. Löfdahl (2010) argues that children who exclude others from play are likely to do this on the basis of differences of age, gender and ethnicity. It seems likely that some young children will also use their power to include or exclude others based on social class and ability/disability.

Extend your knowledge

There are a number of information sources to consult to extend your knowledge and understanding of this area and to identify strategies to improve practice.

- See Grieshaber, S. and McArdle, F. (2010) *The Trouble with Play*, Maidenhead: Open University and McGraw-Hill, Chapter 6. You will find several scenarios exemplifying unfair play in early years settings. The authors encourage practitioners to reflect on the complexities of play, and to develop policies for fairer play.
- Find out about ways of positioning adults in order to support inclusive play in Chapter 12 of MacNaughton, G. and Williams, G. (2009) *Teaching Young Children: Choices in Theory and practice* (2nd edn), Maidenhead: Open University and McGraw-Hill.
- Chapter 7 'Gender performativity in early childhood education', in Robinson, K. H. and Jones-Diaz, C. (2006) *Diversity and Difference in Early Childhood*, Maidenhead: Open University Press.
- Lane, J. (2007) 'Culture, ethnicity, language, faith and equal respect in early childhood – does "getting it" matter?', *Education Review*, vol. 20, no. 1, pp. 101–7.
- Lane, J. (2008) *Young Children and Racial Justice: Taking action for racial equality in the early years – understanding the past, thinking about the present, planning for the future*, London: The National Children's Bureau.

Children often exercise power to enhance their own position and exclude children whom they position as being of lower status. However, practitioners' own commitment to pedagogies of play can raise further diversity issues, as explained below.

Contemporary research

Liz Brooker (2002) began her career as an early years teacher and went on to undertake an important study of children's transition from home to the reception class of an inner-city primary school. She researched the experiences of children and their families in a largely 'Anglo' and Bangladeshi working-class community. A key finding was that mothers brought up in the UK were likely to share the school's belief that play was important to children's development, providing educational toys similar to those of the school, while Bangladeshi parents were more likely to instruct their children in the academic skills that they deemed important to school success. The school's lack of recognition of these cultural differences appeared to disadvantage many of the Bangladeshi children.

Brooker (2002) draws on a range of theories from the fields of sociology and psychology to make sense of the relative difficulties that Bangladeshi families experienced in understanding the potential value of play in the reception class curriculum. The study raises challenging questions about how the traditional 'child-centred' and play-based curriculum of early years settings meets the needs of children growing up in culturally diverse communities.

Extend your knowledge

You may want to find out more about this study and the issues raised for the position of play in early education: Brooker, L. 2002, *Starting School: Young Children Learning Cultures*. Buckingham: Open University Press.

- See pp. 51–5 for a short account of the different views about play and early learning of the parents of children starting school.
- See pp. 167–8, which explains Vygotsky's account of play and early learning; Brooker compares this with Piaget's approach.
- See Brooker, L. and Woodhead, M. (eds.) (2010) *Culture and Learning*, Milton Keynes: The Open University. Available from: http://www.bernardvanleer.org/Culture-and-learning (accessed 1/8/12). This short book includes a succinct account of cross-cultural understandings of play (pp. 24–7).

A risk-averse society?

Many adults have memorable experiences of play involving physical challenges outdoors, for example climbing the highest tree or sliding head first down the playground's steepest slide. Children vary in how far they seek out such adventures but the most intrepid seek out such play repeatedly. They are likely to continue their daring exploits into adulthood, for example pursuing adventurous sports such as water skiing or activities such as bungee jumping. Caillois (2001) identifies four motivations for play (see Table 9.1, page 189), and includes a category described as dizziness or ilinx, the Greek term for whirling water. He explains how children and adults seek out experiences of physical dizziness, for example swinging, sliding, spinning or falling, often at great speed.

The most thrilling experiences for young children, for example climbing on rocks or being close to fire, all raise issues of risk. However, as adults, we feel a responsibility to protect young children from any potential harm. The wide media publicity now given to what are rare tragedies, for example a child snatched from a playground, heighten our sense of the dangers that beset children today and increase our concern to keep children safe. However, there is a danger that a heightened perception of risk will lead us to limit the experiences that children value, and those that promote important aspects of learning and development.

Contemporary research

The Norwegian researcher, Sandseter (2009), has examined the affordances for risky play of two preschools for children of four and five years. The first preschool was a typical municipal preschool, providing some fixed playground equipment, trees and with a surrounding fence. In contrast, the second preschool was located in a forest, with no fixed equipment or barriers to exploration of the forest. Sandseter (2009) undertook extensive observations of outdoor play and interviewed children in both settings. She concluded that the two environments offered a similar range of opportunities for risky play and that children participated in a similar number of episodes of risky play in each. However, she claims that the forest offered more challenging and therefore more valuable experiences than the traditional playground.

What is interesting from a UK perspective is that both preschools offered a wider range of risky play experiences than found in most UK settings for this age group, suggesting significant cultural differences in attitudes to risk. It is therefore useful to review the categories of risky play found in the Norwegian preschools and to consider the extent to which we offer children similar opportunities. Table 9.3 charts the risky play features used and enjoyed by children in the two settings.

	Ordinary preschool	Nature and outdoor preschool
Climbable features	Climbing tower Play hut Two or three climbable trees	Several trees, including taller trees than in the ordinary preschool Cliffs and climbable big rocks Hillside with projecting stone edges
Jump-down-off-able features	Climbing tower Play hut Trees Large wooden storage box	Several climbing trees Several cliffs and big rocks (2–3 metres high)
Balance-on-able features	The rim of a wooden boat used as a sand pool Branches in the climbing trees	Several big rocks, cliff edges, wind-fallen logs and branches
Flat, relatively smooth surfaces	Flat surface with grass, gravel, two sand pools, asphalted paths Small skating rink in winter	Natural forest areas with grass, bushes, trees Gravel yard outside the preschool house
Slopes and slides	Two small grassy hills	Hills, cliffs and slopes in the terrain
Swing-on-able features	Two playground swings made with tractor tyres	Rope swing from a tree
Graspable/detached objects	Plastic buckets and spades Wind-fallen wooden sticks	Plastic buckets and spades Wind-fallen wooden sticks
Dangerous tools	Whittling tools used under adult supervision	Whittling tools and saws used under adult supervision
Dangerous elements	None	Cliffs Pond/small lake 50 metres from preschool house Fire pit on the gravel yard (not always with fire)

Table 9.3 The affordances for risky play in two Norwegian preschools (Sandseter, 2009)

Extend your knowledge

You may want to review the approach to risky play in your setting to ensure that health and safety policies are proportional to actual risks and do not unnecessarily limit children's opportunities for learning.

- For a comprehensive review of the potential benefits and dangers of risky play, see Tovey, H. (2007) *Playing Outdoors: Spaces and Places, Risk and Challenge*, Maidenhead: Open University Press, Chapter 6.
- Read Sara Knight's suggestions for creating and managing riskier outdoor play for under-fives, including ways to deal with mud, wet and cold, in 'Forest School: Playing on the wild side', Chapter 12 of Moyles, J. (ed.) (2010) *The Excellence of Play* (3rd edn), Maidenhead: Open University and McGraw-Hill.

Practical information to facilitate creative outdoor play

Table 9.3 suggests some environmental features that can support challenging physical play outdoors for three- to five-year-olds, although some features would probably not be acceptable in a UK context. Scenarios introduced earlier in the chapter also offer suggestions for facilitating creative outdoor play. Table 9.4 will help you to recall these scenarios and the relevant resources.

Scenarios	Environmental features and resources
Physical play	Grassy area and football
Object play	Grassy area, autumn leaves, tractor tyres, wheelbarrows, buckets, spades
Westwold Kindergarten	Sandpit, flower and vegetable gardens, winding path, clump of birch trees
Forest school visit	Forest, woodland or small clump of trees Fire for cooking Blindfolds to wear when feeling trees
Potion play	Plants and fallen petals, jugs, bowls, spoons, whisks, sieves and a big bucket of water

Table 9.4 Outdoor play features and resources

Anna Craft (2002: 91) argues that 'possibility thinking' lies at the heart of children's creativity; this can be supported outdoors by provision of loosely defined spaces and open-ended resources, offering a range of possibilities for play. The scenarios listed above each demonstrate young children's engagement in outdoor areas with a range of low-cost resources, for example the tractor tyres and leaves in the Object play Scenario. These include open-ended natural resources and environmental features that children can use in varied and flexible ways. Maxwell (2007) also explains the importance of private spaces, as seen in the Potion play Scenario, spaces that allow children relative control over social experiences

Contemporary research

Garrick *et al.* (2010) contributed to a review of the EYFS (DCSF, 2008a), which included research into children's experiences of play. They describe how a childminding setting successfully supported free-flow play between indoor and outdoor environments for children from three to five years. Three girls developed their shared interest in schools through pretend play over a period of several weeks. The setting had French windows from the playroom into the garden and children had ongoing access to outdoor play. The pretend play began indoors, where children collected resources from the home corner, including pretend packed lunches, a satchel, writing book and mark-making materials. Then they raced outdoors with these, setting up a school at a small table at the end of the garden (see Figure 9.1 on the next page). The girls played together, absorbed in their imaginative world, until called in for tea.

Figure 9.1 Childminder's garden

This corner of this suburban garden, with the small table and stools, was a partly bounded, semi-private space, offering varied possibilities for play. The case exemplifies how practitioners can develop flexible outdoor environments, supporting young children's creative play, over time and with relatively modest resources.

Extend your knowledge

There is a wide range of information sources you can consult to help you evaluate the outdoor environment of your setting, with many ideas to support development planning.

- For detailed and practical guidance on low-cost resources for a wide range of categories of outdoor play, see White, J. (2008) *Playing and Learning Outdoors: Making provision for high-quality experiences in the outdoor environment*, London: Routledge.
- To get started on plans to develop your own outdoor area, look at Watts, A. (2011) *Every Nursery Needs a Garden*, London: Routledge. There are inspiring photographs and detailed resource lists.

Many environmental organisations offer useful information and practical support in developing outdoor areas. A very good starting point is *Learning through Landscapes* [online] http://www.ltl.org.uk (accessed 31/7/2012).

Conclusion

This chapter began by introducing the ideas of three pioneers of early years education who included play as an essential element of their innovative curricula. It went on to introduce the work of contemporary researchers who examine the nature and role of play in early education today from different perspectives, including the perspective of children. The chapter explained the different ways in which play has been categorised, and examined five main categories of play: physical play, object play, pretence/socio-dramatic play, symbolic play and games with rules. Free-flow play was also introduced as a broad category of play that shows children playing with intensity and at their highest level.

Following this, the chapter reviewed the features of indoor and outdoor learning environments that support young children's learning and development. Turning to outdoor play, the chapter identified some important features of forest school and nursery garden traditions. Acknowledging that adults tend to take a nostalgic view of play, the chapter raised important diversity and inclusion issues concerning play in early years settings. The issue of risk in children's play and varying attitudes to risk across time and cultures was also considered. Throughout the chapter, you were encouraged to extend your knowledge and understanding of play in the early years through further reading and reflection on your own practice. Finally, you were encouraged to apply your knowledge and understanding of play to practice, to develop and enhance play opportunities for young children.

Evaluate your...

Knowledge and understanding of play as a key element of early years practice

■ How do you review the range and quality of play provision for different kinds of play in your setting?

■ Can you identify examples of children who appear to be playing at their highest level during episodes of free-flow play? What are the enablers and barriers to free-flow play in your setting?

■ In what ways do you share responsibilities with colleagues for the development of your setting's learning environment?

■ How do you plan for the longer-term development of your outdoor learning environment? Who have you involved in these plans?

■ Do you have a health and safety policy and have you reviewed it to ensure that you provide opportunities for children to experience appropriate physical challenges?

■ How do you share your knowledge and understanding of the value of play with parents and carers?

■ In what ways do you support parents and carers in providing appropriate play experiences for children at home?

■ How do you support students and new members of staff to understand the value of play in your setting?

■ Take your professional development needs in relation to play to your next supervision or appraisal meeting with your line manager.

■ What kind of play interests you most? Become a champion for this kind of play in your setting.

Next steps

- Identify the opportunities you provide, both indoors and outdoors, for children to engage in the five main types of play (physical play, play with objects, pretend play, symbolic play and games with rules).
- Which types of play will you prioritise for development indoors and which will you prioritise outdoors to ensure children's access to a wide range of opportunities?
- Write a development plan to introduce or enhance provision to support these types of play.
- Identify staff training needs to ensure practitioners understand their role, both in planning play environments and in promoting children's inclusion in engaging play.

Further reading

Brock, A., Dodds, S., Jarvis, P. and Olusoga, Y. (2009) *Perspectives on Play: Learning for life*. Harlow: Pearson Education.

Bruce, T. (2011) *Early Childhood Education* (4th edn), London: Hodder.

Carr, M. and Lee, W. (2012) *Learning Stories: Constructing Learner Identities in Early Education*, London: SAGE.

Fjortoft, I. (2001) 'The natural environment as a playground for children: The impact of outdoor play activities in pre-primary school children', *Early Childhood Education Journal*, vol. 29, no. 2, pp. 111–17.

Manning-Morton, J. and Thorp, M. (2003) *Key times for play: The first three years*, Maidenhead: Open University Press and McGraw-Hill.

Meade, A. and Cubey, P. (2008) *Thinking Children: Learning About Schemas*, Maidenhead: Open University Press and McGraw-Hill.

Rogers, S. (ed.) (2011) *Rethinking Play and Pedagogy in Early Childhood Education: Concepts, Contexts and Cultures*, London: Routledge.

Vallberg Roth, A. and Månsson, A. (2011) 'Individual development plans from a critical didactic perspective: Focusing on Montessori- and Reggio Emilia-profiled preschools in Sweden', *Journal of Early Childhood Research*, vol. 9, no. 3, 247–61.

10

Observation and record keeping
Ioanna Palaiologou

Introduction

The role of observation in early years practice has been of great importance both in understanding children's development, learning and behaviours, and in informing pedagogy and practice. Since the introduction of the Early Years Foundation Stage (EYFS) in September 2008, observation has become a requirement in the early years sector. The EYFS (DCSF, 2008a) was revised in March 2012, and the new version of the EYFS (DfE, 2012a) has been implemented in early years sector practice since September 2012. Here, the centrality of observation is emphasised as a key element of children's assessment and of early years practice in general. Within the EYFS (DfE, 2012a) it is stressed that there is a need to observe children in order for early years practitioners to be able to identify their needs and interests. Also, practitioners will gain first-hand knowledge of what children can do and how they may respond to certain situations (Early Education, 2012).

Equally important within EYFS (DfE, 2012a) is the need for early years practitioners to be able to record systematically children's responses, behaviours and learning. Furthermore, practitioners must be able to analyse this information in order to inform their knowledge and work. All early years settings that care for children from birth to five years old must demonstrate the ways in which they record and share information about the children's progress in development and learning. Contemporary thinking, including the idea of children's participation, is in line with the key principles of the early years curriculum to create a unique child and positive relationships, enabling environments where children develop and learn in different ways at different rates, and to develop the role of parents in ongoing observations of children. All these are and should be part of the observation process (DfE, 2012a). In light of such changes, there is a need for early years practitioners to have training so that they learn ways to observe systematically.

This chapter aims to explore the role of observation in early years, and then to discuss the variety of observation tools available for recording purposes, as well as ways of analysing and recording from observation. The ethical issues governing observation, and the limitations of observation, will also be addressed.

Learning outcomes

By the end of this chapter you will be able to:

- Understand the role and value of observation in early years practice, and the different types of observation.
- Understand the observation process (aims, objectives, planning, recording, analysis and documenting).
- Understand the role of the observer.
- Consider the ethical implications involved in observation.
- Develop a critical approach to observation in early years practice.

Historical perspectives of observation

Observation as a systematic tool for collecting information is a method developed and used for research within a number of disciplines: sociology, anthropology, psychology and education, for example. Observation captures what humans actually do, and means that various phenomena can be captured as they occur, such as children playing outdoors and discovering ants for the first time – practitioners can observe how children behave in these situations.

Because psychology is a key discipline closely related to education, it relies heavily on the observation of humans or phenomena. The field of child development has used observation in order to study children's development in their natural environment or in clinical/laboratory situations.

Many different theoretical approaches – including behaviourism, psychoanalysis, cognition and ethology – have used observation in order to develop an in-depth understanding of children's development and learning. In brief, behaviourism was concerned with how a human learns; it embarked upon a number of experiments on humans and on children's responses to certain stimuli, which in turn led behaviourists to suggest key terms such as classical conditioning (Pavlov), operant conditioning and reinforcement (Skinner).

Psychoanalysis and the pioneering work of Esther Bick (1964) introduced infant observation in a naturalistic environment. Bick was interested in observing infants in the family environment. As a consequence of her work, a model of infant observation was integrated into various forms of psychoanalytical training. The methodology developed by Bick was later adapted by Bowlby (1969, 1973, 1980, 2005) and other attachment theorists such as Ainsworth (1969, 1979, 1985, 1989); both developed further observational tests in naturalistic and controlled environments. Their findings about children (and others) enhanced our knowledge in the field of social and emotional development of children.

Alongside these theorists, Piaget (1952, 1954, 1962) made use of observations mainly in a laboratory situation (the Piagetian tests) to formulate his theory of children's cognitive development. Cognitive psychology is concerned with patterns of behaviour and attempts to identify those aspects of cognition that interact with the environment in order for humans to grow cognitively. This work was later extended through observations of children in early years settings by Athey (1990) and Nutbrown (1999).

Traditions in early years

The transition of observation from a research tool to observation for early years practice was introduced mainly by two pioneers in early years education and care: Susan Isaacs and Maria Montessori.

Susan Isaacs (1930, 1933, 1935, 1948, 1952) was trained in the field of psychoanalysis, influenced by the work of Melanie Klein. Klein's work (1927) on infant analysis through play focused on attempting to gain access to the unconscious of very young children, and showed play as a form of natural self-expression. Under Klein's influence, Isaacs developed her ideas about play as a way for children not only to understand the world, but also – and equally importantly – as a means of expression. Isaacs' main contribution to early childhood education was the blending of psychoanalysis and education. She brought psychoanalytical ideas and methods into education. She viewed the education of young children as a 'place' where children should feel they were in as natural an environment as possible: 'Experience has shown that it can be looked upon as a normal institution in the social life of any civilised community' (Isaacs, 1952: 31). She transformed the early years setting into an environment reflecting love and warmth; also, she emphasised opportunities and resources to which children might not have access at home. Isaacs believed that 'the nursery school is an extension of the function of the home, not a substitute for it' (Isaacs, 1952: 31). Her ideal early years setting was one that provided opportunities for children to have social experiences, to play and to explore the outdoor environment. She used psychoanalytical techniques in the observation of children in education in order to develop a method of pedagogy from the psychoanalysis of children. Its predominant hypothesis was that intellectual development is interrelated with emotional development, and the importance of play was a key function.

Maria Montessori (1912, 1967, 1969) was invited in 1906 to oversee the care and education of young children whose parents were working. Her work in Italy in her *Casa dei Bambini* ('Children's house' or 'household') has left an influential legacy. Most importantly, though, she changed the way early childhood education and care were perceived. Her interest in young children led her to develop a theory about young children's education based on the idea that children are the best directors of their own development and learning (Montessori, 1967 and 1969). From that idea she created an appropriate environment in which children were able to direct their own needs, and to gain access to materials, activities and situations. Montessori introduced the notion of observation in the early years environment as a crucial part of the everyday life of practitioners. She supported the idea of observing individual children daily and, at regular intervals, for a whole week at a time. She believed that these observations should be shared with the parents in a number of ways, through regular meetings with them or frequent short discussions of day-to-day issues when necessary (Montessori, 1967 and 1969).

Her work on creating an environment for children where each learns to take responsibility has become influential. A number of Montessori schools were established and still flourish across the world.

Extend your knowledge

To develop a better understanding of Montessori you might find it helpful to study:
■ Isaacs, B. (2011) *Understanding the Montessori Approach*, London: Routledge.

To develop an understanding of the relationships between home and early years settings, you might find it helpful to study:
■ Siraj-Blatchford, I. and Siraj-Blatchford, J. (2010) *Improving children's attainment through a better quality of family-based support for early learning*, London: Centre for Excellence and Outcomes in Children and Young People's Services (C4EO). Available from: http://www.c4eo.org.uk/themes/earlyyears/familybasedsupport/files/c4eo_family_based_support_full_knowledge_review.pdf.

Both Isaacs and Montessori, pioneers in early years education, have made observation a key element of everyday life in early years settings. Today, we have a number of curricula, such as Reggio Emilia in Italy and Te Whāriki in New Zealand, which have made observation an integral part of early years practice. Observation is now seen as paving the way towards improving practice, designing an ever-improving early years environment and sustaining growth of practice.

Extend your knowledge

Read further about the Reggio Emilia and the Te Whāriki approaches to observations. You will find the following books helpful in explaining these two approaches:

- Thorton, L. and Burton, P. (2009) *Understanding the Reggio Approach,* London: Routledge.
- Lee, W., Mitchell, I. and Soutar, B. (2012) *Understanding the Te Whāriki Approach: Early Years Education in Practice,* London: Routledge.

Compare and contrast how the two approaches observe children, and then evaluate your professional practice. Ask yourself:

- What am I doing well?
- Where can I improve?
- What can I learn from other practices in early years?

EYFS and observation

As mentioned in the introduction, observation holds a central role in the EYFS. The *Statutory Framework for the Early Years Foundation Stage* (DfE, 2012a) emphasises that children's assessment is a key part of the framework. It states that:

> Providers must maintain records and obtain and share information (with parents and carers, other professionals working with the child, and the police, social services and Ofsted as appropriate) to ensure the safe and efficient management of the setting, and to help ensure that the needs of all children are met. Providers must enable a regular two-way flow of information with parents and/or carers, and between providers, if a child is attending more than one setting. If requested, providers should incorporate parents' and/or carers' comments into children's records.
>
> (DfE, 2012a: 26)

It is clear that within EYFS observation is considered a tool to record children's development and learning but also a way of communicating children's experiences in the setting with the parents and other professionals if necessary. In a previous work I have stated that observing for a curriculum:

> ... is not only an activity that describes what happens between the observer and the observed event/child, but also a process that involves clear aims and objectives, ethical considerations, planning, analysis and documentation.
>
> (Palaiologou, 2012a: 144)

The statutory requirements of the summative assessment requests mean that it is important to link observations with the early years curriculum in order to meet these standards. EYFS guidance (Early Education, 2012) suggests that all early years practitioners should report formally to the parents/carers on their children's progress in two stages, when the children are at the ages of 24 and 36 months, then at the end of EYFS with the Early Years Foundation Stage Profile. Observation helps the early years practitioners to collect information about each child (as illustrated in the scenario provided below) and communicate this information to parents and other professionals, such as health visitors or social workers, when necessary, for example during children's transitions.

Scenario

Study Table 10.1 and consider other reasons why it is important to link observations with the EYFS.

Date completed: April 2012	Child's name: Harry Date of birth: 13 June 2009
Area of learning and development	**Comments**
Prime areas	
Personal, social and emotional development	Harry has a strong exploratory nature within his environment. He is self-confident and has belief in himself. We are working with Harry to show how some actions towards others may hurt them. He is mostly managing his own personal hygiene with a little adult support. **Ways forward:** Continue to give clear boundaries and adult support where needed, especially in expressing his own feelings through language.
Physical development	Harry has fine motor skills as seen in his threading or manipulation of dough. He enjoys large motor play outside and is increasing his skills in control. He will persist at a chosen activity for a sustained period of time. He does not hesitate to climb and follow older children in physical activities and, in some cases, he puts himself in dangerous situations. **Ways forward:** Continue to refine motor activities (especially with scissors). Develop his control and coordination with large operations (bikes, trikes, scooters, etc). Develop an understanding of safety.
Communication and language	Harry is bilingual (speaks German with Mum). If he cannot communicate his needs he has the confidence to take an adult to what he wants or where he wants to go. He makes a sentence, but if he does not know the English word, he uses the German word in his sentence. **Ways forward:** Extend English vocabulary through conversation and his love of books.
Specific areas	
Literacy	He thoroughly enjoys sharing books with adults one-to-one, also in small groups and on his own. He is beginning to develop more of an interest with mark-making. **Ways forward:** Encourage him with activities in relation to mark-making.

(continued)

Mathematics	Harry uses numbers up to ten during his play. He has a very good understanding of the numbers one to five. He can count up to ten if he wants to. Knows some 2D spaces and mathematical language.
	Ways forward:
	More exposure to patterns/shapes/counting in play. Build on measure knowledge through water play, which Harry loves.
Understanding the world	Harry loves to be outdoors and explore nature. He will often be seen getting a closer look with a magnifying glass. Really enjoyed watching the tadpoles grow and he participated in their care. Enjoys model making with support; he has clear ideas of what he wants to make. He uses a computer to play games ('Dora the Explorer') on his own and with the assistance of an adult, yet he is competent in using the computer (mouse and keyboard).
	Ways forward:
	Encourage him with his ICT skills. Continue to develop his curiosity for the natural world. Let him investigate various construction materials.
Expressive arts and design	Harry enjoys role play, fantasy play usually on his own with toys and rarely with adult support. He has started to involve other children in his role play. Loves small wood toys from dinosaurs to police station; he plays with them all. Participates in painting and collage activities. Harry is beginning to join in singing activities.
	Ways forward:
	Encourage more music and movement, collaborative play.

Table 10.1 Harry's Early Years Transfer Record: Areas of learning and development

Extend your knowledge

Transitions in young children's lives are important. Study the following article and reflect how observations can help you to support children's transitions into and out of the EYFS.

- Kennedy, E. K., Cameron, E. J. and Greene, J. (2012) 'Transitions in the early years: Educational and child psychologists working to reduce the impact of school culture shock', *Educational and Child Psychology*, vol. 29, no. 1, pp. 19–31.

What is observation?

Observation is, as we saw above, a tool traditionally used by researchers. In that context it is described as the method where researchers record what actually happens (Plowright, 2011; Gillham, 2008). For example, Plowright states (2011: 64): 'Observation generally takes place concurrently with activities of the cases involved in the observed event. In other words, observation is very much about the here and now.' He claims that a number of senses other than merely the visual are involved in observation – hearing, touch, smell and taste. Similarly, Palaiologou (2012: 9) states that 'observation is a systematic method of studying human behaviour or a phenomenon within a specific context and should always have a precise purpose'.

A definition of observation for early years practice is similar to these definitions, in that observation means the systematic collection of data/information on human behaviour. However, observation for practice goes beyond the act of recording what children actually do – it is a longer, deeper process. This chapter will suggest that observation for early years practice consists not only of the actual action/activity of observing, but also involves planning, clarifying clear aims and objectives, recording through using observation techniques, analysing what has been recorded and, finally, documenting these findings in order to communicate them with the parties involved, such as the rest of the team, children, parents/carers and other professionals.

Before all the steps of the observation process are discussed, it is important to explore the value of observation for early years practice. As mentioned previously, observation informs all daily activities with children in the curriculum for early years. It underpins all the activities in the classroom and outdoors; it may become a valid communication tool and a form of evidence. It helps practitioners to collect information offering an accurate, up-to-the-minute picture of children, their activities, their interests, their likes and dislikes, and helps us to understand why certain behaviours occur. It is a valid tool for monitoring the progress of children, and for recognising at which phase they are in their development. This is essential information, as it enables the professionals to evaluate their practice by providing a focus for discussion and improvement.

Reflective task

- How do you observe children? What format do you use? How often do you undertake observations and what do you observe?
- What do you do with the observations made? Who do you share the observations with? Why? How often?
- Do you invite and consider children's/carers'/colleagues' feedback on your observations?

Learning Walks

Observation plays a dual role in early years practice: we observe children for all of the above reasons, while we also observe our own practice in order to reflect upon and improve it. This is a continuous process informing our curriculum planning and daily practice. Although each individual tries to improve her/his own practice, this cannot happen in isolation. It requires the cooperation found in teamwork. Throughout the literature, peer observation or collaborative observation, collegial observation and peer-to-peer reflection have been discussed as valid tools through which to share ideas about what works, what we do well in our practice, and how we may enhance practice.

A very interesting approach to peer collaborative observation as a learning activity is found in the Learning Walks (DCSF, 2007b). A Learning Walk is a pre-scheduled, organised visit among the staff of a setting to each other's rooms, using specific pre-agreed criteria against which to focus on the teaching and learning taking place there. It has been used widely in schools as a technique for peer observation, although not to assess the staff's performance. It is, rather, a way of opening dialogue among staff about the teaching and learning that take place in the classrooms. Reciprocal learning takes place, as the discussions stimulated after a Learning Walk are usually very interesting, evaluative and helpful to all staff. However, for Learning Walks to be successful they need to take place in an environment of collaboration, mutual respect, trust, collegial amity and security. They do not aim to be a tool assessing the performances of individuals; instead, they are a valuable way of reflecting upon our own practice.

Example of a Learning Walk in an early years setting

Preparation

Prior to the Learning Walk the team meet and discuss who will participate, which rooms will be observed and who is to observe in which rooms. The manager of the setting and the 'key person' from the toddlers' room would visit all the rooms for a ten-minute period over two days. It had been agreed that this would take place during the arrival time of the children, as the focus of this particular Learning Walk was on the interactions of staff with the parents and the children at this moment. The setting wanted to improve communication with parents and to investigate the level of interaction taking place during arrival time. It was discussed and agreed that:

- Observations would be reported to the staff generally (and anonymously) on the kinds of activities that were noted.
- All staff would be given the opportunity to discuss these activities, for consistency of practice within the early years setting to be gained.
- As these observations are merely 'snapshots' of the practice in each room, further discussion and comment from all staff would follow, in order to stimulate self-evaluation.
- It was emphasised that the purpose of the Learning Walk was not to generate professional criticism of individuals; rather, it was to become a means of generating self-evaluation of the practice in a sensitive and open atmosphere, sharing good practice and enriching a culture of learning.

Scenario

Observation extracts from a Learning Walk in an early years setting

Summary of Observation 1

Room one (three years)

Before arrival time the early years practitioners had created a very tidy, bright room by putting the lights on. The displays were very inviting; they had children's photographs of activities done in the class, with small comments on what each activity was. The early years practitioners had placed wooden toys on the tables, and encouraged children on their arrival to go and play with them.

However, the displays looked 'too' tidy – as though the children were not allowed to touch them. There were far too many photographs for anyone to see in only two or three minutes, the time that the parents were usually in the room before they left.

The children were exceptionally quiet. Two children queued at the practitioner's table as she was writing the names of the children on their drawings. The practitioner appeared to have a good, calm relationship with the children and the parents.

Summary of Observation 2

Room two (three years)

The second room drew the parents' enthusiasm as they were walking in: in the middle of the room there was a very large lion that the children had made the previous day. Children were dragging their parents to see the big lion. The practitioners were explaining to the parents how the children had made it, and what activities they planned to do today in relation to the lion.

Children were busily and independently engaged in group work while the practitioners were talking to the parents. The walls had a good variety of materials on display, incorporating 3D work, and a couple of parents were looking at it.

Summary of Observation 3

Room three (toddlers' room)

The room appeared to be 'empty' as there was not much material displayed on the walls (apart from a drawing of balloons by adults and some figures of Winnie the Pooh). There was no display as such, although some photographs of children were pinned on a noticeboard. However, these were not labelled and had no explanation of what was happening in the photographs. During the children's arrival time, the practitioners were comforting toddlers who were crying or feeling unsettled. There was a warmth in the atmosphere of the room, yet it lacked strong visual stimulation for the parents.

Post-Learning Walks discussion

The discussion focused on the use of displays as a way of sharing the everyday life of the setting with the parents in a snapshot. It was found that in rooms where the displays were well organised, tidy and not overcrowded with information, the parents took a couple of minutes to look at them. It was also found that having something created by the children themselves as the central focus in the class during arrival time increases the parents' engagement when they bring their children into the room (lion observation).

Overall, it was agreed that in the setting there was not yet enough focus on the use of displays, at least in terms of wall displays, although there was evidence from conversations that this focus was beginning to emerge.

The team decided to work on displays and in a month's time to plan new Learning Walks to monitor the changes in the displays and children's active engagement in sharing their own learning.

Extend your knowledge

- Although no Primary National Strategy exists, in 2007 *Primary National Strategy: Learning Walks: Tools and templates for getting started* was published. It is available from: http://webarchive.nationalarchives. gov.uk/20110202093118/http:/nationalstrategies.standards.dcsf.gov.uk/node/88674.
- A really good website with lots of practical tips about Learning Walks is: http://learningwalks.com.

Research and study the Learning Walks and consider whether you can implement them in an early years setting. What changes would you make? Create your own ways of learning journeys or design your own template to do peer observation.

Planning for observation

Observation in early years settings is a process that starts with good, clear planning. It is important that all parties involved contribute what they can: all staff as a team, plus the children and parents/carers. During this process it is necessary to discuss and agree the aims and objectives of the observations that will take place. The key element in the planning process is to identify how to gain rich information on what you want to observe, then choose the most appropriate and potentially rewarding techniques.

The methods and techniques are determined by what you wish to observe, as derived from the aims and objectives of the observation. The methods that will be used to collect the information vary depending on the aims and objectives of the observation.

Some of the key questions in the planning process should be:
- Why do you want to observe (aims)?
- What do you want to observe (objectives)?
- What techniques shall be used – how to record, and how to gain rich information?
- How do you want to analyse the recordings of the observation?
- How do you want to document the findings?
- How do you want to share the information, for example informally among the team, children and parents, and formally through the EYFS Profile?

These questions may form the starting point of the planning process. Within the EYFS (DfE, 2012a), observation is linked with the assessment of children's progress. Observation is more than simply the act of observing – it is also used to assess and evaluate the everyday practice of the setting. Observation of the children and the practice informs future planning for practice. It is essential in the planning process to consider both of the main functions of the observation process: the well-being of the children themselves, and collaborative observations on practice.

Aims and objectives

The identification of the aims and objectives of the observation process is key to observation planning. The aims and objectives of the observation need to be clear to all members of staff, parents and children.

Aims are the general area upon which you wish to focus. These are precise and are usually determined from the curriculum. For example, in the EYFS guidance (Early Education, 2012: 4) the main aims of the observation planning are the Learning and Development areas:

- **Prime areas are fundamental, work together, and are moved through to support developments in all other areas.**
  - Personal and Social Development
  - Communication and Language
  - Physical Development
- **Specific areas include essential skills and knowledge for children to participate successfully in society:**
  - Literacy
  - Mathematics

– **Understanding the World**

– **Expressive Arts and Design**

Early years practitioners may apply these areas to arrive at their objectives, which are the specific areas, skills or behaviours you wish to observe. These should be detailed, realistic and possible to observe.

Scenario

Study the following observations and try to identify the aim and the objectives of the observations. Which areas of the EYFS can the observations be linked to?

7 January 2012 (inside)

Francis makes a boat from magnets, says it does not need a driver because it is magnetic.
He uses his fingers to manipulate the magnet.

10 January 2012 (outside)

Francis is outside and he shouts:
'I can jump high, look'
as he jumps up and down.

11 January 2012 (outside)

Francis tells me that he has a tree in his garden. I ask him:
'What sort of tree?'
'It has branches and leaves and
I climb.' He goes on the slide and climbs from the side 'like this'.
'I have two gardens, one has a tree.
And I have a tomato tree, it has tomatoes and I have a magic egg tree. It only works when I go to bed.'

14 January 2012 (inside)

Francis is drawing on blackboard. 'It's a boat, now I am taking it away'– rubs it out with board rubber.

14 January 2012 (outside)

Francis is pushing a bike, pushing it in circles; he goes around four times.

Figure 10.1 Snapshots from Francis's profile (two years and 10 months)

Recording: observation methods

The next step in planning observations is to choose the appropriate methods or techniques to gain rich information about precisely what you want to observe (aims and objectives). In the literature (see the Further reading section at the end of chapter) a range of observation techniques have been described. The most popular techniques to use to observe children are listed here, divided into structured or non-participant observation, and non-structured or participant observation. The former is where the practitioner does not participate in the observed activity, and the latter is where the observation occurs at the same time as the practitioner is participating in an activity.

Structured observation or non-participant observation

Written observation (commonly known as narrative)

This is one of the most popular methods within early years practice. It is a written description of what happens, at the time it happens: for example, what a child does at a particular time or during a particular activity. It has to be both accurate and comprehensive. However, since recording the details takes place during a busy early years setting, the information may, unless full and accurate, be taken out of context and thus misinterpreted. It is therefore important in the early years setting to have developed a system for how this information is gathered. For example, early years practitioners can have a pro forma, to which they can then add information very quickly, writing details in specific boxes.

Child's name	Nelly
Date	April 2012
Name of the observer	Wendy
Starting time	9:55
Finishing time	10:06
No. of adults present	None
No. of other children present	None
Area of observation	Outside area
Description of activity observed	Nelly comes running outside, kicks the sticks over, then sees the ball. She stands the sticks up again and bowls the ball over-arm at them. She walks over to the nature table and uses the magnifying glass to look at the bottles of lentils. She shakes them and looks at them. Then she moves to the playhouse, sits at the table, uses the knife and fork and pretends to eat, picks up the teapot and pretend-pours into a teacup, bringing the cup to her lips as if drinking. She says 'Aaah' and smiles. Goes out of the house and picks up the train track, 'Come on,' she says. On the way there her shoe comes off. 'Where is my shoe, where is it gone?' she says, then laughs when she sees it a couple of steps back. She picks up her shoe and goes back to the playhouse. She sits at the table and picks up the teapot, pouring a cup of tea. She sings: 'Neenaw, neenaw.'

Additional comments (I think…)	Nelly engages in role play, shows signs of curiosity. She has observed adults at teatime and imitates what is observed, doing it spontaneously when adults are absent.
Links with EYFS	Playing and exploring: initiating activities, acting out experiences.
What next?	Extend interest in exploring. Encourage playing with others.

Table 10.2 Observation of Nelly playing

Next steps

When you are in a setting, try to write two or three narrative observations. Reflect on your observations and ask:

- Have you written down what has actually happened or have you used comments and judgements to describe what happened?
- Were you able to make any additional comments?
- Were you able to link your observations with the Learning Areas of the EYFS?
- Identify you own next steps.

Checklists

Usually, checklists are a helpful tool for collecting information on standardised procedures. Once they are created you can use them time and again. We do need to be careful on the length of checklists. Include items that are representative of the behaviour on which you are focusing and are representative of the age of the children you are observing, and ensure that the whole team and users of the checklists understand their function. The checklists may be created in such a way that children can understand them and thus participate in the observation. It is suggested that you create a system of labelled in-trays to help you organise your findings.

Aim: Understanding the world	Pictographic items	Child's response
Objective: Look closely at similarities and differences, patterns and change		
I recognise		
This is a sunny day		
This is a cloudy day		

This is at night		
This is rain		
This is wind		
This is snow		
This is ice		

Table 10.3 Pictographic checklist

In this example, children can complete the checklist with the help of an adult or on their own – if the pictures have been explained to the children. You can also choose, with the children, the pictures that go into your own checklist.

Diagrammatic techniques

These include tracking, sociograms and histograms. The main focus of these techniques is purpose specific, for example duration or frequency. They usually offer an indicative picture of how long children spend in an activity or in an area, or how often a certain behaviour has occurred, although the results are not intended to explain *why* this is happening.

Tracking

Tracking records the time that a child spends with an activity either of their choice or something they have been asked to do. The focus is on the time and the frequency. Such checklists can be used to track the involvement of children in particular activities.

Sociogram

This tool helps the observer to focus on children's social skills. It observes a child's relationships with others. It can show children's popularity among their peers. However, we need to note that the information they provide may be misleading, as children's social relationships change rapidly;

therefore, the information gathered from this method is indicative only and needs the support of other observation techniques.

Histograms

A very helpful technique, especially within the EYFS framework, as it keeps track of the history of a child, following their development over a period of time. Usually, practitioners observe over time certain behaviours that may offer an accurate profile of a child.

Again, as in all other methods, this is not to be used alone; other forms of observation need to be considered to gain a complete and holistic picture of a child and its environment (Bronfenbrenner, 1979).

Sampling

There are various forms of sampling and different approaches. You can use one or more to gather a more rounded idea of a child's and children's learning and development through sampling observations.

Time sampling

The observer records whether or not certain behaviours occur during a sample of a short time period. The observer may have prepared a form covering behaviours of interest. The observation period is defined and the observer collects data watching the child and checking off behaviours.

Example of time sampling

Aim: Physical development

Objective: Can catch a large ball

Area: Outdoors; four children and one adult playing with a large ball

Time	Frequency of behaviour
10:02	2
10:05	1
10:08	0
10:11	1
10:15	2

Event sampling

The observer records all events/instances of a particular behaviour during a specified period, where the focus is on a certain behaviour or pattern of behaviour.

Example of event sampling

Aim: Social development

Objective: How many times a child has cried during the day

Time	Area	Observation of behaviour
9:05	Painting area	Tom cries when Mum kissed him and left
10:45	Outside	Tom and Gabby are putting the wooden blocks into a tray. Tom wants to carry them but Gabby wants to carry them, too. Gabby takes the tray and Tom cries.
11:21	Inside: snack time	Tom wants to stay outside. He gets very upset, tries to take the door keys, cries and throws toys onto the floor.
12:30	Story time	He sits down and asks for a story to be read. A 'key person' asks him to wait his turn; he cries.

Digital media techniques

This is one of the most popular techniques and is widely used in early years settings. The variety of methods adds another dimension to the observations recorded, as they provide the visual and auditory aspects that written observations cannot offer. This technique can be used both by the practitioners taking photos or videos of the children's activities or work, as well as by the children taking photos or making their own videos of their environment and what they perceive they have found, done or learned (see Clark and Moss, 2001).

Extend your knowledge

Study Clark, A. and Moss, P. (2001) *Listening to Young Children: The Mosaic approach*, London: National Children's Bureau.

■ How have digital media been used in the Mosaic approach?
■ Reflect on your own early years practice. How do you use the digital media techniques?
■ In what ways could children participate? How will you rate the children's participation?
■ How do the children's observations match yours?
■ How do you take the children's observations into account when you write their developmental profile?

It is important to stress that when using digital techniques, we need to consider that, for some children and early years practitioners, photographs or videos may make the observation seem intrusive because the subjects might object to being photographed or videoed. Such observation also eliminates the anonymity and confidentiality factors and might affect behaviour as spontaneity might be lost. It is worth mentioning that using digital media for observation serves as a representation of a narrative. We cannot ignore the fact that the digital media illustrate a narrative sequence: their interpretation is subject to individual experience. Pink (2007) addresses this in the following extract:

> Visual research methods [in our case visual observation techniques] are not purely visual. Rather they pay a particular attention to visual aspects of culture. Similarly, they cannot be used independently of other methods; neither a purely visual ethnography nor an exclusively visual approach to culture exists.

> (Pink, 2007: 21 *cited in* Palaiologou, 2012a: 82)

When you attempt to use photographs or videos, it must be borne in mind that these photographs or videos convey meanings that need to be analysed, in a similar way to all other observation techniques.

Unfortunately, since the serious case review of the nursery in Plymouth, many early years settings have become worried about issues of safeguarding and changed their policies and procedures in favour of not allowing or using digital equipment. However, you might wish to rethink your practice, because a rich amount of information about children's learning and development can be gathered by using digital observation techniques. For good practice examples see Chapter 14.

Unstructured observation or participant observation

These observations are part of the daily routine of the early years setting. The observations will be recorded when the practitioners are working directly with children. Unstructured observations tend to be brief comments (snapshots) composed in the present tense as they capture what happens at a given moment. In a typically busy day the practitioners need to be well organised: they have with them prepared forms for when they want to observe an incident as it occurs. This obviously speeds up the recording process, facilitates the filing of recordings and, when the recordings are revisited, makes the retrieval and interpretation of the full information much easier.

> Name of the observer: ....
> Name of the child: ....
> Date of observation: ....
> Starting time: .... Finishing time: ....
> No of adults present: ....
> Description of the activity observed: ....
> Additional comments: ....
> I think: ....
> ....
> ....
> ....
>
> (IN THIS SECTION YOU ADD YOUR THOUGHTS AS THEY OCCUR DURING THE OBSERVATION, SINCE THEY MIGHT LATER HELP YOU TO INTERPRET YOUR RECORDINGS)
>
> **NOTE:** IT MAY BE HELPFUL TO CREATE IN-TRAYS IN WHICH TO CATEGORISE AND ORGANISE YOUR OBSERVATIONS SHEETS.

Figure 10.2 Example format for unstructured observation (adapted from Palaiologou, 2012a)

Self-observation

Another way for practitioners to observe their own practice is systematic self-observation. Systematic self-observation aims to capture the everyday life of individuals. It involves noting a selected feature of your own everyday experience, for example how you interact with parents during the arrival time of children, how you react when children are outdoors, or how you react when you try to resolve an argument among children. This is a very helpful way of evaluating and monitoring your own practice and reflecting on your actions (Schön, 1983 and 1987), as discussed in Chapter 2 about reflective practice.

In your setting, the steps to follow when implementing systematic self-observation can be translated into the following questions and agreements:

- What are the situations, behaviours or aspects of daily life in the setting which it is important to gain an understanding of?
- What explanations have you formulated for the focus of the self-observation?
- Who is going to participate in the self-observation? Is the team involved?
- Is everybody involved clear about the objectives, or do they need to be guided in order to use a similar approach? It may be that those involved need to be guided in order to use a similar approach that has clear objectives.
- Agree that everybody involved in the self-observation will be reliable, consistent and accurate in the aspect to be observed.
- Agree the ways in which all participants will record and report their observations.
- Have some trials first and evaluate and modify as suitable. You might like to use one of the reflective models (Gibbs, 1998; Kolb, 1984) as discussed in Chapter 2.

There are different ways to record self-observations, such as diaries or digital media (digital voice recorder or digital video). The most common methods of self-observation may be periodical (for example, every two hours) or at a given frequency of selected everyday events, whether specifically targeted at sampling a particular practical activity during your day, or event related – as and when an event happens, you record your reactions.

Systematic self-observation is a requirement of early years settings (DfE, 2012a). It involves the observation of selected aspects of practitioners' own everyday experience and practice, as can be demonstrated by Learning Walks (see page 216 above). This is frequently asked of students when they create their portfolios and of practitioners while they are collecting evidence through which their performance may be evaluated.

It is a useful tool for early years practitioners when they wish to gain an in-depth understanding of their practice within the everyday life of their setting. It is a tool that can be applied to a number of different situations that arise in early years settings. An in-depth understanding is essential for reflecting and evaluating on practice. By doing this, we can give better provision for the children whom we care for and educate in the setting.

The role of the observer

There is a wide range of literature regarding the role of the observer in research (Junker, 1960; Rodriguez and Ryave, 2002; Gillham, 2008; Plowright, 2011). The relevant key trends in the research categorise observers as participant and non-participant observers, depending on the type of observation and the involvement of the observer. The literature discusses the emotional involvement of the researcher, the physical distance from the participants involved in an observed activity, the setting – whether it be naturalistic or laboratory, real-life activities, locations, the objectivity versus the subjectivity of the researcher, as well as the prior knowledge of the researcher of the observable event, the activity and the participant.

However, when observation is used in early years settings, the people performing the observations are usually the early years practitioners. The EYFS guidance clearly states: 'Observe children as they act in their play, everyday activities and planned activities, and learn from parents about what the child does at home' (Early Learning, 2012: 3) . This needs, evidently, to be implemented by the early years practitioners. The Statutory Framework (DfE, 2012a: 10) states unequivocally that each assessment 'involves practitioners observing children to understand their level of achievements, interests and learning styles, and then [to] shape learning experiences for each child reflecting those observations'.

In early years practice the observations, although taken from the field of research, are slightly different. One can claim that early years observations constitute a research tool in the hands of the early years practitioners, as indeed they do. In that sense the issues around observation and observer are essentially the same. The main difference lies in the fact that the observer in early years practice is not emotionally detached; consequently, the observers are participating in the activities they are observing, as they are part of the daily life of the setting.

This can be a key advantage, as the observers have a very good knowledge of the whole picture of the activity, and not only of the instance they observe. While this may be a great advantage, it may at the same time be a disadvantage: the observers, because of their knowledge of the whole picture, might arrive at conclusions that are derived not from valid explanations of the observation but from prior knowledge – which may not be a completely accurate interpretation of one individual event. To reduce bias and subjectivity in your observations you can ask team members to undertake observations of the same child and situation parallel to your observation, and compare notes on what you have observed and how you have interpreted your observations. Reflective peer discussions are vital to your own professional development and enhancement of quality childcare provision.

In early years practice the observer is a full participant and the observations are taking place in a naturalistic environment. As a result, the observer could find it difficult or even impossible to maintain emotional distance from what is observed.

The following paragraphs discuss the role of the observer in terms of participant, non-participant and self-observations, the three key aspects of the role adopted by early years practitioners in the settings.

The role of the observer and analysis of observations

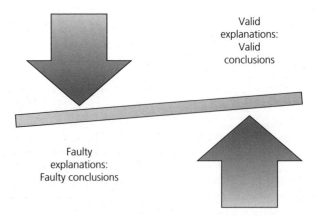

Figure 10.3 Analysis of observations

Once you have recorded all your observations and comments, it is necessary to make sense of what you have collected. The process of analysing requires taking all the pieces of information you have collected and putting them together in order to form a holistic picture of the child's progress or your own practice. You need to take all your observations and start arriving at explanations. There are two types of explanations (as illustrated in Figure 10.3): valid explanations are possible explanations based on the observations recorded, while faulty explanations are possible explanations based on personal opinions. If faulty explanations arise, there is an unbalanced understanding of the children and the early years practice; this results in the aims and objectives of the observation not being met. It is thus important to use a number of different observation techniques to ensure that there is supporting information and you do not rely only on one method. It is equally important to compare the observations recorded with the systematic self-observation of the practitioners and with the observations of colleagues as suggested earlier. That way you may accumulate rich information in order to meet the planned aims and objectives of the observation.

As mentioned above, the knowledge that practitioners have about the children will help them to understand the children very well; however, when they are in the role of observer, this knowledge may mislead the practitioners in their analyses of observations recorded. It is therefore very important for all of the team to be involved in the analysis process – as well as the parents and, if the age of the children allows, the children themselves.

Scenario

Study the following observations and try to extract some valid explanations, based on what these observations have captured and what actually happened.

Observation 1

Child's name	George
Date	15 March
Name of the observer	Liz
Starting time	10:15
Finishing time	10:25
No. of adults present	None
No. of other children present	Two
Area of observation	Outdoors: free play
Description of activity observed	George is in the sand area with two other children. George uses a scoop to fill a pot with sand; he continues filling up the pot. 'Bigger, bigger, bigger,' he says as he fills it. 'Wet sand,' he says as he digs deeper in the sand to where it is wet. The pot is nearly full. George adds more sand by gently using his fingertips, sprinkling it on top. Watching it fall on the top, Tom says to him: 'You make a monster.' George says: 'No, I baby monster, grrr.' George puts some people (toys) on top of his pot of sand; Tom tries to take it. 'No, stop it,' says George, very clearly. 'I don't like it.' He pulls the pot closer and holds it tight. George takes an empty pot and he continues filling the pot with sand on his own.
Additional comments (*I think…*)	'Bigger' demonstrates a beginning of an understanding of mathematical language Engage in activity requiring hand–eye coordination Use one-handed tools and equipment

Observation 2

Child's name	George
Date	17 March
Name of the observer	Liz
Starting time	10:15
Finishing time	10:25
No. of adults present	None
No. of other children present	None
Area of observation	Indoors: free play
Description of activity observed	George picks up the puzzle with the numbers and begins to make the numbered (1–9) crocodile puzzle. 'I make crocodile.' He tries again: 'I make a crocodile.' Picks up no. 2 and puts it in no. 1. 'I doing this number.' This number (picks up no. 6) does not fit. He tries it in another place (head of crocodile). 'I cannot do it,' he points and says correctly 'This is 1, 2, 6, 7', right to left. Keeps trying other pieces, moving them around to try and get them to fit. He slowly puts the puzzle together, not talking, but looking at the pieces and trying to fit them in the right places. He finishes the puzzle. 'I done it, long crocodile, sharp teeth, grrrr,' he says, looking at the puzzle (*which is completed correctly*).
Additional comments (*I think…*)	George was very involved in the puzzle; he was concentrating fully. Beginning to recognise numbers Enjoying engaging in activities that require hand–eye coordination

Observation 3

Child's name	George
Date	20 March
Name of the observer	Liz
Starting time	10:05
Finishing time	10:15
No. of adults present	None
No. of other children present	Three
Area of observation	Outdoors

Description of activity observed	George is outside with Tom, Mary and Francis.
	They go to the slide on the climbing frame and George says 'big boat' (*I think that they pretend the slide is a boat*). 'Come on, let's go beach,' George shouts as he climbs up. The other three join him. 'Come on, everybody, it is a rocket to seaside.'
	'I found a shark,' he says. Very excited/animated he watches the faces of the other children.
	Francis asks, 'Where?'
	'Going to spider's man's house. Me still going to seaside, who wants to come on the boat?'
	Tom: 'Me.'
	Francis runs to sand area.
	George: 'Francis, come back, we go … go to the beach. Let's go: 5, 4, 2, 1.' He jumps off the slide, hops over the top and runs to the sand area, looking back to see whether the others are following him.
Additional comments (*I think…*)	Plays alongside and with other children
	Jumps off slide confidently
	Uses numbers to count backwards

Observation 4

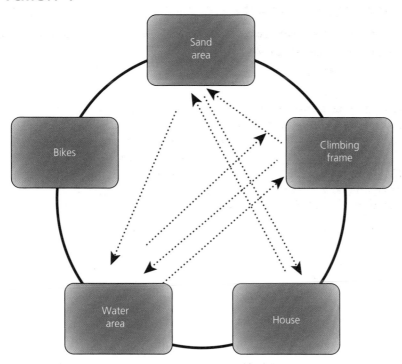

Figure 10.4 Tracking: How George spends time when outside (observation over a period of 30 minutes)

From the observations above, can you make any links with the prime areas of learning and development of the EYFS? Try to complete the following table:

Prime areas of learning	Aspects	Your comments
Personal, social and emotional development	Making relationships Self-confidence and self-awareness Managing feelings	
Physical development	Moving and handling Health and self-care	
Communication and language	Listening and attention Understanding Speaking	
Child's involvement	Very high High Medium Low No involvement	
What next?		

Table 10.4 Prime areas of learning for George

Documenting observations

There are a number of different ways of documenting the findings of the observations recorded. One of the most popular approaches is through learning stories. Carr (1998, 1999 and 2001) introduced the learning stories as a means of ongoing observation and assessment in early years in New Zealand. This process reflects the principles of the Te Whāriki curriculum in New Zealand.

Learning stories (or learning journeys, as they are known in the EYFS) aim to document the learning experiences of children in their daily lives, in the children's own words. Practitioners gather information (stories) over time for either a single child or for a group of children, so that learning story becomes a way into understanding children's development. The learning stories inform planning, help early years practitioners to share information with the parents and, most importantly, become a useful tool through which to discuss this planning with the children.

Example from a learning journey: trying my first steps

I am ready to crawl

... and now I am doing it!

Figure 10.5 and Figure 10.6 Crawling off a step

Extend your knowledge

Read and research further about learning journeys and consider how you can use them in your practice:
- Carr, M. (1999) *Learning and Teaching Stories: New Approaches to Assessment and Evaluation* [online]. Available from: http://www.aare.edu.au/99pap/pod99298.htm.

Capturing children's experiences

Similar to learning stories, introduced by the Te Whāriki curriculum in New Zealand and Margaret Carr, Reggio Emilia in Italy has demonstrated an alternative and flexible pedagogical approach within early years education. Central to the philosophy of Reggio Emilia is the engagement of children, parents and teachers. They all work together through a variety of activities, with the main emphasis on arts and creativity. The Reggio Emilia philosophy is concerned with how children's progress may be assessed through their attempts to explore the world. They have introduced an innovative way of documenting observation recordings: the pedagogical documentation.

The Reggio Emilia method makes full use of digital technologies (photographs, videos and audio recordings) and notes to observe children's daily life. The teachers, with the children and the parents equally involved, make the information collected available through exhibitions and displays. This way, all the information about the children's activities is visibly communicated, allowing everyone to review the observations as and when they wish, in order to assess and evaluate their children's activities and progress.

In England, a similar approach to pedagogical documentation and learning stories was developed by Clark and Moss (2001), known as the Mosaic approach. Within this approach the emphasis was on children's participation in observations. The researchers used photographs and videos as an observation tool and introduced the creation of portfolios as a way of documenting the observations recorded. The children themselves take photos of their environment and their areas of interest. In this way, it is not only the adult who observes and documents learning and development, but children themselves (see Chapter 3 of this book).

In early years practice there are a number of creative approaches to how to document recorded observations. These range from visual portfolios that include photo sequences, through child profiles, to children's books designed with children where the practitioners have helped them to write notes. The most important factor is that, when documenting recorded observations, these reports need to be:

- consistent
- understood by all – children, parents and the team
- accessible to all concerned
- useful and practical in their application
- linked into curriculum practices.

The documentation of recorded observations exists to make the growing archive of material available to the children, the parents – and, according to the EYFS (DfE, 2012a), to other professionals if required. This final step in the observation process is significant because, through the documentation of the recorded observations, early years practitioners should expect to return to the planned aims and objectives of the observation. They must investigate whether the aims and objectives of each session were indeed met, and determine the ways in which a particular observation was successful or otherwise. Such knowledge and understanding form the foundations for planning ways forward.

As is illustrated in Figure 10.7, planning observation is an ongoing process. The aims and objectives are the starting, the ending and the restarting points. Reflecting upon the past in order to refine future plans is continuous in early years practice, similar to Kolb's model of reflection (1984).

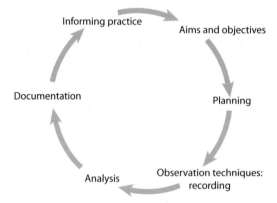

Figure 10.7 The continuous observation process in early years practice

Ethical implications

Ethical considerations are an essential part of the observation process. As observation by its very nature captures what actually happens, observing can intrude into children's lives. For example, when children are playing on their own, we need to consider whether we have the right to capture their private dialogues. It is common practice in early years settings to request parents' permission to observe children using a variety of methods, yet the early years practitioners need to perceive the observation process as a potential problem area with regard to any ethical implications there might be.

There is a need to move beyond merely obtaining the consent of the parents towards discussing the ethical aspects of the observation process with the whole team, the children and the parents.

Ethical practice in your observations is concerned with key questions about the responsible exercise of judgement on the part of early years practitioners, who have to reflect on issues concerning the nature of the observations. It is always essential to question the aims and objectives of your observations, and to what extent observation forms a key element of your practice, rather than just being conducted routinely because it is a policy requirement. All observations that take place in an early years setting should be based on valid reasons. There are questions about whether we should observe certain activities. Children's welfare and development, or any safeguarding concerns, should be the absolute priority in early years practice.

Key questions to ask are whether the observation is needed and why; questions should be underpinned with respect for all those involved in the process. Constant dialogue and discussion with all involved are necessary for ethical practice when we carry out observation in early years settings.

We should not forget that:

> **Children are likely to see the adults as the authoritative figure as in their role they are the ones who create the environments, the ones who set the rules, organise their daily programme and the ones who are responsible for them.**

> (Palaiologou, 2012b: 39)

The power held by the adults should not be underestimated when planning observations.

There is also the issue of accountability. We do encourage and promote children's participation in all daily activities involving them; however, early years practitioners hold a great degree of accountability in terms of what children do and how children spend their day. This accountability is to the children, to the parents, to the other team members and to the community.

When choosing observation methods, a connection must be made between the aim of the observation and the methods chosen. All methods are helpful if the aim of the observation is clear. As mentioned throughout the chapter, observation in early years practice is a process that involves planning, recording, analysis, documentation and sharing information. The teams in the early years settings are responsible for deciding how the observation process is going to be implemented in their settings. They should also ensure that they have considered the ethical issues, including the key question of whether the observation process is reflecting the causality among children's interests, as well as questions around the observation methods chosen, the ways early years practitioners are sharing information, and the programme delivery within the setting. Ethical practice is concerned with the context in which the observations take place. Observation is determined not by the methods employed to collect the information about children, but by the ethical implications of the nature of the use of those observations. Ethical implications go beyond the traditional ways of simply ensuring consent and children's participation; they concern respecting the children's, parents' and practitioners' actions, emotions, dignity and privacy, as well as the 'autonomy and freedom to have opinions on all matters affecting them and these to be given due weight' (Palaiologou, 2012b: 39).

Reflective task

How do you overcome these potential ethical dilemmas? Discuss with your fellow students and your team in your setting.

Limitations of observation

Although observation is a valid tool in early years practice, it is important to identify and acknowledge the limitations of observation. By definition observations capture what is actually happening, and one of the key issues is that observers may have different perceptions of what they see. Due to our respective experiences, emotions and different levels of qualifications, for example, each individual may see things differently and arrive at different conclusions or explanations.

Another limitation of observation is that the emotions of the actions observed might be lost. Although observation results in a record of what actually happens, there is nevertheless the risk that the context, the history of how we arrived at the event being observed, influences the perceptions. It is important in recording observations to acknowledge these issues, and for these reasons to use more than one method of observation in practice. Also, a rigorous plan of the observation process, in which this limitation is addressed, must be thought through in advance of carrying out the process.

Reflective task

Critically reflect on the observation process you use in your setting and try to identify whether it has any limitations, and what these might be.
- Have you considered ways to minimise or eliminate these limitations?
- Have you considered the emotions of the children, parents and staff who are involved?
- Have you considered whether a sufficiently wide variety of methods is used to collect rich information on the everyday life of your setting?

Conclusion

This chapter has explored the role of observation in early years practice. It began by discussing the historical origins of observation, and the fact that observation is a research tool transferred into early years practice as a valid pedagogical tool. In early years practice there is a need for the systematic collection of information in order to assess children's development and learning, as well as to inform the creation and refinement of our learning environment.

The importance of observation was emphasised and this was extended to the importance of planning for observation. Observation planning involves aims and objectives, observation techniques, including ways of recording, analysis and documentation. All of these aspects of the observation process are directly relevant for effective practice in early years settings. Through the findings and information gained from the observation process, the early years practitioners and setting are able to:
- further inform practice
- continuously refine and meet the perceived needs of the setting
- communicate with children, parents and the team effectively
- achieve the outcomes set for the early years setting
- meet the statutory requirements of the EYFS.

Evaluate your...

Practice

Consider the observation practices you use in your early years setting:

■ What methods do you use to observe children?

■ Are all members of staff enabled in the observation process?

■ What observation process(es) do you have in place?

■ How do you involve children in the observation process?

■ How do you involve parents in the observation process?

■ How do you link recorded observations with the EYFS Profile?

■ How do you link recorded observations with EYFS learning and developmental areas?

■ How do you use the documentation resulting from your observation to provide a focus for discussion and the development of your practice?

■ How do you use the documentation resulting from your observation to provide opportunities for collaboration with parents and other services?

■ What collaborative observation do you have in place?

■ How do you use the collaborative observations to inform your practice? Are all staff involved?

■ Make a SWOT analysis to help you identify which areas you are good at (strengths), areas of improvement (weaknesses), and what opportunities and potential threats or barriers there are.

Further reading

Clark, A. and Moss, P. (2001) *Listening to Young Children: The Mosaic approach*, London: National Children's Bureau.

Clark, A., Kjørholt, A. and Moss, P. (eds.) (2005) *Beyond Listening: Children's Perspectives on Early Childhood Services*, Bristol: Policy Press.

Gillham, B. (2008) *Observation Techniques: Structured to Unstructured*, London: Continuum.

Luff, P. (2012) 'Observations: Recording and analysis in Early Years Foundation Stage', in I. Palaiologou (ed.) (2012) *Early Years Foundation Stage: Theory and Practice* (2nd edn), London: SAGE.

Palaiologou, I. (2012) *Child Observation for the Early Years* (2nd edn), Exeter: Learning Matters.

Papatheodorou, T., Luff, P. and Gill, J. (2011) *Child Observation for Learning and Research*, Harlow: Pearson Education.

Plowright, D. (2011) *Using Mixed Methods: Frameworks for an Integrated Methodology*, London: Sage.

Podmore, V. N. and Luff, P. (2011) *Observation*, Maidenhead: Open University Press.

Riddall-Leech, S. (2008) *How to Observe Children* (2nd edn), Oxford: Heinemann Educational Publishers.

Rodriguez, N. and Ryave, A. (2002) *Systematic Self-observation*, London: Sage.

Salaman, A. and Tutchell, S. (2005) *Planning Educational Visits for the Early Years*, London: Sage.

Smidt, S. (2005) *Observing, Assessing and Planning for Children in the Early Years*, London: Routledge.

Equality and inclusion
Penny Mukherji

Introduction

All children and adults have the right to live in a society where there are equity and respect for diversity. Children's rights are to be respected 'without discrimination of any kind, irrespective of the child's or his or her parent's or legal guardian's race, colour, sex, language, religion, political or other opinion, national, ethnic or social origin, property, disability, birth or other status' (Article 2, United Nations *Convention on the Rights of the Child*, 1989).

In this chapter we will be looking at the impact of inequality on young children and we will investigate the role that good-quality, inclusive early childhood care and education play in promoting equality and improving the life chances of children. We shall explore how prejudice and racism can lead to discrimination and we will investigate ways in which settings can celebrate diversity.

Learning outcomes

In this chapter we will:

- Investigate what are meant by 'equality' and 'diversity'.
- Explore the concept of inclusion for children in early childhood settings.
- Discuss how early childhood practitioners can celebrate and manage diversity.
- Discuss ways in which early childhood practitioners can tackle prejudice.
- Describe how poverty has an adverse effect on children's life chances and the role of early years provision.
- Suggest ways in which practitioners can evaluate their practice.

What do we mean by 'equality'?

We live in a world where the life chances of individuals depend, not upon individual effort, but upon the part of the world and the circumstances into which they have been born and the characteristics of their family.

Reflective task

Consider these four children, all born on the same day.

■ Rani, born into a family of agricultural labourers in rural India. The family are not literate.

■ Thomas, born into a Polish family, newly arrived in the UK. At six months old, he was diagnosed with cerebral palsy. Both parents are university graduates, but are working in manual occupations in the UK, while they learn English.

■ Brad, born into a British family living in a local authority housing estate in inner London. No one in his family has been in paid employment for two generations. Both parents dropped out of school at fifteen.

■ Uchenna, born into a wealthy British African family, where both parents are medical practitioners. There is great emphasis placed on education in the family.

How might the circumstances into which they are born affect their future life chances?

You will probably have made a list of many factors that could affect the lives of these children. Factors could include whether the child was born in the majority or minority world, the child's gender, race, social class, the economic position of the family, the educational background and aspirations of parents, and the presence or absence of disability.

For early childhood practitioners 'equality' entails valuing all children as individuals, recognising that children have individual needs and that their rights as individuals need to be respected and upheld. Occasionally the word 'equality' causes confusion because it could be thought that it means that everyone should be treated in the same way. This is not the case as, although the concept of 'equality' encompasses an understanding that children and families should be treated fairly and that services should be accessible to all, it is acknowledged that individuals are all very different from one another and will have diverse and different needs. Within this definition of equality is an understanding that diversity should be not only be acknowledged, but should be respected and valued.

Equality of opportunity and anti-discriminatory practice are a key tenant of the Early Years Foundation Stage (EYFS) (DfE, 2012a: 2), where they are defined as 'ensuring that every child is included and supported'.

Reflective task

At the end of the Foundation Stage, children are observed and assessed to produce a profile that sums up their progress and learning needs. By analysing the results of children across the country it is possible to determine which groups of children may not be progressing as well as the majority of children of their age.

Look at the following report: *Early Years Foundation Stage Profile Attainment by Pupil Characteristics* (DfE, 2011c).

1 What do the statistics tell us about the achievement of children according to:
   – gender
   – ethnicity
   – eligibility for free school meals
   – special educational needs?
2 Explain the relationship between social inequality and children's achievement.

That certain groups of children achieve better within our care and educational system is an ongoing concern. In 2010 Coghlan *et al.* undertook a review of the literature and identified factors that had a positive impact on children's outcomes and those that had a negative impact.

Children do better when:

■ there is a positive home learning environment; the educational level of the mother was very powerful in predicting success
■ they have the opportunity to attend some sort of preschool provision
■ the quality of the preschool provision is high.

These findings have been supported by the Effective Provision of Pre-School Education (EPPE) study (Sylva *et al.*, 2004, 2010) as well as by research into the home learning environment by Siraj-Blatchford and Siraj-Blatchford (2010).

The review by Coghlan *et al.* (2010) found that children do less well when they are raised in poverty, or have English as an additional language (EAL), although the EAL effect disappears by the age of seven as children become competent English users.

Extend your knowledge

Both of these documents look at social inequality and the benefits of early intervention. What evidence is there that early childhood services have a positive impact on the life chances of children from disadvantaged backgrounds?

■ Allen, G. (2011) *Early Intervention: The Next Steps. An Independent Report to Her Majesty's Government,* London: HM Government. Available from: http://www.dwp.gov.uk/docs/early-intervention-next-steps.pdf.
■ Field, F. (2010) *The Foundation Years: preventing poor children becoming poor adults. The report of the Independent Review on Poverty and Life Chances,* London: HM Government. Available from: http://www.nfm.org.uk/component/jdownloads/finish/74/333.

Special educational needs and disability

There is sometimes confusion as to what is meant by a child who has a 'special educational need' or who has a 'disability'. The term 'special' is confusing because all children are 'special' in one way or another, and all have specific and different learning needs. There are, however, certain legal or accepted definitions. The following definition for children with special educational needs comes from the Department for Education and Skills 2001 Code of practice (DfES, 2001: 11):

Children have special educational needs if they have a learning difficulty which calls for special educational provision to be made for them. Children have a learning difficulty if they:

(a) have a significantly greater difficulty in learning than the majority of children of the same age; or

(b) have a disability which prevents or hinders them from making use of educational facilities of a kind generally provided for children of the same age in schools within the area of the local education authority

(c) are under compulsory school age and fall within the definition at (a) or (b) above or would so do if special educational provision was not made for them.

Under the 2010 Equality Act (para 4) a person has a disability if 'they have a physical or mental impairment' and 'the impairment has a substantial and long-term adverse effect on their ability to perform normal day-to-day activities'.

It should be noted that not all children who have a disability would be considered to have a special educational need; for example, a child may use a wheelchair, but, as long as there was access, this would not hinder his or her learning.

Incidence

Overall approximately 20 per cent of children have a special educational need, either segmented or in the process of being assessed. In 2011 there were 9,675 children in England under the age of five with a statement of special educational need (DfE, 2011a).

Next steps

If you are working in an early years setting find out:
- How many children have been identified, or are in the process of being identified, as having a special educational need or a disability?
- In what ways do the children need support (i.e. language delay, learning difficulty etc.)?
- How many of these children have a statement of special educational need?

Extend your knowledge

In 2011 the DfE published a Green Paper outlining proposed changes to the assessment and provision for children with special educational needs or disabilities. Within this paper it was identified that the numbers of children, without statements, identified as having special educational needs had risen from 10 per cent in 1995 to 18.5 per cent in 2010 (DfE, 2011b). What could be the possible reasons for this? The Green Paper can be found at the following website (you will find page 20 helpful):
- https://www.education.gov.uk/publications/eOrderingDownload/Green-Paper-SEN.pdf

Historical background

Before industrialisation, most people worked on the land and the need for a formal education was less important than it is today. Thus children who would be considered to have a special educational need today faced few barriers. It was only with the growing need for an educated, literate workforce that the concept of 'special educational need' arose.

Gradually the awareness that some children needed specialist support was recognised and by the 1970s there was a complex arrangement of separate special schools for children with learning difficulties. Parallel to this was separate provision for children with chronic illnesses or physical disabilities. Often such provision was residential. However, although there was much good practice and undoubted expertise in meeting the needs of these children, there was a growing awareness that separate provision for children with special educational needs and disability was a form of discrimination.

In 1978 Baroness Warnock reviewed provision and her recommendations, contained in what is commonly known as the Warnock Report (Department of Education and Science, 1978), included the following (summarised by Joshi and Mukherji, 2005):

1 Children should be integrated into mainstream schooling as far as possible.
2 Parents should be more involved in consultation and decision making.
3 A multi-professional assessment of children's needs should be undertaken as soon as possible and reviewed annually.
4 Families of children under five should be given a named person such as a health visitor or a social worker to support the family.

The Education Act 1981 gave Local Education Authorities (LEAs) statutory responsibility to meet children's learning needs by arranging special provision and stated this should be provided for children, as far as possible, within mainstream provision. The Act also introduced the process of 'statementing' whereby children would be assessed by multidisciplinary teams and a legally binding statement drawn up, which would include details about how the LEA would meet the children's needs (Joshi and Mukherji, 2005). The Act also made provision for parental views to be taken into account when decisions were being made about children. The Children Act 1989 (section 17) consolidated the duty for local authorities to assess children with disabilities and provide services so that they have the opportunity to develop as well as children without disabilities. The duty to work in partnership with parents and other agencies to support children was also outlined in the Children Act 1989.

Present-day legislation

In 2001 the Special Educational Needs Code of Practice (DfES, 2001) was introduced which included a section on the identification, assessment and provision of special educational needs in early years settings.

Next steps

If you are employed or have a placement in an early years setting find out:

- Who is your Special Educational Needs Coordinator (SENCO)?
- What do her/his responsibilities include?
- What procedures are set in motion if a practitioner or parent has concerns about a particular child, including the drawing up of Individual Education Plans and the system put in place for reviewing children's progress?
- If the setting has recourse to outside professionals, who can help/advise?
- Does the SENCO feel that there is sufficient support for children, parents and practitioners if there are concerns about a child's progress?

Although many parents and practitioners have found the procedures set out in the Special Educational Needs Code of Practice (DfES, 2001) to be helpful and supportive, there have been growing concerns about the system. Parents often find the process bureaucratic, bewildering and difficult to access. Some parents feel that they have to fight for provision for their children and do not feel that their children are sufficiently supported at school (Evans, 2011). In response to some of these concerns the government issued a Green Paper (DfE, 2011b), outlining a radical overhaul in the way that children with special educational needs and disabilities are to be assessed and supported. From 2014, there is to be a single, birth-to-25 assessment process and a single education, health and care plan. In addition parents in England are to be given control over their children's special educational needs budgets, allowing them to choose expert support rather than local authorities being the sole provider (DfE, 2012b).

Parallel to legislation and guidance about provision for children with special educational needs, there have been developments in the legislation surrounding individuals with disabilities. In 1995 the Disability Discrimination Act (DDA) was passed that related to employment and the provision of services. In 2001 the Special Educational Needs and Disability Act extended the coverage of the DDA to education. Since the act was implemented in 2002 it has been against the law to discriminate against disabled children in the provision of services. Stobbs (2008: 9) highlighted two key duties: that disabled children should not be treated 'less favourably', and that 'reasonable adjustments' for disabled children should be made.

The Disability Discrimination Act 2005 was further extended to include services and provision commissioned by local authorities from other agencies, for example where private companies run provision for children's centres or out-of-hours provision run by private or voluntary organisations. Furthermore, the Equality Act 2012 requires all employers to have policies and procedures in place to act on any form of discrimination and promote equality in their provision.

The inclusion debate

By the time that Warnock was looking into the provision for children with special needs and disabilities in the 1970s there was already a groundswell of opinion that they should be educated with their peers rather than in separate specialist facilities. At first this was accomplished by accommodating children with special needs within mainstream provision, but educating them apart from their peers for part of the day. This was known as integration.

True inclusion involves children being taught in the same class as their peers, experiencing the full curriculum. Instead of the focus being on the child to try and adapt to the needs of the setting, inclusion implies a willingness of the setting to adapt to the needs of the child.

There have, however, always been voices raised against the assumption that all children 'do better' included in mainstream provision. Indeed Mary Warnock herself declared that the policy of inclusion could harm some pupils. She acknowledged that in early years settings and primary school most children can be successfully included, but that in secondary schools, as children move into adolescence, difference is less well tolerated and some children can find themselves excluded from friendship groups (Warnock, 2005). In addition it has been claimed that the policy of inclusion has led to increasing numbers of pupil exclusions (Leslie and Skidmore, 2008) and to some children being less prepared to face adult life (Joshi and Mukherji, 2005).

The debate is a complex one; at its heart is our understanding of the concept of inclusion and our understanding of what is best for each individual child. Sadly, in times of economic austerity, another factor has to be taken into account: the resources available to support individual children, train practitioners and modify settings.

The wider context of inclusion

So far we have taken 'inclusion' to be a concept relating to children with special educational needs and disabilities. Nowadays we use the term 'inclusive education' to mean the provision of a framework which encompasses and values all children, regardless of their background and circumstances.

In this definition it is clear that 'inclusion' is a process rather than a 'state', one that, according to the Early Childhood Forum (2003), includes the processes of identification, understanding and removing barriers to full participation and belonging.

It is some of these processes that we will be discussing later in this chapter when we look at other groups of children who are often marginalised, or whose needs are frequently overlooked.

Reflective task

Reflect and take stock of how inclusive your early years provision is for children, their parents/carers and your staff team. Make a SWOT analysis to help you identify the areas you are good at (strengths) and the areas of improvement (weaknesses), and look for opportunities for, and potential threats or barriers to, inclusion.

Adults' attitudes affect the way children learn

Jensen (2009) undertook research with early years practitioners in Denmark. The findings appear to indicate that some early years practitioners hold a deficit model about 'socially endangered children', that is:

> ... children that are at risk of being in or being placed in a vulnerable position, personally, socially and societally, as a consequence of being brought up in families marked by poverty and other vulnerable living conditions, and as a consequence of how they are greeted from a very early age by society's children's institutions.
>
> (Jensen, 2009: 18)

Holding a deficit model may lead us to expect that some children will progress less well in educational settings than others, expectations that may be based on our past experiences and the realities that many of these children perform poorly in the Foundation Stage Profile. Our negative expectations can lead to self-fulfilling prophesies.

Classic research

The Pygmalion effect or the power of the self-fulfilling prophecy

In 1968 Rosenthal and Jacobson (cited in Brain and Mukherji, 2005) looked at the effect of teachers' expectations on pupils' performance. At the beginning of a school year they tested the IQ of primary school-aged children. They informed teachers that they had identified 20 children who would make remarkable progress during the coming academic year. At the end of the school year the children's IQ was retested and the children predicted to make remarkable progress had, indeed, achieved greater gains in IQ than the other children.

It was then revealed to the teachers that the children predicted to progress well had been chosen completely at random. *There should have been no difference in the way these children progressed when compared to the rest of the class.* It seems that the teachers must have treated these children differently (Brain and Mukherji, 2005).

The study shows us that our preconceived ideas, or stereotypes, about certain children can have a powerful effect on both our expectations and our treatment of those children. In the same way that positive expectations can lead to positive outcomes, negative expectations can lead to negative outcomes (also known as self-fulfilling prophecies).

In the study we have just discussed, teachers were completely oblivious to the fact that they were treating the two groups of children differently. If this is so, how can we avoid our negative attitudes adversely affecting the children in our care? The most powerful tools we have are reflection and observation, as you will have read and learned about in some of the other chapters in this book. By observing children and reflecting upon our practice we can go a long way to identifying negative attitudes. There is, as well, a role for managers and leaders of early childhood settings: an environment of psychological safety needs to be established where individual practitioners can share experiences and observations with others, who can act as critical friends to aid self-reflection.

Scenario

It is September and the nursery teacher and early years practitioner are looking over the details of the new children about to start. They have worries about Darrell. On the home visit the first impression was that he was unable to focus very long on any activity and his language appeared delayed. This was hardly surprising, they thought, because the 52-inch TV was left on while they were there and Darrell's mother spent most of her time answering her mobile phone. Darrell's mother told them that his father had left shortly after Darrell's birth and that she found the boy's behaviour difficult to handle. The teacher and early years practitioner discuss their worries as experience has told them that Darrell will find learning a struggle.

- What factors may be operating in Darrell's life which may have a negative effect on his learning and development?
- How might the attitudes of the nursery staff affect his progress in nursery?
- What suggestions do you have for building an effective partnership with Darrell's mother?

Children's attitudes about themselves affect the way they learn

What children think about themselves will also have an effect upon their progress. As practitioners we need to be vigilant for children whose previous life experiences have led them to have negative expectations about their own abilities.

As children grow and develop they begin to form ideas about what they are like as people. This is sometimes referred to as the self-concept (Mukherji, 2001). If their self-concept is positive, that is they feel that they are loved, worthwhile and able to achieve what they want to achieve, then children are said to have high self-esteem. If they do not think very much of themselves and their abilities, as compared to others, or they think that they are not liked or are unlovable, then children are said to have low self-esteem (Brain and Mukherji, 2005).

Children's evaluations about themselves, either positive or negative, are influenced by their attachment experiences, as well as the social context in which they live. If children are cared for in an environment where they are loved and cherished for who they are, and if they are encouraged to take risks and those around them have high, but realistic, expectations of them, then these children are likely to feel positively about themselves. Conversely if children are neglected, feel unloved or are given negative messages about themselves and their abilities, they are likely to develop negative feelings about themselves.

It is not only close family or educational settings that influence children's evaluations of themselves. Children take their identity from the groups to which they perceive they belong. The first group that young children associate with is gender: are they a boy or a girl? Later on, they may categorise themselves according to their ethnic and cultural heritage, whether they are from a working-class family or from a professional family. In the same way that children's self-esteem is influenced by what others think of them as individuals, children's self-esteem is also influenced by what others think about the groups which they use to define their identity.

These factors all contribute to the way children think of their abilities as learners. Dweck (2010) calls the ideas that children hold about their learning capabilities as 'mindsets'. She suggests that children hold one of two different mindsets. Some children have 'fixed' mindsets, that is they believe that they have been born with a certain level of intelligence and that this is fixed throughout life. Other children have 'growth' mindsets where they believe that their level of intelligence is not fixed, but can grow over time. The different types of mindset characteristically lead to different sorts of learning behaviour. According to Dweck (2010) children with a *fixed mindset* value looking 'smart' and will not put themselves in situations where they may fail. Children with a *growth mindset* do not believe that their intelligence is fixed. They believe that their intelligence will grow over time and often relish challenges and even failure, as they can see opportunities to learn from these experiences.

Other groups

Gifted and talented children

The Department for Children, Schools and Families (DCSF, 2008f: 1) defines children as being gifted and talented if they have 'one or more abilities developed to a level significantly ahead of their year group (or with the potential to develop those abilities)'. This aspect of working with very young children has been relatively neglected (Walsh *et al.*, 2010). One possible reason may be that it is difficult to identify children with exceptional gifts and talents in early childhood. There is one indicator, however, that appears to identify gifted children and that is the unique way that some children use their creativity and imagination to make innovative connections in their learning (DCSF, 2010c).

At the beginning of the chapter it was noted that, by the time children are assessed for their Foundation Stage profile, certain groups of children seem to do less well than others. Children from poor families and vulnerable groups are already at a disadvantage. However, within this group are some children whose exceptional abilities are masked by socio-economic factors that have affected their development. It is the responsibility of all early years practitioners to be alert for such children and provide an environment that addresses barriers to development, provides access to experiences that will engage the children and provide opportunities to extend their learning (DCSF, 2010c).

Reflective task

Freeman (2002:2) identifies five major social barriers to achievement: 'political and social attitudes, poverty, gender, social disapproval and handicap [sic]'.

- In what ways may these five barriers have a negative impact on the achievement of children who are gifted and talented? Consider the community and families in which the children live, and the early childhood setting that they attend.
- In what ways can early childhood settings act to remove some of these barriers?

Addressing barriers and providing enriching experiences and opportunities are, of course, at the heart of what we provide (or should be providing) for all children – how is provision for gifted and talented children any different?

The answer to this is that what is good provision for children who are gifted and talented is good provision for all children. However, as we have seen, sometimes our expectations of what children can do or may be able to do in the future are clouded by our own preconceived ideas and negative attitudes about certain groups of children.

Dweck (2010) recommends that adults who support gifted and talented children in their learning should create a culture of risk-taking and identify children who are finding tasks easy and present them with new challenges. If children find a challenge difficult, Dweck (2010) suggests discussing the strategies they have used so far, helping them to identify why the strategy did not work and supporting them in thinking of new strategies they could try. Children should be helped to see how their strategies and hard work have led to improvement and it is this that should be praised, rather than a successful end result. Children should be praised for how they approach a task, for their persistence, motivation, the choices they make and the strategies they use. In particular older children can be encouraged to see that 'fast learning is not always the deepest learning' (Dweck, 2010: 17).

Reflective task

- How do you nurture and support children's self-image and self-esteem?
- Think about how and when you praise children in your setting.
- What strategies do you offer children to problem-solve and develop strategies to master tasks?
- How do you differentiate activities to suit individual children's needs and at the same time manage activities for groups of children?

Children from black and minority ethnic backgrounds (BME)

The population of the UK is ethnically very diverse, with about one in six of the population of England and Wales being non-white (Office for National Statistics, 2011). The term 'black and minority ethnic' (BME) is used to describe people from 'so-called' minority groups, who experience racism or who are in the minority because of their skin colour and/or ethnicity in the country they are living. Commonly, when using this term it is understood to include individuals who are Black African, Black Caribbean, Pakistani, Indian and mixed race (Ipsos MORI, 2005). However, in this chapter a widened definition will be used that includes all those who may be at risk of racism because of their ethnic background or their nationality. This will include those from Arab and Eastern European countries, from South Asia and China, and from any other European countries.

What are racism and discrimination?

Racist attitudes imply that it is possible to divide human beings into races and that some races are inherently superior to others. These attitudes lead to unequal treatment or discrimination towards members of those groups deemed to be inferior. There is a historical background to racism as it is generally accepted that racism is, at least in part, a product of colonialism where Britain and other white Western countries subjugated non-white populations in Asia and Africa. In more recent times, there has been a rise in racist attitudes towards Muslims because of conflict in places such as Afghanistan and fear of terrorist attacks.

Reflective task

In 1978 UNESCO adopted the Declaration on Race and Racial Prejudice (UNESCO, 1978). Look at the declaration and consider your own definition of 'racism' and 'racial prejudice':

- Take stock of your setting and the children's, parents'/carers' and staff's ethnic backgrounds, their belief systems and the languages they speak.
- Look at your setting's policies and procedures and evaluate whether they are inclusive or not in practice when working with children and their families.
- Create an action plan where you consider that your practice and the setting could improve to be more inclusive.

Ethnicity and life chances

In 2008 Johnson and Kossykh conducted a literature review for the Human Rights Commission and found that children from most ethnic groups have lower educational achievement than white British children. However, when socio-economic factors are taken out of the equation, children from minority ethnic groups (with the exception of Black Caribbean boys) make better progress within the school system and achieve better than expected educational outcomes compared to white British children. However, in adulthood individuals from ethnic minorities are more likely to be unemployed and to receive lower wages (Johnson and Kossykh, 2008).

The failure of Black Caribbean boys to do well within the school system has been attributed to a variety of factors which include poor-quality schools, low teacher expectations and the children's views that even if they do well at school they will not find a job afterwards (Tackey et al., 2011).

Extend your knowledge

Read the following article and decide how you can make a positive contribution to enhance children's life chances regardless of their origin.

- Ouseley, H. and Lane, J. (2006) 'We've got to start somewhere: what role can early years services and settings play in helping society to be more at ease with itself?', *Race Equality Teaching*, vol. 24, no. 2, pp. 39–43.

Racism and discrimination in early childhood

Talking to early childhood practitioners and reading policies laid out by early childhood settings it is all too easy to think that we no longer have a 'problem' with racist attitudes and discrimination in the sector. All early childhood courses have anti-racism as a central tenet, and it is extremely rare for any early childhood practitioner to express overtly racist views or discriminate between children on racial or ethnic grounds. However, Lane (2008) points out that racism can be very subtle, and practitioners may fail to realise the extent that racism pervades society and can affect the children and families they care for. It is easy to think that we have fought and won the battle against racism and that there is no more to do. However, it is hard to ignore reports about the rise in anti-Semitism and 'Islamophobia' in the press, and the reality is that children and families from ethnic minorities face racism and discrimination on a regular basis.

In order for us to become aware of the insidious nature of racism, early childhood practitioners need to *know* and *understand* about racism. Lane (2008) suggests this involves knowing what it is, how to recognise it and how it arose. If one truly understands racism, then the apprehensions, fear of using the wrong words and guilt that sometimes surround the issue will be removed, and it will be easier to notice when practices and policies are discriminatory.

Research has shown that if children have the experience of attending quality early childhood provision, then they achieve better in later life (Sylva *et al.*, 2004, 2010). Research has also shown us that families from some ethnic minority groups, for example the Bangladeshi community, do not use formal childcare for their children as much as some other groups (Daycare Trust, 2008). There are several reasons why this should be. One is that there is more of a tradition of informal family care within families, fewer mothers are in employment and there is a language barrier. The Daycare Trust (2008) reports that parents are reluctant to use childcare where there is no member of staff who speaks the child's language. The report concludes that to increase the numbers of children from ethnic minority families accessing formal childcare there needs to be targeted outreach and strong parental partnership work; and that settings should employ practitioners who are able to speak the languages represented in the community (Daycare Trust, 2008). However, in many rural areas of the UK there is less diversity and it is often difficult to find other professionals and/or parents who might be able to assist breaking down potential communication barriers.

Extend your knowledge

Extend your knowledge and understanding by reading and reflecting on your own preconceived ideas and prejudices when it comes to other cultures:

- Lane, J. (2006) *Right From The Start: A commissioned study of antiracism, learning and the early years*, Focus Institute for Regeneration and Social Transformation (FIRST). Available from: http://www.focus-consultancy.co.uk/pdfs/first4.pdf.
- McIntosh, P. (1988) 'White Privilege: Unpacking the Invisible Knapsack', Working Paper 189, Wellesley, MA: Wellesley College Center for Research on Women. Available from: http://ted.coe.wayne.edu/ele3600/mcintosh.html.

Children with English as an Additional Language (EAL)

As we have seen previously, children with EAL do less well on the Foundation Profile than children who speak English fluently, but by the time they are seven years this difference has disappeared (Datta, 2007). Early childhood is the ideal age to learn an additional language. Although relatively uncommon in the UK, most children in the world grow up in a multilingual society and can speak two or more languages fluently, either learning more than one language at the same time from birth, or learning one language first followed by another (Datta, 2007).

Reflective task

- If you are involved in an early childhood setting, count how many different languages the children and families using the setting speak. How many languages do the staff speak?
- What may be the benefit to children, families and staff of having children in the setting who speak more than one language?
- If you live in a rural community there may be no children or staff who speak an additional language. In what ways may these children be at a disadvantage? How may you introduce different languages into the setting?

When this exercise was carried out in one London inner-city setting it was found that the children and their families spoke over 30 different languages, and the staff spoke 11. One practitioner revealed that she could speak five languages: English, French and three different languages that she learned while growing up in Nigeria. In rural areas, there is less diversity among the community and the practitioners.

Children entering settings aged three, unable to speak English, were once considered to be a problem. However, now it is recognised that, far from being a problem, there are social and cognitive benefits attached to learning more than one language (DCSF, 2007c). Children learn an additional language in much the same way as they learn to speak their first language, which is in social situations with the support of adults and older children (Browne, 2001). It is not necessary to give children 'formal' EAL instruction at this age, as sensitive, reciprocal interactions with their 'key persons' and social contact with other children will help them learn through everyday life of the nursery (Browne, 2001).

The principles of inclusive practice apply to these children as they learn English, and they should be supported to access all aspects of the curriculum, ideally through bilingual support, using their first language to help explain activities (DCSF, 2007c).

It used to be common practice not to allow children who were learning English to speak their first language in nursery. However, it is recognised that it is important that children continue to develop their first language as they learn English, as the aim is for them to become fully bilingual, eventually being able to speak, read and write in both languages. Close partnership with parents is needed, as sometimes they are concerned that speaking to their children in their first language will hinder the children learning English.

Reflective task

- What creative measures can you think of to bridge the communication gap if staff do not speak parents' languages?
- What resources are available to help you in your community or from your local authority?
- There is a useful document containing guidance on how to support children with English as an additional language: DCSF (2007c) *Supporting Children Learning English as an Additional Language: Guidance for Practitioners in the Early Years Foundation Stage*, Nottingham. DCSF. Available from: http:// webarchive.nationalarchives.gov.uk/20110208164652/http:/nationalstrategies.standards.dcsf.gov. uk/node/84861. Using this guidance as a guide, write a policy document for an early years setting outlining the practical support that children whose first language is not English, and their families, will be given within the setting.

Asylum seekers and refugees

Many asylum seekers and refugees have very young children who will be eligible for early years provision. Refugee children often share certain experiences. Many will have experienced horrific events which may affect their ability to settle and rebuild their lives. They may have faced disruption in their education and a drop in living standards. Many children have had secure attachment relationships with family members disrupted and trauma may have resulted in their parents being unable to be emotionally available for them (Rutter, 2003).

Refugee families often suffer racism because they may be visibly different from the general population. They often live in poverty and most are in the process of learning English and learning how to live in a new country. They are particularly vulnerable and their children could be described as socially endangered (Jensen, 2009). For all these reasons it is important that they are given places in good-quality early years provision.

Previously we have seen how some ethnic minority groups do not make use of formal early years care and education. The findings are similar for refugee families (Tyler, 2010). When refugee children manage to access early years settings they may be faced with negative attitudes from other parents, or subtle racism by practitioners.

Extend your knowledge

Islington Early Years Foundation Stage Team (2011) wrote the following guide. Read through it and make a set of 'good practice' points when looking after refugee children in your setting.

- Islington Early Years Foundation Stage Team (2011) *Refugee and asylum seeker support and advice pack for early years practitioners.* Available from: http://www.islington.gov.uk/publicrecords/documents/ EducationandLearning/pdf/eyfst/EY-Refugee-pack-2011.pdf.

Gypsy and traveller children

Although we have noted that racism towards ethnic minorities is more subtle and covert than it was, Cemlyn *et al.* (2009) point out that the exception seems to be for gypsies and travellers, who still face overt racism and discrimination from the settled communities around them. Public attitudes and prejudices frequently go unchallenged in a way that would be unthinkable if directed towards other minority groups. As a group gypsy and traveller children are vulnerable and often experience profound inequalities and disadvantage. Cemlyn *et al.* (2009) point out that, although there is great value placed on family cohesion and relationships within communities, the realities of a travelling life lead to a less than ideal environment for children to develop. The constant threat of eviction has direct and indirect effects on children who experience both the trauma of eviction and the distress of the adults who care for them. Often children do not have a safe place to play, and access to early years provision, which may give the children opportunities for physical play, is prevented because of family mobility. Access is further prevented because traveller families are reluctant to use provision if they perceive that there are negative attitudes towards them.

Cemlyn *et al.* (2009) suggest that there needs to be more targeted outreach for these communities and the provision of onsite facilities such as play buses. They suggest that training for early childhood practitioners is vital, so that provision is designed with these children's needs specifically in mind (Cemlyn *et al.*, 2009). Greater use of the travelling community themselves is suggested for the delivery of this training, together with the fostering of strong parental links.

Extend your knowledge

Read the following conference paper and write down action points for how you can be inclusive in your practice with children from gypsy, Roma and traveller backgrounds in your setting.
- Save the Children UK (2007) 'Working Towards Inclusive Practice in the Early Years': Inclusion of Gypsy, Roma and Traveller culture in early years settings, conference proceedings, 20/6/2007, Birmingham Hippodrome. Available from: http://www.savethechildren.org.uk/sites/default/files/docs/Working_Towards_Inclusive_Practice_Conference_Papers_1.pdf.

Poverty

Four million children – one in three – live in poverty in the UK. Children are classified as being in poverty if they live in families in receipt of out-of-work benefits or in receipt of in-work tax credits where their reported income is less than 60 per cent of median income (Child Poverty Action Group, 2012).

Reflective task

Look at the Child Poverty Action Group website and investigate the figures for child poverty in your area. *End Child Poverty Now* [online] http://www.endchildpoverty.org.uk/why-end-child-poverty/poverty-in-your-area.
- How do they compare with other areas in the UK?
- Which areas have the highest and lowest levels of child poverty?
- Using the website, write a paragraph on the effects of child poverty.

Which families are most at risk of living in poverty? In 2007 the charity Barnardo's commissioned a study which identified five groups most at risk of living in poverty. These were: lone parents, large families, parents or children with disabilities, black and minority ethnic groups, and working families on low incomes. Other vulnerable groups included asylum seekers, workless households, young people living independently, and children living in poor housing (Sharma, 2007).

The Child Poverty Action Group (2012) outlines the following effects of poverty on children in the UK:

■ Children are more likely to be cold and hungry. They are less likely to be able to join in activities with their friends and are less likely to go away on holiday.

■ Poor children leave school with lower qualifications than their peers, are less likely to find employment and when in employment will earn less than their peers.

■ Poor children are more likely to suffer ill health, and as adults will die earlier than their peers.

From this we can see that there is a direct link between poverty and inequality. In 2010 UNICEF published a report that ranked child poverty in the UK as 19th out of 24 OECD (Organisation for Economic Co-operation and Development) countries. There was a direct link between material inequality and inequalities in education and health.

Impoverished families can find themselves victims of discrimination, including being the recipients of negative language and experiencing barriers when struggling to access their basic rights (Davies, 2008).

Reflective task

The Joseph Rowntree Foundation has produced a document explaining the effects of 'povertyism' on impoverished families: Davies, M. (2008) *Eradicating child poverty: The role of key policy areas: The effects of discrimination on families in the fight to end child poverty*, York: Joseph Rowntree Foundation. Available from: http://www.jrf.org.uk/sites/files/jrf/2271-poverty-exclusion-discrimination.pdf.

■ Explain what is meant by 'povertyism'.
■ What are the effects of 'povertyism'?
■ How might 'povertyism' impact the lives of very young children?

As we saw at the beginning of this chapter, poverty and disadvantage are the main factor influencing poor attainment in the EYFS profile at the end of the Foundation Stage, so by the time children reach the age of five one can see the powerful negative effects of poverty and a 'poor start' in life (Allen, 2011; Field, 2010; Sylva *et al.*, 2004). Previous and current governments have emphasised that the best way to help children from impoverished backgrounds is to give them access to high-quality early childhood provision, and to target resources to the most disadvantaged children in the first five years of their life (Department of Work and Pensions and DfE, 2011).

The Early Years Foundation Stage (DfE, 2012a) is key to providing quality care and education for children in the earliest years and it is clear that at its heart are the principles of equity and inclusion.

Tackling prejudice

Abrams (2010: 3) defines prejudice as 'bias which devalues people because of their perceived membership of a social group'. In this chapter we have looked at a number of different groups who may, at some time in their lives, experience prejudice.

Prejudice involves stereotyping and prejudging people. A stereotype is a highly simplified idea held about a group. For example, if you ask people what they think of rugby players they may talk about them as tough, strong men who like beer and are not very good at talking about their feelings. This is nonsense, of course, because there are women rugby players, teetotal rugby players and rugby players who are in touch with their emotions. When we hold stereotypical ideas we take short cuts in our thinking which, in some situations, can be damaging (Brain and Mukherji, 2005).

Prejudice and discrimination are very harmful. Children's sense of identity and self-esteem can be affected if they are at the receiving end of negative attitudes towards themselves and/or the group to which they belong. They may feel that certain options are not available or open to them; for example, Black Caribbean boys may not work hard at school because they feel that, however hard they work, they are unlikely to get a job.

It is clear that very young children can hold prejudicial views, which are often transmitted by their friends and families or the communities in which they live, or negative media portrayal of minority groups.

Extend your knowledge

This article looks at the origins of prejudice in children and describes research into attempts to use television to alter children's attitudes:

■ Persson, A. and Musher-Eizenman, D. (2003) 'The impact of a prejudice prevention program on young children's ideas about race', *Early Childhood Research Quarterly*, vol. 18, no. 4, pp. 530–46.

After having read the article, ask yourself the following questions:
■ What evidence is there that young children show prejudicial attitudes?
■ How may television affect the development of prejudicial attitudes in children?
■ What are the possible implications for your practice?
■ How can you help staff, children and parents counteract prejudicial attitudes?

Is it possible to stop people holding prejudicial views? Abrams (2010) conducted an excellent review of the literature and concludes that the more contact there is with people from other groups and cultures and the more understanding there is, the more likely prejudice and discrimination will be reduced.

Reducing prejudice and discrimination in early childhood settings

Throughout this chapter we have noted how the attitudes of adults can have a profound effect on children. We looked at how negative attitudes can lead to self-fulfilling prophecies and we discussed Lane's suggestions (2008) about helping early childhood practitioners understand about racism. There is, therefore, an ongoing need for everyone involved in early childhood to receive high-quality training and education in this area, in a whole-team approach to changing practice. Training is not enough on its own, as there are personal qualities or competencies that those working with very young children need. Diversity in Early Childhood Education and Training (DECET) and the International Step by Step Association (ISSA) (2012: 4) have identified that staff should be empathetic, understanding and non-judgemental with a willingness to accept diversity.

Staff need to be sensitive to the needs of children and parents should be responsive and creative in meeting those needs.

Knowing that young children will sometimes demonstrate prejudice should inform our practice. Young children should be gently shown the effects that their attitudes and actions have on other children. Explanations, at a developmentally appropriate level, and the opportunities to mix with and get to know children from other groups will help to reduce prejudice in children.

Staff are not the only adults within a setting; we also have the opportunity to help the parents and families of the children understand and get to know other groups better. We read previously about how the families of gypsy and traveller children were reluctant to take up provision within communities which they perceived as having prejudiced views about them. Any parent who is considered to be 'different' from the majority of parents in a setting may find themselves at the receiving end of prejudicial views and behaviour from other parents. Depending on the socio-cultural profile of an early childhood setting, gay or lesbian parents, single parents, older parents or parents from different racial or socio-economic groups may all face prejudice. We know prejudice is reduced by contact with different groups, and early childhood settings are ideally placed to help parents meet each other both formally and informally.

At an institutional level we need to be vigilant that our policies and procedures do not discriminate against any particular group. In 2010 the Equality Act became law and early childhood settings now need to show that their policies and procedures meet the requirements of the Act.

Lane and Parkes (2012: 25) outline the three main duties to which settings have to pay 'due regard to the Equality Act by':

1 Eliminating discrimination and other conduct that is prohibited by the Act.
2 Advancing equality of opportunity between people who share a protected characteristic (age, disability, religion or belief, gender or sexual orientation) and people who do not share it.
3 Fostering good relations between people who share a protected characteristic and people who do not share it.

Most settings will already be compliant with the Act because they are subject to the regulatory frameworks of the EYFS (DfE, 2012a) and Ofsted and will already be subject to the previous equality legislation.

Celebrating and managing diversity

Far from diversity being a 'problem', practitioners who work in areas where the children and families come from diverse backgrounds will tell you that this is an enriching experience, full of opportunity for all children. Children thrive when they feel safe and secure, and feel that what matters to them matters to us as well. They thrive when things that they are familiar with in the home can be found in the setting and they thrive when they know that their parents feel comfortable and welcomed. Most of all they thrive within close warm relationships, where their 'key person' and their friends in the setting value them for who they are and support them in developing a positive sense of identity.

When we think of celebrating diversity, it is all too easy to fall into the mindset of thinking that this is to do with celebrating festivals such as Chinese New Year, and holding an international evening where parents are encouraged to come dressed up in national dress and bring a dish from their culture. This is exoticising or 'othering' different cultures and reinforces stereotypical thinking. If these activities are based on the individual needs and interests of the children and their families, then such celebrations may be appropriate. It is the underpinning thinking behind such events that is important.

> **The concept of respecting every child's heritage encompasses more than just having appropriate resources and celebrating some relevant festivals. It involves the whole ethos that surrounds all the children. It includes which children are present in the first place; the knowledge, understanding and commitment of the staff; the racial attitudes and behaviour of the children, their families and staff; and the policies, practices and procedures that underpin everything that goes on.**
>
> (Lane, 2007: 105)

Planning with and for individual children is key to managing diversity. Siraj-Blatchford and Clarke (2000: 70) suggest that the curriculum should:

- foster children's self-esteem
- acknowledge the cultural and linguistic background of all children
- actively maintain or develop the children's first or home languages
- promote the learning of English as an additional language
- value bilingualism as an asset
- value what boys and girls can do equally
- support families in their efforts to maintain their languages and culture
- foster an awareness of diversity in class, gender, ability and culture
- promote respect for similarity and difference
- challenge bias and prejudice
- promote a sense of fairness
- promote principles of inclusion and equity
- support the participation of parents in the children's learning.

Next steps

Using the points outlined by Siraj-Blatchford and Clarke (2000):

- Investigate the EYFS curriculum (DfE, 2012a) and identify whether all these recommendations can be found within the curriculum.
- If you are involved in a setting, lead a discussion with your colleagues about whether your practice needs reviewing in the light of these recommendations.

Conclusion

In this chapter we have investigated why there is a gap in attainment between certain socially endangered groups of children and other children at the end of the Foundation Stage. We looked at the role of early childhood settings in promoting equality for all children by promoting inclusive care and education. The pernicious effect of prejudice, racism and discrimination was discussed and how early childhood practitioners can help tackle prejudice by looking at their own attitudes and by providing a curriculum that celebrates diversity.

Evaluate your...

Practice

The following is a list of questions to help you evaluate your practice. It is suggested that you discuss these questions with your colleagues.

- Does your setting have a written equality statement that conforms to the EYFS requirement?
- Does the setting comply with the requirements of the Equality Act 2010?
- Do the staff represent the ethnic and religious make-up of the local community and speak some of the community languages?
- Does the recruitment and selection process encourage applications from all?
- Is information for parents produced in community languages and is there provision for parents who cannot hear, have difficulties seeing or who have learning needs?
- Are staff trained to understand diversity and are there open, ongoing discussions about how to improve provision?
- Are staff and children encouraged to learn and use Makaton, or some other form of signing?
- Are 'key persons' encouraged to develop close relationships with parents so that they can work in partnership with the setting to plan appropriate experiences for the children's culture and needs?
- Are there books in the first languages of the children in the setting and are they read to all children?
- Do books, posters and toys reflect positive images of different ethnic groups, genders, ages and abilities? Are children with disabilities represented and do resources also reflect a variety of different sorts of family (including gay and lesbian parents)?
- Does the role-play area contain resources that reflect those found in the children's homes? Are children observed regularly and are activities and planning differentiated to meet the needs of all children?
- Is difference discussed in a positive way with children and are any negative attitudes towards others talked about sensitively?
- Are community festivals recognised and celebrated, with input from parents?
- Does the setting work closely with outside agencies to support families in need?

Further reading

Baldock, P. (2010) *Cultural Diversity in the Early Years*, London. Sage.

Lane, J. (2008) *Young Children and Racial Justice: Taking action for racial equality in the early years – understanding the past, thinking about the present, planning for the future*, London: The National Children's Bureau.

Siraj-Blatchford, I. and Clarke, P. (2000) *Supporting Identity, Diversity and Language in the Early Years*, Buckingham: Open University Press.

Wall, K. (2010) *Special Needs and Early Years* (3rd edn), London: Sage.

Walsh, R., Hodge, K., Bowes, J. and Kemp, C. (2010) 'Same age, different page: Overcoming the barriers to catering for young gifted children in prior-to-school settings', *International Journal of Early Childhood*, vol. 42, no. 1, pp. 43–58.

12 Behaviour and behaviour management in early years

Eleni Kanira and Karen Ward

Introduction

Exploring the issues surrounding behaviour and behaviour management as it relates to the development of young children is high on the government agenda. Through recent publications (DfE, 2012c; Teaching Agency, 2012) the government has issued guidelines concerning the knowledge, skills and understanding that trainees and practitioners will need to improve behaviour in schools. By implication this will impact upon all settings that are involved in the care and education of children and young people. Behaviour cannot be seen in isolation, but within the social, cultural and environmental context of the child. 'Behaviour' should always be seen in association with other concepts (attachment, transitions and resilience) and it is for this reason that it is a challenging concept to explore. This chapter adopts the view that learning and managing behaviour are fluid and socially constructed concepts – that there are interrelation and interconnection between the child, the adult(s) and the social and cultural environment.

The purpose of behaviour management is to secure effective learning behaviour (Powell and Tod, 2004). The development of learning behaviour and behaviour management requires practitioners to be knowledgeable and confident in theory and its application in order to be able to support the child's social, emotional and behavioural needs. Failure to do so may affect learning outcomes for the individual child and the group.

This chapter will introduce and explain a variety of theoretical perspectives, strategies and approaches to child development and how they relate to behaviour. You will be encouraged to evaluate and reflect upon your own practice.

Learning outcomes

This chapter will help you to:

- Reflect upon and evaluate previous learning.
- Understand theoretical perspectives on behaviour.
- Recognise the underlying factors influencing children's behaviour.
- Build a repertoire of practical strategies for managing the behaviour of individuals and groups of children.
- Understand the benefits of working in partnership with parents.

Theoretical perspectives on behaviour

The notion of appropriate and inappropriate or disruptive behaviour is context-specific and varies according to different theoretical schools of thought. In most cases, behaviour is associated with learning in classroom and home environments but can be observed in any personal or social activities that individuals are involved in, such as relationships with family, peers and partners, with the self and the social world.

Learning in its broadest sense is a process of change in people's knowledge, attitudes or behaviour and it is associated with human interaction and experience. This change can be intentional or unintentional, conscious or subconscious, for better or worse. Personal motivation and environmental issues, such as chronological and emotional maturity, family life and experiences, play a major role in personality development (Woolfolk *et al.*, 2008).

The selected theories in this section adopt the perspective that behaviour is learned and in most cases associated with specific people and environments which trigger change in its positive or negative manifestation, development, growth or disappearance.

Psychoanalytic theory

Classic research

Psychoanalysis focuses upon the impact that unconscious (repressed) pressures and early experiences have on an individual's decisions. This theory is based on the work of Sigmund Freud (1856–1939), who suggested that all mental behaviours are primarily unconscious and that experience is gained from painful causes and frequent and powerful impulses in the external world.

Freud described unconscious behaviour as a condition that is related to dominance of pleasure, fantasy as opposed to reality. Understanding of the unconscious in the psychoanalytical process is strongly connected to the motive that caused the individual to forget something or to misinterpret something else. Dreams, fantasies and symptoms give an indirect but important insight into the content of unconscious and intrinsic representations (Freud, 1953, 1962).

Freud's stages of individual development (id: the instinctive needs, ego: the socially constructed real self, and superego: the ideals and principles that we inherit from our parents) and his psychosexual stages of development (oral, anal and phallic) provide a deeper understanding of the importance of early childhood in the emotional life of older children, adolescents and adults (Freud, 1923).

Contemporary research

Gardner (2010) views the unconscious as having a dynamic sense, a sense of motivation, a cause of mental conflict which is presented as resistance and transference behaviour and which manifests itself in dreams. Dreams are closely related to memory. At an early stage memory operates at a neural level where the unconscious is conceptualised. Key characteristics of the unconscious are that it is autonomous, relative to the development of the brain and driven by instinct and emotions.

Attachment theory

The process of bonding between a mother and her infant soon after birth has been described by John Bowlby (1907–90) and Mary Ainsworth (1913–99) as an intimate attachment. Mogi *et al.* (2010: 1) define it as a 'universal' concept to all mammals and a significant one in the formation of 'self'.

Attachment is demonstrated in maternal behaviour through physical contact, the suckling of the nipple and the warmth of the mother's breasts, massage – like stroking, eye contact, facial expressions and body language.

Based on the infant's responsiveness to maternal expression of feelings and emotions, the infant may or may not respond to her signals. As stated by Van IJzendoorn (2001: 864), 'attachment describes the enduring affective bond between children and their primary caregivers; from this bond children derive comfort in times of stress'.

Any form of disruption of mother–infant bonding in the early period of their communication can have serious consequences on the developing infant and their later life experiences, such as anxiety-related behaviour, aggressive behaviour (Van IJzendoorn, 2001). It may result in disorganised attachment relationships, where infants seem unable to find a solution when they experience distress and may display 'bizarre or contradictory behaviour instead' (Shuengel *et al.*, 1999: 54).

Attachment in the relationship between a mother or any primary carer and a newborn infant can be achieved through mutual recognition and reciprocity, and it is an important foundation for future relationships and the future social and emotional development of the child.

Extend your knowledge

Many researchers have reflected upon the work of Bowlby and Ainsworth. See, for example:

■ Van IJzendoorn, M. H. (2001) 'Attachment theory: psychological 2', in Smelser, N. J. and Baltes, P. B. (eds.), *International Encyclopedia of the Social and Behavioral Sciences*, pp. 846–68, London: Pergamon.

■ Schuengel, C., Bakermans-Kranenburg, M. J. and Van IJzendoorn, M. H. (1999) 'Frightening maternal behavior linking unresolved loss and disorganized infant attachment', *Journal of Consulting and Clinical Psychology*, vol. 67, no. 1, pp. 54–63.

Moral reasoning

Morality explains a set of personal principles conforming to social standards of behaviour, such as emotions, guilt, shame and pro-social activities like empathy, generosity and enthusiasm. Understanding of morality involves the development of cognitive and social factors that impact on young people's recognition and acknowledgement of the consequences of their behaviour for the self and for others (Schofield, 2006, cited in Aldgate *et al.*, 2006). This is a cognitive process that develops over time but early years are an important stage for the foundations and development of personal principles and ideas, and coincide with the formation of 'self' and 'identity'.

In early years children develop a sense of 'right' and 'wrong'. They identify feelings, develop responsibility, cultivate positive qualities, manage emotions, seek help and learn how to communicate effectively. This is the time when they actively construct their moral judgements in their family environments, childminder settings, playgroups and nursery education. Distributive justice and the morality of cooperation are communicated in children's social activities through the moral beliefs, perspectives, actions and interactions of the adults who are responsible for their care and learning. Although they experience it from the time they are born, children from around the age of five or six years become more consciously aware of equality through fair distribution of rights and understanding of rules. Piaget (1965) called 'moral realism' the cognitive developmental stage where children accept rules without challenging them.

Classic research

The psychologist Lawrence Kohlberg (1927–87) built on Piaget's concept of 'moral realism' and developed it further by proposing that both children and adults should be exposed to moral dilemmas, or hypothetical situations in which they are required to make difficult decisions and give their reasons (moral reasoning) (Kohlberg, 1975). Moral reasoning demands both emotional and cognitive development (abstract thinking) which matures as children move from decisions based on unquestionable truths to communicating and debating about conceptual moral principles (Kohlberg, 1975).

Schofield (2006, cited in Aldgate *et al.*, 2006) highlights that Kohlberg's theory (1975) of moral reasoning develops in three levels:

- Level 1: Pre-conventional reasoning: personal needs together with the rules set by others provide for judgement to be made.
- Level 2: Conventional moral reasoning: judgements are made based on expectations of others (family and society).
- Level 3: Post-conventional moral reasoning: individual rights are socially agreed and the individual uses his/her personal conscience to decide on abstract concepts (justice) and moral principles.

Behavioural learning theory

From the psychology of consciousness to psychology as the 'science of human behaviour', behaviourism focused on what can be observed, and its theoretical goal was to predict and control behaviour. The learning outcome in the behavioural learning theories was a change of behaviour through observation of external proceedings (actions and events) that impacted upon an individual's life. This learning theory used objective methods (observations, tests and laboratory experiments on animals) to interpret human behaviour. Behaviourist studies explored issues such as sense, perception, instinct, habits, the learning process and conditioning, and this work has influenced classroom practices, psychology and biology.

Behavioural theories explore and practise in learning environments four key principles (Woolfolk *et al.*, 2008):

1 Contiguity (one event is associated with another because they are presented together and later the presence of one event (stimulus) is sufficient for a response.
2 Classical conditioning (automatic responses to stimuli are due to learned behaviours).
3 Operant conditioning (goal-directed behaviour is strengthened or weakened by consequences or antecedents).
4 Reinforcement (consequences that follow a behaviour strengthen the behaviour).

Classic research

Behaviourism is centred on research by John B. Watson (1878–1958), who began his career as an animal psychologist and worked later in the field of child psychology. For Watson (1914) psychology should not be limited to the study of consciousness and human experience as such, but stimulus (episode that activates behaviour) and response (observable reaction to a stimulus) in the context of habit formation and learning by association as performed by animals and humans. The behaviourists' aim was to learn general and particular methods by which behaviour might be controlled and, for Watson, behaviour and consciousness were mutually exclusive.

Watson's predecessor Edward Thorndike (1874–1949) experimented on animal instinct and learning, and posed the possibility that animals might use ideas either in reasoning, in association (through imitation) or by trial and error. He excluded by definite experimental evidence two out of the three possibilities and was left with trial and error as the only animal method of learning, stating that animals learned not by watching, not by considering, but by doing (Goss, 1961; Rolls, 2005).

Ivan Pavlov (1849–1936), a Russian neurologist, invented the term 'conditioned reflex' to describe the response that had become attached to some substitute for the natural stimulus, by observing the reflex flow of a dog's saliva at the sight or hearing of a stimulus related to food. He also studied differentiations in these responses. Pavlov's results generalised a theory of the functions of the brain on the sensory and motor sides (Pavlov, 1960; Castro and Wasserman, 2010).

Reflective task

- Explain which of the four key principles (Woolfolk *et al.*, 2008) relate to the work of Watson, Thorndike and Pavlov, and why.
- Explore if and how they might be related and what relevance they have to your practice.

Maturation and interaction with the environment, or nature and nurture

When focusing on maturation and development there is an underlying belief (Gesell, 1933, cited in Murchison, 2007) in a sequence of developmental phases: changes that occur naturally through which children are genetically programmed to pass over time. This particular school of thought explains that the environment will not affect these changes as most people's physical development will be unaffected unless a serious illness or malnutrition occurs. The theory also allows for the effects of the environment on children's development as it recognises changes that are brought about through learning. However, when attempting to explain the development of thinking and personality, most psychologists debate strongly about where the emphasis should be placed: maturation or interaction with the environment – nature or nurture (Woolfolk *et al.*, 2008).

This debate mainly centres on who we are, what we become and how this is determined. Those on the nature side of the debate suggest that it is what we inherit genetically that influences our prospects (genotype), and those on the nurture side that we are products of our environment (phenotype). To suggest that issues are a matter of either nature or nurture oversimplifies the complex interaction of many factors.

The nurture debate has been strongly influenced by Bowlby's attachment theory (1969, cited in Gerhardt, 2004) and the importance of developing strong, secure and warm relationships with a primary carer as a basis for future learning and development. Also key to this debate is the socio-cultural perspective (Vygotsky, 1987), and the idea that learning is guided, supported and 'scaffolded' (Bruner, 1987) by a more able other. This acts as a model for learning and the development of learning behaviour. This view underpins the Nurture Group type provision developed in the 1960s and 1970s (Bennathan and Boxall, 2000) as an intervention which can support those individual children whose behaviour does not meet with the expectations of the setting or is developmentally inappropriate.

Although there is debate about what constitutes development and how it takes place, the following general principles are supported by almost all theorists and inform our understanding of behaviour (as adapted from Woolfolk *et al.*, 2008):

1 There are different developmental rates in people's thinking. Maturity in thinking and social relations plays an important role in the development of behaviour.
2 There is a relatively logical but not necessarily linear progression in development: 'people might advance, stay the same for some time or go backwards' (Woolfolk *et al.*, 2008: 31).
3 Development takes place over a period of time.

Social learning theory

Classic research

The psychologist Albert Bandura (1925–) identified limitations in the behavioural principles of reinforcement and punishment in his early work and developed the behaviourist thinking further, focusing on social influences of learning and how actions are shaped by feelings through observing and imitating others. He distinguished between learning as acquisition of knowledge, and behaviour as observable performance based on acquired knowledge, and suggested that we may be aware of more than we show in our behaviour (Woolfolk *et al.*, 2008).

Bandura's early example (1961) of the 'Bobo doll' experiment, when preschool children were exposed to aggressive behaviour in a film showing adults kicking and punching a model, resulted in a recognition that learners may display performance that is not enhanced by rewards and sanctions. Instead, performance can be affected by incentives through imitating the adults (Bandura, 1986). The outcome of this experiment suggests that learners may not perform 'bad behaviours' like swearing or hitting, even if they are modelled by adults, peers and the media, because they are aware of personal consequences which may encourage or discourage them from doing so (Bandura, 1986).

Bandura's recent research (1986) focuses on how cognitive factors, such as self-perceptions, beliefs and expectations, influence learning. His social cognitive theory identifies two modes of learning: enactive and vicarious. Enactive learning is active and experiential and the learner learns from the consequences of his/her actions. Vicarious learning like attention, construction of images, remembering, analysing and making decisions that affect their learning involves observing others. 'Thus, much is going on mentally before performance and reinforcement can even take place' (Bandura, 1986: 272).

Socio-cultural perspective

Classic research

This is drawn from developmental psychology and the work of Lev Vygotsky (1896–1934), suggesting that childhood, behaviour and family life are social constructions and they should be viewed within the historical context and the uniqueness of the social and cultural environment. Vygotsky (1978: 57) believed that 'every function in a child's cultural development appears twice: first, on the social level and later on the individual level; first between people (inter-psychological) and then inside the child (intra-psychological)'. In other words, understanding, thinking and other cognitive higher mental processes are co-constructed through usually verbal communication and negotiation during shared activities between the child and another person. According to Vygotsky (1978), culture is mediated through cultural tools (tools that allow people to communicate in a society, such as symbols, numbers and language).

Language is the most important tool for cognitive development. It is not only a way of expressing ideas, asking questions and making connections, but it also signifies change and communicates cultural meanings (people's needs, values and ideas) over time. Language can be used by adults to positive effect (as in Vygotsky's theory) or negative effect as highlighted earlier in the introduction with the example that the adult world and media in current societies portray children as being 'out of hand', lacking in discipline and the victims of a way of family life that is breaking down.

A particularly interesting concept in Vygotsky's theory and a relevant one to our understanding of how children learn (including about behaviour) is the concept of 'private speech'. Private speech is the child's self-talk which guides their thinking and action (Vygotsky, 1986). These verbalisations regulate children's thinking as they are eventually internalised and become the understanding of a concept or skill.

The adult's role in this process of learning is to identify what the individual has learned and can do ('zone of actual development') and what they are not yet able to learn, and then to assist the child to master the task in a way that enables them to engage with the task. The term that Vygotsky (1978) used to describe the phase of mastery of the skill by the learner is described as the 'zone of proximal development'.

Ecological systems theory

An ecological perspective considers that children within an environment are surrounded by layers of complex social groupings which influence them. These include family and extended family, friendship networks, school, neighbourhood, work influences and the family's place within the community (Aldgate *et al.*, 2006).

In Bronfenbrenner's theory (1979), the family is seen as a system with each individual family member interacting with each other. Families are interacting systems which in turn interact with other systems, early years settings, school, the community and the wider world (see figure 7.1 on page 148). Each interaction is influenced by previous interactions – changes in one member of the system affect the other members. To understand the child, it is imperative that we understand the family. This theory helps in considering the relationship between individuals and their environment and how society's expectations are transmitted to individuals and groups.

Reflective task

Reflecting on theories around development, learning and behaviour, consider your answers to the following questions:

■ What do these theories tell you about children's learning, development and behaviour?
■ Which theories would more influence the way you work with children in your setting, and why?
■ Identify a particular child in your setting who experiences an emotional, social or behavioural difficulty. Which of the theories discussed in this chapter would provide you with relevant knowledge and skills to support your chosen child and why?

(Allow 30 minutes for this task.)

Underlying factors influencing behaviour

Culture influences how children experience their childhood, and beliefs and practices influence the meaning we attribute to childhood and behaviours. This meaning affects how we react to these behaviours (Timimi, 2005).

There are many factors that could affect children's behaviour: risk factors, such as those which increase the likelihood of antisocial behaviour, and protective factors, such as resilience and self-control (Sutton et al., 2006). There are multiple risk factors associated with antisocial behaviour that may lead to children experiencing problems adapting to the environment of the setting (Sutton et al., 2006). An understanding of these factors is crucial (Hartman et al., 2003). Children with behaviour issues are more likely to experience social isolation and peer rejection. Practitioners need to be able to act to ensure that all children's experiences in early years settings are positive.

The following factors (not necessarily exhaustive) are considered of paramount importance in children's social and emotional development, and how it influences on behaviour:
■ parenting style
■ attachment issues
■ marital relationships
■ prime carer's mental state
■ child's temperament
■ teacher/practitioner perceptions
■ poverty
■ transitions.

Parenting style

According to Baumrind (1967, 1971, 1973, 1975, 1991, cited in Ding and Littleton, 2005), there are four broad styles of parenting characterised by the degree to which emotional warmth and firmness are present:
■ authoritarian – valuing obedience, lacking emotional warmth, distant but firm, possibly harsh, even coercive

- authoritative – emotionally warm, supportive and encouraging, firm and assertive
- permissive – non-intrusive, lacking in firmness but emotionally available
- non-conformist – opposed to authority, less passive than permissive.

Parental attitudes to children shape their social experiences and are essential in terms of personal, social and emotional development as children obtain feedback from the adults in their environment about their own characteristics, self-concept and self-worth (being and/or feeling acceptable) (Roberts, 2006). This feedback can be positive or negative, dependent upon parenting styles and other factors, affecting self-esteem, self-concept, confidence and resilience, which in turn have an impact upon behaviour and the ability to function in that and other contexts.

Reflective task

Choose a parenting style and consider:
- What are the benefits and negative aspects of that style?
- What ideas/beliefs may be held by parents adopting the style you have chosen?
- What factors do you think will influence parenting?

Think about the parental role, the nature of childhood and the context, and reflect upon how this is relevant to your practice.

Attachment issues

The affectionate bonding between child and adult develops over time and it is mutually recognised between the people involved in the attachment relationship. Contemporary developmental psychologists (Wood *et al.*, 2004) recognise the importance of the bonding between immediate care-giver(s) and the child, but they view attachment more broadly: as the child's ability to recognise 'the other' and develop a relationship in infancy. These bonds can exist between children and other individuals in their lives, including friends and relatives and are emotionally significant to a child. However, Wood *et al.* (2004: 246) explain that:

> Although attachment theory predicts that early insecure parent–child attachment will result in poor peer relations and peer rejection, few studies have actually examined that.

Sometimes, the child's difficulty or inability to see themselves in relation to others and form a reciprocal relationship can be recognised in the ways that children organise their own worlds through solitary and cooperative play in early years environments. Sharing of space and toys can become a stressful experience for young children. In addition, a child may feel distressed when separated from the person with whom they have an involuntary attachment. The ways that children's patterns of attachment will develop will be influenced by the sensitive and nurturing behaviour of their carers (parents, early years practitioners, teachers and any other significant adults in their lives).

Marital relationships

According to Liu *et al.* (1999), parental interaction shapes children's behaviour. Behaviour is likely to be adversely affected by social stress and family discord. Taylor (2001) quotes UNICEF's 'Progress of Nations Report' (1996), which suggests that poor school performance has been linked to separation and divorce, and this has been shown to affect the mental health of both mothers and children. According to Fagan and Barnett (2003), divorce and separation affect a child's behaviour; however, the effects of adverse family experiences can be lessened by the child's ability to cope, the foundations for which are laid with the development of warm and secure relationships with their main carer. Through these relationships, practitioners can foster resilience in children to enable them to cope with the adversities of life (Newman, 2002).

Extend your knowledge

Newman's research (2002) poses the question of how children and young people resist and overcome stressful episodes while others suffer long-term damage. Follow the link below to develop your understanding of how practitioners may support the development of resilience in young children.

■ Newman, T. (2002) *Promoting Resilience: A Review of Effective Strategies for Child Care* [online]. Available from: http://www.barnardos.org.uk/resources/researchpublications/documents/RESILSUM. PDF.

Prime carer's mental state

The prime carer's mental state and the relationship between the mental health of the carers and the child can have an impact upon the child's behaviour and language development (Stein *et al.*, 2008). Research by Murray *et al.* (1999) suggests that postnatal depression and the associated difficulties experienced in those early months of life can affect the social and emotional development of the child. This is concerned with the emotional availability of the prime carer and their ability to support and meet the physical, social and emotional needs of the child.

Carers' antisocial behaviour (alcohol, drugs, absence, crime, unavailability or distance in the relationship) is linked to behavioural difficulties in children (Ding and Littleton, 2005). In families where there is a history of antisocial behaviour children are more likely to develop conduct problems (Sutton *et al.*, 2006).

Child's temperament

A child's temperament is born of elements of nature and nurture, and can be difficult or irritable (Gerhardt, 2004). The child's temperament and the parental response interact, thus resulting in positive or negative feedback for the child, which influences the child's behaviour.

Teacher/practitioner perceptions

The research of McCready and Soloway (2010) offers an interesting perspective on the perceptions of teachers which can also be applied to practitioners in the field of early years. They suggest that, rather than looking to the field of psychology, the literature on leadership offers an alternative view. McCready and Soloway (2010) cite the research of Heifetz (1996) and Heifetz and Linsky (2004), who discuss the importance of being able to distinguish between technical and adaptive problems. The former require the knowledge of experts and the latter require individuals themselves to reexamine their own values, beliefs and ways of working in the socio-cultural context of the setting and the children and families which it serves. This requires reflective, innovative and creative practitioners who have the confidence to examine their practice and the knowledge, skills and understanding to seek solutions to these problems and adapt practice where necessary. This is consistent with Steiner Waldorf education where practitioners are expected to advance their own self-development (Nicol and Taplin, 2012).

The Social and Emotional Aspects of Learning programme (SEAL), a curriculum resource designed to develop children's social, emotional and behavioural skills in early years and the primary school, was researched as part of the Primary Behaviour and Attendance Pilot funded by the Department for Education and Skills (DfES, 2005a). The findings of the pilot study in 25 local authorities in the UK revealed that 90 per cent of school staff agreed that the programme had been at least relatively successful. All responding head teachers, 87 per cent of teachers and 96 per cent of non-teaching staff agreed that the programme promoted the emotional well-being of children, while 82 per cent of teachers agreed that it increased pupils' ability to control emotions such as anger. Only 48 per cent of teachers agreed that it reduced bullying, although this rose to 74 per cent of non-teaching staff, suggesting that there was a greater impact on playground as opposed to classroom behaviour (Hallam, 2009).

The interview data indicated that the programme had increased staff understanding of the social and emotional aspects of learning and helped them to better understand their pupils, which changed their behaviour, enhanced their confidence in their interactions with pupils, and led them to approach behaviour incidents in a more thoughtful way. The children's questionnaires revealed a range of complex relationships between age, gender, questionnaire responses and school factors (Hallam, 2009).

Poverty

Multiple risk factors are associated with poverty that can affect the health and well-being of all family members impacting upon the foundations that are laid for future development through attachment. Health and well-being affect behaviour and subsequent cognitive development. For these reasons recent policy suggests targeted support aimed at the most vulnerable should seek to ameliorate these factors (Field, 2010; Allen, 2011). It is their view that the 'Foundation Years' from pregnancy to five years are the most influential in determining future success. During this stage the important issues to consider are a healthy pregnancy, a positive authoritative parenting style leading to resilience, and parental aspirations using a systems approach working in partnership with and responding to the needs of families. The British Cohort Study (BCS) and National Child Development Study (NCDS), whose data span several decades, indicate that skills and abilities acquired in early years are influential in determining success in later life (Johnson and Kossykh, 2008) and that poverty has a negative impact. Feinstein (2006) offers a cautionary note, suggesting that risk is not always indicative of negative future outcomes, but neither can it be ignored – there can be some mobility. There is a risk of stigmatising families who are targeted directly as 'problem' and so the guiding principles are (Feinstein, 2006):

- the rights of children
- supporting parents to enable them to fulfil their responsibilities
- 'progressive universalism' where there is support for all, but more for those who need it most
- early intervention, working to ameliorate against poor outcomes for children and families, both now and in the future.

Transitions

Transitions can be defined as changes in children's lives and it is a term with multiple meanings. In early years these include milestones in children's overall physical, emotional and social development, spatial and chronological changes, evolving capacities and emerging maturity, and geographic and social movements, such as migration (Lansdown, 2011). Some common transitions in early years are as follows:

- bringing a baby home for the first time after a hospital birth
- weaning (moving from milk to other foods)

- migrating between countries
- entering early years care and education.

While growth and change are pleasurable experiences, they can at the same time be difficult and frightening for young children and families. Unsuccessful transitions through education and social systems might influence the development of children who may exhibit behaviour problems including violent impulses and antisocial behaviour.

Practitioners need to have an understanding of development and change, and sensitively facilitate a multi-agency approach (Arai, 2011), and information sharing outlined by the Children Act 2004 and the Early Years Foundation Stage (EYFS) (DfE, 2012a).

Gender issues

Gender issues considered here continue the theme which is that gender identity, roles, stereotypes, behaviours and ways of being male or female are learned.

Gender identity is being aware of being either male or female which is evident in most by the age of two (Jordan, 1995). This is something endowed by nature.

Gender roles are 'attributes, behaviours and attitudes that are associated with being male or female' (Ding and Littleton, 2005: 147). These gender roles are culturally specific and are acquired by observing and imitating adults through their environment, modelling and reinforcing, observing and selecting behaviour (Bandura, 1986). In this context the social environment is influential (Bronfenbrenner, 1979).

Gender stereotypes are 'commonly held beliefs about the characteristics of males and females, including abilities and skills, psychological dispositions, physical appearance and patterns of behaviour' (Ding and Littleton, 2005: 147). Lloyd and Duveen (1992, cited in Jordan, 1995) suggested in their research that children aged four were already aware of their gender identity, but not the stereotypes associated with their gender groups by adults.

Gender behaviour is socially constructed through interactions and practices in the home and setting. There is a variety of discourses associated with the behaviour of boys within their play: the 'warrior' (Jordan, 1995) evident in their superhero play, and 'boys will be boys' (Bhana, 2009) are some examples. The warrior discourse refers to 'action' play themes involving 'goodies and baddies'. These discourses, subsequent interactions and adult reinforcement can perpetuate certain types of behaviour and marginalise boys who do not conform to these ways of behaving. This has implications for practice. As practitioners we have a responsibility to convey to boys and girls that there is a variety of ways of being that are acceptable to their gender identity (Jordan, 1995).

Contemporary research

Bhana (2009) suggests that the 'boys will be boys' discourse serves to overshadow girls and encourages boys to be boisterous and disruptive which compromises their route to academic success, particularly when studiousness is seen as effeminate. While Bhana's research (2009) was conducted in South Africa under a very different social and political agenda, there are lessons to be learned about the ways in which we construct gender in early years settings.

Key issues to consider are:

- differences between boys and girls
- gender and superhero play
- the impact of the elimination of risk on boys' play.

Gender differences

To ensure real equality of opportunity there is a need to understand the similarities and differences between the needs of boys and girls, as well as the different ways in which they learn and the different ways in which their brains develop. These differences have been attributed to hormones and evolution. Historically, nature has required men and women to take differing roles (Gurian, 2001). The use of magnetic resonance imaging (MRI) and positron emission tomography (PET) scans has enabled us to see the structure of the brain, which has confirmed these fundamental differences (Gurian, 2001). In all children the left hemisphere of the brain grows more slowly than the right, but in boys this growth is slower (Featherstone and Bayley, 2005). Broadly speaking, the left hemisphere of the brain is responsible for language development with this difference being apparent as early as in the first few months after birth. Girls tend to outperform boys in measures of reading, writing and language ability (Doherty and Hughes, 2009), while boys tend to perform better at spatial tasks. Readiness to read and write depends upon the brain's readiness to decode and encode print and being physically able to manipulate mark-making tools. This maturity occurs later in boys than girls. Boys' activity levels tend to be higher than girls'. They are more likely to respond to distractions in the environment, while girls seem to find it easier to conform to class rules and routines (Gurian, 2001).

Expectations are built upon culturally specific assumptions and norms which may need to be challenged (Featherstone and Bayley, 2005). The learning environment provided in settings should cater for the needs of both girls and boys, and it is important that the physical environment (both indoors and outdoors), the emotional environment and ethos of the setting reflect these differing needs. It is vital that reflective practitioners use their knowledge of child development, and support children (both girls and boys) to manage their own behaviour and make appropriate choices, ensuring that there are many acceptable ways of being male and female.

Reflective task

Is the culture of our early years settings and classrooms advantaging girls and disadvantaging boys? Consider some examples and justify your reasoning.

Superhero play

This can be defined by the 'warrior' discourse (Jordan, 1995). The research by Holland (2003) suggests that, rather than adopting a 'zero tolerance' approach to superhero play, there should be a consideration of the themes and learning opportunities which are woven into this type of play. She also argues that there should be equal concern about the 'zero tolerance' approach to superhero play and the positive rewards vested upon those girls who play 'nicely' in the home corner (Holland, 2003). This sends out messages which offer less choice about the acceptable ways in which it is possible to be male and female, thus perpetuating gender stereotypes. Both of these approaches are limiting experiences for both girls and boys and the opportunities they have to explore gender. Superhero play should be seen as a form of imaginative play and as such can support the development of socially acceptable behaviour, exploration of gender roles and conflict resolution (Holland, 2003).

High/Scope (Holt, 2009) uses a problem-solving approach to conflict to support resolution. Research shows that supporting children to discuss their problems and generate solutions in a non-punitive environment is effective (Siraj-Blatchford and Sylva, 2004). It is the responsibility of reflective and evaluative practitioners to value and sensitively support children's play interests in the area of superhero play in the same way that other play themes are supported.

Elimination of risk

Much has been said about the importance of child safety – and its importance is undeniable. However, the focus upon the prevention of injury has engendered a fear of risk-taking and has ignored the positive developmental outcomes that can accrue from managed risk-taking. In denying children the opportunity to take risks, we are denying them the opportunity to reach their potential (Greenfield, 2004). There has been a focus on the negative consequences, rather than the positive outcomes, of risk-taking behaviour (Greenfield, 2004). A focus on the former rather than the latter has limited the potential for learning and development. Boys are more likely to engage in negative risk-taking behaviour as a consequence of a lack of challenge and subsequent boredom (Little, 2006). In addition, if children are denied the opportunity to experience managed risk, then they are being deprived of the opportunity to learn about risk and practise the evaluation of risk (Lindon, 2011; Ouvry, 2003), which is an important life skill.

Reflective task

Consider how practitioners may ensure indoor and outdoor provision caters for gender ensuring:

- all forms of play are valued
- there are opportunities for problem solving
- managed risk-taking is encouraged for both boys and girls
- gender barriers and stereotypes are challenged.

Practical strategies for managing individual children and groups

The suitability of strategies is dependent upon the age and developmental stage of the child or children. Management of behaviour, as with all learning and development, begins with reflective practitioners observing children. Practitioners should be aware that there is a subjective element to these observations (Degotardi and Davis, 2008). Much of this will be influenced by personal and professional philosophies rooted in theory but also influenced by adults' perceptions as a result of their own experience and environmental context. Analysis of these observations may suggest that particular strategies may be more suitable than others. Factors influencing behaviour are both environmental (nurture) and genetic (nature). The purpose of behaviour management is to implement strategies that seek to address the environmental (nurture) factors that impact upon and interact with behaviour.

Strategies identified for managing individual children can also be used or modified for use with groups. All work with children that involves supporting their learning and development begins with building strong, secure and supportive relationships as a basis for learning. Supporting children's learning and development, including those children with behavioural needs, is no exception. Adults are the most important influence upon behaviour. Reflective practitioners examine their influences upon the dynamics of the environment. Knowledge of individuals enables adults to manage small groups and the whole class. This is not the whole picture as group dynamics should be taken into account. Behaviour expectations should be taught, and there is much that the adult can do to ensure positive behaviour management.

Practitioners as role models

Practitioners are, at the same time, role models for children and parents in terms of all interactions and behavioural expectations and, as such, their conduct should be exemplary (even in terms of the way in which they resolve conflict with adults and children).

Adults in the setting are likely to have varying views on what constitutes appropriate and inappropriate behaviour and this, in turn, is likely to vary with context (for example, indoors and outdoors). It is important that, prior to the formulation of any policy or rules, adults within the setting discuss their views and come to a shared understanding of:

- What is our shared image of the child?
- What is acceptable and unacceptable behaviour?
- What rewards and sanctions are developmentally appropriate?
- How will children with social, emotional and behavioural difficulties be included and supported in order that their experience is a positive one?
- Which resources are useful in supporting children with social, emotional and behavioural needs within the group?
- Who identifies and assesses those children with behavioural difficulties?

The answers to these questions and the discussion engendered can be used to formulate a policy which will ensure consistency of approach

Reflective task

Consider your setting and the answers to the bullet points above. Note any similarities and differences and record your answers. Discuss with fellow students in groups of four.

Behaviour plans

A set of rules, stated positively, should be developed collaboratively by staff and children together for all those in the setting. It is important that children, as a group and individually, are part of the discussion as it gives them a voice (Brunton, 2007) and takes account of their right to be involved in matters that affect them (UNICEF, 1989). If children are consulted and understand the reasons for the rules, they are more likely to comply because it encourages a problem-solving approach and teaches children responsibilities (Brunton, 2007). Equally, parents/carers need to be involved in the discussion, to ensure (as much as possible) consistency and continuity between the setting and home.

Ensure self-esteem remains intact

Be aware of how the adult can exacerbate a situation by either a confrontational approach or a lack of understanding. Adopt a calm, respectful manner which seeks to acknowledge feelings, and seek a solution where self-esteem can remain intact for all parties. Children exhibiting challenging behaviour often have low self-esteem for many reasons linked to their contexts and the feedback they have received from interactions with key adults in their lives. These children are often not held in high regard by their peers. The key for these children is to raise their self-esteem and their standing with the other children in the group. Such children need to believe that they can be successful and are worthy. Children who receive positive messages about the value of self, have clear messages in early childhood about what is expected, and are supported to be independent, have internalised standards and manage their own behaviour.

Observation and information gathering

As soon as a perceived behavioural issue arises, a period of information gathering should take place which includes observations conducted in a variety of forms by a variety of staff:

- ABC approach – the practitioner records the Antecedent (what led to the behaviour?); the Behaviour (what exactly did the child do?); the Consequence (what happened afterwards?).
- Continuous narrative observation – this takes the form of writing down everything the child does for a set period of time.
- Tracking observation – useful for tracking a child in a free-play situation. This will track the activities the child visits and for how long. This can help practitioners to decide what does and does not motivate a child (Drifte, 2008).

Gradually, practitioners gather a wealth of information about an individual child. Following this, judgements can be made about a child's emotional, social and behavioural needs. Steiner (cited in Nicol and Taplin, 2012: 111) described the child as 'a riddle that the practitioner works to solve'. The more information practitioners have, the more detailed their evaluations and reflections, and the greater the likelihood that they can support the learning and development of all the children in their care. Knowledgeable practitioners using their theoretical knowledge can begin to consider the issues and the strategies which may support learning and development.

A simple question such as 'Why is he/she doing that?', when considering the evidence from observations, may point to a particular special educational need (SEN) linked to child development issues, speech and language needs, sensory needs and personal/social needs such as frustration or low self-esteem. These issues will be considered below as issues arising from SEN and may be due to some of the underlying factors discussed above. It is important to work in partnership with parents, carers and families when addressing the individual needs of children and young people.

Strategies for managing behaviour

The EYFS (DfE, 2012a), Tickell's recommendations (2011) and the Allen Report (2011) are clear about the importance of early intervention, advocating development checks at age two. The principles are also clear: that all children are unique and learn at different rates and in different ways. It is the responsibility of the adults to adapt the environment and their own practice to support children's emerging needs. Possible strategies to consider:

- Making adjustments to the timetable (making time and space for play and ensuring the rhythm of the day is predictable leading to security). Staffing and/or resources should be flexible (Nicol and Taplin, 2012).

- Distraction can prove useful for younger children and can be a positive way of focusing a child's attention on something more appropriate (Nicol and Taplin, 2012).
- Consistency between staff is essential as mixed messages confuse children. The behaviour plan and policy will go some way towards ensuring this. Working in partnership with parents to share strategies can also be beneficial.

It is of paramount importance for practitioners to ensure that they are critical of the behaviour and not the individual. This is important for self-esteem so that children are not labelled as 'bad' or 'naughty'. Adult guidance empowers children to make choices about their behaviour and take responsibility for their actions through ongoing dialogue about what is and is not acceptable. Here are some practical strategies to facilitate and encourage positive behaviour:

- **Give clear and concise instructions**. These should be communicated through modelling mutual respect, and there should be an expectation that they should be followed. Praise those who are following expectations stating clearly and calmly what you wish them to do, e.g. 'I need you to…'. If the child does not comply you should make it clear that it is their choice. Offer the child the request and the sanction (from agreed behaviour plan or policy), making it clear that it is their choice to comply or continue with the behaviour and face the consequences. This encourages children to make choices and take responsibility for their behaviour. Think about the way in which instructions are issued, taking account of the points made above and allow processing time; if necessary, break instructions into smaller phrases.
- **Body language and tone of voice**. Verbal exchanges and body language, including facial expressions, should communicate the same powerful message; that of the assertive adult who expects that their requests are carried through. Confident practitioners give clear instructions calmly and assertively. In early years, body language and the voice can be used in many positive ways to communicate messages and engage children, for example whispering to draw children in, leaning forward and lowering voice to convey mystery.
- **Be specific about rewards and sanctions**. These will have been agreed in advance and reflect the behaviour plan and policy. When giving rewards or praise ensure that the specific reason for the reward or praise is communicated. In doing so you are restating expectations in a positive way and illustrating how individuals can replicate appropriate behaviour in future. As with rewards, sanctions will have been agreed and reflect the behaviour plan and policy. Following this, it is important to 'catch the child being good' and give some genuine praise (Canter and Canter, 2001).
- **Physical proximity**. This strategy is useful in a small or large group situation. The adult moves towards the individual whose behaviour is deemed inappropriate. Moving closer is often enough to let the child know that their behaviour has been noticed and will encourage them to respond to the expectations.
- **Use of the child's name**. This can be used to refocus a child who has become distracted.
- **Proximity praise**. Where a child is in a small or large group and not fulfilling expectations, this is a useful strategy. The adult 'notices' another child in close proximity who is conforming and offers genuine praise stating why praise is due. For example, 'I like the way you are…'. This is often enough to ensure the child off-task follows suit in an attempt to seek recognition (reinforcement) from the adult (Canter and Canter, 2001).
- **Tactical ignoring**. This is an important strategy in terms of positive behaviour management. The suggestion is that adults should ignore the low-level disruption where there is no risk to the child or others and focus on the positive – 'catch them being good'. For this strategy to work adults have to be positive and proactive in identifying and praising appropriate behaviour immediately (Canter and Canter, 2001).
- **Empathy**. In situations where there is a sense of injustice and emotions are running high it may be helpful to acknowledge feelings by restating expectations in a way that acknowledges this. For example, 'I can see that you are feeling … but I need you to …'.

- **Share expectations with all stakeholders (all adults working with the children, the children and the parents)**. Brooker (2002) suggests all families provide different early experiences which equip children for the preschool world in very different ways socially, culturally and linguistically. Failure on the part of practitioners to share expectations with parents may lead to children and families having negative early experiences in settings.
- **Differentiation**. Activities provided should match the learning needs and capabilities of the children where there is an appropriate level of challenge for both child-initiated and adult-led learning, where adults can extend children's thinking in both types of activity (Siraj-Blatchford and Sylva, 2004).

Next steps

- What is your setting's policy or procedure to deal with behaviour issues?
- What do you do when a child displays unacceptable or disruptive behaviour?

Give reasons for your answers.

Play therapy strategies

There seems to be an over-reliance on behaviourist type approaches, which have their place; however, Powell and Tod (2004) suggest that practitioners should have a range of approaches at their disposal for effective behaviour management. The field of play therapy provides various strategies which can support individual children's emotional and social well-being in educational settings.

Inspired by Virginia Axline (1911–88) and the field of non-directive play therapy situations (Axline, 1969), play-based methods of teaching and learning are used to support children's and young people's behaviour and communication skills. This area provides strategies for dealing with children (three to eleven years) with emotional difficulties in one-to-one sessions. Children's experiences are often communicated through play. The following play therapy principles could help to guide practitioners, when applied in an environment where there is a genuine respect for the child and knowledge of the value of limitations:

- establish rapport
- accept the child completely
- allow the child to lead the way
- recognise and reflect on feelings that the child may display through role play, painting and drawing.

Ayling (2012) proposes a range of techniques using the framework for teaching communication skills with children identified by Lefevre *et al.* (2008). Some of these strategies are: symbolic drawing, project play using small-world toys, sand-tray play, role play, music making and storytelling.

Educational drama or drama for learning

Pioneered by Dorothy Heathcote (1926–2011), this operates best in a whole-class shared meaning-making experience. The learning context can emerge from the children (for example, bullying, if this issue occupies their minds) or the practitioner (for example, a theme, a story, a project or a cross-curricular opportunity). The teacher/practitioner as facilitator and his/her skilful use of role and fiction excite, engage and at the same time help the children to self-reflect. The practitioner's responsibility is to empower the class and abandon the regular teacher/pupils relationship for one with different and varied dynamics, such as the colleague/artist. The best way to achieve this is by operating from 'within the drama' (adopting a role, a viewpoint) and not outside it (Heathcote and Bolton, 1995). The creative use of dramatic conventions by the expert facilitator creates meaningful learning environments where children are excited to learn and engage, and behavioural issues diminish. Some of the conventions which are based on theatre practice are as follows:

- **Teacher-in-role**. A powerful and interactive strategy which enables the adult (practitioner) to play with the children and be alongside them as a fellow participant while modelling, mediating and facilitating in a shared imagined drama experience.
- **Still image and freeze-frame**. Freezing the action enables a moment in the drama to be held physically still for a purpose. This can act as a control strategy when the pace is too fast and enables the participants to offer a shared visual focus and focus their attention.
- **Mantle of the expert**. It encourages speaking and listening with partners, gives children a responsible role, such as curators, gardeners and vets, and through their 'expert' role they share the fiction.
- **Hot-seating**. This helps participants to engage, discover and understand the thoughts and motives of a particular character through a shared aural and visual focus. The convention provides opportunities for character development and active thinking.
- **Role on the wall**. A visual way of gathering together and recording what the children feel about a character in the drama.
- **Conscience alley**. This enables children to work as a team, have a shared ownership and hold still a key moment at which an important decision should be made.
- **Thought tracking**. This helps children to hold a moment still and engage deeply with a character. It also models active listening to the thoughts of others.
- **Collective role**. This offers context for active listening and can take place with children seated in a circle and taking turns to speak or pass if they do not wish to contribute.
- **Improvisation**. This enables children to focus their attention on a situation or event.

Group drama is a behaviour-management strategy that engages children in collective role responsibility and consequently enables them to express emotions, feelings and thoughts in a secure, protective and meaningful environment (Baldwin, 2004).

Children with special educational needs

The term special educational needs (SEN) refers to children who 'have a learning difficulty which calls for special educational provision to be made for them' (DfES, 2001: 6), for example language or developmental delays, disabilities such as attention deficit disorder or attention deficit hyperactivity disorder, dyslexia or dyspraxia. Special educational provision means 'for children of two or over … provision which is additional to or different from' the general provision offered to other children of the same age (DfES, 2001: 6). SEN provision also applies to children who are classified as gifted who also have additional needs in comparison to those whose development is typical for their age.

Taylor (2001) suggests that the number of children with pervasive developmental disorders is increasing, but acknowledges that this is due to advances in neonatal and paediatric services; more children survive birth and early trauma. In addition to advances in medical science, there are also better recognition and diagnosis of medical issues. Although this study was undertaken in

Australia she believes that it has global relevance. The research draws on data from the Western Australia Health Survey (1995, 1996 and 1997) involving a random sample of 1,776 households.

According to Taylor (2001), boys have higher levels of disability than girls. The study notes that at least one in four children had difficulties with motor or sensory functioning and nearly 18 per cent of children in the survey had mental health issues (Taylor, 2001). Asperger's syndrome is nine times more likely in boys and attention deficit hyperactivity disorder (ADHD), dyslexia and dyspraxia affect four times more boys than girls (Taylor, 2001). Developmental disorders have both a neurological and a social component (Palmer, 2006). This has implications for practitioners and teachers working with children in settings because children's thinking and development are linked to both nature (genetic inheritance) and nurture (environmental contexts), according to Taylor (2001).

Practitioners should take account of the diverse backgrounds of children and seek to support them in their development. We are moving towards a pedagogy where children are viewed as active participants, co-constructing learning in a reciprocal relationship, where children's rights are both acknowledged and respected. The EYFS (DfE, 2012a) have a principled approach where children are viewed as competent learners who are capable of learning and succeeding. For these reasons we start from where the child is at and use the same approach discussed earlier where there is a period of information gathering to ascertain strengths, areas for development and the most appropriate strategies to move forward. As Taylor (2001) suggests, practitioners should recognise and celebrate difference, accept that children learn and develop in different ways and that all children can succeed. The responsibility lies with the adult to make adaptations to the environment, methods and resources they use to accommodate all. This supports the view that practitioners should have the relevant knowledge and understanding of a variety of children's conditions. To this end, professional development and training are important to enable practitioners to meet individual children's needs. Furthermore, partnership with the parents/carers and other professionals through the sharing of information about individual children enables suitable provision to be made (EYFS, DfE, 2012a).

Speech and language needs

Language development is an important predictor of academic achievement. Positive parenting and maternal care-giving are associated with improved language and communication skills (Stein *et al.*, 2008). Children who have specific language needs, whether receptive or expressive, have difficulty in functioning in the early years environment. Difficulty in understanding and processing information (receptive language) can mean that children are unable to respond to instructions or questions and adhere to rules and routines, and find it difficult to make sense of the environment. As a result, adults may perceive their behaviour to be deviant rather than attributing non-conformity to a lack of understanding. Developing a set of rules with the children can support their understanding of what is acceptable and help them to meet expectations (Brooker, 2002). Gestures and prompts are also useful. Children and families from ethnic minority groups, whether recently arrived or from established communities, whose cultural view of childhood, education and pedagogy differs from Western settings, can find settling in and making sense of their new environment particularly challenging.

Attention deficit disorder (ADD) and attention deficit hyperactivity disorder (ADHD)

ADD and ADHD are medical disorders that can only be diagnosed by a qualified clinician; they are complex and often exist alongside other conditions (Wheeler, 2010). Children present with inattention, hyperactivity and impulsivity (Thorell and Rydell, 2008) and the disorders are more common in boys than girls. Children with these disorders display both internalising and externalising behaviours that are inappropriate to their stage of development; that is to say that they can be aggressive and defiant (externalising) and anxious and withdrawn, even moody (internalising). It is the former (found in ADHD) that presents most difficulties in terms of behaviour management; however, in meeting the needs of all children attention should also be given to support those with internalising behaviours.

The origins of ADHD- and ADD-associated difficulties are not clear, but it is thought that there are both biological and environmental components that interact (Wheeler, 2010). Strategies can be implemented to ameliorate the latter, but it would be dangerous to suggest that it is that simplistic. However, what is clear is that it provides barriers for interaction and functioning in both the life of the family and the early years setting.

Children who are temperamentally difficult (such as can be the case with some babies, toddlers and those with ADHD) receive negative responses from carers which can perpetuate the cycle (Patterson, 1982, cited in Thorell and Rydell, 2008). These children can suffer rejection by peers and, as a result, can lack opportunities to practise their social skills. It is important that a variety of approaches is employed for supporting these children; specific targeted support including modelling, conflict resolution, development of social skills which offer children alternatives to the externalising behaviours, and behaviourist strategies may also have a part to play. It may be necessary to employ interventions such as Nurture Groups (Bennathan and Boxall, 2000), where there is a focus on small groups, on predictable routine with opportunities to practise interaction and opportunities for play-based activities which can be replicated in the home and early years setting.

It is important that successful use of these alternative strategies meets with approval from adults at home and in the setting to break the cycle of negativity. Parents and staff should work together in mutually supportive and consistent ways to mirror the Nurture Group model within the setting and the home environment.

Scientific studies suggest that diet may have a role to play in ameliorating the effects of ADHD, but this has been inconclusive (Wheeler, 2010). Limiting fat, sugary foods, artificial colours, preservatives and monosodium glutamate has been helpful in some cases (Stevens, 2000). Elimination of certain foods and ascertaining efficacy take time and require adults to record diet and any subsequent behaviours.

Gifted and talented

The term 'giftedness' refers to academic skills and 'talent' is mostly associated with non-academic abilities, such as the arts (Porter, 2005: 4). Young, gifted children can potentially develop into talented performers if they live in a supportive environment where stimulating tasks can trigger their intellectual processing skills, including motivation, and eventually enhance the performance of their thought, feeling or behaviour.

The emotional adjustment of gifted children into educational environments can be challenging for adults responsible for their learning and development as well as for other children. Gifted individuals are often emotionally and socially vulnerable and their nervous system contributes to both advanced learning and emotional intensity (Porter, 2005). Their perfectionist drive stimulates feelings of anxiety and stress. If not adapted to the environment and stimulated sufficiently they may demonstrate behavioural difficulties as a way of coping with boredom or to prove to their peers that they are smart.

Cooperation between home and the educational setting is of paramount importance. Thorough assessment as a systematic way of collecting information about the children's learning skills and styles is necessary. Educational as well as psychometric testing can help parents and practitioners to design a programme of differentiated curriculum content that aims to stimulate, engage and develop the gifted child.

Next steps

- Identify the range of children you support with SEN.
- What is the setting's policy for working with children with SEN?
- What strategies do you use to support these children?
- Identify any training needs and where you might go for support, for example portage, speech and language therapists, others?

Working in partnership with parents

The EYFS (DfE, 2012a) stresses the importance of working in partnership with parents. Taylor (2001) suggests that in order to understand children's thinking and being, parent partnership is vital. The Allen Report (2011), *Every Child Matters* (DfES, 2003), the Tickell Report (2011) and Sylva *et al.* (2004) also concur with the need to collaborate. In order for consistency, practitioners and parents should work together exchanging information and sharing strategies about children's individual needs. Parent information and practitioner information are both different and complementary, contributing to the holistic view of the child. For children with conduct problems there is a variety of parenting programmes available, for example the Incredible Years programme developed by Webster-Stratton. However, research by Broadhead *et al.* (2009), Holland (2003) and Hyder (2005) suggests that play can do much to support children's social and emotional development and the ability to resolve conflict.

Being a parent can be a happy time in people's lives, but also a very stressful experience, especially when children demonstrate emotional or behavioural difficulties. Parents can be vulnerable and can rely on practitioners in the same way as do their children. According to The Tavistock and Portman clinical research (2012), the most recent government statistics suggest that one in five children experience emotional or behavioural difficulties. There are many difficulties that may create tension within families:

- Pregnancy can itself be stressful especially for those who experience the loss of a baby or infant.
- Early days with a newborn baby can be emotionally complex for parents and siblings.
- Transitions from home to care and educational settings can be unknown experiences for many new parents.
- Parents experience difficulties such as arguments, bereavement, divorce, consequences of war and dislocation from home, imprisonment, poverty and financial constraints.

Collaborating with parents should not be seen as an additional task, but as a natural process. Practitioners should respect parents and have the skills to engage with them in a warm and supportive atmosphere. They should empower them and support them in meeting their children's needs. Practitioners need to provide parents with information about health, education and financial support services which will enable them to be confident in their role as successful parents.

Some collaborative practices are:

- Active listening to what they have to say: try to be supportive and non–judgemental.
- Show genuine interest and warmth, and that you really care.
- Respect privacy and confidentiality. Although you should not be expected to agree with all their views, you should show recognition and respect for their experiences as well as a positive attitude towards managing their family situation.
- Refer parents to other professionals who can provide expert advice and support. Talking therapies can be successful in treating well–being issues.

Scenario

Holly is a four-year-old child from a traveller family who attends nursery full time. She appears to be happy and charming in the setting and has settled in well, but she has tantrums when she does not get what she wants.

- How should the practitioner support Holly?
- What theories are useful in this situation?
- What strategies does the practitioner need in order to foster well-being and development?
- How should the practitioner work with the parent(s)/carer(s) to ensure consistency?

Work together in a group to consider these questions. Spend 45 minutes on this task.

Conclusion

This chapter has explored some of the theoretical concepts and principles that underpin behaviour management together with a selection of strategies that can be applied practically. You have been encouraged to reflect upon the practical application of these theoretical perspectives and how this supports children's social, emotional and behavioural development in early years.

Early childhood can be described as a significant stage of an individual's learning and development. It is a process that is characterised by change and growth. The following principles are founded within the context of the child's family and social environment:

- attachment to carers
- communication and early language
- complex expressions of emotions
- development of gross and fine motor skills
- differentiation of self from others
- self-compliance and control.

Young children need affectionate, engaging and stimulating learning environments which meet their individual needs and build upon their strengths. Play matters; it is the way in which children rehearse their thinking and learn to interact with others. The development of emotional health and well-being relies on active stimulation: mental, physical and cognitive challenges that take account of gender differences and diversity. This is facilitated by mutually supportive relationships between parents and practitioners who share a common bond – the well-being of the child.

Evaluate your...

Knowledge of behaviour management
- How do you recognise a child who has behaviour problems?
- In what ways do you support the social, emotional and behavioural development of babies, children and/or young people in your working environment?
- How do you encourage children to manage their own behaviour?
- How can the behaviour of adults in a setting affect children's individual and group responses?
- What are the key features of a behaviour policy? What would you include and why?

Further reading

Aldgate, J., Jones, D. P. H., Rose, W. and Jeffery, C. (eds.) (2006) *The Developing World of the Child*, London: Jessica Kingsley.

Broadhead, P. (2009) 'Conflict resolution and children's behaviour: Observing and understanding social and cooperative play in early years educational settings', *Early Years*, vol. 29 no. 2, pp. 105–18.

Cooper, P. and Whitebread, D. (2007) 'The effectiveness of nurture groups on student progress: Evidence from a national research study', *Emotional and Behavioural Difficulties*, vol. 12, no. 3, pp. 171–90.

Degotardi, S. and Davis, B. (2008) 'Understanding infants: Characteristics or early childhood practitioners' interpretations of infants and their behaviours', *Early Years*, vol. 28, no. 3, pp. 221–34.

Drifte, C. (2008) *Encouraging Positive Behaviour Management in the Early Years* (2nd edn), London: Sage.

Featherstone, S. and Bayley, R. (2005) *Boys and Girls Come Out to Play*, Husband's Bosworth: Featherstone Educational.

Foley, P. and Leverett, S. (eds.) (2011) *Children and Young People's Spaces*, Milton Keynes: The Open University.

Powell, S. and Tod, J. (2004) *A systematic review of how theories explain learning behaviour in school contexts*, London: EPPI-Centre, Social Science Research Unit, Institute of Education, University of London. Available from: http://eppi.ioe.ac.uk/cms/LinkClick.aspx?fileticket=xjNFKFrgr G8%3D&tabid=123&mid=928.

Safeguarding children

Francisca Veale

Introduction

This chapter will explore the issues of safeguarding children, and the duty for early years practitioners to safeguard children and promote their well-being under current legislation in Great Britain (Children Act 1989, Education Act 2002, Children Act 2004, Childcare Act 2006). All legislation and guidance referring to children and young people is based on the legal definition of a child, which means a child ceases to be a child on their 18th birthday. Wider reading and research, as well as reflection on your practice, will be encouraged throughout the chapter. Safeguarding children and child protection are not simply a textbook exercise; they require practitioners to be knowledgeable in theory and competent in practice to confidently help and support children to be and stay safe. This chapter will give you a theoretical and statutory knowledge base and encourages you to reflect on your practice, to ensure that children's well-being and safety are paramount, and safeguarding is promoted as part of your everyday practice.

Learning outcomes

This chapter will introduce, explain and invite you to read further on the following areas of safeguarding children. It will encourage you to critically evaluate your own working practices and how you work with other professionals to safeguard children around the following learning objectives:

- Safeguarding children in the historical context.
- Traditional and contemporary theories and current research.
- Safeguarding legislation and regulatory guidance and the EYFS.
- Children Act 1989 and Children Act 2004.
- What are abuse and neglect?
- Domestic violence and the impact on children.
- Multi-agency working and information sharing.
- Assessment frameworks and team around the child.
- Fostering resilience and helping children to protect themselves.

Safeguarding is an overarching and all-encompassing umbrella term which includes general health and safety issues when working with children, from an early intervention and preventative stage at one end of the spectrum, to the more high-risk end of child protection. Safeguarding and promoting the welfare of children are defined as (DCSF, 2010a: 34):

- protecting children from maltreatment
- preventing impairment of children's health or development

- ensuring that children are growing up in circumstances consistent with the provision of safe and effective care
  undertaking that role so as to enable those children to have optimum life chances and to enter adulthood successfully.

The figure below illustrates the wide range of safeguarding provision from universal and preventative services for all children and young people's needs to more specialist services for complex, high-risk or vulnerable children and young people.

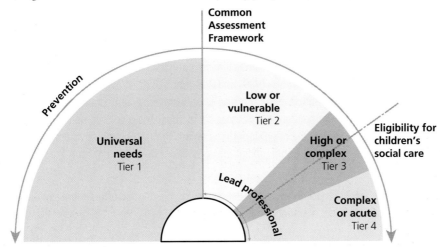

Figure 13.1 Children's needs and multi-agency tiers of intervention

Child protection is a part of safeguarding and promoting children's welfare under the Children Act 1989, section 47, and it refers to the activity that is undertaken to protect 'children who are suffering, or are likely to suffer, significant harm' (DCSF, 2010a: 35). The previous Early Years Foundation Stage's (EYFS) Welfare Requirements (DCSF, 2008a) expected that practitioners should be able to respond appropriately to any significant changes in children's behaviour, or a deterioration in their general well-being, and show vigilance towards any unexplained bruising, marks or signs of possible abuse or signs of neglect, as well as any comments children make which give cause for concern. The importance of safeguarding and keeping children safe was highlighted as 'a non-negotiable element of any early years framework' in the Tickell Report (Tickell, 2011) that influenced the new Safeguarding and Welfare Requirements for the EYFS (DfE, 2012a) which will be discussed later.

The historical emergence of safeguarding

The concept of protecting children has only been acknowledged and addressed in society in the last century, as new views and concepts of childhood emerged. In 1924 the need for the special safeguarding of children was expressed in the Geneva Declaration of the Rights of the Child, and then further recognised in the Universal Declaration of Human Rights and in the statutes of agencies and international organisations concerned with the welfare of children. In 1959 the Declaration of the Rights of the Child was proclaimed by the United Nations stating:

The child, by reason of his physical and mental immaturity, needs special safeguards and care, including appropriate legal protection, before as well as after birth.

However, the internationally accepted UN Convention on the Rights of the Child (United Nations, 1989) was not declared until 1989 and signed by the UK in 1991. The only two countries still not to have signed the convention are the United States and Somalia.

Classic and contemporary research

Attachment

Research into the psychological or mental health illnesses and their underlying causes was undertaken by psychoanalysts Sigmund Freud (1856–1939) and Carl Jung (1875–1961). They found that childhood trauma had a detrimental effect on adult life and relationships, as subconscious processes could lead to 'dissociation' from traumatic experiences, such as abuse, as a coping mechanism. If a child's development of trust and a healthy attachment is impaired through abuse or trauma, it will impact on the child's behaviour, their personal, social and emotional development, and their openness to learning.

Also, John Bowlby's research (1969) highlighted the significance of good attachment in childhood and the otherwise negative effects of attachment disorders.

Current research and contemporary theories by Zeanah and Fox (2004), and Zeanah *et al.* (2004) explore the effects of child abuse trauma and the impaired relationships for children.

Extend your knowledge

Undertake further reading and research into contemporary attachment theory and current research. Compare and contrast the different theoretical concepts and discuss their interrelatedness.

- Zeanah, C. and Fox, N. (2004) 'Temperament and attachment disorders', *Journal of Clinical Child Adolescence Psychology*, vol. 33, no. 1, pp. 32–41.
- Zeanah, C., Scheeringa, M., Boris, N., Heller, S., Smyke, A. and Trapani, J. (2004) 'Reactive attachment disorder in maltreated toddlers', *Child Abuse & Neglect: The International Journal*, vol. 28, no. 8, pp. 877–88.

What are the theoretical assumptions about children and parent relationships in light of safeguarding children?

The first awareness that safeguarding and protection of children needed addressing goes back to the case of Mary Ellen Wilson in New York in 1874. Mary Ellen suffered physical abuse by her foster parents and was only saved by a neighbourhood nurse pleading protection under animal cruelty legislation (Airdrie, 2009). In the UK, similarly to America, animal protection laws were in place in 1849, before child protection laws were introduced with the Prevention of Cruelty to, and Protection of, Children Act 1889.

The first publicly reported child abuse case in the UK was of Dennis O'Neil in 1945, which subsequently led to a public inquiry, resulting in the Monckton Report published by the Home Office in 1945. The Monkton Report highlighted the miscommunications of the professionals involved. The creation of the Parliamentary Care of Children Committee in 1945 led to the Children Act 1948. With this, children's committees and children's officers were established in each local authority, thereby legitimising state intervention to help and support children who were subjects of abuse and mistreatment. Historically, concepts of childhood and family matters were seen as private concerns, neither requiring nor warranting state intervention – in a similar way to how today domestic violence is sometimes considered a private family matter. It could be argued that state intervention poses an ethical dilemma between the individual's right of privacy and the human right of protection, in particular the protection of children (United Nations, 1989).

The death of Maria Colwell in 1973 led to another public inquiry, resulting in recommendations for agencies to share information and to communicate more effectively, and for professionals to be trained to deal with child protection issues (Scott, 1975). Child abuse was identified not just as a social issue but also as a political issue, and the protection of children became an item on the political agenda (Parton, 2003). In 1974, child abuse registers were introduced; however, this in itself did not prevent children dying through abuse and neglect by their parents or step-parents, as evident in the series of high-profile cases which made public headlines between 1984 and 1987: Jasmine Beckford, Tyra Henry, Heidi Koseda, Kimberley Carlile, Doreen Mason and Charlene Salt.

Possibly, it was public and professional heightened alertness that contributed to the Cleveland child abuse scandal in 1987. The 121 cases of suspected child sexual abuse were diagnosed by Dr Marietta Higgs and Dr Geoffrey Wyatt, and consequently the children were taken out of their families by social services and the police. This was a twofold scandal, firstly because so many of the cases were wrongly diagnosed as sexual abuse, and secondly because social services and police, without questioning the medical decision and without their own investigation, removed so many children from their families. Again, the ensuing inquiry evidenced the lack of communication between agencies, and the recommendations emphasised the need for better communication between professionals in a multi-agency approach and the necessity for training (BMJ, 1988).

Reflective task

- Find out more about the individual cases of reported child abuse and identify the causes of what went wrong. Facilitate a debate within your classroom.
- Reflect on what you think is the role of society, government and professionals in safeguarding children.
- What are the underlying theoretical concepts of safeguarding and how are these applied in safeguarding practice in your setting?

As a consequence of high-profile child abuse cases and scenarios, the current Children Act 1989 came into force in 1991. The Act focuses on the welfare and safety of children, outlining the duties and responsibilities of the local authorities in providing services to protect children from harm. The legislation was followed by a guidance document called *Working together to safeguard children*, which clarified the roles and responsibilities of professionals in protecting children from harm. It was first published in 1999, revised in 2006, with the current version being published in 2010 (DCSF, 2010a).

Despite the Children Act 1989 outlining that children's safety and welfare are paramount, Victoria Climbié and Lauren Wright both died in 2000. Lord Laming's inquiry (2003) into the death of Victoria Climbié concluded with 108 recommendations, some of which pointed out again, as in previous cases, the importance of communications within agencies as well as information sharing between agencies. In 2003, the government published the Green Paper *Every Child Matters* (DfES, 2003), setting out five outcomes, which gives everybody working with children and young people the responsibility to proactively promote their safety and well-being.

The Children Act 2004 subsequently became law and set out the Five Outcomes Framework in statute. The introduction of children's centres and extended school services was aimed to support children and their families to achieve the outcomes and promote well-being and safeguarding through early intervention and prevention. Despite new legislation, and the attempts by government to place safeguarding on everyone's top-priority agenda, young children like Baby P (Peter Connelly) in 2007 and Khyra Ishaq in 2008 both died, even though both were known to the local authorities. Subsequently, in November 2008 the Secretary of State for Children, Schools and Families requested Lord Laming to provide an urgent report on the progress being made across the country to implement effective arrangements for safeguarding children. Lord Laming (2009) published *The Protection of Children in England: A Progress Report*, where he confirmed that robust legislative, structural and policy foundations are in place, but commented that, although progress has been made in protecting children from harm, 'much more needs to be done to ensure that … services are as effective as possible at working together to achieve positive outcomes for children'. Lord Laming (2009) made 58 recommendations to improve safeguarding children, which related to leadership, accountability, support for children, inter-agency working, children's workforce training, organisations' finance, and the legal framework.

However, Munro (2011, 2012) and other experts in the field have criticised Laming's approach and recommendations (2009), not only because of his bias, as he reviewed his own recommendations, but more importantly, the fact that the safeguarding systems are far too bureaucratic. Munro (2011, 2012) points out that the demands on social workers to follow timelines and computer systems, rather than dealing with individuals (children and families) in face-to-face contact, or telephone conversations between professionals rather than emails, are problems where the over-bureaucratic systems let children down. Another perspective on the failures of professionals to prevent the death of Victoria Climbié, offered by Ferguson (2005), highlights the emotional and psycho-social dynamics of child protection.

Extend your knowledge

Read the Ferguson (2005) journal article and identify what emotional issues workers are faced with when working with child protection cases, and what recommendations are made:

- Ferguson, H. (2005) 'Working with violence, the emotions and the psycho-social dynamics of child protection: Reflections on the Victoria Climbié case', *Social Work Education*, vol. 24, no. 7, pp. 781–95.

Wrennall (2010) suggested a very different view on the subject of safeguarding children and the role or purpose of state intervention. She asserts that child protection and information sharing have led to expansive data collection and surveillance which are 'used to provide an ostensible rationale for other policies, practices and expenditure that further commercial, political, economic and other interests, rather than the interests of children' (Wrennall, 2010: 305).

Wrennall (2010) based her critical view on questioning the effectiveness of safeguarding children through electronic systems and information and communication technology (ICT) in child protection cases, as recommended by Laming. This is further supported by Munro (2011, 2012) who criticises the fact that social workers are overloaded with managerial, bureaucratic, computer-based assessments and case recording, thus no longer have time for face-to-face contact with children and families.

Reflective task

- Undertake further reading and research into both of Lord Laming's reports and identify recommendations related to early years practice.
- Compare and contrast the different theoretical assumptions and concepts that underpin the approaches to safeguard and protect children by examining the different opinions expressed by Laming, Munro, Wrennall and Ferguson.

Current legislative frameworks and regulatory guidance

The UN Convention on the Rights of the Child (United Nations, 1989), states in Article 4 that all children require protection, and further postulates in Article 19 that children need to be protected from all forms of violence. This is reflected in the UK laws protecting children and promoting their welfare: the Children Act 1989 and the Children Act 2004. Section 11 of the Children Act 2004 and Section 175 of the Education Act 2002 place the duty on organisations and individuals to ensure that their functions are exercised with regard to the need to safeguard and promote the welfare of children. Therefore, all organisations working with children and young people are required to have a child protection policy in place.

The Children Act 1989 obliges local authorities to work in partnership with parents and, provided this is consistent with the child's safety and welfare, to promote the upbringing of children by their families, where appropriate and safe, instead of removing children from their families (as exercised in the Cleveland case). The local authority has a duty to provide services appropriate to the child's needs. The Children Act 1989 also defined **parental responsibility**, which has since been amended by the Adoption and Children Act 2002 (Part 2 of the Children Act 1989) and came into force in December 2003. The amendment takes into account unmarried fathers taking up their parental responsibility in the upbringing of their children. The amendment to the Act means that the mother can agree for her partner (regardless of whether he is the biological father, or as to whether or not they are married) to jointly register the child's birth, therefore agreeing to take up legal parental responsibility. Parental responsibility cannot be lost through separation or divorce of the parents, and can only be abdicated or renounced through a family court decision.

The duty to safeguard children and promote their welfare is further highlighted in the Childcare Act 2006. Early years providers and their staff, including volunteers, have a duty under Section 40 of the Childcare Act 2006 to take necessary steps to safeguard children and have to know how they should respond to any child protection concerns (DCSF, 2010a: 85).

The current working document, which guides all practitioners and should be used in every setting working with children and young people, is *Working Together to Safeguard Children: A guide to inter-agency working to safeguard and promote the welfare of children* (DCSF, 2010a). As suggested in the subtitle, the emphasis is on working together collaboratively in an inter-agency approach to safeguard children, to promote their welfare and to learn from the mistakes of the past.

For health and social care professionals and organisations *The National Service Framework for Children, Young People and Maternity Services* (DoH, 2004) provides guidance about meeting Standard Five on safeguarding and promoting the welfare of children and young people. Furthermore, *The Common Core of Skills and Knowledge for the Children's Workforce* (Children's Workforce Development Council, 2010) guidance document sets out six areas of expertise that everyone working with children, young people and families should be able to demonstrate; it includes safeguarding and promoting the welfare of children.

Above all, any organisation working with children must ensure it has in place safe recruitment policies and practices, including enhanced Criminal Records Bureau (CRB) checks for all staff working with children, whether paid staff, students or volunteers. It is an offence to knowingly employ a person who has been barred by the Independent Safeguarding Authority (ISA) from working in positions which involve caring for or treating children. All employing and voluntary agencies must act in line with the *Safeguarding Children and Safer Recruitment in Education* (DCSF, 2010b) guidance, as well as their Local Safeguarding Children's Boards (LSCB) policies and procedures. All staff, paid or unpaid, working with children need to attend safeguarding children training and to update their training every three years.

Whistleblowing

Furthermore, organisations are required to have policies and procedures in place for whistleblowing (DCSF, 2010a). The underpinning legislation is the Public Interest Disclosure Act 1998, also known as the 'Whistleblowing' Act. The Act is intended to promote internal and regulatory disclosures, thus to encourage workplace accountability, self-regulation and a culture that enables issues about safeguarding to be addressed. The Public Interest Disclosure Act 1998 protects the public interest by providing a route for individuals who suffer workplace reprisals for raising a genuine concern, whether it is a concern about child safeguarding and welfare systems, financial malpractice, danger, illegality or other wrongdoing.

Research published by the Department of Health, *Towards safer care training and resource pack* (DoH, 1999), and the Waterhouse Inquiry (Waterhouse, 2000) into the children in care in North Wales, who were abused by those supposed to care for them, identified that practitioners often chose not to believe the 'worst-case scenario', but rather want to believe that child abuse is not happening until it is often too late. The advice is, if somebody is concerned about a child being abused by anybody, including those who are professionals and caring for them: 'Suspend disbelief, believe the unbelievable, imagine the unimaginable and don't think what if I am wrong, but think "What if I am right?"' (Waterhouse, 2000).

The importance of whistleblowing has become even more imperative in the light of the serious case review by the Plymouth Safeguarding Children Board (2010) with regard to the arrest of the nursery worker Vanessa George, who had circulated indecent pictures of children in her care which she had taken with her mobile phone.

Ofsted

The responsibility for the regulation and inspection of day care and children's social care, and the inspection of local authority children's services and schools rest with the Office for Standards in Education (Ofsted), and provide an independent, external evaluation of the quality and standards of provision. Ofsted's role in relation to local authority safeguarding services is to evaluate and report on the extent to which children's services improve the safeguarding and well-being of children and young people. If during an inspection general safeguarding does not appear to be in place and staff lack appropriate knowledge then this may limit the judgement – meaning that the outcome grade may only be satisfactory or even inadequate. Therefore, it is imperative that all staff are trained and have up-to-date safeguarding knowledge, as well as working to the setting's Code of Conduct (DCSF, 2009a; DCSF, 2010b; DfE, 2012a; Ofsted, 2012).

From September 2012 Ofsted registration continues to focus on safeguarding, with the aim of preventing those who are unsuitable to work with children from any access. Also, the new regulations aim to 'minimise risks to children so that they thrive in a safe environment when in registered early years provision' (Ofsted, 2012:5).

Scenarios

1 The mother of a child in your care has phoned to say that she will not be able to collect the child and that her boyfriend will come to collect the child. The child does not want to go with the boyfriend and demands to be collected by the mother. What do you do?
2 The boyfriend asks about the child's friends and their parents' telephone numbers to call. Can you share this information with him? Who can you share information with?
3 A member of staff wants to take photos of the children's work and put these on the setting's website as they do every Friday afternoon, but the setting's camera is not working. A parent volunteer offers their camera and suggests staff could also use their mobile phone cameras instead. What do you do?

Having reflected on and discussed the above scenarios in small groups, questions for more information might have evolved before you felt comfortable or confident to give an answer. It is not unusual that you, or in fact any lone professional, might not always have all the information and feel reluctant to act. However, safeguarding children is everybody's responsibility, and in case of doubt, appropriate actions should be taken by contacting another child protection or safeguarding professional within your setting, or the local authority, to ensure that the child will be safe from any potentially harmful situations.

Next steps

Safeguarding practice in your setting

Locate and read the following documents in your setting. Check if the content is current and up-to-date with your local authority's recommended guidance and policies.
- The setting's child protection/safeguarding policies and procedures.
- A copy of *Working Together to Safeguard Children* (DCSF, 2010a).
- A copy of the *Guidance for Safer Working Practice for Adults who Work with Children and Young People* (DCSF, 2009a).
- The safer recruitment policy of your setting.
- The use of ICT in your setting, including mobile phones.
- The whistleblowing policy in your setting.
- Your setting's Ofsted report safeguarding judgement.

Research good-practice examples of safeguarding, then compare, contrast and identify gaps in your practice before developing your own action plan for improvement of safeguarding practice in your setting.

The Children Act 1989

The Children Act 1989 outlines the duty of local authorities to assess children in need (Section 17) and children at risk of significant harm (Section 47). Children who are defined as being 'in need', under Section 17 of the Children Act 1989, are those whose vulnerability is such that they are unlikely to reach or maintain a satisfactory level of health or development, or their health and development will be significantly impaired, without the provision of services (Section 17(10) of the Children Act 1989), and those who are disabled. The critical factors to be taken into account in deciding whether a child is in need under Section 17 of the Children Act 1989 are: a) what will happen to a child's health or development without services being provided; and b) the likely effect the services will have on the child's standard of health and development.

Reflective task

Section 17 Children Act 1989

Children in need as classified under Section 17 of the Children Act 1989 can have a wide range of needs, which will require the local authority to provide help, assistance or financial support such as:

1 A child has a disability and needs walking aids or transport.
2 A child with autism or attention deficit hyperactivity disorder (ADHD) needs specialist therapeutic interventions.
3 A child's parent has mental health issues and respite childcare is needed.
4 A child is seeking asylum.
5 A child and parent fled domestic violence and have no clothes or toys.

Reflect and think about what assistance or service would be required to help the child in each of the examples to meet their developmental and health needs. What are your role and responsibility? If applicable, how could you work together with outside agencies?

Local authorities have a duty to safeguard and promote the welfare of children in need. However, some children are in greater need because they are 'suffering, or likely to suffer, significant harm', which is defined under the Section 47 of the Children Act 1989. An investigation under Section 47 justifies compulsory intervention by the local authority into family life in the best interest of children. Furthermore, it establishes a duty for the local authorities to make enquiries to decide whether they should take action to safeguard or promote the welfare of a child who is suffering, or likely to suffer, significant harm (DCSF, 2010a: 35).

Reflective task

Section 47 Children Act 1989

Children suffering, or likely to suffer, significant harm, as classified under Section 47 of the Children Act 1989, can be in different situations that will require the local authority to investigate and intervene such as:

1 A child has sustained non-accidental bruises and cuts.
2 A child has been exposed to or involved in sexually explicit materials or situations.
3 A child is not taken to vital life-enhancing medical appointments.

4 A child's basic needs are not met.

5 A child is living in a violent domestic environment.

6 A child has made an allegation or disclosure of abuse.

Reflect and think about what information you might hold that could support the investigation, and how you could share this with the relevant persons. Why is the sharing of information important? What are potential issues that you need to consider?

What are abuse and neglect?

Working Together to Safeguard Children (DCSF, 2010a) and the EYFS Safeguarding and Welfare Requirements (DfE, 2012a) both state that everybody who has contact with children should be able to recognise, and know how to act upon, evidence that a child's health or development is or might be impaired – especially when they are suffering, or likely to suffer, significant harm through abuse or neglect. Furthermore, the fact is highlighted that children can be, and are more likely to be, abused by someone known to them, rather than a stranger.

> **Abuse and neglect are forms of maltreatment of a child. Somebody may abuse or neglect a child by inflicting harm, or by failing to act to prevent harm. Children may be abused in a family or in an institutional or community setting, by those known to them or, more rarely, by a stranger for example, via the internet. They may be abused by an adult or adults, or another child or children.**
>
> (DCSF, 2010a: 37)

All children are potentially at risk of becoming victims of abuse, regardless of their socio-economic, family, ethnic, religious, racial or disabled status, in particular in light of the potential dangers connected to the social networking accessible via the internet (Byron, 2010). However, research into serious case reviews (DoH, 1995) identified predictive factors that are indicative of children being more likely to be at risk of abuse – if there is a family history or consistent 'cycle of abuse' in the family. Furthermore, statistically, children are more likely to be at risk of significant harm if they are growing up in a household with someone with a known violent or criminal past, where domestic violence is present, where there are concerns over substance abuse (drugs or alcohol) by the carers, or mental health problems are impacting the parenting skills and responsibilities. Equally, children who are looked after and cared for in children's homes, or in foster placements, have often been identified at higher risk of abuse or neglect. In particular babies and children with disabilities are at high risk, because of their inability to articulate. Significantly, the probable major long-term effects of all maltreatment and abuse on children and young people can perpetuate and persist in adulthood:

> **The immediate and longer-term impact can include anxiety, depression, substance misuse, eating disorders and self-destructive behaviours, offending and anti-social behaviour. Maltreatment is likely to have a deep impact on the child's self-image and self-esteem, and on his or her future life. Difficulties may extend into adulthood: the experience of long-term abuse may lead to difficulties in forming or sustaining close relationships, establishing oneself in work, and to extra difficulties in developing the attitudes and skills necessary to be an effective parent.**
>
> (DCSF, 2010a: 258)

In addition, current research and reports (Field, 2010; Allen, 2011) highlight the importance of the Foundation Years in child development, in particular the detrimental influence of poverty and childhood neglect on children's life chances. Both Field (2010) and Allen (2011) argue that preventative and early intervention services, such as children's centres, are vital to support children and families. The impact of neglect on a child's brain development is graphically illustrated in Figure 6.3 on page 133, which compares the brains of a healthy three-year-old with a child who suffered extreme neglect.

Extend your knowledge

Undertake further reading and research about children's development and behaviours which could be linked to child abuse trauma through abuse or neglect, by reading and reflecting on the following reports and journal article. What are the messages conveyed and how can you relate the new learning to your practice?

- Allen, G. (2011) *Early Intervention: The Next Steps. An Independent Report to Her Majesty's Government,* London: HM Government. Available from: http://www.dwp.gov.uk/docs/early-intervention-next-steps.pdf.
- Field, F. (2010) *The Foundation Years: preventing poor children becoming poor adults.* The report of the Independent Review on Poverty and Life Chances, London: HM Government. Available from: http://www.nfm.org.uk/component/jdownloads/finish/74/333.
- Batchelor, J. (2008) '"Failure to thrive" revisited', *Child Abuse Review,* vol. 17, no. 3, pp. 147–59.

Categories of abuse

Below is a brief summary of the four categories of abuse. The detailed definitions of the categories can be found in *Working Together to Safeguard Children* (DCSF, 2010a: 38), which should be available in every setting and can also be easily accessed online.

Physical abuse involves any form of causing physical harm to a child, such as external bruising or deliberately caused illness in a child, or not seeking medical help to prevent and stop the sickness of a child.

Sexual abuse involves all forms of explicit or implicit inappropriate forms of sexually abusive and harming activities, behaviours or witnessing and viewing materials of a sexual nature, whether or not the child is aware of what is happening. This also includes encouraging children to behave in sexually inappropriate ways, or grooming a child in preparation for abuse (including via the internet). Sexual abuse is not solely perpetrated by adult males. Women can also commit acts of sexual abuse, as can other children.

Neglect is defined as a *persistent* failure to meet or respond to a child's basic physical and/or psychological needs which is likely to result in the serious impairment of the child's health or development. Neglect also includes the carer's inability to care for or protect a child from physical and emotional harm or danger, as well as denying or preventing the child access to appropriate medical care or treatment.

Emotional abuse is defined as the *persistent* emotional maltreatment of a child such as to cause severe and persistent adverse effects on the child's emotional development. Emotional abuse involves making a child feel unloved or unwanted and undermining the child's self-worth or self-esteem, conveying that they are inadequate. Furthermore, emotional abuse involves serious bullying (including cyber-bullying), causing children to feel frightened or in danger, or the exploitation or corruption of children. It is important to note that some level of emotional abuse is involved in all of the categories of abuse and in any types of maltreatment of a child. However, emotional abuse can occur on its own.

Scenarios

Case scenarios and categories of abuse

Having read the above definitions, now explore the different scenarios and try to identify the potential category/categories of abuse for each of these. Ask yourself what the signs and symptoms are and what the underlying cause could be. What would you do and why?:

1　A child while playing with others always appears very boisterous and pushes them aside to get to the play area. The parents are separated and you know the child spends alternate weekends with the biological father, who apparently has a bit of a temper.

2　While changing a baby's nappy you notice bruises on the inner thighs and around the tummy button.

3　A child is brought to your setting and appears frequently overtired and not dressed appropriately for the time of year. The child is very clingy to any adult, but does not like socialising with other children, who often call the child 'smelly'.

4　A girl, who has been coming to your setting for a long time, appears to be less outgoing and happy than she used to be. She just recently started to wet herself and does not want to go back home when picked up by her father, but happily goes home with the mother.

Domestic violence and the impact on children

It is important to note that children living in environments of domestic violence are deemed to be at risk of significant harm and would meet the criteria for the categories of emotional abuse, as well as being at high risk of physical abuse. This was validated by the Adoption and Children Act 2002 amendment of the definition of significant harm, as provided by the Children Act 1989, adding a new classification of 'impairment suffered from seeing or hearing the ill-treatment of another'. The Home Office (2009) defines domestic violence as:

> **Any incident of threatening behaviour, violence or abuse (psychological, physical, sexual, financial or emotional) between adults who are, or have been, intimate partners or family members, regardless of gender or sexuality.**

Nearly a quarter of adults in England are victims of domestic violence and it affects both adults and children within the family. An analysis of serious case reviews found evidence of past or present domestic violence present in over half (53 per cent) of the cases of child abuse (DCSF, 2010a: 264). Research by the NSPCC (Cawson, 2002) has shown the links between domestic violence and child abuse as being connected to the emotional maltreatment of children and young people. Further research highlights the interrelatedness between domestic violence, child abuse and the abuse of an animal or the family pet (NSPCC, 2005). Moreover, Calder (2004) identified the impact of domestic violence on children's personal, social and emotional development and behaviour, which can lead to low self-esteem, self-blame, emotional insecurity, low social competence, eating disorders, mental health problems, academic underachievement, as well as antisocial behaviour, delinquency and violence towards others. Children living in households of domestic violence are potentially subjected to physical abuse or violence. Links to 'aggressive behaviour in children, emotional and behavioural problems and educational difficulties' have been identified (DCSF, 2010a: 259).

Aldgate (2006) discussed the effects of maltreatment and child abuse on the development of children and young people, their health and well-being, by taking the wider view of the family and the sources of stress that can have detrimental impacts on children's and young people's developmental progress. Considering domestic violence and the adult role models children are subjected to, it seems unsurprising when children copy the behaviours, as found by Bandura (1976) in his social learning through imitation theory and research into aggression.

Extend your knowledge

- Undertake further reading and research into the impact of domestic violence on children by reading NSPCC and government publications, as well as current research findings from journal articles.
  - Bourassa, C., Lavergne, C., Damant, D.; Lessard, G. and Turcotte, P. (2008) 'Child welfare workers' practice in cases involving domestic violence', *Child Abuse Review*, vol. 17, no. 3, pp. 174–190.
  - Sousa, C., Herrenkohl, T. I., Moylan, C. A., Tajima, E. A.; Klika, J. B.; Herrenkohl, R. C. and Russo, M. J. (2011) 'Longitudinal study on the effects of child abuse and children's exposure to domestic violence, parent-child attachments, and antisocial behavior in adolescence', *Journal of Interpersonal Violence*, vol. 26, no. 1, pp. 111–36.
- Find out what support is available in your area for children and their families fleeing domestic violence.
- Reflect on how you can model and promote positive behaviour for children in your setting.

Recognising and responding to suspected child abuse

Recognising child abuse is not easy and not always clear. However, the impact of neglect as illustrated by the brain scan image on page 133 (Figure 6.3) has devastating and long-lasting effects on the child. If you have any concern about a child's welfare or safety, you have a duty and a responsibility to act in line with your organisation's policies and the procedures of your local authority's LSCB. Although the signs do not necessarily indicate that a child has been abused, they may help practitioners to recognise that something is wrong. Keeping in mind the messages from research (DoH, 1999), practitioners should always anticipate the 'worst-case scenario' rather than let a child suffer. Therefore, the possibility of abuse should be investigated if a child shows a number of signs and symptoms, or any one of them to a notable degree, as outlined by the NSPCC (2010) or your local authority guidance.

As a general rule, any bruises in unusual places, in particular with babies, unexplained injuries or sudden changes in a child's behaviour should be addressed and the possible underlying causes reviewed. Practitioners, and in particular the 'key person', know the children in their care quite well and can detect if a child is not happy or something has happened in a child's life (Lindon, 2009). Depending on their age or ability, children cannot always articulate and communicate what worries them or is happening in their lives. It is important to record, monitor, evaluate and cross-reference observation records to identify changes in a child's behaviour, not just in their individual behaviour, but also in their interactions with peers or other adults, as well as any injuries. It is important to remember that many children may exhibit some signs and symptoms at some time, and that the presence of one or more should not automatically be taken as evidence that the child is suffering abuse. However, there may well be other reasons for changes in behaviour and it will be the task of the investigation agency to establish the reasons and causes when an assessment is made.

If there are obvious physical marks or unexplainable bruises, immediate actions need to be taken in referring suspected abuse and suffering of a child to the local authority. Less obvious are often the signs and symptoms of emotional abuse, neglect or failure to thrive which only become more noticeable through close observation and getting to know a child.

Remember, it is not the childcare practitioner's role to ask questions or investigate further than what the child is telling, because this is the role of the investigating agency. However, the child needs to know that it is likely that the information will need to be shared with other professionals and what will happen next, and with whom the information will be shared. Recording in writing what was said by using only the child's own words as soon as possible, with date, time and names mentioned, is vital information that needs to be shared and forwarded to either the designated safeguarding person in your setting, or directly referred to the local authority. Settings are required to have clear policies and procedures in place for responding to disclosure of abuse, or allegations of abuse, and all staff need to be familiar with these and be proactive in safeguarding children.

Reflective task

- Check your policies and procedures about what to do if you suspect a child is suffering abuse.
- Who would be the appropriate professionals or agencies to support children who have suffered a child abuse trauma?

Diversity and safeguarding

Further factors needing to be considered when working with and caring for children are about their individual and diverse needs as well as life experiences or circumstances they grow up with. Even though most people might think that girls are more vulnerable to abuse, this is not the case. Boys and girls are at equal risk of potentially suffering harm. However, very young babies and children who are disabled are at greater risk of suffering abuse, because they depend on physical and intimate care by others (DCSF, 2009b). Furthermore, because of their age, developmental stage or mental capacity, they are not able to communicate that they are being abused (Lindon, 2009; Powell and Uppal, 2012). Also, children whose first language is not English could be potentially at higher risk, in particular as cultural norms and expectations of children vary in different countries. The pertinence of the cultural context in correlation to responding to child abuse cases was evidenced in an international study of seven countries conducted by Madrid et al. (2002). The study found that, depending on the cultural expectations and norms of a country, social work involvement would either be required, or not even be considered, subject to meeting a country's thresholds granting intervention (Madrid et al., 2002).

It is imperative that you learn about the children in your care, their lives and their cultural influences. Reflect and ask yourself, honestly, what you know about children from different countries, cultures or faith communities. You do not need to look too far afield, because you can think about children from traveller families or from neighbouring European countries.

Read the two-page summary of the international research project by Madrid *et al.* (2002) and reflect on how the different countries responded differently to the case of a child that sustained accidental injuries:

■ Madrid, B., Alma de Ruiz, Z., Andreva, I., Davis, R., Lunden, K., Kaonoparat, W., Lui, P., Johnson, M. (2002) 'Case example offers responses from 7 diverse cultures', *The Link: The Official Newsletter of the International Society for Prevention of Child Abuse and Neglect (ISPCAN)*, vol. 11, no. 2. Available from: http://www.ispcan.org/resource/resmgr/link/link11.2.english.pdf.

Discuss with the rest of the class how family circumstances and cultural norms impact on children's health and well-being. Identify how this is relevant to your early years practice.

The Assessment Framework

If you suspect child abuse, or have safeguarding concerns, you have to remember that it is your duty to act in line with the policies and procedures of your setting and inform the designated or responsible person within the setting. According to Powell and Uppal (2012: 127), a referral which leads to a formal assessment can 'facilitate documentation of your concern and allows a full assessment of events'. The professionals that have a legal duty and responsibility to lead and undertake an investigation are: the local authority's children services (i.e. social services), the police and the NSPCC. The government guidance *What to do if you're worried a child is being abused* (DfES, 2006a) outlines the steps to take when making a referral and addresses issues of confidentiality and data protection, which are secondary to the duty of sharing information when child abuse is being suspected. In order to establish the safeguarding needs of a child, and to assist the decision about which category of abuse the child is suffering, an allocated social worker undertakes the assessment by following the Assessment Framework (DoH, 2000). The assessment enables a holistic view of the context in which the child is living, by taking into account the child's developmental needs, alongside family and environmental factors, and parenting capacity, as illustrated in Figure 13.2.

Figure 13.2 Assessment Framework Triangle (DoH, 2000)

The Children Act 2004

The Children Act 2004 stands alongside the Children Act 1989, and it outlines further aspects of safeguarding children, based on Lord Laming's recommendations (2003), as well as taking the Five Outcomes Framework of *Every Child Matters* (DfES, 2003) into account.

The principles of the Children Act 2004 are to improve opportunities for children and young people through meeting the five outcomes by providing universal services for all children and families. The Act emphasises a shift from crisis intervention towards prevention and early intervention through initiatives such as children's centres or extended schools offering, for example, positive parenting programmes. Most significantly, the Children Act 2004 makes information sharing, collaborative and interdisciplinary working imperative for all professionals and agencies in the quest to safeguard and to promote the well-being of children.

As recommended by Laming (2003), and consolidated in the Children Act 2004, all professionals working with children and young people should safeguard children as everyday practice, and more importantly should prevent children from becoming subject to child protection. In order to assist practitioners to work in a preventative approach and initiate early intervention measures, the **Common Assessment Framework** (CAF) was introduced in 2006. The CAF (DfES, 2006b) is a tool to enable early and effective assessment of children and young people who need additional services or support from more than one agency. The CAF requires that professionals from different agencies coordinate their interventions and offer integrated and personalised services for families.

The practitioners involved in the CAF assessment have to discuss and decide together with the family the course of action and support services required. They constitute the team around the child (TAC), which is a multidisciplinary team of practitioners who, through joined-up working and information sharing, aim to provide early intervention strategies to coordinate service assisting children to reach their full potential (Siraj-Blatchford *et al.*, 2007). It is important to distinguish the difference of assessments, because the CAF (DfES, 2006b) *is not* a referral form for children who would fall under Section 17 or Section 47 of the Children Act 1989, where the local authority has a duty to undertake an assessment and investigation, as discussed earlier. All practitioners working with children and young people should have attended CAF training, because it is more likely that they would be involved in a CAF assessment than an assessment of a child in need under Section 17 or a child at risk under Section 47 of the Children Act 1989.

Reflective task

The following exercises could be used as whole-classroom or group work and even be rehearsed in a CAF role-play scenario.

- For the purpose of this exercise complete a CAF assessment form on an 'imaginary' child and consider what information you could contribute and who would hold other relevant information about the child.
- What support from what agency would be required to assist the child to develop to its full potential and meet the five outcomes of *Every Child Matters* (DfES, 2003)?
- Who would need to be part of the team around the child (TAC) and who would need to offer which services to the child and family?

Multi-agency and integrated working in early years

The theoretical model underpinning multi-agency, interdisciplinary and integrated working is based on the holistic model of child development by Bronfenbrenner (1979), as illustrated in Figure 7.1 on page 148. He asserted that the child should be seen in the context of its immediate family as well as the wider community and environment. Bronfenbrenner's ecological systems model (1979) is mirrored in both the CAF (DfES, 2006b) and the Assessment Framework (DoH, 2000) as it takes a perspective on childhood that cannot be captured from a single professional assessment and evaluation, but instead requires multiple perspectives of the child and its context. Moreover, it describes the interconnectedness of the systems as well as the idea of the different agencies operating within these structures all working together. Consequently, a child and its family need to be seen and worked with in a holistic way, through joined-up services, working towards the five outcomes of *Every Child Matters* (DfES, 2003), in its framework of integrated strategy and governance, as illustrated in Figure 13.3.

Figure 13.3 Framework for integrated strategy and governance: *Every Child Matters* (DfES, 2003)

Guidance in *Working Together to Safeguard Children* (DCSF, 2010a: 112) indicates that all practitioners and managers must be able to work and communicate effectively with others, both within their own agency and across organisational boundaries, which can be initiated through joint training of practitioners across agencies, as recommended by Laming (2003 and 2009).

> **Safeguarding and promoting the welfare of children – and in particular protecting them from significant harm – depends on effective joint working between agencies and professionals that have different roles and expertise. Individual children, especially some of the most vulnerable children and those at greatest risk of suffering harm and social exclusion, will need co-ordinated help from health, education, early years, children's social care, the voluntary sector and other agencies.**
>
> (DCSF, 2010a: 31)

Effective information sharing is the key to joint and integrated working, and is a vital element of both early intervention and safeguarding children. The cross-government guidance *Information Sharing: Guidance for practitioners and managers* (DCSF, 2008h) provides advice on when and how frontline practitioners can share information in a professional capacity within legal requirements. The guidance also covers how organisations can support practitioners and build their confidence in making information-sharing decisions, which should be in line with the setting's organisational policies and procedures about data protection, confidentiality and information sharing. From the first point of contact with children and their families, parents or those with parental responsibility should be made aware that the setting has a duty to share information if they are concerned about the welfare of a child. Powell and Uppal (2012: 152) acknowledge that, once a safeguarding concern has been raised, it can become difficult 'balancing the maintenance of a positive relationship with parents or carers while meeting the needs of the child'.

Reflective task

In the light of the importance placed on information sharing, consider the following points:
- When can or should you share information?
- Who can or should you share information with?
- How do you listen to children and take their views into account?
- Who are the professionals you have shared information with in the last 12 months?
- Who is the professional you work together with on a regular basis?
- What have been or are the challenges when working with other professionals? How can you overcome these?

Examples of poor practice in inter-agency working were found by Ofsted (2009) in an evaluation of 173 serious case reviews which identified weaknesses, with over a third of the reviews (34 per cent) judged as inadequate. The 173 serious case reviews, carried out and completed between April 2008 and March 2009, related to 219 children and included 113 cases of child deaths (Ofsted, 2009). Of the 219 children identified, 68 per cent were known to social care services at the time of the incident. The findings highlighted weaknesses in practice, such as weak management and lack of joint working within and across agencies (Ofsted, 2009). Other examples of poor practice included: failure to focus on the needs of the child, insufficient staff expertise, lack of training, not undertaking adequate risk assessments, and poor identification of ethnic or social cultural issues (Ofsted, 2009). To improve and assist better inter-agency working and communication, each local authority has the duty to oversee and regulate all safeguarding children issues. This duty is coordinated through the LSCB, which consists of professionals from all organisations that work with children in education, social care and health, police, youth services, the voluntary sector and community organisations. The functions of the LSCB are to develop policies and procedures for safeguarding children and promoting their welfare, as well as to define thresholds for intervention and to disseminate all relevant information and procedures through multi-agency training to all professionals working with children. Furthermore, the LSCB has the duty to regulate the safer recruitment and supervision of professionals, and to investigate any allegations made against persons working with children.

Reflective task

- Undertake further research and read about successful examples of effective working together and communication between agencies. Access information from current research as published in peer-reviewed journals and search out government publications or websites such as the National College (see Smith, 2010a).
- Compare these examples with publications from other professional organisation such as the Department of Health or social work publications.
- Identify the areas for learning in your practice and how you can share these with your colleagues in the setting.

Links to the EYFS and the role of the practitioner

As stated at the beginning of the chapter, the responsibilities and obligations of practitioners are reiterated in the EYFS under Safeguarding and Welfare Requirements (DfE, 2012a).

> **Providers must take all necessary steps to keep children safe and well. The requirements in this section explain what early years providers must do to: safeguard children; ensure the suitability of adults who have contact with children; promote good health; manage behaviour; and maintain records, policies and procedures.**

(DfE, 2012a: 13)

Practitioners should be able to respond appropriately to any significant changes in children's behaviour or deterioration in their general well-being. Practitioners have to act in accordance with their policies and procedures for reporting suspected abuse when they see unexplained bruising, marks or signs of possible abuse, or when they see or presume signs of neglect, or when children make any comments which give cause for concern. *Working Together to Safeguard Children* (DCSF, 2010a: 80) outlines early years providers' and practitioners' roles and responsibilities with regard to safeguarding children:

- All registered providers, excepting childminders, must have a practitioner who is designated to take lead responsibility for safeguarding children within each early years setting …. This lead must also attend a child protection course. In addition, all early years settings must implement an effective safeguarding children policy and procedure.
- The EYFS also makes clear that registered early years providers should follow the guidance 'What to do if you're worried a child is being abused'. Such providers must notify local child protection agencies of any suspected child abuse or neglect in line with LSCB local guidance and procedures.

The government recognises that the various early years providers and services ranging from nurseries, preschools, childminders, out-of-school clubs and holiday schemes or children's centres all play a vital role in children's lives. Practitioners are at the forefront of children's learning and development. They hold trusting relationships with the children in their care and often spend more time with them than maybe any other adult in the child's life. Therefore, practitioners are required to take necessary steps to safeguard and promote the welfare of children in their care, as well as support children's good health and well-being. Equally, practitioners are expected to manage children's behaviour effectively and in a manner appropriate for their stage of development by 'taking into account their particular and individual needs' (DCSF, 2010a: 80). The responsibility for observing and recording children's overall learning and development is everyday practice in childcare settings as required by Ofsted, but becomes imperative in cases where a child is in need or perceived as being at risk. Powell and Uppal (2012: 73) highlight that professionals have to develop 'watchfulness' and apply the safeguarding guidance and frameworks available, as well as share information appropriately.

The changes to the EYFS (DfE, 2012a) place emphasis on the protection of children as outlined in the Safeguarding and Welfare Requirements and include examples of adults' behaviour which might be signs of abuse and neglect. Also the EYFS (DfE, 2012a) requires that safeguarding policies and procedures must cover the use of mobile phones and cameras in childcare settings (see also DCSF, 2009a). The overall safety and suitability of the premises, environment and equipment are down to the judgement of the childcare provider as to whether or not risk assessments need to be recorded in writing. The most significant change to the Safeguarding and Welfare Requirements for the EYFS (DfE, 2012a) is the requirement that providers must give staff opportunities for supervision, coaching, training and continuous improvement (see Chapter 5).

Fostering resilience in children and helping children to protect themselves

A much underestimated aspect of the practitioner's role is the preventative and supportive aspect of their work in engaging with children. International research (Benard, 1995; Glover, 2009; Kordich-Hall and Pearson, 2005; Newman, 2002, 2004) has highlighted the important role practitioners can take in helping vulnerable children and young people to bounce back from serious problems in life, such as child abuse trauma. A resilient child is one who exhibits positive adaptation and coping strategies in stressful and adverse situations (Newman, 2004). The international research found that positive and 'unconditional regard' (Rogers, 1967) by a significant adult can assist children in building resilience. This significant adult in a child's life can be an early years practitioner, a teacher or any other professional, as well as a relative or family friend. As professionals, early years practitioners can assist vulnerable children to cope with the risk factors in their life by offering protective factors, such as social competence and problem-solving skills in creating strategies to cope with and overcome difficulties. Benard (1995) suggests that supporting children's self-esteem and self-efficacy promotes their autonomy and their ability to distance themselves from any dysfunctions in their life. If children and young people do not possess coping or problem-solving skills in dealing with the risk factors in their lives (poverty, child abuse, carers with alcohol and drug misuse habits, parental depression or disability, domestic violence), then they are more likely to develop psychological and conduct disorders, such as eating disorders, self-harming behaviours, depression, antisocial behaviour, such as bullying, or the use of physical violence to settle conflicts (Newman, 2004; Glover, 2009).

Furthermore, Kordich-Hall and Pearson (2005) propose that practitioners can teach children and young people to learn and develop 'resilient thinking behaviours'. This is the ability to reframe negative events by searching for a perspective that is truthful as well as favourable, which can help children to maintain a realistic and positive perspective and positive behaviours. Research by Seligman *et al.* (1995, cited in Kordich-Hall and Pearson, 2005: 13) found that 'children as young as two or three years can mimic the thinking style of their primary caregiver'. Resilient thinking behaviours influence decision-making processes and problem solving, encouraging children to persevere, rather than give up, and to interpret challenges as opportunities for new learning and personal growth (Kordich-Hall and Pearson, 2005). In relation to child abuse trauma, it is important for children to be able to realise that it was not their fault that they have been subjected to abuse. Therefore, resilient thinking which evaluates the facts of what has happened can assist children not to develop a self-blaming 'thinking error'. Newman (2002, 2004) emphasises that the key quality needed to trigger resilience and recovery to overcome adversities and trauma is for the child to recognise that they are not powerless victims of the actions by others.

As practitioners caring for and working with children, you are in a unique position to offer children unconditional regard and you can foster resilience to help children to bounce back from the adversities of life. You might have to reflect on your personal values and how you feel about children who have suffered abuse or childhood trauma. You might feel more or less compassionate, or even shy away, because you might not feel confident or competent working with these children. Individually, or as a team, you can create a safe yet challenging environment for children, which is loving and nurturing, as well as supporting children's self-esteem and self-worth. Programmes that promote children's *Social and Emotional Aspects of Learning* (SEAL, DfES, 2005a) or *Social and Emotional Aspects of Development* (SEAD, DCSF, 2008d), emotional intelligence, emotional literacy and empathy can help children to survive and thrive. However, it is disappointing to note that neither the new statutory framework for the EYFS (DfE, 2012a), nor the non-statutory guidance materials produced to support practitioners in implementing the statutory requirements, *Development Matters in the Early Years Foundation Stage* (Early Education, 2012), address how practitioners can promote resilience in children.

Next steps

Fostering resilience in everyday early years practice

- Develop activities for children in your care that foster resilience, enable them to protect themselves and bring out their potential.
- The activities should also include staff in your setting and raise awareness with parents.
- You might find some of the NSPCC, Barnardo's or Kidscape resources very useful.

Challenges and opportunities for early years practice – striving for excellence in safeguarding practice

The most important aspect in safeguarding children and promoting their welfare is that you do your best to keep yourself up to date with the topic. It is not enough to attend child protection or safeguarding training every three years. In order to provide excellent and high-quality childcare, you need to stay abreast of all new research findings (in peer-reviewed journals) and publications by the government as well as independent organisations such as Ofsted or the NSPCC.

It needs to be acknowledged that childcare is a low-paid profession which often does not receive the recognition it deserves from other professionals working in the field. However, if you have chosen to work with and care for children, you need to have the passion and enthusiasm to do your best possible to support children in developing to their best potential in a safe and nurturing environment. Therefore, it is paramount that you gain the relevant knowledge and understanding of how to promote the welfare of children and safeguard them, by gaining confidence and competence in your own practice as a professional.

Extend your knowledge

■ Read Aldgate, J., Jones, D. P. H., Rose, W. and Jeffery, C. (eds.) (2006) *The Developing World of the Child*, London: Jessica Kingsley.
■ Reflect on the implications for your early years practice by linking it to the EYFS.
■ Outline an 'ideal' safeguarding practitioner's role and responsibilities, and match these to your current practice.

Information and Communication Technology (ICT) safety

The EYFS (DfE, 2012a) and *Development Matters in the Early Years Foundation Stage* (Early Education, 2012) require that children learn about and use ICT equipment in preparation for school. At the same time, practitioners need to be aware of the potential dangers when using electronic and intelligent information and communication technology. Regardless of whether your setting is connected to the internet or not, it is important that you know how to protect yourself and the children in your care, as well as educating parents about the potential 'e-dangers' (Byron, 2010). Parents need to be aware that even their very young children learn incredibly quickly how to use electronic devices such as mobile phones, laptops or games consoles by watching and copying their parents or older siblings. Also, you can make yourself potentially vulnerable by using social networking sites that are also used by the parents of your children.

The UK was the first country to demonstrate its commitment to child digital safety by setting up the multi-stakeholder UK Council for Child Internet Safety (UKCCIS), thus it established the UK as a world leader in child digital safety. The Child Exploitation and Online Protection (CEOP) Centre has developed a range of guidance for children, parents and practitioners on how to use the internet safely and report any concerns with the click of a button. Furthermore, the CEOP has developed a very user-friendly website, *Think You Know*, for children of all ages, parents and practitioners, which shows educational video clips and provides information on keeping safe from e-dangers.

Next steps

- Educate yourself and others about e-dangers and how to keep everybody safe by checking out the following websites:
  - Child Exploitation and Online Protection (CEOP) Centre: http://www.ceop.police.uk/
  - *Think You Know*: http://www.thinkuknow.co.uk/
- If not already in place, develop an ICT safety policy as well as practice guidance for your setting.
- Educate staff and parents about e-safety by inviting a local safeguarding police officer to talk about CEOP.
- Produce an information leaflet for parents.
- Dedicate a display board in the entrance of your setting to e-safety issues.
- Organise a discussion group with children about the safe use of the internet/games consoles/mobile phones etc.

Finally, it is important that you move safeguarding visibly to the forefront in your setting. Policies and procedures which are just sitting on a shelf in the office do not keep children safe. In order to promote the welfare of children and exercise safe practice, you need to exercise 'watchfulness' (Powell and Uppal, 2012: 73). Imagine your setting is like a group of meerkats looking out for each other – you should watch out over the children in your care and know how to apply the safeguarding framework. Figure 13.4 is a good example from practice: a display board in the entrance of a nursery which sends out a clear message to children, parents and other professionals that the welfare and safety of the children are paramount at the setting and that they are everybody's responsibility.

Figure 13.4 Good-practice example: Safeguarding display in a nursery

Conclusion

This chapter explored the pertinent issues around safeguarding, protecting children and promoting their well-being. You were provided with a brief overview of the historical and political context, the legislative requirements and practice guidance. The chapter has offered you ample opportunities to read and research further to expand your knowledge and understanding about safeguarding children, as well as reflecting on your current practice. The message that it is everybody's duty to safeguard children should have encouraged you to improve and enhance your current practice and become a proactive champion of safeguarding in your setting.

Evaluate your...

Safeguarding practice

- Have you read the *Guidance for Safer Working Practice for Adults who Work with Children and Young People* (DCSF, 2009a) document and discussed it with your team?
- When was your safeguarding policy last updated?
- When did you last attend safeguarding training?
- Have you attended CAF training?
- What would be your role in a team around the child (TAC) scenario?
- What do you do when you suspect a child is failing to thrive?
- What do you do when you observe or suspect a child is being abused?
- What is your policy on parents or members of staff bringing cameras or mobile phones into the setting?
- Do you know the parents of the children in your setting who have legal 'parental responsibility' and whom you can share confidential information with?
- How do you promote and make safeguarding visible in your setting?
- What activities do you undertake with children, staff and parents in your setting to promote and foster resilience?
- Take your professional development needs to your next supervision or appraisal with your line manager.
- Make 'safeguarding' visible throughout your setting.
- Become a safeguarding champion in your setting.

Further reading

Anning, A., Cottrell, D., Frost, N., Green, J., Robinson, M. (2006) *Developing Multi-professional Teamwork for Integrated Children's Services*, Maidenhead: Open University Press.

Axford, N. (2008) *Exploring concepts of child well-being: Implications for children's services*, Bristol: Policy Press.

Barker, R. (2008) *Making Sense of Every Child Matters: Multi-professional Practice Guidance*, Bristol: Policy Press.

Charles, M. and Horwath, J. (2009) 'Investing in interagency training to safeguard children: An act of faith or an act of reason?' *Children & Society*, vol. 23, no. 5, pp. 364–76.

Cheminais, R. (2009) *Effective Multi-Agency Partnerships: Putting Every Child Matters into Practice*, London: SAGE.

Hughes, L. and Owen, H. (eds.) (2009) *Good Practice in Safeguarding Children: Working Effectively in Child Protection*, London: Jessica Kingsley Publishers.

Working with parents and families

Cath Arnold and Margy Whalley

14

Introduction

In 1979, Christian Schiller, by then an Inspector of Schools (HMI) for many years, wrote of his vision for the future:

> When I peer into the future I don't see any army of professionals at all. I doubt very much if we shall need primary schools as we think of them today. What I see, in every small community (a few streets, maybe one street) is a building, the community's building, and in it will be a place to which young children come to play, to explore, to learn. There will be facilities there, resources there, far greater than can be provided in any one home. And there will be teachers there to help, teachers who are there as leaders.
>
> And Mum will come there and feel at home, and Dad and the neighbour next door, and they'll understand and they will help from time to time.
>
> (Schiller, 1979: 104)

Schiller's comments (1979) are important because he reveals his vision and values. When thinking about working with families, it is important to have a vision of what we want to achieve and what is the core purpose. Crucially, ideas about what services to develop need to come from the parents themselves. That vision needs to be underpinned by shared values. How do we view children and their families? What sorts of relationships do we build in our settings? Schiller presents a world in which adults work closely together to support children's development and learning with no artificial divide between professionals and parents. In reality, even today, many settings are hard for parents to access and many professionals report that they find parents 'hard to reach'. Why has a vision like Schiller's not yet been realised?

This chapter will explore how working with parents and families has evolved in England over the last century. It will consider the recurring themes and the values and principles that underpin work with parents and families today and make links to the EYFS (DfE, 2012a).

Most studies on partnership with parents have been carried out in schools and many assumptions are made that in early years settings and services, staff automatically work more closely and effectively with parents. However, until quite recently there were very few professional development opportunities focusing on work with parents and families in the early years phase and very little theory about what works.

Being a parent is a difficult and complex task. No one can tell you in advance how to be an effective parent. All parents need support along the way. On the whole, all parents want the best for their children, and families deserve the best services the state can offer. 'Parents' means fathers as well as mothers, and often means the extended family and other carers, for example childminders. When thinking about children, it is important to consider them within the context of their family and all important adults in their lives (Bronfenbrenner, 1979; Whalley, 2007).

Learning outcomes

By the end of this chapter, you will be able to:

- Reflect on attitudes to parents within the English education system over a number of years and your own attitudes to parents.
- Understand issues around power differentials when working with families in early years settings.
- Increase your understanding of working with adults.
- Be familiar with some techniques designed to engage families in their children's learning.

An overview of how work with parents has evolved

One hundred years ago

In 1914, Margaret and Rachel McMillan set up an open-air nursery in order to improve the health and life chances of the poorest children in London, England (Steedman, 1990; Kwon, 2002). The sisters were Christian Socialists and worked hard to promote ideas of equality, particularly in relation to poverty and health. They saw nursery as an 'extension of home and encouraged teachers to forge links with parents' and 'encouraged parents to come into the nursery and learn alongside their children' (Curtis and O'Hagan, 2003: 138).

The Hadow Report 1931

In the Hadow Report on 'The Primary School', published in 1931, parents are referred to only a few times and are spoken of with the kind of pejorative tone that characterised this period. There was a recognition of the 'emotional effects' on the child of 'slackness or irregularity within the home' (Hadow, 1931, cited in Gillard 2006: 58). The tone implies that if there is any problem with a child, the fault lies within the home. It is reported that it is 'sometimes hard to persuade parents to act on the advice of the school Medical Officer' with regard to sleep, exercise and diet. The report's intention, however, was to 'stimulate the interest of parents in their children's progress' (Hadow, 1931, cited in Gillard, 2006: 58).

There is one statement in Hadow that remains critically important for us today: 'What a good and wise father desires for his children, a nation must desire for all its children' (Hadow, 1931, cited in Gillard 2006: 58). All parents want their children to have positive experiences within the education system.

The Plowden Report 1967

The next major report on primary schooling in England was the Plowden Report, published in 1967, by which time Jean Piaget's research was beginning to influence educational thinking. Schooling became more child centred, and the environment began being considered to be as important to development as inherited intellect (Brearley and Hitchfield, 1966). The Plowden Report (1967: 37) stated: 'There is certainly an association between parental encouragement and educational performance.' However, the report also suggested that parents quite possibly became interested because their children were doing well.

The Plowden Report gives a picture of what parental involvement or partnership looked like in the mid-1960s. The authors praised schools that offered as many as nine or ten meetings a year for parents and those schools that had very active parent-teacher associations, many of which did fundraising or helped the school in practical ways. They did note, however, that: 'About half of the parents said they would have liked to be told more about how their children were getting on at school' (Plowden, 1967: 38).

There was also mention of a small number of mothers who, after helping in school, went on to train as teachers. It was noted that parents who helped or supported the school in practical ways often learned about the curriculum informally and were able to help their children more effectively.

The report (Plowden, 1967: 462) recommended half-time nursery education for 'nearly all 4 years olds and a good many 3 year olds' and suggested that 'it may sometimes be right for a mother to be with her child in the classroom until he has settled down' and that this would be 'a symbol of the partnership between schools and parents'. The Plowden Report was an important step towards acknowledging the vital role of parents in their children's transition.

Research during the 1970s, 1980s and 1990s

Most of the subsequent research on home–school partnerships was undertaken during the 1970s, 1980s and 1990s. There are over 13,000 papers and books on home–school partnerships written during that period, with the 1990s being the most prolific. The majority of the studies were carried out in the United States or Britain, with some from Australia, New Zealand and South Africa. There are some recurring themes:

- Literacy and its promotion through parental involvement have been well researched (Hannon et al., 1991).
- Children with additional needs need their parents to provide information about their development for professionals and this may be why researchers like Sheila Wolfendale (a specialist in working with children with additional needs and their families) led the way in England and in other countries with regard to home–school partnerships.
- Behaviour problems, which may link with additional needs, require professionals and parents to work together for the benefit of children who are struggling within the education system.
- Homework – if parents are committed to the idea of the importance of homework, children are more likely to do their homework and to comply with the school's aims.
- Attendance – similarly schools need parents 'on board' to ensure children's attendance is high. Nowadays, this is a critical factor in school inspection.
- Social class and ethnicity in relation to parental involvement have been widely researched, especially in the United States. The focus of this research has been the realisation of children's potential (Chrispeels, 1996; Chrispeels and Rivero, 2001).

Think about these questions in relation to your setting:

■ To what extent is our current work on involving parents primarily designed to serve the organisation of which we are part, or the local authority or central government policy?

■ Alternatively, is the primary purpose of engaging with parents to serve the needs of the child and their family?

■ Are we really committed to improving outcomes for children and their families?

Some significant research and practice

The Plowden Report (1967) was significant in many ways. The government set up 'Educational Priority Areas' where more resources, better ratios and more funding were available in order to provide more equal opportunities for children from more disadvantaged families (Plowden, 1967: 57). Following the report, a small number of 'Nursery Centres' were set up where the child was seen as part of their family and the staff provided flexible services and support for families (Gilkes, 1987; Whalley, 1993). The staff in these centres also worked closely with their colleagues in social care and health to provide an improved service for children and families in need (Gilkes, 1987: 105). There was a realisation that early years services needed to provide for the needs of parents as well as children. However, workers were rarely trained to work with adults (Gilkes, 1987: 109).

Malcolm Knowles (1990) shared a theory of adult learning, known as andragogy, and he claimed that adults learned differently from children, having more experience, being self-motivated and usually able to identify their own learning needs. He recommended an informal learning environment for adults in which teachers were facilitators of learning (Knowles, 1990).

Based on the principles of andragogy, Bastiani and colleagues developed the 'Nottingham approach' to working with parents (Atkin and Bastiani, 1988; Bastiani, 1989). The group developed a 'parent-centred' approach in which the following andragogical principles were adhered to:

■ the experience of parents was recognised

■ parents' rights and responsibilities were acknowledged

■ the belief that, when professionals and parents work collaboratively, the outcomes for children are better

■ that parents have knowledge and can be a 'resource' for professionals.

The group was 'centrally concerned with respect for the everyday lives of ordinary people' (Atkin and Bastiani, 1988: 13). They resisted anecdotal stereotypes of parents which are still frequently heard in educational settings such as the comment 'You never see the ones you really want to see' (Atkin and Bastiani, 1988: 14).

At the same time as researchers in the UK were thinking deeply about parent–professional partnerships, there was a plethora of research going on in the United States. One of the leaders in the field was Joyce Epstein. She expressed the view that professionals, parents and children would all benefit if professionals engaged with parents. Epstein has written over a hundred books and papers on home, school and community partnerships (http://www.cpirc.org). Epstein believed that work with parents needed to be embedded into every aspect of school life, including the school/centre development plan (Desforges and Abouchaar, 2003).

More recently, there has been a realisation of the importance of the home learning environment and the difference that parental interest and home practices can make to children's outcomes within our education system (Siraj-Blatchford and Siraj- Blatchford, 2010; Sylva et al., 2010).

Fröbel Project

A study that proved to be very important to early years education in this country was carried out in the early 1970s. This was the Fröbel Early Education Project reported in a powerful book *Extending Thought in Young Children: A Parent–Teacher Partnership* (Athey, 1990 and 2007). The team studied two groups of ten young children and collaborated with their families. One group was from an Educational Priority Area and the other from a more advantaged area. The project was planned as a direct result of the Plowden Report's desire to 'increase knowledge of cognitive functioning in young children' (Athey, 1990: 218). Athey revisited Piaget's theory of constructivism and schemas (or repeated patterns of action) and gathered examples of young children's spontaneous learning along with their parents. The parents in this study observed their children at home and shared their observations with the project team. Although it could be argued that the professionals' agenda was followed, this was a 'shared search' for knowledge (Athey, 1990: 206; Easen *et al.*, 1992).

Knowing how to share theoretical frameworks with parents can be difficult at first. Concerns can arise about whether a setting is following its own agenda and telling parents what staff know, without taking parents' own particular expertise into account. Appearing to be the 'experts' might undermine parents' confidence. However, Easen and his colleagues (1992) allay these anxieties, describing their conceptualisation of a 'developmental partnership'. This is a partnership in which early educators, with their expertise as professionals and knowledge of child development theory, and parents, with their knowledge of their own particular child, bring their expertise together. With both sets of information, a reasonably equal partnership can be developed, and both parties can do their best for the children.

Other shifts in thinking

Two other studies from the 1980s began to shift thinking about both the role of parents and the value of parents' contribution in terms of their child's learning at home. First, Tizard and Hughes (1984) studied 30 four-year-old girls, half from working-class backgrounds and half from middle-class backgrounds. They chose girls because their focus was on adult–child interactions in the home and at nursery and it was well known that girls were likely to talk more. Following the Bullock Report (1975: 519), there was a concern that working-class children were disadvantaged in learning to read because 'many young children do not have the opportunity to develop at home the more complex forms of language which school demands'. This idea was, in the main, based on tests that had been carried out on children rather than on observation of the children using language at home. There was also a reference to involving parents in the early years to specifically improve the reading scores of the children of semi-skilled or unskilled workers. What Tizard and Hughes's research team (2002: xv) found shocking was that 'the richness, depth and variety which characterised the home conversations was sadly missing' in the nursery. Furthermore, they found that all the 'children's intellectual and language needs are much more likely to be satisfied at home than at school' (Tizard and Hughes, 2002: 215). The final sentence in their report is extremely powerful, even today:

> It is time to shift the emphasis away from what parents should learn from professionals, and towards what professionals can learn from studying parents and children at home.
>
> (Tizard and Hughes, 2002: 225)

Second, a larger longitudinal study of young children using language was carried out in Bristol and written up by Gordon Wells (1986). In total, 128 children were studied, 32 of those from just after their first birthday until the last year of elementary schooling. The sample included an equal number of boys and girls and 'the full range of family background' (Wells, 1986: 14). The language of 32 children was compared at home and at school by looking at adult–child conversations. The researchers found that the children seemed a lot more passive at school and that teachers often dominated with their agenda, initiating and expanding on their own learning intentions more often than identifying the learning intentions of the children (Wells, 1986). At home children were much more likely to initiate conversations about what they were trying to understand and to pursue those topics. Again, these researchers were indicating the importance of the home learning environment (Siraj-Blatchford and Siraj-Blatchford, 2010; Sylva *et al.*, 2010).

Extend your knowledge

Read more about the two research studies described above.

- Tizard, B. and Hughes, M. [1984] (2002) (2nd edn) *Young Children Learning*, Oxford: Blackwell Publishers.
- Wells, G. (1986) *The Meaning Makers: Children Learning Language and Using Language to Learn*, London: Hodder and Stoughton.

Identify areas of learning for your early years practice and your setting.

Reflective task

- How are you currently planning for children's learning?
- Are you identifying children's deep interests? Discuss examples from your practice with your fellow students or your team.
- To what extent are you tapping into the knowledge that parents hold about their own children and how they learn at home?
- Evaluate the effectiveness of your contact with the home setting and your information sharing with parents.
- Ask yourself: What would I do differently? How can I achieve this? What do I need in order to implement changes to working with the parents/carers of the children I look after?

Other influences

Parents themselves became active and the Playgroup Movement began in England in 1961 in response to a shortage of nursery places. For the first ten years or so, playgroups were run by parents, 'to provide social and learning experiences for their (own) children' (http://www. playgroupmovement.org.uk). During the 1970s playgroups began to be run by a mix of professionals and parents. Parents began playing other roles in managing, running and fundraising, and also took turns on the 'rota'. A similar movement called Playcentre sprang up in New Zealand during the 1930s and is still a powerful strand of their early years service today. The emphasis in New Zealand is on 'children's development and parent education' and also on parents as educators of their own children (Cubey, 2012: 143).

Families during this period became increasingly diverse. Increasing numbers of children were being raised by single parents or by parents sharing the care of their children (Dawson, 1991). The trend was also towards more mothers working and fathers playing a more significant role in their children's care.

Looking back over a hundred years or more, it might seem that early years educators have not learned a great deal about involving parents in their children's learning. Margaret McMillan was using a model of engaging with parents and children that many settings still find it hard to achieve today. It seems to be the case that as professionals we resist change and are fearful of 'new' ways of working.

Reflective task

- Think about what would happen if parents had more 'say' in what happens in your setting.
- Try to identify your worst fears and talk about them.
- If you are a parent yourself, how would you want to be involved in your child's learning?

Much of the innovative practice seems to take place in small projects, which are often not embedded in mainstream practice. Athey (1990, 2007) listened to what parents had to tell her about their children at home and, possibly inadvertently, engaged the parents in learning for themselves. So it seems that in the early years, the educational needs of children *and* their parents can be met through small-scale interventions, such as Athey's, but we struggle to transfer that learning to the rest of the education system.

Reflective task

- How might you, as a team, begin sharing ideas with parents about their child's learning in the setting?
- How can you find ways of listening to parents talk about what they observe their children engaging in at home?

Contemporary research and current debates

Recent political context

With the election of a Labour government in 1997, the needs of children and their families came to the fore, really for the first time in the UK. The Department for Education and Skills (DfES) became the Department for Children, Schools and Families (DCSF) and there was unprecedented investment in the early years and integrated working with families and communities. The new Labour government looked to research to inform its policy. Research on brain development had taught us that early experiences are important in developing 'neuronal connections' resulting in 'more richly networked brains' (Gerhardt, 2004: 43). This confirmed the early years phase as the most critically important phase of education. Governments across Western Europe, the UK, New Zealand and Australia finally became convinced that, if families are supported during children's early years, children are likely to do better.

Pen Green Centre

Research into 'Involving Parents in Their Children's Learning'

Just as the new Labour government took over, the Pen Green Centre was embarking on a three-year study, funded by the Esmee Fairbairn Trust, called 'Involving Parents in Their Children's Learning' (Whalley, 2007). Having worked closely with parents for 14 years, running health, educational and therapeutic groups and a comprehensive adult community education service, staff at the Pen Green Centre turned their attention to gaining new insights into children learning alongside their parents. Since the nursery opened in 1983, it had used a 'key person' system, similar to the Early Years Foundation Stage 'key person' system (DCSF, 2008a; DfE, 2012a). Keyworkers are called Family Workers and they consistently build close relationships with families by doing home visits several times each year, greeting children on arrival, sharing documentation with families and generally being a 'special person' to that child and family (Whalley and Arnold, forthcoming 2013). There are few 'rules' at Pen Green but the Centre insists on a 'settling-in' period of at least two weeks when children first begin attending the nursery. Parents or carers stay in the vicinity of the nursery for those first few sessions. This is another opportunity for Family Workers and the important people in children's lives to get to know each other and develop a trusting relationship.

Staff at the Pen Green Centre had begun engaging in a dialogue with parents about their children during earlier studies. Paulo Freire, the renowned Brazilian educator defined 'dialogue':

> *... dialogue cannot be reduced to the act of one person's 'depositing' ideas into another, nor can it become a simple exchange of ideas to be 'consumed' by the discussants ... Because dialogue is an encounter among women and men who name the world, it must not be a situation where some name on behalf of others.*

> (Freire, 1970: 70)

Parents kept diaries about what their children were doing at home but the Centre wanted further information about *how* parental involvement benefits children (Whalley, 2007).

As Tizard and Hughes (2002) suggested, early years professionals are just as likely to learn from parents, as parents are to learn from professionals. The Pen Green Centre wanted to work in partnership with parents and with nursery staff. The Centre also had to convey the idea that it was not using a 'deficit' model in which the professional assumes they know what is best for the child in all circumstances. Pen Green offered parents video cameras to film their children at home but without explicit instructions about what to film. The parents were extremely enthusiastic and committed but the results were variable. In the early days, the Centre often got hours of Halloween parties or birthdays, and not much material that helped them to support and extend children's learning in nursery.

The Pen Green Centre tried again the following year, with funding from the Teacher Training Agency, and a tighter focus. A small number of parents agreed to be filmed settling their child into nursery and to film or audiotape their child at home. Staff at the Centre shared with the parents the concept of 'involvement' which signifies 'deep level learning' (Laevers, 1997). Parents immediately grasped the idea of filming their child when he or she was totally absorbed and they began to notice these incidents. Staff had already been sharing ideas about schema theory with parents, so were now beginning to construct a 'shared conceptual framework' that enabled them to enter into a deeper dialogue about children's learning.

During the following three years (1997–2000), the Pen Green Centre extended its approach to the whole nursery (approximately 60 families each year). Of the total families, 84 per cent became involved in a dialogue with staff about their children's learning. Study groups were set up, which ran during a morning, afternoon and evening each week so that parents on shiftwork could attend. Family Group meetings were held once every three months, and there were key concept sessions, during which the Centre's conceptual framework for understanding the children was shared with the parents. In addition to 'schemas' and 'involvement', staff also began sharing ideas about 'emotional well-being' (Bowlby, 1969; Laevers, 1997). They also developed, alongside the parents, a framework for thinking about 'adult pedagogic strategies' (Whalley, 2007). They discovered that they needed a shared conceptual framework in order to engage in a 'dialogue' about children's learning, and also began to appreciate the fact that 'parents are not an homogenous group' and that many different ways of involving them (Whalley, 2007: 53) were needed.

The study groups were (and still are) very exciting. The groups watch video vignettes together of each child 'deeply involved' either at home or at nursery (Laevers, 1997). The study groups consist of parents and workers discussing and trying to tease out the learning and how it might be supported and extended at home and at nursery. This results in much more 'joined-up' and meaningful curriculum content for each child.

While this approach may not be practicable for all early years settings, it provides an interesting alternative perspective on how parents can be engaged in their children's learning.

Scenario

Nathan is four years old and is in his second year at nursery. Nathan has cerebral palsy and is cared for by his grandparents. What follows are his grandmother's words:

*I came to nursery with Nathan, expected to stay for two weeks to settle him in … I actually stayed for five weeks as I couldn't see anyone who understood Nathan's needs as I did … The nursery was full of risks … and I was panic stricken as to how Nathan would cope on his own … I don't think **he** needed me to stay but **I** needed to stay …*

*Home visits from Nathan's Family Worker, Louise, have given me strategies for supporting and coping with Nathan in a positive way … I also help her to plan for Nathan by sharing what we've been doing at home … talking through his assessment … and **together** we plan how to move him forward.*

I joined the PICL group (Parents Involved in Children's Learning) … this is a study group where we look at a video of our own children … and discuss children's well-being … involvement … their communication with adults and children … and think about what they have been doing at home … and how we can move it on.

Now I know why Nathan always runs … throws balls … turns the taps on etc. … it's all part of his trajectory schema … I learnt about well-being and was able to cope better with his screaming … as I understood that he got frustrated in his play … especially when I was trying to intervene and divert his attention to other things … I removed my precious things from around the house … and now we have balls … balloons … buckets … and targets on the door … and all really focused on his play.

*Where am I now? I am continually looking for things for Nathan to express himself and play … I can now play alongside him … letting **him** take the lead … showing me he can do it. I can now say 'Go on, give it a go. Try it!' I now know that I have to give him a chance to work it out for himself … Sometimes he can't … sometimes he can …*

In dialogue with other parents/carers and workers at the study group, Nathan's grandmother has learnt to relax and allow Nathan to fulfil his potential alongside other children in nursery. She expresses a deep understanding of his learning and has adjusted the home environment in order to encourage him even more.

Figures 14.1 and 14.2 Nathan exploring at nursery

Reflective task

- Having read the case study, can you think about similar situations in your setting with children and their carers?
- How can you negotiate with parents/carers and communicate their expectations and encourage learning alongside each other?

Reflective task

You may have a range of languages spoken in your setting. To get an idea of what parents want for their child, you need to communicate with them.

- Think about how you can use video/photos or other methods to communicate with families whose first language is not English.
- Think about whether there is a predominant second language. Could you run groups for parents in that language? If not, what other provision could you offer to include these parents?
- Could you ask parents to help other parents?
- Who else could help? Where could you locate resources (e.g. internet)?

'Growing Together' project: working with parents and children up to three years

The knowledge-sharing approach that Pen Green adopted with the nursery parents was so successful that it extended its study to include the youngest children and their families. The Centre set up a weekly group for parents or carers to attend with their children, called 'Growing Together', during which workers could 'dialogue with parents about their child's development' (Tait, 2007: 142). Staff quickly realised that the shared conceptual framework they were using with the parents of the nursery children (schemas, involvement, well-being and adult pedagogic strategies) was useful, but when it came to the relationships between 'very young infants and their parents, they needed to draw on a number of psychoanalytic theories', as partly summarised from Tait (2007):

- **Holding** refers initially to the physical holding of a young infant so that the infant gradually internalises the feeling of being safely held. Holding also describes the emotional holding parents can give their baby by holding him or her in mind, so that the baby does not feel abandoned when their parent leaves the room (Winnicott, 1991).
- **Containment** describes the parent taking in the baby's distress, understanding it and responding so that the baby feels emotionally looked after and contained (Bion, 1962).
- **Attachment** describes how adults and children form reciprocal relationships and how feeling securely attached enables children to explore and to move away from their carers (Bowlby, 1969).
- **Companionship** describes the relationship between parent and child that involves 'interest and pleasure in shared experiences' (Powers and Trevarthen, 2009: 210).

The weekly drop-in group for infants and their parents or carers now runs three times a week due to the demand from parents. During the 90-minute session, one worker films either a child at play or a parent–child interaction and then watches the filmed sequence with the parent on a computer in one corner of the busy room. This creates an opportunity for dialogue. The worker can introduce some theory (whatever seems pertinent to the piece filmed) and the parent can talk about their child at home and can choose some still images from the film and some language to describe what is happening. The parent takes home this one page created during the session and can start their own child's portfolio.

Parents choose to attend 'Growing Together' at the Pen Green Centre and opt for a turn to be filmed. Seeing oneself on film is an eye opener for anyone, parent or professional. It is unnecessary to point out to parents, in a patronising way, when they are doing something well or not so well. They can see and judge for themselves just as workers, seeing themselves in action, can decide what worked and what did not work with a particular child or group of children. The process of dialogue and reflection results in learning for the adults both about themselves and about the children's learning.

The psychoanalytic concepts drawn on by the Pen Green Centre affect other aspects of their work in the group. In order to 'hold parents in mind' from one week to the next, they 'spend time as a staff team planning and reflecting on what happens each week' (Tait, 2007: 155). They phone parents they have not seen for a couple of weeks to make contact and to let them know they are concerned about them and 'holding them in mind' even though they have not seen them (Tait, 2007: 143). The Centre also provides continuity in the set-up for the children and for their parents, for example sand, water, dough, train set, trucks, a baby area for the children, and comfortable chairs and a warm drink for their parents. The parents attending the group are experiencing all of the usual stresses of being parents and a proportion would also be suffering from postnatal depression sometime during their attendance at the group. The group is well staffed and this enables practitioner–parent conversations, as well as parent-to-parent support.

Reflective task

- Think about how you interact with the parents of the youngest children in your setting.
- How could you 'grow together' with children and parents?
- How do you keep in contact with parents over time?
- What kind of a 'welcome' do you provide for parents who may be feeling tired and stressed?

Working with parents means fathers and mothers

As many settings have a predominantly female workforce, they will often have to work extra hard to engage with fathers as well as with mothers in their daily practice.

During the three-year research study on 'Involving Parents in Their Children's Learning' at the Pen Green Centre, staff monitored all involvement, noting down who attended or contributed to the dialogue. During the first year of the study, they noticed that fewer fathers/male carers were becoming directly involved. They asked a small number of fathers why this was the case. It seemed they needed a reason to come and, in many cases, an invitation. Meetings would usually be advertised in a non-threatening way, inviting parents for 'a coffee and a chat'. This made the meetings sound unimportant to fathers. 'These fathers wanted to know that they could make a difference to their child's education' (Tait, 2007: 46).

In order to invite fathers living apart from their children but with parental responsibility to meetings, it is important to have a record of each child's family situation and addresses, and to offer fathers equal opportunities to be involved in their children's education (for more information on 'parental responsibility', see http://www.direct.gov.uk, or Chapter 13.

The Pen Green Centre differentiated between mothers and fathers in how it advertised events, emphasising the importance and the underpinning research findings to fathers. Staff also sent out invitations by post to the parent who was not collecting their child from nursery. This approach worked well, although fathers are still in the minority. In an American study involving 213 early childhood educators, Green (2003) found that:

> Three factors significantly accounted for early childhood educators' success at involving fathers: (1) including the father's name on the enrollment form; (2) sending written correspondence to fathers even if they live apart from their children, and (3) inviting fathers to the centre to participate in educational activities with their children.

More recently, the Pen Green Centre has set up Fathers' Groups that run on Saturday and Sunday when fathers can come with their children and enjoy time together. The fathers seem to enjoy using the whole provision. One father, Jimmy, who came with his children found it to be a real lifeline at a difficult time.

Scenario

I've had a very difficult time in my life over the past four years – my family was ready for a break-up, so we asked Sure Start for help and my Family Visitor, Christine, said I should start taking the kids to dads' group on a Sunday at Pen Green.

The first time I went to the Sunday dads' club, it was a proper nightmare – I couldn't get into the place! But Christine persuaded me to try again and it worked out better after that. When I first went, I had all sorts of stuff going on in my life and I found it very hard to speak to people or to go out of the house but gradually, as the time went on, I started to feel better in myself.

My kids won't let me miss a single Sunday and it has definitely brought us closer as a family. It started with Christine hounding me – I mean hounding! – to get involved with my kids and take them to dads' group and after two years of asking, I said I would give it a try and see if my kids liked the group. They did like it and I've been a regular there for three and a half years.

I have started getting involved in what's going on in the group, what activities we do and they are always open to ideas that could be fun or exciting for the kids. My boy, Bobby, he loves anything to do with getting in a mess.

We also try and take the kids on as many educational trips as possible. One of the best times was when we took the group to Twin Lakes Park. The kids got to play on the rides and then see a falconry display and got to pet some of the farm animals like the sheep and the pigs. And my kids loved it when we went to the fire station and they got to sit in the fire engine and meet the firefighters.

We do loads of fun things at Pen Green with our children and it's all memories for my kids to look back on when they are older and I hope one day my boy will take his kids to Pen Green dads' group.

Important points in Jimmy's story seem to be:
- Services being available so that families know they can ask for help when they need it.
- The persistence of the worker – this was a long process and not an issue that could be solved in six to ten weeks.
- The group met the children's and parents' needs. Jimmy welcomed the company and support of other dads and the children loved the experiences offered to them.
- Despite severe problems in his own life, Jimmy was interested in his children's learning. He knew what they liked doing and wanted to encourage them.

Reflective task

- Think about the last conversation you had with a parent or carer: who offered information to whom?
- Did you find yourself doing most of the listening or were you mostly talking?
- Did you find yourself 'talking down' to the parent/carer?
- Think about how the parent/carer might have experienced the conversation.
- When given the choice do you prefer to talk to mothers or fathers? Why is that?
- Explore your insecurities when talking to a parent/carer.
- What do you need to feel confident and competent talking to children's carers?
- How do you involve fathers in your setting? There is lots of practical advice available on the internet.

The political context of the late 1990s and early 2000s

What became very significant to the new government in the UK were the long-term findings of the Head Start programme launched in the United States in 1965. Although early evaluations of this huge project indicated that the short-term intellectual and social gains did not seem to last, by the 1990s it had become apparent that children whose families were involved in Head Start had cost the US government much less money in the long term than families not involved. There were some clues about why that was the case in some of the follow-up studies. Although the researchers were largely using a deficit model of families, and Head Start was considered to be a war on poverty rather than a parent involvement programme, Lazar (1983: 463) noted that these sorts of programmes 'change parental aspirations for the child'.

The actual outcomes were 'higher rates of school completion and what these mean in terms of later chances for employment and self-sufficiency' (Datta, 1983: 475). By the late 1990s even more data on the long-term success of Head Start existed and economists had begun doing cost–benefit analysis and came up with the finding that a dollar spent during a child's early years meant seven dollars saved (by government) during their lifetime. This strapline and outcome appealed to the Labour government and the decision was made to invest £540 million in the Sure Start Programme, setting up the first few projects in 1999 (Glass, 1999). A community development model was used and projects were developed locally and steered by management boards often consisting of more parents than workers. Parents were more in control than in previous projects. Initially children's centres were set up in disadvantaged areas, but the services in those communities were universal and, therefore, not stigmatised. From 2006 children's centres were opened in all communities regardless of their specific need, thus to offer all children under five and their families free access to services. Sure Start was designed 'to prevent social exclusion [...] to improve the life chances of younger children through better access to early education and play, health services for children and parents, family support and advice on nurturing' (Glass, 1999: 257). They were a kind of 'one-stop shop' for young children and their families. Furthermore, children's centres offer outreach worker services, thus they 'break down barriers' and help to build trusting relationships with parents/carers and their children.

Recent research

A very influential study in recent years was commissioned by the Department for Education and Skills, and ran from 1997 until 2011, making it a large longitudinal study. The Effective Provision of Pre-school Education (EPPE, Sylva *et al.*, 2010) has studied a range of different types of preschool and 3,000 children from differing social backgrounds. When comparing preschools, the team found that there were better outcomes for children when there were qualified teachers in the setting and leading the learning (Sylva *et al.*, 2010). They also found that the quality of the home learning environment improved outcomes for children. So, for the first time, they state that 'what parents do is more important than who they are' (Sylva *et al.*, 2004: 1), whereas previously better outcomes for children were strongly associated with the education and socio-economic status of the parents. Further to this, they found that there were cognitive gains for children when parents were involved in decision making (Sylva *et al.*, 2010).

Based on some of the EPPE findings Siraj-Blatchford and Siraj-Blatchford (2010) further explored the importance of the home learning environment and the positive impact on children's attainment through a better quality of family-based support for early learning. The finding about the value of the home learning environment may have prompted those people with a deficit view of families to think that, as professionals, we now need to teach parents to carry out 'school-like' activities at home, which is very different from sharing ideas with parents about their children's schemas, interests and spontaneous learning at home. For more information on sharing ideas about schemas with parents, see Athey (2007), or Mairs and the Pen Green Team (2012).

Two other studies also influenced policy during the early 2000s. Firstly, using part of the 1970s birth cohort data, Feinstein showed that within our education system children from low socio-economic status families are likely to do less well than their peers and that the gap widens when children start school (Feinstein, 2003; Feinstein and Sabates, 2006). Feinstein supported the idea of Sure Start and argued that support for poorer families should continue into primary school, that staff should be well trained, 'motivated and well paid; and that turnover of staff should be kept to a minimum' (Feinstein, 2003: 30).

Secondly, Blanden (2006: 1), using the same data set from the 1970s birth cohort, examined what happened when 'children buck that trend' and do better than expected. Blanden's analysis found that 'parental interest' is crucial in helping children to achieve better outcomes and, interestingly, she says (2006: 2):

> My results show that the level of parental interest is very important; with father's interest having a large influence on their sons, and mother's interest most important for their daughters.

However, Blanden (2006: 16) also found that 'the mother's education dominates for sons while the father's education dominates for daughters, the opposite result to that obtained for parental interest'. A proxy for doing better academically was 'being read to at age 5' resulting in the promotion nationally of reading and books for young children (Blanden, 2006, referring to the Book Start initiative, see http://www.bookstart.org.uk).

Desforges and Abouchaar (2003: 4) undertook a review of English-language literature 'to establish research findings on the relationship between parental involvement, parental support and family education on pupil achievement and adjustment in schools'. The most significant finding was that:

> ... parental involvement in the form of 'at-home good parenting' has a significant positive effect on children's achievement and adjustment even after all other factors shaping attainment have been taken out of the equation.
>
> (Desforges and Abouchaar, 2003: 4)

This finding was replicated in all studies across social classes and ethnic groups. Parents who are interested and encourage their children's efforts at home indirectly support their children in developing a positive view of themselves as learners. This review supported the early findings from the EPPE study that 'what parents do is more important than who they are' (Sylva *et al.*, 2004: 1). Desforges and Abouchaar (2003) went on to look at various interventions, designed to enhance parenting and to increase parental involvement. According to Desforges and Abouchaar (2003), in all but a few studies surveyed, there was a lack of evidence of a direct link between becoming more involved and children's attainment. Most studies used anecdotal or self-reports of increased involvement but there was rarely what they considered a rigorous measure. One of the few small studies that linked parents' increase in participation with children's achievement was the Raising Early Achievement in Literacy (REAL) in poor areas of Sheffield, where it was reported that:

> The gains did not result from a teaching or training programme as normally understood ... we [provided] parents with ways of thinking about their roles ... the differences [between programme and control children] reflect socio-cultural change in family literacy produced through teacher–parent interaction and parent–child interaction.
>
> (Hannon and Nutbrown, 2001: 12)

Other issues touched on in the report were: parents, wary of school and authority, who are reluctant to become involved because of their negative experiences of school; and meeting the educational needs of parents as well as children (Desforges and Abouchaar, 2003).

How parents are represented in early years curricula frameworks in England

At roughly the same time as the Labour government was putting money into early years services, early years curricula were being developed for the first time in this country.

Year and Curriculum or Report	What is said about parents
1996 Desirable Learning Outcomes (SCAA, 1996)	Parent involvement should be a two-way process: 'Experiences initiated at home are sometimes used as stimuli for learning in the setting' (SCAA, 1996: 9).
2000 Curriculum Guidance for the Foundation Stage (QCA, 2000)	Acknowledged that learning took place at home as well as in the setting: 'A successful partnership needs a two-way flow of information, knowledge and expertise' (QCA, 2000: 9).
2002 Birth to Three Matters (DfES, 2002)	The emphasis was slightly different and on children's emotional well-being, rather than explicitly on their learning.
2008 Statutory Framework for the Early Years Foundation Stage (DCSF, 2008a)	The 'key person' was seen as important (Elfer, Goldschmied and Selleck, 2003). An emphasis on parents and practitioners 'learning from each other' but most strategies were to do with making children more comfortable in the setting.
2011 An Independent Report on the Early Years Foundation Stage by Dame Clare Tickell (Tickell, 2011)	The role of parents and the home learning environment was recognised. It was recommended that the curriculum be simplified and made more accessible to parents, for example on the internet.

Table 14.1 (Adapted from Medhurst, J. (2011), 'Working with Families', unpubl. assignment, MA in Integrated Provision for Children and Families, validated by the University of Leicester)

There seemed to be a steady trickle of information through curriculum documents about the importance of parents in their children's learning. The new version of the *Statutory Framework for the Early Years Foundation Stage* (EYFS) (DfE, 2012a) also mentions parents several times, mostly in relation to the setting 'informing', 'reporting' and 'discussing' children's progress with parents and other professionals. 'Strong partnership' with parents is encouraged and there is a stronger focus on identifying additional needs whether it be developmental or language.

Learning at home is referred to twice in the EYFS:

> When a child is aged between two and three practitioners must review their progress, and provide parents and/or carers with a short written summary of their child's development in the prime areas. Practitioners must discuss with parents and/or carers how the summary of development can be used to support development at home.

(DfE, 2012a: 10–11)

Further on in the document, 'providers must make the following information available to parents and carers … how parents and carers can share learning at home' (DfE, 2012a: 27). So the acknowledgement that parents are already engaging in learning with their children at home seems to have diminished and the tone suggests that professionals need to tell parents how to share learning at home with their children – in fact it is a requirement that providers do this.

Frank Field was the author of an *Independent Review on Poverty and Life Chances*, published in 2010 in which recommendations were made to provide:

> ... high quality and consistent support for parents during pregnancy, and in the early years, support for better parenting; support for a good home learning environment; and high quality childcare.

> (Field, 2010: 7)

His report emphasised the importance of a phase called the Foundation Years (from birth to five) and also recommended that 'settings should be held to account on their engagement with parents', again making it more of a requirement rather than just desirable (Field, 2010: 8).

This report was followed by Graham Allen's report (2011) on *Early Intervention*, which referred back to his earlier report on the same issues (Allen and Duncan Smith, 2008). Allen (2011) reviewed a range of interventions and made recommendations that several strategies were put in place to ensure that all children get the best early start in life. These were to be low-cost strategies, including:

> ... a new National Parenting Campaign [...] to ensure that the public, parents, health professionals and, especially, newly pregnant women are aware of the importance of developing social and emotional capability in the first years of life, and understand the best ways of encouraging good later outcomes for their children.

> (Allen, 2011: 58)

Allen's emphasis (2011) was very much on targeting disadvantaged children and families and on the savings that could be made by government in the long term. He used the term 'school ready' and 'life ready' and by that he seemed to mean socially and emotionally capable (Allen, 2011).

Following the Field (2010) and Allen (2011) reports and at a time of austerity, the recently elected coalition government (Conservative and Liberal Democrat) seems to be shifting the focus from providing universal services to a more targeted approach with an exclusive focus on vulnerable families. The Department for Education and Department of Health (DfE and DoH, 2011) worked together to develop a document entitled *Supporting Families in the Foundation Years*, outlining how the coalition government will support families of young children. Inevitably there is a huge demand for all high-quality early years services but not all families know how to access these services or have the funds to pay for them. The outcomes of recent and radical cuts to early years budgets may well be that we return to a 1970s model where poor families get the poorest services.

Looking back over the last 15 years, there seems to be an increasing recognition in England (and elsewhere) that being a parent is difficult and that all parents need support, particularly during their children's early years. Research has shown that what has the most impact on children's outcomes is the home learning environment (Siraj-Blatchford and Siraj-Blatchford, 2010). In the drive to offer a more equal education system, could that piece of critical information get 'lost in translation' and become prescriptive and top-down now that the government has become involved?

Reflective task

- What is your view? Discuss with your fellow students or your team.
- How valuable do you consider the work with parents and the home learning environment to be for children and for your setting?

One plan is to offer home visits to the most vulnerable families. Home visiting is one of the strategies that has worked well at children's centres that offer Outreach Workers visiting families in their home.

Reflective task

Consider how you and your setting staff build trusting and understanding relationships with the children and their families?

- Do you visit families at home?
- Do children visit your setting prior to their attendance?
- What sorts of other experiences do you provide for staff and parents to get to know each other?
- How could you improve on what you are currently doing?

One concern is that what families already engage in – everyday tasks that are significant to young children – may not be valued, and parents could become undermined by being told to carry out 'school-like activities' with their children at home.

Extend your knowledge

Read and research more about the benefits of the home learning environment by studying the following knowledge review:

- Siraj-Blatchford, I. and Siraj-Blatchford, J. (2010) *Improving children's attainment through a better quality of family-based support for early learning*, London: Centre for Excellence and Outcomes in Children and Young People's Services (C4EO). Available from: http://www.c4eo.org.uk/themes/earlyyears/familybasedsupport/files/c4eo_family_based_support_full_knowledge_review.pdf.

Conclusion

This chapter has explored how working with parents and families has evolved in England over the last hundred years or so. Since the innovative work by Margaret and Rachel McMillan early in the 20th century, and Plowden's recognition (1967) that attitudes to parents were beginning to change and that parental interest in education might be a factor in children achieving well in school, there has been a growing acknowledgement of the influence parents have over their children's learning.

The chapter emphasises the role we as professionals have in building relationships with the important people in children's lives. However, it is important not to forget that parents are experts on their own children. We need to listen to and respect what parents tell us about their child (Whalley, 2007), as well as offering many different ways that parents can be involved in their children's learning.

While the coalition government seems to be shifting the focus from providing universal services to a more targeted approach, with an exclusive focus on vulnerable families, the early years curricula for England reflect, to some extent, the messages from research about the value of the 'home learning environment' (DfE and DoH, 2011; DfE, 2012a). There is also a recognition of the importance of supporting children and parents in the early years in order to increase the life chances of all children (Field, 2010).

Next steps

- A good first step is to carry out an audit of your current work with parents. Ask yourselves, as a team: What are we already doing that engages parents? Then perhaps, ask yourselves: How are we interacting with parents? Are we genuinely interested in what they can tell us? How could we do a better job?
- Invite parents in to tell you how it felt to walk into your setting for the first time and listen carefully to what they tell you. Give a voice to staff members who currently have young children and are using services, so they can tell you what it is really like. Try to stand in their shoes.
- Carry out a SWOT analysis (individually or as a team) to identify your strengths (what are we good at), weaknesses (where can we improve), the opportunities (who can we work with, how can we make ourselves heard, e.g. organise 'family fun days') and the threats (finance, time and staffing) that impact on your partnership work with parents. Draw up an Action Plan with SMART targets and resources that are required in order to enhance your existing good work with parents.

Evaluate your...

Practice

- There is a huge amount of powerful literature on 'involving parents'. A good starting point might be to share your vision and values with the rest of your team and discuss how and why you want to develop new ways of working with parents.
- Use the value statements you have drawn up as a starting point when reading about work with parents. This will help you to sieve out judgemental attitudes and imposed top-down over-professionalised ways of working.
- Go to peer-reviewed journals for the most recent research, for example the Special Issue of the *European Early Childhood Education Research (EECER) Journal* on Children's and Parents' Perspectives on Diversity published in June 2009.

Further reading

Brooker, L. (2010) 'Learning to play, or playing to learn? Children's participation in the cultures of homes and settings', in Brooker, L. and Edwards, S. (2010) (eds.) *Engaging Play*, Maidenhead: Open University Press.

Cubey, P. (2012) 'Transforming Learning for Children and Their Parents', in Mairs, K. and the Pen Green Team (2012) *Young Children Learning Through Schemas: Deepening the dialogue about learning in the home and in the nursery*, London: Routledge.

Desforges, C. and Abouchaar, A. (2003) *The Impact of Parental Involvement, Parental Support and Family Education on Pupil Achievements and Adjustment: A Literature Review*, DfES, Research Report RR433.

DfE and DoH (2011) *Supporting Families in the Foundation Years*, London: DfE and DoH. Available from: http://www.parliament.uk/deposits/depositedpapers/2011/DEP2011-1250.pdf.

Douglass, A. (2011) 'Improving family engagement: The organisational context and its influence on partnering with parents in formal childcare settings', *Early Childhood Research and Practice*, vol. 13, no. 2. Available from: http://www.ecrp.uiuc.edu.

Goldman, R. (2005) *Fathers' Involvement in Their Children's Education*, London: National Family and Parenting Institute.

Hannon, P., Morgan, A. and Nutbrown, C. (2006) 'Parents' perspectives on a family literacy programme', *Journal of Early Childhood Research*, vol. 3, no. 3, pp. 19–44.

Hughes, M. and MacNaughton, G. (2002) 'Preparing early childhood professionals to work with parents: The challenges of diversity and dissensus', *Australian Journal of Early Childhood*, vol. 27, no. 2, pp. 14–20.

Morrison Gutman, L. and Feinstein, L. (2007) *Parenting Behaviours and Children's Development from Infancy to Early Childhood: Changes, Continuities, and Contributions*, London: Centre for Research on the Wider Benefits of Learning, Institute of Education. Available from: http://www.learning-benefits.net.

Leadership and management in early years

Joy Scadden

Introduction

This chapter will explore the concepts of leadership and management which have become increasingly significant within the early years domain. In the recent document, *Supporting Families in the Foundation Years* (DfE and DoH, 2011), the government stresses the need for 'strong leadership' across the sector. However, the nature of this 'strong leadership' is not evident, due to confusion within the sector about the two types of leadership: leadership of practice and leadership of the organisation. Indeed, Whalley (2008: 2) stated the need for 'urgent clarification of the two types of leadership'. Although a number of courses and qualifications have been established to support leadership of practice, there is little available to improve weak leadership of the organisation in the sector, despite the findings of a recent report, *Improving business skills in the early years and childcare sector* (Sarwar and Grewal, 2011), in which providers specifically request support with business skills.

This chapter will discuss the potentially conflicting concepts of leadership and management and encourage you to reflect on your own practice experience. Past and current government strategies regarding leadership and management will be noted and their value considered in relation to the quality of early years practice. Also leadership and management across the public and private sectors will be acknowledged. Finally, practical issues will be examined that make everyday leadership and management truly challenging.

Learning outcomes

By the end of this chapter, you will be able to:

- Reflect on the concepts of leadership and management and evaluate these in relation to your role.
- Identify the features of the 'strong leadership' required in early years.
- Recognise the challenges of the management role in an early years organisation.
- Understand the need for effective teamwork.
- Demonstrate your ability to think strategically.
- Acknowledge the significance of managing change in an ever-developing sector.
- Debate the concept of 'quality' within early years.
- Understand the role of the 'pedagogue' within 'leadership for learning'.
- Show an awareness of the current qualifications which exist to promote leadership within the sector and evaluate their effectiveness.
- Discuss the role and purpose of Early Years Professional Status (EYPS).

What is leadership and what is management?

To begin this section we will examine the two concepts in a general sense and then apply these thoughts to the early years sector. In summary, leadership is about having a 'vision', and 'followers' – people who believe in the 'vision'.

Reflective task

- Is there someone is your professional life who has inspired you?
- What was it about them that inspired you?
- How have they affected your professional journey?

Historically, putting the responsibility and accountability on a single leader in an organisation has led to a whole raft of theories examining the idea of leadership and its differing styles. A well-published theory by Weber (1947, cited in Fiol *et al.*, 1999) describes three leadership styles: charismatic, bureaucratic and traditional. Weber believed that most leaders exhibited characteristics of all three styles and were most effective when their visions were based on everyday and easily identifiable values, while at the same time presenting pioneering solutions to highly significant issues (Fiol *et al.*, 1999).

Fundamental to Weber's approach, therefore, were innovation and the process of change. This important feature of leadership, 'managing change', will inevitably be explored throughout the chapter. Bolden and Kirk (2006) proposed that leadership itself is a process rather than an individual and it is the quality of the relationship between the 'leaders' and the 'followers' which is significant in terms of 'leadership'. This relationship approach is further supported by Gardner (2011), when he states that the effectiveness of a leader relies on the power of his or her message and whether or not it is positively received or believed by the followers. So if it is the 'buy in' that makes 'leadership' within an organisation, then it must be viewed as a collective experience.

Bolden and Kirk (2006) use a 'weaving' analogy, rather similar to the 'woven mat' of the Te Whāriki approach, to describe the interdependent leadership relationship. They describe the senior management as the 'warp' running lengthwise through the organisation – they have essential roles of implementation or 'making it happen' – whereas the 'weft' applies to all the people who collaborate across the organisation and thereby help to generate the 'fabric'. Without the 'weft', Bolden and Kirk (2006) state that the senior management would become 'warped' and the organisation untenable.

Certainly this emphasis on a collective approach to leadership is one that is most appropriate currently within early years, with the focus being on integrated working and collaboration between all the stakeholders: children, parents, practitioners and multi-agency organisations. Indeed, as Rodd (2010: 29) states: 'Notions of trust, sharing, collaboration and empowerment also appear to be central to successful leadership.'

This approach is further supported by Jackson (2006: 3) when he talks about the importance of *distributed leadership* within the 'learning organisation', leading to shared values and consensus and therefore providing an 'energy' for schools to 'transform themselves' and at the same time bind the institution together, bringing us back to the role or purpose of leadership to manage change.

Extend your knowledge

For further discussion and reference about 'learning organisations' read Senge, P. (2006) *The Fifth Discipline: The Art and Practice of the Learning Organization*, London: Random House.

Then consider whether your setting is a 'learning organisation', where the people are motivated to develop themselves, and thereby contribute to the overall creativity and innovation within the setting.

Using this *collective* or *collaborative* model of leadership, which sits well within the early years sector, it seems the role of management can be easily identified as providing the 'warp' threads across the organisation. But what exactly is management? Peter Drucker (1909–2005) is famously quoted as saying, 'Management is doing things right; leadership is doing the right things' (Cohen, 2010: 57). While this slogan may oversimplify two complex concepts, it does sum up the management focus on *implementation*. Indeed it also emphasises the management focus on the drive for quality and a 'zero defects – getting it right the first time' philosophy (Crosby, 1979).

While a leader may inspire and motivate, it is the manager who must put this inspiration and motivation into everyday practice. Fayol's definition (1916, cited in Cole and Kelly, 2011: 23) of management 'to forecast and plan, to organise, to command, to coordinate and to control' essentially is still current today. However, Peters (1988, cited in Cole and Kelly, 2011: 118) takes this definition of management further, towards our 'fabric' model of collaboration, when he talks about 'innovation', 'leadership that loves change' and 'partnership – the wholesale participation of and gain sharing with all people connected with the organisation'.

It could be summarised, therefore, that management is a dynamic process whereby, through effective planning and functioning of resources, the vision of the organisation and its leaders is implemented.

Leadership and management roles

Mintzberg (1973) compounds this definition in his study of managerial work where he identified 'sets of behaviour' of a manager and grouped these under three roles as below.

Interpersonal roles	Informational roles	Decisional roles
Figurehead	Monitor	Entrepreneur
Leader	Disseminator	Disturbance handler
Liaison	Spokesman	Resource allocator
		Negotiator

Table 15.1 Management roles

While these descriptors remain very broad, notably a number of these roles incorporate acknowledged leadership skills – certainly the interpersonal roles do, for example. The 'entrepreneur' aspect of the decisional roles conjures up an image of captains of industry like Sir Richard Branson and Lord Sugar – not people who would relish the title of 'manager'. However, as we will see further in the chapter, to be an effective manager in early years one must be prepared to lead a team of people and effect change in an inspirational and innovative way, which would certainly tick the entrepreneurship box. Thus, we cannot ignore the inescapable interdependent relationship between leadership and management.

Leadership and management in early years

The concept of leadership exists on many levels within the early years sector, and is therefore often confused, as previously highlighted by Whalley (2008). This may be due to the often perceived subjective and individual nature of 'leadership' and, with the increasing emphasis on integrated working, the difficulties in agreeing the methods to be employed across multi-agencies, let alone the private, voluntary, independent (PVI) and maintained settings. Furthermore, the terminology 'leading early years practice', with the expectation of practitioners with Early Years Professional Status (EYPS) to take up the task, has instigated discussions within the sector.

In order to establish some clarification, leadership for the purposes of this chapter has been divided into two sections – organisation and practice. Meanwhile management, based on its definition of 'implementation', will be evident in both sections.

Reflective task

- Identify who are the leaders and who are the managers in your setting.
- Is there a potential discrepancy between their job role/title and their *actual* practice? If so, explore the reasons behind this further.
- Write down the qualities and skills you would like to see in a manager and in a leader.

Leadership of the organisation

The key to leading a successful childcare organisation, be it a maintained or PVI setting, is to have a clear vision and that clear vision must involve striking a successful balance between the quality of the organisation and its sustainability. It is important to think about sustainability issues not only from the position of the childcare provider, but also for the benefit of children and their families. As emphasised in the recent report, *Improving business skills in the early years and childcare sector*, undertaken by Sarwar and Grewal (2011) for the organisation 4Children and the Department for Education, the sustainability of good-quality early years and childcare provision is critical to both the development and education of young children and to the wider economy, by enabling parents to work and train. However, in early years, sustainability and what is effectively good business management have often been viewed as an ancillary factor to running the organisation for the 'social good'.

Clearly the government wishes to look at new ways of promoting sustainability through encouraging cooperation between the PVI and maintained sectors. The publication *Supporting Families in the Foundation Years* (DfE and DoH, 2011: 34) encourages a desire to develop 'shared ambitions' and to 'foster a sector' which is:
- entrepreneurial
- sustainable
- socially responsible.

In 2010 the *Childcare and early years providers survey* (Brind *et al.*, 2011) recorded 105,100 providers of childcare and early years education, of which 15,700 were early years providers in maintained schools and 89,500 were childcare providers. The overwhelming majority of private day nurseries are small businesses – businesses operating just one or two settings make up 80 per cent of the market. Notably, there were more childminders than any other type of provider, with the survey recording a total of 47,400 working childminders in 2010, most of these being self-employed.

The manager's role

With such a variety of organisation types it is essential that the management is flexible to suit the needs of the organisation. However, this is based on style or behaviours; the 'nuts and bolts' of basic organisational management will remain the same. Whether PVI or maintained, the manager is the owner, a preschool leader, a childminder or head teacher; at the centre is the 'vision' of the organisation which the manager must embody and from which he or she leads. Then the manager's role is to disseminate this vision through all the resources which he or she manages, as shown in the diagram.

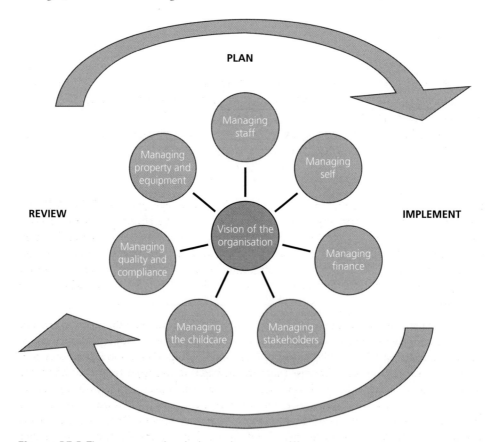

Figure 15.1 The manager's role in early years settings

The style or behaviour of management will vary but this is not just according to the type of organisation, but also according to the demands of the organisation. These demands will fluctuate as the organisation experiences change, a dynamic and cyclical process as shown by the arrows in the diagram.

To examine 'management' within early years further it is helpful to identify the knowledge and skills required to manage an early years organisation:

Knowledge

- Believe in and implement the 'vision' of the sector/setting leader
- Know how to manage resources – staff, finance, property
- Knowledge of market and customer needs
- Knowledge of the early years industry, legislative requirements and curriculum
- Knowledge of employment and health and safety legislation

Skills/abilities

- Engage/lead others to 'follow'
- Strong communicator
- Strategic thinker
- Use resources effectively and efficiently
- Monitor and improve quality
- Good organiser of self and others

Reflective task

- Looking at the specification above, which areas of knowledge and which skills/abilities do you have?
- If you are you in a management role within your organisation identify what your job description or person specification requires you to do.
- What are your responsibilities for managing any of the resources in the diagram above?
- Identify your areas for development and discuss with your line manager.

From these lists it could be argued that, as most of the knowledge and all of the skills are transferable, then a manager from any business background has the ability to be an effective manager in an early years setting, as long as they are willing to build up knowledge of the early years industry, the legislative requirements and the curriculum. It is, therefore, the business and management skills which are important here as highlighted in the report by Sarwar and Grewal (2011) identifying the need and a demand for more business skills training across the whole of the early years sector.

Traditionally, managers in early years settings, mostly women, have come up through the nursery nurse 'ranks' and will have a good knowledge of the industry and service. They will be 'principle-centred' in their leadership (Covey, 1992, cited in Cole and Kelly, 2011) but most often they will lack business and management skills, because there are limited training opportunities available for the sector. As the emphasis of the available training is on what is effectively 'leadership of practice' this skills gap will remain unfilled. Interestingly, this was not an area examined by Nutbrown (2012) within her review of Early Years qualifications. Indeed Nutbrown (2012: 56) even refers to 'highly qualified, talented practitioners that spend too much time behind a desk'. This further reinforces one of the key findings by Sarwar and Grewal (2011: 4) that 'the culture of the sector has meant that business skills are not as highly valued as the ability to provide safe and secure provision for children'.

Rodd (2005: 1) acknowledged this issue when she stated, 'Given the challenge and complexity of current multi-disciplinary service provision, early years practitioners need to be well prepared to function as skilled administrators, managers and leaders in order to fulfil their roles and responsibilities effectively.'

Sustainability issues in early years

It must be acknowledged that within any organisation, whether in the PVI or maintained sector, the money is the life blood, a vital resource. In order to survive, this vital resource must be well managed, another reason to be clear about the interdependent roles of leadership and management.

Despite the effects of the current recession, the results of the *Childcare and early years providers survey 2010* (Brind, 2011) show that full-day care and sessional providers, with the exception of full-day care providers operating in children's centres, are making small profits. A minority are struggling to fill places, however, which inevitably results in financial difficulties.

These findings and those in Sarwar and Grewal's report (2011) underline the need for good management skills within the sector. Arguably any manager in any organisation has to perfect the art of 'plate-spinning' but in early years this is even more relevant as the profit margins are so tight, with staffing costs being anything from 50 per cent to 80 per cent of turnover (Aubrey, 2011). Another feature of the sector is the large numbers of debtors and difficulties in collecting the fees. Parents/carers either cannot afford to pay for childcare or they can afford to pay but choose not to, not believing it to be 'a priority spend'. It is this difficulty in viewing the service as a 'business' which lies at the root of the issue and of course any business must be managed and managed well if it is to survive, especially in this tough economic climate.

Extend your knowledge

Read the following publication and write down the main messages and how you can apply this or learn from it for your practice:

- Sarwar, S. and Grewal, S. (2011) *Improving business skills in the early years and childcare sector*, London: Office for Public Management. Available from: http://www.4children.org.uk/Resources/Detail/Improving-business-skills-in-the-early-years-and-childcare-sector.

Next steps

In 2004 Moyles and Yates published *The Effective Leadership and Management Evaluation Scheme* (ELMS) (Moyles, 2010) as a tool to support practitioners in a managerial role. Research this further and use it to evaluate your skills and knowledge.

Managing an early years organisation

As a manager within an early years organisation, staffing is a challenging resource to manage. Despite the fact that early years practitioners are renowned for being poorly paid, staff ratios as stated in the statutory requirements mean that this is an expensive part of any manager's budget and, as such, must be managed efficiently to ensure sustainability. This is particularly significant with the up-skilling of the workforce and one has to carefully consider how to pay for highly qualified professionals, and where additional funding can be sourced from.

In order to provide good-quality and efficient services a manager needs a good-quality team to lead, as illustrated by the findings of the Effective Provision of Pre-school Education (EPPE) Project report (Sylva *et al.*, 2004). However, it is not just a question of staff being highly qualified; the team must share the vision and values of the organisation, as projected by the team leader or manager. Therefore, the manager must be able to identify individuals' skills and motivations to ensure sound recruitment, an effective deployment and group dynamic, thus promoting a positive and productive culture. Referring back to Mintzberg's sets of behaviour of a manager (1973), these abilities would cut across all three 'roles'.

As a manager, a good knowledge of the people who are working under you is essential in order to be effective. Goleman (1999) emphasises the need for organisations to encourage the 'soft skills' and states that emotional intelligence is 'a vital component of any organisation's management philosophy'. Having this emotional intelligence, which Goleman (2012: 1) describes as a 'one-person psychology', later enlarges into social intelligence, 'a two-person psychology: what transpires as we connect'. Pink (2005) concurs with this approach when he talks about emotional intelligence and empathy being greater success factors at work and for organisations than financial gain. Once again, we see here the emphasis on a *collective* or *collaborative* experience.

Social intelligence inevitably helps managers to manage and participate within groups, be these formal or informal groups, within or outside the organisation. According to Goleman (1999), research has consistently shown that well-performing groups or teams perform much better than even outstanding individuals. In the classic study of group intelligence by Williams and Sternberg (1988, cited in Goleman, 1999), the social skills and collaboration of the group members proved vital to their performance. Group motivation is significant and if all members are committed to the cause then the effort to succeed is there. It is the leader's or manager's role, therefore, to ensure that all the members of the group are committed to the cause, in order to maximise performance and effort. Thus, a good manager will understand each group member well and know 'what makes them tick'.

An effective manager must 'get to know' their staff team to understand what motivates each of them. Pink (2005) talks about the 'drive' model of motivation, which is divided into three elements: autonomy, mastery and purpose. Pink (2005) believes that autonomy, mastery and purpose are the motivators for people to work, rather than money.

Then again, in her study of staff in private day nurseries, Simms (2006: 1) found that 'quality, from the practitioners' point of view, relates to conditions of work, salary, management style, training and opportunities for progression'. However, she adds that 'many practitioners feel undervalued by their current managers but nevertheless remain in the setting because they love the children' (Simms, 2006: 1). Although this may be seen as a perturbing feature of vocational work which can leave workers open to abuse, studies have shown that 'happiness' in the workplace is significant, thus management style is central (Simms, 2006).

Reflective task

- How well do you know the members in your team?
- What motivates them in their work?
- What methods are used within your organisation for team members to 'get to know' one another?
- How effective are these?

Traditional management style theories

Late 19th-century management theorist F. W. Taylor (cited in Cole and Kelly, 2011) believed that simplifying tasks and giving workers little room for initiative made them more efficient – management was highly structured and controlling. While this approach may have been effective for shop-floor workers at that time it would certainly not be viewed as the ideal management strategy today. Indeed, in her study Simms (2006: 4) noted, 'Where dissatisfaction appeared to creep in, [it] was in relation to job aspects such as the lack of variety in their work and job security.'

In 1960 McGregor developed his Theory X and Theory Y approach whereby he identified two different sets of management beliefs which were directed towards their workforce and thereby made a significant impact on motivation. Simply explained, in Theory X management assumes that the workforce is lazy and purely driven by money and therefore manages through intimidation and control; in Theory Y management views its workforce positively and provides good working conditions, inspiring initiative and creativity. There are similarities between Taylor's approach and that of Theory X management, while Theory Y could be compared to that of Maslow (1967) and his theory of the hierarchy of needs; see Figure 2.1, page 21.

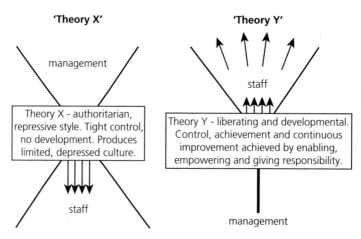

Figure 15.2 McGregor's Theory X and Theory Y model

Maslow's theory (1967) has become very well established not only within management theory but also within early years, particularly with reference to personal, social and emotional development. In his theory he identifies groups of needs which must be systematically satisfied before progression to the next set of needs, finally resulting in self-actualisation or realising your potential. Although Maslow's pyramid suggests a 'one-way ticket' to the point of self-actualisation, in reality this hierarchy can be applied as a circular process as, once having reached the pinnacle of the pyramid, if an unsettling life event or change such as death or divorce is experienced, you may again return to the base in order to recommence the climb. Applying Maslow's theory, a good manager will work hard to ensure that all the worker's basic needs are met to enable them to perform 'worry free' and thus to their full potential.

In the mid-20th century Herzberg (cited in Cole and Kelly, 2011) undertook studies to identify certain factors within the workplace which generated feelings of satisfaction or dissatisfaction. He called the terms and conditions of work that generated negative feelings 'hygiene factors' and those that generated positive feelings 'motivators'.

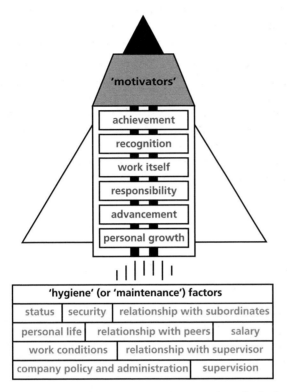

Figure 15.3 Herzberg's motivators and hygiene factors

Again it is possible to see the similarities between Herzberg's hygiene factors and Taylor's approach to management, while the motivators link strongly with the approaches of McGregor's Theory Y and Goleman's emphasis on the use of 'soft skills' within the organisation. Simms's findings (2006: 1) appear to support the idea that 'being valued, listened to and appreciated and knowing that they are having a positive effect on the development of children in their care' are of the utmost importance for early years practitioners.

This approach is further reinforced by Likert's work (1932) in the mid-20th century when he studied the relationship between management styles and productivity. He established that the managers with the highest productivity also had the highest levels of employee motivation and vice versa. Within Likert's ideal organisation the management is supportive and consultative with high levels of employee participation. He identifies four styles of management as seen in Figure 15.4.

	Direction of power	Management methods	Communication	Teamwork	Productivity
Exploitative-authoritative	One direction from the top downwards	Punishment Threats	Poor	None	Low
Benevolent-authoritative	Some consultation Some delegation	Threats Some rewards	Weak	Weak	Fair but high turnover and absenteeism
Consultative	All involved in agreeing and setting goals	Some involvement of employees	Good in both directions	Encouraged	Good with moderate absenteeism
Participative-group	Participation at all levels	Fully cooperative leading to commitment to the goals	Good upwards, downwards, and laterally	Excellent	Excellent and turnover and absenteeism are low

Figure 15.4 Likert's four styles of management

In contrast, McClelland's research (1978) focused on the needs of individuals. He identified three sets of needs:

- the need for achievement (n–Ach)
- the need for power (n–Pow)
- the need for affiliation or belonging (n–Aff).

Significantly, McClelland (1978) highlighted 'n–Ach' as a key human need and states that it is strongly influenced by personality and by environment. Individuals with a high 'n–Ach' consistently show certain personality characteristics such as desiring tasks where they can take on a high level of personal responsibility, enjoying realistic challenges, seeking feedback on their results and having little interest in affiliation or social needs. Such individuals with a high 'n–Ach', while exhibiting drive and ambition for themselves, will not fit well within a team or group which will only perform well when the overriding need is to achieve goals through shared values and commitment.

Extend your knowledge

Investigate staff motivation further by reading about Pink's drive model in Pink, D. (2005) *A Whole New Mind*, New York: Penguin Books.

Interestingly, a significant feature of the current environment within early years is the up-skilling of the workforce and the emphasis on achieving higher educational qualifications with a view to increased professionalism.

Brock (2006) identified seven dimensions of professionalism within early years:

Knowledge	Specialist knowledge, unique expertise, experience
Education and training	Higher education, qualification, practical experience, obligation to engage in CPD
Skills	Competence and efficacy, task complexity, communication, judgement
Autonomy	Entry requirement, self-regulation and standards, voice in public policy, discretionary judgement
Values	Ideology, altruism, dedication, service to clients
Ethics	Codes of conduct, moral integrity, confidentiality, trustworthiness, responsibility
Reward	Influence, social status, power, vocation

Table 15.2 Brock's seven dimensions of professionalism in early years (2006)

Applying McClelland's theory (1978) to Brock's dimensions (2006), we note that, while there are the 'n-Ach' dimensions of knowledge, education and training, and skills; as well as the 'n-Pow' dimensions of autonomy and reward, these are counterbalanced by the 'n-Aff' dimensions of values and ethics which remain strong within early years. Further to this Brock (2006: 8) noted: 'EYEs' (Early Years Educators') professional knowledge needs to be recognised for its importance and complexity, incorporating knowledge of child development, pedagogy and curriculum; the integration of disciplines of care, education and health; management of people; knowledge of children, families and communities.'

Indeed, the *Researching Effective Pedagogy in the Early Years* (REPEY) study (Siraj-Blatchford *et al.*, 2002: 43) showed that the effectiveness of the settings did not just relate to the educational performance but moreover to the 'sound leadership, good communications, and shared and consistent ways of working amongst the staff'.

A leadership theory which supports this outcome well is that of Adair (1973), who developed the action-centred leadership approach or the contingency theory of leadership. Adair's approach identifies three factors to be managed in order to achieve a task effectively:

a Group/team – the needs of the group/team must be met in order that they can perform to maximum potential through team building, strong communication, self-discipline and boundaries.

b Task – needs to be well planned and resourced with a clear set of objectives.

c Individual – the needs of the individual must be taken into account: they must have a good understanding of the objectives in order to undertake the task.

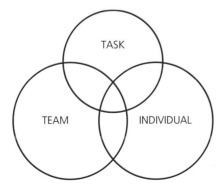

Figure 15.5 Adair's three factors involved in achieving tasks

Effective management will ensure that all three factors are taken into consideration when planning the task. Here, the real leadership skill lies in prioritising whichever factor indicates that its needs are not being fully met, in order to achieve the task, and this will, of course, change according to the situation, therefore requiring a flexible and dynamic behavioural approach.

Reflective task

- Which management style theory would best describe the style of management used within your setting organisation?
- Describe the effectiveness of this style. What works well and where are there gaps?

Group and team development

As seen above, the value of a well-managed group or team is undeniable. To assist in this, it is helpful to understand how groups develop and form. Tuckman (1965) identified five stages of development:

1 Forming – initially the group is finding out about what is involved in the task, each other and the resources required, as well as detecting a leader.
2 Storming – then there is a 'flexing of muscles', with internal conflict and everyone testing the boundaries.
3 Norming – then members are settling down and starting to communicate, exchange ideas and agree a method of working together to achieve the task.
4 Performing – now the group members are working effectively as a team, everyone is cooperating, there is flexibility and tolerance and the task is being achieved.
5 Adjourning – the task has been achieved and the group disbands.

The collaboration that Williams and Sternberg (1988, cited in Goleman, 1999) identified would start taking place at the Norming stage in Tuckman's model. It could be said that stages 1 and 2 are where the social intelligence is being gathered but stage 3 is where we start to see the social intelligence being implemented. In a typical working environment, assuming the group has been formed for a long-term purpose, stage 5 may never be reached but inevitably stage 4 will be difficult to maintain consistently as the group will change, for example if new members join the group or if working requirements change – especially relevant in the early years sector! Then the stages will have to be rebuilt once more. Although all group members have a role to play in this process, the key member is the leader or manager, because they are responsible for achieving accord and consensus so the group can perform to the best of its ability and realise the task effectively.

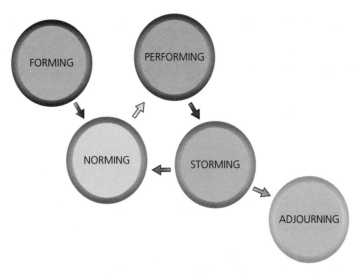

Figure 15.6 Tuckman's stages of group development

Reflective task

Reflect on a team you work in or are familiar with.

- Consider which stage of Tuckman's model the team is in.
- Why is this?
- How could the next stage be achieved?

Effective teamwork

According to Cole and Kelly (2011: 90), a 'team' suggests a small group that has bonded well together and is focused on performing a task well as 'a single unit', thus creating effective teamwork as depicted in stage 4 of Tuckman's model. Cole and Kelly (2011: 90) identify the features of effective teamwork as:

- clear objectives and agreed goals
- openness and confrontation
- support and trust
- cooperation and conflict
- sound procedures
- appropriate leadership
- regular review
- individual development
- sound inter-group relations.

In order to maintain effective teamwork a manager must continually monitor team cohesion and the performance of individuals within a team as a dynamic process. It is therefore useful to apply team roles, such as those identified by Belbin, first in 1981 and since then refined:

> A team is not a bunch of people with job titles, but a congregation of individuals, each of whom has a role which is understood by other members. Members of a team seek out

certain roles and they perform most effectively in the ones that are most natural to them.

(Belbin Associates, 2012)

We see here that a skilful manager, through a good knowledge of the individuals in his or her team, can deploy the team members according to their team roles to effect best performance. Belbin identified the following roles:

Team role		Contribution	Allowable weaknesses
Plant		Creative, imaginative, free-thinking. Generates ideas and solves difficult problems.	Ignores incidentals. Too preoccupied to communicate effectively.
Resource Investigator		Outgoing, enthusisatic, communicative. Explores opportunities and develops contacts.	Over-optimistic. Loses interest once initial enthusiasm has passed.
Co-ordinator		Mature, confident, identifies talent. Clarifies goals. Delegates effectively.	Can be seen as manipulative. Offloads own share of the work.
Shaper		Challenging, dynamic, thrives on pressure. Has the drive and courage to overcome obstacles.	Prone to provocation. Offends people's feelings
Monitor Evaluator		Sober, strategic and disceming. Sees all options and judges accurately.	Lacks drive and ability to inspire others. Can be overly critical.
Teamworker		Co-operative, perceptive and diplomatic. Listens and averts friction.	Indecisive in crunch situations. Avoids confrontation.
Implementer		Practical, reliable, effcient. Turns ideas into actions and organises work that needs to be done.	Somewhat inflexible. Slow to respond to new possibilities.
Completer Finisher		Painstaking, conscientious, anxious. Searches out errors. Polishes and perfects.	Inclined to worry unduly. Reluctant to delegate.
Specialist		Single-minded, self-starting, dedicated. Provides knowledge and skills in rare supply.	Contributes only on a narrow front. Dwells on technicalities.

Figure 15.7 The Belbin® Team Roles, reproduced by kind permission of Belbin – please visit www.belbin.com

Reflective task

Reflect on a team you work in or are familiar with and apply these team roles to each individual in the team.

- Are they in the most appropriate job role to perform effectively?
- How could you change their job roles to better suit the Belbin® Team Roles?
- What would be the implications?

Performance appraisal

When focusing on managing staff teams, an invaluable tool for getting to know the individual and monitoring performance is that of the appraisal. While the performance appraisal originated as a 'business tool', it is nevertheless an effective way to manage an individual's performance in an early years 'culture' through a process of reflection, feedback and agreeing performance targets and development goals to enable improvements. Moreover, this is an ideal time for a manager to assess an individual's commitment to the objectives of the setting and promote consensus. Also, it provides an occasion to encourage staff with their professional development. As Nutbrown (2012: 40) states: 'Good leaders in positions of management in a setting can create opportunities for new leaders to emerge from those with lower level qualifications in the workforce.'

The value of the appraisal process was endorsed in the Statutory Framework for the Early Years Foundation Stage (DCSF, 2008) and has been further reinforced following the review of the Early Years Foundation Stage (EYFS) undertaken by Dame Clare Tickell (2011). In Section 3 of the EYFS (DfE, 2012a: 17), under the safeguarding and welfare requirements, it is specified that: 'Providers should ensure that regular staff appraisals are carried out to identify any training needs, and secure opportunities for continued professional development for staff.'

The appraisal process should not be confused, however, with that of professional supervision which is a new requirement specified in the reformed framework (DfE, 2012a) – see more about supervision in Chapter 5.

Reflective task

- Is the performance appraisal currently used within your organisation?
- How effective is it in improving performance and goal setting?
- How are you involved in the process?
- Do you feel it is a fair process that reflects your performance?
- If not, how could it be improved?

Scenario

Rosie, an apprentice in the nursery setting, had just had her first appraisal with her Room Supervisor, Elsa. Following this, Sally, the setting manager, was given the appraisal paperwork to read through as part of her regular monitoring process and she was disappointed to see that a number of performance issues, such as poor attendance, punctuality, untidy hair and uniform, had not been raised with Rosie by Elsa. The feedback generally from Elsa was positive and encouraging but Sally knew that if these issues were not dealt with then Rosie's weak performance areas would not improve, especially since, as a student, Rosie needed clear guidance.

Sally spoke with Elsa about the appraisal feedback and asked her why she had not tackled these issues with Rosie. Elsa explained that she did not want to be negative towards Rosie as she thought it might demotivate and upset her. Sally arranged to meet with Rosie and Elsa to follow up on the appraisal but also to model to Elsa how to deal effectively with 'negative' issues. Having acknowledged the positive feedback from Elsa, Sally then talked through the 'negative' issues with Rosie and they agreed some specific targets and achievement dates. After the meeting Elsa thanked Sally and reflected that she had not helped Rosie to progress by ignoring her weak performance areas. Sally decided to organise some training for her supervisors on appraisals and how to give effective feedback.

Extend your knowledge

- Well-established management tools can be used to develop the performance appraisal process. Examine the SWOT analysis and download a free template from: http://www.businessballs.com/swotanalysisfreetemplate.htm.
- Read about the Kirkpatrick Model, a tool designed to measure the impact of training on staff and to what extent it improves their performance: http://www.kirkpatrickpartners.com/OurPhilosophy/tabid/66/Default.aspx.

Next steps

- Using the EYFS (DfE, 2012a), undertake a Training Needs Analysis for you and your team. You may wish to seek advice from your local authority's Early Years Development Officer or Consultant regarding available continuing professional development opportunities in your area.
- Check your team's qualifications against this list: https://www.education.gov.uk/eypqd/qualification-search.

Professional supervision

Once again under safeguarding and welfare requirements in the reformed EYFS it states that:

> Providers must put appropriate arrangements in place for the supervision of staff that has contact with children and families. Effective supervision provides support, coaching and training for the practitioner and promotes the interests of children. Supervision should foster a culture of mutual support, teamwork and continuous improvement which encourages the confidential discussion of sensitive issues.

(DfE, 2012a: 17)

The guidance document, *Development Matters* (Early Education, 2012), goes on to specify that supervision should provide opportunities for staff to:
- discuss any issues – particularly concerning children's development or well-being
- identify solutions to address issues as they arise
- receive coaching to improve their personal effectiveness.

Inevitably, there are similarities between the two support processes of appraisal and supervision; however, they do come from two distinct directions. As noted previously, the appraisal process has its roots in business and performance management, while professional supervision stems from a health and social care background and offers the opportunity to bring an employee and a skilled supervisor together to reflect on work practice. Supervision aims to identify solutions to problems, improve practice and increase understanding of professional issues. Undeniably both will improve quality of practice.

Reflective task

- How is professional supervision currently delivered within your organisation?
- How are solutions to problems identified?
- How does it improve practice and increase understanding of professional issues?

Diversity in the team

As already acknowledged, when building a team, a manager has to get the right dynamic in order to maximise team performance and effectiveness. However, a further consideration for the manager of an early years setting is that of diversity, in the sense of promoting positive role models to children and families, and this is no easy task in an industry still dominated by white females. In 2010 no more than 1 or 2 per cent of staff were male in early years settings.

Often a concern of potential male practitioners is the vulnerability of their role. Rising awareness of allegations of child abuse in care settings promotes suspicion of male carers in non-traditional occupations such as early years. These reactions to men within early years settings often deters them from entering the profession. Ironically, 'Were there to be more male workers, status queries may become less frequent' (Cameron *et al.*, 1999, cited in Cameron, 2006: 69). However, the case of the female nursery worker in Plymouth provided sad and concerning evidence that women are able to abuse the children in their care, thus contradicting the stereotypes perceived by the public.

Further under-representation within the children's and young people's workforce exists from the black and minority ethnic (BME) groups and the disabled across all providers. The highest proportions of BME staff were employed in full day care in Children's Centres (17 per cent) and therefore more likely to be in disadvantaged areas (Brind, 2011). Disabled staff also remain poorly represented at 1 per cent across the early years workforce (Brind, 2011).

In her interim review of early years qualification, Nutbrown (2012: 24) found that 60 per cent of her respondents 'felt that the workforce itself is not sufficiently inclusive and diverse, with obvious issues around the lack of men working in the sector, and concerns over under-representation of black and minority ethnic groups in managerial and leadership positions. In the final report she recommends the Department for Education conducts research 'to ensure BME groups are not being excluded from more senior roles' (Nutbrown, 2012: 7).

Within the *Supporting Families in the Foundation Years* document (DfE and DoH, 2011) these issues of under-representation in the workforce were highlighted for further discussion. It could be seen to be to the detriment of our children's early years education to experience such a narrow range of practitioners, limiting their exposure to a diversity of values and cultures, not providing a true reflection of their own backgrounds and communities.

Reflective task

- How diverse is your team?
- Why do you think black and minority ethnic groups are under-represented in managerial and leadership positions?

Implementing change

Improving diversity is just one of the many changes expected of managers and early years practitioners by the government to raise quality throughout the sector. Essentially, change is a fundamental leadership function to ensure success and the management of change is an important process. The requirement for change often implies that something is not working efficiently or effectively, or new findings from research suggest the need for change of current practices. An important aspect of this process is that the managers must understand *what* it is that needs to change. This can only be achieved through a sound knowledge of the requirements of the industry as well as those of the setting or business. Here, we see the need for good leadership skills – the ability to analyse and then 'strategise', that is put a plan in place to implement the change, which motivates the staff team who want to be involved. Managers are encouraged to 'think outside the box', a phrase which relates to strategic thinking or taking a long-term overview of the organisation rather than being confined within the present situation. When undertaking strategic thinking, it is essential to consider all perspectives, to critically analyse and to problem-solve. A useful tool to support the strategic thinking process is the Six Thinking Hats® by Edward de Bono (2011), which is particularly supportive when planning for the group thinking process or collaboration towards an end goal such as change.

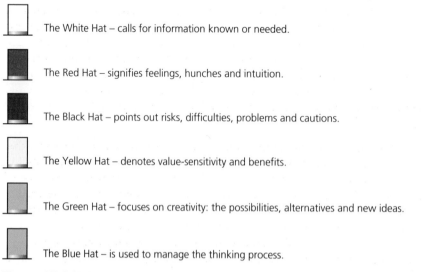

The White Hat – calls for information known or needed.

The Red Hat – signifies feelings, hunches and intuition.

The Black Hat – points out risks, difficulties, problems and cautions.

The Yellow Hat – denotes value-sensitivity and benefits.

The Green Hat – focuses on creativity: the possibilities, alternatives and new ideas.

The Blue Hat – is used to manage the thinking process.

Figure 15.8 Six Thinking Hats® by Edward de Bono © IP Development Corporation Edward de Bono hereby asserts his moral right to be known as the author of this work. For copyright permissions and enquiries, please contact de Bono Global Pty Ltd, ipenquiries@debonoglobal.com

Reflective task

Put on a 'blue hat' and explore the Six Thinking Hats® approach in your next team meeting. Give each team member a 'hat' (if you have actual coloured hats to use, even better!!), preferably one that is different from their usual way of thinking and insist that they wear that 'hat' during the course of the meeting.

■ How did this change the dynamic of the meeting?

■ How did this widen your team members' perspectives and encourage their critical thinking?

■ Why and how could this tool be useful when preparing for your next multi-agency meeting?

Explore creative thinking further by visiting this website: www.debono.com.

Communicating and implementing change

Once the strategy or plan for change is in place then it must be implemented. Kotter (2007) established an eight-stage process for implementing major changes:

1 Create, and sustain, a sense of urgency about the future.
2 Create and empower a leadership team (a 'guiding coalition').
3 Develop an end goal (a 'vision') and a strategy for achieving it.
4 Constantly communicate the new vision and set out what changes in behaviour are required.
5 Empower employees to help change happen by removing obstacles.
6 Generate benefits in the short term so that people can see tangible improvements.
7 Consolidate short-term gains and produce more change by continuing the actions.
8 Embed the new approaches in the organisation's culture ('anchoring') so as to avoid eventual regression into previous practices.

In stage 4 of Kotter's theory we see the need for constant communication, and conveying the correct feelings and attitudes through communication will certainly affect a manager's credibility, particularly when trying to implement a change. Through his research, Mehrabian (1981, cited in Chapman, 2012) showed that only 7 per cent of our feelings and attitudes are transmitted through words, whereas 38 per cent are transmitted through tone of voice and 55 per cent are based on facial expression. However, with an emphasis on integrated working and increasing technological interactions, such as the use of ICT as a means of communicating and recording, there are concerns that the basics of effective communication skills are not understood and addressed. Indeed, Munro (2011) warned about using ICT systems rather than dealing with individuals (children and families) in a human face-to-face contact or with telephone conversations between professionals rather than emails. It is a problem when over-bureaucratic and non-personal systems let children down.

While working in a multi-agency and integrated team approach it is important to remember that in the process of communication we send and receive messages. It is everybody's responsibility, and even more so the manager's role within the organisation, to ensure that the quality of communication is good so that the messages sent are received and understood in the correct context. Furthermore, it is vital to ensure that any barriers to communication are broken down, such as language and cultural issues. Knowing the correct type of communication to use in a certain situation, and how to respond in difficult circumstances, can be quite a challenge, not to mention the process of collaboration and participating in multidisciplinary meetings. It is here that emotional and social intelligence really shines.

Emotional and social intelligence is essential to stage 5 of Kotter's theory, where we see the need to understand the impact of change on individuals in order to motivate and empower them. The curve of transition developed by Fisher in 1999 and revised 2012 aptly illustrates the effects the change process can have on the individual, and it can help to assist managers (and staff) to plan ahead, support individuals and each other, and negotiate potential obstacles to change.

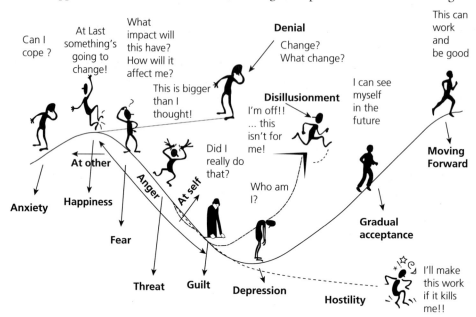

Figure 15.9 Fisher's process of transition (2012)

Reflective task

Think about a situation in your personal or professional life where you have undergone change.
- Reflect about how you felt at the time and how you managed and coped with the changed circumstances.
- Looking at the transition curve above, what stages did you go through?
- How can you learn from past experiences and apply coping mechanism in the future to make change situations easier to manage?

Here we return to the point made earlier that a manager must understand their team really well in order to effect change positively. Having that emotional and social intelligence identified by Goleman (1999: 7) is fundamental, and as he notes that research found that 'women, on average, are more aware of their emotions, show more empathy, and are more adept interpersonally'. However, he adds that men are 'more self-confident and optimistic, adapt more easily, and handle stress better' (Goleman, 1999: 7).

Identified at stage 8 in Kotter's theory, a manager's role is not only to identify what must be changed but also to build a team which responds positively towards change and actively welcomes it, effectively changing the culture. A manager can only achieve this through successful recruitment and deployment decisions. Returning to Tuckman's model, at stage 4 – Performing – the group members are working effectively as a team, everyone is cooperating, there is flexibility and tolerance and the task is being achieved. It is in this stage that change is welcomed and successfully implemented.

Reflective task

- How long have you been involved in the early years industry? Produce a timeline for the period that you have been working in early years.
- Reflect on your experience of the changes from government over that time period, and how they have been implemented by your local authority, and subsequently within your setting.
- How could the implementation have been improved?

Extend your knowledge

- In an industry that is ever changing and improving it is important to keep abreast of all the changes. The best way to do this is to keep a close eye on these websites:
  - http://www.education.gov.uk
  - http://www.foundationyears.org.uk
  - http://www.ofsted.gov.uk
- Choose some professional organisations to join, such as TACTYC (http://www.tactyc.org.uk) and subscribe to their journals or newsletters.

Next steps

Seek out management training opportunities – this may inevitably mean seeking training beyond that which is currently available via your setting or local authority, but it will extend your knowledge and develop your transferable skills whatever your role. Furthermore, check with your local authority as funding may be available.

Leadership of practice

Without a doubt the most significant change that leaders and managers have had to effect within early years within the past 12 years has been a massive improvement in the quality of practice in the setting. This change was essentially underpinned by the findings of the EPPE (Sylva *et al.*, 2004) and other studies undertaken in the United States (Mooney, 2007), which showed that high quality early years experiences led to positive outcomes in children's development at school.

> In leading practice we are inevitably leading and managing quality. Leadership is a vital ingredient in the pursuit of quality in early years service provision.
>
> (Rodd, 2005: 3)

What is quality?

An important factor to consider, however, is that there are many different definitions of the term 'quality'. Mooney (2007) talks of the established indicators of quality being staff–child ratios, staff qualifications, training and working conditions, continuity of care, staff–child and staff–parent interactions and so on, all of which are regulated and inspected in England by Ofsted, whereas, Mathers (2012) identifies the stakeholders (parents, children, practitioners and policymakers) within the early years sector and researches their individual perceptions of the concept of 'quality'. This represents 'blue-hat' thinking (de Bono, 2011), as discussed earlier. Furthermore, Mathers (2012) examines the tools that have been used to measure quality and thus guide the various stakeholders, such as the Ofsted grades, the *Early Childhood Environmental Rating Scales* (ECERS) (Harms *et al.*, 2004) and quality improvement schemes. Not only does Mathers (2012) note the fact that the quality improvement schemes have been initiated based on the Ofsted grades, but she also highlights the purposes and vested interests that each quality measure may serve.

Interestingly, and in line with other previous research, Mathers (2012) establishes that there was consensus among stakeholders as they all placed staffing firmly at the centre of their 'concept of quality'. However, differences did occur in relation to roles, priorities and knowledge. Parents' main focus was what was best for their child, whereas providers were focused on their success as a provider in areas such as training and development. Furthermore, providers recognised the value of strong leadership and management, noting that 'without self-reflective managers leading quality improvement "from the top" it would be difficult for settings to achieve high quality' (Mathers, 2012: 86).

To lead this change managers have participated in quality improvement programmes, such as the Investors in Children initiative or other sector-endorsed programmes. These programmes have often been linked to a financial incentive or government funding to encourage participation. According to Mooney (2007), quality improvement schemes involve practitioners undergoing a process of reflection and self-evaluation leading to continuous improvement. What has proved important, though, is the support provided to effect this improvement: 'the quality of support providers receive while going through quality improvement or quality assurance procedures is key' (DfEE, 2001: 12, cited in Mooney, 2007). Since the Childcare Act 2006 it has been incumbent on local authorities to provide this support.

The REPEY study (Siraj-Blatchford *et al.*, 2002) and *Study of Pedagogical Effectiveness in Early Learning* (SPEEL) (Moyles *et al.*, 2002) identified six Key Elements of Effective Practice (KEEP) (DfES, 2005b), which were developed to support and guide local authorities in their role to support and promote good-quality practice in settings:
- Relationships with both children and adults
- Understanding of the individual and diverse ways that children develop and learn
- Knowledge and understanding in order to actively support and extend children's learning in and across all areas and aspects of learning
- Practice in meeting all children's needs, learning styles and interests
- Work with parents, carers and the wider community
- Work with other professionals within and beyond the setting.

It is easy to see the relationship between KEEP (DfES, 2005b) and the SPEEL wheel (Moyles *et al.*, 2002), which was designed to explain the contents of their framework of effective pedagogy and which formed the basis of criteria for quality assessment. Furthermore, KEEP were developed in conjunction with the *Common Core of Skills and Knowledge for the Children's Workforce*, in order to identify the skills and attitudes required to be an early years practitioner and in doing so support recruitment, training and development (CWDC, 2010a).

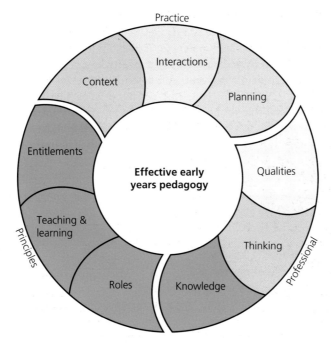

Figure 15.10 SPEEL wheel

In 2008 a new set of tools was introduced as part of the *Early Years Quality Improvement Support Programme* (EYQISP) (DCSF, 2008e). These tools were developed to facilitate local authorities meeting their duties to improve outcomes for children, as specified in the Childcare Act 2006. Based on the cycle of improvement and in conjunction with the EYFS (DCSF, 2008a) the tools were aligned with the principles of leadership, self-improvement, support and strong partnerships with local authorities, settings and communities.

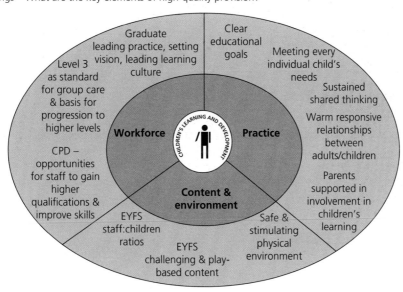

Figure 15.11 What quality looks like (EYQISP diagram)

Clearly this programme has been developed based on the EPPE (Sylva *et al.*, 2004) and SPEEL (Moyles *et al.*, 2002) outcomes and there is a strong focus on the need for leadership. However, within this process the leadership clearly refers to 'leadership for learning – focusing on the key role of leaders in building capacity and ensuring high quality learning development and provision' (DCSF, 2008e). The government's response and solution were the introduction of the Early Years Professional Status (EYPS), which will be discussed later. The EPPE study (Sylva *et al.*, 2004) acknowledges the vital role of the leader in achieving quality improvements through the Setting Improvement Cycle (SIC), which is the familiar process of self-evaluation, identifying and prioritising improvements, agreeing an action plan (or FIP – Focused Improvement Plan) (DCSF, 2008e), implementation and review.

Reflective task

Other than by the Ofsted inspection process:
- How do you assess for quality in your setting?
- How does this quality assessment cover all perceptions?
- Does the assessment provide clear guidance for improvements, and how are practitioners supported to achieve these?
- Looking at the different models for quality such as the SPEEL wheel and the EYQISP diagram, can you identify areas of your work where you contribute or have achieved good-quality practice?

Extend your knowledge

Read this report and write down areas of learning and improvement for your practice:
- Mathers, S. K. (2012) *Improving Quality in the Early Years*, Oxford: The Daycare Trust.

Are you familiar with the ECERS and ITERS quality audit tool? If not, try these:
- Harms, T., Clifford, R. M. and Cryer, D. (2004) *Early Childhood Environment Rating Scale (ECERS-R)*, Teachers' College Press.
- UK ECERS Network Resource: http://www.ecersuk.org

Leadership for learning

In 2006 the *Effective Leadership in the Early Years Sector* (ELEYS) study (Siraj-Blatchford and Manni, 2006) identified the fundamentals required for effective leadership for learning as:
- Contextual literacy
- Commitment to collaboration
- Commitment to the improvement of children's learning outcomes.

Reflective task

Can you identify these fundamentals for effective leadership for learning within your current practice? Give examples.

These three fundamentals for effective leadership for learning had been encapsulated within the EYFS (DCSF, 2008a), the first statutory curriculum for under-fives in England. The reformed EYFS (2012a) offers a framework for all practitioners to follow, setting the minimum standard for the learning, development and care of children under five years. It was envisaged that this standard would demand consistency of approach and provide a baseline for quality, giving parents an assurance that whichever setting they chose for their child, the quality would remain the same.

Grouped under four themes of Unique Child, Enabling Environment, Learning and Development and Positive Relationships, the early curriculum draws from a wide range of endorsed international theories, approaches and research, such as those of Piaget, Vygotsky, Bruner, Skinner, Bowlby, Dewey, Fröbel, Montessori, Steiner, Athey, Reggio Emilia, Te Whāriki, Carr, Donaldson, Gardner, Bronfenbrenner, Forest Schools and High/Scope, in order to provide the best practice guidance for early years practitioners. Essentially there was nothing new within the EYFS (DCSF, 2008a), it was simply setting the context. It seems the government was being innovative in its leadership, taking a 'story' that had been latent since Hadow in 1933:

> **The innovative leader takes a story that has been latent in the population, or among the members of his or her chosen domain, and brings new attention or a fresh twist to that story.**
>
> (Gardner, 2011: 496)

Significantly this framework was developed following the body of research commissioned by the government at the end of the 1990s, namely the EPPE project (Sylva *et al.*, 2004), SPEEL (Moyles *et al.*, 2002) and REPEY (Siraj-Blatchford *et al.*, 2002). Although the research remains ongoing at present with regard to the long-term benefits, the outcomes of the EPPE project (1997–2004) (Sylva *et al.*, 2004) did provide the necessary evidence to justify the government's renewed focus on early years. Through this five-year longitudinal study across a range of preschool settings, using the quality measure ECERS (Harms *et al.*, 2004) and subsequent studies the team established a number of the recommendations which we see ultimately being implemented through government strategies, such as the up-skilling of the workforce and the EYFS curriculum (DfE, 2012a). Indeed, findings from the EPPE suggest that:

> **All the managers took a strong lead, especially in curriculum and planning. In most of the settings the strong leadership was characterised by a strong philosophy that was shared by everyone working in the centre.**
>
> (Sylva *et al.*, 2004: 35)

According to EPPE (Sylva *et al.*, 2004), however, a central contributing factor to the quality within the 'effective' settings was having a 'trained teacher' as manager. It is important to note here that throughout the REPEY (Siraj-Blatchford *et al.*, 2002) and EPPE (Sylva *et al.*, 2004) reports the term 'manager' is used to describe what is effectively the 'pedagogista', to use the term reminiscent of the Reggio Emilia approach, or 'curriculum leader' in the setting. This point was clarified by Kathy Sylva when questioned by the author at a conference at Bridgewater College in 2011. This clarification of terms does not take place anywhere in the REPEY or EPPE reports and therefore it could be argued that this mixed use of terminology has added to the confusion regarding leadership roles within early years.

Conversely SPEEL examines the relationship between setting management and curriculum leadership, and refers to the management roles within a school setting as being a vital part of the overall construct to *enable* effective pedagogy (Moyles *et al.*, 2002). Indeed, REPEY (Siraj-Blatchford *et al.*, 2002) refers to two types of 'pedagogy' within these settings: 'pedagogical interactions' (specific behaviours on the part of adults)' and 'pedagogical framing' (the behind-the-scenes aspects of pedagogy which include planning, resources, and establishment of routines). In this 'framing' description it would be easy to confuse this with the role of the 'manager' of the organisation; however, this is specifically referring to management of the curriculum (Siraj-Blatchford *et al.*, 2002).

Reflective task

- How is 'leadership for learning' managed in your setting?
- Is there one named person with responsibility for the curriculum?
- How does this work and how is it communicated with the team?
- Are there any benefits or potential pitfalls to this?

Pedagogy

It would seem appropriate at this point to return to the term 'pedagogy', which is generally understood to be the art or science of teaching but, according to more classical roots, the term refers to being led along a path of learning. It is a process which has direct links with 'pedagogical interactions' and we can witness this process taking place in practice through sustained shared thinking (Siraj-Blatchford *et al.*, 2002). In reconsidering the 'pedagogical framing' (Siraj-Blatchford *et al.*, 2002) aspect, this would bring to mind the role of the pedagogue or 'pedagogista', a vision the government held for those practitioners with Early Years Professional Status (EYPS).

Within the Reggio Emilia approach the pedagogistas are extremely knowledgeable about the curriculum and the approach, providing a 'leading' role, planning and guiding the teachers within the preschools, as well as having a coordinating role for a small group of preschools – which helps to maintain consistency and quality. According to Papatheodorou (2006: 3), 'By going through the process of careful planning, the adults know well what they expect the children to achieve; the children have to find this out for themselves through the facilitation of the adults.' Similarly the ELEYS study found 'a clear vision, especially with regard to pedagogy and curriculum, which was shared by everyone working within the setting' (Siraj-Blatchford and Manni, 2006: 16) as being the most significant feature.

In Europe the term 'pedagogy' is more frequently used than in the UK and has a holistic connotation to a child's development. According to Petrie *et al.* (2009: 3), 'Our European neighbours often apply it to a much broader set of services, covering, for example, childcare and early years, youth work, parenting and family support services, secure units for young offenders, residential care and play work.' Read more about pedagogy in Chapter 5.

Early Years Professional Status (EYPS)

In 2007 the government restated their strategy to 'up-skill' the workforce in *The Children's Plan* (DCSF, 2007a: 2): 'Leadership and highly skilled and committed staff are key to improving and maintaining high quality practice.' They also launched their Graduate-Led Workforce proposal in the form of the Early Years Professional Status (EYPS): 'the only professional graduate accreditation for the early years workforce, endorsed by government and increasingly recognised as the credential for leading practice in early years provision' and New Leaders in Early Years, 'a three year pilot programme seeking to attract top graduates to work and become strategic and practice leaders in the early years sector' (CWDC, 2012).

These graduates who are envisaged as 'agents of change' undertake a short programme or full pathway to gain EYPS, intended to hone and ratify their leadership skills within the realm of early years practice. Based on a set of National Standards developed originally by the CWDC, candidates are required to demonstrate that they can lead and support effective practice (CWDC, 2008). These standards are grouped within the Key Elements of Effective Practice (KEEP) (DfES, 2005b) and designed around working safely with babies, toddlers and young children from birth to five years within the context of the EYFS (DfE, 2012a). Interestingly, the emphasis of the programme is on what are seen as the transferable skills of leadership, such as reflection, decision making, support and communication.

Initially, it was envisaged that the accreditation would have equivalency with the Qualified Teacher Status (QTS), but this did not transpire, much to the dismay of many of those who undertook the EYPS. Indeed, in her recently published report Nutbrown (2012: 61) recommends strongly that the access routes to QTS be made available to those with EYPS. Despite this, the EYPS programme has made an impact on the early years workforce and, according to figures in 2011, over 8,300 EYPs are already working across England. There are some positives as highlighted in the *First National Survey of Practitioners with EYPS* (Hadfield *et al.*, 2011): newly qualified practitioners felt more positive about their career prospects since attaining EYPS and felt they had more credibility, 76 per cent of practitioners felt obtaining EYPS had improved their sense of professional status, and 80 per cent felt it had increased their confidence as practitioners.

However, a large proportion of the practitioners who achieved EYPS, according to Hadfield *et al.* (2011), were fitting the stereotypical demographics of the early years sector:
- white British (87 per cent)
- female (98 per cent)
- aged between 36 and 45 years (31 per cent)
- established in their career (34 per cent had 8–15 years' experience)
- the owner or manager of a setting (40 per cent) that is rated good by Ofsted (55 per cent)
- having been in their current role for one to three years (38 per cent).

This suggests that the programme was effectively 'preaching to the converted' by simply ratifying already established 'leaders' in settings and reinforcing the existing stereotypes within the workforce.

The government's response to this within the revision of the EYPS programme is to reduce the amount of funding available and make the application process much more rigorous. Additionally, there will inevitably be positive discrimination to increase access for under-represented groups into the workforce, such as ethnic minorities and men. Another major difficulty that has emerged within settings has been the acceptance and credibility of graduates entering the workforce via the full pathway route. Practitioners have been reluctant to 'follow' these EYPs due to their lack of experience. While leadership skills may be transferable between industries, as Gardner (2011: 167) argues, 'It is important that a leader be a good storyteller but equally crucial that the leader embody that story in his or her life.'

A concern is that the 'role' of the EYP within the setting was never fully considered by the CWDC, leadership or otherwise. At the National Day Nurseries Association conference in 2007, Jane Haywood of the CWDC was asked by the author: 'While it is feasible to envisage a role for the EYP within a public-sector setting (i.e. children's centre), what is the role of the

EYP considered to be within a PVI setting where a clearly defined structure will already exist?' Ms Haywood responded by saying that it was unknown but they would see over time how it developed. This lack of clarity and strategic 'blue-hat' thinking has had a significant impact on the training that EYPs have received and the way they are perceived within the industry. Confusion around 'leadership' and 'management' roles has further added to this. Hadfield *et al.* (2011: 24) state in their report:

> EYPs occupied a range of positions in settings' leadership and management structures. Many practitioners were already experienced leaders before gaining EYPS; others remained emerging leaders. Such variations may explain the fact that only around a quarter of practitioners felt they were more able to influence change at work or had more opportunities to show leadership since gaining EYPS.

It is the lack of clarity when the programme was conceived and perhaps a misunderstanding of the 'leadership of practice' role in the first place which have led to this outcome.

Extend your knowledge

In 2012 the EYPS programme and funding criteria have been revised. Keep abreast of this programme and the New Leaders in Early Years pilot by visiting: http://www.education.gov.uk/childrenandyoungpeople/ earlylearningandchildcare/delivery/b00201345/graduate-leaders.

Reflective task

- Do you aspire to the role of Early Years Professional in your setting?
- How do you see a future for this role in early years?
- How do you think the role can be developed to ensure highly trained professionals remain in early years by leading on and offering good-quality services for children and their families?

Is the quality of practice improving?

Despite the acknowledged fact that Ofsted's assessment of quality may be somewhat limited in perspective, it is all that we have, at this point in time, on which to base settings' progress since the introduction of the EYFS (DCSF, 2008a) and the EYPS programme. The 2010/11 findings point to an increase in performance for providers being judged good or outstanding against the EYFS requirements from 68 per cent in 2009/10 to 74 per cent (Ofsted, 2011a, b). It seems there has been an increase in the effectiveness of self-evaluation and that the 'better providers have a planned and systematic approach to children's learning and development' (Ofsted, 2011a: 3). Although there is no specific mention of the impact of EYPs within settings in the report, it does state that settings with a strong culture of professional development provided better outcomes for children and therefore attained higher grades:

Inspectors found that outcomes for children were good or outstanding where practitioners were well-qualified or trained. They used more than intuition; they knew why they were doing what they were doing, and what they needed to do next to promote children's learning.

(Ofsted, 2011a: 21)

Conclusion

Until relatively recently, leadership and management were not significant concepts within early years. However, over the past decade this has changed along with so much else within the sector. The government is driving these changes forward as a 'direct' leader, telling the 'story' in a 'clear and persuasive' way (Gardner, 2011: 6091), to improve quality. To support the changes, it has put in place 'indirect' leaders, who will ensure implementation from the ground floor up through, ideally, a collaborative leadership approach. What is important, however, is that we ensure all involved are clear about their roles and are trained appropriately to implement these changes effectively.

To improve quality we are witnessing the professionalisation of the sector and we appear to be heading towards a teaching leadership as identified by Tickell in her report (2011) and more recently by Nutbrown (2012) in her review of qualifications in the sector when she states:

The sector seems to support the idea of strong leadership at all levels, but in particular recognises the impact that those with teaching qualifications can deliver. This is supported by research evidence linking qualified teacher leadership with better outcomes for young children.

(Nutbrown, 2012: 9)

At the same time we must achieve sustainability and to do this the training needs, as identified in the report by Sarwar and Grewal (2011), must be met to ensure strong management underpins the strong leadership.

Next steps

- Identify your leadership and management role within your setting – are you leading the organisation or practice or both?
- If you are not already in a designated leadership or management role within your setting, seek to gain leadership experience through opportunities such as supporting/mentoring new staff, leading in areas of practice such as outdoor play, inclusive practice and so on.
- Having undertaken the reflective tasks throughout the chapter, you should have identified targets for development for yourself and your setting. Structure your thoughts with reflective cycles and develop an action plan for achieving these targets. Ensure your targets are SMART – see templates and guidance at http://www.businessballs.com/goal_planning.htm.
- Investigate *your* next steps. See Nutbrown (2012) and consider which qualification route or professional development route is right for you.

Evaluate your...

Practice

- What leadership or management training have you undertaken?
- What leadership opportunities do you have in your current role?
- How do you demonstrate good leadership in your setting?
- How do you keep abreast of sector changes and updates?
- How do you know where to find out about these and advise others?
- How do you plan for change within the setting?
- When planning, do you consider all perspectives?
- How do you support staff in the setting?
- How do you participate in staff and team meetings?
- How do you contribute to the development of the team?
- How do you contribute to staff development?
- When was the last time you had an appraisal?
- Have you ever participated in professional supervision?
- Do you participate in multi-agency meetings?
- What do you do to communicate effectively?
- How do you assess the quality of practice in your setting?

Finally, by taking some of the responsibility for the work in the setting and the quality of provision, you can support your manager/leader and work collaboratively:

- Think about an area of interest or expertise in your practice which you would like to be responsible for (manage) and/or you would like to be in charge of (lead), i.e. managing activities for children, or leading a project such as redesigning the outdoor space, enhancing partnership work with parents, etc.
- How can this be implemented within your organisation and what needs to change?

Further reading

Daly, M., Byers, E. and Taylor, W. (2009) *Early Years Management in Practice*, Oxford: Heinemann.

Johnson, S. (1999) *Who Moved My Cheese?*, Reading: Ebury Publishing.

Jones, C. and Pound, L. (2008) *Leadership and Management in the Early Years: From principles to practice*, Maidenhead: Open University.

Kotter, J. and Rathgeber, H. (2006) *Our Iceberg Is Melting: Changing and succeeding under any conditions*, London: Macmillan.

Lindon, J. and Lindon, L. (2011) *Leadership and Early Years Professionalism*, London: Hodder Education.

Miller, T. (1992) 'A customer's definition of quality', *The Journal of Business Strategy*, vol. 13, no. 1, pp. 4–7.

Myrna, J. (2009) 'Turning the tables on performance reviews: How to create a better process that empowers, energizes and rewards your employees', *Business Strategy Series*, vol. 10, no. 6, pp. 366–73.

O'Sullivan, J. (2009) *Leadership Skills in the Early Years*, London: Network Continuum.

Robins, A. and Callan, S. (2010) *Managing Early Years Settings*, London: Sage Publications.

Senge, P. (2006) *The Fifth Discipline: The Art and Practice of the Learning Organization*, London: Random House.

Early years research
Ann Farrell

Introduction

Early years research is increasingly concerned with the everyday lives of young children and adults in the cut-and-thrust of early years contexts. It is concerned with what happens *in situ*, that is, in the everyday lives of those within the context.

> **We must learn to live in the middle of things, in the tension of conflict, confusion and possibility; and we must become adept at making do with the messiness of that condition.**
>
> (Merriam, 2002: 401)

Early years research is concerned with understanding young children and adults in the contexts of their lives, but it goes beyond understanding to transforming their contexts, such that children and adults have the best possible chances, now and in the future. The dual focus of understanding and transforming makes early years research a powerful force for change.

This chapter explores key theoretical underpinnings of early years research and presents key aspects of conducting research in ethical and sustainable ways. Early years research, here, refers to research conducted by early years practitioner researchers in the context of their own setting. It may involve research around their own practice and/or research around a particular issue or phenomenon of importance in their setting – the focal point may be children, families or practitioners or combinations thereof. The research may be a seamless part of the daily routine of the setting or it may be a discrete project, clearly delineated with a timeframe for commencement and conclusion. The research may be used for ongoing reflection and planning within the setting and/or for dissemination in research reports or scholarly publications.

Learning outcomes

In this chapter, you will have the opportunity to tackle the key features of early years research, such that you will be in a position to explain:

- Early years research as a priority.
- International agendas of starting strong, accountability and children's rights.
- Conceptual underpinnings of early years research.
- Child participation in research.
- Ethical issues in early years research.
- Action research in the early years.
- Disseminating research.

Early years research: a priority

The field of early years has become a priority in a range of countries. In the UK, for example, it has come to prominence particularly with the onset of the Early Years Foundation Stage (EYFS) (DfE, 2012a). The UK's focus on young children's learning and development and on empirically informed early years programmes and resources is providing a timely impetus for early years research (Brooker *et al.*, 2010).

Approaches and methods used in early years research vary, from large-scale work such as the Effective Provision of Pre-School Education (EPPE) study (1997–2003) (Sylva *et al.*, 2004) to fine-grained nested studies conducted *in situ* within the actual sites where a particular phenomenon is seen to be occurring. Very often these research sites, nested within a larger study, are designed to complement, illuminate, challenge or counterpoint the wider corpus of data. There may be longitudinal cohort studies such as the Avon Longitudinal Study of Parents and Children (since 1991) and the Longitudinal Study of Australian Research (LSAC) (since 2004) which may not be located primarily in the early years setting but which, nonetheless, impact the setting.

Studies may draw upon different research methods or upon mixed methods, which may be described broadly as qualitative and quantitative or as involving textual and numeric data (Danby and Thorpe, 2006). Whether large or small scale or described as qualitative, quantitative or mixed method, early years research characteristically relies upon the early years practitioner for its effective design, implementation and dissemination. While much research is now being led by practitioners within the setting, early years research may include projects undertaken by those who are external to the setting, that is, researchers contracted by funding bodies or other organisations. Also, research undertaken by higher degree research students who come into the setting for the express purposes of conducting research. While the chapter provides insights that may be of merit for researchers who are external to the setting, the main focus here is the work of the practitioner researcher operating within their own setting.

Practitioner research

Accompanying the UK's Early Years Foundation Stage (EYFS) is a growing interest in practitioner research, with an ensuing raft of research resources for use by early years practitioners (Arnold, 2012; Mukherji and Albow, 2009; Roberts-Holmes, 2005). Australian researcher Goodfellow (2005: 48) defines practitioner research as 'systematic inquiry-based efforts directed towards creating and extending professional knowledge and associated understandings of professional practice'. Collaborative inquiry processes provide opportunities for practitioners to deconstruct some of the taken-for-granted practices found within many early childhood services.

So prominent is the profile of early years practitioner research that it is now a named category of research award sponsored by the British Educational Research Association (BERA) (2012) and SAGE Publications, and a similar award sponsored by the European Early Childhood Education Research Association and Routledge (2012). The BERA award reflects the association's commitment to quality in ethical educational research, to independent debate about the quality, purpose and methodologies of educational research, and to improving the conditions of work and rights of educational researchers.

So too, in countries such as Australia and New Zealand, there is mounting interest in early years practitioner research (see, for example, Goodfellow and Hedges, 2007), with practitioner research featured in the Research in Practice series published by Early Childhood Australia (Goodfellow, 2009). These initiatives are emblematic of the status of early years practitioner research within our scholarly and professional communities.

Early years research on the international agenda

Early years research is squarely on the international agenda. The agenda has three discrete yet converging facets that can be seen to frame early years research:

1 the starting strong agenda
2 the accountability agenda
3 the children's rights agenda.

First, the starting strong agenda has a focus on a strong start for children's life chances and life outcomes. Its nomenclature has been used by the Organisation for Economic Co-operation and Development (OECD) in a series of international comparative reports on Early Childhood Education and Care (ECEC) in developed countries (OECD, 2001, 2006 and 2012). Evidence provided in these reports, along with evidence from cost–benefit studies (Cunha *et al.*, 2005) has been a driver for investment in quality ECEC in a range of countries (Council of Australian Governments, 2009; Moss, 2007). So too, UNICEF's Innocenti Research Centre has provided international benchmarks for ECEC and 'minimum standards for protecting the lives of children in their most vulnerable and formative years' (UNICEF, 2008: 8). Such initiatives serve to profile the provision and practice of ECEC as potential sites of early years research.

The second agenda of accountability is concerned with assessing and reporting academic achievement against international benchmarks. The accountability agenda is exemplified in the OECD's *Programme for International Student Assessment* (2011), known as PISA, and in the work of the International Association for the Evaluation of Educational Achievement (2007) in reports such as *Trends in International Mathematics and Science Study* (TIMSS). While ostensibly focusing on the school sector, standardised assessment of children's educational attainment, using such measures and publication of results on international league tables, has the potential to forcibly push the early years sector to mimic what is happening in the school sector with respect to assessment, measurement and reporting of children's learning. British educational researcher Pat Petrie (2005: 179) refers to a process of 'schoolification', whereby the cultural and pedagogical practices of the school push down on the everyday experience of young children in prior-to-school contexts. The accountability agenda of the school sector has the potential to coerce the early years sector into practices which may be counterproductive or even harmful to young children's learning and to the pedagogical work undertaken in the early years.

An interesting convergence of the starting strong agenda and the accountability agenda, albeit pursuing accountability for different purposes within the early years field, is the EPPE study

(Sylva *et al.*, 2004 and 2010) with a concern for children's achievement in relation to the quality of childcare provision. Moreover, the EPPE study combines the starting strong and accountability agendas with the third agenda, that of children's rights.

The agenda of children's rights was articulated in the *UN Convention on the Rights of the Child* (United Nations, 1989) and gave impetus to early years research and to children's rights in research, as inalienable human rights of children, as people in their own right and people to whom dignity should be accorded (Alderson, 2002). The two key elements of the Convention which have come to underpin early years research are (Farrell, 2006 and 2010; Morrow, 2010):

1 children's right to participation within the arenas of their everyday lives
2 children's right to protection from harm and danger from adverse people and experiences within those arenas.

These elements were used, in turn, to underpin the UK's *Every Child Matters: Change for Children* framework (DfES, 2004a) and the Children Act 2004. The framework for children and young people features five outcomes that are seen to be key to well-being in childhood and later life, which are:

■ being healthy
■ staying safe
■ enjoying and achieving
■ making a positive contribution
■ achieving economic well-being.

The main focus areas within the framework are:

■ early intervention
■ a shared sense of responsibility
■ information sharing
■ integrated front-line services.

The enactment of children's rights in the contexts of their lives can be seen to operate within risk-conscious and risk-producing global societies, in what Beck (1992: 1) labels the 'risk society'. Social and personal well-being is seen to be under serious threat from adverse social conditions and dangerous people (Giddens, 2001; Bessant *et al.*, 2003). Bessant *et al.* (2003: 1) argue that: 'Risk now embodies an anxiety that social order and personal well-being alike are under threat.' Ironically, risk-oriented measures, administered under the adult gaze, may serve to limit the opportunities for young children to participate in early years settings and, in turn, may stunt children's own protective resources. Moreover, adults' pursuit of children's safety may, inadvertently, curb the potential for children's productive experiences with other children and adults (Jenks, 1996). It 'may turn into its opposite, namely a convenient tool to protect the adult world against the intrusion of children' (Qvortrup, 1994: 21).

We see, therefore, the three major agendas of starting strong, accountability and children's rights as framing the contexts in which early years research is designed, conducted and disseminated.

Conceptual underpinnings of early years research

A conceptual impetus for early years research is a field of work known broadly as the new social studies of childhood and the sociology of childhood, which is being applied in various forms in the UK (Alanen and Mayall, 2001; Alderson, 2002; James and Prout, 2004; Tisdall, 2012) and in countries such as Australia (Danby and Baker, 2001; Danby and Farrell, 2005; MacNaughton *et al.*, 2007; Tayler *et al.*, 2008). It sees children as active participants and interpreters of their own worlds, persons with the right to be seen and heard about issues that affect them. It is concerned with children's sites of experience (Qvortrup, 2000), where children have the opportunity to operate as competent informants on their lives (Christensen and James, 1998; Mayall, 2003).

Childhood, within this framework, is not seen as universal, but is jointly constructed within specific places, times and settings. Research in the settings, in turn, claims to listen to what children say and how they say it (Morrow, 2010). This approach can be seen to contrast traditional developmental perspectives on children, where children may have been seen as either 'precompetent' (Danby, 2002; Mackay, 1991), or as 'underdeveloped ... thus *not something* rather than *something*' (Wacksler, 1991: 63), or as 'human becomings' (Phillips and Alderson, 2002: 6) – that is, as one day, becoming adult humans.

Extend your knowledge

- Find a piece of research that acknowledges children as competent informants and seeks their views on matters that affect them. For example, look at National Children's Bureau (2011) *Listening as a way of life* [online]. Available from: http://www.ncb.org.uk/ycvn/resources/listening-as-a-way-of-life.
- Describe your current practice and consider how you might develop children's involvement in the design and operation of the early years service.
- How do children share their views on matters that affect them?
- How can adults help children to express their ideas and feelings on these matters?
- What are the benefits of listening to children – for children and for adults?
- What are the challenges to listening and how can they be tackled?

Child participation in research

Recent decades have seen a growing interest in participatory approaches and methods in early years research, whether in free-standing or nested studies. The participatory remit, according to Kellett (2005), is for research *with* children, rather than research *on* or *about* children. A related yet distinct field of enquiry is concerned with children's learning as participation (Berthelsen *et al.*, 2009). Both of these strands of research call for children to be both seen and heard, that is, for their everyday lives to be made visible and audible to those around them. In broad terms, participatory research involving children is the research-oriented engagement of children with adults and/or other children that asks them to account for or contribute views on their experience of a particular phenomenon or set of phenomena. Such activities are labelled variously as child participation, child consultation or child participatory research.

While child participation in research is on the international agenda (OECD, 2006), it faces the problem of little empirical evidence of how children *themselves* see their involvement in such activities. So too, there is scant evidence of how adults (who have responsibility for governing and conducting child research) see children in these activities and what principles they employ to make decisions with and about children in these contexts.

Reflective task

- How do others on your team seek to involve children?
- How do parents/families see children's involvement?
- How do the children themselves see their involvement?
- How do you communicate children's involvement to others?

The growth of participatory research has been accompanied by a sense of optimism about children's capacities to participate and the merit of their participation for themselves and those around them. Relatively little attention, however, has been given to dealing with its challenges: conceptual, methodological and analytical. Challenges may ensue from diverse or competing understandings of the research held by approving bodies and gatekeepers, as well as by practitioner researchers, families and the children themselves. Challenges may also relate to research methods, mechanisms for gaining consent/dissent, judgements about children's competence or otherwise to participate, temporal aspects such as the nature and duration of the research, as well as issues of beneficence (that is, the relative benefit versus the risk for those participating in and/or conducting the research). There are also the challenges of risk-minimisation and heightened surveillance of children and researchers, where legislation and policy seek to protect children from harm and danger, but may also limit children's opportunities for participation (Farrell, 2010). Thus, any consideration of research, be it labelled participatory or otherwise, needs to include both the possibilities and challenges inherent in the design, methodology and context.

Reflective task

- What are the key ethical considerations in research with children?
- Do children want to be involved and how do we know they want to be involved?
- Is the research of benefit to children, now and in the future? If so, what are the benefits?
- What if children want to be involved but their parents do not?
- What if parents want their children to be involved and the children do not?

A persistent challenge is that, despite the rhetoric of child participation and the keenness of the field to espouse it, there is scant evidence of whether child participation goes beyond mere rhetoric. So too, there is little evidence of the ways in which institutional contexts and practices operate in sites that purport to practise child participation. The Australian research of Theobald and Kultti (2012) makes a contribution here by showing child participation as constrained by the institutional categories of *teacher* and *student* that were jointly produced in their talk. So too, their analysis revealed tensions that arose for teachers as they balanced the pedagogical intent of *teaching* with its associated institutional expectations (Theobald *et al.*, 2011). David *et al.* (2001: 347), in turn, refer to school-based pedagogic approaches that are 'inscribed with differential power relations'. These are matters ripe for further research.

We need, also, to consider a range of conceptual and operational matters relevant to the design and planning phase as well as to approval-seeking and approval-gaining, implementation, analysis and dissemination. Ethics are at the core of such considerations.

Ethical issues in early years research

First, we need to consider ethics as an overarching concern in early years research. Ethics, in its colloquial sense, is concerned with moral principles or codes of human conduct which are seen to govern what people do. When applied to research and, in this chapter, when applied to research with children, there are moral principles and codes of human conduct which have come to govern and regulate research.

The British Educational Research Association (BERA) (2011), for example, has in common with numerous other countries a set of guidelines for research with children and, more specifically, research with young children in education contexts, such as early years services. BERA (2011) articulates a widely held ethic involving respect for: the person, knowledge, democratic values, the quality of educational research and academic freedom. Guidelines for ethical research with children, such as those codified by BERA (2011) are seen to comply with Articles 3 and 12 of the *UN Convention on the Rights of the Child* (United Nations, 1989). Article 3 concerns the best interests of the child as a primary consideration and Article 12 acknowledges that children who are capable of forming their own views should be granted the right to express their views on matters that affect them.

Moreover, the purpose of most codes of ethics is to improve knowledge in the pursuit of democracy and social well-being. Despite the rhetoric around the purposes of research ethics, it is important to be mindful that:

> **Research related to education is varied and complex, rarely amenable to precise measurement or given to all-encompassing solutions to its many challenges. Nevertheless, the continued pursuit of improved knowledge and understanding of all aspects of education is vital for our democracy and social well-being. To this end, guidelines are designed to support educational researchers in conducting research to the highest ethical standards in whatever context it is needed.**
>
> (BERA, 2011: 1)

In short, consideration of research ethics is central to early years research. Wellington (2000: 3) argues: 'Ethical concerns should be at the forefront of any research project and should continue through to the write-up and dissemination stages.'

A rudimentary step is to consider the ethical issue of consent and dissent. Fundamentally, this is how we conceptualise and operationalise the participation of children (and/or adults) and how they come to communicate their agreement to be involved in the research, that is, the protocols and processes for informed voluntary consent (decision to participate) and dissent (decision to withdraw) (BERA, 2011; Farrell, 2005).

Alderson and Morrow (2011) note that much research underestimates children and their capacity to agree to being involved in it. So too, adults may rely on stereotypic views of children's competence or lack thereof and, so doing, close off opportunities for children's active participation in matters that affect their lives. Conversely, Australian research undertaken by Danby and Farrell (2005) demonstrated the capability of young children to agree to participate in research and to conceptualise their role as research participants.

The challenge is to see consent/dissent as a multifaceted exchange of information that requires the researcher to listen to children and those around them and to seek to make meaningful decisions with children, not merely for them (Alderson and Morrow, 2011). It is a process that requires interactive dialogue, negotiation and renegotiation, over time. The exchange typically involves children, parents/guardians and the practitioner researcher, operating within the legislative and policy requirements of their particular jurisdiction and within the institutional culture of the setting.

Adults need to be conversant with protocols around privacy, confidentiality and disclosure in the use of digital images and the role of social media in data collection, analysis and sharing (Data Protection Act 1998). We need to be mindful, as well, of possible resistance to the use of digital images of children, emanating from high-profile cases of serious child abuse such as that of the Plymouth nursery in 2009 (reported by Morris, 2009). Such cases and their adverse consequences for children, families and the early years profession serve to limit legitimate uses of digital images for pedagogical practice and reflection, both for children and for adults.

Reflective task

Consider your institutional context:

- What institutional agendas are at work here (e.g. agenda of compliance, democracy)?
- How do the institutional agendas operate?
- How do children and adults operate here?
- What makes children visible and audible in this context?
- How do we know that children want to be seen and heard?
- How do children communicate their willingness to be involved in adult agendas?
- What are the opportunities for participation and decision making, and how are they negotiated?
- What measures are in place to do no harm or to minimise harm in the research?
- Is there a gap between the rhetoric of children's rights and the reality of children's rights in this context?

Second, we consider the perennial issue of power differentials in early years research. As Edwards and Alldred (1999: 267) argue, it is 'not simply a matter of transferring power from one group (researchers/adults) to another (research participants/children), where the group with the power perceives this as beneficial. Power is not packageable and, therefore, givable in this sense.' Nor is it a matter of simplifying or downsizing, for young children, procedures used with adults (Koocer and Keith-Spiegel, 1994). Rather, it is a process that acknowledges that children are persons in their own right who may (or may not) decide to contribute to research. A corollary is for the researcher to consider carefully their roles and responsibilities in research.

Respect for children's status as social actors does not diminish adult responsibilities. It places new responsibilities on the adult community to 'structure children's environments, guide their behaviour and enable their social participation in ways consistent with their understanding, interests and ways of communication, especially in the issues that most directly affect their lives' (Woodhead and Faulkner, 2008: 31–3). Power differentials may also apply to adults within the setting, that is, within and between early years personnel and families.

A third consideration that relates to the previous two is the weighing up of the ethical principles in research. Across most codes of ethics pertaining to research with children, there is an expressed consideration of ethical principles, such as research integrity, justice, respect and beneficence (benefit versus risk). While such principles may be inherent within statutory directives and policy guidelines, there may be conflict between or within these principles, such as the weighing up of benefits against risk or the weighing up of justice against benefits to participants and those around them. Inherent here is the tension between affording children (and adults) opportunities for participation, and ensuring mechanisms for protecting participants. There may be instances where the child wants to be involved in the research but the parent/guardian does not; or, alternatively, where the parent/guardian wants the child to be involved but the child does not. In both instances, there may be legitimate reasons for involvement or non-involvement and decisions may change from consent to dissent (withdrawal or cessation of research involvement). These are the tensions that the practitioner researcher manages on an almost daily basis in the cut and thrust of the early years service.

Fourth, we consider strategies for ongoing negotiation with parents and families about the research, ensuring ample opportunities for informal focused discussion about the research, before, during and after data collection. Related to negotiation is considering ways in which children can be invited to indicate, in appropriate ways, their willingness to be involved. In an Australian study (Farrell and Danby, 2007) children were invited to indicate their consent (to participation in the research) with their special mark (for example, a thumbprint, a signature, a verbal or non-verbal gesture). Such an activity afforded the children opportunity to exercise their decision making in a safe and familiar context. While the study focused on children's everyday decision making in home and school contexts, there was an analytic focus on children's communicative competence in the opening phase of the research conversation (Danby and Farrell, 2005). Our analysis showed that, during the opening moments of the interview, the purpose and conditions of the conversation were established and clarified by both the child participant and the researcher. Analysis showed that, within this phase of the conversation, children established *themselves* as gatekeepers, deciding whether or not to proceed with the research conversation.

In research involving audio-recorded or video-recorded data, researchers may consciously involve children in starting and stopping the recorder. Rather than contaminating the research record, such a practice of involving children may demonstrate their ownership within the research. In an Australian study of young children's peer interaction, Cobb-Moore (2008) undertook a period of ethnographic observation (including observations of drop-off and pick-up times), prior to video recording, to allow staff, parents and children to feel comfortable with her presence. In other work, such as that of Kelly-Byrne's ethnographic study (1989), the researcher engaged in play with the child. In Corsaro's study (1985), participant observation was used, along with video recording. In short, the researcher needs to negotiate with the setting on the data collection methods used, ensuring that they are fit for purpose. A prime example is video recording as a method for studying talk-in-interaction, where 'actions are central to the way that participants, themselves, produce and understand conduct, they are a fundamental part of the meaningfulness on conduct' (Pomerantz and Fehr, 1997: 72).

Fifth, we seek to ensure that the research design, implementation and dissemination are as seamless as possible so as to reduce any demarcation between programmatic practice and research. To this end, we need to take into account children's daily routines, transition times and family participation patterns so that research ambitions are aligned to the reality of the everyday lives of those in the setting and have the least disruptive impact on their lives. We might encourage children and/or adult participants to review and critique the research data (for example, video-recorded data) in which they feature and to build in opportunities for reflecting with children and adults on the experience of the research as part of their everyday routine. 'Unless adults are alert to children's own ways of seeing and understanding and representing the world to themselves, it is unlikely that the child will ever manage to identify with the school's and teacher's ways of seeing' (Brooker, 2002: 171).

Mosaic approach

Using multiple ways of engaging with and listening to children is a key underpinning of the 'Mosaic' approach, a framework championed by Alison Clark and colleagues (2005) in the UK.

While the Mosaic approach was developed originally in the context of research, it has now penetrated everyday early years practice such that research/practice boundaries have been blurred. As Seidel (2001: 333) notes: 'The actions of instruction, assessment, documentation and research have come to contain each other. They cannot be pulled apart in any practical sense; they are a piece. No dichotomy between teaching and research remains.'

The Mosaic approach has key elements. It is (Clark *et al.*, 2005: 31):
- *multi-method:* recognises the different 'voices' or languages of children;
- *participatory:* treats children as experts and agents in their own lives;
- *reflexive:* includes children, practitioners and parents in reflecting on meanings, and addresses the question of interpretation;
- *adaptable:* can be applied in a variety of early childhood institutions;
- *focused on children's lived experiences:* can be used for a variety of purposes including looking at lives lived rather than knowledge gained or care received;
- *embedded into practice:* a framework for listening that has the potential to be both used as an evaluative tool and to become embedded into early years practice.

The Mosaic approach was epitomised in the early study, *Spaces to play* (Clark and Moss, 2001), and involved three inter-related stages. Stage 1 involved gathering children's and adults' perspectives; stage 2 involved discussing and reviewing the material; and stage 3 involved deciding on areas of continuity and change. Discussion and review permeated the entire process, with children's documentation being used to inform this discussion and review. Clark *et al.* (2005) refer to the introduction, in story form, of Barney the dog as the main character together with a cartoon caterpillar, serving as an intermediary in many of the conversations with children. The Mosaic design used in the original spaces study showed the use of multiple methods of data collection and analysis to generate a comprehensive picture of spaces for children.

The Mosaic approach has a focus on listening (Clark *et al.*, 2005):
- **Internal listening** or self-reflection as a strategy for children to make sense of their world. Internal listening is a reflective process enabling children to consider a range of meanings, to make new connections and to express new understandings. It asks questions such as 'What does it mean to be in this place?' 'What does it mean *to be you* in this place?'
- **Multiple listening** or openness to other perspectives, affording opportunities for practitioners, individual children and groups of children to listen to each other and themselves. Multiple listening is a complex web of interactions that involves time and resources, allowing children to reflect on their ideas and experiences with peers and adults.
- **Visible listening** includes documentation and interpretation through digital images, note taking and map making. Visible listening is a platform for communication at individual, organisational and community levels.

Getting started in early years research

The first step in getting started in early years research is establishing the need for the research. The need for the research may come from either reflection on practice, or an awareness of an issue or set of issues from what others have said or done, and/or a review of the literature. Whether it is from one's own practice or that of others, a review of the literature can serve to illuminate or clarify the issue or phenomenon being researched, the research method(s) that may be used and the goals of the research. In this respect, conducting a literature review is an important rudimentary step in getting started.

A **literature review** involves a systematic critique of research on a particular topic. It goes beyond mere description of the research to provide a critical discussion and synthesis of its underlying assumptions, purposes and affordances, showing its themes, gaps and absences. In short, it provides a rationale for the proposed research, building a systematic case for the research, locating the research in its conceptual and/or historical contexts and demonstrating its significance.

According to Burton and Bartlett (2009), reviewing the literature is crucial to:

- provide background information on the general area of study
- describe and evaluate the context of the research (social, political, economic, educational, environmental)
- consider and comment on what has already been written within the general area of investigation, looking particularly at the relationships (differences and similarities) between studies
- discuss the relevance of existing research to the research focus and methodology (including any impact on the intended research questions).

Reflective task

When undertaking a literature review, ask the following questions:
- What was the purpose of the research?
- How was it conducted?
- What were the key findings?
- Was the research rigorous?
- What is its relevance for the proposed research?

Action research in the early years

The next step is to plan and conduct the research. While early years research features a range of research approaches and methods (such as ethnography and case study), action research is an approach which has come to prominence in the early years and one which aligns well with the UK's EYFS (DfE, 2012a).

Kurt Lewin coined the term 'action research' in his paper 'Action research and minority problems' (1946), theorising social action and the ways in which research can drive social action. Action research, by definition, uses research for action and improvement (Lewin, 1948). As Carr and Kemmis (1986: 162) argue:

> Action research is simply a form of self-reflective enquiry undertaken by participants in social situations in order to improve the rationality and justice of their own practice, their understanding of these practices, and the situations in which the practices are carried out.

Action research requires a clear research design, plan and strategy. The researcher and research team need to establish the purpose, rationale and vision for change that are being pursued within the research. In turn, the research plan needs to be mindful of the context, participants and practicalities of conducting research of this kind.

Reflective task

Consider, as a team, the following elements of action research:

Rationale
- What is the rationale or justification for the research?
- Why does it need to be done?
- What would happen if it were not done?
- Whose interests will be served by the research; those of the child, the practitioner researcher, the family, the early years service?

Research problem
- What is the problem/issue/phenomenon that needs to be researched and improved?
- Is the problem able to be tackled?

Literature review
- What does the literature say about the problem/issue/phenomenon and how it might be researched and improved?

Methodology
- What conceptual and methodological approach is necessary (qualitive/quantitive)?
- How will the action research be conducted?
- What resources will be needed for its conduct?

Analysis
- What analytical approach will be used and how will analysis be conducted?
- What resources will be needed for analysis?

Dissemination
- How, when, why and with whom will the findings be disseminated?
- How will findings drive change?

Action
- What will you do differently as a result of the research?
- What will you do that is the same as before?
- With whom will you collaborate?
- How might you learn from others?

Action research is cyclical, involving a cycle of reflection, action, discussion and reflection. Typically, it begins with an awareness of a problem or challenge being faced by the practitioner. Stake (2010: 158) argues that action research 'usually starts with a practitioner realising things could be better and setting out to look into the mirror'. McNiff and Whitehead (2002) emphasises the importance of discussion among colleagues, first to establish what needs to be done, how it will be done and when it will be done. This phase may involve information seeking from stakeholders (children, families, staff) through observation, focus groups and surveys. Once the vision for the action research is cast, the action cycle begins. Here again, the research itself may involve observation, focus groups, digital recordings and surveys.

Educational change theorist Fullan (2003) calls for consideration of the core elements of practice within the setting. This includes: the context-specific moral purpose, or desired direction; developing a collaborative learning culture; ensuring that reflective practice infuses discussion and decision making; and building a team culture that celebrates incremental gains (Fullan, 2003).

Action research does not preclude a mixture of qualitative and quantitative approaches, and when each is conducted with systematic rigour, the mixed method can generate findings that illuminate the complexity of the situation and can, in turn, drive change. Traditional understandings of qualitative and quantitative approaches as conceptual and operational binaries have given way to new understandings of the ways in which both textual and numeric data (Danby and Thorpe, 2006) can, together, be used to complement the data set.

Action research, by definition, is concerned with action and, as such, carries an ethical responsibility to act upon findings and to enact practices which will improve the everyday experience of those within the context.

A case of action research

A case of action research impacting practice is the Australian research of Julie Davis (2008), which focused on education for sustainability in an early childhood service. The Sustainable Planet Project (Davis, 2008), conducted in a full-day care centre (with staff and children from two and a half to five years), was concerned with creating cultural change. The complexity of the problem being tackled and the scale of the change being sought within the action research project required a whole-of-setting approach, rather than a room-based or group-based approach.

A focus on 'the environment' grew from the desire among staff to strengthen home–centre links. Working under the broad banner of the Sustainable Planet Project, early years staff consciously brought to their roles as early childhood educators, personal interests such as gardening, wildlife conservation and recycling. From its inception, the project had an action-oriented focus, exemplified in its subtitle, 'Saving our planet: Become a conscious part of the solution'. Davis (2008) describes the way in which, initially, the staff worked with the children on mini-projects aligned to their own environmental interests, such as environmental aesthetics, litter-less lunches, efficient use of natural resources, reusing, recycling and composting.

Over time, the mini-projects became embedded into the everyday practice of the centre and, in turn, gave rise to child-initiated projects, such as water conservation where children themselves identified instances of water wastage. Over time, a whole-of-setting water conservation programme took hold. There were collaborative enquiries into the origins of household and centre water, discussions around drought/flood, and examination of archival material and media sources on water. Davis (2008) notes that, with children's increased knowledge of and interest in water issues, their enquiries were transformed into *actions*. Concrete actions included the creation of signs about water and its usage, and installation of a water barrel for children to access for water play and sand play. Not only did water consumption in the centre change, so too did attitudes to water change, and its use gave rise to practical action at home, with parents noting children's greater care in using water. Actions with respect to water usage combined with actions with respect to the outdoor environment as a habitat for local flora and fauna, and curiosity about the natural environment.

We may well ask: What made this project 'action research' rather than merely a focused programme of learning and teaching? Its claim of being action research can be substantiated by a clear *prior* plan for change, born of heightened awareness of sustainability within the centre. There was also a clear plan to use data to drive the change. Data sources included observations, diaries, interviews and digital images, which together generated evidence of practice and highlighted the areas in need of change. Data generation methods, as well as the data themselves, were the focus of discussion, reflection and collaboration and involved both adults and children.

Extend your knowledge

- Read and reflect on the following example of action research: Davis, J. (2008), 'What might education for sustainability look like in early childhood? A case for participatory, whole-of-settings approaches', in *The contribution of early childhood education to a sustainable society*, Paris: UNESCO, pp.18–24.
- What was it that made the project 'action research' as distinct from a learning and teaching programme that typically might occur in an early childhood setting?
- What were the features of the action research?
- What were the enablers of the action research?
- What were the challenges to the action research?

Scenario

In a similar way to the example of Davis's (2008) Sustainable Planet Project, a centre might come up with a specific focus on water use as one part of the action research cycle, as in the following scenario.

Your community is experiencing record low rainfall, drought has been declared and water restrictions are now in place. Your early childhood setting, like all other water users, is moving to water rationing and hefty fines apply to those who breach the policy.

Children and adults alike have been used to a plentiful water supply and are finding it difficult to change their water-use habits. Many children are accustomed to running the tap in the bathroom, even when they are not washing their hands and staff are accustomed to using a large volume of water for everyday activities such as washing paintbrushes and glue containers. You realise that water use has reached a critical point and you will need to implement a water-wise strategy.

Your strategy is likely to include:
- consultation with families about being water wise
- modelling and reinforcing the wise use of water
- discussion about appropriate and inappropriate uses of water
- use of resources (hand-made, commercial and online) about water and its usage with children, staff and families
- development of a water-wise policy and mechanisms for judging its effectiveness
- placing water use on the agenda of your staff meeting
- exploring ways to optimise learning and teaching around water, sustainability and social responsibility.

Dissemination

Dissemination is also a crucial part of the research cycle, i.e. the Sustainable Planet Project could have been shared with the local community. So important is dissemination that an entire SAGE research handbook has been devoted to communication and dissemination in the behavioural sciences (Welch-Ross and Fasig, 2007). While the handbook addresses interdisciplinary research and professional contexts such as journalism, mass media, social commentary and advocacy, its dual focus on 'doers' and 'thinkers' demonstrates the importance of practitioners (who can be seen as both 'doers' and 'thinkers') sharing their research findings and insights with others.

Dissemination, in its broadest sense, may be either internal to the setting and/or external to the setting. Internal dissemination may occur through discussion groups with staff, websites, blogs or other social networking media, involving adults and/or children. Shared stories of learning and teaching may be generated to inform ongoing planning, implementation and reflection. External dissemination may also draw upon internally disseminated findings or insights, and may be augmented by conventional forms of dissemination such as scholarly articles, books or reports. The genre or form of dissemination depends, to a degree, on the intended audience and purpose for which dissemination is designed. There may well be different dissemination modes and artefacts to capture the different types of data sources, participants, stakeholders and contexts.

An example of early years research being disseminated to both internal and external audiences was the Hubs research on integrated child and family services in rural and disadvantaged communities in Australia (Farrell *et al.*, 2004). The research, funded by the Australian Research Council and six industry partners (including commonwealth and state government departments), involved more than 1,100 participants (adults and children) across six integrated hubs (Tayler *et al.*, 2008). Findings were shared through various media with participants, with their Hubs and with key government departments. Venues for dissemination included a website, workshops, technical reports, leaflets, newsletters and focus groups. A key outcome of dissemination was its contribution to the national rollout of the Hubs strategy and adoption of key empirically informed lessons around integrating child and family services.

Conclusion

This chapter has considered early years research as part of the reflective practice of the early years professional. The chapter has introduced early years research as an international and national priority, fuelled by the international agendas of starting strong, accountability and children's rights. It has considered the conceptual underpinnings of early years research, understandings of child competence and the merits of child participation on matters that affect them. The entire enterprise of early years research is imbued with ethical responsibilities at each stage of the research, from design to implementation and dissemination – each stage needing to recognise and afford opportunities for both children and adults to participate. The chapter has concluded with a consideration of action research, an approach aligned with the EYFS (DfE, 2012a).

In conclusion, as early years researchers, we need to enact our professional, ethical and legal obligations to give children (and adults) authentic opportunities to have their views heard, considered respectfully and acted upon appropriately. Despite the affordances of early years research, the challenge is to listen in ways that both respect the competence of children (and adults) and to recognise possible power differentials between children and adults (as well as among children and among adults). When well designed, implemented and disseminated, early years research can accrue significant benefits to participants as well as to the early years contexts within which it operates and to the broader arenas that are part of children's everyday lives.

By engaging in research and reflecting on research practice in a systematic manner, the practitioner can gain a clearer understanding of their transformative work with children and families. Research insights have the capacity to challenge received wisdom and conventional practice in ways that bring about change in the lives of children and adults, for good.

Evaluate your...

Understanding of research

- Are you engaged in practitioner research? If so, how would you describe it (e.g. case study, action research)?
- What is the focus of your research? Why have you taken such a focus?
- What impact is your research having in the short term and in the longer term?
- Who are the beneficiaries of the research?
- Who has a say in the research, in its design, implementation and evaluation?
- Who disseminates or shares the research, how and with whom?
- What advice might you give to a practitioner aspiring to conduct practitioner research? What might be a focus? What are the pitfalls and how might they be avoided or minimised?

Next steps

You are planning to conduct a new research project in your centre.

- Consider the practical steps you will need to take to begin and sustain a research project (e.g. bring together a team, appoint a leader, consult with team about approach and analysis).
- Consider the logistics, such as the timeline and resources (human and material) needed to conduct the research.
- Consider how the research will complement the ongoing conduct of the programme.
- Consider how you will be able to judge the success of the research, in the short and longer term. Consider the use of milestone targets and reports.
- Consider how the research will align with the United Nations *Convention on the Rights of the Child* (United Nations, 1989) and other documents relevant to children's participation in research.
- Consider any ethical processes and approvals that may need to be obtained before the research can begin.

Further reading

British Educational Research Association (BERA) (2011) *Revised Ethical Guidelines for Educational Research* [online]. Available from: http://www.bera.ac.uk/publications/ethical-guidelines.

Christensen, P. and Prout, A. (2002) 'Working with ethical symmetry in social research with children', *Childhood*, vol. 9, no. 4, pp. 477–97.

Farrell, A. (2004) 'Ethical dimensions of practitioner-research in the early years', *Early Childhood Practice: The Journal for Multi-Professional Partnerships*, vol. 6, no. 2, pp. 18–27.

Goodfellow, J. and Hedges, M. (2007) 'Practitioner research "centre stage": Contexts, contributions and challenges', in Keesing-Styles, L. and Hedges, H. (eds.), *Theorising Early Childhood Practice: Emerging dialogues*, Castle Hill, NSW: Pademelon Press.

Kellett, M., Forrest, R., Dent, N. and Ward, S. (2004) '"Just teach us the skills please, we'll do the rest": Empowering ten-year-olds as active researchers', *Children & Society,* vol. 18, no. 5, pp. 329–43.

Mayall, B. (2002) *Towards a Sociology for Childhood: Thinking from children's lives*, Buckingham: Open University Press.

Mayall, B. (2008) 'Conversations with children: Working with generational issues' in Christensen, P. and James, A. (eds.), *Research with Children: Perspectives and Practices* (2nd edn), London: Routledge, pp. 109–22.

United Nations (1989) *Convention on the Rights of the Child*, Geneva: United Nations. Available from: http://www2.ohchr.org/english/law/crc.htm.

Play and creativity in early years
Tina Bruce

This chapter takes a slightly different approach to other chapters in this book, offering a personal perspective on play and creativity in early years.

Introduction: What is creativity?

Layer upon layer of creativity

Creativity is a word that has layers of meaning. Some kinds of creativity result in world-shattering acts of creation, which mean that those involved in them will view and act on the world in completely new ways. When that happens, things will never be the same again. Newton's Laws of Motion were in that category in the world of science. Sir William Beveridge's vision of the National Health Service in the UK in the 1940s is an example from the world of humanities. In the world of the arts, Maria Taglione's father invented point shoes, and changed the world of dance. World-changing transformations, through the creativity of individuals or groups working together, can be found across time in science, the arts and the humanities.

But there is layer upon layer of creativity. Very little of the creativity found in the world is in fact of the world-shattering kind. Creativity of the next layer down (after the world-shattering layer) would be the sort that makes an impact on a particular field of endeavour, specialism or expertise. Replacing the familiar idea of seating an audience in a theatre auditorium to watch a performance with encouraging the audience to follow the performers around different parts of a building is an example of something which creatively changes the nature of the drama or dance.

The main focus of this chapter is on the third layer of creativity, which can be called everyday creativity. Those involved in education will focus on this because it opens up possibilities for every child to engage in their creative possibilities. It locates creativity, the process of it as well as the results of it, at the centre of education. Something as simple as setting the table for a meal to share with family and friends is often an act of creation. The way flowers, ornaments, candles are placed, made or chosen, the folding of napkins, who is seated next to whom, and the carefully made, even artistic, placeholders all give possibilities for creativity of the everyday kind. Ideas, feelings and relationships with others are an important part of creativity in its process of development and in the ways it bursts out on occasions. Creativity also depends on the physical coordination of the creator. The whole child is involved in the process of creativity. Pentti Hakkarainen and Milda Bredikyte (Hakkarainen, 2009) emphasise the importance of emotional and intellectual engagement in their role play if creativity is to develop. This is called *perezhivanie*. We shall see later in this chapter that play and creativity are very closely linked and at times it is not possible to separate the two. The younger the child, the more this is so, as anyone who has observed babies, toddlers and young children will recognise.

Learning objectives

This chapter will help you to:

- Understand how to tune into a child's thoughts and feelings, and to get to know them as a unique person, enabling the child to develop their creativity.
- Learn that developing a good relationship with the child can help their creative ideas to develop and help them to express themselves in creative ways.
- Realise that it is important to avoid imposing your own ideas or insisting that every child must do the same thing.
- Recognise how you can support a child's emerging thoughts and feelings, which are the beginnings of creative processes, or acts of creation.

It is true that chimpanzees, such as Ida in an observational study (Matthews, 2011: 341), are capable of creative drawings. It is also a fact that, although bird calls are innate and pre-scripted, if birds hear fellows of their species sing, they become more experimental and show a degree of creativity, developing their song verse by verse in original ways (Sample, 2000: 8). However, acts of creation, and the processes which lead to these, form a part of humanity which sets the human being apart from the rest of the animal kingdom. To neglect creativity in the way we bring up children and educate them is to neglect human possibilities, and to cause lives to be constrained in ways which lead to a lack of fulfilment, but also have implications for the future of this planet.

Historical development of creativity in early years

Classic research

Friedrich Fröbel (1782–1852) pioneered creativity in the early childhood curriculum through emphasising the importance of play in the educational process. He also developed materials which would support play, called the Gifts (wooden blocks designed to relate to each other mathematically). These are found in current early childhood settings as unit blocks and hollow blocks, in large- or small-scale sets. At first, he prescribed their use, but his observations of children demonstrated to him that children worked at a higher level and showed more creative thinking and ideas when using the blocks in free play. The Occupations (such as clay, sewing, weaving, shape boards, drawing, chalking on slates, painting, making things from recycled materials, stick laying to make patterns and pictures, tessellation boards with geometric wooden shapes, cooking – to give some examples) gave children further opportunities for creativity. Movement games, finger plays and action songs (in the Mother Songs of 1844, which were illustrated songs with finger rhymes and actions about everyday life which families – children, parents, grandparents – were encouraged to sing and act out together in the home) and literature were further developments, offering children possibilities to imagine and feed creative ideas, and to make variations on themes of music and dance. His emphasis on children learning actively, using the senses and freedom of movement, with rich direct experiences in nature out of doors, as well as indoors, laid the foundations for the higher-level symbolic life (Bruce, 2011b) of more abstract ideas, to which he gave a central place in education.

Fröbel's groundbreaking thinking in relation to creativity emphasised the development of the child's understanding and use of symbols. Steiner (1861–1925) also gave a central place to the creativity of children, working with ecology, rhythm and repetition as aids to learning (Oldfield, 2003). Both Fröbel and Steiner understood the importance of first-hand experience, nature, movement, the arts and freedom to learn through activity. Steiner gave a greater place to imitation. They saw the adult as a facilitator of the child's inner creativity.

Extend your knowledge

To find out more on Fröbel, read:

- Bruce, T. (2011b) *Cultivating Creativity for Babies, Toddlers and Young Children* (2nd edn), London: Hodder Education.
- Tovey, H. (2012) *Bringing the Fröebel Approach to your Early Years Practice,* London: Routledge.

Find out more about the historical journey in the thinking of creativity.

For Fröbel and Steiner and the philosophical approach of the late 19th and early 20th centuries:

- Miller, L. and Pound, L. (eds.) (2011) *Theories and Approaches to Learning in the Early Years*, London: SAGE.

For the mid- to end of the 20th century – the impact of philosophy with the development of psychology:

- Barron, F. (1955) 'The disposition toward originality', *Journal of Normal and Social Psychology*, vol. 51, pp. 478–88.
- Greenspan, S. and Lieberman, A. (1994) 'Representational Elaboration and Differentiation: A Clinical-Quantitative Approach to the Assessment of 2–4 year olds', in Slade, A. and Palmer Wolf, D., *Children at Play: Clinical and Developmental Approaches to Meaning and Representation*, Oxford: Oxford University Press.
- Koestler, A. (1964) *The Act of Creation*, London: Pan Books.

For the early 2000s and onwards – socio-cultural and biological approaches:

- Craft, A. (2002) *Creativity and Early Years Education: A lifewide foundation,* London and New York: Continuum.
- Dowling, M. (2012) *Young Children's Thinking*, London: SAGE.
- Dweck, C. (2000) *Self Theories: Their Role in Motivation, Personality and Development*, London: Psychology Press.
- Fumoto, H., Robson, S., Greenfield, S. and Hargreaves, D. (2012) *Young Children's Creative Thinking*, London: SAGE.
- Malloch, S. and Trevarthen, C. (2009) *Communicative Musicality: Exploring the Basis of Human Companionship,* Oxford: Oxford University Press.

Current views of creativity

Feeling separate but connected to other people

Children growing up need to feel loved and they need to feel that they matter to someone. Warm, affectionate companionship is part of this, and contributes to a feeling of belonging and of being acknowledged and affirmed (Maslow, 1943). Human beings are social animals, and not feeling isolated is part of this. The psycho-dynamic theory of Winnicott (1971: 29) suggests that a child who enjoys his or her own company is emotionally well developed. This is not an argument for leaving children on their own, which causes loneliness. Vygotsky (1978) suggests that the highest forms of thinking and creativity begin in social relationships. This does not mean that children never need personal space. Some cultures encourage personal space more than others, but crowded living through economic circumstances can also make this difficult. The important thing is that children have both a sense of belonging and are aware of themselves as separate, creative individuals. Damasio (1999) sees self-awareness as important in developing creativity.

Doing something different from the rest of the group is central to creativity. Overdependence on others and always following the crowd limit creativity. This has implications for creativity and play.

Not knowing what will happen next: uncertainty is part of creativity

Creative children are able to move out of their comfort zone, supported in doing so because they feel comfortable in themselves to explore something that interests, frightens or puzzles them. The creative process opens up possibilities to experiment with new ways of exploring the deeper aspects of life. These might include examining what is fair, being hard-working, lazy, kind or cruel. This might be a very long process, and the child might return again and again to an idea or thought, and only gradually does a creative process develop into a creative act.

Making new connections – new ways of doing things – transformations

Creativity involves transformation in the way we feel, think and act. Being creative means that we will never be the same again. The cliché 'Dare to be different' is at the heart of the creative process. In the next section of this chapter, we will look at the important ways in which play and creativity are linked. Imaginative play makes a powerful contribution to the development of creativity. Being able to transform and change things, to experiment and adapt, find new possibilities and rearrange how things are in a play scenario equip children to take their findings into the world of reality.

Reflective task

- How do you define creativity?
- In your setting, what are your colleagues' and the parents' views of what constitutes creativity?
- How do you encourage creativity in your work with children?
- What opportunity do children in your setting have to express their creativity?

Creativity, imagination and play

Creativity, imagination and play are at the heart of human development and education. Creativity, imagination and play are connected to each other in important ways. It is a bit like asking the question: Which comes first, the chicken or the egg?

Play – first, second and last

If we think of babies, then we would say that play comes first, before imagination and creativity. But this will not yet be the kind of play that involves a symbolic life. That will develop later, along with talking, walking and pretending – unless there are extreme circumstances of abuse, neglect or deprivation, or some specific complex needs. The kind of play we see in the early period of life will be sensory and movement play. But this kind of play sets the scene for the later development of symbolic play (Vygotsky, 1978). A symbol is something which stands for something else. Children see others using symbols, and they begin to imitate, and to develop pretend play and imaginative ideas which are creative. The important thing about early sensory and movement play is that babies have wide-ranging opportunities to socialise with people, and in doing so to see, hear, smell, taste and touch, with freedom of movement. Babies benefit from having time on their tummies, and from kicking their limbs (Greenland, 2010). They like to look at faces and be talked to, and to engage in proto-conversations (Malloch and Trevarthen, 2009). They begin to hold objects in their hands, and always put things in their mouths, which is a major way of learning about the world they are experiencing. By the fifth month they are, typically, coordinating looking at an object they grasp, and drawing it into their mouth (known as hand–eye–mouth coordination).

For their play to be rich, babies need time with people and time to enjoy and explore objects without distraction, with family and loved ones nearby, but respecting their need for times when they have personal space, as well as the baby's need for social play and the company of others. Sitting babies will play for long periods with objects in a treasure basket pioneered by Elinor Goldschmied (Forbes, 2004). However, babies are very dependent at this time on adults providing interesting objects for them to play with. In most parts of the world, babies do not play with toys. They are presented with everyday and non-cost objects. It is important to remember that play does not cost money. It is only those who wish to profit from play commercially who argue that children need expensive toys to play with in order for their brains to develop maximally.

As babies begin to crawl, they have a newfound independence. They do not rely any longer on others bringing objects for play to them. They can go to objects, or fetch them for themselves. They can pull on a tablecloth and objects will come crashing on the floor beside them – or

Figure 17.1 The baby is exploring the objects in a treasure basket (developed by Elinor Goldschmied, a Fröbelian pioneer of the education of babies and toddlers)

on them! Some babies are adventurous enough to climb onto chairs and up bookcases. The joy of movement is deep, but as yet the baby has no understanding of what might be dangerous.

A further development in play takes place when the baby becomes a toddler. This is the time which typically marks the transition to an explosion of language development, and symbolic behaviour in general. The toddler becomes a symbol maker and a symbol user (Bruce, 2004; Bruce, 2012). One thing stands for another. This shows in the play. At first the symbolic play is very literal. We see the toddler pretending to eat, sleep, put the teddy to bed, do the ironing, prepare the food, use the mobile phone, computer, go shopping, swipe the credit card in the machine, drive the car – to give a few examples. The pretend play during this time of development is scarcely removed from self. 'I' am pretending to eat. 'I' am pretending to feed the baby, or mend the car, or write the bill. The young child is imitating what he or she sees others doing. Young children are not being someone else in this kind of literal play. During this time of literal play (Greenspan and Lieberman, 1994), children are being like the mother, father, shopkeeper, car mechanic etc. Gradually, but only if this is encouraged, the young child develops from literal play to a more complex and sophisticated kind of symbolic play. Narrative develops, and so do characters of imagined people. Imagination kicks in, and this is the point that most theories of play emphasise. Pentti Hakkarainen (2009) and Milda Bredikyte (2011) have been interested in the way literal play can be encouraged to develop into what they describe as more mature forms of play. These are the basis of creativity. Children who have developed rich play have the possibility of being very creative in a range of ways:

- spanning the sciences through hypothesis making and mathematical problem solving
- in creative story making
- in music making
- in their paintings and drawings, constructions and model making
- as they create dances
- in the creative ways in which they negotiate and solve conflicts and find ways of cooperating with others.

Figure 17.2 With the support of an adult, these children are learning to negotiate and cooperate when making models out of recycled materials

Contemporary research

Milda Bredikyte (2011) and Pentti Hakkarainen (2009) have developed work in Finland, Moscow and Lithuania training early childhood practitioners to help them become supporters of children's creativity. They believe that the child's point of view is more important than the mastery of subject knowledge, and so they encourage practitioners to enter into dramatic story/art/puppet scenarios with children from toddlers to about seven years of age. The creativity is developed as adults and children take their unique and individual themes and begin to learn together how to tune into each other, to make a single creative endeavour. The more experienced both children and adults become, the more long lasting the creative growth becomes. In order to become imaginative and creative, children need adults who know how to participate in their play, art experiences or small world/puppets/dolls rather than taking over, or invading the children's possibilities for creativity.

Extend your knowledge

To find out more about creativity in the way children develop characters and storylines see section 7 (Discussion) of Bredikyte, M. (2011) *The Zones of Proximal Development in Children's Play*, Finland: University of Oulu.

Just as Piaget (1968) saw the interconnectivity of thought and feelings in young children, but always used the term thinking (assuming emotion to be present in every thought), so many writers on play assume the connection with creativity, and use the words play and creativity with considerable interchange.

The following 12 features of play (Bruce, 2012) encapsulate different aspects of play. It is important to bear in mind that although sensory and movement play are often seen as an early kind of play, they also continue throughout our lives. They are part of a larger possibility for play, rather than the only possibility for it, as is the case during babyhood. These 12 features of play also give an important place to the contribution of imagination and creativity, for play that is sophisticated depends on these. The pioneer educator Friedrich Fröbel saw play as the highest level of learning, and in doing so anticipated the later theory of Lev Vygotsky (1978). One of the challenges to modern educators is that creativity is very underdeveloped, because play is not developed as it needs to be. Unless the play is rich, the creativity is absent. Desultory play means constrained creativity, and the lack of imagination in a child's development and learning.

Twelve features of play (Bruce, 1991 and 2012)

1. The crucial contribution of first-hand and direct experience of life and the natural world

The first-hand and direct experiences children participate and engage in are at the heart of play. Often these are of the everyday life kind: eating, sleeping, going to the shops, going to the park, travelling in a pushchair, car or bus, on a scooter or bike, and visiting Grandma would be typical examples. Children use first-hand experience as a rich resource, which they draw upon and make use of in their play. We often see three-year-olds pretending to prepare a meal, or a two-year-old pushing a pram with a doll in it and a shopping bag draped over the handle. Five-year-olds are hopefully engaged in more sophisticated use of first-hand experiences, perhaps creating a marketplace complete with stalls, and playing at stall keepers and customers who visit these to buy food, clothes, and other purchases, with different children taking different roles. This contrasts with the earlier use of first-hand experiences that we see during babyhood (Manning-Morton and Thorp, 2003), before children develop speech and walking. The baby who has fed from the breast, drunk water from a bottle, and juice from a lidded cup has more experience to draw upon and enrich their play than the baby who has only one of these ways of drinking.

2. Play depends on rules – but who makes the rules?

Children do not like to be in situations where they feel boundary-less. This frightens them, and they begin to behave in ways in which they try to find out if there are any boundaries, because they expect to find some. This often leads to unacceptable behaviour, because they feel very insecure. It is a widespread misconception among those who are uninformed about the important contribution that play makes to development and learning that play is a free-for-all, with no shape or purpose, and with no rules to guide children or adults. In fact, play, as Vygotsky (1978) explained, helps children to tease out the importance of having rules. It provides a space in a child's life in which to test and experiment, explore, analyse and make decisions about the importance of rules. During play, children are subject to two rules. They must not damage or hurt each other, and they must not damage materials and the physical environment. (This also applies when children are given professional therapy.) Children learn, through their imaginative play, that there are social rules and moral rules (Turiel and Weston, 1983). As well as this, they see the differences between mathematical rules, cultural conventions, rules in musical notations, and the conventions of writing (sometimes in different languages if they speak several). Different rules are explored in play (Kallialla, 2005), and children begin to develop their ideas (Holland, 2003) about fairness, justice, kindness, being caring or being cruel, the need for rules and laws, whose rules matter, and that rules can be made by people (which people?). Rules can be changed and altered, or modified. They can be ignored, or abandoned. They can be broken. This kind of thinking requires children to engage and participate in the play with the whole of themselves, and it leads children into being creative. Creative thinking of this kind spills over into their real lives as they begin to apply the learning they have established and consolidated. Just as first-hand experiences are a resource children draw on in their play, so their creative experiments with rules and moral issues during play lead them to trying out their findings in real-life situations that are about kindness, not being cruel, being fair and more. This is being researched by Milda Bredikyte (2011) in Finland and Pentti Hakkarainen (2009) at the University of Vilnius in Lithuania.

3. Play props – representing – making one thing stand for another

Some play props contribute in deep ways to the imaginative and creative development and learning of the child. Some do not. Plastic fruits and vegetables are constraining to the imagination and creativity. They exert a constant 'pull' on the child to represent an apple, or a carrot, because they look so realistic. A lump of dough, on the other hand, can be made into any shape and can be a potato, apple, swede, cake, scone, bread roll, or rolled to look like a carrot or turnip, or flattened to become a plate, pizza or pancake. The best play props are those which can be transformed to represent all sorts of different things. Young children do need objects which are literal likenesses of what they represent. The examples here do that. The transformations into different representations (making one thing stand for another) will depend on the first-hand experience of the child. The child who has not seen a sweet potato, or a star fruit, will not transform dough creatively into either of these. Similarly, a child who has seen and used a mobile phone will be able to engage with a set of wooden blocks, and select one which can be a play prop, and represent a mobile phone by holding a wooden block to their ear. This is creative, but creativity depends on first-hand experience and understanding that one thing can be used as a symbol to represent another. Seeing the creative possibilities for symbolic representation in the use of play props means rich and sophisticated play develops. The richer the play, the more the development and learning can be seen in life beyond the play.

Figure 17.3 The best play props are those which can be transformed to represent all sorts of different things. This girl is using blocks to make a road. She has experience of roads in real life. Children use their real experiences in their creative play

4. The moment and conditions must be right in order for play to develop

Play cannot be forced on children. A child needs to be in the right frame of mind, because play cannot be timetabled. Having adults who support and help play along will make all the difference. Children are likely to choose to play, and to play with greater quality, if they feel supported to play by the adults they spend time with. Under these circumstances, play begins to flourish.

5. Play allows children to escape from the here and now, and to move in time and space

In the early life of a child, or until the symbolic development is present, children exist in the present. Their play is dictated by the senses, seeing, smelling, tasting, touching and hearing, and by the way they move and explore with people and objects. Typically, we see babies and toddlers combining people and objects in their play. They grab the necklace from their mother's neck, or the glasses from their father's nose. They anticipate the 'tickly under there' from the adult playing with them, singing 'Round and round the garden'. Psycho-dynamic theories emphasise this relationship with people and objects (Slade and Palmer Wolf, 1994) and Piaget (1968) illuminated the importance of the sensorimotor period. Vygotsky (1978) focused on the way in which early social relationships form the basis of higher-level thinking and functioning, as in imaginative play. Piaget also showed the importance of the symbolic life of the child in creative, imaginative play. Language, walking and becoming a symbol maker and symbol user emerge along with greater possibilities for creativity and imagination. Freedom from the constraints of living in the here and now means that children move from literal play to more advanced, sophisticated forms of play.

6. Literal play changes into symbolic, pretend play

The toddler who is ironing the clothes in the home corner, who says out loud to herself, 'I ironing for the baby' is on the edge of pretend play. She is imitating the adult she sees doing the family ironing. As she enters further into the world of pretending, she will move into the role of the person ironing for the baby. She will create a character to become. She will use the personalities of people she has met, and the moods people have at different moments. She might be the cross mother, the inexperienced father, who is learning how to iron because he wants to be a modern father! There are many possibilities, depending on the experiences the child has had of different people. Into this mix, there will also be possibilities of different characters from literature and television. Children bring into their play the people they meet in stories. They begin to explore and experiment if encouraged to do so. The play becomes more abstract in the use of symbolic representations, and less rooted and trapped in reality and so is less literal or real, and more engaged with imaginative possibilities, and alternative ways of living and being.

7. Playing alone helps children to reflect and know themselves

Solitary play makes an important contribution to later creativity. Children need personal space, just as they need companionship and collaborative, social play. Solitary play is very different from being lonely. Children need time and possibilities to develop their ideas, and to do this they need time with themselves. They often like to be near others when they do so, but they need to be free from interruption. One of the problems of modern life, outlined earlier in this chapter, suggests that life in crowded situations means there is often a lack of space to allow for this kind of reflective play.

8. Play with one other child, or one other adult, has an important contribution to make

Children seem to benefit from playing with one other, providing they do not feel invaded or dominated by the co-player. Stephen and Ann (both five years of age) enjoyed playing together. Ann would take her dolls-house dolls and some of the furniture to Stephen's house, and they would make a train scenario using his miniature train set. There were different towns, which connected, with characters who lived in different places travelling on the train.

Grandma and Joanna (four years) played jumble sales together. Joanna sold the articles, and Grandma came into the room as a different character each time.

The important thing is that each of the play partners in these examples is emotionally engaged (Bredikyte, 2011) with their character, and the narrative. This made the play of a deeper and more sophisticated kind.

9. Collaborative, social play demands each player can develop and sustain their play agenda, and make it resonate and chime with that of others so that the play flows

One afternoon, in the Festival Hall, on the South Bank in London, it was pouring with rain outside. Many families sheltered and ate picnics in the large open space inside known as the ballroom. There is a small platform at one end, with ropes around it. Two girls, aged about seven years, ran over and climbed on it. Together they performed a complex movement rather like an advanced from of 'pat-a-cake'. A younger child (about four years) joined them, and watched. Other girls arrived. The younger children tried to echo what the older girls did, and gradually about eight girls formed a row and all made variations, some watching, some doing. The girl who had led the way to the platform was the leader. She then began a complex snaking movement and led everyone off the platform, weaving about, behind curtains, in and out of families, and back to the platform where once again pat-a-cakes in various forms were performed. It was like a chorus with the snaking dance as a variation in between. It was as if the older girl instinctively knew that the younger children could not perform the movements accurately enough to hold their attention and keep them satisfied, and so she choreographed easier sections in between which they thoroughly enjoyed and wanted to participate in. This was free-flow group play. It was very creative too.

Gradually boys arrived. They were older. About nine to eleven years of age. The lead girl tried to control the situation by indicating that the complex pat-a-cake movements were the secret code of the play. But the boys began to weave in and out of the girls, as if inviting them to snake dance on the platform (rather than in the room as they had been doing). The lead girl stood as if trying to decide what to do, seeing she was losing control of the group of girls. She made a huge movement, with a large leap, and then led the girls off the platform, and then the boys and girls snake-danced together. The lead boy and the lead girl seemed to take it in turns to be at the head of the snaking meandering dancers.

10. Deep play means deep involvement in the play by the players

The girls (four- to seven-year-olds) in the play above concentrated for over an hour. The play showed no sign of disintegrating after the arrival of the boys, and was still flowing when I left the Festival Hall. Involvement means great concentration in the play, and can be described as children wallowing in their play, because they are so engaged they are difficult to distract.

It is not only the older children who are involved in free-flow play. Babies and toddlers are too. On the same occasion as in the above observation, a toddler followed his grandmother who ran across the ballroom and hid behind a screen. They played peek-a-boo. He looked at the girls on the platform, and it felt as if he was interested in being up there too. His grandmother ran back to his parents, and he followed her. The next time, she ran to the platform, and up the steps, ran across the back, so as not to disturb the girls, and then down the steps on the other side of the platform, across the hall, and back to the parents. He followed. During the hour that followed he began to develop routes and to initiate these. His grandmother, and then later his father, followed him. Then his baby brother (an advanced crawler on the brink of walking) followed him, with grandmother supporting the teamwork. Interestingly, he allowed his baby brother to lead the crawling as often as he expected the baby to follow him. He seemed to understand that grandmother or father could follow his lead every time, but his baby brother would need to lead the play or would lose concentration too quickly for the play to flow.

11. Play helps children to apply their learning

Fröbel believed that play helps children to make the inner outer and the outer inner (Bruce, 2012). Children use what they know and understand and have been learning form their first-hand experiences of people, culture and the physical world of nature, and they take these into their play scenarios. They apply what they know inside the play situations they create. In this way, the outer becomes inner. But play also involves the child in making what becomes inner outer. This is supported by recent work by Kravtsova (2010 cited in Bredikyte, 2011) which suggests that children, through their play, become able to view themselves in the play role and narrative of the play scenario, and at the same time, to view themselves from the outside. Play allows the child to be both subjective and objective at the same time. Hakkarainen (2009) and Bredikyte (2011) call these mature forms of play. Mature play opens up the possibilities for creativity.

12. Play is an integrating mechanism, which unleashes creativity

We talk about the importance of people being grounded, centred, together. Having a rich inner life, which is able to link with and connect to the outer world, and to use this as a tool through which to experiment safely with life, ways of living and being, possible alternatives, and impossibilities make free-flowing play an important contributor to creativity. Evil, wickedness, forces of good and kindness introduce moral aspects. Doing things in different ways frees the mind and emotions to invent, create and be innovative in the arts, sciences and humanities. The kind of play reflected upon through the 12 features identified has the possibility to develop deep thinking, thoughtful feelings and creativity.

Scenario

You see three-year-old Zac going to the shelf and taking a box of small-world animals. How conducive is this to encouraging the child's creativity?

- Are the animals a mix of prehistoric, farm, African, Indian, insects, sea etc?
- How much does this child know about different categories of animals and where and how they live, feed, what they do? Could the animals be sorted into separate boxes so that they are presented to children in a more logical way?
- Has the child any experience of the living animals in real life? At a zoo, lakeside, nature in a park?
- Could you provide any real experiences to give children a firm foundation from which they can create themes and creative play scenarios?
- More specifically, which animals in the box are attracting the attention of Zac? The crocodile? Are you wondering why? Is it the linear shape, the snapping jaws?
- Could you develop Zac's understanding of crocodiles by creating the pretend habitat, river, or showing interest in the teeth. Look at your teeth, teeth of other children, watching a film about crocodiles (say five minutes maximum) and talking about it. Ideally a visit to the zoo. Sing an action song about crocodiles, and make a home-made book about crocodiles.

Imagination – part of play and so much more – inseparably connected with creativity

A convincing definition of imagination is given by Peter McKellar (1957), who argues that imagination is the rearrangement of past experience in new and fascinating ways. Imagination gives the young child the possibility to live outside the present, and to use past experience as a resource, which can transform the present and also create alternative and wide-ranging futures. Imagination, as Bruner (1996) argued, allows human beings to think beyond the here and now. Imagination is rooted in real experience. But it does allow for the possibility of making new connections between those experiences. In this respect, it makes powerful links with creative processes and creative acts.

Imagination is anchored in images formed in the brain. These might be visual images, sound images, or images of taste, smell and touch. Or they might be images stored through movement feedback that are called kinaesthetic. Images of all kinds serve an important purpose. They help us to keep hold of past experiences, and to use them as a resource. As the brain develops, images become more mobile, and can be manipulated more readily.

Piaget (1952b) pioneered the view that images, imitation and symbolic representation are linked as language, walking and pretending emerged and made a major contribution to our understanding of imaginative play in young children. Images are very internal, however, and so it is a huge challenge for those spending time with young children to try and work out what is in their minds, and what is in their imagination. Fröbel (Bruce, 2012) believed that one of the main tasks of the educator is to support children as they strive to make the inner outer, and to transform these feelings and thoughts, ideas, relationships and physical learnings in ways which are conducive to making them internalised again. The flow of inner images, transformed to be shared with others into outer forms, but returned to an inner life once again and held inwardly, is at the heart of the deeper kinds of learning.

Creativity – catching clouds and pinning them down

Images are internal, and so are creative processes. But when the imagination feeds creativity, the processes of creativity are at times pinned down and become acts of creation. There is tangible form in an act of creation, whether it is a scientific theory, invention of the world wide web, developing a welfare state with a national health service, or creating a sculpture, choreographed dance or musical composition. Acts of creation occur in science and technology, the humanities and the arts.

Creative processes are, in important ways, about what can be done with the imagination (the internal images developed during early childhood). Different writers on creativity seem to agree that neither children nor adults are aware of how they came to have an idea. There is agreement that certain things have to happen in order for a creative idea to emerge. During the creative process thinking is allowed to drift and meander. It is as if thinking becomes dream-like, and does not obey the rules of logic and common sense. Then thinking is pulled together by the thinker (who may be a child or an adult), and a creative act takes place. The creative process results in a creation. The drifting, meandering and dreamlike thinking opens up the possibilities for new connections and creative thoughts to be made. Many of these will remain as thoughts, internal and private, unexpressed or shared. Sometimes creative processes take tangible form so that creativity (the process) becomes a creation which moves from being internal to becoming externally formed and possible to place in the outside world.

Frank Barron (1955: 281) suggested that creative people embrace 'complexity of outlook, independence of judgement and originality'. His research with those involved in the arts and sciences found that original and creative thinkers used richness of experiences to the full, even though this often led them into discord and disorder of thought as a result. Those who resisted allowing themselves to embrace experiences which caused them discomfort and a feeling of disorder preferred to be in their comfort zone and to lead a simpler life, even though this excluded them from some aspects of reality. Barron (1955: 286) hypothesises that creative thinkers produce 'adaptive responses which are unusual'. The range of experiences in which this occurs depends on the degree of freedom and independence that exists in the community or social world of the person.

This has deep implications for the kind of family life structure and atmosphere and the educational setting that a child experiences. Barron states (1955: 286): 'There are at hand enough case histories of both organisations, political and private, to make it clear that the sort of unity and balance that depends upon suppression of the claims of minority affects and opinions is maladaptive in the long run.' He goes on to say that creative thinking and acts of creation flourish 'where suppression is at a minimum and where some measure of disintegration is tolerable in the interests of the higher levels of integration' (Barron, 1955: 286). Higher levels of integration mean children need to be supported in learning to become, as educated people, able to self-regulate, rather than always depending on being regulated by others.

In other words, Frank Barron is typical of writers on creativity in taking the view that creative thinking involves messy thinking, which defies the usual rules of logic and common sense, and meanders and drifts. He is also typical in emphasising that thoughts are later drawn together in what he terms 'final form', resulting in 'independence of judgement, freedom of expression, and novelty of construction and insight' (Barron, 1955: 287).

Unlike most writers on creativity, he does not place all the emphasis on creativity in individuals. He believes that the conditions which cultivate creativity in individuals can be applied more broadly in order to develop creative societies and creative epochs. 'Freedom of expression and movement, lack of fear of dissent and contradiction, a willingness to break with custom, a spirit of play as well as of dedication to work, purpose on a grand scale' (Barron, 1955: 288).

These themes arise time and again in the literature on creativity so that, as stated in Bruce (2011b), a pattern emerges (see Wallas in Storr, 1989; Koestler, 1964; Howkins, 2001; Craft, 2002; Duffy, 2009). More recently the writings on the subject of creativity by Fumoto *et al.* (2012) and Dowling (2012 in press) also chime with those that have gone before.

There is a serious problem in the history of education across the world, in that adults who hold power often favour a simple approach to life, with clear answers and a lack of ambiguity, complexity or uncertainty. This means that creativity is not understood or encouraged in general. Early childhood education has always led the way in the cultivation of creativity, but more often than not it comes under threat as children begin statutory education. Creativity cannot be taught. It can only be cultivated. The conditions for its cultivation have to be right, or it cannot develop and flourish. See Chapter 5 on creativity, pages 108–111.

Reflective task

Look at the provision indoors and outdoors in your setting.

- How much opportunity do children have to choose how they use materials or experiences they are offered?
- Is the focus on narrow, adult-led activities, or offering broad experiences?
- What constraints do you put on the way materials are used?

Constraints on creativity

The idea still lurks that some people are born creative and others are not. It is true that not many people compose music, choreograph dances, write poetry, make original paintings or sculptures, weavings or knittings. Few people pioneer new theories or projects of science and mathematics, engineering, technology or medicine. Those who develop new ways of working in the humanities, in social justice, reconciliation or ethics are few.

It is important to look at how children are encouraged, or not, to be creative from an early age. It could well be that more people could be creative if their early childhood experiences cultivated their creativity.

Figure 17.4 Children need to be encouraged to be creative from an early age

We hear people say, 'They are a very musical family.' The grandparents, their children and grandchildren all seem to play musical instruments, to read music, and to improvise, and even to turn the improvisations into musical composition. It is likely that, in such families, ways of encouraging musical creativity have developed. The family is probably unaware that they are doing this. Perhaps more families could be creative in the arts, sciences and humanities, given more help in knowing how to encourage it.

The first Elizabethan age in England is often referred to as the Golden Age of English Music, when madrigals thrived. Ordinary people sang and sight-read music in the evenings as a community. Singers could hold a part and beautiful music was created both at court and in country life. For the first time, complex music, such as madrigals, was sung by ordinary people. Previously, the more sophisticated music was confined to those at court or aristocrats in their grand houses. This was an epoch of musical creativity. Although by modern standards there was constraint in freedom of expression, there was less fear in Elizabeth's reign than in the earlier reigns of the boy King Edward VI, when there was fierce enforcement of Protestantism by those in charge, or of the ardently Roman Catholic Queen Mary, when there were many burnings at the stake. In comparison, Elizabeth I was more moderate, and through her visits staying in stately houses around the country (known as Royal Progresses), she encouraged secular country music/dance and court music/dance, as well as music for the church. She introduced music from ordinary people to the court, and there was a flow between the two contexts, which enriched both. This happens when music and dance are not elitist, and instead are inclusive and embrace diversity.

In the late 1960s most of the funding for the arts from the Arts Council was allocated to the Royal Opera House, the major orchestras and the Royal Ballet, and art galleries and museums with collections of the works of dead artists (painters, sculptors etc). There were two strands in this. One was the emphasis on funding the arts that appeal to a small elite. The second strand showed an overwhelming lack of funding for living artists (Bruce *et al.*, 1972). During the 1980s funding for the arts was cut dramatically, but since then there has been a steady trend towards funding community arts with the meagre amounts of funding available. This leaves little opportunity for professionally trained dancers or artists (including painters, sculptors, ceramicists), musicians or film-makers to contribute to the arts.

The elite forms of art have been greatly reduced, and community arts groups are often peopled by those working as unpaid volunteers. Creativity in the arts flourishes when there is a strong tradition through the more elite forms, with schools of dance, music and art handing on techniques which can be used, rejected or expanded and developed by those trained in them. Alongside this there need to be possibilities for choreographers, composers and artists to experiment in smaller, less traditional and more open contexts. Third, the community needs encouragement and opportunity to participate in the arts, with funding to bring this about, while many taking part will do so as volunteers. Currently the middle strand is neglected and seriously underfunded. The traditional, more elite strand is shrinking, and this is unhealthy for the future. It is important to remember that one of the hallmarks of a civilisation lies in the way that it values creativity in the arts.

Creativity does not have to be the gift of a few. Neither is it necessary to be a genius in order to be creative. It is certainly true that only a few people will be creative to the extent that their ideas and actions bring about world-shaking impact from their creativity. But they might make a worthwhile and very useful contribution to their field of work, or their favourite pastimes. However, as suggested earlier in this chapter, most creativity is of the everyday kind. Everyday creativity leads to fulfilled lives, and fulfilled people contribute more to their families, communities and the world in general. They have interests and concerns. They care deeply, and engage with life. They are prepared to venture outside their comfort zone, and are tolerant of other points of view. They will not be pushed into accepting the ideas of others in order to conform. They dare to be different. These are good citizens because they reflect and participate in their community, making it a better place to live.

Often, and this is made worse by the fact that official curriculum documents tend to place creative development within the arts, creativity is presented as an artistic aspect of human behaviour. We see terms such as the 'expressive and creative arts' in curriculum documents, but we don't see references to 'expressive and creative science', or 'expressive and creative humanities'. Until we see creativity as central to the arts, sciences and humanities, creativity will not be fully encouraged in young children in family and community life, in the wider world, or in their education beyond the home. Until then, creativity will not be given the status it should have throughout each phase of education and life.

The arts, sciences and humanities

Performing art and creative art – there is a difference

In the countries where there is a national curriculum, there is emphasis, almost exclusively, on creativity in the arts, and neglect of its contribution in the sciences and the humanities. However, within the confines of this emphasis on creativity in the arts, there is also confusion about the difference between performance art and creative art. Perhaps some of the confusion arises because it is often the case that the performer and the creator are the same person. It is easier to see the difference between the two if an example is taken from a painter such as Raphael. In art galleries it is not unusual to see a painting labelled 'the school of Raphael'. The painter Raphael created the idea for the painting and then showed his students how to paint in his style. The students are performing a task set by the master painter. Another example would be the designer Cath Kidston, who created the design for a handbag, and the performance task in this case is in the manufacture of the patterns, using machinery to do so.

Children who are required to copy a painting in the style of Monet, or to write a story in the style of 'Once upon a time …', or to learn the steps for a country dance and then to perform it, are performing a task. They are not being creative in the strict sense.

There can be a degree of creativity within a task, and this is called interpretation. When an actor 'performs' the role of Hamlet in Shakespeare's play, or Darcy Bussell 'performs' the role of Giselle in the ballet of that name, they are interpreting, and will inevitably bring something of their own to their performance. Nowadays, there is greater coming together of performance, creativity and interpretation . Some choreographers encourage dancers to contribute their ideas during the creating process, and before the creation of a piece. Examples of this way of creating dance would be the well-established work of Siobhan Davies.

Mixed media

Many artists nowadays use a mixture of forms in their creations. Dance choreographers, for example, use film, and text, drama and music in a balanced way as in the recent work of Hannah Bruce at Clarence Mews, or at the Hoxton Arts Centre or the Langford Courtyard, where attention is given to film, music, architecture, text, narration and dance. Both performance and creativity are important.

Appreciating creativity in the arts and in science – who cares? Are audiences necessary?

Creative people are usually autonomous, self-regulating and self-disciplined. They do not do their work for external reward, or in order to receive public praise. However, most artists appreciate an audience to view their work, whether they be potters, choreographers, composers, film-makers or sculptors. Creativity in the arts is more likely to be appreciated by audiences if it is in tune with group thinking. A postmodern art object is more likely to be applauded and placed in an art gallery during the period when postmodernism is the zeitgeist. But art often challenges audiences because it takes people out of their comfort zones, and away from what has gone before, such as the work of Damien Hirst or Tracey Emin.

In the world of science, a new hypothesis might lead to an important impact on the world, such as a cure for malaria, or the invention of plastic. A new drug may be created by scientists, but the drug company funding this might exert power and influence the promotion of it. When looking at scientific research it is important to look first at who is funding it. Scientists need a different sort of appreciative audience from that of the artist. There needs to be agreement between scientists that the tests they have carried out are valid, reliable and robust. Scientists need as their audience other scientists. Often their work is too specialised for the general population to be able to form a view. Those who hold specialist knowledge which can have the power of life and death over others can be held in awe, or they can be seen as dangerous. The witch doctor who could cure certain illnesses would often be seen as the wise man or woman, who would live in a separate place from the rest of the community, held in deep respect and often fear. The scientific theory of evolution developed by Darwin (who acknowledged the work of Wallace) was so dangerous in exploding traditional thinking about the evolution of the animal world, including the origins of human beings, that it was not published until after his death in order to protect his family. Creativity requires courage, both in the arts and the sciences.

The humanities

Something very important is becoming established, in that the humanities are making greater and greater contributions to developments in sciences of all kinds. During the Second World War scientists working on nuclear fission realised that the act of developing a nuclear bomb would be appalling in its consequences. They held back from sharing their work with politicians so that a bomb of this kind was delayed. This is explored in a play called *Copenhagen* by Michael Frayn. The humanitarian aspect and impact of creations in science were given focus. This coming together of science and the humanities is becoming increasingly apparent.

Scientists in Africa had the creative idea that animals such as gorillas or elephants should be protected. Areas were fenced off in order to preserve the habitat of these animals. People were kept out, and sometimes whole communities were moved from their homes. This caused poverty, and destroyed traditional ways of living. With specialists in the humanities working together with creative conservationist scientists, ways forward are being found. The habitats of the animals are not destroyed, and the people living there can do so in harmony, with no need to poach if careful consideration is given to the needs of both animals and people together. This kind of creative thinking could literally save the future of our planet.

One of the great challenges for those involved in creative thinking in the humanities is the inevitable clashes that occur between the humanities and politics. The humanities look to the long term. A creative idea might take 20 years (typically) to be understood and to begin to take root. Politicians may begin with a long-term vision, but the pressures upon them in gaining and holding power usually take over, and in the main they come to look at issues in short-term ways. Another problem for creative thinkers in the humanities is that the original idea, across the 20 or so years, becomes reinterpreted and distorted, so that it no longer remains in its original conceptualisation.

An example is found in the welfare state concept of council housing. Originally the creative idea was that hard-working people could not afford a mortgage, but with a bit of help by having low-rent housing they would be able to contribute as good citizens living respectable lives in communities, relieved of the anxieties of making ends meet with a mortgage or having to pay high rents. Then it became possible for families to buy their council houses, thus reducing the stock available, while across time this creative idea has been transformed into economically poor and vulnerable families being placed in council houses, when, without this support, they might become homeless. Recently this creative idea has again been transformed to suggest that families might only be allowed to stay in council houses for a set period before being required to move out. Having a creative idea in the humanities carries with it the challenge of how that idea is interpreted and implemented across quite long periods of time.

Creative people dare to be different

When we look across time at the arts, humanities and sciences, we see that people who were creative thinkers have often been branded as revolutionary. They have taken us out of our comfort zones, and we have had to look at things in a different way. They have dared to be different. It is not unusual for someone who is being creative to need to show some courage. This applies at all levels of creativity, from world-shattering creative acts, to creativity in specialist fields of work, and even in everyday creativity.

The creative process and the creative act

Different writers on creativity have suggested similar features of its processes (see Bruce, 2011b for more details on this). Adults play a critical role in supporting and encouraging creativity in babies, toddlers and young children. Adults who respect and tune into what interests a child are off to a good start. It is also important not to invade the child's space and take over the child's interest by over-organising. Children flourish in their creativity when they spend time with adults who are good observers, and who are sensitive to their personal space and autonomy. Adults who cultivate creativity in babies, toddlers and young children are aware of their need for supportive companionship. They arrange and organise the learning environment indoors and outdoors in ways which are conducive to the child's possibilities to incubate and hatch out creative ideas, thoughts, feelings and relationships.

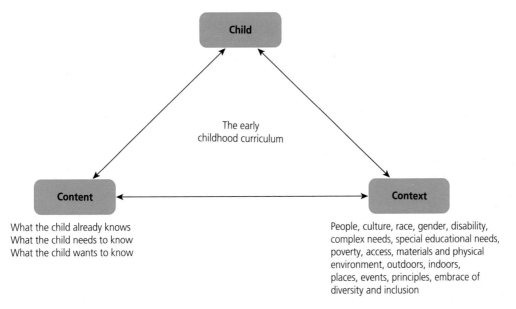

Figure 17.5 The three Cs of the early childhood curriculum (Bruce, 2011c)

Some children are fortunate enough to grow up in families which support and encourage creativity. Other children meet educators who cultivate their creativity, and who actively engage in seeking out and developing the creativity in the family too. Working with other people's children requires mature, well-educated, appropriately and highly trained educators (Tickell, 2011; Nutbrown, 2012). This involves using observation skills developed from knowledge of child development, which allow the adult to tune into the child's interests and needs, and to offer well-matched, supportive and extending educationally worthwhile experiences. This chimes with the tip of the triangle in Figure 17.5.

Much of the discussion in this chapter gives focus to the context in which this takes place. The materials and resources provided indoors and outdoors are of central importance. So are the people children spend time with. Creativity depends on the way adults develop the autonomy, interests and needs of children. If adults treat children as unique individuals, they are much more likely to cultivate creativity in them. If they recognise that creativity is a strong urge in human beings, they will look out for its processes and find it in all children, including those with special educational needs and complex needs, those from vulnerable families, or economic poverty. They will cultivate creativity in boys and girls, and will use diversity as a resource to enable creativity to flourish. The triangle in Figure 17.5 summarises the contextual aspects of creativity.

Reflective task

Observe a child aged two to five years in a garden. Using the triangle in Figure 17.5 as a navigational tool to guide you, analyse your observation. Are you seeing any creative learning?

The third point of the triangle in Figure 17.5 emphasises that there are aspects of knowledge and understanding that children already know about and find fascinating, and other areas that children want to learn about. Creativity depends deeply on these established and emergent interests being cultivated. The content of learning is also about what society and the culture in which the child is growing up deem to be important. This is important too, although it is necessary to bear in mind that in some countries, such as those in the UK, this has become increasingly politically driven since the late 1980s. This only emphasises that, despite this situation, it is the responsibility of educators to ensure that cultivating creativity is at the heart of the third point in the triangle diagram. This is needed across the teaching of the arts, sciences and humanities.

Cultivating creativity – the heart of the curriculum and pedagogy

A good companion who cultivates creativity

Throughout this chapter the need for children to be with adults they trust and feel comfortable with through a warm, affectionate, attached relationship is highlighted. Being connected in this way allows children to become confident about trying new ways of doing things, and experimenting with their own ideas, thoughts, feelings and relationships, which is crucial if they are to be creative. The 'key person' of the Early Years Foundation Stage or EYFS (DfE, 2012a) can make an important contribution in this within the English context. In Finland, Milda Bredikyte (2011) is further developing her work on the role of the educator in cultivating play in toddlers and young children. This is closely linked to creativity.

Creative ideas that fall by the wayside – part of life

One of the things that adults find difficult when working with young children is the way many creative ideas look as if they are leading to something tangible as the play flows along, only to evaporate and fade suddenly. For every creative idea, there will be many that fall by the wayside. The whole point of free-flowing play is that it cannot be pinned down. The same can be said of the processes involved in creative thinking.

Meandering – but is this always purposeless?

Children sometimes look as if they lack purpose, when in fact they are following through an idea. They need to meander when they do this. Chris Athey (1990) suggests that when children do so they are fitting ideas together, and it is not 'flitting about' without any focus. Part of the skill of the adult is to recognise when a child is incubating and simmering ideas as part of the creative process, and needing to meander though materials seeking what is needed.

Cultivating creativity indoors and outdoors

Both the atmosphere and the physical environment are central to the cultivation of creativity. The way that materials and resources are offered indoors and outdoors is as important as the material and resources themselves. The way that adults interact with children as they explore, experiment and discover these is equally important.

Children arrive at a setting with the expectation that there will be interesting things to do. Planning the environment will be of a general nature, but it should also offer individual experiences to children. These will be based on the observation of children. If children are to be encouraged in their creativity, the emphasis will need to be on offering experiences which will help children to further develop what they can do and what they find interesting. Planning which focuses on what the child cannot do is based on a deficit model of the child. It is more efficient and impactful to work on the strengths of the child, and usually this means the weaker aspects of the child's learning are tackled in a positive atmosphere. Read more about outdoor play in Chapter 9.

Reflective task

- How do you create learning environments indoors and outdoors which encourage creativity?
- How open-ended are your materials?
- Do you offer broad, enriching experiences or tightly adult-controlled activities?

Conclusion

Creativity does not happen unless it is cultivated. Children need to spend time with adults who, as a team, share the view that creativity is important and who actively promote it. Typically, it is thought that babies are too underdeveloped to be creative. Not so long ago people used to laugh at the idea that babies could enjoy books. It is now a well-established fact that they do. The more that is understood about human development, the more it is becoming realised that babies can be creative. It is exciting to work with babies precisely because they are at the emergent stages of their possibilities of becoming creative.

It is not necessary to wait until a child can perform certain techniques for creativity to be present. It is important not to place the main focus on the products of creation, rather than the processes which cultivate it. The processes of creativity explored in this chapter open up the educational possibilities for children (and throughout life). The emphasis in this chapter on creativity needing to be at the heart of education throughout life gives an inclusive approach, and rejects the view that children with special needs, disabilities or complex needs, children with health problems or who are vulnerable cannot be creative.

Evaluate your...

Learning

Whichever country in the world you are working in, take another look at the national framework document if there is one (for example, in England, Scotland, Wales, Northern Ireland, Ireland, New Zealand) and examine it from the point of view of how it helps you to encourage and cultivate the creativity of the young children you work with.

- ■ Is there more emphasis on some areas than others?
- ■ Is it possible to introduce an emphasis on creativity in every aspect of the framework?
- ■ Do you think it is important to try and do this?

Further reading

Brooker, L. and Edwards, S. (eds.) (2010) *Engaging Play*, Maidenhead: Open University and McGraw-Hill.

Craft, A. (2011) *Creativity and Early Years Education*, London: Continuum.

Duffy, B. (2009) *Supporting Creativity and Imagination in the Early Years* (2nd edn), Maidenhead: Open University Press.

Rogers, S. (2011) 'Play and pedagogy: A conflict of interest?', in Rogers, S. (ed.) (2011) *Rethinking Play and Pedagogy in Early Childhood Education: Concepts, Contexts and Cultures*, London: Routledge.

Tims, C. (2010) (ed.) *'Creative learning in the early years is not just child's play...': Born creative*, London: DEMOS. Available from: http://www.demos.co.uk.

Tovey, H. (2007) *Playing Outdoors: Spaces and Places, Risk and Challenge*, Maidenhead: Open University Press.

Bibliography

Tip: check with your training provider if any of these books are available as e-books, or if they can get books on loan for you from other libraries.

All internet references were last accessed in August 2012.

Abrams, D. (2010) *Processes of prejudice: Theory, evidence and intervention*, Manchester: Equality and Human Rights Commission Research report 56. Available from: http://www. equalityhumanrights.com/uploaded_files/research/56_processes_of_prejudice.pdf.

Adair, J. E. (1973) *Action-Centred Leadership*, London: McGraw-Hill, in Cole, G. A. and Kelly, P. (2011) *Management Theory and Practice* (7th edn), Singapore: Cengage Learning.

Ainsworth, M. D. (1962) *Deprivation of Maternal Care: A reassessment of its effects*, Geneva: World Health Organization.

Ainsworth, M. D. (1969) 'Object relations, dependency, and attachment: A theoretical review of the infant–mother relationship', *Child Development*, vol. 40, pp. 969–1025.

Ainsworth, M. D. (1979) 'Attachment as related to mother–infant interaction', *Advances in the Study of Behavior*, vol. 9, pp. 2–52.

Ainsworth, M. D. (1985) 'Attachments across the lifespan', *Bulletin of the New York Academy of Medicine*, vol. 61, pp. 792–812.

Ainsworth, M. D. (1989) 'Attachment beyond infancy', *American Psychologist*, vol. 44, pp. 709–16.

Ainsworth, M. D. and Bell, S. (1970) 'Attachment, exploration, and separation: Illustrated by the behavior of one-year-olds in a strange situation', *Child Development,* vol. 41, no. 1. pp. 49–67.

Ainsworth, M. D. and Bowlby, J. (1991) 'An ethological approach to personality development', *American Psychologist*, vol. 46, no. 4, pp. 333–41.

Ainsworth, M. D., Blehar, M. C., Waters, E., and Wall, S. (1978) *Patterns of Attachment: A psychological study of the strange situation*, Hillsdale, NJ: Lawrence Erlbaum Associates.

Airdrie, K. (2006) 'Abused Child Mary Ellen Wilson' [online]. Available from: http://historicalbiographies.suit101.com/article.cfm/abused_child_mary_ellen_wilson.

Alanen, L. and Mayall, B. (eds.) (2001) *Conceptualising child–adult relations*, London: Routledge Falmer.

Albright, T., Jessell, T., Kandel, E. and Posner M. (2000) 'Neural science: A century of progress and the mysteries that remain', *Cell*, vol. 100, *Neuron*, vol. 25, no. 1, S1–55.

Alderson, P. (2002) 'Children, healing, suffering and voluntary consent', in Bendelow, G., Carpenter, M., Vautier, C. and Williams, S. (eds.) *Gender Health and Healing: The public/private divide*, London: Routledge Falmer.

Alderson, P. and Morrow, V. (2011) *The Ethics of Research with Children and Young People: A practical handbook*, London: SAGE Publications.

Aldgate, J. (2006) 'Children, Development and Ecology', in Aldgate, J., Jones, D., Rose, W. and Jeffery, C. (eds.) *The Developing World of the Child*, London: Jessica Kingsley Publishers.

Aldgate, J., Jones, D. P. H., Rose, W. and Jeffery, C. (eds.) (2006) *The Developing World of the Child*, London: Jessica Kingsley.

Alexander, R. (2010) *The Independent Review of the Primary Curriculum*, Nottingham: Department for Children, Schools and Families.

Allen, G. (2011) *Early Intervention: The Next Steps. An Independent Report to Her Majesty's Government*, London: HM Government. Available from: http://www.dwp.gov.uk/docs/early-intervention-next-steps.pdf.

Allen, G. and Duncan Smith, I. (2008) *Early Intervention: Good Parents, Great Kids, Better Citizens*, London: Centre for Social Justice and the Smith Institute.

Allerton, M. (1993) 'Am I asking the right questions? What teachers ask of children', *International Journal of Early Childhood*, vol. 25, no. 1, pp. 42–8.

Allington, S. (2011) *Transitions in the Early Years: A practical guide to support transitions between early years settings and into Key Stage 1*, London: Practical Pre-school.

Anning, A. and Ring, K. (2004) *Making Sense of Children's Drawings*, Maidenhead: Open University.

Anning, A., Cottrell, D., Frost, N., Green, J., Robinson, M. (2006) *Developing Multi-professional Teamwork for Integrated Children's Services*, Maidenhead: Open University Press.

Arai, L. (2011) 'Growing up: moving through time, place and space from babyhood to adolescence', in Foley, P. and Leverett, S. (eds.) *Children and Young People's Spaces*, Milton Keynes: The Open University.

Archard, D. and Skiveness, M. (2009) 'Hearing the child', *Child and Family Social Work*, vol. 14, no. 4, pp. 391–9.

Argyris, C. and Schön, D. (1974) *Theory in Practice: Increasing Professional Effectiveness*, San Francisco: Jossey-Bass.

Arling, G. L. and Harlow, H. F. (1967) 'Effects of social deprivation on maternal behavior of rhesus monkeys', *Journal of Comparative and Physiological Psychology*, vol. 64, no. 3, pp. 371–7.

Arnold, C. (ed.) (2012) *Improving Your Reflective Practice through Stories of Practitioner Research*, London: Routledge.

Ashiabi, G. (2000) 'Promoting the emotional development of preschoolers', *Early Childhood Education Journal*, vol. 28, no. 2, pp. 79–84.

Athey, C. (1990) *Extending Thought in Young Children: A Parent–Teacher Partnership*, London: Paul Chapman.

Athey, C. (2007) *Extending Thought in Young Children: A Parent–Teacher Partnership* (2nd edn), London: Paul Chapman.

Atkin, J. and Bastiani, J. with Goode, J. (1988) *Listening to Parents: An approach to the improvement of home–school relations*, London: Croom Helm.

Atkinson, T. (2003a) 'Learning to teach: Intuitive skills and reasoned objectivity', in Atkinson, T. and Claxton, G. (2003) *The Intuitive Practitioner*, Maidenhead: Open University Press.

Atkinson, T. (2003b) 'Trusting your own judgement (or allowing yourself to eat the pudding)', in Atkinson, T. and Claxton, G. (2003) *The Intuitive Practitioner*, Maidenhead: Open University Press.

Aubrey, C. (2011) *Leading and Managing in the Early Years*, London: SAGE Publications.

Aubrey, C. and Dahl, S. (2006) 'Children's voices: the views of vulnerable children on their service providers and the relevance of services they receive', *British Journal of Social Work*, vol. 36, no. 1, pp. 21–9.

Aubrey, C., David, T., Godfrey, R. and Thompson, L. (2000) *Early Childhood Educational Research: Issues in Methodology and Ethics*, London: The Falmer Press.

Avon Longitudinal Study of Parents and Children (2012) University of Bristol [online]. Available from: http://www.bristol.ac.uk/alspac.

Axford, N. (2008) *Exploring concepts of child well-being: Implications for children's services*, Bristol: Policy Press.

Axline, V. M. (1969) *Play Therapy*, New York: Ballantine Books.

Ayling, P. (2012) 'Learning through playing in Higher Education: Promoting play as a skill for social work students', *Social Work Education: The International Journal*, vol. 31, no. 6., pp. 764–77.

Ayres, A. J. (1972) *Sensory Integration and Learning Disorders*, Los Angeles, CA: Western Psychological Services.

Ayres, A. J. (1989) *Sensory Integration and Praxis Test*, Los Angeles, CA: Western Psychological Services.

Ayres, A. J. (2005) *Sensory Integration and the Child: 25th Anniversary Edition*, Los Angeles, CA: Western Psychological Services.

Bailey, R. (2011) *Letting Children Be Children: Report of an Independent Review of the Commercialisation and Sexualisation of Childhood*, London: Department for Education.

Bainbridge-Cohen, B. (2008) *Sensing, Feeling and Action* (2nd edn), Berkeley, CA: North Atlantic Books.

Baldock, P. (2010) *Cultural Diversity in the Early Years*, London. Sage.

Baldwin, P. (2004) *With Drama in Mind: Real Learning in Imagined Worlds*, London and New York: Continuum.

Ball, S. C. (1994) *Start Right Report*, London: RSA.

Bandura, A. (1976) *Social Learning Theory*, Englewood Cliffs, NJ: Prentice Hall.

Bandura, A. (1986) *Social Foundations of Thought and Action*, Englewood Cliffs, NJ: Prentice Hall.

Bandura, A., Ross, D. and Ross, S. A. (1961) 'Transmission of aggression through imitation of aggressive models', *Journal of Abnormal and Social Psychology*, vol. 63, pp. 575–82.

Barker, R. (2008) *Making Sense of Every Child Matters: Multi-professional Practice Guidance*, Bristol: Policy Press.

Barker, R. (2011) *Every Child Matters and the Coalition Government* [Kindle edn].

Barnsley, R. and Thompson, A. (1988*)* 'Birthdate and success in minor hockey: The key to the NHL', *Canadian Journal of Behavioural Science*, vol. 20, no. 2, pp. 167–76.

Barron, F. (1955) 'The disposition toward originality', *Journal of Normal and Social Psychology*, vol. 51, pp. 478–88.

Bastiani, J. (1989) *Working with Parents: A whole-school approach*, London: Routledge.

Batchelor, J. (2008) '"Failure to thrive" revisited', *Child Abuse Review*, vol. 17, no. 3, pp. 147–59.

Bayley, N. (1935) *The Development of Motor Abilities During the First Three Years*, in Gallahue, D. L., Ozmun, J. C. and Goodway, J. (2011) *Understanding Motor Development: Infants, children, adolescents, adults* (7th edn), New York: McGraw-Hill.

Bear, M., Connors, B. and Paradiso, M. (2001) *Neuroscience: Exploring the brain*, London: Lippincott Williams & Wilkins.

Beck, U. (1992) *Risk Society: Towards a new modernity*, London: SAGE Publications.

Beckley, P. (2012) (ed.) *Learning in Early Childhood*, London: SAGE.

Belbin Associates (2012) *Belbin Team Roles* [online]. Available from: http://www.belbin.com/rte.asp.

Belsky, J. and Fearon, R. (2002) 'Infant–mother attachment security, contextual risk, and early development: a moderational analysis', *Development and Psychopathology*, vol. 14, pp. 293–310.

Benard, B. (1995) *Fostering Resilience in Children*, Urbana, IL: ERIC Clearinghouse on Elementary and Early Childhood Education. Available from: http://www.edpsycinteractive.org/files/resilience.html.

Benjamin, A. C. (1994) 'Observations in early childhood classrooms: Advice from the field', *Young Children*, vol. 49, no. 6, pp. 14–20.

Bennathan, M. and Boxall, M. (2000) *Effective Intervention in Primary Schools: Nurture Groups* (2nd edn), London: Fulton.

Bennett J. (2011) 'Early childhood education and care systems: Issue of tradition and governance' (rev. edn), in Tremblay, R. E., Boivin, M., Peters, R. de V. (eds.), *Encyclopedia on Early Childhood Development* [online], Montreal, Quebec: Centre of Excellence for Early Childhood Development and Strategic Knowledge Cluster on Early Child Development, 1–5. Available from: http://www.child-encyclopedia.com/documents/BennettANGxp2.pdf.

Bernstein, N. (1967) *The Co-ordination and Regulation of Movements*, Oxford: Pergamon Press, in Gallahue, D. L., Ozmun, J. C. and Goodway, J. (2011) *Understanding Motor Development: Infants, children, adolescents, adults* (7th edn), New York: McGraw-Hill.

Berthelsen, D., Brownlee, J. and Johansson, E. (eds.) (2009) *Participatory Learning in the Early Years: Research and Pedagogy*, London: Routledge.

Bertram, T. and Pascal, C. (1997) *Effective Early Learning: Case Studies in Improvement*, London: SAGE.

Bessant, J., Hill, R. and Watts, R. (2003) *Discovering Risk: Social Research and Policy Making*, New York: Peter Lang.

Bhana, D. (2009) 'Boys will be boys': what do early childhood teachers have to do with it?' *Educational Review*, vol. 61, no. 3, pp. 327–39.

Bick, E. (1994) 'Notes on infant observation in psychoanalytical training', in *Psychoanalytical Study of Child*, vol. 45, pp. 558–66.

Bion, W. (1962) *Learning Through Experience*, London: Heinemann.

Blackwell, P. (2000) 'The influence of touch on child development: Implications for interventions', *Infants and Young Children*, vol. 13, no. 1, pp. 25–39.

Blackwell, S. and Pound, L. (2011) 'Forest schools in the early years', in Miller, L. and Pound, L. (eds.) *Theories and Approaches to Learning in the Early Years*, London: SAGE Publications.

Blade, H. and Wolf, A. (1990) *Knowledge and Competence*, London: HMSO.

Blakeslee, S. and Blakeslee, M. (2007) *The Body Has a Mind of Its Own*, New York: Random House.

Blanden, J. (2006) *'Bucking the trend': What enables those who are disadvantaged in childhood to succeed later in life?* Working Paper No. 31, Department for Work and Pensions.

BMJ (British Medical Journal) (1988) 'Summary of the Cleveland Inquiry', *British Medical Journal*, vol. 297, no. 6642, pp. 190–1.

Bolden, R. and Kirk, P. (2006) 'From leaders to leadership: Nurturing a leadership culture', *Effective Executive*, vol. 8, no. 10, pp. 27–33.

Borton, T. (1970) *Reach, Teach and Touch*, London: McGraw-Hill.

Boud, D. (2001) 'Using journal writing to enhance reflective practice', in English, L. M. and Gillen, M. A. (eds.) *Promoting Journal Writing in Adult Education. New Directions in Adult and Continuing Education*, no. 90, pp. 9–18.

Bourassa, C., Lavergne, C., Damant, D.; Lessard, G. and Turcotte, P. (2008) 'Child welfare workers' practice in cases involving domestic violence', *Child Abuse Review*, vol. 17, no. 3, pp. 174–190.

Bowlby, J. (1951) *Maternal Care and Mental Health*, World Health Organization Monograph (Serial No. 2), Geneva: World Health Organization, in (1986) 'Citation Classic, *Maternal Care and Mental Health*', Citation Classic, no. 50 [online]. Available from: http://www.garfield.library.upenn.edu/classics1986/A1986F063100001.pdf.

Bowlby, J. (1969) *Attachment and Loss. Vol. I: Attachment*, London: Hogarth Press.

Bowlby, J. (1973) *Attachment and Loss. Vol. II: Separation: Anxiety and Anger*, London: Hogarth Press.

Bowlby, J. (1979) *The Making and Breaking of Affectional Bonds*, New York: Brunner-Routledge.

Bowlby, J. (1980) *Attachment and Loss. Vol. III: Loss: Sadness and Depression*, London: Hogarth Press.

Bowlby, J. (1983) [1969] *Attachment and Loss. Vol. I: Attachment* (2nd edn), New York: Basic Books.

Bowlby, J. (2005) *The Making and Breaking of Affectional Bonds* (new edn), London: Routledge.

Brady, L., Gibbs, J., Henshall, A. and Lewis, J. (2008) *Play and Exercise in Early Years: Physically active play in early childhood provision*, London: Department for Culture, Media and Sport.

Brain, C. and Mukherji, P. (2005) *Understanding Child Psychology*, Cheltenham: Nelson Thornes.

Braungart-Rieker, J. M., Garwood, M. M., Powers, B. P. and Wang, X.-Y. (2001) 'Parental sensitivity, infant affect, and affect regulation: predictors of later attachment', *Child Development*, vol. 72, no. 1, pp. 252–70.

Brazelton, T. B. (1969) *Infants and Mothers*, New York: Dell Publishing.

Brazelton, T. B. (1973) *Neonatal Behavioural Assessment Scale.* Clinics in Developmental Medicine, No. 50, London: Heinemann Medical Books.

Brazelton, T. B. (1992) *Touchpoints*, New York: Guilford Press.

Brazelton, T. B. and Sparrow, J. (2006) *Touchpoints: Birth to Three: Your child's emotional and behavioral development*, Cambridge, MA: Da Capo Press.

Brearley, M. and Hitchfield, E. (1966) *A Teacher's Guide to Reading Piaget*, London: Routledge and Kegan Paul.

Bredikyte, M. (2011) *The zones of proximal development in children's play*, Doctoral Thesis, Finland: University of Oulu, Faculty of Education.

Brennan, K. A., Wu, S. and Love, J. (1998) 'Adult romantic attachment and individual differences in attitudes toward physical contact in the context of adult romantic relationships', in Simpson, J. A. and Rholes, W. S. (eds.), *Attachment Theory and Close Relationships*, New York: Guilford Press.

Bretherton, I. (1992) 'The origins of attachment theory: John Bowlby and Mary Ainsworth', *Developmental Psychology*, vol. 28, no. 5, pp. 759–75.

Brind, R. *et al.* (2011) *Childcare and early years providers survey 2010*, London: Department for Education.

British Educational Research Association (BERA) (2011) *Revised Ethical Guidelines for Educational Research* [online]. Available from: http://www.bera.ac.uk/publications/ethical-guidelines.

British Educational Research Association (BERA) (2012) *Research Practitioner Awards* [online] Available from: http://www.bera.ac.uk/news/berasage-practitioners-award.

Broadhead, M. A., Hockaday, A., Zahra, M., Francis, P. J. and Crichton, C. (2009) 'Scallywags – an evaluation of a service targeting conduct disorders at school and at home', *Educational Psychology in Practice*, vol. 25, no. 2, pp. 167–79.

Broadhead, P. (2009) 'Conflict resolution and children's behaviour: Observing and understanding social and cooperative play in early years educational settings', *Early Years*, vol. 29, no. 2, pp. 105–18.

Broadhead, P. and Burt, A. (2012) *Understanding Young Children's Learning Through Play: Building Playful Pedagogies*, Abingdon: Routledge.

Brock, A. (2006) *Elliciting Early Years Educators' Thinking: How do they define and sustain their professionalism?* Paper presented to the *European Early Childhood Education Research Association* (EECERA) conference, Reykjavik, Iceland.

Brock, A., Dodds, S., Jarvis, P. and Olusaga, Y. (2009) *Perspectives on Play: Learning for Life*, Harlow: Pearson Education.

Bronfenbrenner, U. (1979) *The Ecology of Human Development: Experiments by Nature and Design*, Cambridge, MA: Harvard University Press.

Brooker, L. (2002) *Starting School: Young Children Learning Cultures*. Buckingham: Open University Press.

Brooker, L. (2010) 'Learning to play, or playing to learn? Children's participation in the cultures of homes and settings', in Brooker, L. and Edwards, S. (eds.) *Engaging Play*, Maidenhead: Open University Press.

Brooker, L. and Edwards, S. (eds.) (2010) *Engaging Play*, Maidenhead: Open University and McGraw-Hill.

Brooker, L. and Woodhead, M. (2010) *Culture and Learning*, Milton Keynes: Open University. Available from: http://www.bernardvanleer.org/Culture-and-learning.

Brooker, L., Rogers, S., Ellis, D., Hallet, E., Roberts-Holmes, G. (2010) *Practitioners' Experience of the Early Years Foundation Stage*, London: Department for Education.

Brookfield, S. D. (1995) *Becoming a Critically Reflective Teacher*, San Francisco, CA: Jossey-Bass.

Brooks, D. (2011) *The Social Animal: A Story of How Success Happens*, New York: Random House.

Brooks, L. (2006) *The Story of Childhood*, London: Bloomsbury.

Browne, A. (2001) *Developing Language and Literacy 3–8*, London. SAGE.

Browne, N. (2004) *Gender Equity in the Early Years*, Maidenhead: Open University Press.

Brownhill, S. (2010) *The 'brave' man in the early years: examining the ambiguities of being a male role model*, University of Derby, BERA conference paper. Available from: http://www.beraconference.co.uk/2010/downloads/abstracts/pdf/BERA2010_0219.pdf.

Bruce, I., Castillejo, D., Cornford, C., Gosford, C., Routh, F. (1972) *Artists Now: Patronage of the Creative Artist*, London: Artists Now (107 Arlington Road, NW1).

Bruce, T. (1991) *Time to Play in Early Childhood Education and Care*, London: Hodder and Stoughton.

Bruce, T. (2004) *Developing Learning in Early Childhood*, London: SAGE.

Bruce, T. (2006) *Early Childhood: A guide for students* (2nd edn), London: Sage.

Bruce, T. (2010) 'Play, the universe and everything!', in Moyles, J. (ed.) *The Excellence of Play* (3rd edn), Maidenhead: Open University and McGraw-Hill.

Bruce, T. (2011a) *Learning through Play: For Babies, Toddlers and Young Children* (2nd edn), London: Hodder Education.

Bruce, T. (2011b) *Cultivating Creativity for Babies, Toddlers and Young Children* (2nd edn), London: Hodder Education.

Bruce, T. (2011c) *Early Childhood Education* (4th edn), London: Hodder Education.

Bruce, T. (ed.) (2012) *Early Childhood Practice: Fröbel today*, London: SAGE.

Brühlmeier, A. (2010) *Head, Heart and Hand: Education in the Spirit of Pestalozzi*, Cambridge: Sophia Books. Available from: http://www.pestalozziworld.com/images/HeadHeartandHand.pdf.

Bruner, J. (1975) 'From communication to language: A psychological perspective', *Cognition*, vol. 3, pp. 225–89.

Bruner, J. (1987) 'The transactional self', in Cooper, P. and Whitebread, D. (2007) 'The effectiveness of nurture groups on student progress: Evidence from a national research study', *Emotional and Behavioural Difficulties*, vol. 12, no. 3, pp. 171–90.

Bruner, J. (1996) *The Culture of Education*, Cambridge, MA: Harvard University Press.

Brunton, P. (2007) *Bringing the Reggio Emilia Approach to Your Early Years Practice*, London: Routledge.

Buchanan, A. and Hudson, B. (2000) *Promoting Children's Emotional Well-being: Messages from research*, Oxford: Oxford University Press.

Bullock Report (1975) *A Language for Life. Report of the Committee of the Inquiry into Reading and the Use of English*, London: HMSO.

Burns, T. and Sinfield, S. (2008) *Essential Study Skills: The Complete Guide to Success at University* (2nd edn), London: SAGE [available as e-book and Kindle edn].

Burton, D. and Bartlett, S. (2009) *Key Issues for Education Research*, London: SAGE.

Butler, I., Scanlan, L., Robinson, M., Douglas, G. and Murch, M. (2002) 'Children's involvement in their parents' divorce', *Children & Society*, vol. 16, no. 2, pp. 89–102.

Buzan , T. (2006) *Mind Mapping: Kickstart Your Creativity and Transform your Life*, Harlow: BBC Active.

Byron, T. (2010) *Do we have safer children in a digital world? A review of progress since the 2008 Byron Review*. Nottingham: DCSF. Available from: https://www.education.gov.uk/publications/eOrderingDownload/DCSF-00290-2010.pdf.

Caillois, R. (2001) *Man, Play and Games*, Urbana and Chicago: University of Illinois Press.

Caine, R., and Caine, G. (1991) *Making Connections: Teaching and the human brain*, Alexandria, VA: Association for Supervision and Curriculum Development.

Calder, M. (2004) *Children Living with Domestic Violence: Towards a framework for assessment and intervention*, Lyme Regis: Russel House Publishing.

Cameron, C. (2006) 'Men in the nursery revisited: Issues of male workers and professionalism', *Contemporary Issues in Early Childhoold*, vol. 7, no. 1, pp. 68–79.

Canter, L. and Canter, M. (2001) *Assertive Discipline: Positive Behavior Management for Today's Classroom* (3rd edn), Bloomington: Solution Tree.

Carr, M. (1998) *Assessing Children's Learning in Early Childhood Settings: A development programme for discussion and reflection*, Wellington: New Zealand Council for Educational Research.

Carr, M. (1999) *Learning and Teaching Stories: New Approaches to Assessment and Evaluation* [online]. Available from: http://www.aare.edu.au/99pap/pod99298.htm.

Carr, M. (2001) *Assessment in Early Childhood Settings*, London: Paul Chapman Publishing.

Carr, M. and Lee, W. (2012) *Learning Stories: Constructing Learner Identities in Early Education*, London: SAGE.

Carr, W. and Kemmis, S. (1986) *Becoming Critical: Education, knowledge and action research*, Geelong, VIC: Deakin University Press.

Caspi, A., Taylor, A., Moffitt, T. and Plomin, R. (2000) 'Neighborhood deprivation affects children's mental health: Environmental risks identified in a genetic design', *Psychological Science*, vol. 1, no. 4, pp. 338–42.

Castro, L. and Wasserman, E. A. (2010) 'Animal learning', *Wiley Interdisciplinary Reviews: Cognitive Science*, vol. 1, no. 1, pp. 89–98.

Cawson, P. (2002) *Child maltreatment in the family: The experience of a national sample of young people*, London: NSPCC. Available from: http://www.nspcc.org.uk/Inform/research/findings/childmaltreatmentinthefamily_wda48240.html.

Claxton, G. (2006) *Expanding the Capacity to Learn: A new end for education?* Opening Keynote Address British Educational Research Association Annual Conference, 6 September 2006, Warwick University. Available from: http://www.tloltd.co.uk/downloads/BERA-Keynote-Update-Feb10.pdf.

Claxton, G. (2007) 'Expanding young people's capacity to learn', *British Journal of Educational Studies*, vol. 55, no. 2, pp. 1–20.

Cemlyn, S., Greenfields, M., Burnett, S., Mathews, Z. and Whitwell, M. (2009) *Inequalities Experienced by Gypsy and Traveller Communities: A review*, Manchester: Equality and Human Rights Commission.

Central Advisory Council for Education (CACE) (1967) *Children and their Primary Schools*, London: HMSO.

Chand, A. (2005) 'Do you speak English? Language barriers in child protection social work with minority ethnic families', *British Journal of Social Work*, vol. 35, no. 6, pp. 807–21.

Chandiramani, R. (2010) 'Shhh…. Every Child Matters lives on', *Children & Young People Now* [online]. Available from: http://www.cypnow.co.uk/cyp/opinion/1053002/shhh-every-child-matters-lives.

Chapman, A. (2012) 'Mehrabian's communication research' [online]. Available from: http://www.businessballs.com/mehrabiancommunications.htm.

Charles, M. and Horwath, J. (2009) 'Investing in interagency training to safeguard children: An act of faith or an act of reason?' *Children & Society*, vol. 23, no. 5, pp. 364–76.

Cheminais, R. (2009) *Effective Multi-Agency Partnerships: Putting Every Child Matters into Practice*, London: SAGE.

Chene, A. (1983) 'The concept of autonomy in adult education: A philosophical discussion', *Adult Education Quarterly*, Fall, vol. 34, no. 1, pp. 38–47.

Childcare Act 2006, London: HMSO. Available from: http://www.legislation.gov.uk/ukpga/2006/21/contents.

Child Poverty Action Group (2012) *End Child Poverty* [online] http://www.endchildpoverty.org.uk.

Children Act 1948 (Curtis Report), London: HMSO.

Children Act 1989, London: HMSO. Available from: http://www.legislation.gov.uk/ukpga/1989/41/contents.

Children Act 2004, London: HMSO. Available from: http://www.legislation.gov.uk/ukpga/2004/31/contents.

Children's Workforce Development Council *see under* CWDC.

Chrispeels, J. (1996) 'Effective schools and home-school-community partnership roles: A framework for parent involvement', *School Effectiveness and School Improvement*, vol. 7, no. 4, pp. 297–323.

Chrispeels, J. and Rivero, E. (2001) 'Engaging Latino families for student success: How parent education can reshape parents' sense of place in the education of their children', *Peabody Journal of Education*, vol. 76, no. 2, pp. 119–69.

Christensen, P. and James, A. (eds.) (1998) *Research with Children: Perspectives and Practices*, London: Falmer Press.

Christensen, P. and Prout, A. (2002) 'Working with ethical symmetry in social research with children', *Childhood*, vol. 9, no. 4, pp. 477–97.

Christie, J. F. and Roskos, K. A. (2009) 'Play's Potential in Early Literacy Development', in Tremblay, R. E., Barr, R. G., Peters, R. De V. and Boivin, M. (eds.) *Encyclopedia on Early Childhood Development* [online], Montreal, Quebec: Centre for Excellence for Early Childhood Development. Available from: http://www.child-encyclopedia.com/documents/Christie-RoskosANGxp.pdf.

Clance, P. R. and Imes, S. (1978) 'The imposter phenomenon in high achieving women: Dynamics and therapeutic intervention', *Psychotherapy Theory, Research and Practice*, vol. 15, no. 3, pp. 241–7.

Clance, P. R. and O'Toole, M. A. (1987) 'The imposter phenomenon: An internal barrier to empowerment and achievement', *Women and Therapy*, vol. 6, no. 3, pp. 51–64.

Clark, A. (2005) 'Ways of seeing: Using the Mosaic approach to listen to young children's perspectives', in Clark, A., Kjørholt A., and Moss, P. (eds.) *Beyond Listening: Children's Perspectives on Early Childhood Services*, Bristol: Policy Press.

Clark, A. (2007) *Early Childhood Spaces: Involving young children in the design process*. Working papers in Early Child Development, The Hague, The Netherlands: Bernard van Leer Foundation.

Clark, A. and Moss, P. (2001) *Listening to Young Children: The Mosaic approach*, London: National Children's Bureau and Joseph Rowntree Foundation.

Clark, A., Kjørholt, A. and Moss, P. (eds.) (2005) *Beyond Listening: Children's Perspectives on Early Childhood Services*, Bristol: Policy Press.

Claxton, G. (2008) *What's the Point of School?* Oxford: Oneworld Publications.

Clay, J. W. (1990) 'Working with lesbian and gay parents and their children', *Young Children*, vol. 45, no. 3, pp. 31–5.

Clutterbuck, D. (1991) *Everyone needs a Mentor: Fostering talent at work*, Institute of Personnel Management, in Gardiner, C. (1998) 'Mentoring: Towards a professional friendship', *Mentoring and Tutoring*, vol. 6, pp. 77–84.

Cobb-Moore, C. (2008) *Young children's social organisation of peer interactions*, Doctoral Thesis, Queensland University of Technology, Brisbane, Australia.

Coghlan, M., Bergeron, C., White, K., Sharp, C., Morris, M. and Wilson, R. (2010) *Narrowing the gap in outcomes for young children through effective practices in the early years*, London: Centre for Excellence and Outcomes in Children and Young People's Services (C4EO).

Cohen, W. A. (2010) *Drucker on Leadership*, San Francisco: Jossey-Bass.

Cole, G. A. and Kelly, P. (2011) *Management Theory and Practice* (7th edn), Singapore: Cengage Learning.

Colwell, S. (1998) 'Mentoring, socialisation and the mentor/protégé relationship [1]', *Teaching in Higher Education*, vol. 3, no. 3, pp. 313–25.

Community Care (2012) *Social pedagogy in the UK: time to reflect*. Available from: http://www.communitycare.co.uk/Articles/02/03/2012/118035/Social-pedagogy-in-the-UK-time-to-reflect.htm.

Condry, G. (1981) 'Towards multi-professional co-ordination: The rationale of an in-service training course' *Early Childhood Development and Care*, vol. 7, no. 4, pp. 371–9.

ContinYou (2012) *Pyramid* [online]. Available from: http://www.continyou.org.uk/what_we_do/pyramid/home.

Cooper, P. and Whitebread, D. (2007) 'The effectiveness of nurture groups on student progress: Evidence from a national research study', *Emotional and Behavioural Difficulties*, vol. 12, no. 3, pp. 171–90.

Copus, J. (2009) *Brilliant Tips for Students*, Basingstoke: Palgrave Macmillan.

Corsaro, W. (1985) *Friendship and Peer Culture in the Early Years*, Norwood, NJ: Ablex.

Corsaro, W. (2011) *The Sociology of Childhood* (3rd edn), London: SAGE.

Costa, A. and Kallick, B. (1993) 'Through the lens of a critical friend', *Educational Leadership*, vol. 51, no. 2, pp. 49–51.

Cottrell, S. (2008) *The Study Skills Handbook* (3rd edn), Basingstoke: Palgrave Macmillan.

Council of Australian Governments (2009) *Belonging, Being and Becoming: The Early Years Learning Framework for Australia*, Department of Education, Employment and Work Relations, Canberra, ACT.

Covey, S. (1992) *Principle-Centred Leadership*, London: Simon & Schuster, in Cole, G. A. and Kelly, P. (2011) *Management Theory and Practice* (7th edn), Singapore: Cengage Learning.

Cox, M. (1991) *The Child's Point of View*, Hemel Hempstead: Harvester Wheatsheaf.

Cozolino, L. (2006) *The Neuroscience of Human Relationships: Attachment and the Developing Social Brain*, London: W. W. Norton and Company.

Craft, A. (2002) *Creativity and Early Years Education: A lifewide foundation*, London and New York: Continuum.

Craft, A. (2003) 'Creative thinking in the early years of education', *Early Years: An International Journal of Research and Development*, vol. 23, no. 2, pp. 143–54.

Craft, A. (2008) *Creativity and Possibility in the Early Years* [online]. Available from: http://www.tactyc.org.uk/pdfs/Reflection-craft.pdf.

Craft, A. (2010) *Creativity and Education Futures: Learning in a Digital Age*, Stoke-on Trent: Trentham Books Ltd.

Craft, A. (2011) *Creativity and Early Years Education*, London: Continuum.

Crittenden, P. M. (1995) 'Attachment and psychopathology', in Goldberg, S., Muir, R. and Kerr, J. (eds.) *Attachment Theory: Social, Developmental and Clinical Perspectives*, Hillsdale, NJ: Analytic Press.

Crittenden, P. M. (1999) 'Danger and development: The organisation of self-protective strategies', *Monographs of the Society for Research in Child Development*, vol. 64, no. 3, pp. 145–71.

Crittenden, P. M. (2000) 'A dynamic-maturational model of the function, development, and organization of human relationships', in Mills, R. S. L. and Duck, S. (eds.) *Developmental Psychology of Personal Relationships*, Chichester: Wiley.

Crittenden, P. M. (2005) 'Attachment and Early Intervention', Keynote address at the German Association of Infant Mental Health, Hamburg. Available from: http://www.iasa-dmm.org/images/uploads/Attachment-and-intervention.pdf.

Crittenden, P. M. (2006a) 'A dynamic-maturational model of attachment', ANZJFT, vol. 27, no. 2, pp. 105–15.

Crittenden, P. M. (2006b) *CARE-Index (birth–15 Months) Coding Manual*, Miami, FL: Family Relations Institute.

Crittenden, P. M. (2008) *Raising Parents: Attachment, parenting and child safety*, Cullompton: Willan Publishing.

Crosby, P. (1979) *Quality Is Free*, New York: McGraw-Hill Books.

Cubey, P. (2012) 'Transforming Learning for Children and Their Parents', in Mairs, K. and the Pen Green Team (2012) *Young Children Learning Through Schemas: Deepening the dialogue about learning in the home and in the nursery*, London: Routledge.

Cunha, F., Heckman, J., Lochner, L. and Masterov, D. V. (2005) *Interpreting the evidence of life-cycle skill formation*, ISA Discussion Paper Series, No. 1575, July, Bonn: Institute for the Study of Labour.

Cunningham, H. (2006) *The Invention of Childhood*, London: BBC Books.

Curran, A. (ed. Gilbert, I.) (2008) *The Little Book of Big Stuff About the Brain*, Bancyfelin: Crown House.

Curtis, A. and O'Hagan, M. (2003) *Care and Education in Early Childhood: A Student's Guide to Theory and Practice*, London: Routledge Falmer.

Cutting, A. and Dunn, J. (2006) 'Conversations with siblings and with friends: Links between relationship quality and social understanding', *British Journal of Developmental Psychology*, vol. 24, pp. 73–87.

CWDC (Children's Workforce Development Council) (2008) *Guidance to the Standards for the Award of Early Years Professional Status*, Leeds: CWDC.

CWDC (2010a) *The Common Core of Skills and Knowledge for the Children's Workforce*, Leeds: CWDC.

CWDC (2010b) *Inspiring practice: A guide to developing an integrated approach to supervision in Children's Trusts*, Leeds: CWDC. Available from: https://www.education.gov.uk/publications/standard/publicationDetail/Page1/IW115/2010.

CWDC (2011) *Early Years Worforce: The Way Forward*, Leeds: CWDC.

CWDC (2012) *About CWDC* [online]. Available from: http://www.cwdcouncil.org.uk/about.

Daly, M., Byers, E. and Taylor, W. (2009) *Early Years Management in Practice*, Oxford: Heinemann.

Damasio, A. (1999) *The Feeling of What Happens: Body, Emotion and the Making of Consciousness*, London: Heinemann.

Danby, S. (2002) 'The communicative competence of young children', *Australasian Journal of Early Childhood*, vol. 27, no. 3, pp. 25–30.

Danby, S. and Baker, C. (2001) 'Escalating terror: Communicative strategies in a preschool classroom dispute', *Early Education and Development*, vol. 12, no. 3, pp. 343–58.

Danby, S. and Farrell, A. (2005) 'Opening the research conversation', in Farrell, A. (ed.) *Ethical Research with Children*, Milton Keynes: Open University Press.

Danby, S. and Thorpe, K. (2006) 'Compatibility and conflict: Negotiation of relationships by dizygotic same-sex twin girls', *Twin Research and Human Genetics*, vol. 9, no. 1, pp. 103–12.

Daniel, M. (2010) *Self-Scoring Emotional Intelligence Tests (Self-Scoring Tests)*, New York: Sterling Publishing.

Datta, L. (1983) 'We Never Promised You A Rose Garden, But One May Have Grown Anyhow', in The Consortium for Longitudinal Studies, *As the Twig is Bent…Lasting Effects of Preschool Programs*, New Jersey: Lawrence Erlbaum Associates.

Datta, M. (2007) *Bilinguality and Literacy: Principles and Practice*, London: Continuum.

David, M., Edwards, R. and Aldred, P. (2001) 'Children and school-based research: "informed consent" or "educated consent"?', *British Educational Research Journal*, vol. 27, no. 3, pp. 347–65.

Davies, M. (2003) *Movement and Dance in Early Childhood* (2nd edn), London: SAGE.

Davies, M. (2008) *Eradicating child poverty: The role of key policy areas: The effects of discrimination on families in the fight to end child poverty*, York: Joseph Rowntree Foundation. Available from: http://www.jrf.org.uk/sites/files/jrf/2271-poverty-exclusion-discrimination.pdf.

Davis, J. (2008) 'What might education for sustainability look like in early childhood? A case for participatory, whole-of-settings approaches', in *The contribution of early childhood education to a sustainable society*, Paris: UNESCO.

Davis, J. and Pratt, R. (2005) 'Creating cultural change @ Campus Kindergarten: The Sustainable Planet Project', *Every Child*, vol. 11, no. 4, pp. 10–11.

Dawson, D. A. (1991) 'Family structure and children's health and well-being: Data from the 1988 National Health Interview Survey on Child Health', *Journal of Marriage and Family*, vol. 53, no. 3, pp. 573–84.

Day, S. (2010) 'Listening to young children: An investigation of children's day care experiences in Children's Centres', *Educational and Child Psychology*, vol. 27, no. 4, pp. 45–55.

Daycare Trust (2008) *Ensuring Equality in Childcare for Black and Minority Ethnic Families: A summary paper*, London: Daycare Trust.

DCSF (Department for Children, Schools and Families) (2007a) *The Children's Plan*, Norwich: TSO.

DCSF (2007b) *Primary National Strategy: Learning Walks: Tools and templates for getting started*, Nottingham: DCSF. Available from: http://webarchive.nationalarchives.gov.uk/20110202093118/http:/nationalstrategies.standards.dcsf.gov.uk/node/88674.

DCSF (2007c) *Supporting Children Learning English as an Additional Language: Guidance for Practitioners in the Early Years Foundation Stage*, Nottingham. DCSF. Available from: http://webarchive.nationalarchives.gov.uk/20110208164652/http:/nationalstrategies.standards.dcsf.gov.uk/node/84861.

DCSF (2008a) *Statutory Framework for the Early Years Foundation Stage*, Nottingham: DCSF.

DCSF (2008b) *Practice Guidance for the Early Years Foundation Stage*, Nottingham: DCSF.

DCSF (2008c) *Child Development Overview Cards*, Nottingham: DCSF.

DCSF (2008d) *Social and Emotional Aspects of Development (SEAD): Guidance for practitioners working in the Foundation Stage*, Nottingham: DCSF.

DCSF (2008e) *Early Years Quality Improvement Support Programme (EYQISP)*, Nottingham: DCSF. Available from: http://www.school-portal.co.uk/GroupDownloadFile.asp?GroupId=716966&ResourceID=2635260.

DCSF (2008f) *Identifying Gifted and Talented Learners: Getting Started*, Nottingham: DCSF.

DCSF (2008g) *The Impact of Parental Involvement on Children's Education*, Nottingham: DCSF.

DCSF (2008h) *Information Sharing: Guidance for practitioners and managers*, Nottingham: DCSF. Available from: https://www.education.gov.uk/publications/standard/publicationdetail/page1/DCSF-00807-2008.

DCSF (2008i) *Every Child a Talker: Guidance for Early Language Lead Practitioners*, Nottingham: DCSF. Available from: https://www.education.gov.uk/publications/standard/publicationDetail/Page1/DCSF-00854-2008.

DCSF (2009a) *Guidance for Safer Working Practice for Adults who Work with Children and Young People*, Nottingham: DCSF. Available from: http://webarchive.nationalarchives.gov.uk/20100202100434/dcsf.gov.uk/everychildmatters/resources-and-practice/ig00311.

DCSF (2009b) *Safeguarding Disabled Children: Practice Guidance*, Nottingham: DCSF. Available from: https://www.education.gov.uk/publications/eOrderingDownload/00374-2009DOM-EN.pdf.

DCSF (2010a) *Working Together to Safeguard Children: A guide to inter-agency working to safeguard and promote the welfare of children*, Nottingham: DCSF. Available from: https://www.education.gov.uk/publications/standard/publicationdetail/page1/DCSF-00305-2010.

DCSF (2010b) *Safeguarding Children and Safer Recruitment in Education*, Nottingham: DCFS. Available from: http://www.education.gov.uk/consultations/downloadableDocs/Safeguarding%20Children%20Guidance.pdf.

DCSF (2010c) *Finding and exploring young children's fascinations: Strengthening the quality of gifted and talented provision in the early years*, Nottingham. DCSF. Available from: http://earlyyearsmatters.co.uk/wp-content/uploads/2011/03/sen_gt_yc_fasc_0010710.pdf.

de Bono Thinking Systems (2011) 'Six Thinking Hats' [online]. Available from: http://www.debonothinkingsystems.com/tools/6hats.htm.

DeGangi, G., Breinbauer, C., Roosevelt, J., Porges, S. and Greenspan, S. (2000) 'Prediction of childhood problems at three years in children experiencing disorders of regulation during infancy', *Mental Health Journal*, vol. 21, no. 3, pp. 156–75.

Degotardi, S. and Davis, B. (2008) 'Understanding infants: Characteristics or early childhood practitioners' interpretations of infants and their behaviours', *Early Years*, vol. 28, no. 3, pp. 221–34.

DeLoache, J. and Gottlieb, A. (2000) *A World of Babies*, Cambridge: Cambridge University Press.

Denham, S. A., Kalb, S., Way, E., Warren-Khot, H., Rhoades, B. L. and Bassett H. H. (2012) 'Social and emotional information processing in preschoolers: indicator of early school success?' *Early Child Development and Care*, forthcoming, Version of record first published: 28 May 2012.

Department for Children, Schools and Families *see under* DCSF.

Department for Education *see under* DfE.

Department for Education and Employment *see under* DfEE.

Department for Education and Skills *see under* DfES.

Department for Work and Pensions (DWP) and the Department for Education (DfE) (2011) *A New Approach to Child Poverty: Tackling the Causes of Disadvantage and Transforming Families' Lives*, London. HMSO.

Department of Education and Science (DES) (1978) *The Report of the Committee of Enquiry into the Education of Handicapped Children and Young People* (Warnock Report), London. HMSO.

Department of Health *see under* DoH.

Derman-Sparks, L. (1989) *Anti-bias Curriculum: Tools for empowering young children*, Washington, DC: NAEYC.

Desforges, C. and Abouchaar, A. (2003) *The Impact of Parental Involvement, Parental Support and Family Education on Pupil Achievements and Adjustment: A Literature Review*, DfES, Research Report RR433.

Dewey, J. (1910) *Educational Essays*, Bath: Cedric Chivers.

Dewey, J. (1933) *How We Think*, Chicago: Regnery.

DfE (Department for Education) (2011a) *Special Educational Needs in England*, London: DfE. Available from: http://www.education.gov.uk/rsgateway/DB/SFR/s001007/sfr14-2011v2.pdf.

DfE (2011b) *Support and aspiration: A new approach to special educational needs and disability: A consultation*, London: DfE. Available from: https://www.education.gov.uk/publications/eOrderingDownload/Green-Paper-SEN.pdf.

DfE (2011c) *Early Years Foundation Stage Profile Attainment by Pupil Characteristics, England 2010/11*, London: DfE. Available from: http://www.education.gov.uk/rsgateway/DB/SFR/s001044/index.shtml.

DfE (2012a) *Statutory Framework for the Early Years Foundation Stage*, London: DfE. Available from: https://www.education.gov.uk/publications/standard/AllPublications/Page1/DFE-00023-2012.

DfE (2012b) *Support and aspiration: A new approach to special educational needs and disability: Progress and next steps*, London: DfE. Available from: https://www.education.gov.uk/publications/standard/publicationDetail/Page1/DFE-00046-2012.

DfE (2012c) Press notice: *'New survey shows school behaviour improvement but with more to do'*, London: DfE. Available from: http://www.education.gov.uk/inthenews/inthenews/a00210695/schbehsur.

DfE (2012d) *'Graduate leaders in Early Years: New Leaders explained'* , London: DfE. Available from: http://www.education.gov.uk/childrenandyoungpeople/earlylearningandchildcare/delivery/b00201345/graduate-leaders/new-leaders.

DfE (2012e) *'The lead professional'* , London: DfE. Available from: http://www.education.gov.uk/childrenandyoungpeople/strategy/integratedworking/a0068961/the-lead-professional.

DfE and DoH (2011) *Supporting Families in the Foundation Years*, London: DfE and DoH. Available from: http://www.parliament.uk/deposits/depositedpapers/2011/DEP2011-1250.pdf.

DfEE (Department for Education and Employment) (1999) *Sure Start: Making a Difference for Children and Families*, London: HMSO.

DfEE (2001) *Childcare Quality Improvement and Assurance Practices*, London: DfEE.

DfES (Department for Education and Skills) (2001) *The Special Educational Needs Code of Practice*, London DfES.

DfES (2002) *Birth to Three Matters: A framework to support under-3s*, London: DfES.

DfES (2003) *Every Child Matters* Green Paper, London: TSO.

DfES (2004a) *Every Child Matters: Change for Children*, London: DfES.

DfES (2004b) *Choice for parents, the best start for children: a ten year strategy for childcare*, Norwich: HMSO.

DfES (2005a) *Social and Emotional Aspects of Learning (SEAL): Improving behaviour, improving learning*, Primary National Strategy, Norwich: HMSO.

DfES (2005b) *Key Elements of Effective Practice (KEEP)*, Primary National Strategy, Norwich: HMSO.

DfES (2006a) *What to do if you're worried a child is being abused*, London: DfES.

DfES (2006b) *The Common Assessment Framework*, London: DfES.

Diamond, L. M. and Fagundes, C. P. (2010) 'Psychobiological research on attachment', *Journal of Social and Personal Relationships*, vol. 27, no. 2, pp. 218–25.

Diamond, M. C., Krech, D. and Rosenzweig, M. R. (1964) 'Effects of an enriched environment on the histology of the rat cerebral cortex', *Journal Comparative Neurology*, vol. 123, no. 1, pp. 111–19.

Ding, S. and Littleton, K. (2005) *Children's Personal and Social Development*, Milton Keynes: Blackwell Publications.

Disability Discrimination Act 1995, London: HMSO.

Disability Discrimination Act 2005, London: HMSO.

Diversity in Early Childhood Education and Training (DECET) and the International Step by Step Association (ISSA) (2012) *Diversity and Social Inclusion: Exploring Competencies for Professional Practice for Early Childhood Education and Care*. Available from: http://www.decet.org/fileadmin/decet-media/publications/Diversity-and-Social-Inclusion.pdf.

DoH (Department of Health) (1991) *The Children Act Guidance and Regulations*, Vol. II: Family Support, Daycare and Educational Provision for Young Children, London: HMSO.

DoH (1995) *Child Protection: Messages from Research*, London: DoH.

DoH (1999) *Towards safer care training and resource pack*, London: DoH.

DoH (2000) *Framework for the Assessment of Children in Need and their Families*, London: DoH.

DoH (2004) *The National Service Framework for Children, Young People and Maternity Services: Core Standards*, London: DoH.

DoH (2004) *Choosing Health* (Public Health White Paper), London: DoH.

DoH (2005) *Choosing Activity: a physical activity action plan*, London: DoH.

Doherty, J. and Hughes, M. (2009) *Child Development. Theory and Practice 0–11*, Harlow: Pearson Education.

Donaldson, M. (1978) *Children's Minds*, London: Croom-Helm.

Douglass, A. (2011) 'Improving family engagement: The organisational context and its influence on partnering with parents in formal childcare settings', *Early Childhood Research and Practice*, vol. 13, no. 2. Available from: http://ecrp.uiuc.edu/v13n2/douglass.html.

Dowling, M. (2010) *Young Children's Personal, Social and Emotional Development* (3rd edn), London: SAGE.

Dowling, M. (2012 in press) *Young Children's Thinking*, London: SAGE.

Drifte, C. (2008) *Encouraging Positive Behaviour Management in the Early Years* (2nd edn), London: SAGE.

Drummond, A. J. and Jenkinson, S. (2009) *Meeting the Child: Approaches to Observation and Assessment in Steiner Kindergartens*, Plymouth: The University of Plymouth.

Dryden, L., Hyder, T. and Jethwa, S. (2003) 'Assessing individual oral presentations', *Investigations in University Teaching and Learning*, vol. 1, no. 1, pp. 79–83.

Dryden, L., Mukherji, P., Forbes, R. and Pound, L. (2005) *Essential Early Years*, London: Hodder Arnold.

Duffy, B. (2009) *Supporting Creativity and Imagination in the Early Years* (2nd edn), Maidenhead: Open University Press.

Duffy, B. (2010) 'Using creativity and creative learning to enrich the lives of young children at the Thomas Coram Centre', in Tims, C. (2010) (ed.) *'Creative learning in the early years is not just child's play…': Born creative*, London: DEMOS. Available from: http://www.demos.co.uk.

Dunn, L., Kontos, S. and Potter, L. (1996) 'Mixed-age interactions in family child care', *Early Education and Development*, vol. 7, no. 4, pp. 349–66.

Dweck, C. (2000) *Self Theories: Their Role in Motivation, Personality and Development*, London: Psychology Press.

Dweck, C. (2010) 'Even geniuses work hard', *Educational Leadership*, vol. 68, no. 1, pp. 16–21.

Early Childhood Australia (ECA) (2012) *Research in Practice* [online]. Available from: http://www.earlychildhoodaustralia.org.au/research_in_practice_series/about_rips.html.

Early Childhood Forum (2003) *Policy Statement: Definition of Inclusion*, London: HMSO.

Early Education (2012) *Development Matters in the Early Years Foundation Stage (EYFS)*, London: Early Education supported by DfE. Available from: http://media.education.gov.uk/assets/files/pdf/d/development%20matters%20in%20the%20eyfs.pdf.

Easen, P., Kendall, P. and Shaw, J. (1992) 'Parents and educators: Dialogue and development through partnership', *Children & Society*, vol. 6, no. 4, pp. 282–96.

Education Act 1944 (Butler Education Act). Available from: http://www.parliament.uk/about/living-heritage/transformingsociety/livinglearning/school/overview/educationact1944/.

Education Act 2002, London: HMSO. Available from: http://www.legislation.gov.uk/ukpga/2002/32/contents.

Edwards, C. P. and Springate, K. W. (1995) 'The lion comes out of the stone: Helping young children achieve their creative potential', *Dimensions of Early Childhood*, vol. 23, no. 4, Fall, pp. 24–9.

Edwards, E. P., Eiden, R. D. and Leonard, K. E. (2006) 'Behavior problems in 18 to 36 month old children of alcoholic fathers: Secure mother–infant attachment as a protective factor', *Development and Psychopathology*, vol. 18, pp. 395–407.

Edwards, R. and Alldred, P. (1999) 'Children and young people's views of social research: A case of research on home–school relations', *Childhood*, vol. 6, no. 2, pp. 261–81.

Eide, B. and Winger, N. (2005) 'From the Children's Point of View: Methodological and Ethical Challenges', in Clark, A., Kjørholt, A. and Moss, P. (eds.) *Beyond Listening: Children's Perspectives on Early Childhood Services*, Bristol: Policy Press.

Eisenstadt, N. (2011) *Providing a Sure Start: How government discovered early childhood*, Bristol: Policy Press.

Elfer, P. and Dearnley, K. (2007) 'Nurseries and emotional well-being: Evaluating an emotionally containing model of professional development', *Early Years*, vol. 27, no. 3, pp. 267–79.

Elfer, P., Goldschmied, E. and Selleck, D. (2003) *Key Persons in the Nursery: Building relationships for quality provision*, London: David Fulton.

Ellis, S., Rogoff, B. and Cromer, C. (1981) 'Age segregation in children's social interactions', *Developmental Psychology*, vol. 17, no. 4, pp. 399–407.

Entwistle, N. (1991) 'Learning and studying: contrasts and influences', John Hopkins University: New Horizons for Learning [online]. Available from: http://education.jhu.edu/PD/newhorizons/future/creating_the_future/crfut_entwistle.cfm.

Epstein, A., Johnson, S. and Lafferty, P. (2011) 'The High/Scope Approach', in Miller, L. and Pound, L. (eds.) *Theories and Approaches to Learning in the Early Years*, London: SAGE.

Equality Act 2010, London: HMSO.

Eraut, M. (1994) *Developing Professional Knowledge and Competence*, Abingdon: Routledge Falmer.

Eraut, M. (1995) 'Schön Shock: A case for reframing reflection-in-action', *Teachers and Teaching*, vol. 1, no. 1, pp. 9–22.

Erikson, E. H. (1963) *Childhood and Society*, New York: W. W. Norton & Company.

Evangelou, M., Sylva, K. and Kyriacou, M. (2009) *Early Years Learning and Development: Literature Review*, Nottingham: DCSF. Available from: https://www.education.gov.uk/publications/eOrderingDownload/DCSF-RR176.pdf.

Evans, M. (2011) 'Analysis: SEN Green Paper: The advent of parent power?' *Nursery World*, 23/3/11. Available from: http://www.nurseryworld.co.uk/news/1061200/Analysis-SEN-Green-Paper---advent-parent-power/?DCMP=ILC-SEARCH12).

Fabian, H. and Mould, C. (2009) *Development and Learning for Very Young Children*, London: SAGE.

Fagan, J. and Barnett, M. (2003) 'The relationship between maternal gatekeeping, paternal competence, mother's attitudes about the father role and father involvement', *Journal of Family Issues*, vol. 24, pp. 1020–43.

Farrell, A. (2004) 'Ethical dimensions of practitioner-research in the early years', *Early Childhood Practice: The Journal for Multi-Professional Partnerships*, vol. 6, no. 2, pp. 18–27.

Farrell, A. (2005) 'New times in ethical research with children', in Farrell A. (ed.) *Ethical Research with Children*, Milton Keynes: Open University Press and McGraw-Hill.

Farrell, A. (2006) 'Transnational displacement of children: An Australian perspective', in Adams, L. and Kirova, A. (eds.) *Global Migration and Education: Schools, Children and Families*, Malwah, NJ: Lawrence Erlbaum Associates.

Farrell, A. (2010) 'Towards beneficence for young children in research: Challenges for bioethics committees', *Medicine and Law*, vol. 29, no. 3, pp. 391–402.

Farrell, A. (ed.) (2005) *Ethical Research with Children*, Milton Keynes: Open University Press and McGraw-Hill.

Farrell, A. and Danby, S. (2007) 'Children making decisions about food and eating practices', *Every Child*, vol. 13, no. 4, pp. 20–21.

Farrell, A., Tayler, C. and Tennent, L. (2004) 'Building social capital in early childhood education and care: An Australian study', *British Educational Research Journal*, vol. 30, no. 5, pp. 623–32.

Featherstone, S. and Bayley, R. (2005) *Boys and Girls Come Out to Play*, Husband's Bosworth: Featherstone Educational.

Feinstein, L. (2003) 'Very early evidence', *CentrePiece*, vol. 8, no. 2, pp. 24–30. Available from: http://cep.lse.ac.uk/pubs/download/CP146.pdf.

Feinstein, L. (2006) *Predicting adult life outcomes from earlier signals: Modelling pathways through childhood*, London: Institute of Education.

Feinstein, L. and Sabates, R. (2006) 'Predicting adult life outcomes from earlier signals: Identifying those at risk', Report for the PMSU, Centre for Research on the Wider Benefits of Learning, London: Institute of Education.

Ferguson, H. (2005) 'Working with violence, the emotions and the psycho-social dynamics of child protection: Reflections on the Victoria Climbié case', *Social Work Education: The International Journal*, vol. 24, no. 7, pp. 781–95.

Field, F. (2010) *The Foundation Years: preventing poor children becoming poor adults. The report of the Independent Review on Poverty and Life Chances*, London: HM Government. Available from: http://www.nfm.org.uk/component/jdownloads/finish/74/333.

Fiol, C. M., Harris, D. and House, R. (1999) *Charistmatic Leadership: Strategies for Effecting Social Change*, Denver: University of Colorado.

Fish, D. and Coles, C. (1998) *Developing Professional Judgement in Health Care: Learning through the critical appreciation of practice*, Oxford: Butterworth-Heinemann.

Fjortoft, I. (2001) 'The natural environment as a playground for children: The impact of outdoor play activities in pre-primary school children', *Early Childhood Education Journal*, vol. 29, no. 2, pp. 111–17.

Fogel, A. (2011) *Infant Development: A topical approach*, Hudson, NY: Sloan Publishing.

Foley, P. and Leverett, S. (eds.) (2011) *Children and Young People's Spaces*, Milton Keynes: The Open University.

Fonagy, P. (2001) *Attachment Theory and Psychoanalysis*, London: Karnac.

Fonagy, P. and Target, M. (2005) 'Bridging the transmission gap: An end to an important mystery of attachment research?', *Attachment and Human Development*, vol. 7, no. 3, pp. 333–43.

Fonagy, P., Steele, M., Steele, H., Leigh, T., Kennedy, R., Matoon, G. and Target, M. (1995) 'Attachment, the reflective self, and borderline states', in Goldberg, S., Muir, R. and Kerr, J. (eds.) *Attachment Theory: Social, Developmental, and Clinical Perspectives*, Hillsdale, NJ: Analytic Press.

Forbes, R. (2004) *Beginning to Play from Birth to Three*, Maidenhead: Open University Press.

Freeman, J. (2002) *Out of School Educational Provision for the Gifted and Talented Around the World*, London: DfES.

Freeman, M. (1999) 'The right to be heard', *Adoption and Fostering*, vol. 22, no. 4, pp. 50–9.

Freire, P. (1970) *Pedagogy of the Oppressed*, London: Penguin.

Freud, S. (1923) *The Ego and the Id* (Standard Edn., 19:1–66), London: Hogarth.

Freud, S. (1953) *The Standard Edition of the Complete Psychological Works of Sigmund Freud*, London: Hogarth.

Freud, S. (1962) *Three Essays on the Theory of Sexuality* (trans. James Strachey), New York: Basic Books.

Friedman, M. (2005) *Trying Hard Is Not Good Enough*, Manchester: Trafford Publishing.

Fullan, M. (2003) *The Moral Imperative of School Leadership*, Thousand Oaks, CA: Ontario Principals' Council/Corwin Press.

Fuller, E. (1951) *The Right of the Child*, London: Gollancz.

Fumoto, H., Robson, S., Greenfield, S. and Hargreaves, D. (2012) *Young Children's Creative Thinking*, London: SAGE.

Furedi, F. (2004) 'Plagiarism stems from a loss of scholarly ideals', *Times Higher Education Supplement*, 6 August.

Furlong, J. (2003) 'Intuition and the crisis in teacher professionalism', in Atkinson, T. and Claxton, G. (2003) *The Intuitive Practitioner*, Maidenhead: Open University Press.

Furlong, J., and Maynard, T. (1995) *Mentoring Student Teachers: The growth of professional knowledge*, London: Routledge.

Gallahue, D. L., Ozmun, J. C. and Goodway, J. (2011) *Understanding Motor Development: Infants, children, adolescents, adults* (7th edn), New York: McGraw–Hill.

Gandini, L. (2012) 'Connecting through caring and learning spaces' in Edwards, C., Gandini, L. and Forman, G. (eds.) *The Hundred Languages of Children: The Reggio Emilia Experience in Transformation* (3rd edn), Santa Barbara, CA: Praeger.

Garbarino, J. and Stott, F. (1992) *What Children Can Tell Us: Eliciting, Interpreting and Evaluating Critical Information from Children*, San Francisco: Jossey-Bass.

Gardiner, C. (1998) 'Mentoring: Towards a professional friendship', *Mentoring and Tutoring*, vol. 6, pp. 77–84.

Gardner, H. (1983) *Frames of Mind: The Theory of Multiple Intelligences*, New York: Basic Books.

Gardner, H. (2011) *Leading Minds: An Anatomy of Leadership*, New York: Basic Books [Kindle edn].

Gardner, H., Kornhaber, M. and Wake, W. (1996) *Intelligence: Multiple Perspectives*, Fort Worth: Harcourt Brace.

Gardner, L. I. (1972) 'Deprivation dwarfism', *Scientific American* (July), in Juhan, D. (2002) *Job's Body: A Handbook for Bodywork*, New York: Barrytown Ltd.

Gardner, S. (2010) 'Eduard von Hartmann's Philosophy of the Unconscious', in Nicholls, A. and Liebscher, M. (eds.) *Thinking the Unconscious: Nineteenth Century German Thought*, New York: Cambridge University Press.

Garrett, P. M. (2009) 'The Case of Baby P: Opening up spaces for debate on the "transformation" of Children's Services?', *Critical Social Policy*, vol. 29, no. 3, pp. 533–47.

Garrick, R. (2009) *Playing Outdoors in the Early Years* (2nd edn), London and New York: Continuum.

Garrick, R., Bath, C., Dunn, K., Maconochie, H., Willis, B. and Wolstenholme, C. (2010) *Children's Experiences of the Early Years Foundation Stage*, Research Report RR071, London: DfE.

Gasper, M. (2010) *Multi-agency Working in the Early Years*, London: SAGE Publications.

Gerber, M. (1977) *A Manual for Parents and Professionals*, Los Angeles: Resources for Infant Educarers.

Gerber, M. and Johnson, A. (1998) *Your Self-confident Baby*, New York: John Wiley & Sons Inc.

Gerhardt, S. (2004) *Why Love Matters: How affection shapes a baby's brain*, Hove: Brunner-Routledge.

Gesell, A. (1928) *Infant Behavior: Its genesis and growth*, New York: McGraw-Hill.

Gesell, A. (1933) 'Maturation and the patterning of behaviour', in Murchison, C. (ed.), (2007) *A Handbook of Child Psychology*, vol. I (2nd edn), New York: Russell & Russell/Atheneum Publishers.

Gesell, A., Ilg, F. L. and Bates Ames, L. (1974) *Infant and Child in the Culture of Today: The guidance of development in home and nursery school*, Oxford: HarperCollins.

Ghaye, T. (2011) *Teaching and Learning Through Reflective Practice: A Practical Guide for Positive Action*, Abingdon: Routledge.

Gibbs, G. (1998) *Learning by Doing: A Guide to Teaching and Learning*, London: FEU.

Giddens, A. (2001) *Sociology*, Cambridge: Polity Press.

Gilkes, J. (1987) *Developing Nursery Education*, Milton Keynes: Open University Press.

Gillard, D. (1987) *Plowden and the Primary Curriculum: Twenty years on* [online]. Available from: http://www.educationengland.org.uk/articles/04plowden.html.

Gillard, D. (2004) 'The Plowden Report', *The encyclopaedia of informal education* [online]. Available from: http://www.infed.org/schooling/plowden_report.htm.

Gillard, D. (2006) 'The Hadow Reports: an introduction' [online]. Available from: http://www.educationengland.org.uk/articles/24hadow.html.

Gillham, B. (2008) *Observation Techniques: Structured to Unstructured*, London: Continuum.

Gilligan, R. (1999) 'Enhancing the resilience of children and young people in public care by mentoring their talents and interests', *Child and Family Social Work*, vol. 4, no. 3, pp. 187–96.

Glass, N. (1999) 'Sure Start: The development of an early intervention programme for young children in the United Kingdom', *Children & Society*, vol. 13, no. 4, pp. 257–64.

Glazebrook, C., Hollis, C., Heussler, H., Goodman, R. and Coates, L. (2003) 'Detecting emotional and behavioural problems in paediatrics clinics', *Childcare Health and Development*, vol. 29, pp. 141–9.

Glover, J. (2009) *Bouncing back: How can resilience be promoted in vulnerable children and young people?*, Ilford: Barnardo's. Available from: http://www.barnardos.org.uk/bouncing_back_resilience_march09.pdf.

Gmitrováa, V. and Gmitrovb, J. (2004) 'The primacy of child-directed pretend play on cognitive competence in a mixed-age environment: Possible interpretations', *Early Child Development and Care*, vol. 174, no. 3, pp. 267–79.

Goddard Blythe, S. (2005) *The Well Balanced Child: Movement and early learning*, Gloucestershire: Hawthorn Press.

Goldman, R. (2005) *Fathers' Involvement in Their Children's Education*, London: National Family and Parenting Institute.

Goldschmied, E. and Jackson, S. (2004) *People under 3: Young children in day care*, Abingdon: Routledge.

Goldsmith, H., Pollak, S. and Davidson, R. (2008) 'Developmental neuroscience perspectives on emotion regulation', *Child Development Perspectives*, vol. 2, no. 3, pp. 132–40.

Goleman, D. (1996) *Emotional Intelligence: Why it can matter more than IQ*, London: Bloomsbury.

Goleman, D. (1999) *Working with Emotional Intelligence*, London: Bloomsbury.

Goleman, D. (2012) *Social Intelligence* [online]. Available from: http://danielgoleman.info/topics/social-intelligence.

Göncü, A. and Gaskins, S. (eds.) (2006) *Play and Development: Evolutionary, Sociocultural and Functional Perspectives*, New Jersey: Lawrence Erlbaum Associates.

Goodfellow, J. (2005) 'Researching with/for whom? Stepping in and out of practitioner research', *Australasian Journal of Early Childhood*, vol. 30, no. 4, pp. 48–57.

Goodfellow, J. (2009) *Early Years Learning Framework: Getting started*, Early Childhood Australia Research in Practice Series, Canberra: ECA.

Goodfellow, J. and Hedges, M. (2007) 'Practitioner research "centre stage": Contexts, contributions and challenges', in Keesing-Styles, L. and Hedges, H. (eds.), *Theorising Early Childhood Practice: Emerging dialogues*, Castle Hill, NSW: Pademelon Press.

Goss, A. E. (1961) 'Early behaviorism and verbal mediating responses', *American Psychologist*, vol. 16, no. 6, 285–98.

Goswami, U. (ed.) (2011) *The Wiley-Blackwell Handbook of Childhood Cognitive Development* (2nd edn), Milton Keynes: Blackwell Publications.

Gottman, J. M. (1983) 'How children become friends', *Monographs of the Society for Research in Child Development*, vol. 48, no. 3, serial no. 201, pp. 1–86.

Gove, M. (2011) 'Review of the National Curriculum' [online]. Available from: http://www.education.gov.uk/schools/teachingandlearning/curriculum/nationalcurriculum.

Graue, M. E. (1992) 'Social Interpretations of Readiness for Kindergarten', *Early Childhood Quarterly*, vol. 7, no. 2, pp. 225–43.

Gray, C. and MacBlain, S. (2012) *Learning Theories in Childhood*, London: SAGE.

Green, S. (2003) 'Reaching out to fathers: An examination of staff efforts that lead to greater father involvement in early childhood programmes', *Early Childhood Research and Practice*, vol. 5, no. 2. Available from: http://ecrp.uiuc.edu/v5n2/green.html.

Greenfield, C. (2004) '"Can run, play on bikes, jump the zoom slide and play on the swings": exploring the value of outdoor play', *Australian Journal of Early Childhood*, vol. 29, no. 2, pp. 1–5.

Greenspan, S. and Lieberman, A. (1994) 'Representational Elaboration and Differentiation: A Clinical-Quantitative Approach to the Assessment of 2–4 year olds', in Slade, A. and Palmer Wolf, D., *Children at Play: Clinical and Developmental Approaches to Meaning and Representation*, Oxford: Oxford University Press.

Greenway, R. (1995) *Powerful learning experiences in management learning and development: A study of the experiences of managers attending residential development training courses at the Brathay Hall Trust (1988–9)*. Unpublished doctoral dissertation. The University of Lancaster, Centre for the Study of Management Learning, Lancaster, England.

Grenier, J., Elfer, P., Manning-Morton, J., Dearnley, K. and Wilson, D. (2008) *The key person in reception classes and small nursery settings*, in DCSF (2008d) *Social and Emotional Aspects of Development: Guidance for practitioners working in the Foundation Stage*, Nottingham: DCSF.

Greenland, P. (2000) *Hopping Home Backwards*, Leeds: JABADAO.

Greenland, P. (2006) *Developmental Movement Play: action research. Cycle one report*, Leeds: JABADAO.

Greenland, P. (2009) *Developmental Movement Play: final report*, Leeds: JABADAO.

Greenland, P. (2010) 'Physical Development', in Bruce, T. (ed.) *Early Childhood: A Student Guide*, London: SAGE.

Greenough, W. T., Black, J. E. and Wallace, C. D. (1987) 'Experience and brain development', *Child Development*, vol. 58, no. 3, pp. 539–59.

Grieshaber, S. and McArdle, F. (2010) *The Trouble with Play*, Maidenhead: Open University and McGraw-Hill.

Grooms, K. (2003) 'A childhood of their own', *A Child's Life,* vol. 25, no. 2. Available from: http://www.indiana.edu/~rcapub/v25n2/corsaro.shtml.

Gurian, M. (2001) *Boys and Girls Learn Differently. A Guide for Teachers and Parents*, San Francisco: Jossey-Bass.

Hackney, P. (2000) *Making Connections: Total Body Integration Through Bartenieff Fundamentals*, Abingdon: Routledge.

Hadfield, M., Jopling, M., Royle, K. and Waller, T. (2011) *First National Survey of Practitioners with Early Years' Professional Status.* Wolverhampton: CeDARE.

Hakkarainen, P. (2009) 'Development of motivation in play and narratives', in Blenkinshop, S. (ed.) *The Imagination in Education: Extending the Boundaries of Theory and Practice*, Newcastle-upon-Tyne: Cambridge Scholars Publishing.

Hall, K., Cremin, T., Comber, B. and Moll, L. (eds.) (2012) *The Wiley Blackwell International Research Handbook of Children's Literacy, Learning and Culture*, Oxford: Wiley Blackwell.

Hallam, S. (2009) 'An evaluation of the Social and Emotional Aspects of Learning (SEAL) programme: Promoting positive behaviour, effective learning and well-being in primary school children', *Oxford Review of Education*, vol. 35, no. 3, pp. 313–30.

Hallinger, P. (1999) 'Conceptual models, methodology, and methods for studying school leadership', in Murphy, J. and Seashore-Louis, K. (eds.), *The 2nd Handbook of Research in Educational Administration*, San Francisco: McCutchan.

Hammond, R. A. (2009) *Respecting Babies: A New Look at Magda Gerber's RIE Approach*, Washington, DC: Zero to Three.

Hanna, T. (1976) 'The field of somatics', *Somatics*, Autumn, pp. 30–4.

Hannaford, C. (2005) *Smart Moves: Why learning is not all in your head* (2nd edn), Arlington, VA: Great Ocean Publishers.

Hannon, P. and Nutbrown, C. (2001) *Outcomes for children and parents of an early literacy education parental involvement programme*, Paper presented at the British Educational Research Association (BERA) Annual Conference, September 2001, Leeds.

Hannon, P., Morgan, A. and Nutbrown, C. (2006) 'Parents' perspectives on a family literacy programme', *Journal of Early Childhood Research*, vol. 3, no. 3, pp. 19–44.

Hannon, P., Weinberger, J., and Nutbrown, C. (1991) 'A study of work with parents to promote early literacy development', *Research Papers in Education*, vol. 6, no. 2, pp. 77–97.

Hargreaves, D. (2005) *About Learning: Report of the Learning Working Group*, London: Demos. Available from: http://www.demos.co.uk/files/About_learning.pdf?1240939425.

Haringey Local Children Safeguarding Board (2009) *Serious Case Review: Baby Peter*, London: Haringey LCSB.

Harms, T., Clifford, R. M. and Cryer, D. (2004) *Early Childhood Environment Rating Scale (ECERS-R)*, New York: Teachers' College Press.

Hartman, R., Stage, S. and Webster-Stratton, C. (2003) 'A growth curve analysis of parent training outcomes: Examining the influence of child risk factors (inattention, impulsivity and hyperactivity problems), parental and family risk factors', *Journal of Child Psychology and Psychiatry*, vol. 44, no. 3, pp. 388–98.

Hatton, N., Smith, D. (1995) *Reflection in Teacher Education: Towards Definition and Implementation*, Sydney: The University of Sydney, School of Teaching and Curriculum Studies.

Havinghurst, R. and Levine, R. (1979) *Society and Education*, Reading, MA: Allyn and Bacon, in Gallahue, D. L., Ozmun, J. C. and Goodway, J. (2011) *Understanding Motor Development: Infants, children, adolescents, adults* (7th edn), New York: McGraw-Hill.

Hayes, M. and Whitebread, D. (2006), *ICT in the Early Years: Learning and Teaching with Information and Communications Technology*, Maidenhead: Open University Press.

Haynes, N. and Orrell, S. (1993) *Maslow in Psychology: An Introduction*, London: Longman Group UK Ltd.

Heathcote, D. and Bolton, G. (1995) *Drama for Learning: Dorothy Heathcote's Mantle of the Expert Approach to Education*, Portsmouth: Heinemann.

Hebb, D. (1949) *The Organisation of Behaviour*, New York: Wiley and Sons.

Hedges, H. and Cullen, J. (2005) 'Subject knowledge in early childhood curriculum and pedagogy: Beliefs and practices', *Contemporary Issues in Early Childhood*, vol. 6, no. 1, pp. 66–79.

Heifetz, R. A. (1996) *Leadership Without Easy Answers*, Cambridge, MA: Harvard University Press.

Heifetz, R. A. and Linsky, M. (2004) 'When leadership spells danger', *Educational Leadership*, vol. 61, no. 7, pp. 33–7.

Hendrick, H. (1997) 'Constructions and reconstructions of British childhood: An interpretative survey, 1800 to the present', in James, A. and Prout, A. (eds.) *Constructing and Reconstructing Childhood*, London: Falmer Press.

High/Scope Educational Research Foundation (2003) *Preschool Child Observation Record* (2nd edn), Ypsilanti, MI: High/Scope Press.

Hill, J. A. (2011) 'Endangered childhoods: How consumerism is impacting child and youth identity', *Media, Culture & Society*, vol. 33, no. 3, pp. 347–62.

Hillman, M. (2006) 'Children's rights and adults' wrongs', *Children's Geographies,* vol. 4, no. 1, pp. 61–7.

Hobart, C., Frankel, J. and Walker, M. (2009) *Good Practice in Safeguarding Children*, Cheltenham: Nelson Thornes.

Holland, P. (2003) *We don't play with guns here: War, weapon and superhero play in the early years*, Maidenhead: Open University and McGraw-Hill.

Holland, P. (2004) *Picturing Childhood*, London: I. B. Taurus and Co. Ltd.

Holt, N. (2009) *Bringing the High/Scope Approach to Your Early Years Practice*, Abingdon: David Fulton Publishers [Kindle edn].

Home Office (2009) *What Is Domestic Violence?* London: Home Office.

Home Office, Lord Chancellor's Department, Crown Prosecution Service, Department of Health and the National Assembly for Wales (2002) *Achieving Best Evidence in Criminal Proceedings: Guidance for Vulnerable or Intimidated Witnesses, Including Children*, London: Home Office.

Hopkin, R., Stokes, L. and Wilkinson, D. (2010) *Quality, Outcomes and Costs in Early Years Education*, London: National Institute of Economic and Social Research. Available from: http://www.niesr.ac.uk/pdf/Quality%20Outcomes%20and%20Costs%20in%20early%20Years%20Education.pdf.

Hornor, G. (2008) 'Reactive attachment disorder', Journal of Pediatric Health Care, vol. 22, no. 4, pp. 234–9.

House of Lords (1986) Ruling on Gillick vs. West Norfolk and Wisbech Health Authority.

Howard, J. and McInnes, K. (2012) 'The impact of children's perception of an activity as play rather than not play on emotional well-being', *Child: care, health and development*. Forthcoming. Available from: http://onlinelibrary.wiley.com/doi/10.1111/j.1365-2214.2012.01405.x/abstract.

Howe, D. (2011) *Attachment across the Lifecourse: A Brief Introduction*, Basingstoke: Palgrave Macmillan.

Howe, D., Brandon, M., Hinnings, D. and Schofield, G. (1999) *Attachment Theory, Child Maltreatment, and Family Support*, Basingstoke: Macmillan.

Howes, C. and Farver, I. (1987) 'Social pretend play in 2-year-olds: Effects of age of partner', *Childhood Research Quarterly*, vol. 2, pp. 305–14.

Howkins, J. (2001) *The Creative Economy: How People Make Money from Ideas*, London: Allen Lane.

Hoyle, E. and John, P. (1995) *Professional Knowledge and Professional Practice*, London: Cassell.

Hughes, A. M. (2006) *Developing Play for the Under 3s*, London: Fulton.

Hughes, C. and Dunn, J. (2000) 'Hedonism or empathy?: Hard-to-manage children's moral awareness and links with cognitive and maternal characteristics', *British Journal of Developmental Psychology*, vol. 18, pp. 227–45.

Hughes, L. and Owen, H. (eds.) (2009) *Good Practice in Safeguarding Children: Working Effectively in Child Protection*, London: Jessica Kingsley Publishers.

Hughes, M. and MacNaughton, G. (2002) 'Preparing early childhood professionals to work with parents: The challenges of diversity and dissensus', *Australasian Journal of Early Childhood*, vol. 27, no. 2, pp. 14–20.

Hyder, T. (2005) *War, Conflict and Play*, Maidenhead: Open University Press.

International Association for the Evaluation of Educational Achievement (2007) *Trends in International Mathematics and Science Study* (TIMSS), Boston: Boston College.

Ipsos MORI (2005) *Black and Minority Ethnic Survey: Research study conducted for the Electoral Commission*, London: Ipsos MORI. Available from: http://www.ipsos-mori.com/Assets/Docs/Archive/Publications/ethnic-minority-voters-and-non-voters.pdf.

Ipsos MORI (2011) *Children's Well-being in UK, Sweden and Spain: The Role of Inequality and Materialism*, London: Ipsos MORI. Available from: http://www.unicef.org.uk/Documents/Publications/IPSOS_UNICEF_ChildWellBeingreport.pdf.

Isaacs, B. (2011) *Understanding the Montessori Approach*, London: Routledge.

Isaacs, S. (1930) *The Intellectual Growth of Young Children*, London: Routledge.

Isaacs, S. (1933) *Social Development in Young Children*, London: Routledge.

Isaacs, S. (1935) *Psychological Aspects of Child Development*, London: Evans.

Isaacs, S. (1948) *Childhood and After*, London: Routledge and Kegan Paul.

Isaacs, S. (1952) 'The Nature and Function of Phantasy', in Riviere, J. (ed.), *Developments in Psycho-analysis*, London: Hogarth Press.

Isaacs, S., Clement Brown, S. and Thouless, R. H. (eds.) (1941) *Cambridge Evacuation Survey*, London: Methuen.

Islington Early Years Foundation Stage Team (2011) *Refugee and asylum seeker support and advice pack for early years practitioners*. Available from: http://www.islington.gov.uk/publicrecords/documents/EducationandLearning/pdf/eyfst/EY-Refugee-pack-2011.pdf.

Jackson, D. (2006) *Distributed Leadership: 'spaces between the pebbles in a jar'*, Manchester: NCSL. Available from: http://networkedlearning.ncsl.org.uk/knowledge-base/research-papers/distributed-leadersip-the-space-between-the-pebbles-in-the-jar.pdf.

James, A., and Prout, A. (eds.) (2004) *Constructing and Reconstructing Childhood*, London: Falmer Press.

James, A., Jenks, C. and Prout, A. (1998) *Theorizing Childhood*, Cambridge: Polity Press.

Jändling, M. (2003) *'Exercises for learning – a Beacon Project between Knowle CE Primary School and Kingsley Preparatory School'* [online]. Available from: http://www.inpp.org.uk/intervention-adults-children.

Jenks, C. (1996) *Childhood*, Routledge, London.

Jensen, B. (2009) 'A Nordic approach to Early Childhood Education (ECE) and socially endangered children', *European Early Childhood Education Research Journal*, vol. 17, no. 1, pp. 7–21.

Jewett, C. (1995) *Helping Children Cope with Separation and Loss*, London: BAAF.

Johns, C. (2000) *Becoming a Reflective Practitioner*, Oxford: Blackwell Science.

Johnson, D. H. (ed.) (1995) *Bone, Breath and Gesture: Practices of embodiment*, Berkeley, CA: North Atlantic Books.

Johnson, D.H. (2000) 'Intricate tactile sensitivity: A key variable in western integrative bodywork', in Saper, C. and Mayer, E. (eds.), *The Biological Basis for Mind Body Interactions*, The Progress in Brain Research Series, vol. 122.

Johnson, J., Ironsmith, M., Whitcher, A., Poteat, M., Snow, C. and Mumford, S. (1997) 'The development of social networks in preschool children', *Early Education and Development*, vol. 8, pp. 389–405.

Johnson, P. and Kossykh, Y. (2008) *Early Years, Life Chances and Equality: A Literature Review*, Manchester: Equality and Human Rights Commission.

Johnson, S. (1999) *Who Moved My Cheese?*, Reading: Ebury Publishing.

Jones, C. and Pound, L. (2008) *Leadership and Management in the Early Years: From principles to practice*, Maidenhead: Open University.

Jones, D. (2003) *Communicating with Vulnerable Children: A Guide for Practitioners*, London: Gaskell.

Jordan, E. (1995) 'Fighting boys and fantasy play: The construction of masculinity in the early years of school', *Gender and Education*, vol. 7, no. 1, pp. 69–86.

Joshi, U. and Mukherji, P. (2005) 'Special Educational Needs, Disability and Inclusion', in Dryden, L., Forbes, R., Mukherji, P. and Pound, L. *Essential Early Years*, London. Hodder Arnold.

Judge, B., Jones, P. and McCreery, E. (2009) *Critical Thinking Skills for Education Students (Study Skills in Education)*, Exeter: Learning Matters.

Juhan, D. (2002) *Job's Body: A Handbook for Bodywork*, New York: Barrytown Ltd.

Junker, B. H. (1960) *An Introduction to Social Sciences*, Chicago: University of Chicago Press.

Kalliala, M. (2006) *Play Culture in a Changing World*, Maidenhead: Open University and McGraw-Hill.

Karen, R. (1994) *Becoming Attached: The unfolding mysteries of the mother–infant bond*, New York: Warner Books.

Katz, L. (1985) *The Nature of Professions: Where is Early Childhood Education?* Washington, DC: Education Resources Information Center (ERIC).

Kellett, M. (2005) *Children as Active Researchers: A new research paradigm for the 21st century?* NCTM Methods Review Papers NCRM/003, London: Economic and Social Research Council National Centre for Research Methods.

Kellett, M., Forrest, R., Dent, N. and Ward, S. (2004) '"Just teach us the skills please, we'll do the rest": Empowering ten-year-olds as active researchers', *Children & Society,* vol. 18, no. 5, pp. 329–43.

Kelley, N. (2006) 'Children's involvement in policy formation', *Children's Geographies*, vol. 4, no. 1, pp. 37–44.

Kelly-Byrne, D. (1989) *A Child's Play Life: An ethnographic study*, New York: Teachers College Press.

Kemmis, S. (1982) *The Action Research Reader*, Geelong, Victoria: Deakin University Press (out of print), in National College for School Leadership (NCSL) (2008) *NPQICL Booklet 1: Module 1 Building the learning community*, Nottingham: NCSL.

Kennedy, E. K., Cameron, R. J. and Greene, J. (2012) 'Transitions in the early years: Educational and child psychologists working to reduce the impact of school culture shock', *Educational and Child Psychology*, vol. 29, no. 1, pp. 19–31.

Kenway, J. and Bullen, E. (2001) *Consuming Children*, Buckingham: Open University Press.

Kinney, L. (2005) 'Small voices, powerful messages', in Clark, A., Kjørholt, A. and Moss, P. (eds.) *Beyond Listening: Children's Perspectives on Early Childhood Services*, Bristol: Policy Press.

Kirkpatrick Partners (2011) *Kirkpatrick Model*. Available from: http://www.kirkpatrickpartners.com/OurPhilosophy/tabid/66/Default.aspx.

Kitson, N. (2010) 'Children's fantasy role play – why adults should join in', in Moyles, J. (ed.) *The Excellence of Play* (3rd edn), Maidenhead: Open University and McGraw-Hill.

Kjørholt, A. (2005) 'The competent child and the right to be oneself: Reflections on children as fellow-citizens in an early childhood centre', in Clark, A., Kjørholt, A. and Moss, P. (eds.) *Beyond Listening: Children's Perspectives on Early Childhood Services*, Bristol: Policy Press.

Kjørholt, A., Moss, P. and Clark, A. (2005) 'Beyond listening: Future prospects', in Clark, A., Kjørholt, A. and Moss, P. (eds.) *Beyond Listening: Children's Perspectives on Early Childhood Services*, Bristol: Policy Press.

Klein, M. (1927) 'The psychological principles of infant analysis', *International Journal of Psychoanalysis*, vol. 8, pp. 25–37.

Klein, M. (1932) *The psycho-analysis of children*, London: Hogarth Press.

Knight, S. (2010) 'Forest school: playing on the wild side', in Moyles, J. (ed.) *The Excellence of Play* (3rd edn), Maidenhead: Open University and McGraw-Hill.

Knowles, G. (2009) *Ensuring Every Child Matters: A critical approach*, London: SAGE Publications.

Knowles, M. (1980) *The Modern Practice of Adult Education: From pedagogy to andragogy* (2nd edn), Englewood Cliffs, NJ: Prentice Hall/Cambridge.

Knowles, M. (1990) *The Adult Learner: A neglected species* (4th edn), Houston: Gulf Publishing.

Koblinsky, S., Gordon, A. and Anderson, E. (2000) 'Changes in the social skills and behavior problems of homeless and housed children during the preschool year', *Early Education & Development*, vol. 11, no. 3, pp. 321–38.

Koestler, A. (1964) *The Act of Creation*, London: Pan Books.

Kohlberg, L. (1975) 'The cognitive-developmental approach to moral education', *Phi Delta*, vol. 56, pp. 670–77.

Kolb, D. A. (1984) *Experiential Learning: Experience as a source of learning and development*, Englewood Cliffs, NJ: Prentice Hall.

Koocer, P. and Keith-Spiegel, P. (1994) 'Children and consent to participate in research', in Melton, G. B., Koocher, G. P. and Saks, M. J. (eds.), *Children's Competence to Consent*, New York and London: Plenum.

Kordich-Hall, D. and Pearson, J. (2005) 'Resilience: Giving children the skills to bounce back', *Health and Education*, vol. 23, no.1, pp. 12–15.

Korthagen, F. A. J. and Wubbels, T. (1995) 'Characteristics of reflective practitioners: Towards an operationalisation of the concept of reflection', *Teachers and Teaching*, vol. 1, no. 1, pp. 51–72.

Kotter, J. and Rathgeber, H. (2006) *Our Iceberg Is Melting: Changing and succeeding under any conditions*, London: Macmillan.

Kotter, J. P. (2007) *Leading Change*, Boston: Harvard Business School Press.

Kramer, P. D. (1995) 'Preface', in Rogers, C., *On Becoming a Person*, New York: Houghton Mifflin Co.

Kugler, P. N., Kelso, J. A. S. and Turvey, M. T. (1980) 'On the concept of coordinative structures as dissipative structures: 1. Theoretical lines of convergence', in Gallahue, D. L., Ozmun, J. C. and Goodway, J. (2011) *Understanding Motor Development: Infants, children, adolescents, adults* (7th edn), New York: McGraw-Hill.

Kurtz, L. (2006) *Visual Perception Problems in Children With AD/HD, Autism and Other Learning Disabilities: A guide for parents and professionals*, London: Kingsley.

Kwon, Y.-I. (2002) 'Changing curriculum for early childhood education in England', *Early Childhood Research and Practice*, vol. 4, no. 2. Available from: http://ecrp.uiuc.edu/v4n2/kwon.html.

Laevers, F. (1997) *A Process-Oriented Child Follow-Up System for Young Children*, Leuven University, Belgium: Centre for Experiential Education.

Laevers, F. and Heylen, L. (2003) *Involvement of Children and Teacher Style: Insights from an International Study on Experiential Education*, Leuven University, Belgium: Leuven University Press.

Laming, W. H. (2003) *The Victoria Climbié Inquiry: Report of an Inquiry by Lord Laming*, Norwich: HMSO.

Laming, W. H. (2009) *The Protection of Children in England: A Progress Report*, London: The Stationery Office.

Lane, J. (2006) *Right From The Start: A commissioned study of antiracism, learning and the early years*, Focus Institute for Regeneration and Social Transformation (FIRST). Available from: http://www.focus-consultancy.co.uk/pdfs/first4.pdf.

Lane, J. (2007) 'Culture, ethnicity, language, faith and equal respect in early childhood – does "getting it" matter?', *Education Review*, vol. 20, no. 1, pp. 101–7.

Lane, J. (2008) *Young Children and Racial Justice: Taking action for racial equality in the early years – understanding the past, thinking about the present, planning for the future*, London: The National Children's Bureau.

Lane, J. and Parkes, B. (2012) 'Acting to end discrimination', *Nursery World*, Spring 2012 Supplement, pp. 25–7.

Lansdown, G. (2011) 'Children's welfare and children's rights', in O'Dell, L. and Leverett, S. (eds.) *Working with Children and Young People: Co-constructing practice*, Basingstoke: Palgrave and Macmillan/Milton Keynes: The Open University.

Layard, R. and Dunn, J. (2009) *A Good Childhood*, London: Penguin Books Ltd.

Lazar, I. (1983) 'Discussion and Implications of Findings', in The Consortium for Longitudinal Studies, *As the Twig is Bent…Lasting Effects of Preschool Programs*, New Jersey: Lawrence Erlbaum Associates.

Learning and Teaching Scotland (2003) *Using ICT creatively with children with communication difficulties* [online]. Available from: http://wayback.archive-it.org/1961/20100802090900/http://www.ltscotland.org.uk/inclusionandequality/ictandinclusion/writingandspeaking/usingictcreatively.asp.

Learning and Teaching Scotland (2005) *Birth to three: supporting our youngest children*, Edinburgh: Scottish Executive. Available from: http://www.educationscotland.gov.uk/images/birth2three_tcm4-161671.pdf.

LeDoux, J. (1998) *The Emotional Brain*, London: Weidenfeld & Nicolson.

Lee, W., Mitchell, l. and Soutar, B. (2012) *Understanding the Te Whāriki Approach: Early Years Education in Practice*, London: Routledge.

Lefevre, M. (2010) *Communicating with Children and Young People: Making a Difference*, Bristol: Policy Press.

Lefevre, M., Tanner, K. and Luckock, B. (2008) 'Developing social work students' communication skills with children and young people: A model for the qualifying level curriculum', *Child and Family Social Work*, vol. 13, no. 2, pp. 166–76.

Lennon, R. and Eisenberg, N. (1987) *Gender and age differences in empathy and sympathy*, in Eisenberg, N. and Strayer, J. (1987) *Empathy and Its Development*, Cambridge: Cambridge University Press.

Leslie, C. and Skidmore, C. (2008) *SEN: The Truth about Inclusion*, London: The Bow Group.

Levine, S. (1960) 'Stimulation in infancy', *Scientific American* (May), in Juhan, D. (2002) *Job's Body: A Handbook for Bodywork*, New York: Barrytown Ltd.

Lewin, K. (1946) 'Action research and minority problems', *Journal of Social Issues*, vol. 2, no. 4, pp. 34–46.

Lewin, K. (1948) *Resolving Social Conflicts: Selected papers on group dynamics*, New York: Harper & Row.

Lieberman, D. A., Fisk, M. C. and Biely, E. (2009) 'Digital games for young children ages three to six: From research to design', *Computers in the Schools*, vol. 26, no. 4, pp. 299–313.

Likert, R. (1932) *A Technique for the Measurement of Attitudes*, New York: Columbia University Press, in Cole, G. A. and Kelly, P. (2011) *Management Theory and Practice* (7th edn), Singapore: Cengage Learning.

Lindon, J. (2003) *Child Care and Early Education: Good practice to support young children and their families*, London: Thomson Learning.

Lindon, J. (2008) *Safeguarding Children and Young People: Child Protection 0–18 Years* (3rd edn), London: Hodder.

Lindon, J. (2009) *Guiding the Behaviour of Children and Young People: Linking Theory to Practice*, London: Hodder Education.

Lindon, J. (2010a) *Reflective Practice and Early Years Professionalism: Linking Theory and Practice*, London: Hodder.

Lindon, J. (2010b) *Understanding Child Development: Linking Theory and Practice* (2nd edn), London: Hodder Education.

Lindon, J. (2011) *Too Safe for Their Own Good: Helping Children Learn About Risk and Lifeskills*, London: National Children's Bureau.

Lindon, J. and Lindon, L. (2011) *Leadership and Early Years Professionalism*, London: Hodder Education.

Linn, S. (2005) *Consuming Kids: Protecting our children from the onslaught of marketing and advertising*, New York: Anchor Books.

Linsey, A. and McAuliffe, A. (2006) 'Children at the Centre? The Children Act 2006', *Children & Society*, vol. 20, no. 5, pp. 404–8.

Little, H. (2006) 'Children's risk-taking behaviour: Implications for early childhood policy and practice', *International Journal of Early Years Education*, vol. 14, no. 2, pp. 141–54.

Liu, X., Kurita, H., Sun, Z. and Wang, F. (1999) 'Risk factors for psychopathology among Chinese children', *Psychiatry and Clinical Neurosciences*, vol. 53, pp. 497–503.

Lloyd, D. and Duveen, G. (1992) *Gender Identities and Education: The impact of starting school*, Hemel Hempstead: Harvester Wheatsheaf, in Jordan, E. (1995) 'Fighting boys and fantasy play: The construction of masculinity in the early years of school', *Gender and Education*, vol. 7, no. 1, pp. 69–86.

Löfdahl, A. (2010) 'Who gets to play? Peer groups, power and play in early childhood settings', in Brooker, L. and Edwards, S. (eds.) *Engaging Play*, Maidenhead: Open University and McGraw-Hill.

Loman, S. with Foley, F. (1996) 'Models for understanding the nonverbal process in relationships', *The Arts in Psychotherapy*, vol. 23, no. 4, pp. 341–50.

Louv, R. (2006) *Last Child in the Woods*, New York: Algonquin Books.

Lown, J. (2002) 'Circle time: The perceptions of teachers and pupils', *Educational psychology in practice*, vol. 18, no. 2, pp. 93–102.

Luff, P. (2007) 'Written observations or walks in the park: Documenting children's experiences', in Moyles, J. (ed.) *Early Years Foundations: Meeting the Challenge*, Maidenhead: Open University Press.

Luff, P. (2012) 'Observations: Recording and analysis in Early Years Foundation Stage', in I. Palaiologou (ed.) (2012) *Early Years Foundation Stage: Theory and Practice* (2nd edn), London: SAGE.

McClellan, D. and Kinsey, S. (1999) 'Children's social behavior in relation to participation in mixed-age or same-age classrooms', *Early Childhood Research and Practice*, vol. 1, no. 1. Available from: http://ecrp.uiuc.edu/v1n1/mcclellan.html.

McClelland, D. C. (1978) 'Managing motivation to expand human freedom', *American Psychologist*, vol. 33, no. 3, pp. 201–10, in Cole, G. A. and Kelly, P. (2011) *Management Theory and Practice* (7th edn), Singapore: Cengage Learning.

McCready, L. T. and Soloway, G. B. (2010) 'Teachers' perceptions of challenging student behaviours in model inner city schools', *Emotional and Behavioural Difficulties*, vol. 15, no. 2, pp. 111–23.

McDowall Clark, R. and Baylis, S. (2012) '"Wasted down there": policy and practice with the under-threes', *Early Years: An International Journal of Research and Development*, vol. 32, no. 2, pp. 229–42.

McGraw, M. B. (1935) *Growth: A study of Johnny and Jimmy*, in Gallahue, D. L., Ozmun, J. C. and Goodway, J. (2011) *Understanding Motor Development: Infants, children, adolescents, adults* (7th edn), New York: McGraw-Hill.

McGregor, D. M. (1960) *The Human Side of Enterprise*, New York: McGraw-Hill, in Cole, G. A. and Kelly, P. (2011) *Management Theory and Practice* (7th edn), Singapore: Cengage Learning.

McInnes, K., Howard, J., Miles, G. and Crowley, K. (2011) 'Differences in practitioners' understanding of play and how this influences pedagogy and children's perceptions of play', *Early Years: An International Journal of Research and Development*, vol. 31, no. 2, pp. 121–33.

McIntosh, P. (1988) *'White Privilege: Unpacking the Invisible Knapsack'*, Working Paper 189, Wellesley, MA: Wellesley College Center for Research on Women. Available from: http://ted. coe.wayne.edu/ele3600/mcintosh.html.

Mackay, R. W. (1991) 'Conceptions of Children and Models of Socialisation', in Wacksler, F. (ed.) *Studying the Social Worlds of Children: Sociological Readings*, London: Falmer Press.

McKellar, P. (1957) *Imagination and Thinking: A psychological analysis*, London: Cohen and West.

McLeod, A. (2008) *Listening to Children: a Practitioner's Guide*, London: Jessica Kingsley.

McMillan, M. (1919) *The Nursery School*, London: Dent.

McMullen, M. B., Addleman, J. M., Fulford, A. M., Moore, S. L., Mooney, S. J., Sisk, S. S. and Zachariah, J. (2009) 'Learning to be me while coming to understand we: Encouraging prosocial babies in group care settings', *Young Children*, vol. 64, no. 4, pp. 20–8.

MacNaughton, G. (2003) *Shaping Early Childhood*, Maidenhead: Open University Press.

MacNaughton, G. and Williams, G. (2009) *Teaching Young Children: Choices in Theory and practice* (2nd edn), Maidenhead: Open University and McGraw-Hill.

MacNaughton, G., Hughes, P. and Smith, K. (2007) 'Young children's rights and public policy: Practices and possibilities for citizenship in the early years', *Children & Society*, vol. 21, pp. 458–69.

McNiff, J. and Whitehead, J. (2002), *Action Research: Principles and practices* (2nd edn), London: Routledge.

Madrid, B., Alma de Ruiz, Z., Andreva, I., Davis, R., Lunden, K., Kaonoparat, W., Lui, P., Johnson, M. (2002) 'Case example offers responses from 7 diverse cultures', *The Link: The Official Newsletter of the International Society for Prevention of Child Abuse and Neglect (ISPCAN)*, vol. 11, no. 2. Available from: http://www.ispcan.org/resource/resmgr/link/link11.2.english.pdf.

Maguire, M. and Dunn, J. (1997) 'Friendships in early childhood and social understanding', *International Journal of Behavioral Development*, vol. 21, no. 4, pp. 669–86.

Main, M. and Solomon, J. (1986) 'Discovery of an insecure-disorganized/ disoriented pattern', in Brazelton, T. B. and Yogman, M. (eds.) *Affective Development in Infancy*, Norwood, NJ: Ablex Publishing Corporation.

Main, M. and Solomon, J. (1990) 'Procedures for identifying infants as disorganized/ disorientated during Ainsworth Strange Situation', in Greenberg, M. T., Cicchetti, D. and Cummings, E. M. (eds.), *Attachment in the Preschool Years: Theory, research, and intervention*, Chicago, IL: University of Chicago Press.

Mairs, K. and the Pen Green Team (2012) *Young Children Learning Through Schemas: Deepening the dialogue about learning in the home and in the nursery*, London: Routledge.

Malaguzzi, L. (1993) 'History, ideas and basic philosophy', in Edwards, C., Gandini, L. and Forman, G. (eds.) *The Hundred Languages of Children*, Norwood, NJ: Ablex Publishing Corporation.

Malloch, S. and Trevarthen, C. (2009) *Communicative Musicality: Exploring the basis of human companionship*, Oxford: OUP.

Manning-Morton, J. and Thorp, M. (2003) *Key Times for Play*, Maidenhead: Open University Press.

Marmot, M. (2010) *Fair Society, Healthy Lives (The Marmot Review): A Strategic Review of Health Inequalities in England Post-2010*, London: The Marmot Review. Available from: http://www.instituteofhealthequity.org/projects/fair-society-healthy-lives-the-marmot-review.

Maslow, A. (1943) 'A theory of human motivation', *Psychological Review*, vol. 50, no. 4, pp. 370–96.

Maslow, A. (1967) 'A Theory of Metamotivation: The Biological Rooting of the Value-life', *Journal of Humanistic Psychology*, vol. 7, pp. 93–127.

Mathers, S. K. (2012) *Improving Quality in the Early Years*, Oxford: The Daycare Trust.

Matthews, J. (2003) *Drawing and Painting: Children and Visual Representation* (2nd edn), London: SAGE.

Matthews, J. (2011) *Starting from Scratch*, London and New York: Psychology Press.

Maxwell, L. (2007) 'Competency in child care settings: The role of the physical environment', *Environment and Behaviour*, vol. 39, no. 2, pp. 229–245.

Maxwell, L., Mitchell, M. and Evans, G. (2008) 'Effects of play equipment and loose parts on preschool children's outdoor play behaviour: An observational study and design intervention', *Children, Youth and Environments*, vol. 18, no. 2, pp. 36–63.

Mayall, B. (2002) *Towards a Sociology for Childhood: Thinking from children's lives*, Buckingham: Open University Press.

Mayall, B. (2003) *Sociologies of childhood and educational thinking*, professorial lecture, Institute of Education, University of London.

Mayall, B. (2008) 'Conversations with children: Working with generational issues' in Christensen, P. and James, A. (eds.), *Research with Children: Perspectives and Practices* (2nd edn), London: Routledge, pp. 109–22.

Mayer, J., Caruso, D. and Salovey, P. (1999) 'Emotional intelligence meets the traditional standards for intelligence', *Intelligence*, vol. 27, no. 4, pp. 267–98.

Mayer, J., Caruso, D. and Salovey, P. (2004) 'Emotional intelligence: Theory, findings and implications', *Psychological Inquiry*, vol. 15, no. 3, pp. 197–215.

Meade, A. and Cubey, P. (2008) *Thinking Children: Learning About Schemas*, Maidenhead: Open University Press and McGraw-Hill.

Meggitt, C., Kamen, T., Bruce, T. and Grenier, J. (2001) *Early Learning and Child Care*, London: Hodder and Cache: Children and Young People's Workforce.

Melhuish, E., Belsky, J., MacPherson, K. and Cullis, A. (2010) *The quality of group childcare settings used by 3-4 year old children in Sure Start Local Programme Areas, and the relationship with child outcomes*, Nottingham: DfE.

Melton, G. and Thompson, R. (1978) 'Getting out of a rut: Detours to less travelled paths in child witness research', in Ceci, S., Toglia, M. and Ross, D., *Children's Eye-witness Memory*, New York: Springer–Verlag.

Mercurio, C. (2003) 'Guiding boys in the early years to lead healthy emotional lives', *Early Childhood Education Journal*, vol. 30, no. 4, pp. 255–8.

Merriam, S. B. (ed.) (2002) *Qualitative Research in Practice*, San Francisco: Jossey-Bass.

Mezirow, J. (2000) *Learning as Transformation: Critical Perspectives on a Theory in Progress*, San Francisco: Jossey-Bass.

Miller, L. and Pound, L. (2011) 'Taking a critical perspective', in Miller, L. and Pound, L. (eds.) *Theories and Approaches to Learning in the Early Years*, London: SAGE Publications.

Miller, S. (1978) 'The facilitation of fundamental motor skill learning in young children', in Gallahue, D. L., Ozmun, J. C. and Goodway, J. (2011) *Understanding Motor Development: Infants, children, adolescents, adults* (7th edn), New York: McGraw-Hill.

Miller, T. (1992) 'A customer's definition of quality', *The Journal of Business Strategy*, vol. 13, no. 1, pp. 4–7.

Mindham, C. (2005) 'Creativity and the young child', *Early Years: An International Journal of Research and Development*, vol. 25, no. 1, pp. 81–4.

Minik, N. (1997) 'The Early History of the Vygotskian School', in Cole, M., Engestrom, Y., Vasquez, O. (eds.) *Mind, Culture, and Activity: Seminal Papers from the Laboratory of Comparative Human Cognition*, Cambridge: Cambridge University Press.

Ministry of Education (1996) *Te Whāriki*, Wellington, New Zealand: Learning Media.

Mintzberg, H. (1973) *The Nature of Managerial Work*, New York: Harper and Row.

Mogi, K., Nagasawa, M. and Kikusui, T. (2010) 'Developmental consequences and biological significance of mother–infant bonding', *Progress in Neuro-psychopharmacology and Biological Psychiatry*, vol. 35, no. 5, pp. 1232–41.

Montague, A. (1971) *Touching: The Human Significance of Skin*, in Juhan, D. (2002) *Job's Body: A Handbook for Bodywork*, New York: Barrytown Ltd.

Montessori, M. (1912) *The Montessori Method* (trans. A. E. George), New York: Frederick A. Stokes Company.

Montessori, M. (1967) *The Absorbent Mind*, New York: Delta.

Montessori, M. (1969) 'The four planes of development', *AMI Communications* (2/3), pp. 4–10.

Moon, J. (2004) *A Handbook of Reflective and Experiential Learning: Theory and Practice*, London: Routledge Falmer.

Mooney, A. (2007) *The Effectiveness of Quality Improvement Programmes for Early Childhood Education and Childcare*, London: Thomas Coram Institute.

Mooney, C. H. (2010) *Theories of Attachment*, St Paul, MN: Red Leaf Press.

Morgan, A. and Siraj-Blatchford, J. (2009) *Using ICT in the Early Years: Parents and practitioners in partnership*, London: Practical Pre-school.

Moritz Rudasill, K. and Konold, T. (2008) 'Contributions of children's temperament to teachers' judgments of social competence from kindergarten through second grade', *Early Education & Development*, vol. 19, no. 4, pp. 643–66.

Morris, J. (2009) 'Nursery abuser's trail of damage', *BBC News* [online]. Available from: http://news.bbc.co.uk/2/hi/uk_news/england/8380975.stm.

Morrison Gutman, L. and Feinstein, L. (2007) *Parenting Behaviours and Children's Development from Infancy to Early Childhood: Changes, Continuities, and Contributions*, London: Centre for Research on the Wider Benefits of Learning, Institute of Education. Available from: http://www.learningbenefits.net.

Morrow, G. and Malin, N. (2004) 'Parents and professionals working together: Turning the rhetoric into reality', *Early Years: Journal of International Research and Development*, vol. 24, no. 2, pp. 163–77.

Morrow, V. (2010) 'Child poverty, social exclusion and children's rights: A view from the sociology of childhood', in Vandenhole, W., Vranken, J. and Boyser, K. De (eds.) *Poverty and Children's Rights*, Belgium: Intersentia Publishing.

Moss, E., Smolia, N., Cyr, C., Dubois-Comtois, K., Mazzarello, T. and Berthiaume, C. (2006) 'Attachment and behavior problems in middle childhood as reported by adult and child informants', *Development and Psychopathology*, vol. 18, no. 2, pp. 425–44.

Moss, P. (2001) 'The otherness of Reggio', in Abbott, L. and Nutbrown, C. (eds.) *Experiencing Reggio Emilia*, Buckingham: Open University Press.

Moss, P. (2007) 'Starting strong: An exercise in international learning', *International Journal of Child Care and Education Policy*, vol. 1, no. 1, pp. 11–21.

Moyles, J. (2010) *Effective Leadership and Management in the Early Years*, Maidenhead: Open University Press.

Moyles, J. (ed.) (2010) *The Excellence of Play* (3rd edn), Maidenhead: Open University and McGraw-Hill.

Moyles, J. and Worthington, M. (2011) *The Early Years Foundation Stage through the daily experiences of children*, TACTYC, Occasional paper no. 1. Available from: http://www.tactyc.org.uk/occasional-papers.asp.

Moyles, J., Adams, S. and Musgrove, A. (2002) *Study of Pedagogical Effectiveness in Early Learning (SPEEL)*, Research report 363, London: DfES.

Mukherji, P. (2001) *Understanding Children's Challenging Behaviour*, Cheltenham: Nelson Thornes.

Mukherji, P. and Albow, P. (2009) *Research Methods in Early Childhood: An introductory guide*, London: SAGE.

Munro, E. (2001) 'Empowering looked-after children', *Child and Family Social Work*, vol. 6, no. 2, pp. 129–37.

Munro, E. (2007) *Child Protection*, London: SAGE.

Munro, E. (2011) *The Munro Review of Child Protection: Final Report: A child-centred system*, London: DfE. Available from: http://www.education.gov.uk/munroreview/downloads/8875_DfE_Munro_Report_TAGGED.pdf.

Munro, E. (2012) 'Munro review progress report: Moving towards a child-centred system', London: DfE. Available from: http://www.education.gov.uk/childrenandyoungpeople/healthandwellbeing/safeguardingchildren/a00209245/munro-progress.

Murray, L., Sinclair, D., Cooper, P., Ducournau, P., Turner, P. and Stein, A. (1999) 'The socioemotional development of 5-year-old children of postnatally depressed mothers', *Journal of Child Psychology and Psychiatry*, vol. 40, no. 8, pp. 1259–71.

Myrna, J. (2009) 'Turning the tables on performance reviews: How to create a better process that empowers, energizes and rewards your employees', *Business Strategy Series*, vol. 10, no. 6, pp. 366–73.

National Children's Bureau (2011) *Listening as a way of life* [online]. Available from: http://www.ncb.org.uk/ycvn/resources/listening-as-a-way-of-life.

National College for School Leadership (NCSL) (2008a) *Impact of NPQICL research project: Case study 2*, Nottingham: NCSL.

National College for School Leadership (NCSL) (2008b) *NPQICL Booklet 1: Module 1 Building the learning community*, Nottingham: NCSL.

National Health and Medical Research Council (NHMRC) (2007), *National Statement on Ethical Conduct in Human Research*, NHMRC, Canberra, ACT.

Neumann, M., Hood, M. And Ford, R. (2012) 'Mother–child joint writing in an environmental print setting: Relations with emergent literacy', *Early Child Development and Care*, vol. 182, no. 10, pp. 1349–69.

Newman, T. (2002) *Promoting Resilience: A Review of Effective Strategies for Child Care Services* [online]. Available from: http://www.barnardos.org.uk/resources/researchpublications/documents/RESILSUM.PDF.

Newman, T. (2004) *What Works in Building Resilience?* Barkingside: Barnardo's.

Newton, E. and Jenvey, V. (2011) 'Play and theory of mind: Associations with social competence in young children', *Early Child Development and Care*, vol. 181, no. 6, pp. 761–73.

Nicol, J. (2007) *Bringing the Steiner Waldorf Approach to your Early Years Practice*, London: David Fulton.

Nicol, J. and Taplin, J. T. (2012) *Understanding the Steiner-Waldorf Approach: Early Years Education*, Abingdon: Routledge.

Nolan, A. and Kilderry, A. (2010) 'Postdevelopmentalism and professional learning', in Brooker, L. and Edwards, S. (eds.) *Engaging Play*, Maidenhead: Open University and McGraw-Hill.

NSPCC (2005) *Understanding the links: child abuse, animal abuse and domestic violence: Information for professionals*, London: NSPCC. Available from: http://www.nspcc.org.uk/Inform/research/findings/understandingthelinks_wda48278.html.

NSPCC (2010) *The definitions and signs of child abuse*, London: NSPCC. Available from: http://www.nspcc.org.uk/inform/trainingandconsultancy/consultancy/helpandadvice/definitions_and_signs_of_child_abuse_pdf_wdf65412.pdf.

Nutbrown, C. (1999) *Threads of Thinking*, London: Paul Chapman.

Nutbrown, C. (2012) *Foundations for Quality: The independent review of early education and childcare qualifications: Final report*, London: DfE.

Nutbrown, C. and Page, J. (2008) *Working with Babies and Children*, London: SAGE.

Nutbrown, C., Clough, P. and Selbie, P. (2008) *Early Childhood Education: History, philosophy and experience*, London: SAGE Publications.

Nutbrown, C., Hannon, P. and Morgan, A. (2005) *Early Literacy Work with Families: Policy, Practice and Research*, London: SAGE Publications.

OECD (Organisation for Economic Co-operation and Development) (2004) *Starting Strong: Curricula and pedagogies in early childhood education and care. Five curriculum outlines*, Paris: OECD.

OECD (2006) *Starting Strong II: Early childhood education and care*, Paris: OECD. Available from: http://www.oecd.org/dataoecd/14/32/37425999.pdf.

OECD (2011) *Programme for International Student Assessment* (PISA), Paris: OECD.

OECD (2012) *Starting Strong III: A quality toolbox for ECEC*, Paris: OECD.

Office for National Statistic (ONS) (2011) *Population Estimates by Ethnic Group 2006–2009*. Cardiff. ONS.

Ofsted (2009) *Serious Case Reviews: Lessons being learnt but more still to do*. Available from: http://www.ofsted.gov.uk/Ofsted-home/Publications-and-research/Browse-all-by/Documents-by-type/Thematic-reports/Learning-lessons-from-serious-case-reviews-year-2.

Ofsted (2010) *Learning Lessons from serious case reviews 2009–2010*. Available from: http://www.ofsted.gov.uk/Ofsted-home/Publications-and-research/Browse-all-by/Documents-by-type/Statistics/Other-statistics/Learning-lessons-from-serious-case-reviews-2009-2010.

Ofsted (2011a) *Annual Report 2010/11 Early Years and Childcare*, London: The Stationery Office. Available from: http://www.ofsted.gov.uk/resources/annualreport1011.

Ofsted (2011b) *Report Summary: The impact of the Early Years Foundation Stage* [online]. Available from: http://www.ofsted.gov.uk/resources/impact-of-early-years-foundation-stage.

Ofsted (2012) *Early Years Register inspection and regulation from September 2012* [online]. Available from: http://www.ofsted.gov.uk/resources/early-years-register-inspection-and-regulation-september-2012-presentation-speakers-notes.

Oldfield, L. (2003) *Free to Learn*, Sussex: Hawthorne Press.

Opie, I. and Opie, P. [1959] (1977) *The Lore and Language of Schoolchildren*, Oxford: Oxford University Press.

Organisation for Economic Co-operation and Development *see under* OECD.

Ostrov, J. and Keating, C. (2004) 'Gender differences in preschool aggression during free play and structured interactions: An observational study', *Social Development*, vol. 13, no. 2, pp. 255–77.

O'Sullivan, J. (2009) *Leadership Skills in the Early Years*, London: Network Continuum.

Ouseley, H. and Lane, J. (2006) 'We've got to start somewhere: what role can early years services and settings play in helping society to be more at ease with itself?', *Race Equality Teaching*, vol. 24, no. 2, pp. 39–43.

Ouvry, M. (2003) *Exercising Muscles and Minds*, London: National Children's Bureau.

Paige-Smith, A. and Craft, A. (eds.) (2008) *Developing Reflective Practice in the Early Years*, Maidenhead: Open University Press.

Paige-Smith, A. and Rix, J. (2011) 'Researching early intervention and young children's perspectives – developing and using a "listening to children approach"', *British Journal of Special Education*, vol. 38, no. 1, pp. 28–36.

Palaiologou, I. (2012a) *Child Observation for the Early Years* (2nd edn), Exeter: Learning Matters.

Palaiologou, I. (ed.) (2012b) *Ethical Practice in Early Childhood*, London: SAGE.

Paley, V. G. (2004) *A Child's Work*, Chicago: Chicago University Press.

Palmer, S. (2006) *Toxic Childhood: How the modern world is damaging our children and what we can do about it*, London: Orion.

Palmer, S. (2007) *Detoxing Childhood: What Parents Need to Know to Raise Happy, Successful Children*, London: Orion.

Palmer, S. (2009) *21st Century Boys: How modern life is driving them off the rails and how we can get them back on track*, London: Orion.

Papatheodorou, D. T. (2006) *Seeing the Wider Picture - Reflections on the Reggio Emilia Approach*, Cambridge: Anglia Ruskin University.

Papatheodorou, T., Luff, P. and Gill, J. (2011) *Child Observation for Learning and Research*, Harlow: Pearson Education.

Parker-Rees, R., Leeson, C., Savage, J. and Willan, J. (eds.) (2010) *Early Childhood Studies Book* (3rd edn), Exeter: Learning Matters.

Parton, N. (2004) 'From Maria Colwell to Victoria Climbié: Reflections on public inquiries into child abuse a generation apart', *Child Abuse Review*, vol. 13, no. 2, pp. 80–94.

Pauk, W. and Owens, R. J. Q. (2011) *How to Study in College* (10th edn), Boston, MA: Wadsworth Cengage Learning.

Pavlov, I. P. (1960) *Conditioned Reflexes*, Oxford: Oxford University Press.

Pears, R. and Shields, G. (2010) *Cite Them Right: The Essential Reference Guide* (8th edn), Basingstoke: Palgrave Macmillan.

Peck, J. and Coyle, M. M. (2005) *Write it Right*, Basingstoke: Palgrave Macmillan [available in Kindle edn].

Perry, B. (2001a) *Bonding and Attachment in Maltreated Children: Consequences of Emotional Neglect in Childhood*, Houston, TX: The Child Trauma Academy.

Perry, B. (2001b) 'The neurodevelopmental impact of violence in childhood', in Schetky, D. and Benedek, E. P. (eds.), *Textbook of Child and Adolescent Forensic Psychiatry*, Washington, DC: American Psychiatric Press.

Perry, B. (2002) 'Studies of childhood abuse and neglect have important lessons for considerations of nature and nurture', *Brain and Mind*, vol. 3, pp. 79–100.

Perry, B. and Szalavitz, M. (2006) *The Boy Who Was Raised as a Dog*, New York: Basic Books.

Persson, A. and Musher-Eizenman, D. (2003) 'The impact of a prejudice prevention program on young children's ideas about race', *Early Childhood Research Quarterly*, vol. 18, no. 4, pp. 530–46.

Peters, J. M. (1994) 'Instructors as researchers-and-theorists: faculty development in a community college', in Benn, R. and Fieldhouse, R. (eds.) *Training and Professional Development in Adult and Continuing Education*, Exeter: CRCE.

Petrie, P. (2005) 'Schools and support staff: Applying the European pedagogic model', *Support for Learning*, vol. 20, no. 4, pp. 176–180.

Petrie, P., Boddy, J., Cameron, C., Heptinstall, E., McQuail, S., Simon, A. and Wigfall, V. (2009) *Pedagogy: A holisitic, personal approach to work with children and young people, across services*, London: TCRU.

Pfeifer, J., Iacoboni, M., Mazziotta, J. and Dapretto, M. (2008) 'Mirroring others' emotions relates to empathy and interpersonal competence in children', *Neuroimage*, vol. 39, no. 4, pp. 2076–85.

Phillips, B. and Alderson, P. (2002) *Beyond 'anti-smacking': Challenging violence and coercion in parent–child relations*, London: The Children's Society.

Piaget, J. (1952a) *The Origins of Intelligence in Children*, New York: International Universities.

Piaget, J. (1952b) *Play, Dreams and Imitation*, transl. C. Gattegno and F. Hodgson, London: Routledge and Kegan Paul.

Piaget, J. (1954) *The Construction of Reality in the Child*, New York: Basic Books.

Piaget, J. (1959) *The Language and Thought of the Child*, London: Routledge and Kegan Paul.

Piaget, J. (1962) *Play, Dreams, and Imitation in Childhood*, New York: W. W. Norton.

Piaget, J. (1965) *The Moral Judgement of the Child*, New York: Free Press.

Piaget, J. (1968) *Six Psychological Studies*, London: University of London Press.

Piaget, J. (1972) *The Psychology of the Child*, New York: Basic Books.

Piaget, J. and Inhelder, B. (1969) *The Psychology of the Child*, New York: Basic Books.

Pikler, E. (1945) *There Is No Orphanage in Socialism*, Budapest: Department of Sociology, Karl Marx University.

Pink, D. (2005) *A Whole New Mind*, New York: Penguin Books.

Play England (2007) *Charter for Children's Play* [online]. Available from: http://www.playengland.org.uk/media/71062/charter-for-childrens-play.pdf.

Plowden, B. (1967) *Children and their Primary Schools: A Report of the Central Advisory Council for Education (England)* (Plowden Report), London: HMSO.

Plowman, L. and Stephen, C. (2005) 'Children, play and computers in pre-school education', *British Journal of Educational Technology*, vol. 36, no. 2, pp. 145–57.

Plowman, L. and Stephen, C. (2007) 'Guided interaction in pre-school settings', *Journal of Computer Assisted Learning*, vol. 23, no. 1, pp. 14–26.

Plowright, D. (2011*) Using Mixed Methods: Frameworks for an Integrated Methodology*, London: SAGE.

Plymouth Safeguarding Children Board (2010) *Serious Case Review Overview Report: Executive Summary in respect of Nursery Z*. Available from: http://www.plymouth.gov.uk/serious_case_review_nursery_z.pdf.

Podmore, V. N. and Luff, P. (2011) *Observation*, Maidenhead: Open University Press.

Polanyi, M. (1967) *The Tacit Dimension*, New York: Doubleday Anchor.

Pollard, A. (2002) *Reflective Teaching: Effective and evidence-informed professional practice*, London and New York: Continuum.

Pollard, A. (2008) *Reflective Teaching: Evidence Informed Practice* (3rd edn), London, New York: Continuum.

Pomerantz, A. and Fehr, B. J. (1997) 'Conversation analysis: An approach to the study of social action as sense making practices', in van Dijk, T. A. (ed.) *Discourse as Social Interaction*, London: SAGE.

Porter, L. (2005) *Gifted Young Children: A guide for teachers and parents* (2nd edn), Berkshire: Open University Press.

Postman, N. (1996) *The Disappearance of Childhood*, London: Vintage Press.

Pound, L. (2005) *How Children Learn*, Leamington Spa: Step Forward Publishing.

Pound, L. (2008) *How Children Learn: From Montessori to Vygotsky – Educational Theories and Approaches Made Easy*, London: Step Forward [available in Kindle edn].

Pound, L. (2009) *How Children Learn 3: Contemporary thinking and theorists*, London: Practical Pre-School Books.

Pound, L. (2011) *Influencing Early Childhood Education*, Maidenhead: Open University Press.

Pound, L. and Harrison, C. (2003) *Supporting Musical Development in the Early Years*, Maidenhead: Open University and McGraw-Hill.

Pound, L. and Miller, L. (2011) 'Critical issues', in Miller, L. and Pound, L. (eds.) *Theories and Approaches to Learning in the Early Years*, London: SAGE Publications.

Powell, J. and Uppal, E. (2012) *Safeguarding Babies and Young Children*, Maidenhead: Open University Press.

Powell, S. and Tod, J. (2004) *A systematic review of how theories explain learning behaviour in school contexts*, London: EPPI-Centre, Social Science Research Unit, Institute of Education. Available from: http://eppi.ioe.ac.uk/cms/LinkClick.aspx?fileticket=xjNFKFrgrG8%3D&tabid=123&mid=928.

Powell, T. (2012) 'The impact of being homeless on young children and their families', NHSA Dialog, *A Research-to-Practice Journal for the Early Childhood Field*, vol. 15, no. 2, pp. 221–8.

Powers, N. and Trevarthen, C. (2009) 'Voices of shared emotion and meaning: Young infants and their mothers in Scotland and Japan', in Malloch, S. and Trevarthen, C. (2009) *Communicative Musicality: Exploring the basis of human companionship*, Oxford: Oxford University Press.

Preedy, P., O'Donovon, C., Scott, J., Wolinski, R. (2003) 'Releasing educational potential through movement', *Child Care in Practice*, vol. 11, no. 4, pp. 415–32.

Public Interest Disclosure Act 1998, London: HMSO. Available from: http://www.legislation.gov.uk/ukpga/1998/23/contents.

Puffett, N. (2010) 'Government clarifies ban on Every Child Matters', *Children & Young People Now* [online]. Available from: http://www.cypnow.co.uk/cyp/news/1053008/government-clarifies-ban-every-child-matters.

Pugh, G. and Duffy, B. (2006) *Contemporary Issues in the Early Years* (3rd edn), London: SAGE.

Pugh, G. and Selleck, D. (1996) 'Listening to and communicating with young children', in Davie, R., Upton, G. and Varma, V. (eds.) *The Voice of the Child: A handbook for professionals*, London: Falmer Press.

QCA (Qualifications and Curriculum Agency) (2000) *Curriculum Guidance for the Foundation Stage*, London: QCA/ DfEE.

Qvortrup, J. (1994) 'Childhood and modern society: A paradoxical relationship?', in Branner, J. and Brien, M. (eds.), *Childhood and Parenthood: Proceedings of ISA Committee for Family Research Conference on Children and Families*, London: Institute of Education.

Qvortrup, J. (2000) 'Macroanalysis of childhood', in Christensen, P. and James, A. (eds.), *Research with children: Perspectives and practices*, London: Falmer Press.

Reed, M. and Canning, N. (eds.) (2010) *Reflective Practice in the Early Years*, London: SAGE.

Riddall-Leech, S. (2008) *How to Observe Children* (2nd edn), Oxford: Heinemann Educational Publishers.

Riley, D. (1983) *War in the Nursery*, London: Virago Press.

Rinaldi, C. (2005) 'Documentation and Assessment: What is the Relationship?', in Clark, A., Kjørholt, A. and Moss, P. (eds.) *Beyond Listening: Children's Perspectives on Early Childhood Services*, Bristol: Policy Press.

Rinaldi, C. (2007) 'Preface', in Dahlberg, G., Moss, P. and Pence, A. (eds.) *Beyond Quality in Early Childhood Care and Education*, London: Routledge.

Ritchie, J. (2005) 'Implementing Te Whāriki as postmodernist practice: a perspective from Aotearoa/New Zealand', in Ryan, S. and Grieshaber, S. (eds.) *Practical Transformations and Transformational Practices: Globalisation, postmodernism and early childhood education*, Oxford: Elsevier Ltd.

Roazzi, A. and Bryant, P. (1998) 'The effects of symmetrical and asymmetrical social interaction on children's logical inferences', *British Journal of Developmental Psychology*, vol. 16, pp. 175–81.

Roberts, R. (2006) *Self Esteem and Early Learning: Key People from Birth to School*, London: SAGE.

Roberts, R. D., Zeidner, M. and Matthews, G. (2001) 'Does emotional intelligence meet traditional standards for an intelligence? Some new data and conclusions', *Emotion*, vol. 1, no. 3, pp. 196–231.

Roberts, W. and Strayer, J. (1996) 'Empathy, emotional expressiveness, and prosocial behaviour', *Child Development*, vol. 67, no. 2, pp. 449–70.

Roberts-Holmes, G. (2005) *Doing your Early Years Research Project: A step-by-step guide*, SAGE, London.

Roberts-Holmes, G. (2012) '"It's the bread and butter of our practice": Experiencing the Early Years Foundation Stage', *International Journal of Early Years Education*, vol. 20, no. 1, pp. 30–42.

Robins, A. (ed.) (2007) *Mentoring in the Early Years*, London: Paul Chapman Publishing.

Robins, A. and Callan, S. (2010) *Managing Early Years Settings*, London: Sage Publications.

Robinson, K. (1999) *All Our Futures: Creativity, Culture and Education*, London: National Advisory Committee on Creativity and Cultural Education.

Robinson, K. (2010) *Changing education paradigms* [online talk]. Available from: http://www.ted.com/talks/ken_robinson_changing_education_paradigms.html.

Robinson, K. H. and Jones-Diaz, C. (2006) *Diversity and Difference in Early Childhood*, Maidenhead: Open University and McGraw-Hill.

Rodd, J. (2005) 'Leadership: an essential ingredient or an optional extra in quality early childhood provision?' A discussion paper. Available from: http://www.tactyc.org.uk/pdfs/Reflection-rodd.pdf.

Rodd, J. (2010) *Leadership in Early Childhood*. Maidenhead: Open University Press.

Rodriguez, N. and Ryave, A. (2002) *Systematic Self-observation*, London: SAGE.

Roe, V. (1994) 'Silent voice', *Child Education*, vol. 71, no. 6, pp 62–3.

Rogers, C. R. (1967) *On Becoming a Person*, London: Constable.

Rogers, C. R. [1967] (2004) *On Becoming a Person* (new edition of original print), London: Constable.

Rogers, S. (2010) 'Powerful pedagogies and powerful resistance', in Brooker, L. and Edwards, S. (eds.) *Engaging Play*, Maidenhead: Open University and McGraw-Hill.

Rogers, S. (ed.) (2011) *Rethinking Play and Pedagogy in Early Childhood Education: Concepts, Contexts and Cultures*, London: Routledge.

Rogers, S. and Evans, J. (2008) *Inside Role-Play in Early Childhood Education: Researching young children's perspectives*, London: Routledge.

Rolfe, G., Freshwater, D. and Jasper, M. (2001) *Critical Reflection in Nursing and the Helping Professions: A User's Guide*, Basingstoke: Palgrave Macmillan.

Rolls, E. T. (2005) *Emotion Explained*, Oxford: Oxford University Press.

Rose, J. and Rogers, S. (2012) *The Role of the Adult in Early Years Settings*, Maidenhead: Open University Press.

Rosenshine, B. and Meister, C. (1992) 'The use of scaffolds for teaching higher-level cognitive strategies', *Educational Leadership*, vol. 49, no. 7, pp. 26–33.

Ross, E. (1996) 'Learning to listen to children', in Davie, R., Upton, G. and Varma, V. (eds.) *The Voice of the Child: A handbook for professionals*, London: Falmer Press.

Rumbold, A. (1990) *Starting with Quality*, London: HMSO.

Rutter, J. (2003) *Working with Refugee Children*, York: Joseph Rowntree Foundation.

Rutter, M. (2000) 'Children in substitute care: Some conceptual considerations and research implications', *Children and Youth Services Review*, vol. 22, nos. 9–10, pp. 685–703.

Salaman, A. and Tutchell, S. (2005) *Planning Educational Visits for the Early Years*, London: SAGE.

Salovey, P., and Mayer, J. (1990) 'Emotional intelligence', *Imagination, Cognition, and Personality*, vol. 9, pp. 185–211.

Saluja, G., Scott-Little, C. and Clifford, R. M. (2000) 'Readiness for School: A survey of state policies and definitions', *Early Childhood Research and Practice*, vol. 2, no. 2, Fall 2000. Available from: http://ecrp.uiuc.edu/v2n2/saluja.html.

Samaras, A. P., Freese, A. R., Kosnik, C. and Beck, C. (2008) *Learning Communities in Practice*, Dordrecht: Springer.

Sample, G. (2000) *Garden Birdsongs and Calls*, London: HarperCollins.

Sandseter, E. (2009) 'Children's expressions of exhilaration and fear in risky play', *Contemporary Issues in Early Childhood*, vol. 10, no. 2, pp. 92–106.

Sargent, P. (2005) 'The gendering of men in early childhood education', *Sex Roles*, vol. 52, nos. 3/4, pp. 251–9.

Sarwar, S. and Grewal, S. (2011) *Improving business skills in the early years and childcare sector*, London: Office for Public Management. Available from: http://www.4children.org.uk/Resources/Detail/Improving-business-skills-in-the-early-years-and-childcare-sector.

Save the Children UK (2007*) 'Working Towards Inclusive Practice in the Early Years': Inclusion of Gypsy, Roma and Traveller culture in early years settings*, conference proceedings, 20/6/2007, Birmingham Hippodrome. Available from: http://www.savethechildren.org.uk/sites/default/files/docs/Working_Towards_Inclusive_Practice_Conference_Papers_1.pdf.

SCAA (School Curriculum and Assessment Authority) (1996) *Nursery Education: Desirable Learning Outcomes on Entering Compulsory Education*, London: SCAA.

Schiller, C. (1979) *Christian Schiller in his own words*, London: published by private subscription through A&C Black.

Schofield, G. (2005) 'The voice of the child in family placement decision-making', *Adoption and Fostering*, vol. 29, no. 1, pp. 29–44.

Schofield, G. (2006) 'Middle Childhood: 5–11 Years', in Aldgate, J., Jones, D., Rose, W. and Jeffery, C. (eds.), *The Developing World of the Child*, London. Jessica Kingsley Publishers.

Schön, D. A. (1983) *The Reflective Practitioner: How Professionals Think in Action*, London: Temple Smith.

Schön, D. A. (1987) *Educating the Reflective Practitioner*, San Francisco: Jossey-Bass.

Schore, A. (2001) 'Effects of a secure attachment relationship on right brain development, affect regulation, and infant mental health', *Infant Mental Health Journal*, vol. 22, nos. 1–2, pp. 7–66.

Schratz, M. and Walker, R. (1995) *Research as Social Change*, London: Routledge.

Schuengel, C., Bakermans-Kranenburg, M. J. and Van IJzendoorn, M. H. (1999) 'Frightening maternal behavior linking unresolved loss and disorganized infant attachment', *Journal of Consulting and Clinical Psychology*, vol. 67, no. 1, pp. 54–63.

Schweinhart, L. J. and Weikart, D. P. (1997) 'The High/Scope preschool curriculum comparison through age 23', *Early Childhood Research Quarterly*, vol. 12, pp. 117–143, in Siraj-Blatchford, I., Sylva, K., Muttock, S., Gilden, R. and Bell, D. (2002) *Researching Effective Pedagogy in the Early Years (REPEY),* DfES Research Report 356, London: DfES, HMSO.

Schweinhart, L., Montie, J., Xiang, Z., Barnett, W., Belfield, C. and Nores, M. (2005) *Lifetime Effects: the High/Scope Perry Preschool study though age 40*, Ypsilanti, MI: High/Scope Press.

Scott, P. (1975) 'The tragedy of Marie Colwell', *British Journal of Criminology*, vol. 13, no. 2, pp. 88–90.

Sears, W. and Sears, M. (2001) *The Attachment Parenting Book*, New York: Little, Brown and Co.

Sears, W. and Sears, M. (2003) *The Baby Book*, New York: Little, Brown and Co.

Seidel, S. (2001) 'Perspectives on research in education', in Giudici, C., Rinaldi, C. and Krechevsky, M. (eds.) *Making Learning Visible: Children as individual and group learners*, Reggio Children, Reggio Emilia.

Seligman, M., Reivich, K., Jaycox, L, Gilham, J. (1995)*The Optimistic Child*, New York: Houghton-Mifflin, in Kordich-Hall, D. and Pearson, J. (2005) 'Resilience: Giving children the skills to bounce back', *Health and Education*, vol. 23, no.1, pp. 12–15.

Senge, P. (2006) *The Fifth Discipline: The Art and Practice of the Learning Organization*, London: Random House.

Sfard, A., and Prusak, A. (2005) 'Telling identities: In search of an analytic tool for investigating learning as a culturally shaped activity', *Educational Researcher*, vol. 34, no. 4, pp. 14–22.

Shah, P. E., Fonagy, P. and Strathearn, L. (2010) 'Is attachment transmitted across the generations? The plot thickens', *Clinical Child Psychology and Psychiatry*, vol. 15, no. 3, pp. 329–45.

Sharma, N. (2007) *It doesn't happen here: The reality of child poverty in the UK*, Ilford: Barnado's. Available from: http://www.barnardos.org.uk/poverty_executive_summary.pdf.

Shemmings, D. (2000) 'Professionals' attitudes to children's participation in decision-making: Dichotomous accounts and doctrinal contests', *Child and Family Social Work*, vol. 5, pp. 235–43.

Sheridan, M. (2008) *From Birth to Five Years: Children's Developmental Progress* (3rd edn), London: Routledge.

Shields, P. (2009) '"School doesn't feel as much of a partnership": Parents' perceptions of their children's transition from nursery school to reception class', *Early Years: An International Journal of Research and Development*, vol. 29, no. 3, pp. 237–48.

Shirley, M. M. (1931) *The First Two Years: A Study of Twenty-Five Babies*, in Gallahue, D. L., Ozmun, J. C. and Goodway, J. (2011) *Understanding Motor Development: Infants, children, adolescents, adults* (7th edn), New York: McGraw-Hill.

Simms, M. (2006) 'Retention of early years and childcare practitioners in private day nurseries: Is love enough?', paper presented at the BERA New Researchers/Student Conference, University of Warwick. Available from: http://www.leeds.ac.uk/educol/documents/157460.htm.

Sinclair, R. (2000) *Quality Protects Research Briefing No 3: Young People's Participation*, London: DoH.

Singer, E. (1998) 'Shared care for children', in Woodhead, M., Faulkner, D. and Littleton, K. (eds.) *Cultural Worlds of Early Childhood*, London: Routledge/ Open University.

Siraj-Blatchford, I. (2005) 'Quality Interactions in the Early Years', TACTYC Annual Conference *Birth to Eight Matters! Seeking Seamlessness – Continuity? Integration? Creativity?*, 5 November 2005, Cardiff. Available from: http://www.tactyc.org.uk/pdfs/2005conf_siraj.pdf.

Siraj-Blatchford, I. (2007) 'Creativity, communication and collaboration: The identification of pedagogic progression in sustained shared thinking', *Asia-Pacific Journal of Research in Early Childhood Education*, vol. 1, no. 2, pp. 3–23.

Siraj-Blatchford, I. (2009) 'Conceptualising progression in the pedagogy of play and sustained shared thinking in early childhood education: A Vygotskian perspective', *Educational & Child Psychology*, vol. 26, no. 2, pp 77–89.

Siraj-Blatchford, I. (2010) 'Learning in the home and in school: How working-class children succeed against the odds', *British Educational Research Journal*, vol. 36, no. 3, pp. 463–82.

Siraj-Blatchford, I. and Clarke, P. (2000) *Supporting Identity, Diversity and Language in the Early Years*, Buckingham: Open University Press.

Siraj-Blatchford, I. and Manni, L. (2006) *Effective Leadership in the Early Years Sector (ELEYS) Study*, London: Institute for Education. Available from: http://acecqa.gov.au/storage/eleys_study.pdf.

Siraj-Blatchford, I. and Manni, L. (2008) '"Would you like to tidy up now?" An analysis of adult questioning in the English Foundation Stage', *Early Years: An International Journal of Research and Development*, vol. 28, no. 1, pp. 5–22.

Siraj-Blatchford, I. and Siraj-Blatchford, J. (2009). *Improving children's attainment through a better quality of family-based support for early learning*, Research Review 2, London: Centre for Excellence and Outcomes in Children and Young People's Services (C4EO). Available from: http://www.c4eo.org.uk/themes/earlyyears/familybasedsupport/files/c4eo_family_based_support_kr_2.pdf.

Siraj-Blatchford, I. and Siraj-Blatchford, J. (2010) *Improving children's attainment through a better quality of family-based support for early learning*, Knowledge Review 2, London: C4EO. Available from: http://www.c4eo.org.uk/themes/earlyyears/familybasedsupport/files/c4eo_family_based_support_full_knowledge_review.pdf.

Siraj-Blatchford, I. and Sylva, K. (2004) 'Researching pedagogy in English pre-schools', *British Educational Research Journal*, vol. 30, no. 5, pp. 713–30.

Siraj-Blatchford, I., Clarke, K. and Needham, M. (eds.) (2007) *The Team Around the Child: Multi-agency Working in the Early Years*, Stoke-on-Trent: Trentham Books.

Siraj-Blatchford, I., Sylva, K., Muttock, S., Gilden, R. and Bell, D. (2002) *Researching Effective Pedagogy in the Early Years (REPEY)*, DfES Research Report 356, London: DfES, HMSO.

Skills for Care and the Children's Workforce Development Council (2007) *Providing effective supervision: A workforce development tool, including a unit of competence and supporting guidance*, Leeds: Skills for Care and CWDC. Available from: https://www.education.gov.uk/publications/standard/Childrensworkforce/Page1/SCF01/0607.

Slade, A. and Palmer Wolf, D. (1994), *Children at Play: Clinical and Developmental Approaches to Meaning and Representation*, Oxford: Oxford University Press.

Smidt, S. (2005) *Observing, Assessing and Planning for Children in the Early Years*, London: Routledge.

Smit, A. G. and Liebenberg, L. (2003) 'Understanding the dynamics of parent involvement in schooling within a poverty context', *South African Journal of Education*, vol. 23, no. 1, pp. 1–5.

Smith, A. (2011) 'Relationships with people, places and things – TeWhāriki', in Miller, L. and Pound, L. (eds.) *Theories and Approaches to Learning in the Early Years*, London: SAGE Publications.

Smith, M. K. (1996) 'David A. Kolb on experiential learning', *The encyclopaedia of informal education* [online]. Available from: http://www.infed.org/biblio/b-explrn.htm.

Smith, M. K. (1996, 2000) 'Curriculum theory and practice', *The encyclopaedia of informal education* [online]. Available from: http://www.infed.org/biblio/b-curric.htm.

Smith, P. (2010a) 'BEST case scenario: A case study of effective multi-agency working at Malvin's Close Primary School, Blyth', Nottingham: National College for School Leadership and Children's Services. Available from: http://www.nationalcollege.org.uk/docinfo?id=73876&filename=best-case-scenario.pdf.

Smith, P. (2010b) *Children and Play*, Chichester: Wiley-Blackwell.

Social Services Committee (1984) *Children in Care,* HC 360, London: HMSO.

Soler, J. and Miller, L. (2003) 'The struggle for early childhood curricula: A comparison of the English Foundation Stage Curriculum, Te Whāriki and Reggio Emilia', *International Journal of Early Years Education*, vol. 11, no. 1, pp. 57–68.

Sossin, K. M. and Birklein, S. B. (2006) 'Nonverbal transmission of stress between parent and young child: Considerations and psychotherapeutic implications of a study of affective movement patterns', *Journal of Infant, Child and Adolescent Psychotherapy*, vol. 5, pp. 46–69.

Sousa, C., Herrenkohl, T. I., Moylan, C. A., Tajima, E. A.; Klika, J. B.; Herrenkohl, R. C. and Russo, M. J. (2011) 'Longitudinal study on the effects of child abuse and children's exposure to domestic violence, parent-child attachments, and antisocial behavior in adolescence', *Journal of Interpersonal Violence*, vol. 26, no. 1, pp. 111–36.

Spartacus Educational. *McMillan* [online]. Available from: http://www.spartacus.schoolnet.co.uk/Wmcmillan.htm.

Special Educational Needs and Disability Act 2001, London: HMSO.

Spitz, R. A. (1945) 'Hospitalism: An inquiry into the genesis of psychiatric conditions in early childhood', *Psychoanalytic Study of the Child*, vol. 1, pp. 53–74.

Stainthorp, R. (2003) 'Use it or lose it' [online]. Available from: http://www.literacytrust.org.uk/Pubs/stainthorp.html.

Stake, R. (2010) *Qualitative Research: Studying how things work*, New York: Guilford Press.

Stalker, K. and Connors, C. (2003) 'Communicating with disabled children', *Adoption and Fostering*, vol. 27, no. 1, pp. 26–35.

Steedman, C. (1990) *Childhood, Culture and Class in Britain: Margaret McMillan, 1860–1931*, London: Virago.

Stein A., Malmberg, L. E., Sylva, K., Barnes, J., Leach, P. and the Family and Childcare Project Team (2008) *Child: Care, Health and Development*, vol. 34, no. 5, pp. 603–12.

Steiner Waldorf Education (2009) *Guide to the Early Years Foundation Stage in Steiner Waldorf Early Childhood Settings*, Isle of Harris: White Horse Press.

Steiner Waldorf Schools Fellowship (2012) *The Early Years in Steiner Waldorf Education* [online]. Available from: http://www.steinerwaldorf.org.uk/earlyyears.html.

Stephen, C. (2010) 'Pedagogy: The silent partner in early years learning', *Early Years: An International Journal of Research and Development*, vol. 30, no. 1, pp. 15–28.

Stern, D. N. (1985) *The Interpersonal World of the Infant*, New York: Basic Books.

Stevens, L. J. (2000) *Effective Ways to Help Your ADD/ADHD Child*, New York: Penguin.

Stewart, N. (2011) *How Children Learn: The characteristics of effective early learning*, London: BAECE.

Stobbs, P. (2008) *Extending inclusion: Access for disabled children and young people to extended schools and children's centres: A development manual*, London: Council for Disabled Children. Available from: http://www.councilfordisabledchildren.org.uk/media/56642/extending_inclusion.pdf.

Storr, A. (1989) *Solitude*, London: HarperCollins.

Sunderland, M. (2007) *What Every Parent Needs To Know* , London: Dorling Kindersley.

Sutton, C., Utting, D. and Farrington, D. (2006) 'Nipping criminality in the bud', *The Psychologist*, vol. 19, no. 8, pp. 470–5.

Sweet, J. (2006) *Beyond reflection dogma*, Cardiff University. Available at: http://www.leeds.ac.uk/medicine/meu/lifelong06/P_JohnSweet.pdf.

Sylva, K., Siraj-Blatchford, I. and Taggart, B. (2003) *The Early Childhood Environmental Rating Scale*: 4 Curricular Subscales, Stoke-on-Trent: Trentham Books.

Sylva, K., Melhuish, E., Sammons, P., Siraj-Blatchford, I. and Taggart, B. (2004) *The Effective Provision of Pre-school Education (EPPE) Project: Technical Paper 12 – The Final Report: Effective Pre-school Education*, London: DfES/Institute of Education.

Sylva, K., Melhuish, E., Sammons, P., Siraj-Blatchford, I. and Taggart, B. (eds.) (2010) *Early Childhood Matters: Evidence from the Effective Pre-School And Primary Education Project*, London: Routledge.

Tackey, N., Barnes, H. and Khambhaita, P. (2011) *Poverty, Ethnicity and Education*, York: Joseph Rowntree Foundation.

Tait, C. (2007) 'Getting to Know the Families', in Whalley, M. (2007) *Involving Parents in their Children's Learning* (2nd edn), London: Paul Chapman.

The Tavistock and Portman NHS Foundation Trust (2012) *Your Child*. Available from: http://www.tavistockandportman.nhs.uk/yourchild.

Tayler, C., Cloney, D., Farrell, A. and Muscat, T. (2008) *Hubs Report: Child care and family services hubs. Impact study in rural and regional communities*, Brisbane: QUT.

Taylor, C. (2001) 'Australian early childhood milieu: Teacher challenges in promoting children's language and thinking', *European Early Childhood Education Research Journal*, vol. 9, no. 1, pp. 41–56.

Taylor, C. (2004) 'Underpinning knowledge for child-care practice: Reconsidering child development theory', *Child and Family Social Work,* vol. 9, pp. 225–35.

Teaching Agency (2012) *Improving Teacher Training for Behaviour*. Available from: http://media.education.gov.uk/assets/files/pdf/i/improving_teacher_training_for_behaviour.pdf.

Te One, S. (2006) 'Setting the context for children's rights in early childhood', *ChildreNZ Issues*, vol. 10, no. 1, pp. 18–22.

Theobald, M. and Kultti, A. (2012) 'Investigating child participation in the everyday talk of teacher and children in a preparatory year', *Contemporary Issues in Early Childhood*, vol. 13, no. 3, pp. 210–25.

Theobald, M., Danby, S. and Ailwood, J. (2011) 'Child participation in the early years: Challenges for education', *Australasian Journal of Early Childhood*, vol. 36, no. 3, pp. 19–26.

Thomas, M. (2010) 'Sensitive periods in brain development: Implications for language and literacy', Psychological Aspects of Education Current Trends Conference Series, 23 June. Available from: http://www.educationalneuroscience.org.uk/files/BJEP-CEN%20Conference/Thomas_BJEP_2010.pdf.

Thomas, M. and Knowland, V. (2009) 'Sensitive periods in brain development: Implications for education policy', *European Psychiatric Review*, Touch Briefings, vol. 2, no. 1, pp. 17–20.

Thomas, N. (2002) *Children, Family and the State: Decision-making and children's participation*, Bristol: Policy Press.

Thompson, S. and Thompson, N. (2008) *The Critically Reflective Practitioner*, Basingstoke: Palgrave Macmillan.

Thorell, L. B. and Rydell, A. M. (2008) 'Behaviour problems and social competence deficits associated with symptoms of attention-deficit/hyperactivity disorder: Effects of age and gender', *Child: care, health and development*, vol. 34, no. 5, pp. 584–95.

Thorton, L. and Burton, P. (2009) *Understanding the Reggio Approach,* London: Routledge.

Thwaites, J. (2008) *100 Ideas for Teaching Personal, Social and Emotional Development (100 Ideas for the Early Years)*, London: Continuum.

Tickell, C. (2011)*The Early Years: Foundations for life, health and learning. An Independent Report on the Early Years Foundation Stage to Her Majesty's Government*, London: DfE. Available from: http://media.education.gov.uk/assets/Files/pdf/F/Foundations%20for%20life%20health%20and%20learning.pdf.

Timimi, S. (2005) *Naughty Boys: Anti-social behaviour, ADHD and the role of culture*, London: Palgrave McMillan.

Tims, C. (2010) (ed.) *'Creative learning in the early years is not just child's play…': Born creative*, London: DEMOS. Available from: http://www.demos.co.uk.

Tisdall, K. (2012) 'Children's services: Working together', in Hill, M., Head, G., Lockyer, A., Reid, B. and Taylor, R. (eds.)*Taking Forward Children's and Young People's Participation in Decision-making*, New York and London: Pearson Longman.

Tizard, B. and Hughes, M. [1984] (2002) *Young Children Learning* (2nd edn), Oxford: Blackwell Publishers.

Tobin, J. (2004) 'The disappearance of the body in early childhood education', in Bresler, L. (ed.) *Knowing Bodies: Moving Minds*, Dordrecht, The Netherlands: Kluwer Academic Publishers.

Törnebohm, H. (1986) *Caring, Knowing and Paradigms, Report 10/12*. Sweden: Department of Theory of Science, University of Goteborg.

Tovey, H. (2007) *Playing Outdoors: Spaces and Places, Risk and Challenge*, Maidenhead: Open University Press.

Tovey, H. (2012) *Bringing the Fröbel Approach to your Early Years Practice*, London: Routledge.

Trevarthen, C. and Aitkin, K. (2001) 'Infant intersubjectivity: Research, theory, and clinical implications', *Journal of Child Psychology and Psychiatry*, vol. 42, no. 19, pp. 3–48.

Trevarthen, C. and Marwick, H. (2002) *Review of childcare and the development of children 0–3: Research evidence and implications for out-of-home provision*, Edinburgh: Scottish Executive.

Tronick, E. Z. (1989) 'Emotions and emotional communication in infants', *American Psychologist*, vol. 44, pp. 112–19.

Tuckman, B. W. (1965) 'Developmental sequence in small groups', *Psychological Bulletin*, vol. 63, pp. 384–99, in Cole, G. A. and Kelly, P. (2011) *Management Theory and Practice* (7th edn), Singapore: Cengage Learning.

Turiel, E. and Weston, D. (1983) 'Act-rule relation: children's concept of social rules', in Donaldson, M., Grieve, R. and Pratt, C. (eds.), *Early Childhood Development and Care*, Oxford: Blackwell.

Tyler, R. W. (1949) *Basic Principles of Curriculum and Instruction*, Chicago: University of Chicago Press.

Tyler, P. (2010) *Safer, Healthier and Integrated Faster: Improving outcomes for families seeking sanctuary by addressing child care difficulties*, Northern Refugee Centre and the Tudor trust. Available from: http://www.nrcentre.org.uk/downloads/women/Safer%20Healthier%20and%20Integrated%20Faster.pdf.

UNESCO (United Nations Educational Scientific and Cultural Organization) (1978) *Declaration on Race and Racial Prejudice*, Paris: UNESCO. Available from: http://www.unesco.org/webworld/peace_library/UNESCO/HRIGHTS/107-116.HTM.

UNICEF (2002) *For Every Child*, London: Red Fox Books.

UNICEF (2007) *An overview of child well-being in rich countries*, UNICEF Innocenti Research Centre, Report Card 7, Florence: UNICEF. Available from: http://www.unicef.org/media/files/ChildPovertyReport.pdf.

UNICEF (2008) *The child care transition: A league table of early childhood education and care in economically advanced countries*, UNICEF Innocenti Research Centre, Report Card 8, Florence: UNICEF. Available from: http://www.unicef-irc.org/publications/pdf/rc8_eng.pdf.

UNICEF (2010) *The children left behind: A league table of inequality in child well-being in the world's rich countries*, UNICEF Innocenti Research Centre, Report Card 9, Florence. UNICEF.

UNICEF (2012a) *Early childhood education and school readiness* [online]. Available from: http://www.unicef.org/education/bege_61627.html.

UNICEF (2012b) *School Readiness: A conceptual framework* [online]. Available from: http://www.unicef.org/education/index_44888.html.

United Nations (1959) *Declaration of the Rights of the Child*, Geneva: United Nations. Available from: http://www.un.org/cyberschoolbus/humanrights/resources/child.asp.

United Nations (1989) *Convention on the Rights of the Child*, Geneva: United Nations. Available from: http://www2.ohchr.org/english/law/crc.htm.

University of Cambridge (2009) *Introducing The Cambridge Primary Review*, Cambridge: University of Cambridge. Available from: http://www.primaryreview.org.uk/Downloads/Finalreport/CPR-booklet_low-res.pdf.

Urban, M. (2008) 'Dealing with uncertainty: Challenges and possibilities for the early childhood profession', *European Early Childhood Education Research Journal*, vol. 16, no. 2, pp. 131–5.

Usher, R. and Edwards, R. (1994) *Postmodernism and Education*, London: Routledge.

Usher, R., Bryant, I. and Johnston, R. (2002) 'Self and Experience in Adult Learning', in Harrison, R., Reeve, F., Hanson, A. and Clarke, J. (eds.), *Supporting Lifelong Learning*, London: Routledge-Falmer/Open University.

Vallberg Roth, A. and Månsson, A. (2011) 'Individual development plans from a critical didactic perspective: Focusing on Montessori- and Reggio Emilia-profiled preschools in Sweden', *Journal of Early Childhood Research*, vol. 9, no. 3, 247–261.

van der Eyken, W. and Turner, B. (1969) *Adventures in Education*, Harmondsworth: Penguin Press Ltd.

Vandermaas-Peeler, M., Boomgarden, E., Finn, L. and Pittard C. (2012) 'Parental support of numeracy during a cooking activity with four-year-olds', *International Journal of Early Years Education*, vol. 20, no. 1, pp. 78–93.

Van IJzendoorn, M. H. (2001) 'Attachment theory: psychological 2', in Smelser, N. J. and Baltes, P. B. (eds.), *International Encyclopedia of the Social and Behavioral Sciences*, London: Pergamon.

Vygotsky, L. S. (1978) *Mind in Society: The development of higher mental processes*, Cambridge, MA: Harvard University Press.

Vygotsky, L. S. (1986) *Thought and Language*, Cambridge, MA: MIT Press.

Vygotsky, L. S. (1987) *Collected Works*, New York; Plenum, in Cooper, P. and Whitebread, D. (2007) 'The effectiveness of nurture groups on student progress: Evidence from a national research study', *Emotional and Behavioural Difficulties*, vol. 12, no. 3, pp. 171–90.

Wacksler, F. (1991) 'Studying children: Phenomenological insights', in Waksler, F. (ed.) *Studying the Social Worlds of Children: Sociological readings*, London: Falmer Press.

Wall, K. (2006) *Special Needs and Early Years* (2nd edn), London: Paul Chapman Publishing.

Walsh, R., Hodge, K., Bowes, J. and Kemp, C. (2010) 'Same age, different page: Overcoming the barriers to catering for young gifted children in prior-to-school settings', *International Journal of Early Childhood*, vol. 42, no. 1, pp. 43–58.

Warnock, M. (2005) *Special educational needs: a new look. Impact No 11*, London: The Philosophy Society of Great Britain.

Warren, H. and Stifter, C. (2008) 'Maternal emotion-related socialization and preschoolers' developing emotion self-awareness', *Social Development*, vol. 17, no. 2, pp. 239–58.

Waterhouse, R. (2000) *Lost in care, report of the tribunal of inquiry into the abuse of children in care in the former county council areas of Gwynedd and Clwyd since 1974*, London: DoH.

Watson, J. B. (1914) *Behavior: An introduction to comparative psychology*, New York: Holt.

Watson, J. (2006) '*Every Child Matters* and children's spiritual rights: Does the new holistic approach to children's care address children's spiritual well-being?' *International Journal of Children's Spirituality*, vol.11, no. 2, pp. 251–63.

Watts, A. (2011) *Every Nursery Needs a Garden*, London: Routledge.

Welch-Ross, M. and Fasig, L. (eds.) (2007) *Handbook of Communicating and Disseminating Behavioural Science*, Thousand Oaks, CA: SAGE.

Wellington, J. (2000) *Educational Research: Contemporary issues and practical approaches*, London: Continuum.

Wells, G. (1986) *The Meaning Makers: Children Learning Language and Using Language to Learn*, London: Hodder and Stoughton.

Wenger, E. (2006) *Communities of practice: A brief introduction*. Available from: http://www.ewenger.com/theory/index.htm.

West, M. and Prinz, J. (1987) 'Parental alcoholism and childhood psychopathology', *Psychological Bulletin*, vol. 102, no. 2, pp. 204–18.

Whalley, M. (1993) *Fathers and childcare services*, paper for the International Seminar of the European Commission Childcare Network.

Whalley, M. (1994) *Learning to Be Strong*, Sevenoaks: Hodder and Stoughton.

Whalley, M. (2006) *Children's Centres: The new frontier for the welfare state and the education system?* Nottingham: National College for School Leadership.

Whalley, M. (2007) *Involving Parents in their Children's Learning* (2nd edn), London: Paul Chapman.

Whalley, M. (2008) *Leading Practice in Early Years Settings*, Exeter: Learning Matters Limited.

Whalley, M. and Arnold, C. (forthcoming 2013) *Working with Families in Children's Centres*, London: Hodder Education.

Whalley, M., Peerless, S., Lawrence, P. and Arnold, C. (forthcoming 2012) 'How did we make a difference? A Tracer Study engaging with children and families who used the centre 8–20 years ago: families, practitioners and researchers developing emancipatory methodologies', *European Early Childhood Education Research Journal*.

Wheeler, L. (2010) *The ADHD Toolkit*, London: SAGE.

White, J. (2008) *Playing and Learning Outdoors: Making provision for high-quality experiences in the outdoor environment*, London: Routledge.

Whitebread, D. (2012) *Developmental Psychology and Early Childhood Education: A Guide for Students and Practitioners*, London: SAGE.

Whitebread, D. and Bingham, S (2011) *School Readiness: A critical review of perspectives and evidence*, TACTYC, Occasional paper no. 2. Available from: http://www.tactyc.org.uk/occasional-papers.asp.

Whitehead, M. (2009) *Supporting Language and Literacy Development in the Early Years* (2nd edn), Maidenhead: Open University and McGraw-Hill.

Wild, M. (2011) 'Thinking together: Exploring aspects of shared thinking between young children during a computer-based literacy task' *International Journal of Early Years Education*, vol. 19, no. 3/4, pp. 219–31.

Wing, L. (1995) 'Play is not the work of the child: Young children's perceptions of work and play', *Early Childhood Research Quarterly*, vol. 10, pp. 223–47.

Winnicott, D.W. (1971) *Playing and Reality*, London: Penguin.

Winnicott, D.W. (1991) *Playing and Reality*, East Sussex: Brunner-Routledge.

Winsler, A., Caverly, S., Willson-Quayle, A., Carlton, M., Howell, C., and Long, G. (2002) 'The social and behavioral ecology of mixed-age and same-age preschool classrooms: A natural experiment', *Applied Developmental Psychology*, vol. 23, pp. 305–30.

Winter, K. (2009) 'Relationships matter: The problems and prospects for social workers' relationships with young children in care', *Child and Family Social Work*, vol. 14, no. 4, pp. 450–60.

Winter, K. (2010) 'The perspectives of young children in care about their circumstances and the implications for social work practice', *Child and Family Social Work*, vol. 15, no. 2, pp. 186–95.

Wittmer, D. and Honig, A. (1991) 'Convergent or divergent? Teacher questions to 3 year old children in day care', *Early Childhood Development and Care*, vol. 68, pp. 141–8.

Wood, E. (2010a) 'Developing integrated pedagogical approaches to play and learning', in Broadhead, P., Howard, J. and Wood, E., *Play and Learning in Education Settings*, London: SAGE.

Wood, E. (2010b) 'Reconceptualising the play–pedagogy relationship: From control to complexity', in Brooker, L. And Edwards, S. (eds), *Engaging Play*, Maidenhead: Open University Press.

Wood, E. (2012) 'The state of play', *International Journal of Play*, vol. 1, no. 1, pp. 4–5.

Wood, E. and Attfield, J. (2005) *Play, Learning and the Early Childhood Curriculum* (2nd edn), London: Paul Chapman.

Wood, J. (2007) 'Academic competence in preschool: Exploring the role of close relationships and anxiety', *Early Education & Development*, vol. 18, no. 2, pp. 223–42.

Wood, J. J., Emmerson, N. A. and Cowan, P. A (2004) 'Is early attachment security carried forward into relationships with preschool peers?', *British Journal of Developmental Psychology*, vol. 22, pp. 245–53.

Woodhead, M. and Faulker, D. (2008), 'Subjects, objects or participants? Dilemmas in psychological research with children', in Christensen, P. and James, A. (eds.) *Research with Children: Perspectives and practices* (2nd edn), Abingdon: Routledge.

Woods, J. (2012) 'Knickers to the "nappy curriculum"', 8 Feb., *Telegraph.co.uk* [online]. Available from: http://www.telegraph.co.uk/education/9066921/Knickers-to-the-nappy-curriculum.html.

Woolfolk, A., Hughes, M. and Walkup, V. (2008) *Psychology in Education*, Harlow: Pearson Education Ltd.

Worthington, M. (2006) 'Creativity meets mathematics', *Practical Pre-school*. Available from: http://www.childrens-mathematics.net/creativity_meets_mathematics.pdf.

Wrennall, L. (2010) 'Surveillance and child protection: De-mystifying the Trojan horse', *Surveillance and Society*, vol. 7, nos. 3/4, pp. 304–24.

Wyse, D. (2007) *The Good Writing Guide for Education Students* (2nd edn), London: SAGE.

Yarrow, M. and Waxler, C. (1979) 'Observing Interaction: A Confrontation with Methodology', in Cairns, R. (ed.) *The Analysis of Social Interactions: Methods, Issues and Illustrations*, Hillsdale, NJ: Lawrence Erlbaum Associates.

YoungMinds (2004) *Mental Health in Infancy*, London: YoungMinds. Available from: http://www.youngminds.org.uk/assets/0000/1332/YM_Infancy_Policy.pdf.

Zeanah, C. and Fox, N. (2004) 'Temperament and attachment disorders', *Journal of Clinical Child Adolescence Psychology*, vol. 33, no. 1, pp. 32–41.

Zeanah, C., Scheeringa, M., Boris, N., Heller, S., Smyke, A. and Trapani, J. (2004) 'Reactive attachment disorder in maltreated toddlers', *Child Abuse & Neglect: The International Journal*, vol. 28, no. 8, pp. 877–88.

Zeichner, K. and Liston, D. (1987) 'Teaching student teachers to reflect', *Harvard Educational Review*, vol. 57, no. 1, pp. 23–48.

Zeitlin, H. (1994) 'Children with alcohol misusing parents', *British Medical Bulletin*, vol. 50, no. 1, pp. 139–51.

Zimmerman, F. and Christakis, D. (2005) 'Children's television viewing and cognitive outcomes' *Archives of Pediatrics and Adolescent Medicine*, vol. 159, no. 7, pp. 619–25.

Websites

Brain Gym: http://www.braingym.org.uk

Burns and Sinfield (2012) *Essential Study Skills: Succeeding at University: Quick Steps to Success.* Available from: http://www.youtube.com/watch?v=JMvvnNsZenM&feature=relmfu (uploaded by SAGE Publications on 6/3/2012)

Centre for Research on the Wider Benefits of Learning: http://www.learningbenefits.net

The Child Trauma Academy: http://www.childtrauma.org

Department for Education: http://www.education.gov.uk

Early Childhood Research and Practice (ECRP): http://ecrp.uiuc.edu

European Early Childhood Education Research Association (EECERA): http://www.eecera.org

Foundation Years: http://www.foundationyears.org.uk

International Neuro Developmental Delay (INPP): http://www.inpp.org.uk/intervention-adults-children

Learning through Landscapes: http://www.ltl.org.uk

Learning Walks: http://learningwalks.com

Media Education Formation: http://www.mediaed.org/cgi-bin/commerce.cgi?preadd=action&key=134-cfc-d&preadd=action

Ofsted: http://www.ofsted.gov.uk

Open University: http://www.open.ac.uk/skillsforstudy

Palgrave Macmillan: http://www.palgrave.com/skills4studycampus

Ken Robinson (2012) *Changing education paradigms.* Available from: http://www.ted.com/talks/ken_robinson_changing_education_paradigms.html

TACTYC: http://www.tactyc.org.uk

UK ECERS Network Resource: http://www.ecersuk.org

Zero to Three: http://www.zerotothree.org

Films/videos

Changing Education Paradigms. Available from: http://www.youtube.com/watch?V=zdzfcdgpl4u.

Community Playthings (2012) *Blocks.* Available from: http://www.communityplaythings.co.uk/products/blocks/index.html.

Fröbel Kindergarten Gifts Early Childhood Education History of Toys. Available from: http://www.youtube.com/watch?v=LNBzmCKLNdU.

JABADAO (2000) *Missing Piece of the Jigsaw*.

Jack's heuristic play with his treasure basket. Available from: http://www.youtube.com/watch?v=uCW7jZIWZ18&feature=related.

Kindergarten Nov18. Available from: http://www.youtube.com/watch?v=GMRyN3I8-Xo.

Move, Play and Learn – Physical Activity in North Dakota Child Care Programs. Available from: http://www.youtube.com/watch?v=4XtaotPsu4M&feature=plcp.

Siren Films, *Pretend play: twenty months to seven years*.

Index